MAGILL'S CINEMA ANNUAL

1986

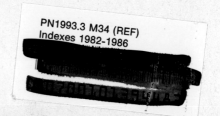

MAGILL'S
CINEMA ANNUAL
CUMULATIVE INDEXES
1982-1986

Edited by

FRANK N. MAGILL

SALEM PRESS
Pasadena, California and Englewood Cliffs, New Jersey

Library of Congress Catalog Card No. 83-644357
ISBN 0-89356-405-2
ISSN 0739-2141

First Printing

PRINTED IN THE UNITED STATES OF AMERICA

PUBLISHER'S NOTE

Magill's Cinema Annual Cumulative Indexes, 1982-1986 provides references for the nine hundred films that have been reviewed in the Magill's cinema annuals from 1982 to 1986. There are nine indexes: Title Index, Director Index, Screenwriter Index, Cinematographer Index, Editor Index, Art Director Index, Music Index, Performer Index, and Subject Index. Any film covered at length in an essay-review in an annual has been referenced under all nine indexes. Those films which appear in a section of the annual known as "More Films of..." are referenced only by title, director, performer, and subject. In addition, pseudonyms, foreign titles, and alternate titles are all cross-referenced. Each entry is followed by the year of the annual where discussion of the film can be found. Foreign and retrospective films are also provided with the year of their original release in brackets. Thus, the researcher may approach a film in a variety of ways, through its credits or even its subject matter.

As well as a listing of all the films reviewed in the annuals, the indexes include those films and artists discussed at some length in the annual's general essays (such as the Life Achievement Award essay or an interview with a film industry notable). Indexes other than the Title and Subject are arranged by the artist's name, which is followed by a listing of the films on which he or she worked and/or the general essays in which that artist is discussed. Finally, in the extensive subject index, each film covered in the annuals has been categorized under several headings, providing yet another access point to the information in Magill's cinema annuals.

CONTENTS

MAGILL'S CINEMA ANNUAL

1986

TITLE INDEX

À nos amour [1983] (85) 509
Absence of Malice (82) 57
Acqua e sapone. *See* Water and Soap.
Addition, L'. *See* Patsy, The.
Adolescente, L' [1979] (83) 53
Adventures of Buckaroo Banzai, The (85) 47
After Hours (86) 51
After the Rehearsal (85) 52
Against All Odds (84) 509
Agnes of God (86) 56
Airplane II (83) 417
Alamo Bay (86) 436
All of Me (85) 58
All Quiet on the Western Front [1930] (86) 13, 14
All the Right Moves (84) 41
Alley Cat (85) 509
Almost You (86) 436
Alphabet City (84) 509
Altars of the World [1976] (86) 18, 19
Always (86) 60
Amadeus (85) 63; (86) 26
Amateur, The (83) 417
American Dreamer (85) 509
American Flyers (86) 436
American in Paris, An [1951] (86) 6, 7
American Ninja (86) 435
American Pop (82) 62
American Taboo (85) 509
American Werewolf in London, An (82) 66
Amin—The Rise and Fall (84) 479
Amityville II (82) 417
Amityville 3-D (84) 479
Amour de Swann, Un. *See* Swann in Love.
Anchors Aweigh [1945] (86) 3, 4
And Nothing but the Truth (85) 510
And the Ship Sails On [1983] (85) 69
Android (85) 510
Angel (85) 510
Angelo My Love (84) 47
Animal Kingdom, The [1932] (86) 469
Annie (83) 56
Another State of Mind (85) 510
Another Time, Another Place [1983] (85) 510
Antarctica (85) 511
Apache [1954] (82) 395
Arch of Triumph [1948] (84) 501
Argent, L' [1983] (85) 74
Arrangement, The [1969] (86) 474
Arthur (82) 26, 71
Atlantic City (82) 74

Author! Author! (83) 417
Avenging Angel (86) 436
Aviator, The (86) 437

Baby (86) 437
Baby, It's You (84) 479
Bachelor Party (85) 511
Back to the Future (86) 65
Backstage at the Kirov (85) 511
Bad Boy, The (86) 437
Bad Boys (83) 479
Bad Medicine (86) 437
Bal, Le [1983] (85) 18, 80
Balance, La [1982] (84) 52
Bambi [1942] (85) 543
Band Wagon, The [1953] (82) 4
Bar Esperanza [1983] (86) 437
Barbarosa (83) 60
Barbary Coast [1935] (84) 506
Barefoot Contessa, The [1954] (82) 399
Basileus Quartet (85) 511
Bastille [1984] (86) 437
Battletruck (83) 417
Beach Boys, The (86) 438
Beach Girls, The (83) 417
Bear, The (85) 511
Beast Within, The (83) 418
Beastmaster, The (83) 418
Beat Street (85) 512
Beau Mariage, Le (83) 65
Beau Pere (82) 78
Becky Sharp [1935] (82) 403
Bedtime for Bonzo [1951] (84) 512
Beguiled, The [1971] (83) 37
Bells Are Ringing [1960] (84) 517
Beloved Rogue [1927] (84) 522
Berlin Alexanderplatz [1980] (84) 57
Berry Gordy's The Last Dragon (86) 438
Best Defense (85) 512
Best Friends (83) 68
Best Little Whorehouse in Texas, The (83) 72
Best Years of Our Lives, The [1946] (82) 23
Betrayal (84) 67
Better Off Dead (86) 438
Beverly Hills Cop (85) 88
Beyond Reasonable Doubt [1980] (84) 74
Beyond the Limit (84) 479
Big Chill, The (84) 78
Billy Budd [1962] (82) 11
Birdy (85) 93
Birth of a Nation, The [1915] (83) 25
Bizet's Carmen [1983] (85) 98

1

Black Cat, The (85) 512
Black Cauldron, The (86) 75
Black Peter [1964] (86) 22, 23
Black Stallion Returns, The (84) 479
Blade Runner (83) 76
Blame It on Rio (85) 512
Blame It on the Night (85) 512
Blood Simple (86) 438
Blood Wedding [1981] (83) 418
Blow Out (82) 37, 83
Blue Skies Again (84) 479
Blue Thunder (84) 84
Boat Is Full, The [1981] (83) 82
Boat, The. See Boot, Das.
Bob le Flambeur [1955] (84) 526
Body and Soul (83) 418
Body Double (85) 513
Body Heat (82) 32, 87
Body Rock (85) 513
Bohème, La [1926] (83) 27
Bolero [1981] (83) 418
Bolero (85) 513
Bon Plaisir, Le [1983] (85) 513
Boot, Das [1981] (83) 86
Boot Ist Voll, Das. See Boat Is Full, The.
Border, The (83) 418
Bostonians, The (85) 14, 105
Boum, La [1980] (84) 480
Bounty, The (85) 513
Boys from Brazil, The [1978] (86) 480
Brady's Escape (85) 514
Brainstorm (84) 480
Brazil (86) 80
Breakfast Club, The (86) 85
Breakin' (85) 514
Breakin' 2 (85) 514
Breathless (84) 89
Brewster McCloud [1970] (86) 484
Brewster's Millions (86) 438
Bride, The (86) 438
Bridge of San Luis Rey, The [1929] (82) 408
Brimstone and Treacle (83) 91
Bring on the Night (86) 439
Brittania Hospital (84) 480
Broadway Danny Rose (85) 112
Broken Blossoms [1919] (85) 6
Broken Rainbow (86) 439
Brother from Another Planet, The (85) 118
Buddy Buddy (82) 34, 93
Buddy System, The (85) 514
Bulldog Drummond [1929] (83) 17
Bullshot [1983] (86) 439
By Design (83) 418

Caddie [1976] (83) 439
Caged Fury (85) 514
Cal (85) 124

Came a Hot Friday (86) 439
Campanadas a medianoche. See Falstaff.
Can She Bake a Cherry Pie? (84) 95
Cannery Row (83) 95
Cannonball Run II (85) 514
Care Bears Movie, The (86) 439
Careful He Might Hear You [1983] (85) 130
Carmen (84) 101
Cat People [1942] (82) 13
Cat People (83) 100
Cattle Annie and Little Britches (82) 97
Cave Girl (86) 439
Cease Fire (86) 440
Céleste [1981] (83) 104
Ceravani tanto Amati. See We All Loved
  Each Other So Much.
Certain Fury (86) 440
Chained Heat (84) 480
Challenge, The (83) 109
Champions (85) 515
Chan Is Missing (83) 113
Chaos. See Ran.
Chariots of Fire (82) 30, 101
Chattanooga Choo Choo (85) 515
Cheech and Chong Still Smokin' (84) 480
Cheech and Chong's The Corsican Broth-
  ers (85) 515
Chère Inconnue. See I Sent a Letter to My
  Love.
Chèvre, La. See Goat, The.
Chimes at Midnight. See Falstaff.
Choose Me (85) 135; (86) 36
Chorus Line, A (86) 91
Chosen, The (83) 116
Christine (84) 106
Christine F. [1981] (83) 419
Christmas Story, A (84) 110
Chronos (86) 440
C.H.U.D. (85) 515
Circle of Deceit [1981] (83) 419
Città della donne, La. See City of Women.
City Girl, The (85) 516
City Heat (85) 141
City Limits (86) 440
City of Women (82) 106
Clash of the Titans (82) 111
Class (83) 480
Class of 1984 (83) 419
Clean Slate. See Coup de torchon.
Cloak and Dagger (85) 516
Clock, The (82) 46
Clue (86) 440
Coca-Cola Kid, The (86) 440
Cocoon (86) 96
Code of Silence (86) 440
Cold Feet (85) 516
Colonel Redl [1984] (86) 100

Color Purple, The (86) 105
Colorado Territory [1949] (86) 489
Come and Get It [1936] (82) 412
Come Back to the 5 & Dime Jimmy Dean,
 Jimmy Dean (83) 120
Comfort and Joy (85) 146
Commando (86) 111
Company of Wolves, The [1984] (86) 115
Competition [1963] (86) 22
Compromising Positions (86) 120
Conan the Barbarian (83) 419
Conan the Destroyer (85) 516
Confidentially Yours [1983] (85) 516
Continental Divide (82) 115
Coogan's Bluff [1968] (83) 37
Cotton Club, The (85) 150
Country (85) 156
Coup de foudre. See Entre nous.
Coup de torchon [1981] (83) 124
Cover Girl [1944] (86) 3
Cowboy [1958] (82) 417
Crackers (85) 516
Creator (86) 441
Creature from the Black Lagoon, The
 [1954] (82) 422
Creepshow (83) 419
Crimes of Passion (85) 161
Cross Country (84) 481
Cross Creek (84) 116
Crossover Dreams (86) 441
Cruel Story of Youth [1960] (85) 517
Cujo (84) 481
Curse of the Pink Panther (84) 481
Curtains (84) 481
Cutter and Bone. See Cutter's Way.
Czlowiek z Marmuru. See Man of Marble.
Czlowiek z Zelaza. See Man of Iron.

Dance with a Stranger [1984] (86) 125
Dangerous Moves [1984] (86) 129
Daniel (84) 481
Danny Boy (85) 517
Danton [1982] (84) 121
Dark Crystal, The (83) 130
Dark Star [1975] (86) 494
D.A.R.Y.L. (86) 441
Day of the Dead (86) 441
D. C. Cab (84) 481
Dead Men Don't Wear Plaid (83) 134
Dead Zone, The (84) 481
Deadly Eyes (83) 482
Deal of the Century (84) 482
Death of Mario Ricci, The [1983] (86) 133
Death Valley (83) 419
Death Wish II (83) 420
Death Wish III (86) 441
Deathstalker (85) 517

Deathtrap (83) 137
Deep in the Heart (85) 517
Deer Hunter, The (82) 24
Def-Con 4 (86) 441
Demons in the Garden [1982] (85) 517
Dernier Combat, Le [1983] (85) 517
Desaparecidos, Los. See Official Story, The.
Desperately Seeking Susan (86) 33, 34, 35,
 137
Detective (86) 442
Detour [1946] (86) 498
Devotion [1944] (82) 7
Diagonale du fou. See Dangerous Moves.
Dim Sum (86) 141
Dimanche a la Campagne, Un. See A Sunday
 in the Country.
Diner (83) 142
Dirty Dishes [1978] (84) 482
Dirty Harry [1971] (83) 37
Disraeli [1929] (82) 426
Diva [1980] (83) 147
Divorcée, The [1930] (82) 429
Doctor and the Devils, The (86) 442
Dr. Butcher, M.D. [1980] (83) 420
Doctor Detroit (84) 482
Don't Cry, It's Only Thunder (83) 420
Door to Door (85) 518
Dorm That Dripped Blood, The (84) 482
Dorothy and Alan at Norma Place (82) 40
Double Indemnity [1944] (82) 32
Dragonslayer (82) 125
Draughtsman's Contract, The [1982] (84)
 126
Dreamchild (86) 146
Dreamscape (85) 166
Dresser, The (84) 130
Drifting (85) 518
Duel in the Sun [1946] (83) 29
Dulcy [1923] (82) 432
Dune (85) 171

E la nave va. See And the Ship Sails On.
Earthling, The [1980] (82) 130
Easy Money (84) 482
Eating Raoul (83) 420
Echoes (84) 483
Eddie and the Cruisers (84) 483
Eddie Macon's Run (84) 483
Edith and Marcel [1983] (85) 518
Educating Rita (84) 136
Efter Repetitionen. See After the Rehearsal.
Eine Liebe in Deutchland. See Love in Ger-
 many, A.
Electric Dreams (85) 518
Eleni (86) 151
Emerald Forest, The (86) 156
Enchanted Cottage, The [1945] (82) 9

Endangered Species (83) 420
Enemy Mine (86) 161
Enigma [1982] (84) 483
Enter the Ninja (83) 420
Entity, The (84) 483
Entre nous [1983] (85) 176
Erendira [1983] (85) 181
Escape Artist, The (83) 421
Escape from Alcatraz [1979] (83) 33, 38
Escape from New York (82) 35, 133
Escape 2000 (84) 483
E. T.: The Extra-Terrestrial (83) 151
Étoile du nord, L' (84) 484
Eureka (86) 442
Every Man for Himself [1979] (82) 139
Evil Dead, The (84) 484
Evil That Men Do, The (85) 518
Evil Under the Sun [1981] (83) 421
Excalibur (82) 28, 144
Experience Preferred ... but Not Essential
  [1982] (84) 141
Explorers (86) 442
Exposed (84) 484
Eye of the Needle (82) 148

Falcon and the Snowman, The (86) 165
Falling in Love (85) 519
Falstaff [1966] (83) 443
Fandango (86) 442
Fanny and Alexander [1982] (84) 146
Fanny och Alexander. *See* Fanny and
  Alexander.
Fantasies [1973] (83) 421
Fast Forward (86) 442
Fast Times at Ridgemont High (83) 156
Fat City [1972] (84) 5
Father of the Bride [1950] (83) 20
Femme d'à côté, La. *See* Woman Next Door,
  The.
Femme de mon pote, La. *See* My Best
  Friend's Girl.
Fever Pitch (86) 443
Fighting Back (83) 421
Final Option, The (84) 484
Finders Keepers (85) 519
Fire and Ice (84) 153
Firefox (83) 160
Firemen's Ball, The [1967] (86) 24, 25
Firestarter (85) 519
First Blood (83) 164
First Monday in October (82) 151
First Name, Carmen [1983] (85) 186
Firstborn (85) 519
Fitzcarraldo (83) 167
Five Days One Summer (83) 421
Flaming Star [1960] (83) 36
Flamingo Kid, The (85) 192

Flanagan (86) 443
Flash of Green, A (86) 443
Flashdance (84) 158
Flashpoint (85) 519
Flaxfield, The [1983] (86) 443
Flesh and Blood (86) 443
Fleshburn (85) 519
Fletch (86) 169
Flight of the Phoenix, The [1966] (85) 549
Flowing [1956] (86) 444
Fool for Love (86) 172
Footloose (85) 198
For Me and My Gal [1942] (86) 2, 3
For Your Eyes Only (82) 155
Forbidden World (83) 421
Forced Vengeance (83) 422
Fort Apache [1948] (84) 530
Fort Apache, the Bronx (82) 159
48 HRS. (83) 173
Foster Daddy, Tora! [1980] (82) 163
Four Friends (82) 167
Four Seasons, The (82) 171
4th Man, The [1983] (85) 203
Fox and the Hound, The (82) 26
Frances (83) 178
Fraternity Vacation (86) 444
French Connection, The [1971] (83) 37
French Lieutenant's Woman, The (82) 32,
  174
Freud [1962] (84) 6, 535
Friday the 13th—Part III (83) 422
Friday the 13th—The Final Chapter (85)
  520
Fright Night (86) 444
Front, The [1976] (86) 502
Full Moon in Paris (85) 208
Funny Farm (84) 484

Gabriela [1983] (85) 213
Gallipoli [1980] (82) 179
Gandhi (83) 183
Garbo Talks (85) 520
Garde à vue [1981] (83) 189
Gay Divorcée, The [1934] (82) 2
Get Crazy (84) 484
Ghare Bhaire. *See* Home and the World,
  The.
Ghost Story (82) 183
Ghostbusters (85) 219
Gift, The (84) 484
Giornata speciale, Una. *See* Special Day, A.
Girl with the Red Hair, The (84) 484
Give My Regards to Broad Street (85) 520
Goat, The [1981] (86) 444
Gods Must Be Crazy, The [1980] (85) 224
Godzilla 1985 (86) 444
Going Berserk (84) 484

TITLE INDEX

Golden Seal, The   (84) 485
Gone with the Wind [1939]   (82) 28; (83) 19
Good Bye Cruel World   (85) 520
Good Marriage, A. *See* Beau Mariage, Le.
Goodbye, New York   (86) 444
Goonies, The   (86) 176
Gorky Park   (84) 162
Gospel   (85) 520
Gotcha!   (86) 444
Grace Quigley   (86) 444
Grandview, U.S.A.   (85) 520
Grease 2   (83) 422
Great Muppet Caper, The   (82) 183
Gregory's Girl [1981]   (83) 193
Gremlins   (85) 230
Grey Fox, The   (84) 168
Greystoke   (85) 236
Gringo   (86) 445
Guerre du feu, La. *See* Quest for Fire.
Guest, The   (85) 520
Guy Named Joe, A [1943]   (82) 435
Gwendoline [1983]   (85) 521
Gymkata   (86) 445

Hadley's Rebellion   (85) 521
Hail Mary   (86) 182
Halloween III   (83) 422
Hammett   (84) 174
Hanky Panky   (83) 422
Hanna K.   (84) 177
Hard to Hold   (85) 521
Hard Traveling   (86) 445
Hard Way, The [1942]   (85) 555
Hardbodies   (85) 521
Harriet Craig [1950]   (85) 30
Harry and Son   (85) 521
Hatchet Man, The [1932]   (83) 447
Heads or Tails [1980]   (84) 485
Heart Like a Wheel   (84) 182
Heart of a Stag   (85) 522
Heartaches [1981]   (83) 197
Heartbreaker   (84) 485
Heartland   (82) 191
Heat and Dust [1982]   (84) 187; (85) 15
Heat of Desire [1981]   (85) 522
Heatwave   (84) 485
Heaven Help Us   (86) 445
Heavenly Bodies   (85) 522
Heavenly Kid, The   (86) 445
Heaven's Gate   (82) 195
Hecate [1982]   (85) 522
Heller Wahn. *See* Sheer Madness.
Henry IV [1983]   (86) 446
Hercules   (84) 485
Hercules II   (86) 446
Here Come the Littles   (86) 446
High Road to China   (84) 486

History Is Made at Night [1937]   (84) 542
Hit, The   (86) 446
H. M. Pulham, Esq. [1941]   (82) 439
Holcroft Covenant, The   (86) 446
Holiday [1938]   (86) 15
Holiday Inn [1942]   (82) 443
Holy Innocents, The   (86) 447
Hombre [1967]   (84) 547
Home and the World, The [1984]   (86) 447
Home Free All   (85) 522
Homework [1979]   (83) 422
Hondo [1953]   (83) 452
Honky Tonk Freeway   (82) 199
Honkytonk Man   (83) 200
Honorable Mr. Wong, The. *See* Hatchet Man, The.
Horse of Pride, The   (86) 447
Hot Dog . . . The Movie   (85) 522
Hotel New Hampshire, The   (85) 243
Hound of the Baskervilles, The [1978]   (82) 203
House Where Evil Dwells, The   (83) 423
Householder, The   (85) 12
Howling, The   (82) 207
Humongous   (83) 423
Hunger, The   (84) 486
Hunters of the Golden Cobra, The [1982]   (85) 523

I Know Where I'm Going [1945]   (83) 456
I Love You   (83) 423
I Married a Shadow   (84) 486
I Ought to Be in Pictures   (83) 423
I Remember Mama [1948]   (82) 10
I Sent a Letter to My Love [1980]   (82) 214
I, the Jury   (83) 423
Ice Pirates, The   (85) 523
Iceman   (85) 248
If You Could See What I Hear   (83) 423
I'm Dancing as Fast as I Can   (83) 423
I'm No Angel [1933]   (85) 561
Imperative [1982]   (86) 447
Impulse   (85) 523
In Our Hands   (84) 486
Inchon   (83) 424
Incubus, The [1980]   (83) 424
Indiana Jones and the Temple of Doom   (85) 253
Insignificance   (86) 447
Into the Night   (86) 186
Invasion of the Body Snatchers [1956]   (83) 33, 35
Invasion U.S.A.   (86) 447
Invitation au voyage [1982]   (84) 486
Invitation to the Dance [1956]   (86) 8, 9, 507
Irreconcilable Differences   (85) 523
It Happened One Night [1934]   (83) 3

5

It Happened Tomorrow [1944]   (84) 552
It's a Wonderful Life [1946]   (83) 4, 8, 12

Jagged Edge   (86) 190
J'ai épousé une ombre. *See* I Married a
    Shadow.
James Joyce's Women   (86) 193
Jaws 3-D   (84) 486
Jazzman   (85) 523
Je tu il elle [1974]   (86) 447
Je vous salue, Marie. *See* Hail Mary.
Jeanne Dielman, 23 Quai du Commerce,
    1080 Bruxelles [1976]   (82) 44
Jekyll and Hyde . . . Together Again   (83)
    424
Jewel of the Nile, The   (86) 448
Jigsaw Man, The [1983]   (85) 524
Jimmy the Kid   (84) 486
Jinxed   (83) 206
Joey   (86) 448
Johnny Dangerously   (85) 524
Joke of Destiny, A [1983]   (85) 259
Joshua Then and Now   (86) 198
Journey into Fear [1943]   (86) 511
Journey of Natty Gann, The   (86) 203
Joy of Sex   (85) 524
Joysticks   (84) 487
Jument vapeur, La. *See* Dirty Dishes.
Just One of the Guys   (86) 448
Just the Way You Are   (85) 524

Karate Kid, The   (85) 264
Keep, The   (84) 487
Kerouac, the Movie   (86) 448
Key Exchange   (86) 448
Kid Colter   (86) 449
Killing Fields, The   (85) 270
Killpoint   (85) 524
King David   (86) 449
King Kong [1933]   (82) 20
King of Comedy, The   (84) 192
King of Jazz [1930]   (86) 515
King Solomon's Mines   (86) 449
Kipperbang [1983]   (85) 524
Kiss Me Goodbye   (83) 209
Kiss of the Spider Woman   (86) 209
Kitty and the Bagman [1982]   (84) 487
Klynham Summer   (84) 487
Koyaanisqatsi   (84) 197
Krull   (84) 487
Krush Groove   (86) 449

Lady Sings the Blues [1972]   (85) 565
Ladyhawke   (86) 214
Lassiter   (85) 524
Last American Virgin, The   (83) 424
Last Hunter, The   (85) 525

Last Starfighter, The   (85) 277
Late Chrysanthemums [1954]   (86) 449
Legend of Billie Jean, The   (86) 450
Let's Spend the Night Together   (84) 487
Lianna   (84) 201
Liar's Moon   (83) 424
Life and Times of Judge Roy Bean, The
    [1972]   (84) 7, 509
Lifeforce   (86) 450
Light Ahead, The [1939]   (83) 460
Lili Marleen   (82) 222
Lily in Love   (86) 450
Liquid Sky   (84) 487
Little Drummer Girl, The   (85) 525
Little Jerk [1984]   (86) 450
Little Sex, A   (83) 424
Little Women [1933]   (83) 18
Local Hero   (84) 206
Lola [1981]   (83) 215
Lone Wolf McQuade   (84) 488
Lonely Guy, The   (85) 525
Lonely Hearts [1982]   (84) 212
Lonely Lady, The   (84) 488
Long Good Friday, The [1980]   (83) 220
Long Gray Line, The [1955]   (82) 447
Lookin' to Get Out   (83) 424
Lords of Discipline, The   (84) 488
Losin' It   (84) 488
Lost in America   (86) 219
Lost Moment, The [1947]   (83) 465
Louis Bluie   (86) 450
Loulou [1980]   (82) 226
Love Child   (83) 425
Love in Germany, A [1983]   (85) 283
Love Letters   (85) 288
Love Streams   (85) 293
Loveless, The   (85) 525
Lovelines   (85) 525
Loves of a Blonde [1965]   (86) 23, 24
Lovesick   (84) 488
Lust in the Dust   (86) 450

Macaroni   (86) 451
MacArthur's Children   (86) 451
Maccheroni. *See* Macaroni.
Macomber Affair, The [1947]   (83) 20
Mad Max Beyond Thunderdome   (86) 223
Madman   (84) 488
Make Way for Tomorrow [1937]   (82) 30
Making Love   (83) 425
Making the Grade   (85) 526
Makioka Sisters, The [1983]   (86) 451
Maltese Falcon, The [1941]   (84) 4, 506
Man from Snowy River, The   (83) 425
Man Hunt [1941]   (85) 570
Man of Iron   (82) 230
Man of Marble [1977]   (82) 234

Man Who Fell to Earth, The [1975]   (83) 469

Man Who Loved Women, The   (84) 218

Man Who Wasn't There, The   (84) 488

Man Who Would Be King, The [1975] (84) 5

Man with One Red Shoe, The   (86) 451

Man with Two Brains, The   (84) 223

Man, Woman and Child   (84) 489

Maria's Lovers   (86) 451

Marie   (86) 227

Marvin & Tige   (84) 489

Mask   (86) 231

Mass Appeal   (85) 303

Matter of Struggle, A   (86) 451

Max Dugan Returns   (84) 228

Maxie   (86) 452

Me and My Gal [1932]   (83) 17

Mean Season, The   (86) 452

Meatballs Part II   (85) 526

Meet John Doe [1941]   (83) 3, 8, 14

Megaforce   (83) 425

Melvin and Howard [1980]   (82) 453

Mephisto   (82) 237

Merry Christmas, Mr. Lawrence   (84) 231

Metalstorm   (84) 489

Micki & Maude   (85) 308

Midsummer Night's Sex Comedy, A   (83) 228

Mike's Murder   (85) 526

Mikey and Nicky [1976]   (85) 576

Miracle Woman, The [1931]   (83) 473

Mischief   (86) 452

Misfits, The [1961]   (84) 5, 507

Mishima   (86) 236

Mrs. Soffel   (85) 314

Missing   (83) 232

Missing in Action   (85) 526

Missing in Action 2   (86) 452

Mission, The   (84) 489

Missionary, The   (83) 233

Mr. Deeds Goes to Town [1936]   (83) 3

Mr. Mom   (84) 489

Mr. Smith Goes to Washington [1930] (83) 3

Misunderstood   (85) 526

Mixed Blood   (86) 452

Modern Romance   (82) 241

Mommie Dearest   (82) 245

Monsignor   (83) 425

Montenegro   (82) 250

Monty Python's The Meaning of Life   (84) 489

Moon in the Gutter   (84) 490

Moonlighting   (83) 237

Moriarty. See Sherlock Holmes.

Morons from Outer Space   (86) 452

Mort de Mario Ricci, La. See Death of Mario Ricci, The.

Moscow on the Hudson   (85) 321

Most Dangerous Game, The [1932]   (86) 519

Mother Lode   (84) 490

Mothering Heart, The [1913]   (85) 4

Movers and Shakers   (86) 453

Moving Violations   (86) 453

Muppets Take Manhattan, The   (85) 526

Murphy's Romance   (86) 242

Mutiny on the Bounty [1962]   (85) 581

My Best Friend's Girl [1983]   (85) 326

My Cousin Rachel [1952]   (82) 458

My Dinner with André   (82) 255

My Favorite Year   (83) 241

My First Wife   (86) 453

My Foolish Heart [1949]   (84) 13

My New Partner [1984]   (86) 246

My Other Husband   (86) 453

My Reputation [1946]   (85) 586

My Science Project   (86) 453

My Tutor   (84) 490

Napoleon [1927]   (82) 461

Nate and Hayes   (84) 236

National Lampoon's Class Reunion   (83) 425

National Lampoon's European Vacation   (86) 453

National Lampoon's Vacation   (84) 241

Natural, The   (85) 329

Neil Simon's The Slugger's Wife   (86) 454

Nell Gwyn [1934]   (84) 24, 26, 557

Never Cry Wolf   (84) 247

Never Say Never Again   (84) 252

Neverending Story, The   (85) 527

New Babylon, The [1929]   (84) 561

New Kids, The   (86) 454

New York, New York [1977]   (84) 567

Next Stop, Greenwich Village [1976]   (85) 592

Next Year if All Goes Well   (84) 490

Night Crossing   (83) 426

Night in Heaven, A   (84) 490

Night of the Comet   (85) 527

Night of the Hunter, The [1955]   (83) 30

Night of the Iguana, The [1964]   (84) 6

Night of the Shooting Stars, The [1982]   (84) 258

Night Patrol   (86) 454

Night Shift   (83) 426

Night Song [1947]   (82) 10

Nighthawks   (82) 259

Nightmare on Elm Street, A   (85) 527

Nightmare on Elm Street, Part 2, A   (86) 454

Nightmares   (84) 490
9 Deaths of the Ninja   (86) 454
1918   (86) 454
1984   (85) 335
1990   (84) 491
No Small Affair   (85) 527
Norte, El   (84) 265
North Star, The [1943]   (83) 476
Nostalghia. *See* Nostalgia.
Nostalgia [1983]   (85) 340
Not for Publication   (85) 527
Notte di San Lorenzo, La. *See* Night of the Shooting Stars, The.
Nuit de Varennes, La [1982]   (84) 270; (85) 21
Nuits de la pleine lune, Les. *See* Full Moon in Paris.

Oasis, The   (85) 528
Oberst Redl. *See* Colonel Redl.
Octopussy   (84) 276
Odd Man Out [1947]   (86) 30
Oedipus Rex [1967]   (85) 528
Of Unknown Origin   (84) 491
Officer and a Gentleman, An   (83) 246
Official Story, The   (86) 249
Oh God, You Devil   (85) 528
O'Hara's Wife   (83) 426
On Golden Pond   (82) 29, 263
On the Town [1949]   (86) 6
Once Bitten   (86) 455
Once upon a Time in America   (85) 345
One Flew Over the Cuckoo's Nest [1975]   (86) 24, 26
One from the Heart   (83) 250
One Magic Christmas   (86) 455
Only Emptiness Remains   (86) 455
Only When I Laugh   (82) 268
Ordeal by Innocence [1984]   (86) 455
Orphans of the Storm   (85) 8
Osterman Weekend, The   (84) 491
Otac Na Sluzbenom Putu. *See* When Father Was Away on Business.
Our Relations [1936]   (86) 523
Out of Africa   (86) 255
Out of Control   (86) 455
Out of Order   (86) 455
Outland   (82) 272
Outsiders, The   (84) 282
Oxford, Blues   (85) 528

Pale Rider   (86) 261
Paradise   (83) 426
Parasite   (83) 426
Paris, Texas   (85) 359
Parsifal   (84) 491
Partners   (83) 426

Party Animal   (86) 455
Passage to India, A   (85) 365
Passion [1982]   (84) 289
Passion d'amore   (85) 22
Patsy, The   (86) 456
Pauline à la plage. *See* Pauline at the Beach.
Pauline at the Beach [1982]   (84) 296
Pee-wee's Big Adventure   (86) 265
Penitentiary II   (83) 427
Pennies from Heaven   (82) 276
Perfect   (86) 456
Peril   (86) 456
Peril en la demeure. *See* Peril.
Personal Best   (83) 254
Personals, The   (84) 491
Pete Kelly's Blues [1955]   (83) 481
Peter Ibbetson [1935]   (86) 527
Petit Con. *See* Little Jerk.
Petite Bande, Le [1982]   (85) 528
Phar Lap   (85) 528
Philadelphia Experiment, The   (85) 529
Piaf [1980]   (83) 427
Pigs and Pearls. *See* Montenegro.
Pile ou face. *See* Heads or Tails.
Pink Floyd the Wall [1981]   (83) 258
Pirate, The [1948]   (86) 5
Pirate Movie, The   (83) 427
Pirates of Penzance, The   (84) 301
Pixote [1980]   (82) 280
Places in the Heart   (85) 371
Play Misty for Me [1971]   (86) 532
Plenty   (86) 271
Plouffe, Les   (86) 456
Ploughman's Lunch, The [1983]   (85) 377
Police Academy   (85) 529
Police Academy 2   (86) 276
Poltergeist   (83) 263
Pope of Greenwich Village, The   (85) 529
Porky's   (83) 267
Porky's II   (84) 491
Postman Always Rings Twice, The   (82) 32, 284
Power, The   (85) 529
Prenom, Carmen. *See* First Name, Carmen.
Pretty Baby [1978]   (85) 597
Priest of Love   (82) 288
Prince of the City   (82) 292
Private Function, A [1984]   (86) 280
Private School   (84) 491
Private Worlds [1935]   (83) 18, 19
Prizzi's Honor   (86) 285
Protocol   (85) 383
Psycho [1960]   (82) 38
Psycho II   (84) 307
Puberty Blues [1981]   (84) 492
Pumping Iron II   (86) 456
Puppies [1957]   (86) 21, 22

Purple Haze   (84) 492
Purple Hearts   (85) 529
Purple Rain   (85) 389
Purple Rose of Cairo, The   (86) 290

Quartet   (82) 296
Querelle [1982]   (84) 313
Quest for Fire   (83) 271
Question of Silence, A   (85) 530
Quiet Earth, The   (86) 295
Quiet Man, The [1952]   (82) 47

Racing with the Moon   (85) 397
Raggedy Man   (82) 300
Ragtime   (82) 304
Raiders of the Lost Ark   (82) 26, 308
Rainbow Brite and the Star Stealer   (86) 456
Rainy Day Friends   (86) 457
Rambo: First Blood Part II   (86) 299
Ran   (86) 304
Rappin'   (86) 457
Rasputin [1975]   (86) 457
Razorback [1984]   (86) 457
Razor's Edge, The   (85) 402
Real Genius   (86) 309
Re-Animator   (86) 457
Reckless   (85) 530
Red Dawn   (85) 530
Red Sonja   (86) 457
Redl Ezredes. See Colonel Redl.
Reds   (82) 29, 312
Remo Williams   (86) 457
Rent Control   (85) 530
Repo Man   (85) 408
Retour de Martin Guerre, Le. See Return of
   Martin Guerre, The.
Return of Martin Guerre, The   (84) 318
Return of the Jedi   (84) 326
Return of the Living Dead, The   (86) 314
Return of the Secaucus 7 [1980]   (83) 484
Return of the Soldier, The [1982]   (84) 332
Return to Oz   (86) 458
Reuben, Reuben   (84) 337
Revenge of the Nerds   (85) 530
Revenge of the Ninja   (84) 492
Revolution   (86) 458
Rhinestone   (85) 531
Rich and Famous   (82) 33, 316
Richard Pryor Here and Now   (84) 492
Richard's Things   (82) 321
Riddle of the Sands, The [1979]   (85) 531
Right Stuff, The   (84) 342
Riot in Cell Block 11 [1954]   (83) 33, 36, 38
Ripoux, Les. See My New Partner.
Risky Business   (84) 349
River, The   (85) 416
River Rat, The   (85) 531

Road Warrior, The [1981]   (83) 277
Rocky III   (83) 283
Rocky IV   (86) 319
Romancing the Stone   (85) 421
Romantic Comedy   (84) 492
Rough Cut [1981]   (83) 34
Roughly Speaking [1945]   (83) 94
Royal Wedding [1951]   (86) 536
Rumble Fish   (84) 492
Runaway Train   (86) 324
Running Brave   (84) 354
Running Hot   (85) 531
Rustler's Rhapsody   (86) 458

Sahara   (85) 531
St. Elmo's Fire   (86) 330
Sam's Son   (85) 531
Santa Claus   (86) 334
Sauve qui peut (La Vie). See Every Man for
   Himself.
Savage Island   (86) 458
Savannah Smiles   (84) 492
Scandalous   (85) 532
Scarface   (84) 361
Scarlet Letter, The [1927]   (83) 28; (85) 602
Scarlet Street [1946]   (83) 19
Scherzo del destino agguato dietro l'angelo
   come un brigante di strada. See Joke of
   Destiny, A.
School Spirit   (86) 458
Sea Wolves, The [1981]   (83) 427
Second Thoughts   (84) 493
Secret Admirer   (86) 459
Secret Life of Walter Mitty, The [1947]   (86)
   540
Secret of NIMH, The   (83) 288
Secret of the Sword, The   (86) 459
Secret Places [1984]   (86) 459
Secrets   (85) 532
Seduction, The   (83) 427
Sender, The   (83) 427
Sense of Freedom, A   (86) 459
Sesame Street Presents: Follow That
   Bird   (86) 459
Seto uchi shonen yakyudan. See MacArthur's
   Children.
Sharky's Machine   (82) 324
Sheena   (85) 532
Sheer Madness [1983]   (86) 459
Sherlock Holmes [1922]   (83) 494
Shoah   (86) 339
Shoot the Moon   (83) 295
Shooting Party, The [1984]   (86) 27, 28, 334
Shootist, The [1976]   (83) 38
Siberiade [1977]   (83) 299
Sign of the Cross, The [1932]   (85) 607
Silent Madness   (85) 532

Silent Night, Deadly Night   (85) 532
Silent Rage   (83) 428
Silkwood   (84) 367
Silver City [1984]   (86) 460
Silverado   (86) 339
Singin' in the Rain [1952]   (86) 6, 7, 8
Six Pack   (83) 428
Six Weeks   (83) 428
Sixteen Candles   (85) 532
Sixty Glorious Years [1938]   (84) 26
Ski Country   (85) 533
Skyline   (85) 533
Slap Shot [1977]   (82) 467
Slapstick   (85) 533
Slayground [1983]   (85) 533
Smash Palace [1981]   (83) 302
Smithereens   (83) 307; (86) 33, 34, 35
Smokey and the Bandit—Part 3   (84) 493
Smooth Talk   (86) 354
Smurfs and the Magic Flute, The   (84) 493
Snows of Kilimanjaro, The [1952]   (83) 498
S.O.B.   (82) 33, 328
Softly Softly [1984]   (86) 460
Soldier, The   (83) 428
Soldier's Story, A   (85) 427
Solid Gold Cadillac, The [1956]   (85) 615
Some Kind of Hero   (83) 428
Something Wicked This Way Comes   (84) 493
Songwriter   (85) 533
Sophie's Choice   (83) 311
Sotto Sotto. See Softly Softly.
Sound Barrier, The [1952]   (85) 621
Southern Comfort   (82) 35, 332
Spacehunter   (84) 493
Special Day, A   (85) 20
Specter of the Rose [1946]   (83) 504
Spies like Us   (86) 360
Splash   (85) 434
Split Image   (83) 317
Spring Break   (84) 493
Stand der Dinge, Der. See State of Things, The.
Star Chamber, The   (84) 494
Star 80   (84) 374
Star Is Born, A [1954]   (84) 573; (86) 30, 31
Star Trek II—The Wrath of Khan   (83) 321
Star Trek III—The Search for Spock   (85) 439
Starchaser   (86) 460
Stardust Memories [1980]   (85) 626
Starman   (85) 445
Starstruck   (83) 428
State of Things, The   (84) 379
Staying Alive   (84) 386
Stephen King's Cat's Eye   (86) 460

Stephen King's Children of the Corn   (85) 534
Stephen King's Silver Bullet   (86) 460
Stick   (86) 460
Still of the Night   (83) 326
Sting II, The   (84) 494
Stitches   (86) 461
Stone Boy, The   (85) 450
Stop Making Sense   (85) 534
Strange Brew   (84) 494
Strange Invaders   (84) 494
Stranger Is Watching, A   (83) 429
Stranger than Paradise   (85) 455
Stranger's Kiss   (85) 534
Streamers   (84) 391
Streets of Fire   (85) 534
Streetwalkin'   (86) 461
Streetwise   (86) 364
Stripes   (82) 336
Stroker Ace   (84) 494
Stryker   (84) 494
Stuff, The   (86) 461
Suburbia   (85) 534
Subway   (86) 461
Sudden Death   (86) 461
Sudden Impact   (84) 395
Sugar Cane Alley [1983]   (85) 461
Sugarbaby   (86) 461
Summer Lovers   (83) 429
Summer Rental   (86) 462
Summer Stock [1950]   (86) 6
Sunday in the Country, A   (85) 466
Supergirl   (85) 535
Superman II   (82) 339
Superman III   (84) 399
Sure Thing, The   (86) 369
Surf II   (85) 535
Survivors, The   (84) 495
Swamp Thing, The   (83) 429
Swann in Love   (85) 471
Sweet Dreams   (86) 374
Sweet Sixteen   (85) 535
Swing Shift   (85) 535
Sword and the Sorcerer, The   (83) 429
Sylvester   (86) 462
Sylvia   (86) 462

Table for Five   (84) 404
Tag   (83) 429
Take a Letter, Darling [1942]   (85) 632
Taking Off [1971]   (86) 25, 545
Tales of Ordinary Madness   (84) 495
Tank   (85) 535
Taps   (82) 343
Target   (86) 462
Taxi to the Toilet. See Taxi Zum Klo.
Taxi Zum Klo   (82) 346

Teachers (85) 535
Teen Wolf (86) 462
Tempest (83) 331
Tender Mercies (84) 409
Terminator, The (85) 478
Terms of Endearment (84) 414
Tess [1980] (82) 471
Test of Love (86) 462
Testament (84) 420
Tex (83) 335
That Championship Season (83) 338
That Sinking Feeling [1979] (85) 536
That Was Then . . . This Is Now (86) 463
They All Laughed (82) 31, 350
They Call Me Bruce (83) 429
They Drive by Night [1940] (83) 508
They Live by Night (82) 42
They Might Be Giants [1971] (83) 515
They're Playing with Fire (85) 536
Thief (82) 356
Thief of Hearts (85) 536
Thing, The (83) 343
Things Are Tough All Over (83) 429
This Is Elvis (82) 360
This Is Spinal Tap (85) 484
Three Brothers [1980] (83) 349
Threshold (84) 495
THX 1138 [1971] (85) 638
Tightrope (85) 489
Time After Time [1979] (84) 579
Time Bandits [1980] (82) 364
Time Machine, The [1960] (84) 585
Timerider (84) 495
To Be or Not to Be (84) 426
To Begin Again. See Volver a empezar.
To Live and Die in L.A. (86) 379
Tokyo-Ga (86) 463
Tomboy (86) 463
Tomorrow [1972] (84) 589
Too Hot to Handle [1938] (84) 596
Too Scared to Scream (86) 463
Tootsie (83) 353
Top Secret (85) 536
Torajiro Kamone Uta. See Foster Daddy,
   Tora!
Torn Curtain [1966] (85) 644
Tough Enough (84) 495
Toy, The (83) 358
Toy Soldiers (85) 536
Trace, The [1983] (85) 537
Trade Winds [1939] (83) 18
Trading Places (84) 430
Tragedia di un umo riducolo. See Tragedy of
   a Ridiculous Man.
Tragedy of a Ridiculous Man [1981] (83)
   361
Trail of the Pink Panther (83) 430

Trancers (86) 463
Transylvania 6-5000 (86) 463
Traviata, La (83) 366
Tre fratelli. See Three Brothers.
Treasure of the Four Crowns (84) 496
Treasure of the Sierra Madre, The
   [1948] (84) 4, 7
Trenchcoat (84) 496
Trip to Bountiful, A [1953] (83) 29
Trip to Bountiful, The (86) 383
TRON (83) 371
Trouble in Mind (86) 388
Trout, The [1982] (84) 496
True Confessions (82) 368
True Heart Susie [1919] (85) 5
Truite, La. See Trout, The.
Tuff Turf (86) 464
Turk 182 (86) 464
Turtle Diary (86) 464
28 Up [1984] (86) 392
Twice in a Lifetime (86) 397
Twice upon a Time (84) 496
Twilight Zone—The Movie (84) 435
Two of a Kind (84) 496
2010 (85) 494

Uncommon Valor (84) 496
Under Fire (84) 441
Under Suspicion. See Garde à vue.
Under the Volcano (84) 8; (85) 499
Unfaithful, The [1947] (86) 550
Unfaithfully Yours (85) 537
Unfinished Piece for Piano Player, An
   [1977] (83) 430
Until September (85) 537
Up the Creek (85) 537
Utu [1983] (85) 504

Valentina [1982] (84) 496
Valley Girl (84) 447
Venom [1981] (83) 430
Verdict, The [1946] (83) 35
Verdict, The (83) 377
Veronika Voss (83) 382
Vice Squad (83) 430
Victim [1961] (85) 649
Victor/Victoria (83) 387
Victory (82) 374
Videodrome (84) 452
Vie continue, La [1981] (83) 430
Vierde Man, De. See 4th Man, The.
View to a Kill, A (86) 402
Vision Quest (86) 464
Visiting Hours (83) 431
Volunteers (86) 464
Volver a empezar (83) 393
Vulture, The (86) 464

Wagner   (84) 497
Waiting for Gavrilov [1982]   (84) 497
Waitress   (83) 431
Waltz Across Texas   (84) 497
War and Love   (86) 465
WarGames   (84) 458
Warning Sign   (86) 465
Water and Soap   (86) 465
Waterloo Bridge [1940]   (82) 46
Wavelength   (84) 497
Way Down East [1920]   (85) 7
Way We Were, The [1973]   (82) 474
We All Loved Each Other So Much   (85) 20
We of the Never Never [1982]   (84) 497
We're No Angels [1954]   (83) 21
Wedding, A [1978]   (83) 31
Weekend Pass   (85) 537
Weird Science   (86) 465
Wetherby   (86) 406
When Father Was Away on Business
   [1984]   (86) 411
When Nature Calls   (86) 465
Where the Boys Are '84   (85) 537
Where the Green Ants Dream [1984]   (86)
   465
White Nights   (86) 416
White Rose, The   (84) 497
White Sister, The [1923]   (83) 26
Whose Life Is It, Anyway?   (82) 378
Wicked Lady, The   (84) 498
Wicker Man, The [1974]   (86) 555
Wild Duck, The [1983]   (86) 466
Wild Geese II   (86) 466
Wild Horses [1983]   (85) 538
Wild Life, The   (85) 538
Wind, The [1928]   (85) 9

Windy City   (85) 538
Winter of Our Dreams [1981]   (83) 431
Without a Trace   (84) 498
Witness   (86) 416
Wo Die Gruenen Ameisen Traeumen. *See*
   Where the Green Ants Dream.
Wolfen   (82) 382
Woman in Flames, A [1983]   (85) 538
Woman in Red, The   (85) 538
Woman in the Window, The [1944]   (83) 19
Woman Next Door, The   (82) 385
Woman on the Beach, The [1947]   (83) 519
Wombling Free [1979]   (85) 538
World According to Garp, The   (83) 397
World of Henry Orient, The [1964]   (84) 600
Wrong Is Right   (83) 403

Xica [1976]   (83) 407
Xica da Silva. *See* Xica.

Year of Living Dangerously, The
   [1982]   (84) 462
Year of the Dragon   (86) 426
Yellowbeard   (84) 498
Yentl   (84) 468
Yes, Giorgio   (83) 431
Yol   (83) 411
Yor   (84) 498
Young Dr. Kildare [1938]   (86) 16
Young Doctors in Love   (83) 431
Young Sherlock Holmes   (86) 431

Zappa   (85) 539
Zapped!   (83) 431
Zelig   (84) 473
Zoot Suit   (82) 389

DIRECTOR INDEX

AARON, PAUL
  Deadly Force   (84) 482
  Maxie   (86) 452
ABRAHAMS, JIM
  Top Secret   (85) 536
ACKEREN, ROBERT VAN
  Woman in Flames, A   (85) 538
ADLON, PERCY
  Céleste [1981]   (83) 104
  Sugarbaby   (86) 461
AKERMAN, CHANTAL
  Je tu il elle   (86) 447
ALDA, ALAN
  Four Seasons, The   (82) 171
ALDRICH, ROBERT
  Apache [1954]   (82) 395
  Flight of the Phoenix, The [1966]   (85) 549
  "Obituaries"   (84) 607
ALEXANDROV, GRIGORI
  "Obituaries"   (84) 608
ALLEN, WOODY
  Broadway Danny Rose   (85) 112
  Midsummer Night's Sex Comedy, A   (83) 228
  Purple Rose of Cairo, The   (86) 290
  Stardust Memories [1980]   (85) 626
  Zelig   (84) 473
ALSTON, EMMETT
  9 Deaths of the Ninja   (86) 454
ALTMAN, ROBERT
  Brewster McCloud [1970]   (86) 484
  Come Back to the 5 & Dime Jimmy Dean, Jimmy
    Dean   (83) 120
  Fool for Love   (86) 172
  "Interview with Lillian Gish, An"   (83) 31
  Streamers   (84) 391
  Wedding, A [1978]   (83) 31
ALUES, JOE
  Jaws 3-D   (84) 486
AMAR, DENIS
  Patsy, The   (86) 456
AMATEAU, ROD
  Lovelines   (85) 525
ANDERSON, JOHN MURRAY
  King of Jazz [1930]   (86) 515
ANDERSON, LINDSAY
  Brittania Hospital   (84) 480
ANNAKIN, KEN
  Pirate Movie, The   (83) 427
ANNAUD, JEAN-JACQUES
  Quest for Fire   (83) 271
ANTHONY, JOSEPH
  Tomorrow [1972]   (84) 589
ANTONELLI, JOHN
  Kerouac, the Movie   (86) 448
APTED, MICHAEL
  Agatha [1979]   (83) 435
  Bring on the Night   (86) 439
  Continental Divide   (82) 115
  Firstborn   (85) 519
  Gorky Park   (84) 162
  Kipperbang [1983]   (85) 524
  28 Up [1984]   (86) 392

ARAGON, MANUEL GUTIERREZ
  Demons in the Garden [1982]   (85) 517
ARKUSH, ALAN
  Get Crazy   (84) 484
ARMSTRONG, GILLIAN
  Mrs. Soffel   (85) 314
  Starstruck   (83) 428
ARNOLD, JACK
  Creature from the Black Lagoon, The
    [1954]   (82) 422
ASHBY, HAL
  Let's Spend the Night Together   (84) 487
  Lookin' to Get Out   (83) 425
  Neil Simon's The Slugger's Wife   (86) 454
ASHER, WILLIAM
  Movers and Shakers   (86) 453
ATTENBOROUGH, RICHARD
  Chorus Line, A   (86) 91
  Gandhi   (83) 183
ATTIAS, DANIEL
  Stephen King's Silver Bullet   (86) 460
AUGUST, BILLIE
  Zappa   (85) 539
AUZINS, IGOR
  We of the Never Never [1982]   (84) 497
AVEDIS, HOWARD
  They're Playing with Fire   (85) 536
AVERBACK, HY
  Where the Boys Are '84   (85) 537
AVILDSEN, JOHN
  Karate Kid, The   (85) 264
  Night in Heaven, A   (84) 490
AVILDSEN, THOMAS K.
  Things Are Tough All Over   (83) 430

BABENCO, HECTOR
  Kiss of the Spider Woman   (86) 209
  Pixote [1980]   (82) 280
BADAT, RANDALL
  Surf II   (85) 535
BADHAM, JOHN
  American Flyers   (86) 436
  Blue Thunder   (84) 84
  WarGames   (84) 458
  Whose Life Is It Anyway?   (82) 378
BAILEY, PATRICK
  Door to Door   (85) 518
BAKER, GRAHAM
  Impulse   (85) 523
BAKSHI, RALPH
  American Pop   (82) 62
  Fire and Ice   (84) 153
BALDI, FERDINANDO
  Treasure of the Four Crowns   (84) 495
BALLARD, CARROLL
  Never Cry Wolf   (84) 247
BAND, CHARLES
  Metalstorm   (84) 489
  Parasite   (83) 426
  Trancers   (86) 463

13

BARRETO, BRUNO
Gabriela [1983]   (85) 213
BARRON, STEVE
Electric Dreams   (85) 518
BARRON, ZELDA
Secret Places [1984]   (86) 459
BARTEL, PAUL
Eating Raoul   (83) 420
Lust in the Dust   (86) 450
Not for Publication   (85) 527
BARTMAN, WILLIAM S.
O'Hara's Wife   (83) 426
BARTON, CHARLES T.
"Obituaries"   (82) 478
BARWOOD, HAL
Warning Sign   (86) 465
BASSOFF, LAWRENCE
Weekend Pass   (85) 537
BEAIRD, DAVID
Party Animal   (86) 455
BEARDSLY, NICHOLAS
Savage Island   (86) 458
BEATTY, WARREN
Reds   (82) 312
BECKER, HAROLD
Taps   (82) 343
Vision Quest   (86) 464
BEDFORD, TERRY
Slayground [1983]   (85) 533
BEINEIX, JEAN-JACQUES
Diva [1980]   (83) 147
Moon in the Gutter, The   (84) 490
BELL, MARTIN
Streetwise   (86) 364
BELLOCCHIO, MARCO
Henry IV [1983]   (86) 446
BELSON, JERRY
Jekyll and Hyde . . . Together Again   (83) 424
BENJAMIN, RICHARD
City Heat   (85) 141
My Favorite Year   (83) 241
Racing with the Moon   (85) 397
BENTON, ROBERT
Places in the Heart   (85) 371
Still of the Night   (83) 326
BERAUD, LUC
Heat of Desire [1981]   (85) 522
BERESFORD, BRUCE
King David   (86) 449
Puberty Blues [1981]   (84) 492
Tender Mercies   (84) 409
BERGMAN, INGMAR
After the Rehearsal   (85) 52
Fanny and Alexander [1982]   (84) 146
BERKELEY, BUSBY
"Life Achievement Award"   (86) 2
BERMAN, TED
Black Cauldron, The   (86) 75
BERNHARDT, CURTIS
My Reputation [1946]   (85) 586
"Obituaries"   (82) 479
BERNSTEIN, ARMYAN
Windy City   (85) 538
BERTOLUCCI, BERNARDO
Tragedy of a Ridiculous Man [1981]   (83) 361

BESHEARS, JAMES
Homework   (83) 422
BESSIE, DAN
Hard Traveling   (86) 445
BESSON, LUC
Dernier Combat, Le [1983]   (85) 517
Subway   (86) 461
BETANCOR, ANTONIO JOSE
Valentina [1982]   (84) 496
BETUEL, JONATHAN
My Science Project   (86) 453
BIGELOW, KATHRYN
Loveless, The   (85) 525
BILL, TONY
Six Weeks   (83) 428
BILSON, BRUCE
Chattanooga Choo Choo   (85) 515
BIRCH, PATRICIA
Grease 2   (83) 422
BIRD, STEWART
Home Free All   (85) 522
BLACK, NOEL
Private School   (84) 491
BLIER, BERTRAND
Beau Pere   (82) 78
My Best Friend's Girl [1983]   (85) 326
BLUTH, DON
Secret of NIMH, The   (83) 288
BOGART, PAUL
Oh God, You Devil   (85) 528
BOGDANOVICH, PETER
Mask   (86) 231
They All Laughed   (82) 350
BOORMAN, JOHN
Emerald Fores , The   (86) 156
Excalibur   (82) 350
BORIS, ROBERT
Oxford Blues   (85) 528
BORSOS, PHILIP
Grey Fox, The   (84) 168
Mean Season, The   (86) 452
One Magic Christmas   (86) 455
BORZAGE, FRANK
History Is Made at Night [1937]   (84) 542
BOULTING, JOHN
"Obituaries"   (86) 561
BOWERS, GEORGE
Body and Soul   (83) 418
My Tutor   (84) 490
BRABIN, CHARLES
Bridge of San Luis Rey, The [1929]   (82) 408
BRAHM, JOHN
"Obituaries"   (83) 528
BRANDON, THOMAS
"Obituaries"   (83) 528
BREELEY, GIL
Test of Love   (86) 462
BRESSON, ROBERT
Argent, L' [1983]   (85) 74
BREST, MARTIN
Beverly Hills Cop   (85) 88
BRICKMAN, MARSHALL
Lovesick   (84) 488

DIRECTOR INDEX

BRICKMAN, PAUL
  Risky Business   (84) 349
BRIDGES, ALAN
  Return of the Soldier, The [1982]   (84) 332
  Shooting Party, The [1984]   (86) 344
BRIDGES, JAMES
  Mike's Murder   (85) 526
  Perfect   (86) 456
BROOKS, ADAM
  Almost You   (86) 436
BROOKS, ALBERT
  Lost in America   (86) 219
  Modern Romance   (82) 241
BROOKS, JAMES L.
  Terms of Endearment   (84) 414
BROOKS, RICHARD
  Fever Pitch   (86) 443
  Wrong Is Right   (83) 403
BURROWS, JAMES
  Partners   (83) 427
BURTON, TIM
  Pee-wee's Big Adventure   (86) 265
BUTE, MARY ELLEN
  "Obituaries"   (84) 612
BUTLER, GEORGE
  Pumping Iron II   (86) 456
BUTLER, ROBERT
  Up the Creek   (85) 537
BUÑUEL, JOYCE
  Dirty Dishes [1978]   (84) 482
BUÑUEL, LUIS
  "Obituaries"   (84) 611
BYRUM, JOHN
  Razor's Edge, The   (85) 402

CAIN, CHRISTOPHER
  Stone Boy, The   (85) 450
  That Was Then . . . This Is Now   (86) 464
CAMERON, JAMES
  Terminator, The   (85) 478
CAMUS, MARCEL
  "Obituaries"   (83) 529
CAMUS, MARIO
  Holy Innocents, The   (86) 446
CAPRA, FRANK
  "Interview with Fay Wray, An"   (82) 19
  "Life Achievement Award"   (83) 1
  Miracle Woman, The [1931]   (83) 473
CARLE, GILLES
  Plouffe, Les   (86) 456
CARLINO, LEWIS JOHN
  Class   (84) 480
CARPENTER, JOHN
  "American Cinema in 1981, The"   (82) 35
  Christine   (84) 106
  Dark Star [1975]   (86) 494
  Escape from New York   (82) 133
  Starman   (85) 445
  Thing, The   (83) 343
CARPENTER, STEPHEN
  Power, The   (85) 529
CARPI, FABIO
  Basileus Quartet   (85) 511
CARVANA, HUGO
  Bar Esperanza [1983]   (86) 437

CARVER, STEVE
  Lone Wolf McQuade   (84) 488
CASARIL, GUY
  Piaf [1980]   (83) 427
CASSAVETES, JOHN
  Love Streams   (85) 293
CASTELLANI, RENATO
  "Obituaries"   (86) 564
CASTELLAR, ENZO G.
  1990   (84) 491
CASTLE, NICK
  Last Starfighter, The   (85) 277
  Tag   (83) 429
CAVALCANTI, ALBERTO
  "Obituaries"   (83) 529
CHABROL, CLAUDE
  Horse of Pride, The   (86) 447
CHAPMAN, MATTHEW
  Stranger's Kiss   (85) 534
CHAPMAN, MICHAEL
  All the Right Moves   (84) 41
CHOMSKY, MARVIN
  Tank   (85) 535
CHONG, THOMAS
  Cheech and Chong Still Smokin'   (84) 480
  Cheech and Chong's The Corsican
    Brothers   (85) 515
CHOPRA, JOYCE
  Smooth Talk   (86) 354
CHRISTIAN, ROGER
  Sender, The   (83) 427
CIAMPI, YVES
  "Obituaries"   (83) 530
CIMINO, MICHAEL
  "American Cinema in 1981, The"   (82) 24
  Heaven's Gate   (82) 195
  Year of the Dragon   (86) 426
CLAIR, RENÉ
  It Happened Tomrrow [1944]   (84) 552
  "Obituaries"   (82) 483
CLARK, BOB
  Christmas Story, A   (84) 110
  Porky's   (83) 267
  Porky's II   (84) 491
  Rhinestone   (85) 531
  Turk 182   (86) 464
CLARK, GREYDON
  Joysticks   (84) 487
CLARK, RON
  Funny Farm   (84) 484
CLAYTON, JACK
  Something Wicked This Way Comes   (84) 493
CLEMENT, DICK
  Bullshot [1983]   (86) 439
CLIFFORD, GRAEME
  Frances   (83) 178
CLOUSE, ROBERT
  Deadly Eyes   (84) 482
  Gymkata   (86) 445
COATES, LEWIS
  Hercules   (84) 485
COEN, JOEL
  Blood Simple   (86) 438
COHEN, LARRY
  Stuff, The   (86) 461

COHEN, NORMAN
"Obituaries" (84) 614
COHEN, ROB
Scandalous (85) 532
COKLISS, HARLEY
Battletruck (83) 417
COLLINSON, PETER
Earthling, The [1980] (82) 130
COLOMO, FERNANDO
Skyline (85) 533
CONNOR, KEVIN
House Where Evil Dwells, The (83) 423
CONWAY, JACK
Too Hot to Handle [1938] (84) 596
COOLIDGE, MARTHA
City Girl, The (85) 516
Joy of Sex (85) 524
Real Genius (86) 309
Valley Girl (84) 447
COOPER, THOMAS
"Obituaries" (83) 530
COPPOLA, FRANCIS
Cotton Club, The (85) 150
One from the Heart (83) 250
Outsiders, The (84) 282
Rumble Fish (84) 492
COSCARELLI, DON
Beastmaster, The (83) 418
COSMATOS, GEORGE PAN
Of Unknown Origin (84) 491
Rambo: First Blood Part II (86) 299
COSTA-GAVRAS, CONSTANTIN
Hanna K. (84) 17
Missing (83) 232
COX, ALEX
Repo Man (85) 408
COX, PAUL
Lonely Hearts [1982] (84) 212
My First Wife (86) 453
COZZI, LUIGI
Hercules II (86) 446
CRAVEN, WES
Nightmare on Elm Street, A (85) 527
Swamp Thing (83) 429
CREEK, DOUGLAS
C.H.U.D. (85) 515
CROMBIE, DONALD
Caddie [1976] (83) 439
Kitty and the Bagman [1982] (84) 487
CRONENBERG, DAVID
Dead Zone, The (84) 481
Videodrome (84) 452
CROSLAND, ALAN
Beloved Rogue [1927] (84) 522
CUKOR, GEORGE
"American Cinema in 1981, The" (82) 33
Gone with the Wind [1939] (83) 17
"Interview with James Mason, An" (86) 30, 31
"Interview with Joan Bennett, An" (83) 16
Little Women [1933] (83) 18
"Obituaries" (84) 615
Rich and Famous (82) 316
Star Is Born, A [1954] (84) 573
CUNNINGHAM, SEAN S.
New Kids, The (86) 454
Spring Break (84) 494
Stranger Is Watching, A (83) 429

CURTIZ, MICHAEL
Roughly Speaking [1945] (83) 490
DALVA, ROBERT
Black Stallion Returns, The (84) 479
DAMIANI, DAMIANO
Amityville II (83) 417
DAMSKI, MEL
Mischief (86) 452
Yellowbeard (84) 498
DANE, LAWRENCE
Heavenly Bodies (85) 522
DANIEL, ROD
Teen Wolf (86) 462
DANTE, JOE
Explorers (86) 442
Gremlins (85) 230
Howling, The (82) 207
Twilight Zone—The Movie (84) 435
DAVES, DELMER
Cowboy [1958] (82) 417
DAVIDSON, BOAZ
Last American Virgin, The (83) 424
DAVIDSON, MARTIN
Eddie and the Cruisers (84) 483
DAVIS, ANDY
Code of Silence (86) 440
DAVIS, DESMOND
Clash of the Titans (82) 111
Ordeal by Innocence [1984] (86) 455
DAVIS, ROBIN
I Married a Shadow (84) 486
DAWSON, ANTHONY M.
Hunters of the Golden Cobra, The [1982] (85) 523
Last Hunter, The (85) 525
Yor (84) 498
DAY, ERNEST
Waltz Across Texas (84) 497
DEAR, WILLIAM
Timerider (84) 495
DEARDEN, BASIL
Victim [1961] (85) 649
DE CORDOVA, FREDERICK
Bedtime for Bonzo [1951] (84) 512
DE FILIPPO, EDUARDO
"Obituaries" (85) 662
DE GASTYNE, MARC
"Obituaries" (83) 531
DELUCA, RUDY
Transylvania 6-5000 (86) 463
DEMBO, RICHARD
Dangerous Moves [1984] (86) 129
DE MILLE, CECIL B.
Sign of the Cross, The [1932] (85) 607
DEMME, JONATHAN
Stop Making Sense (85) 534
Swing Shift (85) 535
DEMME, JONATHAN
Melvin and Howard [1980] (82) 453
DEMORO, PIERRE
Savannah Smiles (84) 493
DENHAM, REGINALD
"Obituaries" (84) 619

DIRECTOR INDEX

DEPALMA, BRIAN
  "American Cinema in 1981, The"   (82) 37
  Blow Out   (82) 83
  Body Double   (85) 513
  Scarface   (84) 361
DE POLIGNY, SERGE
  "Obituaries"   (84) 619
DEREK, JOHN
  Bolero   (85) 513
  Fantasies   (83) 421
DESCHANEL, CALEB
  Escape Artist, The   (83) 421
DEVENISH, ROSS
  Guest, The   (85) 520
DEVILLE, MICHEL
  Peril   (86) 456
  Petite Bande, La [1982]   (85) 528
DEYRIES, BERNARD
  Here Come the Littles   (86) 446
  Rainbow Brite and the Star Stealer   (86) 456
DICKINSON, THOROLD
  "Obituaries"   (85) 663
DIEGUES, CARLOS
  Xica [1976]   (83) 407
DINNER, MICHAEL
  Heaven Help Us   (86) 445
DONALDSON, ROGER
  Bounty, The   (85) 513
  Marie   (86) 227
  Smash Palace [1981]   (83) 302
DONEN, STANLEY
  Blame It on Rio   (85) 512
  "Life Achievement Award"   (86) 2, 3, 4, 6, 7, 8
  Royal Wedding [1951]   (86) 536
DONNER, RICHARD
  Goonies, The   (86) 176
  Ladyhawke   (86) 214
  Toy, The   (83) 58
DONOHUE, JACK
  "Obituaries"   (85) 663
DONOVAN, PAUL
  Def-Con 4   (86) 441
DONSKOI, MARK
  "Obituaries"   (82) 484
DRAGOTI, STAN
  Man with One Red Shoe, The   (86) 451
  Mr. Mom   (84) 489
DUFFELL, PETER
  Experience Preferred . . . but Not Essential
    [1982]   (84) 141
DUIGAN, JOHN
  Winter of Our Dreams [1981]   (83) 431
DUVALL, ROBERT
  Angelo My Love   (84) 47
DWAN, ALLAN
  "Obituaries"   (82) 485

EASTWOOD, CLINT
  Firefox   (83) 160
  Honkytonk Man   (83) 200
  Pale Rider   (86) 261
  Play Misty for Me [1971]   (86) 532
  Sudden Impact   (84) 395
EBERHARDT, THOM
  Night of the Comet   (85) 527

EDEL, ULRICH
  Christine F. [1981]   (83) 419
EDWARDS, BLAKE
  "American Cinema in 1981, The"   (82) 33
  Curse of the Pink Panther   (84) 481
  Man Who Loved Women, The   (84) 218
  Micki & Maude   (85) 308
  S.O.B.   (82) 328
  Trail of the Pink Panther   (83) 430
  Victor / Victoria   (83) 387
EDWARDS, HILTON
  "Obituaries"   (83) 532
ELLISON, JOSEPH
  Joey   (86) 448
ENRICO, ROBERT
  Heads or Tails [1980]   (84) 485
EPSTEIN, MARCELO
  Body Rock   (85) 513
ESPER, DWAIN
  "Obituaries"   (82) 532
EUSTACHE, JEAN
  "Obituaries"   (83) 532
EVERETT, D. S.
  Running Brave   (84) 354
EYRE, RICHARD
  Ploughman's Lunch, The [1983]   (85) 377

FAIRFAX, FERDINAND
  Nate and Hayes   (84) 236
FANAKA, JAMAA
  Penitentiary II   (83) 427
FARGO, JAMES
  Forced Vengeance   (83) 422
FARROW, JOHN
  Hondo [1953]   (83) 452
FASSBINDER, RAINER WERNER
  Berlin Alexanderplatz [1980]   (84) 57
  Lili Marleen   (82) 222
  Lola [1981]   (83) 215
  "Obituaries"   (83) 532
  Querelle [1982]   (84) 313
  Veronika Voss   (83) 382
FAVRE, BERNARD
  Trace, The [1983]   (85) 537
FELLINI, FEDERICO
  And the Ship Sails On [1983]   (85) 69
  City of Women   (82) 106
  "Interview with Ettore Scola, An"   (85) 22
FERRERI, MARCO
  Tales of Ordinary Madness   (84) 495
FINKLEMAN, KEN
  Airplane II   (83) 417
FIRSTENBERG, SAM
  American Ninja   (86) 436
  Breakin 2   (85) 514
  Revenge of the Ninja   (84) 492
FIRTH, MICHAEL
  Heart of a Stag   (85) 522
  Sylvia   (86) 462
FISHER, DAVID
  Liar's Moon   (83) 424
  Toy Soldiers   (85) 536
FISK, JACK
  Raggedy Man   (82) 300
FLEISCHER, RICHARD
  Amityville 3-D   (84) 479
  Conan the Destroyer   (85) 516

Red Sonja   (86) 457
Tough Enough   (84) 495
FLEMING, VICTOR
  Guy Named Joe, A [1943]   (82) 435
FLORIO, MARIA
  Broken Rainbow   (86) 439
FOLEY, JAMES
  Reckless   (85) 530
FORD, JOHN
  Fort Apache [1948]   (84) 530
  Long Gray Line, The [1955]   (82) 447
  "Modern Cinema and Silent Cinema"   (82) 47
FORDE, WALTER
  "Obituaries"   (85) 666
FORMAN, MILOŠ
  Amadeus   (85) 63
  "Interview with, An"   (86) 1
  Ragtime   (82) 304
  Taking Off [1971]   (86) 545
FORSYTH, BILL
  Comfort and Joy   (85) 146
  Gregory's Girl [1981]   (83) 193
  Local Hero   (84) 206
  That Sinking Feeling [1979]   (85) 536
FOSSE, BOB
  Star 80   (84) 374
FOSTER, NORMAN
  Journey into Fear [1943]   (86) 511
FRANCIS, FREDDIE
  Doctor and the Devils, The   (86) 442
FRANCIS, KARL
  And Nothing but the Truth   (85) 510
FRANKENHEIMER, JOHN
  Challenge, The   (83) 109
  Holcroft Covenant, The   (86) 446
FRANKLIN, RICHARD
  Cloak and Dagger   (85) 516
  Psycho II   (84) 307
FRANKLIN, SIDNEY
  Dulcy [1923]   (82) 432
FRAWLEY, JAMES
  Fraternity Vacation   (86) 444
FREARS, STEPHEN
  Hit, The   (86) 446
FREED, HERB
  Tomboy   (86) 463
FREEMAN, JOAN
  Streetwalkin'   (86) 461
FRICKE, RON
  Chronos   (86) 440
FRIEDKIN, WILLIAM
  Deal of the Century   (84) 482
  To Live and Die in L.A.   (86) 379
FRIEDMAN, ED
  Secret of the Sword, The   (86) 459
FULCI, LUCIO
  Black Cat, The   (85) 512
FURIE, SIDNEY J.
  Entity, The   (84) 483
  Lady Sings the Blues [1972]   (85) 565
  Purple Hearts   (85) 529

GABEL, MARTIN
  Lost Moment, The [1947]   (83) 465
GABOR, PAL
  Brady's Escape   (85) 514

GAGE, GEORGE
  Fleshburn   (85) 519
GANCE, ABEL
  Napoleon [1927]   (82) 461
  "Obituaries"   (82) 487
GARCI, JOSÉ LUIS
  Volver a empezar   (83) 393
GARNETT, TONY
  Deep in the Heart   (85) 517
GASSMAN, VITTORIO
  "Interview with Ettore Scola, An"   (85) 19
GIANNONE, JOE
  Madman   (84) 488
GILBERT, LEWIS
  Educating Rita   (84) 136
GILLARD, STUART
  Paradise   (83) 426
GILLIAM, TERRY
  Brazil   (86) 80
  Time Bandits [1980]   (82) 364
GILLING, JOHN
  "Obituaries"   (85) 669
GIROD, FRANCIS
  Bon Plaisir, Le [1983]   (85) 513
GLEN, JOHN
  For Your Eyes Only   (82) 155
  Octopussy   (84) 276
  View to a Kill, A   (86) 402
GLICKENHAUS, JAMES
  Soldier, The   (83) 428
GODARD, JEAN-LUC
  Detective   (86) 442
  Every Man for Himself [1979]   (82) 139
  First Name, Carmen [1983]   (85) 186
  Hail Mary   (86) 182
  "Modern Cinema and Silent Cinema"   (82) 45
  Passion [1982]   (84) 289
GOLAN, MENAHEM
  Enter the Ninja   (83) 420
GOLDSTEIN, SCOTT
  Flanagan   (86) 443
GORDON, STEVE
  Arthur   (82) 71
  "Obituaries"   (83) 536
GORDON, STUART
  Re-Animator   (86) 457
GÖREN, SERIF
  Yol   (83) 411
GORETTA, CLAUDE
  Death of Mario Ricci, The [1983]   (86) 133
GORRIS, MARLEEN
  Question of Silence, A   (85) 530
GOTTLIEB, LISA
  Just One of the Guys   (86) 448
GRANIER-DEFERRE, PIERRE
  Étoile du nord, L'   (84) 484
GRAY, MIKE
  Wavelength   (84) 497
GREEN, ALFRED E.
  Disraeli [1929]   (82) 426
GREENAWAY, PETER
  Draughtsman's Contract, The [1982]   (84) 126
GREENE, SPARKY
  Oasis, The   (85) 528

GREENWALT, DAVID
Secret Admirer (86) 459
GRIFFITH, D. W.
Birth of a Nation, The [1915] (83) 25
"Interview with Lillian Gish, An" (83) 24
"Life Achievement Award" (85) 1
GRIFFITH, EDWARD A.
Animal Kingdom, The [1932] (86) 469
GRIFFITHS, MARK
Hardbodies (85) 521
Running Hot (85) 531
GROSBARD, ULU
Falling in Love (85) 519
True Confessions (82) 368
GRUYAERT, JAN
Flaxfield, The [1983] (86) 443
GUERRA, RUY
Erendira [1983] (85) 181
GUILLERMIN, JOHN
Sheena (85) 532
GÜNEY, YILMAL
"Obituaries" (85) 670
GUTTMAN, AMOS
Drifting (85) 518
GYLLENHAAL, STEPHEN
Certain Fury (86) 440

HACKFORD, TAYLOR
Against All Odds (85) 509
Officer and a Gentleman, An (83) 246
White Nights (86) 416
HAGGARD, PIERS
Venom [1981] (83) 430
HAHN, STEVEN
Starchaser (86) 460
HAMILTON, GUY
Evil Under the Sun [1981] (83) 421
Remo Williams (86) 457
HAND, DAVID
Bambi [1942] (85) 543
HANSON, CURTIS
Losin' It (84) 488
HARDY, ROBIN
Wicker Man, The [1974] (86) 555
HARE, DAVID
Wetherby (86) 406
HARRIS, FRANK
Killpoint (85) 524
HARRISON, KEN
1918 (86) 454
HART, DEREK
Backstage at the Kirov (85) 511
HARVEY, ANTHONY
Grace Quigley (86) 444
Richard's Things (82) 321
They Might Be Giants [1971] (83) 515
HARVEY, JOAN
Matter of Struggle, A (86) 451
HASHIMOTO, KOHJI
Godzilla 1985 (86) 444
HATHAWAY, HENRY
"Obituaries" (86) 569
Peter Ibbetson [1935] (86) 527

HAWKS, HOWARD
Barbary Coast [1935] (84) 506
Come and Get It [1936] (82) 412
HAYDN, RICHARD
"Obituaries" (86) 570
HECHT, BEN
Specter of the Rose [1946] (83) 504
HECKERLING, AMY
Fast Times at Ridgemont High (83) 156
Johnny Dangerously (85) 524
National Lampoon's European Vacation (86) 453
HEFFRON, RICHARD T.
I, the Jury (83) 423
HENSON, JIM
Dark Crystal, The (83) 130
Great Muppet Caper, The (82) 187
HERZ, MICHAEL
Waitress (83) 431
HERZFELD, JOHN
Two of a Kind (84) 496
HERZOG, WERNER
Fitzcarraldo (83) 167
Where the Green Ants Dream [1984] (86) 465
HESTON, CHARLTON
Mother Lode (84) 490
HIGGINS, COLIN
Best Little Whorehouse in Texas, The (83) 72
HILL, GEORGE ROY
Little Drummer Girl, The (85) 525
Slap Shot [1977] (82) 467
World According to Garp, The (83) 397
World of Henry Orient, The [1964] (84) 600
HILL, WALTER
"American Cinema in 1981, The" (82) 35
Brewster's Millions (86) 438
48 HRS. (83) 173
Southern Comfort (82) 332
Streets of Fire (85) 534
HILLER, ARTHUR
Author
Lonely Guy, The (85) 525
Making Love (83) 425
Romantic Comedy (84) 492
Teachers (85) 535
HITCHCOCK, ALFRED
Torn Curtain [1966] (85) 644
HODGES, MIKE
Morons from Outer Space (86) 452
HOFSISS, JACK
I'm Dancing as Fast as I Can (83) 423
HOLLAND, SAVAGE STEVE
Better Off Dead (86) 438
HOLLAND, TOM
Fright Night (86) 444
HOLLEG, ALAN
School Spirit (86) 458
HOLZMAN, ALLAN
Forbidden World (83) 421
Out of Control (86) 455
HONG, ELLIOTT
They Call Me Bruce (83) 429
HOOL, LANCE
Missing in Action 2 (86) 452

HOOPER, TOBE
Lifeforce (86) 450
Poltergeist (83) 263
HOUGH, JOHN
Incubus, The [1980] (83) 424
HOWARD, RON
Cocoon (86) 96
Night Shift (83) 426
Splash (85) 434
HUBERT, JEAN-LOUP
Next Year if All Goes Well (84) 490
HUDSON, HUGH
Chariots of Fire (82) 101
Greystoke (85) 236
Revolution (86) 458
HUGHES, JOHN
Breakfast Club, The (86) 85
Sixteen Candles (85) 532
Weird Science (86) 465
HUMBERSTONE, H. BRUCE (LUCKY)
"Obituaries" (85) 673
HUNT, PETER
Wild Geese II (86) 466
HUNTER, TIM
Sylvester (86) 462
Tex (83) 335
HUSTON, JOHN
Annie (83) 56
Freud [1962] (84) 535
"Life Achievement Award" (84) 1
Prizzi's Honor (86) 285
Under the Volcano (85) 499
Victory (82) 374
HUTTON, BRIAN G.
High Road to China (84) 486
HUYCK, WILLARD
Best Defense (85) 512
HYAMS, PETER
Outland (82) 272
Star Chamber, The (84) 494
2010 (85) 494

ICHASO, LEON
Crossover Dreams (86) 441
ICHIKAWA, KON
Makioka Sisters, The [1983] (86) 451
IMHOOF, MARKUS
Boat Is Full, The [1981] (83) 82
IRVIN, JOHN
Champions (85) 515
Ghost Story (82) 183
Turtle Diary (86) 464
IRVING, DAVID
Good Bye Cruel World (85) 520
ISRAEL, NEAL
Bachelor Party (85) 511
Moving Violations (86) 453
IVORY, JAMES
Bostonians, The (85) 105
Heat and Dust [1982] (84) 187
"Interview with, An" (85) 11
Quartet (82) 296

JABOR, ARNALDO
I Love You (83) 423
JAECKLIN, JUST
Gwendoline [1983] (85) 521

JAFFE, STANLEY R.
Without a Trace (84) 498
JAGLOM, HENRY
Always (86) 60
Can She Bake a Cherry Pie? (84) 95
JARMUSCH, JIM
Stranger than Paradise (85) 455
JARROTT, CHARLES
Amateur, The (83) 417
JEFFRIES, LIONEL
Wombling Free [1979] (85) 538
JEWISON, NORMAN
Agnes of God (86) 56
Best Friends (83) 68
Soldier's Story, A (85) 427
JOFFE, ROLAND
Killing Fields, The (85) 270
JOHNSON, ALAN
To Be or Not to Be (84) 426
JOHNSON, LAMONT
Cattle Annie and Little Britches (82) 97
Spacehunter (84) 493
JONES, AMY
Love Letters (85) 288
JONES, DAVID
Betrayal (84) 67
JONES, TERRY
Monty Python's The Meaning of Life (84) 489
JORDAN, GLENN
Mass Appeal (85) 303
Only When I Laugh (82) 268
JORDAN, NEIL
Company of Wolves, The [1984] (86) 115
Danny Boy (85) 517
JORDON, GLENN
Buddy System, The (85) 514
JUTRA, CLAUDE
By Design (83) 419

KACHIVAS, LOU
Secret of the Sword, The (86) 459
KAGAN, JEREMY PAUL
Chosen, The (83) 116
Journey of Natty Gann, The (86) 203
Sting II, The (84) 494
KANEW, JEFF
Eddie Macon's Run (84) 483
Gotcha! (86) 444
Revenge of the Nerds (85) 530
KAPLAN, JONATHAN
Heart Like a Wheel (84) 182
KASDAN, LAWRENCE
Big Chill, The (84) 78
Body Heat (82) 87
Silverado (86) 349
KAST, PIERRE
"Obituaries" (85) 675
KAUFMAN, CHARLES
When Nature Calls (86) 465
KAUFMAN, PHILIP
Right Stuff, The (84) 342
KAZAN, ELIA
Arrangement, The [1969] (86) 474
KEIGHLEY, WILLIAM
"Obituaries" (85) 675

20

DIRECTOR INDEX

KELLJAN, ROBERT
"Obituaries" (83) 540
KELLMAN, BARNET
Key Exchange (86) 448
KELLY, GENE
Invitation to the Dance [1956] (86) 507
KENT, GARY
Rainy Day Friends (86) 457
KERSHNER, IRVIN
Never Say Never Again (84) 252
KIERSCH, FRITZ
Stephen King's Children of the Corn (85) 534
Tuff Turf (86) 464
KING, HENRY
"Obituaries" (83) 541
Snows of Kilimanjaro, The [1952] (83) 498
KIZER, R.J.
Godzilla 1985 (86) 444
KLEISER, RANDAL
Grandview, U.S.A. (85) 520
Summer Lovers (83) 429
KLIMOV, ELEM
Rasputin [1975] (86) 457
KOLLEK, AMOS
Goodbye, New York (86) 444
KONCHALOVSKY, ANDREI
Maria's Lovers (86) 451
Runaway Train (86) 324
KONG, JACKIE
Night Patrol (86) 454
KORTY, JOHN
Twice upon a Time (84) 496
KOSTER, HENRY
My Cousin Rachel [1952] (82) 458
KOTCHEFF, TED
First Blood (83) 164
Joshua Then and Now (86) 198
Split Image (83) 317
Uncommon Valor (84) 496
KOWALSKI, LECH
Gringo (86) 445
KOZINTSEV, GRIGORI
New Babylon, The [1929] (84) 561
KRASNA, NORMAN
"Obituaries" (85) 676
KUHN, RODOLFO
Only Emptiness Remains (86) 455
KURAHARA, KOREYOSHI
Antarctica (85) 511
KUROSAWA, AKIRA
Ran (86) 304
KURYS, DIANE
Entre nous [1983] (85) 176
KUSTURICA, EMIR
When Father Was Away on Business
[1984] (86) 411
KWAPIS, KEN
Sesame Street Presents: Follow That
Bird (86) 459
KYROU, ADONIS (ADO)
"Obituaries" (86) 573

LACHMAN, HARRY
Our Relations [1936] (86) 523

LAING, JOHN
Beyond Reasonable Doubt [1980] (84) 74
LAMAS, FERNANDO
"Obituaries" (83) 543
LAMORE, MARSH
Secret of the Sword, The (86) 459
LANDIS, JOHN
American Werewolf in London, An (82) 66
Into the Night (86) 186
Spies like Us (86) 360
Trading Places (84) 430
Twilight Zone—The Movie (84) 435
LANDON, MICHAEL
Sam's Son (85) 531
LANG, FRITZ
"Interview with Joan Bennett, An" (83) 16
Man Hunt [1941] (85) 570
Woman in the Window, The [1944] (83) 19
LANG, MICHEL
Gift, The (84) 484
LANZMANN, CLAUDE
Shoah (86) 339
LATHAN, STAN
Beat Street (85) 512
LAUGHLIN, MICHAEL
Strange Invaders (84) 494
LAUTNER, GEORGES
My Other Husband (86) 453
LAUZIER, GERARD
Little Jerk [1984] (86) 450
LEACH, WILFRED
Pirates of Penzance, The (84) 301
LEAN, DAVID
Passage to India, A (85) 365
Sound Barrier, The [1952] (85) 621
LEENHARDT, ROGER
"Obituaries" (86) 574
LEISEN, MITCHELL
Take a Letter, Darling [1942] (85) 632
LEIVICK, DAVID
Gospel (85) 520
LELOUCH, CLAUDE
Bolero [1981] (83) 418
Edith and Marcel [1983] (85) 518
LEO, MALCOLM
Beach Boys, The (86) 438
This Is Elvis (82) 360
LEONARD, ROBERT Z.
Divorcée, The [1930] (82) 429
LEONE, SERGIO
Once upon a Time in America (85) 345
LEROY, MERVYN
"Modern Cinema and Silent Cinema" (82) 46
LESTER, MARK L.
Class of 1984 (83) 419
Commando (86) 111
Firestarter (85) 519
LESTER, RICHARD
Finders Keepers (85) 519
Superman II (82) 339
Superman III (84) 399
LEVINSON, BARRY
Diner (83) 142
Natural, The (85) 329
Young Sherlock Holmes (86) 431

21

LIEBERMAN, ROBERT
Table for Five   (84) 404
LINDTBERG, LEOPOLD
"Obituaries"   (85) 679
LINSON, ART
Wild Life, The   (85) 538
LIPSTADT, AARON
Android   (85) 510
City Limits   (86) 440
LISBERGER, STEVEN
TRON   (83) 371
LITTMAN, LYNNE
Testament   (84) 420
LO BIANCO, TONY
Too Scared to Scream   (86) 463
LONCRAINE, RICHARD
Brimstone and Treacle   (83) 91
Missionary, The   (83) 233
LORD, JEAN CLAUDE
Visiting Hours   (83) 431
LOSEY, JOSEPH
"Obituaries"   (85) 680
Trout, The [1982]   (84) 496
LOWRY, DICK
Smokey and the Bandit—Part 3   (84) 493
LUCAS, GEORGE
THX 1138 [1971]   (85) 638
LUDWIG, EDWARD
"Obituaries"   (83) 543
LUMET, SIDNEY
Daniel   (84) 481
Deathtrap   (83) 137
Garbo Talks   (85) 520
Prince of the City   (82) 292
Verdict, The   (83) 377
LUSTGARTEN, STEVE
American Taboo   (85) 509
LYFORD, RICHARD H.
"Obituaries"   (86) 574
LYNCH, DAVID
Dune   (85) 171
LYNCH, PAUL
Cross Country   (84) 481
Humongous   (83) 423
LYNE, ADRIAN
Flashdance   (84) 158
LYNN, JONATHAN
Clue   (86) 440

MCBRIDE, JIM
Breathless   (84) 89
MACKENZIE, JOHN
Beyond the Limit   (84) 479
Long Good Friday, The [1980]   (83) 220
Sense of Freedom, A   (86) 459
MCLAGLEN, ANDREW V.
Sahara   (85) 531
MCLAUGHLIN, ANDREW
Sea Wolves, The [1981]   (83) 427
MCLEOD, NORMAN Z.
Secret Life of Walter Mitty, The [1947]   (86) 540
MAGNOLI, ALBERT
Purple Rain   (85) 389

MAKAVEJEV, DUSAN
Coca-Cola Kid, The   (86) 440
Montenegro   (82) 250
MAKK, KAROLY
Lily in Love   (86) 450
MALLE, LOUIS
Alamo Bay   (86) 436
Atlantic City   (82) 74
Crackers   (85) 516
My Dinner with André   (82) 255
Pretty Baby [1978]   (85) 597
MALMUTH, BRUCE
Man Who Wasn't There, The   (84) 489
Nighthawks   (82) 259
MAMOULIAN, ROUBEN
Becky Sharp [1935]   (82) 403
MANKIEWICZ, JOSEPH L.
Barefoot Contessa, The [1954]   (82) 399
MANN, DELBERT
Night Crossing   (83) 426
MANN, MICHAEL
Keep, The   (84) 487
Thief   (82) 356
MARGHERITI, ANTONIO. See DAWSON,
ANTHONY M.
MARKLE, PETER
Hot Dog . . . The Movie   (85) 522
Personals, The   (84) 491
MARQUAND, RICHARD
Eye of the Needle   (82) 148
Jagged Edge   (86) 190
Return of the Jedi   (84) 326
Until September   (85) 537
MARSHALL, GARRY
Flamingo Kid, The   (85) 192
Young Doctors in Love   (83) 431
MARTIN, FRANK
Dr. Butcher, M.D. [1980]   (83) 420
MASTERSON, PETER
Trip to Bountiful, The   (86) 383
MAY, ELAINE
Mikey and Nicky [1976]   (85) 576
MAYLAM, TONY
Riddle of the Sands, The [1979]   (85) 531
MAZURSKY, PAUL
Moscow on the Hudson   (85) 321
Next Stop, Greenwich Village [1976]   (85) 592
Tempest   (83) 331
MEDOWAY, GARY
Heavenly Kid, The   (86) 445
MELVILLE, JEAN-PIERRE
Bob le Flambeur [1955]   (84) 526
MEYER, NICHOLAS
Star Trek II—The Wrath of Khan   (83) 321
Time After Time [1979]   (84) 579
Volunteers   (86) 464
MICHAELS, RICHARD
Blue Skies Again   (84) 479
MIKHALKOV, NIKITA
Unfinished Piece for Piano Player, An
[1977]   (83) 430
MIKHALKOV-KONCHALOVSKY, ANDREY
Siberiade [1977]   (83) 299
MILES, CHRISTOPHER
Priest of Love   (82) 288

DIRECTOR INDEX

MILESTONE, LEWIS
Arch of Triumph [1948]   (84) 501
Mutiny on the Bounty [1962]   (85) 581
North Star, The [1943]   (83) 476
MILIUS, JOHN
Conan the Barbarian   (83) 419
Red Dawn   (85) 530
MILLAR, GAVIN
Dreamchild   (86) 146
Secrets   (85) 532
MILLER, CLAUDE
Garde à vue [1981]   (83) 189
MILLER, GEORGE
Aviator, The   (86) 437
Mad Max Beyond Thunderdome   (86) 223
Man from Snowy River, The   (83) 425
Road Warrior, The [1981]   (83) 277
Twilight Zone—The Movie   (84) 435
MILLER, HARVEY
Bad Medicine   (86) 437
MILLER, JASON
That Championship Season   (83) 338
MILLER, MICHAEL
National Lampoon's Class Reunion   (83) 426
Silent Rage   (83) 428
MILLER, ROBERT ELLIS
Reuben, Reuben   (84) 337
MILLER, WARREN
Ski Country   (85) 533
MINER, STEVE
Friday the 13th—Part III   (83) 422
MINNELLI, VINCENTE
Bells Are Ringing [1960]   (84) 517
"Life Achievement Award"   (86) 5, 7
"Modern Cinema and Silent Cinema"   (82) 46
MIZRAHI, MOSHE
I Sent a Letter to My Love [1980]   (82) 214
Vie Continue, La [1981]   (83) 430
War and Love   (86) 465
MOLINARO, EDOUARD
Just the Way You Are   (85) 524
MONTE, PETER DEL
Invitation au voyage [1982]   (84) 486
MONTGOMERY, MONTY
Loveless, The   (85) 525
MOORE, ROBERT
"Obituaries"   (85) 687
MORA, PHILIPPE
Beast Within, The   (83) 418
MORANIS, RICK
Strange Brew   (84) 494
MOREAU, JEANNE
Adolescente, L' [1979]   (83) 53
MORRIS, DAVID BURTON
Purple Haze   (84) 492
MORRISSEY, PAUL
Hound of the Baskervilles, The [1978]   (82) 203
Mixed Blood   (86) 452
MORSE, TERRY O.
"Obituaries"   (85) 687
MORTON, DEREK
Wild Horses [1983]   (85) 538
MOWBRAY, MALCOLM
Private Function, A [1984]   (86) 280

MUDD, VICTORIA
Broken Rainbow   (86) 439
MULCAHY, RUSSELL
Razorback [1984]   (86) 457
MULLER, EDWARD
Savage Island   (86) 458
MULLIGAN, ROBERT
Kiss Me Goodbye   (83) 209
MUNE, IAN
Came a Hot Friday   (86) 439
MURCH, WALTER
Return to Oz   (86) 458
MURNAU, F. W.
"Modern Cinema and Silent Cinema"   (82) 44
MURPHY, GEOFF
Quiet Earth, The   (86) 295
Utu [1983]   (85) 504
NARUSE, MIKIO
Flowing [1956]   (86) 444
Late Chrysanthemums [1954]   (86) 449
NATTER, DAVID
Cease Fire   (86) 440
NAVA, GREGORY
Norte, El   (84) 265
NEAME, RONALD
First Monday in October   (82) 151
NEEDHAM, HAL
Cannonball Run II   (85) 514
Megaforce   (83) 425
Stroker Ace   (84) 494
NELSON, CARY
Jimmy the Kid   (84) 486
NEWELL, MIKE
Dance with a Stranger [1984]   (86) 125
NEWMAN, PAUL
Harry and Son   (85) 521
NICHOLS, MIKE
Silkwood   (84) 367
NICOLAS, PAUL
Chained Heat   (84) 480
NIMOY, LEONARD
Star Trek III—The Search for Spock   (85) 439
NORTON, B.W. L.
Baby   (86) 437
NOYCE, PHILLIP
Heatwave   (84) 485
NUCHTERN, SIMON
Silent Madness   (85) 532
NUNEZ, VICTOR
Flash of Green, A   (86) 443
O'BANNON, DAN
Return of the Living Dead, The   (86) 314
O'BRIEN, EDMOND
"Obituaries"   (86) 577
OBROW, JEFFREY
Dorm That Dripped Blood, The   (84) 482
Power, The   (85) 529
O'CONNOR, PAT
Cal   (85) 124
OGILVIE, GEORGE
Mad Max Beyond Thunderdome   (86) 223

OLIVER, DAVID
  Cave Girl   (86) 439
O'MALLEY, DAVID
  Kid Colter   (86) 449
O'NEIL, ROBERT VINCENT
  Angel   (85) 510
  Avenging Angel   (86) 436
OSHIMA, NAGISA
  Cruel Story of Youth [1960]   (85) 517
  Merry Christmas, Mr. Lawrence   (84) 231
OZ, FRANK
  Dark Crystal, The   (83) 130
  Muppets Take Manhattan, The   (85) 526
OZU, YASIJURO
  "Modern Cinema and Silent Cinema"   (82) 43

PAKULA, ALAN J.
  Sophie's Choice   (83) 311
PAL, GEORGE
  Time Machine, The [1960]   (84) 585
PALCY, EUZHAN
  Sugar Cane Alley [1983] (85) 461
PALMER, TONY
  Wagner   (84) 497
PALMOS, EDUARDO
  Alley Cat   (85) 509
PALTROW, BRUCE
  Little Sex, A   (83) 424
PARIS, JERRY
  Police Academy 2   (86) 276
PARKER, ALAN
  Birdy   (85) 93
  Pink Floyd the Wall [1981]   (83) 258
  Shoot the Moon   (83) 295
PARKER, ALBERT
  Sherlock Holmes [1922]   (83) 494
PASOLINI, PIER PAOLO
  Oedipus Rex [1967]   (85) 528
PASSER, IVAN
  Creator   (86) 441
  Cutter's Way   (82) 119
PATEL, SHARAD
  Amin—The Rise and Fall   (84) 479
PAUL, STEVEN
  Slapstick   (85) 533
PEARCE, MICHAEL
  James Joyce's Women   (86) 193
PEARCE, PERCE
  Bambi [1942]   (85) 543
PEARCE, RICHARD
  Country   (85) 156
  Heartland   (82) 191
  Threshold   (84) 495
PECKINPAH, SAM
  "Obituaries"   (85) 688
  Osterman Weekend, The   (84) 491
PEERCE, LARRY
  Hard to Hold   (85) 521
  Love Child   (83) 425
PENN, ARTHUR
  Four Friends   (82) 167
  Target   (86) 462
PERRY, FRANK
  Compromising Positions   (86) 120

Mommie Dearest   (82) 245
Monsignor   (83) 425
PETERSEN, WOLFGANG
  Boot, Das [1981]   (83) 86
  Enemy Mine   (86) 161
  Neverending Story, The   (85) 527
PETRI, ELIO
  "Obituaries"   (83) 548
PETRIE, DANIEL
  Bad Boy, The   (86) 437
  Fort Apache, the Bronx   (82) 159
  Six Pack   (83) 428
PIALAT, MAURICE
  À Nos Amour [1983]   (85) 509
  Loulou [1980]   (82) 226
PICHEL, IRVING
  Most Dangerous Game, The [1932]   (86) 519
PILLSBURY, SAM
  Klynham Summer   (84) 487
PINOTEAU, CLAUDE
  Boum, La   (84) 480
POE, AMOS
  Alphabet City   (85) 509
POITIER, SIDNEY
  Fast Forward   (86) 442
  Hanky Panky   (83) 422
POLANSKI, ROMAN
  Tess [1980]   (82) 471
POLIDORO, GIAN L.
  Rent Control   (85) 530
POLLACK, SYDNEY
  Absence of Malice   (82) 57
  Out of Africa   (86) 255
  Tootsie   (83) 353
  Way We Were, The [1973]   (82) 474
POWELL, MICHAEL
  I Know Where I'm Going [1945]   (83) 456
PRESSBURGER, EMERIC
  I Know Where I'm Going [1945]   (83) 456
PRESSMAN, MICHAEL
  Doctor Detroit   (84) 482
  Some Kind of Hero   (83) 428
PRYOR, RICHARD
  Richard Pryor Here and Now   (84) 492
PUENZO, LUIS
  Official Story, The   (86) 249
PYUN, ALBERT
  Sword and the Sorcerer, The   (83) 429

QUINE, RICHARD
  Solid Gold Cadillac, The [1956]   (85) 615

RADFORD, MICHAEL
  Another Time, Another Place [1983]   (85) 510
  1984   (85) 335
RAFELSON, BOB
  Postman Always Rings Twice, The   (82) 284
RAFFHILL, STEWART
  Ice Pirates, The   (85) 523
  Philadelphia Experiment, The   (85) 529
RAIMI, SAM
  Evil Dead, The   (84) 484
RAMIS, HAROLD
  National Lampoon's Vacation   (84) 241

RAY, SATYAJIT
Home and the World, The [1984]   (86) 447
REED, BILL
Secret of the Sword, The   (86) 459
REED, CAROL
"Interview with James Mason, An"   (86) 30
REGGIO, GODFREY
Koyaanisqatsi   (84) 197
REINER, CARL
All of Me   (85) 58
Dead Men Don't Wear Plaid   (83) 134
Man with Two Brains, The   (84) 223
Summer Rental   (86) 462
REINER, ROB
Sure Thing, The   (86) 369
This Is Spinal Tap   (85) 484
REISZ, KAREL
French Lieutenant's Woman, The   (82) 174
Sweet Dreams   (86) 374
REITMAN, IVAN
Ghostbusters   (85) 219
Stripes   (82) 336
RENOIR, JEAN
Woman on the Beach, The [1947]   (83) 522
REYNOLDS, BURT
Sharky's Machine   (82) 324
Stick   (86) 460
REYNOLDS, KEVIN
Fandango   (86) 442
RICH, RICHARD
Black Cauldron, The   (86) 75
RICHARDS, DICK
Death Valley   (83) 419
Man, Woman and Child   (84) 489
RICHARDSON, TONY
Border, The   (83) 418
Hotel New Hampshire, The   (85) 243
RICHTER, BOB
In Our Hands   (84) 486
RICHTER, W. D.
Adventures of Buckaroo Banzai, The
(85) 47
RICKMAN, TOM
River Rat, The   (85) 531
RIPPLOH, FRANK
Taxi Zum Klo   (82) 346
RITCHIE, MICHAEL
Fletch   (86) 169
Survivors, The   (84) 495
RITT, MARTIN
Cross Creek   (84) 116
Front, The [1976]   (86) 502
Hombre [1967]   (84) 547
Murphy's Romance   (86) 242
RITZENBERG, FREDERICK A.
Gospel   (85) 520
RIVETTE, JACQUES
"Modern Cinema and Silent Cinema"   (82) 45
ROBBINS, MATTHEW
Dragonslayer   (82) 125
Legend of Billie Jean, The   (86) 450
ROCHA, GLAUBER
"Obituaries"   (82) 500
RODDAM, FRANC
Bride, The   (86) 438
Lords of Discipline, The   (84) 488

ROEG, NICOLAS
Eureka   (86) 442
Insignificance   (86) 447
Man Who Fell to Earth, The [1975]   (83) 469
ROHMER, ERIC
Beau Mariage, Le   (83) 65
Full Moon in Paris   (85) 208
Pauline at the Beach [1982]   (84) 296
ROMERO, GEORGE A.
Creepshow   (83) 419
Day of the Dead   (86) 441
ROSENBERG, STUART
Pope of Greenwich Village, The   (85) 529
ROSENTHAL, RICK
American Dreamer   (85) 509
Bad Boys   (84) 479
ROSENTHAL, ROBERT J.
Zapped!   (83) 431
ROSI, FRANCESCO
Bizet's Carmen [1983]   (85) 98
Three Brothers [1980]   (83) 349
ROSS, HERBERT
Footloose   (85) 198
I Ought to Be in Pictures   (83) 423
Max Dugan Returns   (84) 228
Pennies from Heaven   (82) 276
Protocol   (85) 383
ROTHA, PAUL
"Obituaries"   (85) 693
RUBEN, JOSEPH
Dreamscape   (85) 166
RUDOLPH, ALAN
Choose Me   (85) 135
Endangered Species   (83) 420
Songwriter   (85) 533
Trouble in Mind   (86) 388
RUGGLES, WESLEY
I'm No Angel [1933]   (85) 561
RUSSELL, KEN
Crimes of Passion   (85) 161
RUST, JOHN
Smurfs and the Magic Flute, The   (84) 493
RYDELL, MARK
On Golden Pond   (82) 263
River, The   (85) 416

SAFRAN, HENRI
Wild Duck, The [1983]   (86) 466
SAGAL, BORIS
"Obituaries"   (82) 501
SANDRICH, MARK
Holiday Inn [1942]   (82) 443
SANTELL, ALFRED
"Obituaries"   (82) 501
SANTIAGO, CIRIO H.
Caged Fury   (85) 514
Stryker   (84) 494
SARAFIAN, RICHARD C.
Bear, The   (85) 511
SARGENT, JOSEPH
Nightmares   (84) 490
SASDY, PETER
Lonely Lady, The   (84) 488
SAURA, CARLOS
Blood Wedding [1981]   (83) 418
Carmen   (84) 101

SAYLES, JOHN
Baby, It's You (84) 479
Brother from Another Planet, The (85) 118
Lianna (84) 201
Return of the Secaucus 7 [1980] (83) 484
SAYYAD, PARVIZ
Mission, The (84) 489
SCHAFFNER, FRANKLIN J.
Boys from Brazil, The [1978] (86) 480
Yes, Giorgio (83) 431
SCHATZBERG, JERRY
Misunderstood (85) 526
No Small Affair (85) 527
SCHENKEL, CARL
Out of Order (86) 455
SCHEPISI, FRED
Barbarosa (83) 60
Iceman (85) 248
Plenty (86) 271
SCHLESINGER, JOHN
Falcon and the Snowman, The (86) 165
Honky Tonk Freeway (82) 199
SCHLÖNDORFF, VOLKER
Circle of Deceit [1981] (83) 419
Swann in Love (85) 471
SCHMID, DANIEL
Hecate [1982] (85) 522
SCHMOELLER, DAVID
Seduction, The (83) 427
SCHOEDSACK, ERNEST B.
Most Dangerous Game, The [1932] (86) 519
SCHRADER, PAUL
Cat People (83) 100
Mishima (86) 236
SCHULTZ, CARL
Careful He Might Hear You [1983] (85) 130
SCHULTZ, MICHAEL
Berry Gordy's The Last Dragon (86) 438
Krush Groove (86) 449
SCHUMACHER, JOEL
D. C. Cab (84) 481
St. Elmo's Fire (86) 330
SCOLA, ETTORE
Bal, Le [1983] (85) 80
"Interview with, An" (85) 18
Macaroni (86) 451
Nuit de Varennes, La [1982] (84) 270
SCORSESE, MARTIN
After Hours (86) 51
King of Comedy, The (84) 192
New York, New York [1977] (84) 567
SCOTT, RIDLEY
Blade Runner (83) 76
SCOTT, TONY
Hunger, The (84) 486
SEASTROM, VICTOR
"Interview with Lillian Gish, An" (83) 28
Scarlet Letter, The [1927] (83) 28; (85) 602
SEIDELMAN, ARTHUR ALLAN
Echoes (84) 483
SEIDELMAN, SUSAN
Desperately Seeking Susan (86) 137
"Interview with, An" (86) 33
Smithereens (83) 307
SELLIER, CHARLES E., JR.
Silent Night, Deadly Night (85) 532

SELZNICK, ARNA
Care Bears Movie, The (86) 439
SHAKHNAZAROV, KAREN
Jazzman (85) 523
SHARP, IAN
Final Option, The (84) 484
SHEBIB, DONALD
Heartaches [1981] (83) 197
SHERMAN, GARY A.
Vice Squad (83) 430
SHERMAN, VINCENT
Hard Way, The [1942] (85) 555
"Interview with, An" (85) 25
Unfaithful, The [1947] (86) 550
SHINODA, MASAHIRO
MacArthur's Children (86) 451
SHOLDER, JACK
Nightmare on Elm Street, Part 2, A (86) 454
SHORE, SIG
Sudden Death (86) 461
SHYER, CHARLES
Irreconcilable Differences (85) 523
SIEGEL, DON
Beguiled, The [1971] (83) 37
Coogan's Bluff [1968] (83) 37
Dirty Harry [1971] (83) 37
Escape from Alcatraz [1979] (83) 33, 38
Flaming Star [1960] (83) 36
"Interview with, An" (83) 33
Invasion of the Body Snatchers [1956] (83) 33, 35
Jinxed (83) 33, 206
Riot in Cell Block 11 [1954] (83) 33, 36, 38
Shootist, The [1976] (83) 38
Verdict, The [1946] (83) 35
SIGNORELLI, JAMES
Easy Money (84) 482
SILBERG, JOEL
Breakin' (85) 514
Rappin' (86) 457
SKOLIMOWSKI, JERZY
Moonlighting (83) 237
SMALL, ADAM
Another State of Mind (85) 510
SMITHEE, ALAN
Stitches (86) 461
SOLT, ANDREW
This Is Elvis (82) 360
SPHEERIS, PENELOPE
Suburbia (85) 534
SPIELBERG, STEVEN
"American Cinema in 1981, The" (82) 26
Color Purple, The (86) 105
E.T.: The Extra-Terrestrial (83) 151
Indiana Jones and the Temple of Doom (85) 253
Raiders of the Lost Ark (82) 308
Twilight Zone—The Movie (84) 435
SPOTTISWOODE, ROGER
Under Fire (84) 441
STALLONE, SYLVESTER
Rocky III (83) 283
Rocky IV (86) 319
Staying Alive (84) 386
STEINBERG, DAVID
Going Berserk (84) 485

DIRECTOR INDEX

STERNBERG, JOSEF VON
"Interview with Fay Wray, An" (82) 19
"Modern Cinema and Silent Cinema" (82) 44
STEWART, DOUGLAS DAY
Thief of Hearts (85) 536
STORM, HOWARD
Once Bitten (86) 455
STREISAND, BARBRA
Yentl (84) 468
STRYKER, JONATHAN
Curtains (84) 481
STUART, PETER
Another State of Mind (85) 510
SUTUS, JIM
Sweet Sixteen (85) 535
SWAIM, BOB
Balance, La [1982] (84) 52
SWENSON, CHARLES
Twice upon a Time (84) 496
SYBERBERG, HANS-JUERGEN
Parsifal (84) 491
SZABÓ, ISTVÁN
Colonel Redl [1984] (86) 100
Mephisto (82) 237
SZWARC, JEANNOT
Enigma [1982] (84) 483
Santa Claus (86) 334
Supergirl (85) 535

TAFT, GENE
Blame It on the Night (85) 512
TANNEN, WILLIAM
Flashpoint (85) 519
TARKOVSKY, ANDREI
Nostalgia [1983] (85) 340
TAUROG, NORMAN
"Obituaries" (82) 504
TAVERNIER, BERTRAND
Coup de torchon [1981] (83) 124
Sunday in the Country, A (85) 466
TAVIANI, PAOLO
Night of the Shooting Stars, The [1982] (84) 258
TAVIANI, VITTORIO
Night of the Shooting Stars, The [1982] (84) 258
TEAGUE, LEWIS
Cujo (84) 481
Fighting Back (83) 421
Jewel of the Nile, The (86) 448
Stephen King's Cat's Eye (86) 460
THALBERG, IRVING G.
"Interview with Lillian Gish, An" (83) 27
THOMAS, DAVE
Strange Brew (84) 494
THOMPSON, J. LEE
Evil That Men Do, The (85) 518
King Solomon's Mines (86) 449
10 to Midnight (84) 495
TILL, ERIC
If You Could See What I Hear (83) 423
Improper Channels (82) 218
TOBACK, JAMES
Exposed (84) 484
TODOROVSKY, PYOTR
Waiting for Gavrilov [1982] (84) 497

TOWNE, ROBERT
Personal Best (83) 254
TOWNSEND, PAT
Beach Girls, The (83) 417
TRAUBE, SHEPARD
"Obituaries" (84) 640
TRAUBERG, LEONID
New Babylon, The [1929] (84) 561
TRENCHARD-SMITH, BRIAN
Escape 2000 (84) 483
TROTTA, MARGARETHE VON
Sheer Madness [1983] (86) 459
TRUFFAUT, FRANÇOIS
Confidentially Yours [1983] (85) 516
"Obituaries" (85) 695
Woman Next Door, The (82) 385
TRUMBULL, DOUGLAS
Brainstorm (84) 480
TSUKERMAN, SLAVA
Liquid Sky (84) 487
TUCHNER, MICHAEL
Trenchcoat (84) 496
TUGGLE, RICHARD
Tightrope (85) 489
TURKIEWICZ, SOPHIA
Silver City [1984] (86) 460
TURMAN, LAWRENCE
Second Thoughts (84) 493

ULMER, EDGAR G.
Detour [1946] (86) 498
Light Ahead, The [1939] (83) 460
UYS, JAMIE
Gods Must Be Crazy, The [1980] (85) 224

VALDEZ, LUIS
Zoot Suit (82) 389
VAN DEN BERG, RUDOLF
Bastille [1984] (86) 437
VAN DUSEN, BRUCE
Cold Feet (85) 516
VEBER, FRANCIS
Goat, The [1981] (86) 444
VERBONG, BEN
Girl with the Red Hair, The (84) 485
VERDONE, CARLO
Water and Soap (86) 465
VERHOEVEN, MICHAEL
White Rose, The (84) 497
VERHOEVEN, PAUL
Flesh and Blood (86) 443
4th Man, The [1983] (85) 203
VIDOR, KING
H. M. Pulham, Esq. [1941] (82) 439
"Obituaries" (83) 553
VIGNE, DANIEL
Return of Martin Guerre, The (84) 318
VON STROHEIM, ERICH
"Interview with Fay Wray, An" (82) 18

WADLEIGH, MICHAEL
Wolfen (82) 382

WAGGNER, GEORGE
"Obituaries" (85) 697
WAJDA, ANDRZEJ
Danton [1982] (84) 121
Love in Germany, A [1983] (85) 283
Man of Iron (82) 230
Man of Marble [1977] (82) 234
WALKER, DORIAN
Making the Grade (85) 526
WALLACE, TOMMY LEE
Halloween III (83) 422
WALSH, RAOUL
Colorado Territory [1949] (86) 489
They Drive by Night [1940] (83) 509
WALTERS, CHARLES
"Obituaries" (83) 554
WALTON, FRED
Hadley's Rebellion (85) 521
WANG, WAYNE
Chan Is Missing (83) 113
Dim Sum (86) 141
WANGER, WALTER
"Interview with Joan Bennett, An" (83) 16
Private Worlds [1935] (83) 18, 19
WARD, DAVID S.
Cannery Row (83) 95
WARNOW, STAN
In Our Hands (84) 486
WATSON, JOHN
Deathstalker (85) 517
WEBB, JACK
"Obituaries" (83) 555
Pete Kelly's Blues [1955] (83) 481
WEBB, PETER
Give My Regards to Broad Street (85) 520
WEIL, SAMUEL
Waitress (83) 431
WEIR, PETER
Gallipoli [1980] (82) 179
Witness (86) 421
Year of Living Dangerously, The [1982] (84)
462
WELLES, ORSON
Falstaff [1967] (83) 443
Journey into Fear [1943] (86) 511
"Obituaries" (86) 585
WELLMAN, WILLIAM A.
Hatchet Man, The [1932] (83) 447
WENCER, SIMON
Phar Lap (85) 528
WENDERS, WIM
Hammett (84) 174
Paris, Texas (85) 359
State of Things, The (84) 379
Tokyo-Ga (86) 463
WERNER, PETER
Don't Cry, It's Only Thunder (83) 420
WERTMULLER, LINA
Joke of Destiny, A [1983] (85) 259
Softly Softly [1984] (86) 459
WESTON, ERIC
Marvin & Tige (84) 489
WETZLER, GWEN
Secret of the Sword, The (86) 459

WHITE, JACK
"Obituaries" (85) 701
WIEDERHORN, KEN
Meatballs Part II (85) 526
WILCOX, HERBERT
Nell Gwyn [1934] (84) 557
WILDER, BILLY
"American Cinema in 1981, The" (82) 34
Buddy Buddy (82) 93
WILDER, GENE
Woman in Red, The (85) 538
WILSON, HUGH
Police Academy (85) 529
Rustler's Rhapsody (86) 458
WINCER, SIMON
D.A.R.Y.L. (86) 441
WINNER, MICHAEL
Death Wish II (83) 420
Death Wish III (86) 441
Wicked Lady, The (84) 497
WOLF, KONRAD
"Obituaries" (83) 556
WYLER, WILLIAM
"American Cinema in 1981, The" (82) 24
Come and Get It [1936] (82) 412
"Obituaries" (82) 507

YABUKI, KIMIO
Rainbow Brite and the Star Stealer (86) 456
YAMADA, YOJI
Foster Daddy, Tora! [1980] (82) 163
YAMAMOTO, SATSUO
"Obituaries" (84) 642
YATES, PETER
Dresser, The (84) 130
Eleni (86) 151
Krull (84) 487
YORKIN, BUD
Twice in a Lifetime (86) 397
YOSHA, YAKY
Vulture, The (86) 464
YOUNG, ROGER
Lassiter (85) 524
YOUNG, TERENCE
Inchon (83) 424
Jigsaw Man, The [1983] (85) 524

ZANUSSI, KRZYSTOF
Imperative [1982] (86) 447
ZEFFIRELLI, FRANCO
Traviata, La (83) 366
ZEMECKIS, ROBERT
Back to the Future (86) 65
Romancing the Stone (85) 421
ZIDI, CLAUDE
My New Partner [1984] (86) 246
ZIEFF, HOWARD
Unfaithfully Yours (85) 537
ZINNEMANN, FRED
Five Days One Summer (83) 421
ZITO, JOSEPH
Friday the 13th—The Final Chapter (85) 520
Invasion U.S.A. (86) 447
Missing in Action (85) 526

DIRECTOR INDEX

SCREENWRITER INDEX

ABERDEIN, KEITH
Utu [1983]   (85) 504
ADLER, FELIX
Our Relations [1936]   (86) 523
ADLON, PERCY
Céleste [1981]   (83) 104
Sugarbaby   (86) 461
AGE
Joke of Destiny, A [1983]   (85) 259
AINSLEE, MARIAN
Bridge of San Luis Rey, The [1929]   (82) 408
AKERMAN, CHANTAL
Je tu il elle [1974]   (86) 447
ALDA, ALAN
Four Seasons, The   (82) 171
ALDEN, ROBERT
Streetwalkin'   (86) 461
ALENCAR, MARTHA
Bar Esperanza [1983]   (86) 437
ALEXANDER, J. GRUBB
Hatchet Man, The [1932]   (83) 447
ALLAN, TED
Love Streams   (85) 293
ALLEN, JAY PRESSON
Deathtrap   (83) 137
Prince of the City   (82) 292
ALLEN, WOODY
Broadway Danny Rose   (85) 112
Midsummer Night's Sex Comedy, A   (83) 228
Purple Rose of Cairo, The   (86) 290
Stardust Memories [1980]   (85) 626
Zelig   (84) 473
ALSTON, EMMETT
9 Deaths of the Ninja   (86) 454
ALTMAN, ROBERT
"Interview with Lillian Gish, An"   (83) 23
Wedding, A [1978]   (83) 31
AMBROSE, DAVID
D.A.R.Y.L.   (86) 441
AMIDEI, SERGIO
Nuit de Varennes, La [1982]   (84) 270
ANHALT, EDWARD
Holcroft Covenant, The   (86) 446
ANTONELLI, JOHN
Kerouac, the Movie   (86) 448
ARCALLI, FRANCO
Once upon a Time in America   (85) 345
ARCE, MANUEL
Crossover Dreams   (86) 441
ARKIN, ADAM
Improper Channels   (82) 218
ARLEN, ALICE
Alamo Bay   (86) 436
Silkwood   (84) 367
ASAMA, YOSHITAKA
Foster Daddy, Tora! [1980]   (82) 163
ASKIN, PETER
Smithereens   (83) 307
AUDIARD, MICHEL
Garde à vue [1981]   (83) 189

AUREL, JEAN
Woman Next Door, The   (82) 385
AURENCHE, JEAN
Coup de torchon [1981]   (83) 124
AUSTIN, MICHAEL
Greystoke   (85) 236
AXELROD, GEORGE
Holcroft Covenant, The   (86) 446
AYKROYD, DAN
Ghostbusters   (85) 219
Spies like Us   (86) 360
AYRES, GERALD
Rich and Famous   (82) 316

BABENCO, HECTOR
Pixote [1980]   (82) 280
BAER, BILL
Quiet Earth, The   (86) 295
BAERE, GEOFFREY
School Spirit   (86) 458
BAKER, GRAHAM
History Is Made at Night [1937]   (84) 542
BANDEIRA, DENISE
Bar Esperanza [1983]   (86) 437
BARBERA, NEAL
Too Scared to Scream   (86) 463
BARISH, LEORA
Desperately Seeking Susan   (86) 137
BARRETO, BRUNO
Gabriela [1983]   (85) 213
BARRON, ZELDA
Secret Places [1984]   (86) 459
BARRY, JULIAN
River, The   (85) 416
BARWOOD, HAL
Dragonslayer   (82) 125
Warning Sign   (86) 465
BAYER, OSVALDO
Only Emptiness Remains   (86) 455
BEAIRD, DAVID
Party Animal   (86) 455
BEAN, HENRY
Running Brave   (84) 354
BEARDSLY, NICHOLAS
Savage Island   (86) 458
BEATTY, WARREN
Reds   (82) 312
BEHR, JACK
Birdy   (85) 93
BEINEIX, JEAN-JACQUES
Diva [1980]   (83) 147
BELLOCCHIO, MARCO
Henry IV [1983]   (86) 446
BENEDEK, TOM
Cocoon   (86) 96
BENNETT, ALAN
Private Function, A [1984]   (86) 280
BENNETT, HARVE
Star Trek III—The Search for Spock   (85) 439

31

BENTON, ROBERT
  Places in the Heart (85) 371
  Still of the Night (83) 326
BENVENUTI, LEONARD
  Once upon a Time in America (85) 345
BERCOVICI, LEONARDO
  Lost Moment, The [1947] (83) 465
BERGMAN, ANDREW
  Fletch (86) 169
BERGMAN, INGMAR
  After the Rehearsal (85) 52
  Fanny and Alexander [1982] (84) 146
BERGREN, ERIC
  Frances (83) 178
BERK, HOWARD
  Target (86) 462
BERN, PAUL
  Beloved Rogue [1927] (84) 522
BERNSTEIN, ARMYAN
  One from the Heart (83) 250
BERNSTEIN, WALTER
  Front, The [1976] (86) 502
BERRIAULT, GINA
  Stone Boy, The (85) 450
BERTOLUCCI, BERNARDO
  Tragedy of a Ridiculous Man [1981] (83) 361
BESSIE, ALVAH
  "Obituaries" (86) 561
BESSIE, DAN
  Hard Traveling (86) 445
BESSON, LUC
  Subway (86) 461
BETUEL, JONATHAN
  Last Starfighter, The (85) 277
  My Science Project (86) 453
BILSON, DANNY
  Trancers (86) 463
BING, STEVE
  Missing in Action 2 (86) 452
BINYON, CLAUDE
  Holiday Inn [1942] (82) 443
  Take a Letter, Darling [1942] (85) 632
BIRKIN, ANDREW
  King David (86) 449
BLACK, NOEL
  Mischief (86) 452
BLANKFORT, MICHAEL
  "Obituaries" (83) 526
BLAUSTEIN, BARRY
  Police Academy 2 (86) 276
BLESSING, BERT
  Jinxed (83) 206
BLIER, BERTRAND
  Beau Pere (82) 78
  My Best Friend's Girl [1983] (85) 326
BLINN, WILLIAM
  Purple Rain (85) 389
BLOOM, STEVEN L.
  Sure Thing, The (86) 369
BLUM, LEN
  Stripes (82) 336
BLUTH, DON
  Secret of NIMH, The (83) 288

BODEEN, DEWITT
  Billy Budd [1962] (82) 11
  Cat People [1942] (82) 8
  Devotion [1944] (82) 7
  Enchanted Cottage, The [1942] (82) 9
  I Remember Mama [1948] (82) 10
  "Interview with, An" (82) 6
  Night Song [1947] (82) 10
BOGDANOVICH, PETER
  They All Laughed (82) 350
BOND, JULIAN
  Shooting Party, The [1984] (86) 344
BOORMAN, JOHN
  Excalibur (82) 144
BORTHWICK, CHRIS
  Test of Love (86) 462
BORTNIK, AIDA
  Official Story, The (86) 249
BOULANGER, DANIEL
  Horse of Pride, The (86) 447
BOX, SYDNEY
  "Obituaries" (84) 610
BRACH, GERARD
  I Sent a Letter to My Love [1980] (82) 214
  Maria's Lovers (86) 451
  My Best Friend's Girl [1983] (85) 326
  Quest for Fire (83) 271
  Tess [1980] (82) 471
BREEN, RICHARD L.
  Bedtime for Bonzo [1951] (84) 512
  Pete Kelly's Blues [1955] (83) 48
BRESSON, ROBERT
  Argent, L' [1983] (85) 74
BRICKMAN, PAUL
  Risky Business (84) 349
BRIDGES, JAMES
  Perfect (86) 456
BRILEY, JOHN
  Gandhi (83) 183
  Marie (86) 227
BROOK, PETER
  Swann in Love (85) 471
BROOKS, ALBERT
  Lost in America (86) 219
  Modern Romance (82) 241
BROOKS, JAMES L.
  Terms of Endearment (84) 414
BROOKS, RICHARD
  Fever Pitch (86) 443
  Wrong Is Right (83) 403
BROWN, HARRY
  Arch of Triumph [1948] (84) 501
BROWN, LEIGH
  Christmas Story, A (84) 110
BROWN, SAM O. See EDWARDS, BLAKE.
BROWNE, EARLE
  Sherlock Holmes [1922] (83) 494
BROWNJOHN, JOHN
  Tess [1980] (82) 471
BRUNER, JAMES
  Invasion U.S.A. (86) 447
BUCHMAN, SIDNEY
  Sign of the Cross, The [1932] (85) 607
BULLUCK, VICANGELO
  Out of Control (86) 455

BUNKER, EDWARD
Runaway Train   (86) 324
BURNETT, W. R.
"Obituaries"   (83) 528
BURROWS, ABE
"Obituaries"   (86) 564
Solid Gold Cadillac, The [1956]   (85) 615
BURTON, VAL
Bedtime for Bonzo [1951]   (84) 512
BUTLER, GEORGE
Pumping Iron II   (86) 456
BUTLER, MICHAEL
Code of Silence   (86) 440
Pale Rider   (86) 261
BYRUM, JOHN
Razor's Edge, The   (85) 402

CALA, JOSEPH M.
Avenging Angel   (86) 436
CAMERON, JAMES
Rambo: First Blood Part II   (86) 299
Terminator, The   (85) 478
CANNON, DORAN WILLIAM
Brewster McCloud [1970]   (86) 484
CAPETANOS, LEON
Moscow on the Hudson   (85) 321
Tempest   (83) 331
CARLE, GILLES
Plouffe, Les   (86) 456
CARLILE, CLANCY
Honkytonk Man   (83) 200
CARNES, CHARLES ROBERT
Gymkata   (86) 445
CARPENTER, JOHN
Dark Star [1975]   (86) 494
Escape from New York   (82) 133
CARRIÈRE, JEAN-CLAUDE
Danton [1982]   (84) 121
Every Man for Himself [1979]   (82) 139
Return of Martin Guerre, The   (84) 318
Swann in Love   (85) 471
Taking Off [1971]   (86) 545
CARSON, L. M. KIT
Breathless   (84) 89
Paris, Texas   (85) 359
CARTER, ANGELA
Company of Wolves, The [1984]   (86) 115
CARVANA, HUGO
Bar Esperanza [1983]   (86) 437
CASTLE, NICK
Escape from New York   (82) 133
CERVARICH, FRANK
Kerouac, the Movie   (86) 448
CHASKIN, DAVID
Nightmare on Elm Street, Part 2, A   (86) 454
CHAYEFSKY, PADDY
"Obituaries"   (82) 482
CHOQUETTE, MICHEL
Stitches   (86) 461
CIMINO, MICHAEL
Heaven's Gate   (82) 195
Year of the Dragon   (86) 426
CLAIR, RENÉ
It Happened Tomorrow [1944]   (84) 552

CLARK, BOB
Christmas Story, A   (84) 110
Porky's   (83) 267
CLARK, BRIAN
Whose Life Is It Anyway?   (82) 378
CLARK, CHRIS
Lady Sings the Blues [1972]   (85) 565
CLARKE, JOHN
Lonely Hearts [1982]   (84) 212
CLINTON, ED
Honky Tonk Freeway   (82) 199
COEN, ETHAN
Blood Simple   (86) 438
COEN, JOEL
Blood Simple   (86) 438
COFFEE, LENORE
"Obituaries"   (85) 659
COHEN, ALBERT
"Obituaries"   (85) 660
COHEN, HOWARD R.
Rainbow Brite and the Star Stealer   (86) 456
COHEN, LARRY
Stuff, The   (86) 461
COHEN, LAWRENCE D.
Ghost Story   (82) 183
COLE, LESTER
"Obituaries"   (86) 565
COLE, TOM
Smooth Talk   (86) 354
COLLIER, CONSTANCE
Peter Ibbetson [1935]   (86) 527
COLLINS, EDMOND
Flanagan   (86) 443
COLUMBUS, CHRIS
Goonies, The   (86) 176
Gremlins   (85) 230
Young Sherlock Holmes   (86) 431
COMDEN, BETTY
Bells Are Ringing [1960]   (84) 517
CONDON, RICHARD
Prizzi's Honor   (86) 285
CONNELL, RICHARD
Our Relations [1936]   (86) 523
CONWAY, GERRY
Fire and Ice   (84) 153
COOK, PETER
Hound of the Baskervilles, The [1978]   (82) 203
COPELAND, MARTIN
Heavenly Kid, The   (86) 445
COPPOLA, FRANCIS
Cotton Club, The   (85) 150
One from the Heart   (83) 250
COSTA, ARMANDO
Bar Esperanza [1983]   (86) 437
COSTA-GAVRAS, CONSTANTIN
Hanna K.   (84) 177
Missing   (83) 232
COSTIGAN, JAMES
King David   (86) 449
COTLER, LANNY
Earthling, The [1980]   (82) 130
COTTON, JOSEPH
Journey into Fear [1943]   (86) 511
COX, ALEX
Repo Man   (85) 408

COX, PAUL
  Lonely Hearts [1982]   (84) 212
  My First Wife   (86) 453
COZZI, LUIGI
  Hercules II   (86) 446
CRAWFORD, WAYNE
  Valley Girl   (84) 447
CREELMAN, JAMES A.
  Most Dangerous Game, The [1932]   (86) 519
CRONENBERG, DAVID
  Videodrome   (84) 452
CRONIN, ISAAC
  Chan Is Missing   (83) 113
CROSS, BEVERLEY
  Clash of the Titans   (82) 111
CROWE, CAMERON
  Fast Times at Ridgemont High   (83) 156
CUCCI, FRANK
  Lily in Love   (86) 450
CUMMINGS, RUTH
  Bridge of San Luis Rey, The [1929]   (82) 408
CURTELIN, JEAN
  Patsy, The   (86) 456
CURTIN, VALERIE
  Best Friends   (83) 68

DABADIE, JEAN-LOUP
  My Other Husband   (86) 453
DAMAMME, ROSALINDE
  Peril   (86) 456
DAVID, MARJORIE
  Maria's Lovers   (86) 451
DAVIS, BILL C.
  Mass Appeal   (85) 303
DAVIS, FRANK
  Woman on the Beach, The [1947]   (83) 519
DE BERNARDI, PIERO
  Once upon a Time in America   (85) 345
DELANEY, SHELAGH
  Dance with a Stranger [1984]   (86) 125
DELUCA, RUDY
  Transylvania 6-5000   (86) 463
DEMBO, RICHARD
  Dangerous Moves [1984]   (86) 129
DE MEO, PAUL
  Trancers   (86) 463
DE NEGRI, GIULIANI G.
  Night of the Shooting Stars, The [1982]   (84) 258
DENNIS, GILL
  Return to Oz   (86) 458
DEPALMA, BRIAN
  Blow Out   (82) 83
DE PASSE, SUZANNE
  Lady Sings the Blues [1972]   (85) 565
DEROCHE, EVERETTE
  Razorback [1984]   (86) 457
DE SOUZA, STEVEN E. See SOUZA, STEVEN
  E. DE.
DEVILLE, MICHEL
  Peril   (86) 456
DIAMOND, I. A. L.
  Buddy Buddy   (82) 93

DIDION, JOAN
  True Confessions   (82) 368
DIEGUES, CARLOS
  Xica [1976]   (83) 407
DILLON, ROBERT
  Revolution   (86) 458
  River, The   (85) 416
DI PEGO, GERALD
  Sharky's Machine   (82) 324
DITILLO, LARRY
  Secret of the Sword, The   (86) 459
DOBAI, PETER
  Colonel Redl [1984]   (86) 100
  Mephisto   (82) 237
DONALDSON, ROGER
  Smash Palace [1981]   (83) 302
DONOVAN, PAUL
  Def-Con 4   (86) 441
DOS SANTOS, JOÃO FELICIO
  Xica [1976]   (83) 407
DOWD, NANCY
  Slap Shot [1977]   (82) 467
DRIEST, BURKHARD
  Querelle [1982]   (84) 313
DRIMMER, JOHN
  Iceman   (85) 248
DUNCAN, DAVID
  Time Machine, The [1960]   (84) 585
DUNNE, JOHN GREGORY
  True Confessions   (82) 368
DURAN, JORGE
  Pixote [1980]   (82) 280
DUSENBERRY, PHIL
  Natural, The   (85) 329
DUVALL, ROBERT
  Angelo My Love   (84) 47

EDMONDS, MICHAEL
  Death Wish III   (86) 441
EDWARDS, BLAKE
  City Heat   (85) 141
  Man Who Loved Women, The   (84) 218
  S.O.B.   (82) 328
  Victor/Victoria   (83) 387
EDWARDS, GEOFFREY
  Man Who Loved Women, The   (84) 218
ELLIS, BOB
  My First Wife   (86) 453
ELLIS, JEFFREY
  D.A.R.Y.L.   (86) 441
ELLISON, JOSEPH
  Joey   (86) 448
EMERSON, JOHN
  Dulcy [1923]   (82) 432
ENGEL, SAMUEL G.
  "Obituaries"   (85) 665
ENGLUND, KEN
  Secret Life of Walter Mitty, The [1947]   (86) 540
EPHRON, NORA
  Silkwood   (84) 367
EPSTEIN, JULIUS J.
  "Interview with, An"   (84) 11
  Reuben, Reuben   (84) 337

ESSEX, HARRY
Creature from the Black Lagoon, The [1954] (82) 422
ESTEVEZ, EMILIO
That Was Then . . . This Is Now (86) 463
ESTIENNE, MARIE-HELENE
Swann in Love (85) 471
ESZTERHAS, JOE
Flashdance (84)158
Jagged Edge (86) 190
EVANS, BRUCE A.
Starman (85) 445
EXTON, CLIVE
Red Sonja (86) 457
EYRE, DAVID
Cattle Annie and Little Britches (82) 97
Wolfen (82) 382

FABIANI, M.
Balance, La [1982] (84) 52
FAIRFAX, F.
Sylvia (86) 462
FAIRFAX, MARION
Sherlock Holmes [1922] (83) 494
FANCHER, HAMPTON
Blade Runner (83) 76
FARAGOH, FRANCIS EDWARD
Becky Sharp [1935] (82) 403
FARQUHAR, RALPH
Krush Groove (86) 449
FASSBINDER, RAINER WERNER
Berlin Alexanderplatz [1980] (84) 57
Lili Marleen (82) 222
Lola [1981] (83) 215
Querelle [1982] (84) 313
FELDMAN, DENNIS
Just One of the Guys (86) 448
FELLINI, FEDERICO
And the Ship Sails On [1983] (85) 69
City of Women (82) 106
FERNANDEZ, GEORGE
Cease Fire (86) 440
FERRINI, FRANCO
Once upon a Time in America (85) 345
Water and Soap (86) 465
FERRIS, BETH
Heartland (82) 191
FINN, WILL
Secret of NIMH, The (83) 288
FIRTH, MICHAEL
Sylvia (86) 462
FISHKIN, JEFFREY ALAN
Cutter's Way (82) 119
FLANAGAN, FIONNULA
James Joyce's Women (86) 193
FLORIO, MARIA
Broken Rainbow (86) 439
FONVIELLE, LLOYD
Bride, The (86) 438
FOOTE, HORTON
1918 (86) 454
Tender Mercies (84) 409
Tomorrow [1972] (84) 589
Trip to Bountiful, The (86) 383

FORMAN, MILOŠ
Taking Off [1971] (86) 545
FORSYTH, BILL
Comfort and Joy (85) 146
Gregory's Girl [1981] (83) 193
FORWARD, BOB
Secret of the Sword, The (86) 459
FOSSE, BOB
Star 80 (84) 374
FRAENKEL, HELENE
It Happened Tomorrow [1944] (84) 552
FRANK, HARRIET
Hombre [1967] (84) 547
Local Hero (84) 206
Murphy's Romance (86) 242
FRANKLIN, JEFF
Just One of the Guys (86) 448
FRASER, GEORGE MACDONALD
Octopussy (84) 276
Red Sonja (86) 457
FREEMAN, EVERETT
Secret Life of Walter Mitty, The [1947] (86) 540
FREEMAN, JOAN
Streetwalkin' (86) 461
FREITAG, HEINZ
Colonel Redl [1984] (86) 100
FREUDBERG, JUDY
Sesame Street Presents: Follow That Bird (86) 459
FRICKE, RON
Chronos (86) 440
Koyaanisqatsi (84) 197
FRIEDKIN, WILLIAM
To Live and Die in L.A. (86) 379
FRIEDMAN, ADAM
Rappin' (86) 457
FRIEDMAN, BRUCE JAY
Splash (85) 434
FRIEDMAN, KEN
Heart Like a Wheel (84) 182
FRINGS, KETTI
"Obituaries" (82) 487
FROHMAN, CLAYTON
Under Fire (84) 441
FRÖLICH, PEA
Lola [1981] (83) 215
Veronika Voss (83) 382
FUCHS, DANIEL
Hard Way, The [1942] (85) 555
FULLER, CHARLES
Soldier's Story, A (85) 427
FURTHMAN, JULES
Come and Get It [1936] (82) 412

GADES, ANTONIO
Carmen (84) 101
GAINES, CHARLES
Pumping Iron II (86) 456
GALE, BOB
Back to the Future (86) 65
GALLO, GUY
Under the Volcano (85) 499
GANCE, ABEL
Napoleon [1927] (82) 461

GANZ, LOWELL
Spies like Us   (86) 360
Splash   (85) 434
GARCÍA MÁRQUEZ, GABRIEL
Erendira [1983]   (85) 181
GEISS, TONY
Sesame Street Presents: Follow That Bird   (86)
459
GELBART, LARRY
Tootsie   (83) 353
GETCHELL, ROBERT
Mommie Dearest   (82) 245
Sweet Dreams   (86) 374
GIDEON, RAYNOLD
Starman   (85) 445
GILER, DAVID
Southern Comfort   (82) 332
GILLIAM, TERRY
Brazil   (86) 80
Time Bandits [1980]   (82) 364
GIPE, GEORGE
Dead Men Don't Wear Plaid   (83) 134
Man with Two Brains, The   (84) 223
GODARD, JEAN-LUC
Detective   (86) 441
Hail Mary   (86) 182
Passion [1982]   (84) 289
GOHRE, FRANK
Out of Order   (86) 455
GOLDBERG, DAN
Stripes   (82) 336
GOLDMAN, BO
Melvin and Howard [1980]   (82) 453
Shoot the Moon   (83) 295
GOLDMAN, GARY
Secret of NIMH, The   (83) 288
GOLDMAN, JAMES
They Might Be Giants [1971]   (83) 515
White Nights   (86) 416
GOLDSMITH, MARTIN
Detour [1946]   (86) 498
GOLDSTEIN, SCOTT
Flanagan   (86) 443
GOODIS, DAVID
Unfaithful, The [1947]   (86) 550
GOODRICH, FRANCES
"Obituaries"   (85) 669
GORDON, DAN
Gotcha!   (86) 444
GORDON, EDWIN
Chosen, The   (83) 116
GORDON, RUTH
"Obituaries"   (86) 567
GORDON, STEVE
Arthur   (82) 71
"Obituaries"   (83) 536
GORDON, STUART
Re-Animator   (86) 457
GORETTA, CLAUDE
Death of Mario Ricci, The [1983]   (86) 133
GOULD, HEYWOOD
Boys from Brazil, The [1978]   (86) 480
Fort Apache, the Bronx   (82) 159

GRACZYK, ED
Come Back to the 5 & Dime Jimmy Dean, Jimmy
Dean   (83) 120
GRAHAM, RONNY
To Be or Not to Be   (84) 426
GRAIS, MICHAEL
Poltergeist   (83) 263
GRANT, JAMES EDWARD
Hondo [1953]   (83) 452
GRAY, MIKE
Code of Silence   (86) 440
GREEN, ADOLPH
Bells Are Ringing [1960]   (84) 517
GREEN, CLIFFORD
Baby   (86) 437
GREEN, ELLEN
Baby   (86) 437
GREEN, JANET
Victim [1961]   (85) 649
GREENAWAY, PETER
Draughtman's Contract, The [1982]   (84) 126
GREENWALT, DAVID
Secret Admirer   (86) 459
GREGORY, ANDRÉ
My Dinner with André   (82) 255
GRIFFITHS, TREVOR
Reds   (82) 312
GRODIN, CHARLES
Movers and Shakers   (86) 453
GROSS, LARRY
48 HRS.   (83) 173
GROVES, PHIL
Cave Girl   (86) 439
GRUYAERT, JAN
Flaxfield, The [1983]   (86) 443
GUARE, JOHN
Taking Off [1971]   (86) 545
GUARE, LOUIS
Atlantic City   (82) 74
GUERRA, TONINO
And the Ship Sails On [1983]   (85) 69
Bizet's Carmen [1983]   (85) 98
Night of the Shooting Stars, The [1982]   (84) 258
Nostalgia [1983]   (85) 340
Three Brothers [1980]   (83) 349
GUEST, CHRISTOPHER
This Is Spinal Tap   (85) 484
GUNN, JAMES
Unfaithful, The [1947]   (86) 550
GYLLENHAAL, STEPHEN
New Kids, The   (86) 454
GÜNEY, YILMAZ
Yol   (83) 411

HAAS, CHARLIE
Tex   (83) 335
HALE, JOE
Black Cauldron, The   (86) 75
HAMILL, DENIS
Turk 182   (86) 464
HAMILL, JOHN
Turk 182   (86) 464
HAMM, SAM
Never Cry Wolf   (84) 247

HANNANT, BRIAN
Road Warrior, The [1981]   (83) 277
HANSARD, PETER
Smash Palace [1981]   (83) 302
HANSON, CURTIS
Never Cry Wolf   (84) 247
HARE, DAVID
Plenty   (86) 271
Wetherby   (86) 406
HARRIS, TIMOTHY
Brewster's Millions   (86) 438
Trading Places   (84) 430
HARRISON, LINDSAY
Fraternity Vacation   (86) 444
HART, MOSS
Star Is Born, A [1954]   (84) 573
HARTMAN, PHIL
Pee-wee's Big Adventure   (86) 265
HARWOOD, RONALD
Doctor and the Devils, The   (86) 442
Dresser, The   (84) 130
HAUSE, JEFFREY
Once Bitten   (86) 455
HAYES, ALFRED
"Obituaries"   (86) 570
HAYES, TERRY
Mad Max Beyond Thunderdome   (86) 223
Road Warrior, The [1981]   (83) 277
HECHT, BEN
Barbary Coast [1935]   (84) 506
Specter of the Rose [1946]   (83) 504
HEDLEY, TOM
Flashdance   (84) 158
HEFFERNAN, TERENCE
Heartaches [1981]   (83) 197
HEIMS, JO
Play Misty for Me [1971]   (86) 532
HELLER, LUKAS
Flight of the Phoenix, The [1966]   (85) 549
HELLMAN, LILLIAN
North Star, The [1943]   (83) 476
"Obituaries"   (85) 671
HENDRYX, SHIRL
Running Brave   (84) 354
HENRY, BUCK
Protocol   (85) 383
HERMAN, JEAN
Garde à vue [1981]   (83) 189
HERTZ, DAVID
History Is Made at Night [1937]   (84) 542
HERZOG, WERNER
Fitzcarraldo   (83) 167
Where the Green Ants Dream [1984]   (86) 465
HIDAKA, SHINYA
Makioka Sisters, The [1983]   (86) 451
HIGGINS, COLIN
Best Little Whorehouse in Texas, The   (83) 72
HILL, ELIZABETH
H. M. Pulham, Esq. [1941]   (82) 439
HILL, WALTER
48 HRS.   (83) 173
Southern Comfort   (82) 332
HINES, DAVID
Once Bitten   (86) 455

HOENIG, MICHAEL
Koyaanisqatsi   (84) 197
HOGAN, J. R. MICHAEL
Woman on the Beach, The [1947]   (83) 519
HOLLAND, AGNIESZKA
Love in Germany, A [1983]   (85) 283
HOLLAND, SAVAGE STEVE
Better Off Dead   (86) 438
HOLLAND, TOM
Fright Night   (86) 444
Psycho II   (84) 307
HOPCRAFT, ARTHUR
Agatha [1979]   (83) 435
HOPE, EDWARD
Long Gray Line, The [1955]   (82) 447
Mommie Dearest   (82) 245
HOPKINS, JOHN
Holcroft Covenant, The   (86) 446
HOROWITZ, MARK
Almost You   (86) 436
HOUSE, RON
Bullshot [1983]   (86) 439
HOWELL, DOROTHY
Miracle Woman, The [1931]   (83) 473
HUGHES, ERIC
White Nights   (86) 416
HUGHES, JOHN
Breakfast Club, The   (86) 85
Nate and Hayes   (84) 236
National Lampoon's European Vacation   (86) 453
National Lampoon's Vacation   (84) 241
Weird Science   (86) 465
HUNTER, JOHN
Grey Fox, The   (84) 168
HUNTER, TIM
Tex   (83) 335
HURD, GALE ANNE
Terminator, The   (85) 478
HUSTON, JOHN
"Life Achievement Award"   (84) 1
HYAMS, PETER
Outland   (82) 272
2010   (85) 494

ICHASO, LEON
Crossover Dreams   (86) 441
ICHIKAWA, KON
Makioka Sisters, The [1983]   (86) 451
IDE, MASATO
Ran   (86) 304
IDE, TOSHIRO
Flowing [1956]   (86) 444
Late Chrysanthemums [1954]   (86) 449
IMHOOF, MARKUS
Boat Is Full, The [1981]   (83) 82
ISAACS, DAVID
Volunteers   (86) 464
ISAACS, SUSAN
Compromising Positions   (86) 120
ISRAEL, NEAL
Moving Violations   (86) 453
Real Genius   (86) 309

IVORY, JAMES
    Quartet   (82) 296

JACKSON, HORACE
    Animal Kingdom, The [1932]   (86) 469
JAGLOM, HENRY
    Always   (86) 60
    Can She Bake a Cherry Pie?   (84) 95
JAKOBY, DON
    Blue Thunder   (84) 84
    Lifeforce   (86) 450
JARMUSCH, JIM
    Stranger than Paradise   (85) 455
JELINEK, HENRIETTE
    Adolescente, L' [1979]   (83) 53
JENKINS, MICHAEL
    Careful He Might Hear You [1983]   (85) 130
JENNINGS, TALBOT
    "Obituaries"   (86) 572
JHABVALA, RUTH PRAWER
    Bostonians, The   (85) 105
    Heat and Dust [1982]   (84) 187
    Quartet   (82) 296
JOHNSON, GEORGE CLAYTON
    Twilight Zone—The Movie   (84) 435
JOHNSON, MONICA
    Lost in America   (86) 219
    Modern Romance   (82) 241
JOHNSON, NORA
    World of Henry Orient, The [1964]   (84) 600
JOHNSON, NUNNALLY
    My Cousin Rachel [1952]   (82) 458
    World of Henry Orient, The [1964]   (84) 600
JOHNSON, TERRY
    Insignificance   (86) 447
JOLIVET, PIERRE
    Subway   (86) 461
JONAS, DAVID
    Black Cauldron, The   (86) 75
JONES, AMY
    Love Letters   (85) 288
JONES, EVAN
    Victory   (82) 374
JONES, GRIFF RHYS
    Morons from Outer Space   (86) 452
JORDAN, NEIL
    Company of Wolves, The [1984]   (86) 115
JOSEPHSON, JULIAN
    Disraeli [1929]   (82) 426
JUHL, JERRY
    Great Muppet Caper, The   (82) 187

KAMEN, ROBERT MARK
    Karate Kid, The   (85) 264
    Split Image   (83) 317
    Taps   (82) 343
KAMINSKY, STUART
    Once upon a Time in America   (85) 345
KANE, MICHAEL
    All the Right Moves   (84) 4
    Southern Comfort   (82) 332
KASDAN, LAWRENCE
    Big Chill, The   (84) 78
    Body Heat   (82) 87

Continental Divide   (82) 115
    Raiders of the Lost Ark   (82) 308
    Return of the Jedi   (84) 326
    Silverado   (86) 349
KASDAN, MARK
    Silverado   (86) 349
KATZ, GLORIA
    Indiana Jones and the Temple of Doom   (85)
      253
KAUFMAN, CHARLES
    Freud [1962]   (84) 535
    When Nature Calls   (86) 465
KAUFMAN, PHILIP
    Right Stuff, The   (84) 342
KAUFMAN, ROBERT
    Split Image   (83) 317
KAZAN, ELIA
    Arrangement, The [1969]   (86) 474
KAZAN, NICHOLAS
    Frances   (83) 178
KEEFFE, BARRIE
    Long Good Friday, The [1980]   (83) 220
KELLEY, WILLIAM
    Witness   (86) 421
KELLY, GENE
    Invitation to the Dance [1956]   (86) 507
KENEALLY, THOMAS
    Silver City [1984]   (86) 460
KENNEDY, WILLIAM
    Cotton Club, The   (85) 150
KENT, GARY
    Rainy Day Friends   (86) 457
KERN, RONNIE
    American Pop   (82) 62
KHMARA, EDWARD
    Enemy Mine   (86) 161
    Ladyhawke   (86) 214
KIBBEE, ROLAND
    "Obituaries"   (85) 676
KING, LARRY L.
    Best Little Whorehouse in Texas, The   (83) 72
KING, STEPHEN
    Stephen King's Cat's Eye   (86) 460
    Stephen King's Silver Bullet   (86) 460
KING, WOODY
    Here Come the Littles   (86) 446
KINGSTON, JAMES GREGORY
    Turk 182   (86) 464
KLANE, ROBERT
    Man with One Red Shoe, The   (86) 451
    National Lampoon's European Vacation   (86)
      453
KLEIN, JOHN
    Taking Off [1971]   (86) 545
KLETTER, RICHARD
    Never Cry Wolf   (84) 247
KLOVES, STEVEN
    Racing with the Moon   (85) 397
KOCH, C. J.
    Year of Living Dangerously, The [1982]   (84)
      462
KOLLEK, AMOS
    Goodbye, New York   (86) 444
KONCHALOVSKY, ANDREI
    Maria's Lovers   (86) 451

KONG, JACKIE
Night Patrol   (86) 454
KONNER, LAWRENCE
Jewel of the Nile, The   (86) 448
Legend of Billie Jean, The   (86) 450
KOSLOW, RON
Into the Night   (86) 186
KOUF, JIM
Secret Admirer   (86) 459
KOZINTSEV, GRIGORI
New Babylon, The [1929]   (84) 561
KOZOLL, MICHAEL
First Blood   (83) 164
KRAMER, ROBERT
State of Things, The   (84) 379
KRASNA, NORMAN
"Obituaries"   (85) 676
KROOPF, SANDY
Birdy   (85) 93
KURLANDER, CARL
St. Elmo's Fire   (86) 380
KUROSAWA, AKIRA
Ran   (86) 304
KURTA, PAUL
Key Exchange   (86) 448
KURYS, DIANE
Entre nous [1983]   (85) 176
KUYCK, WILLARD
Indiana Jones and the Temple of Doom   (85) 253

LANCASTER, BILL
Thing, The   (83) 343
LANDIS, JOHN
American Werewolf in London, An   (82) 66
Twilight Zone—The Movie   (84) 435
LANE, ANDREW
Valley Girl   (84) 447
LANGMANN, ARLETTE
Loulou [1980]   (82) 226
LANGSTON, MURRAY
Night Patrol   (86) 454
LASKER, ALEX
Firefox   (83) 160
WarGames   (84) 458
LATHAM, AARON
Perfect   (86) 456
LAURENTS, ARTHUR
Way We Were, The [1973]   (82) 474
LAUZIER, GERARD
Little Jerk [1984]   (86) 450
LAWRENCE, BRUNO
Quiet Earth, The   (86) 295
Smash Palace [1981]   (83) 302
LAWRENCE, JEROME
First Monday in October   (82) 151
LAWRENCE, VINCENT
History Is Made at Night [1937]   (84) 542
Peter Ibbetson [1935]   (86) 527
LEACH, WILFRED
Pirates of Penzance, The   (84) 301
LEAN, DAVID
Passage to India, A   (85) 365

LE BRETON, AUGUSTE
Bob le Flambeur [1955]   (84) 526
LEDERER, CHARLES
Mutiny on the Bounty [1962]   (85) 581
LEE, ROBERT E.
First Monday in October   (82) 151
LE HENRY, ALAIN
Entre nous [1983]   (85) 176
Subway   (86) 461
LEMELIN, ROGER
Plouffe, Les   (86) 456
LEO, MALCOLM
Beach Boys, The   (86) 438
This Is Elvis   (82) 360
LEONARD, ELMORE
Stick   (86) 460
LEONE, SERGIO
Once upon a Time in America   (85) 345
LEOPOLD, GLENN
Too Scared to Scream   (86) 463
LERNER, ALAN JAY
Royal Wedding [1951]   (86) 536
LEVEN, JEREMY
Creator   (86) 441
LEVEY, BILL
Night Patrol   (86) 454
LEVINE, KEN
Volunteers   (86) 464
LEVINSON, BARRY
Best Friends   (83) 68
Diner   (83) 142
LEVINSON, LARRY
Missing in Action 2   (86) 452
LEWTON, VAL
"Interview with DeWitt Bodeen, An"   (82) 8
LISBERGER, STEVEN
TRON   (83) 71
LITZ, ROBERT
Rappin'   (86) 457
LLORENTE, ANGEL
Volver a empezar   (83) 393
LOEB, JOSEPH, III
Teen Wolf   (86) 462
LONG, JOAN
Caddie [1976]   (83) 439
LOOS, ANITA
Dulcy [1923]   (82) 432
"Obituaries"   (82) 496
LOUGHERY, DAVID
Dreamscape   (85) 166
LOWE, EDWARD T.
King of Jazz [1930]   (86) 515
LUCAS, GEORGE
Return of the Jedi   (84) 326
THX 1138 [1971]   (85) 638
LUEDTKE, KURT
Absence of Malice   (82) 57
Out of Africa   (86) 255
LUKE, ERIC
Explorers   (86) 442
LUMET, SIDNEY
Prince of the City   (82) 292
LUNGHIN, SEMYON
Rasputin [1975]   (86) 457

LYNCH, DAVID
Dune (85) 171
LYNN, JONATHAN
Clue (86) 440

MACARTHUR, CHARLES
Barbary Coast [1935] (84) 506
King of Jazz [1930] (86) 515
MACAULAY, RICHARD
They Drive by Night [1940] (83) 508
MCBRIDE, JIM
Breathless (84) 89
MACCARI, RUGGERO
Bal, Le [1983] (85) 80
Macaroni (86) 451
MCCLOY, TERENCE
Lady Sings the Blues [1972] (85) 565
MCCORMICK, JOHN
Victim [1961] (85) 649
MCDOUGALL, PETER
Sense of Freedom, A (86) 459
MCEWAN, IAN
Ploughman's Lunch, The [1983] (85) 377
MCKEAN, MICHAEL
This Is Spinal Tap (85) 484
MCKEOWN, CHARLES
Brazil (86) 80
MACLAVERTY, BERNARD
Cal (85) 124
MACRAUCH, EARL
New York, New York [1977] (84) 567
MAGNOLI, ALBERT
Purple Rain (85) 389
MAHIN, JOHN LEE
"Obituaries" (85) 682
Too Hot to Handle [1938] (84) 596
MAIBAUM, RICHARD
For Your Eyes Only (82) 155
Octopussy (84) 276
View to a Kill, A (86) 402
MAKAVEJEV, DUSAN
Montenegro (82) 250
MALLESON, MILES
Nell Gwyn [1934] (84) 557
MALTZ, ALBERT
"Obituaries" (86) 575
MAMET, DAVID
Postman Always Rings Twice, The (82) 284
Verdict, The (83) 377
MANDEL, BABALOO
Spies like Us (86) 360
Splash (85) 434
MANKIEWICZ, JOSEPH L.
Barefoot Contessa, The [1954] (82) 399
MANKIEWICZ, TOM
Ladyhawke (86) 214
MANN, ABBY
War and Love (86) 465
MANN, MICHAEL
Thief (82) 356
MANN, STANLEY
Eye of the Needle (82) 148
MARINHO, EUCLIDES
Bar Esperanza [1983] (86) 437

MARION, FRANCES
Scarlet Letter, The [1927] (85) 602
MARK, ROBERT
Split Image (83) 317
MARSHALL, GARRY
Flamingo Kid, The (85) 192
MARSHALL, NEAL
Flamingo Kid, The (85) 192
MARTHESHEIMER, PETER
Lola [1981] (83) 215
Veronika Voss (83) 382
MARTIN, DON
"Obituaries" (86) 575
MARTIN, MARDIK
New York, New York [1977] (84) 567
MARTIN, STEVE
Dead Men Don't Wear Plaid (83) 134
Man with Two Brains, The (84) 223
MASTERSON, PETER
Best Little Whorehouse in Texas, The (83) 72
MATHESON, RICHARD
Twilight Zone—The Movie (84) 435
MATHISON, MELISSA
E.T.: The Extra-Terrestrial (83) 151
MAXWELL, RICHARD
Challenge, The (83) 109
MAYER, EDWIN JUSTUS
Peter Ibbetson [1935] (86) 527
MAYERSBERG, PAUL
Eureka (86) 442
Man Who Fell to Earth, The [1975] (83) 469
Merry Christmas, Mr. Lawrence (84) 231
MAZURSKY, PAUL
Moscow on the Hudson (85) 321
Next Stop, Greenwich Village [1976] (85) 592
Tempest (83) 331
MEDIOLI, ENRICO
Once upon a Time in America (85) 345
MEDOWAY, GARY
Heavenly Kid, The (86) 445
MEEHAN, JOHN
Divorcée, The [1930] (82) 429
Peter Ibbetson [1935] (86) 527
To Be or Not to Be (84) 426
MEEHAN, THOMAS
One Magic Christmas (86) 455
MELVILLE, JEAN-PIERRE
Bob le Flambeur [1955] (84) 526
MEYER, NICHOLAS
Time After Time [1979] (84) 579
MEYJES, MENNO
Color Purple, The (86) 105
MICHALEK, BOLESLAW
Love in Germany, A [1983] (85) 283
MIELCHE, PAUL DE
American Ninja (86) 436
MIEVILLE, ANNE-MARIE
Detective (86) 442
Every Man for Himself [1979] (82) 139
First Name, Carmen [1983] (85) 186
MIKHALKOV-KONCHALOVSKY, ANDREY
Siberiade [1977] (83) 299
MILESTONE, LEWIS
Arch of Triumph [1948] (84) 501

MILICEVIC, DJORDJE
  Runaway Train   (86) 324
MILLER, ALICE DUER G.
  "Obituaries"   (86) 576
MILLER, CLAUDE
  Garde à vue [1981]   (83) 189
MILLER, GEORGE
  Mad Max Beyond Thunderdome   (86) 223
  Road Warrior, The [1981]   (83) 277
MILLER, HARVEY
  Bad Medicine   (86) 437
MILLER, JASON
  That Championship Season   (83) 338
MINION, JOSEPH
  After Hours   (86) 51
MIZRAHI, MOSHE
  I Sent a Letter to My Love [1980]   (82) 214
MONTAGU, IVOR
  "Obituaries"   (85) 686
MOONEY, MARTIN
  Detour [1946]   (86) 498
MOORE, BRIAN
  Torn Curtain [1966]   (85) 644
MOORE, DUDLEY
  Hound of the Baskervilles, The [1978]   (82) 203
MOORHOUSE, FRANK
  Coca-Cola Kid, The   (86) 440
MOREAU, JEANNE
  Adolescente, L' [1979]   (83) 53
MOREY, LARRY
  Bambi [1942]   (85) 543
MORITA, ROY
  Black Cauldron, The   (86) 75
MORRISSEY, PAUL
  Hound of the Baskervilles, The [1978]   (82) 203
  Mixed Blood   (86) 452
MUDD, VICTORIA
  Broken Rainbow   (86) 439
MUNE, IAN
  Came a Hot Friday   (86) 439
MURCH, WALTER
  Return to Oz   (86) 458
  THX 1138 [1971]   (85) 638
MURFIN, JANE
  Come and Get It [1936]   (82) 412
MURPHY, GEOFF
  Utu [1983]   (85) 504
MURRAY, BILL
  Razor's Edge, The   (85) 402

NAGAHARA, SHUICHI
  Godzilla 1985   (86) 444
NAVA, GREGORY
  Norte, El   (84) 265
NEWMAN, DAVID
  Jinxed   (83) 206
  Santa Claus   (86) 334
  Superman II   (82) 339
  Superman III   (84) 399
NEWMAN, LESLIE
  Superman II   (82) 339
  Superman III   (84) 399
NICHOLS, DUDLEY
  It Happened Tomorrow [1944]   (84) 552
  Man Hunt [1941]   (85) 570

NORMAN, MARC
  Aviator, The   (86) 437
NORRIS, CHUCK
  Invasion U.S.A.   (86) 447
NORRIS, WILLIAM J.
  Re-Animator   (86) 457
NORTH, EDMUND H.
  Colorado Territory [1949]   (86) 489
  Cowboy [1958]   (82) 417
NUGENT, FRANK S.
  Fort Apache [1948]   (84) 530
NUNEZ, VICTOR
  Flash of Green, A   (86) 443
NYSWANER, RON
  Mrs. Soffel   (85) 314
  Smithereens   (83) 307

O'BANNON, DAN
  Blue Thunder   (84) 84
  Dark Star [1975]   (86) 494
  Lifeforce   (86) 450
  Return of the Living Dead, The   (86) 314
ODELL, DAVID
  Dark Crystal, The   (83) 130
  Nate and Hayes   (84) 236
O'FLAHERTY, DENNIS
  Hammett   (84) 174
OGUNI, HIDEO
  Ran   (86) 304
OLDOINI, ENRICO
  Softly Softly [1984]   (86) 460
  Water and Soap   (86) 465
O'MALLEY, DAVID
  Kid Colter   (86) 449
O'NEIL, ROBERT VINCENT
  Avenging Angel   (86) 436
OPPER, DON
  City Limits   (86) 440
ORMSBY, ALAN
  Cat People   (83) 100
OSCO, WILLIAM
  Night Patrol   (86) 454
OSHIMA, NAGISA
  Merry Christmas, Mr. Lawrence   (84) 231

PAHVER, CHAVER
  Light Ahead, The [1939]   (83) 460
PAKULA, ALAN J.
  Sophie's Choice   (83) 311
PALCY, EUZHAN
  Sugar Cane Alley [1983]   (85) 461
PALIN, MICHAEL
  Missionary, The   (83) 233
  Time Bandits [1980]   (82) 364
PALLENBERG, ROSPO
  Emerald Forest, The   (86) 156
  Excalibur   (82) 144
PALUMBO, DENNIS
  My Favorite Year   (83) 241
PAOLI, DENNIS
  Re-Animator   (86) 457
PARKER, DEAN
  Came a Hot Friday   (86) 439
PARKES, WALTER F.
  WarGames   (84) 458

PASEORNEK, MICHAEL
  Stitches   (86) 461
PATCHETT, TOM
  Great Mupper Caper, The   (82) 187
PATTERSON, JOHN
  Test of Love   (86) 462
PENCHENAT, JEAN-CLAUDE
  Bal, Le [1983]   (85) 80
PEOPLES, DAVID
  Blade Runner   (83) 76
PERRIER, MARC
  Subway   (86) 461
PERRY, ELEANOR
  "Obituaries"   (82) 500
PETERS, CHARLIE
  Kiss Me Goodbye   (83) 209
PETERSEN, WOLFGANG
  Boot, Das [1981]   (83) 86
PETERSON, DON
  Target   (86) 462
PETIEVICH, GERALD
  To Live and Die in L.A.   (86) 379
PETRIE, DANIEL
  Bad Boy, The   (86) 437
PETRIE, DANIEL, JR.
  Beverly Hills Cop   (85) 88
PHELAN, ANNA HAMILTON
  Mask   (86) 231
PHILLIPS, BILL
  Christine   (84) 106
PIALAT, MAURICE
  Loulou [1980]   (82) 226
PIEDMONT, LEON
  Mean Season, The   (86) 452
PIELMEIER, JOHN
  Agnes of God   (86) 56
PIERSON, LOUISE RANDALL
  Roughly Speaking [1945]   (83) 490
PILLSBURY, SAM
  Quiet Earth, The   (86) 295
PINTER, HAROLD
  Betrayal   (84) 67
  French Lieutenant's Woman, The   (82) 174
  Turtle Diary   (86) 464
PITCHFORD, DEAN
  Footloose   (85) 198
PLATER, ALAN
  Priest of Love   (82) 288
PLATT, POLLY
  Pretty Baby [1978]   (85) 597
POLANSKI, ROMAN
  Tess [1980]   (82) 471
POMEROY, JOHN
  Secret of NIMH, The   (83) 288
PONICSAN, DARRYL
  Brimstone and Treacle   (83) 91
  Gorky Park   (84) 162
  Pennies from Heaven   (82) 276
  Taps   (82) 343
  Vision Quest   (86) 464
POTTER, DENNIS
  Dreamchild   (86) 146
POWELL, MICHAEL
  I Know Where I'm Going [1945]   (83) 456

PREKOP, GABRIELLA
  Colonel Redl [1984]   (86) 100
PRESSBURGER, EMERIC
  I Know Where I'm Going [1945]   (83) 456
PRINCE, PETER
  Hit, The   (86) 446
PROFT, PAT
  Moving Violations   (86) 453
  Real Genius   (86) 309
PROSER, CHIP
  Iceman   (85) 248
PUENZO, LUIS
  Official Story, The   (86) 249
PURPURA, CHARLES
  Heaven Help Us   (86) 445
PURZER, MANFRED
  Lili Marleen   (82) 222
PUZO, MARIO
  Superman II   (82) 339

QUILL, MICHELE
  Sylvia   (86) 462
QUINTANO, GENE
  King Solomon's Mines   (86) 449

RABE, DAVID
  Streamers   (84) 391
RADFORD, MICHAEL
  1984   (85) 335
RAMIS, HAROLD
  Ghostbusters   (85) 219
  Stripes   (82) 336
RAPHAEL, FREDERIC
  Richard's Things   (82) 321
RAPHAELSON, SAMSON
  "Obituaries"   (84) 632
RATTIGAN, TERENCE
  Sound Barrier, The [1952]   (85) 621
RAUCH, EARL MAC
  Adventures of Buckaroo Banzai, The
    (85) 47
RAVETCH, IRVING
  Hombre [1967]   (84) 547
  Murphy's Romance   (86) 242
RAY, SATYAJIT
  Home and the World, The [1984]   (86) 447
REGGIO, GODFREY
  Koyaanisqatsi   (84) 197
REINER, CARL
  Dead Men Don't Wear Plaid   (83) 134
  Man with Two Brains, The   (84) 223
REINER, ROB
  This Is Spinal Tap   (85) 484
REINHARDT, WOLFGANG
  Freud [1962]   (84) 535
REISCH, WALTER
  "Obituaries"   (84) 633
REISMAN, MARK
  Summer Rental   (86) 462
RENOIR, JEAN
  Woman on the Beach, The [1947]   (83) 519
RESNICK, PATRICIA
  Maxie   (86) 452

REUBENS, PAUL
Pee-wee's Big Adventure (86) 265
REYNOLDS, JONATHAN
Micki & Maude (85) 308
REYNOLDS, KEVIN
Fandango (86) 442
RICH, RICHARD
Black Cauldron, The (86) 75
RICHLER, MORDECAI
Joshua Then and Now (86) 198
RIESNER, DEAN
Play Misty for Me [1971] (86) 532
RINCK, JETTE
Tuff Turf (86) 464
RIPPLOH, FRANK
Taxi Zum Klo (82) 346
ROACH, JANET
Prizzi's Honor (86) 285
ROBBINS, MATTHEW
Dragonslayer (82) 125
Warning Sign (86) 465
ROBERTS, BEN
"Obituaries" (85) 691
ROBERTS, JONATHAN
Once Bitten (86) 455
Sure Thing, The (86) 369
ROBERTS, JUNE
Experience Preferred ... but Not Essential
[1982] (84) 141
ROBINSON, BRUCE
Killing Fields, The (85) 270
ROBINSON, CASEY
Snows of Kilimanjaro, The [1952] (83) 498
ROBINSON, PHIL ALDEN
All of Me (85) 58
ROGAN, JOSH
Twilight Zone—The Movie (84) 435
ROHMER, ERIC
Beau Mariage, Le (83) 65
Full Moon in Paris (85) 208
Pauline at the Beach [1982] (84) 296
ROLAND, SANDRA WEINTRAUB
Out of Control (86) 455
ROMERO, GEORGE A.
Day of the Dead (86) 441
RONDI, BRUNELLO
City of Women (82) 106
ROSE, JACK
Great Muppet Caper, The (82) 187
ROSE, REGINALD
Whose Life Is It Anyway? (82) 378
Wild Geese II (86) 466
ROSENBERG, JEANNE
Journey of Natty Gann, The (86) 203
ROSENTHAL, JACK
Yentl (84) 468
ROSENTHAL, MARK
Jewel of the Nile, The (86) 448
Legend of Billie Jean, The (86) 450
ROSI, FRANCESCO
Bizet's Carmen [1983] (85) 98
Three Brothers [1980] (83) 349
ROSS, ARTHUR
Creature from the Black Lagoon, The
[1954] (82) 422

ROWELL, KATHLEEN KNUTSEN
Outsiders, The (84) 282
RUBEN, JOSEPH
Dreamscape (85) 166
RUDOLPH, ALAN
Choose Me (85) 135
Trouble in Mind (86) 388
RUSKIN, HARRY
King of Jazz [1930] (86) 515
RUSSELL, CHUCK
Dreamscape (85) 166
RUSSELL, WILLY
Educating Rita (84) 136
RUVINSKY, MORRIE
Improper Channels (82) 218
RYSKIND, MORRIE
"Obituaries" (86) 581

SACKHEIM, WILLIAM
First Blood (83) 164
SAFRAN, HENRI
Wild Duck, The [1983] (86) 466
SANDER, PETER
Care Bears Movie, The (86) 439
SANDLER, BARRY
Crimes of Passion (85) 161
SARDE, ALAIN
Detective (86) 442
SAURA, CARLOS
Carmen (84) 101
SAYLES, JOHN
Brother from Another Planet, The (85) 118
Challenge, The (83) 109
Howling, The (82) 207
Lianna (84) 201
Return of the Secaucus 7 [1980] (83) 484
SCARPELLI, FURIO
Bal, Le [1983] (85) 80
Macaroni (86) 451
SCHENKEL, CARL
Out of Order (86) 455
SCHIFFMAN, SUZANNE
Woman Next Door, The (82) 385
SCHISGAL, MURRAY
Tootsie (83) 353
SCHLÖNDORFF, VOLKER
Swann in Love (85) 471
SCHMIDT, SOPHIE
Subway (86) 461
SCHRADER, CHIEKO
Mishima (86) 236
SCHRADER, LEONARD
Kiss of the Spider Woman (86) 209
Mishima (86) 236
SCHRADER, PAUL
Mishima (86) 236
SCHRANK, JOSEPH
"Obituaries" (85) 693
SCHULMAN, ARNOLD
Chorus Line, A (86) 91
SCHUMACHER, JOEL
St. Elmo's Fire (86) 380
SCIBOR-RYLSKI, ALEKSANDER
Man of Iron (82) 230
Man of Marble [1977] (82) 234

SCOLA, ETTORE
  Bal, Le [1983]   (85) 80
  Macaroni   (86) 451
SCOTT, ALLAN
  D.A.R.Y.L.   (86) 441
SCOTT, JEFFREY
  Starchaser   (86) 460
SCOTT, KEVIN
  Key Exchange   (86) 448
SELTZER, DAVID
  Table for Five   (84) 404
SELTZER, TERREL
  Chan Is Missing   (83) 113
  Dim Sum   (86) 141
SEMPLE, LORENZO, JR.
  Gabriela [1983]   (85) 213
  Never Say Never Again   (84) 252
SETBON, PHILIPPE
  Detective   (86) 442
SHABER, DAVID
  Nighthawks   (82) 259
SHAFFER, ANTHONY
  Wicker Man, The [1974]   (86) 555
SHAFFER, PETER
  Amadeus   (85) 63
SHANE, MAXWELL
  "Obituaries"   (84) 635
SHAW, IRWIN
  "Obituaries"   (85) 694
SHAWN, WALLACE
  My Dinner with André   (82) 255
SHEARER, HARRY
  This Is Spinal Tap   (85) 484
SHEARMAN, ALAN
  Bullshot [1983]   (86) 439
SHEFFIELD, DAVID
  Police Academy 2   (86) 276
SHELTON, RON
  Under Fire   (84) 441
SHEPARD, SAM
  Fool for Love   (86) 172
  Paris, Texas   (85) 359
SHEPHERD, JEAN
  Christmas Story, A   (84) 110
SHORE, SIG
  Sudden Death   (86) 461
SHRYACK, DENNIS
  Code of Silence   (86) 440
  Pale Rider   (86) 261
SIDRAN, ABDULAH
  When Father Was Away on Business
  [1984]   (86) 411
SILKE, JAMES R.
  King Solomon's Mines   (86) 449
SILVER, ARTHUR
  Missing in Action 2   (86) 452
SIMON, NEIL
  Max Dugan Returns   (84) 228
  Neil Simon's The Slugger's Wife   (86) 454
  Only When I Laugh   (82) 268
SINCLAIR, JOSHUA
  Lili Marleen   (82) 222
SKOLIMOWSKI, JERZY
  Moonlighting   (83) 237

SMITH, MEL
  Morons from Outer Space   (86) 452
SOBIESKI, CAROL
  Annie   (83) 56
  Sylvester   (86) 462
  Toy, The   (83) 358
SOETEMAN, GERARD
  Flesh and Blood   (86) 443
  4th Man, The [1983]   (85) 203
SOLINAS, FRANCO
  Hanna K.   (84) 177
SOLT, ANDREW
  This Is Elvis   (82) 360
SOUZA, STEVEN E. DE
  Commando   (86) 111
  48 HRS.   (83) 173
SOWARDS, JACK B.
  Star Trek II—The Wrath of Khan   (83) 321
SPENCER, SCOTT
  Split Image   (83) 317
SPIELBERG, STEVEN
  Poltergeist   (83) 263
SPOTTISWOODE, ROGER
  48 HRS.   (83) 173
STALLINGS, LAURENCE
  Too Hot to Handle [1938]   (84) 596
STALLONE, SYLVESTER
  First Blood   (83) 164
  Rambo: First Blood Part II   (86) 299
  Rocky III   (83) 283
  Rocky IV   (86) 319
  Staying Alive   (84) 386
STEINBERG, NORMAN
  My Favorite Year   (83) 241
STEVENS, ART
  Black Cauldron, The   (86) 75
STEVENS, JEREMY
  Summer Rental   (86) 462
STEWART, DONALD
  Missing   (83) 232
STEWART, DOUGLAS DAY
  Officer and a Gentleman, An   (83) 246
STINSON, JOSEPH C.
  City Heat   (85) 141
  Stick   (86) 460
  Sudden Impact   (84) 395
STONE, OLIVER
  Scarface   (84) 361
  Year of the Dragon   (86) 426
STOPPARD, TOM
  Brazil   (86) 80
STREISAND, BARBRA
  Yentl   (84) 468
STUART, ALEXANDER
  Ordeal by Innocence [1984]   (86) 455
SULLIVAN, C. GARDNER
  Dulcy [1923]   (82) 432
SUTHERLAND, IAN
  Improper Channels   (82) 18
SWAIM, BOB
  Balance, La [1982]   (84) 52
SWERLING, JO
  Miracle Woman, The [1931]   (83) 473

SCREENWRITER INDEX

SZABÓ, ISTVÁN
Colonel Redl [1984]   (86) 100
Mephisto   (82) 237

TAMURA, TAKESHI
MacArthur's Children   (86) 451
TANAKA, SUMIE
Flowing [1956]   (86) 444
Late Chrysanthemums [1954]   (86) 449
TARKOVSKY, ANDREI
Nostalgia [1983]   (85) 340
TARSES, JAY
Great Muppet Caper, The   (82) 187
TAVERNIER, BERTRAND
Coup de torchon [1981]   (83) 124
Sunday in the Country, A   (85) 466
TAVERNIER, COLO
Sunday in the Country, A   (85) 466
TAVIANI, PAOLO
Night of the Shooting Stars, The [1982]   (84) 258
TAVIANI, VITTORIO
Night of the Shooting Stars, The [1982]   (84) 258
TAYLOR, PHILIP
Lust in the Dust   (86) 450
TESICH, STEVEN
American Flyers   (86) 436
Eleni   (86) 151
Four Friends   (82) 167
World According to Garp, The   (83) 397
THOMAS, ANNA
Norte, El   (84) 265
THOMAS, DIANE
Romancing the Stone   (85) 421
THOMAS, MICHAEL
Ladyhawke   (86) 214
THOMAS, ROSS
Hammett   (84) 174
THOMAS, ROY
Fire and Ice   (84) 153
THOMPSON, ERNEST
On Golden Pond   (82) 263
THOMPSON, HARLAN
I'm No Angel [1933]   (85) 561
TIDYMAN, ERNEST
"Obituaries"   (85) 695
TOMEI, LISA
Godzilla 1985   (86) 444
TOMSKI, MICHELLE
Savage Island   (86) 458
TOROKVEI, PETER
Real Genius   (86) 309
TOWNE, GENE
History Is Made at Night [1937]   (84) 542
TOWNE, ROBERT
Greystoke   (85) 236
Personal Best   (83) 254
TOWNE, ROGER
Natural, The   (85) 329
TRAUBERG, LEONID
New Babylon, The [1929]   (84) 561
TROTTA, MARGARETHE VON
Sheer Madness [1983]   (86) 459
TRUFFAUT, FRANÇOIS
Woman Next Door, The   (82) 385

TRUMBO, DALTON
Guy Named Joe, A [1943]   (82) 435
TUGGLE, RICHARD
Tightrope   (85) 489
TURKIEWICZ, SOPHIA
Silver City [1984]   (86) 460
TURNEY, CATHERINE
My Reputation [1946]   (85) 586
TWIST, JOHN
Colorado Territory [1949]   (86) 489
TYNAN, KATHLEEN
Agatha [1979]   (83) 435
Gods Must Be Crazy, The [1980]   (85) 224
TYTELL, JOHN
Kerouac, the Movie   (86) 448

ULLMAN, ELWOOD
"Obituaries"   (86) 584

VALDEZ, LUIS
Zoot Suit   (82) 389
VAN DE PUTTE, ANNEMARIE
Bastille [1984]   (86) 437
VAN DEN BERG, RUDOLF
Bastille [1984]   (86) 437
VAN HAMME, JEAN
Diva [1980]   (83) 147
VARHOL, MICHAEL
Pee-wee's Big Adventure   (86) 265
VAZAK, P. H. See TOWNE, ROBERT.
VEBER, FRANCIS
Goat, The [1981]   (86) 444
VENOSTA, LOUIS
Berry Gordy's The Last Dragon   (86) 438
VERDONE, CARLO
Water and Soap   (86) 465
VERHOEVEN, PAUL
Flesh and Blood   (86) 443
VICTOR, MARK
Poltergeist   (83) 263
VIDOR, KING
H. M. Pulham, Esq. [1941]   (82) 439
VIERTEL, PETER
Hard Way, The [1942]   (85) 555
VIGNE, DANIEL
Return of Martin Guerre, The   (84) 318

WADLEIGH, MICHAEL
Wolfen   (82) 382
WAJDA, ANDRZEJ
Love in Germany, A [1983]   (85) 283
WALD, JERRY
They Drive by Night [1940]   (83) 508
WALLACE, EARL W.
Witness   (86) 421
WALPOLE, ALTON
Koyaanisqatsi   (84) 197
WANG, WAYNE
Chan Is Missing   (83) 113
WARD, DAVID
Cannery Row   (83) 95
WARD, ROBERT
Cattle Annie and Little Britches   (82) 97

WATERS, ROGER
Pink Floyd the Wall [1981]   (83) 258
WEBB, JAMES R.
Apache [1954]   (82) 395
WEINGROD, HERSCHEL
Brewster's Millions   (86) 438
Trading Places   (84) 430
WEIR, PETER
Year of Living Dangerously, The [1982]   (84)
462
WEISMAN, MATTHEW
Teen Wolf   (86) 462
WEISMAN, STRAW
When Nature Calls   (86) 465
WELLAND, COLIN
Chariots of Fire   (82) 101
"Obituaries"   (86) 585
Twice in a Lifetime   (86) 397
WELLER, MICHAEL
Ragtime   (82) 304
WELLES, ORSON
Falstaff [1967]   (83) 443
WELLMAN, WENDELL
Firefox   (83) 160
WENDERS, WIM
State of Things, The   (84) 379
Tokyo-Ga   (86) 463
WERTMULLER, LINA
Softly Softly [1984]   (86) 460
WESLEY, RICHARD
Fast Forward   (86) 442
WEST, MAE
I'm No Angel [1933]   (85) 561
WEXLER, MILTON
Man Who Loved Women, The   (84) 218
WEXLER, NORMAN
Staying Alive   (84) 386
WHITE, DIZ
Bullshot [1983]   (86) 439
WHITE, JACK
"Obituaries"   (85) 701
WHITEMORE, HUGH
Return of the Soldier, The [1982]   (84) 332
WILDER, BILLY
Buddy Buddy   (82) 93
WILLIAMS, TENNESSEE
"Obituaries"   (84) 691
WILLIAMSON, DAVID
Gallipoli [1980]   (82) 179
Year of Living Dangerously, The [1982]   (84)
462
WILSON, AL
Black Cauldron, The   (86) 75
WILSON, HUGH
Rustler's Rhapsody   (86) 458
WILSON, MICHAEL G.
For Your Eyes Only   (82) 155
Octopussy   (84) 276
View to a Kill, A   (86) 402

WINKLESS, TERENCE H.
Howling, The   (82) 207
WINTER, LEON
Bastille [1984]   (86)·437
WITTLIFF, WILLIAM D.
Barbarosa   (83) 60
Country   (85) 156
Raggedy Man   (82) 300
WOOD, CHRISTOPHER
Remo Williams   (86) 457

YABLANS, FRANK
Mommie Dearest   (82) 245
YABLONSKY, YABO
Victory   (82) 374
YALLOP, DAVID
Beyond Reasonable Doubt [1980]   (84) 74
YAMADA, YOJI
Foster Daddy, Tora! [1980]   (82) 163
YATES, PETER
Dresser, The   (84) 130
YEZHOV, VALENTINE
Siberiade [1977]   (83) 299
YOSHA, YAKY
Vulture, The   (86) 464
YOUNG, DALENE
Cross Creek   (84) 116
YOUNG, JOHN SACRET
Testament   (84) 420
YOUNG, PETER
Black Cauldron, The   (86) 75
YOUNG, WALDEMAR
Peter Ibbetson [1935]   (86) 527
Sign of the Cross, The [1932]   (85) 607

ZAILLIAN, STEVEN
Falcon and the Snowman, The   (86) 165
ZANUSSI, KRZYSTOF
Imperative [1982]   (86) 447
ZAPPONI, BERNARDINO
City of Women   (82) 106
ZEFFIRELLI, FRANCO
Traviata, La   (83) 366
ZELIG, BEN
Tomboy   (86) 463
ZEMECKIS, ROBERT
Back to the Future   (86) 65
ZIDI, CLAUDE
My New Partner [1984]   (86) 246
ZIMMERMAN, PAUL D.
King of Comedy, The   (84) 192
ZINDEL, PAUL
Maria's Lovers   (86) 451
Runaway Train   (86) 324
ZWEIBACK, A. MARTIN
Grace Quigley   (86) 445

CINEMATOGRAPHER INDEX

ABBOTT, LENWOOD BALLARD
"Obituaries" (86) 559

ABEL, DAVID
Holiday Inn [1942] (82) 443

AGOSTINI, CLAUDE
Bad Boy, The (86) 437
Quest for Fire (83) 271

AHERN, LLOYD
"Obituaries" (84) 607

AHLBERG, MAC
Re-Animator (86) 457
Trancers (86) 463

AITKEN, LEN
Kid Colter (86) 449

ALCAINE, JOSE LUIS
Rustler's Rhapsody (86) 458

ALCOTT, JOHN
Baby (86) 437
Fort Apache, the Bronx (82) 159
Greystoke (85) 236

ALEKAN, HENRI
State of Things, The (84) 379
Under Fire (84) 441

ALLINGHAM, DAN
Reuben, Reuben (84) 337

ALMENDROS, NESTOR
Pauline at the Beach [1982] (84) 296
Places in the Heart (85) 371
Sophie's Choice (83) 311
Still of the Night (83) 326

ALONZO, JOHN A.
Blue Thunder (84) 84
Cross Creek (84) 116
Lady Sings the Blues [1972] (85) 565
Out of Control (86) 455
Scarface (84) 361

ANCHIA, JUAN RUIZ
Maria's Lovers (86) 451
That Was Then . . . This Is Now (86) 463

ANDERSON, MICHAEL
Broken Rainbow (86) 439

ARONOVICH, RICHARD
Bal, Le [1983] (85) 80
Hanna K. (84) 117
Missing (83) 232

ASH, JEROME
King of Jazz [1930] (86) 515

BAER, HANANIA
Always (86) 60
American Ninja (86) 436
Night Patrol (86) 454

BAGGOT, KING
Gotcha! (86) 444
Last Starfighter, The (85) 277

BAILEY, JOHN
Big Chill, The (84) 78
Cat People (83) 100
Continental Divide (82) 115
Honky Tonk Freeway (82) 199
Mishima (86) 236
Racing with the Moon (85) 397
Silverado (86) 349
That Championship Season (83) 338

BAKER, IAN
Barbarosa (83) 60
Iceman (85) 248
Plenty (86) 271

BALLHAUS, MICHAEL
After Hours (86) 51
Sheer Madness [1983] (86) 459

BARTKOWIAK, ANDRZEJ
Deathtrap (83) 137
Prince of the City (82) 292
Prizzi's Honor (86) 285
Terms of Endearment (84) 414
Verdict, The (83) 377

BARTLE, JAMES
Quiet Earth, The (86) 295

BAZZONI, CAMILLO
Joke of Destiny, A [1983] (85) 259

BELL, MARTIN
Streetwise (86) 364

BERN, PAUL
Beloved Rogue [1927] (84) 522

BERTA, RENATO
Every Man for Himself [1979] (82) 139
Full Moon in Paris (85) 208

BIROC, JOSEPH
Flight of the Phoenix, The [1966] (85) 549
Hammett (84) 174

BIZIOU, PETER
Pink Floyd the Wall [1981] (83) 258
Time Bandits [1980] (82) 364

BODE, RALF D.
Bring on the Night (86) 439
Gorky Park (84) 162
Raggedy Man (82) 300

BOLLINGER, ALUN
Beyond Reasonable Doubt [1980] (84) 74
Came a Hot Friday (86) 439

BONT, JAN DE
Flesh and Blood (86) 443

BOREN, LAMAR
Brewster McCloud [1970] (86) 484

BOYD, RUSSELL
Gallipoli [1980] (82) 179
Mrs. Soffel (85) 314
Soldier's Story, A (85) 427
Tender Mercies (84) 409
Year of Living Dangerously, The [1982] (84) 462

BRENNER, JULES
Return of the Living Dead, The (86) 314

BRODINE, NORBERT
Divorcée, The [1930] (82) 429
Dulcy [1923] (82) 432

BROENIG, H. LYMAN
"Obituaries" (84) 610

BRYANT, BAIRD
Broken Rainbow (86) 439

BURKS, ROBERT
Hondo [1953] (83) 452

BURMANN, HANS
Holy Innocents, The (86) 447

BURUM, STEPHEN H.
Bride, The (86) 438

Outsiders, The   (84) 282
St. Elmo's Fire   (86) 330
BUSH, DICK
Crimes of Passion   (85) 161
Hound of the Baskervilles, The [1978]   (82) 203
Journey of Natty Gann, The   (86) 203
Victor/Victoria   (83) 387
BUTLER, BILL
Rocky III   (83) 283
Rocky IV   (86) 319
Stripes   (82) 336

CARDIFF, JACK
Barefoot Contessa, The [1954]   (82) 399
Ghost Story   (82) 183
Rambo: First Blood Part II   (86) 29
Stephen King's Cat's Eye   (86) 460
CHAPMAN, MICHAEL
Dead Men Don't Wear Plaid   (83) 134
Front, The [1976]   (86) 502
Man with Two Brains, The   (84) 22
Personal Best   (83) 254
CHAPUIS, DOMINIQUE
Shoah   (86) 339
Sugar Cane Alley [1983]   (85) 461
CHEA, CLAUDIO
Crossover Dreams   (86) 441
CHIN, MICHAEL
Chan Is Missing   (83) 113
Dim Sum   (86) 141
CIUPKA, RICHARD
Atlantic City   (82) 74
CLARK, CURTIS
Alamo Bay   (86) 436
Draughtsman's Contract, The [1982]   (84) 126
Sesame Street Presents: Follow That
   Bird   (86) 459
CLARKE, CHARLES G.
"Obituaries"   (84) 613
CLERVAL, DENYS
Erendira [1983]   (85) 181
CLOQUET, GHISLAIN
Four Friends   (82) 167
I Sent a Letter to My Love [1980]   (82) 214
"Obituaries"   (82) 484
Tess [1980]   (82) 471
COLLI, TONINO DELLI
Once upon a Time in America   (85) 345
COLLISTER, PETER LYONS
Avenging Angel   (86) 436
CONNELL, DAVID
Aviator, The   (86) 437
CONNELL, DOUG
Def-Con 4   (86) 441
CONTNER, J. BURGI
Light Ahead, The [1939]   (83) 460
CONTNER, JAMES A.
Berry Gordy's The Last Dragon   (86) 438
Flamingo Kid, The   (85) 192
Nighthawks   (82) 259
COOP, DENYS
"Obituaries"   (82) 484
CORRELL, CHARLES
Star Trek III—The Search for Spock   (85) 439
COULTER, MICHAEL
Gregory's Girl [1981]   (83) 193

COUTARD, RAOUL
First Name, Carmen [1983]   (85) 186
Passion [1982]   (84) 289
COWLEY, GRAEME
Smash Palace [1981]   (83) 302
Utu [1983]   (85) 504
CRABE, JAMES
Karate Kid, The   (85) 264
Police Academy 2   (86) 276
CRONENWETH, JORDAN
Best Friends   (83) 68
Blade Runner   (83) 76
Brewster McCloud [1970]   (86) 484
Cutter's Way   (82) 119
CROSBY, FLOYD
"Obituaries"   (86) 566
CUNDEY, DEAN
Back to the Future   (86) 65
Escape from New York   (82) 133
Psycho II   (84) 307
Romancing the Stone   (85) 421
Thing, The   (83) 343
Warning Sign   (86) 465

DAVIAU, ALLEN
Color Purple, The   (86) 105
E.T.: The Extra-Terrestrial   (83) 151
Falcon and the Snowman, The   (86) 165
Twilight Zone—The Movie   (84) 435
DAVIS, BENJAMIN
Sudden Death   (86) 461
DAY, ERNEST
Passage to India, A   (85) 365
DEAKINS, ROGER
1984   (85) 335
DE BESCHE, AUSTIN
Lianna   (84) 201
Return of the Secaucus 7 [1980]   (83) 484
DE BONT, JAN
All the Right Moves   (84) 41
4th Man, The [1983]   (85) 203
Jewel of the Nile, The   (86) 448
DECAE, HENRI
Bob le Flambeur [1955]   (84) 526
Boys from Brazil, The [1978]   (86) 480
My Other Husband   (86) 453
DE GRASSE, ROBERT
Most Dangerous Game, The [1932]   (86) 519
DE KEYZER, BRUNO
Sunday in the Country, A   (85) 466
DELESALLE, BENEDICTE
Je tu il elle [1974]   (86) 447
DEL RUTH, THOMAS
Breakfast Club, The   (86) 85
Fandango   (86) 442
DEMBO, RICHARD
Dangerous Moves [1984]   (86) 129
DE SANTIS, PASQUALINO
Argent, L' [1983]   (85) 74
Bizet's Carmen [1983]   (85) 98
Three Brothers [1980]   (83) 349
DESCHANEL, CALEB
Natural, The   (85) 329
Neil Simon's The Slugger's Wife   (86) 454
Right Stuff, The   (84) 342

DESIDERI, DANILO
  Water and Soap   (86) 465
DICILLO, TOM
  Stranger than Paradise   (85) 455
DICKERSON, ERNEST
  Brother from Another Planet, The   (85) 118
  Krush Groove   (86) 449
DI GIACOMO, FRANCO
  Night of the Shooting Stars, The [1982]   (84) 258
DI PALMA, CARLO
  Gabriela [1983]   (85) 213
  Tragedy of a Ridiculous Man [1981]   (83) 361

EBINGER, ROBERT
  School Spirit   (86) 458
ECO, PETER
  Rich and Famous   (82) 316
EDESON, ARTHUR
  They Drive by Night [1940]   (83) 508
EL KHADEM, CHIRINE
  Smithereens   (83) 307
ELMES, FREDERICK
  Broken Rainbow   (86) 439
  Valley Girl   (84) 447
ELSWIT, ROBERT
  Moving Violations   (86) 453
  Sure Thing, The   (86) 369
ENGIN, ERDOGAN
  Yol   (83) 411
ENGLAND, BRYAN
  Party Animal   (86) 455
ESCAMILLA, TEO
  Carmen   (84) 101

FASH, MIKE
  Betrayal   (84) 67
FERNANDES, JOAO
  Invasion U.S.A.   (86) 447
FERNANDEZ, ANGEL LUIS
  Only Emptiness Remains   (86) 455
FERRUCCI, RAFFI
  Gringo   (86) 445
FIERBERG, STEVEN
  Streetwalkin'   (86) 461
FIGUEROA, GABRIEL
  Under the Volcano   (85) 499
FIGUEROA, HECTOR R.
  Stitches   (86) 461
FILAC, VILKO
  When Father Was Away on Business
  [1984]   (86) 411
FIORE, BOB
  Can She Bake a Cherry Pie?   (84) 95
FIRMANN, JACQUES
  Hail Mary   (86) 182
FISHER, GERRY
  Holcroft Covenant, The   (86) 446
  Victory   (82) 374
  Wolfen   (82) 382
FOLSEY, GEORGE
  Animal Kingdom, The [1932]   (86) 469
  Guy Named Joe, A [1943]   (82) 435
FRAISSE, ROBERT
  Patsy, The   (86) 456

FRAKER, WILLIAM A.
  Best Little Whorehouse in Texas, The   (83) 72
  Fever Pitch   (86) 443
  Murphy's Romance   (86) 242
  Protocol   (85) 383
  Sharky's Machine   (82) 324
  WarGames   (84) 458
FRANCIS, FREDDIE
  Dune   (85) 171
  French Lieutenant's Woman, The   (82) 174
FREUND, KARL
  Guy Named Joe, A [1943]   (82) 435
FRICKE, RON
  Chronos   (86) 440
  Koyaanisqatsi   (84) 197
FRIEDMAN, JOSEPH
  Angelo My Love   (84) 47
FUJIMOTO, TAK
  Heart Like a Wheel   (84) 182
  Melvin and Howard [1980]   (82) 453

GARCIA, RONALD V.
  One from the Heart   (83) 250
  Rainy Day Friends   (86) 457
GARMES, LEE
  Disraeli [1929]   (82) 426
  Secret Life of Walter Mitty, The [1947]   (86) 540
  Specter of the Rose [1946]   (83) 504
GAUTARD, NOELE
  Adolescente, L' [1979]   (83) 53
GERRARD, HENRY
  Most Dangerous Game, The [1932]   (86) 519
GERSTAD, MERRITT B.
  Bridge of San Luis Rey, The [1929]   (82) 408
GEYER, JOHANNES
  Taxi Zum Klo   (82) 346
GLASBERG, JIMMY
  Shoah   (86) 339
GLENN, PIERRE WILLIAM
  Coup de torchon [1981]   (83) 124
  Loulou [1980]   (82) 226
GLENNON, JAMES
  Norte, El   (84) 265
  Smooth Talk   (86) 354
GLICKMAN, PAUL
  Stuff, The   (86) 461
GODAR, GODFREY
  Gymkata   (86) 445
GOLDBLATT, STEPHEN
  Cotton Club, The   (85) 150
  Outland   (82) 272
  Return of the Soldier, The [1982]   (84) 332
  Young Sherlock Holmes   (86) 431
GORNICK, MICHAEL
  Day of the Dead   (86) 441
GREEN, ALLAN
  Tomorrow [1972]   (84) 589
GREENBERG, ADAM
  Once Bitten   (86) 455
  Terminator, The   (85) 478
GREENBERG, ROBBIE
  Creator   (86) 441
  Movers and Shakers   (86) 453
  Sweet Dreams   (86) 374
GRUSZYNSKI, ALEXANDER
  Almost You   (86) 436

GUARNIER, ENNIO
  Traviata, La   (83) 366
GUFFEY, BURNETT
  "Obituaries"   (84) 623
GURFINKEL, DAVID
  Rappin'   (86) 457
GUTHRIE, CARL
  Bedtime for Bonzo [1951]   (84) 512

HAITKIN, JACQUES
  Nightmare on Elm Street, Part 2, A   (86) 454
HALLER, ERNEST
  Unfaithful, The [1947]   (86) 550
HANNAN, PETER
  Brimstone and Treacle   (83) 91
  Dance with a Stranger [1984]   (86) 125
  Insignificance   (86) 447
  Missionary, The   (83) 233
  Razor's Edge, The   (85) 402
  Turtle Diary   (86) 464
HARA, KAZUTAMI
  Godzilla 1985   (86) 444
HARRIS, STUART
  Wetherby   (86) 406
HASEGAWA, HAJIME
  Here Come the Littles   (86) 446
HASEGAWA, KIYOSHI
  Makioka Sisters, The [1983]   (86) 451
HASKIN, BYRON
  "Obituaries"   (85) 671
HEER, JOHANNA
  Sugarbaby   (86) 461
HEICK, SUSAN
  Hard Traveling   (86) 445
HELLER, OTTO
  Victim [1962]   (85) 649
HICKOX, SID
  Colorado Territory [1949]   (86) 489
  Hatchet Man, The [1932]   (83) 447
HILDYARD, JACK
  Sound Barrier, The [1952]   (85) 621
HILLER, ERWIN
  I Know Where I'm Going [1945]   (83) 456
HIRSCHFELD, ALEC
  Love Letters   (85) 288
HIRSCHFELD, GERALD
  My Favorite Year   (83) 241
  To Be or Not to Be   (84) 426
HORA, JOHN
  Explorers   (86) 442
  Gremlins   (85) 230
  Howling, The   (82) 207
  Twilight Zone—The Movie   (82) 435
HOWE, JAMES WONG
  Hard Way, The [1942]   (85) 555
  Hombre [1967]   (84) 547
  My Reputation [1946]   (85) 586
  North Star, The [1943]   (83) 476
HUBBS, GIL
  This Is Elvis   (82) 360
HUME, ALAN
  Eye of the Needle   (82) 148
  For Your Eyes Only   (82) 155
  Lifeforce   (86) 450
  Octopussy   (84) 276

Return of the Jedi   (84) 326
Runaway Train   (86) 324
View to a Kill, A   (86) 402
HUNT, J. ROY
  Sherlock Holmes [1922]   (83) 494
HYAMS, PETER
  2010   (85) 494
HYLAND, EDWARD
  Light Ahead, The [1939]   (83) 460

IBBETSON, ARTHUR
  Santa Claus   (86) 334
IDZIAK, SLAVOMIR
  Imperative [1982]   (86) 447
IMI, TONY
  Enemy Mine   (86) 161
  Nate and Hayes   (84) 236
IRWIN, MARK
  Videodrome   (84) 452
IVANO, PAUL
  "Obituaries"   (85) 673

JAMES, PETER
  Caddie [1976]   (83) 439
  Wild Duck, The [1983]   (86) 466
JESSUP, ROBERT
  Split Image   (83) 317
JONES, JERRY
  Kerouac, the Movie   (86) 448
JUNE, RAY
  Barbary Coast [1935]   (84) 506
  H. M. Pulham, Esq. [1941]   (82) 439

KALASHNIKOV, LEONID
  Rasputin [1975]   (86) 457
KALICINSKI, JANUSZ
  Man of Iron   (82) 230
KAUFMAN, BORIS
  World of Henry Orient, The [1964]   (84) 600
KEMPER, VICTOR J.
  Clue   (86) 440
  Four Seasons, The   (82) 241
  National Lampoon's Vacation   (84) 241
  Pee-wee's Big Adventure   (86) 265
  Secret Admirer   (86) 459
  Slap Shot [1977]   (82) 467
  They Might Be Giants [1971]   (83) 515
KIESSER, JAN
  Choose Me   (85) 135
  Fright Night   (86) 444
KIHN, ALBERT
  THX 1138 [1971]   (85) 638
KIMBALL, JEFFREY L.
  Legend of Billie Jean, The   (86) 450
KLINE, BENJAMIN H.
  Detour [1946]   (86) 498
KLINE, RICHARD H.
  All of Me   (85) 58
  Body Heat   (82) 87
  Breathless   (84) 89
  Man with One Red Shoe, The   (86) 451
KLOSINSKI, EDWARD
  Man of Iron   (82) 230
  Man of Marble [1977]   (82) 234
KNAPP, DOUGLAS
  Dark Star [1975]   (86) 494

KNOOP, JOHN
Louis Bluie (86) 450
KOBAYASHI, KENICHI
Here Come the Littles (86) 446
KOENEKAMP, FRED J.
Adventures of Buckaroo Banzai, The (85) 47
First Monday in October (82) 151
Wrong Is Right (83) 403
KOLTAI, LAJOS
Colonel Redl [1984] (86) 100
Mephisto (82) 237
KOVACS, LASZLO
Frances (83) 178
Ghostbusters (85) 219
Mask (86) 231
New York, New York [1977] (84) 567
Toy, The (83) 358
KRASKER, ROBERT
"Obituaries" (82) 495
KRASNER, MILTON
Bells Are Ringing [1960] (84) 517
KRIZSAN, LES
Def-Con 4 (86) 441
KRUGER, JULES
Napolean [1927] (82) 461
KUHN, TONI
Bastille [1984] (86) 437
KURANT, WILLY
Tuff Turf (86) 464
KURITA, TOYOMICHI
Trouble in Mind (86) 388

LACHMAN, EDWARD
Desperately Seeking Susan (86) 137
"Interview with Susan Seidelman, An" (86) 37
Tokyo-Ga (86) 463
LANCI, GIUSEPPE
Henry IV [1983] (86) 446
Nostalgia [1983] (85) 340
LANG, CHARLES
Peter Ibbetson [1935] (86) 527
Solid Gold Cadillac, The [1956] (85) 615
LARNER, STEVEN
Twilight Zone—The Movie (84) 435
LASHELLE, JOSEPH
My Cousin Rachel [1952] (82) 458
LASSALLY, WALTER
Bostonians, The (85) 105
Heat and Dust [1982] (84) 187
LASZLO, ANDREW
First Blood (83) 164
Remo Williams (86) 457
Southern Comfort (82) 332
LASZLO, ERNEST
Apache [1954] (82) 395
"Obituaries" (85) 677
LATHROP, PHILIP
Hammett (84) 174
LAWTON, CHARLES, JR.
Cowboy [1958] (82) 417
Long Gray Line, The [1955] (82) 447
LEAVITT, SAM
"Obituaries" (85) 678
Star Is Born, A [1954] (84) 573

LEONETTI, MATTHEW F.
Commando (86) 111
Fast Forward (86) 442
Fast Times at Ridgemont High (83) 156
Jagged Edge (86) 190
Poltergeist (83) 263
Weird Science (86) 465
LEWIS, ROBERT
Gods Must Be Crazy, The [1980] (85) 224
LHOMME, PIERRE
Quartet (82) 296
LI, CHRIS
Louis Bluie (86) 450
LIECHTE, HANS
Boat Is Full, The [1981] (83) 82
Death of Mario Ricci, The [1983] (86) 133
LINDLEY, JOHN
Lily in Love (86) 450
LOFTUS, BRYAN
Company of Wolves, The [1984] (86) 115
LOGAN, BRUCE
TRON (83) 371
LOHMANN, PAUL
Lust in the Dust (86) 450
Mommie Dearest (82) 245
Time After Time [1979] (84) 579
LOISELEUX, JACQUES
Loulou [1980] (82) 226
LUBTCHANSKY, WILLIAM
Every Man for Himself [1979] (82) 139
Shoah (86) 339
Woman Next Door, The (82) 385
LUTHER, IGOR
Danton [1982] (84) 121
Love in Germany, A [1983] (85) 283
LUTIC, BERNARD
Entre nous [1983] (85) 176
Revolution (86) 458
LUTIE, BERNARD
Beau Mariage, Le (83) 65

MCALPINE, DON
Earthling, The [1980] (82) 130
King David (86) 449
Moscow on the Hudson (85) 321
Tempest (83) 331
MACDONALD, PETER
Secret Places [1984] (86) 459
MACHUEL, EMMANUEL
Argent, L' [1983] (85) 74
MCLEAN, NICK
City Heat (85) 141
Goonies, The (86) 176
Staying Alive (84) 386
Stick (86) 460
Twice in a Lifetime (86) 397
MCPHERSON, JOHN
Just One of the Guys (86) 448
MALLOY, MIKE
Hit, The (86) 446
MANKOFSKY, ISIDORE
Better Off Dead (86) 438
MARTIN, JURGEN
Céleste [1981] (83) 104

MATÉ, RUDOLPH
  Come and Get It [1936]   (82) 412
  Our Relations [1936]   (86) 523
MAUCH, THOMAS
  Fitzcarraldo   (83) 167
MEDEIROS, JOSÉ
  Xica [1976]   (83) 407
MEHEUX, PHIL
  Experience Preferred ... but Not Essential
    [1982]   (84) 141
  Long Good Friday, The   (83) 220
  Morons from Outer Space   (86) 452
MENGES, CHRIS
  Comfort and Joy   (85) 146
  Killing Fields, The   (85) 270
  Local Hero   (84) 206
  Marie   (86) 227
  Sense of Freedom, A   (86) 459
MÉNOUD, JEAN-BERNARD
  Hail Mary   (86) 182
MESCALL, JOHN
  Take a Letter, Darling [1942]   (85) 632
METCALFE, JOHN
  James Joyce's Women   (86) 193
METTY, RUSSELL
  Arch of Triumph [1948]   (84) 501
MEYERS, DAVE
  THX 1138 [1971]   (85) 638
MIGNOT, PIERRE
  Come Back to the 5 & Dime Jimmy Dean,
    Jimmy Dean   (83) 120
  Fool for Love   (86) 172
  Streamers   (84) 391
MIKHAILOV, EVGENI
  New Babylon, The [1929]   (84) 561
MILLER, ARTHUR
  Man Hunt [1941]   (85) 570
MIYAGAWA, KAZUO
  MacArthur's Children   (86) 451
MOHR, HAL
  King of Jazz [1930]   (86) 515
  Lost Moment, The [1947]   (83) 465
MONTI, FELIX
  Official Story, The   (86) 249
MOORE, RICHARD
  Annie   (83) 56
MOORE, TED
  Clash of the Titans   (82) 111
  Priest of Love   (82) 288
MORGAN, DONALD M.
  Christine   (84) 106
  Starman   (85) 445
MORRIS, OSWALD
  Dark Crystal, The   (83) 130
  Great Muppet Caper, The   (82) 187
MORRIS, REGINALD
  Christmas Story, A   (84) 110
  Porky's   (83) 267
  Turk 182   (86) 464
MOSKVIN, ANDREI
  New Babylon, The [1929]   (84) 561
MOURA, EDGAR
  Bar Esperanza [1983]   (86) 437
MUDD, VICTORIA
  Broken Rainbow   (86) 439

MULLER, ROBBY
  Paris, Texas   (85) 359
  Repo Man   (85) 408
  They All Laughed   (82) 350
  To Live and Die in L.A.   (86) 379
MURPHY, FRED
  Heartland   (82) 191
  Key Exchange   (86) 448
  State of Things, The   (84) 379
  Trip to Bountiful, The   (86) 383
MYERS, DAVID
  Hard Traveling   (86) 445
  Zoot Suit   (82) 389

NAKAI, ASAKAZU
  Ran   (86) 304
NANNUZZI, ARMANDO
  Nuit de Varennes, La [1982]   (84) 270
  Stephen King's Silver Bullet   (86) 460
NARITA, HIRO
  Never Cry Wolf   (84) 247
  Sylvester   (86) 462
NARUSHIMA, TOICHIRO
  Merry Christmas, Mr. Lawrence   (84) 231
NEAU, ANDRÉ
  Return of Martin Guerre, The   (84) 318
NUNEZ, VICTOR
  Flash of Green, A   (86) 443
NUYTTEN, BRUNO
  Detective   (86) 442
  Garde à vue [1981]   (83) 189
NYKVIST, SVEN
  After the Rehearsal   (85) 52
  Agnes of God   (86) 56
  Cannery Row   (83) 95
  Fanny and Alexander [1982]   (84) 146
  Postman Always Rings Twice, The   (82) 284
  Pretty Baby [1978]   (85) 597
  Star 80   (84) 374
  Swann in Love   (85) 471

OKAZAK, KOZO
  Challenge, The   (83) 109
OLIVER, DAVID
  Cave Girl   (86) 439
ONDŘÍČEK, MIROSLAV
  Amadeus   (85) 63
  Heaven Help Us   (86) 445
  Ragtime   (82) 304
  Silkwood   (84) 367
  Taking Off [1971]   (86) 545
  World According to Garp, The   (83) 397
ORNITZ, ARTHUR
  Chosen, The   (83) 116
  Next Stop, Greenwich Village [1976]   (85) 592
  "Obituaries"   (86) 578
  World of Henry Orient, The [1964]   (84) 600

PAATASHVILI, LEVAN
  Siberiade [1977]   (83) 299
PAUL, IAN
  Sylvia   (86) 462
PAYNTER, ROBERT
  American Werewolf in London, An   (82) 66
  Into the Night   (86) 186
  National Lampoon's European Vacation   (86)
    453

Spies like Us   (86) 360
Superman III   (84) 399
Trading Places   (84) 430
PENZER, JEAN
My Best Friend's Girl [1983]   (85) 326
PETERMAN, DONALD
American Flyers   (86) 436
Cocoon   (86) 96
Flashdance   (84) 158
Kiss Me Goodbye   (82) 209
Mass Appeal   (85) 303
Rich and Famous   (82) 316
Splash   (85) 434
PETERSSON, MARK
Matter of Struggle, A   (86) 451
PHILLIPS, ALEX
Goat, The [1981]   (86) 444
King Solomon's Mines   (86) 449
PIERCE-ROBERTS, TONY
Moonlighting   (83) 237
Private Function, A [1984]   (86) 280
PIKE, KELVIN
Bad Medicine   (86) 437
Dresser, The   (84) 130
PINTER, TOMISLAV
Montenegro   (82) 250
Transylvania 6-5000   (86) 463
PIZER, LARRY
Cattle Annie and Little Britches   (82) 97
Grace Quigley   (86) 444
Too Scared to Scream   (86) 463
PLANCK, ROBERT
Royal Wedding [1951]   (86) 536
POSTER, STEVEN
Heavenly Kid, The   (86) 445
New Kids, The   (86) 454
Testament   (84) 420
PRATT, ROGER
Brazil   (86) 80
PROTAT, FRANÇOIS
Joshua Then and Now   (86) 198
Running Brave   (84) 354

RABIER, JEAN
Horse of Pride, The   (86) 447
RAGONA, CLAUDIO
Macaroni   (86) 451
REED, MICHAEL
Wild Geese II   (86) 466
RENNAHAN, RAY
Becky Sharp [1935]   (82) 403
King of Jazz [1930]   (86) 515
RESCHER, GAYNE
Star Trek II—The Wrath of Khan   (83) 321
RICHARD, EDMOND
Falstaff [1967]   (83) 443
RICHMOND, ANTHONY
Improper Channels   (82) 218
Man Who Fell to Earth, The [1975]   (83) 469
ROIZMAN, OWEN
Absence of Malice   (82) 57
Taps   (82) 343
Tootsie   (83) 353
True Confessions   (82) 368
Vision Quest   (86) 464
ROJAS, MANUEL
Volver a empezar   (83) 393

ROSSON, HAROLD
Pete Kelly's Blues [1955]   (83) 481
Too Hot to Handle [1938]   (84) 596
ROTUNNO, GIUSEPPE
And the Ship Sails On [1983]   (85) 69
City of Women   (82) 106
Red Sonja   (86) 457
ROUSSELOT, PHILIPPE
Diva [1980]   (83) 147
Emerald Forest, The   (86) 156
ROY, SOUMENDU
Home and the World, The [1984]   (86) 447
RUBAN, AL
Love Streams   (85) 293
RUIZ-ANCHIA, JUAN
Stone Boy, The   (85) 450
RUTTENBERG, JOSEPH
Invitation to the Dance [1956]   (86) 507
"Obituaries"   (84) 635
RYAN, PAUL
Fraternity Vacation   (86) 444

SAARINEN, ERIC
Lost in America   (86) 219
Modern Romance   (82) 241
SAITO, TAKAO
Ran   (86) 304
SALOMON, AMNON
Goodbye, New York   (86) 444
SÁNCHEZ, RODOLFO
Kiss of the Spider Woman   (86) 209
Pixote [1980]   (82) 280
SARIN, VICTOR
Heartaches [1981]   (83) 197
SARTOV, HENDRIK
Scarlet Letter, The [1927]   (85) 602
SCHELLERUP, HENNING
Cease Fire   (86) 440
SCHIER, HORST
Taxi Zum Klo   (82) 346
SCHMIDT-REITWEIN, JORG
Where the Green Ants Dream [1984]   (86) 465
SCHNALL, PETER
Matter of Struggle, A   (86) 451
SCHULER, FRED
Arthur   (82) 71
Fletch   (86) 169
King of Comedy, The   (84) 192
Maxie   (86) 452
SCHWARTZ, JEAN-PAUL
Little Jerk [1984]   (86) 450
SCHWARZENBERGER, XAVER
Berlin Alexanderplatz [1980]   (84) 57
Lili Marleen   (82) 222
Lola [1981]   (83) 215
Querelle [1982]   (84) 313
Veronika Voss   (83) 382
SEALE, JOHN
Careful He Might Hear You [1983]   (85) 130
Silver City [1984]   (86) 460
Witness   (86) 421
SEAWRIGHT, ROY
Our Relations [1936]   (86) 523
SEMLER, DEAN
Coca-Cola Kid, The   (86) 440

Mad Max Beyond Thunderdome (86) 223
Razorback [1984] (86) 457
Road Warrior, The [1981] (83) 277

SERESIN, MICHAEL
Birdy (85) 93
Shoot the Moon (83) 295

SHAMROY, LEON
Snows of Kilimanjaro, The [1952] (83) 498

SLOCOMBE, DOUGLAS
Freud [1962] (84) 535
Indiana Jones and the Temple of Doom (85) 253
Never Say Never Again (84) 252
Pirates of Penzance, The (84) 301
Raiders of the Lost Ark (82) 308

SMOKLER, PETER
This Is Spinal Tap (85) 484

SNYDER, WILLIAM E.
Creature from the Black Lagoon, The [1954] (82) 422

SOKOL, YURI
Lonely Hearts [1982] (84) 212
My First Wife (86) 453

SONNENFELD, BARRY
Blood Simple (86) 438
Compromising Positions (86) 120

SOPANEN, JERI
My Dinner with André (82) 255

SOVA, PETER
Diner (83) 142

SPAGNOLI, ALBERT
Hercules II (86) 446

SPERA, MIKE
When Nature Calls (86) 465

SPINOTTI, DANTE
Softly Softly [1984] (86) 460

ST. JOHN, TONY
Broken Rainbow (86) 439

STAHL, JORGE
Missing in Action 2 (86) 452

STANIER, JOHN
Death Wish III (86) 441

STEYN, JACQUES
Out of Order (86) 455

STORARO, VITTORIO
Agatha [1979] (83) 435
Ladyhawke (86) 214
One from the Heart (83) 250
Reds (82) 312

STOUT, ARCHIE J.
Fort Apache [1948] (84) 530
Hondo [1953] (83) 452
It Happened Tomorrow [1944] (84) 552

STRADLING, HARRY, JR.
Buddy Buddy (82) 93
Micki & Maude (85) 308
S.O.B. (82) 328
Way We Were, The [1973] (82) 474

STRUSS, KARL
Journey into Fear [1943] (86) 511
"Obituaries" (82) 503
Sign of the Cross, The [1932] (85) 607

SUHRSTEDT, TIMOTHY
City Limits (86) 440
Teen Wolf (86) 462

SURTEES, BRUCE
Beverly Hills Cop (85) 88
Firefox (83) 160
Honkytonk Man (83) 200
Pale Rider (86) 261
Play Misty for Me [1971] (86) 532
Risky Business (84) 349
Sudden Impact (84) 395
Tightrope (85) 489

SURTEES, ROBERT
Arrangement, The [1969] (86) 474
Mutiny on the Bounty [1962] (85) 581
"Obituaries" (86) 584

TAKABA, TETSUO
Foster Daddy, Tora! [1980] (82) 163

TAMAI, MASAO
Flowing [1956] (86) 444
Late Chrysanthemums [1954] (86) 449

TAMMES, FRED
Shooting Party, The [1984] (86) 344

TARBES, JEAN-JAQUES
My New Partner [1984] (86) 246

TAYLOR, DYANNA
Pumping Iron II (86) 455

TAYLOR, RONNIE
Chorus Line, A (86) 91
Gandhi (83) 183

TENNIGLO, BEN
Flaxfield, The [1983] (86) 443

THOMSON, ALEX
Bullshot [1983] (86) 439
Eureka (86) 442
Excalibur (82) 144
Year of the Dragon (86) 426

THORIN, DONALD
Mischief (86) 452
Officer and a Gentleman, An (83) 246
Purple Rain (85) 389
Thief (82) 356

THURY, MARTIAL
Peril (86) 456

TICKNER, CLIVE
Ploughman's Lunch, The [1983] (85) 377

TIDY, FRANK
Code of Silence (86) 440
Grey Fox, The (84) 168
Mean Season, The (86) 452
One Magic Christmas (86) 455

TIRL, GEORGE
1918 (86) 454

TOLAND, GREGG
Come and Get It [1936] (82) 412
History Is Made at Night [1937] (84) 542

TOSI, MARIO
Whose Life Is It Anyway? (82) 378

TOURNIER, JEAN
Target (86) 462

TOVER, LEO
I'm No Angel [1933] (85) 561
Woman on the Beach, The [1947] (83) 519

TUFANO, BRIAN
Dreamscape (85) 166

TURNER, GEORGE JESSE
28 Up [1984] (86) 392

CINEMATOGRAPHER INDEX

TURPIN, GERRY
Doctor and the Devils, The   (86) 442

UNSWORTH, GEOFFREY
Superman II   (82) 339
Tess [1980]   (82) 471

VACANO, JOST
Boot, Das [1981]   (83) 86
VAN BORNEMANN, MARK
Test of Love   (86) 462
VANLINT, DEREK
Dragonslayer   (82) 125
VARINI, CARLO
Subway   (86) 461
VAVRA, JOSEF
Querelle [1982]   (84) 313
VIERNY, SACHA
Beau Pere   (82) 78
VILLALOBOS, REYNALDO
Risky Business   (84) 349
VOGEL, PAUL C.
Time Machine, The [1960]   (84) 585

WAGNER, ROY H.
9 Deaths of the Ninja   (86) 454
WAGREITCH, HERB
Ghostbusters   (85) 219
WAITE, RIC
Brewster's Millions   (86) 438
Footloose   (85) 198
48 HRS.   (83) 173
Summer Rental   (86) 462
Tex   (83) 335
Volunteers   (86) 464
WALKER, JOSEPH
Miracle Woman, The [1931]   (83) 473
"Obituaries"   (86) 584
Roughly Speaking [1945]   (83) 490
WALSH, DAVID M.
Country   (85) 156
Max Dugan Returns   (84) 228
My Science Project   (86) 453
Only When I Laugh   (82) 268
WALTHERS, JUERG
Night Patrol   (86) 454
WARREN, JOHN F.
Torn Curtain [1966]   (85) 644
WATKIN, DAVID
Chariots of Fire   (82) 101
Hotel New Hampshire, The   (85) 243
Out of Africa   (86) 255
Return to Oz   (86) 458
White Nights   (86) 416
Yentl   (84) 468

WATTS, FRANK
D.A.R.Y.L.   (86) 441
Educating Rita   (84) 136
WAXMAN, HARRY
Wicker Man, The [1974]   (86) 555
WAYMAN, JEFF
Matter of Struggle, A   (86) 451
WEIDMAN, JOAN
Broken Rainbow   (86) 439
WETZEL, ALBERT
"Obituaries"   (85) 701
WEXLER, HASKELL
Man Who Loved Women, The   (84) 218
WILCOX, JOHN
Hound of the Baskervilles, The [1978]   (82) 203
WILLIAMS, BILLY
Dreamchild   (86) 146
Eleni   (86) 151
Gandhi   (83) 183
On Golden Pond   (82) 263
Ordeal by Innocence [1984]   (86) 455
WILLIS, GORDON
Broadway Danny Rose   (85) 112
Midsummer Night's Sex Comedy, A   (83) 228
Pennies from Heaven   (82) 276
Perfect   (86) 456
Purple Rose of Cairo, The   (86) 290
Stardust Memories [1980]   (85) 626
Zelig   (84) 473
WOOD, OLIVER
Joey   (86) 448

YARUSSI, DANIEL
Tomboy   (86) 463
YOUNG, FREDDIE
Richard's Things   (82) 321
YOUNG, FREDERICK A.
Invitation to the Dance [1956]   (86) 507
Nell Gwyn [1934]   (84) 557

ZAPASNIK, STEFAN
Mixed Blood   (86) 452
ZIELINSKI, JERZY
Cal   (85) 124
ZITZERMANN, BERNARD
Balance, La [1982]   (84) 52
ZSIGMOND, VILMOS
Blow Out   (82) 83
Heaven's Gate   (82) 195
Jinxed   (83) 206
Real Genius   (86) 309
River, The   (85) 416
Table for Five   (84) 404

EDITOR INDEX

ABROMS, EDWARD
  Blue Thunder   (84) 84
ADAMS, JOHN K.
  Streetwalkin'   (86) 461
AKST, ALBERT
  Royal Wedding [1951]   (86) 536
ALICE, MAURO
  Kiss of the Spider Woman   (86) 209
ALLEN, DEDE
  Breakfast Club, The   (86) 85
  Reds   (82) 312
  Slap Shot [1977]   (82) 467
ALSTON, EMMETT
  9 Deaths of the Ninja   (86) 454
ANDERSON, WILLIAM
  Gallipoli [1980]   (82) 179
  King David   (86) 449
  Razorback [1984]   (86) 457
  Tender Mercies   (84) 409
  Year of Living Dangerously, The
    [1982]   (84) 462
ANDREWS, CHRISTOPHER
  Joey   (86) 448
APPLETON, PETER
  Rainy Day Friends   (86) 457
ARNSTEN, STEFAN
  Arrangement, The [1969]   (86) 474
AUDSLEY, MICK
  Dance with a Stranger [1984]   (86) 125
  Hit, The   (86) 446
AVILDSEN, JOHN G.
  Karate Kid, The   (85) 264

BAIRD, STUART
  Ladyhawke   (86) 214
  Outland   (82) 272
  Revolution   (86) 458
BAKER, NANCY
  Streetwise   (86) 364
BALSAM, ALAN
  Better Off Dead   (86) 438
  To Be or Not to Be   (84) 426
BALSON, MICHAEL
  Road Warrior, The [1981]   (83) 277
BARAGLI, NINO
  Once upon a Time in America   (85) 345
BARNES, PAUL
  Pumping Iron II   (86) 456
BARON, SUZANNE
  Atlantic City   (82) 74
  My Dinner wtih André   (82) 255
BARRAQUÉ, MARTINE
  Woman Next Door, The   (82) 385
BARTON, SEAN
  Eye of the Needle   (82) 148
  Jagged Edge   (86) 190
  Return of the Jedi   (84) 326
BAUCHENS, ANNE
  Sign of the Cross, The [1932]   (85) 607
BEAUMAN, NICHOLAS
  Mrs. Soffel   (85) 314

BENKO, TOM
  Movers and Shakers   (86) 453
BERBER, HELENA
  Boat Is Full, The [1981]   (83) 151
BERGER, PETER E.
  First Monday in October   (82) 151
  Mommie Dearest   (82) 245
BEYDA, KENT
  Fright Night   (86) 443
  This Is Spinal Tap   (85) 484
BEYER, ED
  Too Scared to Scream   (86) 463
BIGGERSTAFF, CAROLINE
  Soldier's Story, A   (85) 427
BIURRUN, JOSÉ MARIA
  Holy Innocents, The   (86) 447
BIXMAN, JERRY
  Krush Groove   (86) 449
BLANGSTED, FOLMAR
  "Obituaries"   (83) 526
  Star Is Born, A [1954]   (84) 573
BLANKETT, BETSY
  Norte, El   (84) 265
BLEWITT, DAVID
  Ghostbusters   (85) 219
BLOOM, JOHN
  Betrayal   (84) 67
  Chorus Line, A   (86) 91
  French Lieutenant's Woman, The   (82) 174
  Gandhi   (83) 183
BOITA, PETER
  Heartaches [1981]   (83) 197
  Jewel of the Nile, The   (86) 448
BONNOT, FRANÇOISE
  Hanna K.   (84) 177
  I Sent a Letter to My Love [1980]   (82) 214
  Missing   (82) 232
  Swann in Love   (85) 471
  Year of the Dragon   (86) 426
BONNOT, MONIQUE
  Bob le Flambeur [1955]   (84) 526
BOOTH, MARGARET
  Annie   (83) 56
  Bridge of San Luis Rey, The [1929]   (82)
    408
  Way We Were, The [1973]   (82) 474
BORDEN, MARSHALL M.
  Wolfen   (82) 382
BOWERS, GEORGE
  Adventures of Buckaroo Banzai, The
    (85) 47
BOYD-PERKINS, ERIC
  Wicker Man, The [1974]   (86) 555
BOYER, LYLE
  Woman on the Beach, The [1947]   (83) 519
BOYLE, PETER
  Morons from Outer Space   (86) 452
  Razor's Edge, The   (85) 402
BRACHT, FRANK
  Hombre [1967]   (84) 547
  "Obituaries"   (86) 561

BRADSELL, MICHAEL
Cal (85) 124
Local Hero (84) 206
BRADY, BOB
Nightmare on Elm Street, Part 2, A (86) 454
BRAM, MARTIN
Wolfen (82) 382
BRETHERTON, DAVID
Baby (86) 437
Best Little Whorehouse in Texas, The (83)
72
Cannery Row (83) 95
Clue (86) 440
BROCHU, DON
Neil Simon's The Slugger's Wife (86) 454
BROWN, O. NICHOLAS
Bad Medicine (86) 437
Heart Like a Wheel (84) 182
Man with One Red Shoe, The (86) 451
Mischief (86) 452
BRUCE, JAMES
Alamo Bay (86) 436
BUBA, PASQUALE
Day of the Dead (86) 441
BUFF, CONRAD
Jagged Edge (86) 190
BURNETT, JOHN F.
Rich and Famous (82) 316
BURNS, MARK
Almost You (86) 436

CAMBAS, JACQUELINE
Cat People (83) 100
City Heat (85) 141
Personal Best (83) 254
Racing with the Moon (85) 397
Zoot Suit (82) 389
CAMBERN, DONN
Excalibur (82) 144
Romancing the Stone (85) 421
Tempest (83) 331
Time After Time [1979] (84) 579
CAMPBELL, MALCOLM
American Werewolf in London, An (82) 66
Into the Night (86) 186
Spies like Us (86) 360
Trading Places (84) 430
Twilight Zone—The Movie (84) 435
CARLISLE, ROBERT
King of Jazz [1930] (86) 515
CARR, ADRIAN
D.A.R.Y.L. (86) 441
CARRUTH, MILTON
Lost Moment, The [1947] (83) 465
CARRUTH, WILLIAM
They All Laughed (82) 350
CARTER, JOHN
Mikey and Nicky [1976] (85) 576
Taking Off [1971] (86) 545
CASTRO, EMMANUELLE
Gabriela [1983] (85) 213
CHANDLER, MICHAEL
Amadeus (85) 63
Mishima (86) 236
Never Cry Wolf (84) 247

CHAVES, JULIO
Cease Fire (86) 440
CHEW, RICHARD
Creator (86) 441
My Favorite Year (83) 241
Real Genius (86) 309
Risky Business (84) 349
CIRINCIONE, RICHARD P.
Target (86) 462
CLANCEY, MARGARET
History Is Made at Night [1937] (84) 542
CLARK, AL
Cowboy [1958] (82) 417
CLARK, JIM
Agatha [1979] (83) 435
Honky Tonk Freeway (82) 199
Killing Fields, The (85) 270
CLARK, LAURENCE MERV
Return of the Soldier, The [1982] (84) 332
CLIFFORD, GRAEME
Man Who Fell to Earth, The [1975] (83)
469
Postman Always Rings Twice, The (82)
284
COATES, ANNE V.
Greystoke (85) 236
Pirates of Penzance, The (84) 301
Ragtime (82) 304
COBURN, ARTHUR
Beverly Hills Cop (85) 88
COLE, STAN
Christmas Story, A (84) 110
Porky's (83) 267
Turk 182 (86) 464
COLLINGWOOD, MONICA
Secret Life of Walter Mitty, The [1947] (86) 540
CONRAD, SCOTT
Stephen King's Cat's Eye (86) 460
CONTE, MARK
Missing in Action 2 (86) 452
Under Fire (84) 441
COOKE, MALCOLM
Sweet Dreams (86) 374
COUSSEIN, SOPHIA
Loulou [1980] (82) 226
COX, JOEL
Honkytonk Man (83) 200
Pale Rider (86) 261
Sudden Impact (84) 395
Tightrope (85) 489
CRAFFORD, IAN
Emerald Forest, The (86) 156
CRAVEN, GARTH
Educating Rita (84) 136
CRISTIANI, GABRIELLA
Tragedy of a Ridiculous Man [1981] (83)
361
CROCIANNI, RAIMONDO
Bal, Le [1983] (85) 80
Nuit de Varennes, La [1982] (84) 270
CROSLAND, ALAN, JR.
Apache [1954] (82) 395
Unfaithful, The [1947] (86) 550
CRUST, ARNOLD
Death Wish III (86) 441

EDITOR INDEX

CRUTCHER, SUSAN
  Pumping Iron II   (86) 456
CSÁKÁNY, ZSUZSA
  Colonel Redl [1984]   (86) 100
CURTISS, EDWARD
  Barbary Coast [1935]   (84) 506
  Come and Get It [1936]   (82) 412

DANEVIC, NENA
  Amadeus   (85) 63
DANTE, JOE
  Howling, The   (82) 207
DAVIES, FREEMAN
  Brewster's Millions   (86) 438
  48 HRS.   (83) 173
  Southern Comfort   (82) 332
DAVIES, PAUL
  Priest of Love   (82) 288
DAVIES, PETER
  Octopussy   (84) 276
  Shooting Party, The [1984]   (86) 344
  View to a Kill, A   (86) 402
DAWSON, RALPH
  Hondo [1953]   (83) 452
DEBRIL, MARIE-AIMÉE
  Woman Next Door, The   (82) 385
DE CASABLANCA, DENISE
  Return of Martin Guerre, The   (84) 318
DECUGIS, CECILE
  Beau Mariage, Le   (83) 65
  Full Moon in Paris   (85) 208
  Pauline at the Beach [1982]   (84) 296
DEDET, YANN
  Loulou   (82) 226
DEL REY, PEDRO
  Carmen   (84) 101
DERUE, EUGENE
  "Obituaries"   (86) 566
DIXON, HUMPHREY
  Heat and Dust [1982]   (84) 187
  Maria's Lovers   (86) 451
  Quartet   (82) 296
DODD, PATRICK
  Smooth Talk   (86) 354
DOLAN, DENNIS
  Repo Man   (85) 408
  Wolfen   (82) 382
DOMMARTIN, SOLVEIG
  Tokyo-Ga   (86) 463
DORNISCH, WILLIAM P.
  Star Trek II—The Wrath of Khan   (83) 321
DOYLE, JULIAN
  Brazil   (86) 80
  Time Bandits [1980]   (82) 364
DUFFY, JOHN
  Stitches   (86) 461
DUNHAM, DUWAYNE
  Mean Season, The   (86) 452
  Return of the Jedi   (84) 326
DUNN, STEVE
  Fool for Love   (86) 172
DUTHIE, MICHAEL J.
  American Ninja   (86) 436
DUTT, DULAL
  Home and the World, The [1984]   (86) 447

ECONOMOU, MICHAEL
  Four Seasons, The   (82) 171
EFFENTERRE, JOELE VAN
  Death of Mario Ricci, The [1983]   (86) 133
ELIAS, LUIZ
  Pixote [1980]   (82) 280
ELIOPOULAS, NICHOLAS
  Best Little Whorehouse in Texas, The   (83) 72
ELLIS, MICHAEL
  Bride, The   (86) 438
  Comfort and Joy   (85) 146
  Jewel of the Nile, The   (86) 448
ERNST, DONALD W.
  Starchaser   (86) 460
ESTRIN, ROBERT
  Breathless   (84) 89

FABRY, CLARA
  Céleste [1981]   (83) 104
FARR, GLENN
  Right Stuff, The   (84) 342
FAZAN, ADRIENNE
  Bells Are Ringing [1960]   (84) 517
  Invitation to the Dance [1956]   (86) 507
FEHR, KAJA
  Prizzi's Honor   (86) 285
FEHR, RUDI
  One from the Heart   (83) 250
  Prizzi's Honor   (86) 285
FENN, SUZANNE
  Pretty Baby [1978]   (85) 597
FERRETTI, ROBERT A.
  Gymkata   (86) 445
  Out of Control   (86) 455
FERRIOL, CAROLINE
  Cutter's Way   (82) 534
FIELD, ROBERT
  Cave Girl   (86) 439
FIELDS, VERNA
  "Obituaries"   (83) 534
FINFER, DAVID
  Lost in America   (86) 219
  Modern Romance   (82) 241
FITZSTEPHENS, JOHN J.
  Deathtrap   (83) 137
  Prince of the City   (82) 292
FOOT, GEOFFREY
  Sound Barrier, The [1952]   (85) 621
FORD, BARBARA
  Mask   (86) 231
FRANCIS-BRUCE, RICHARD
  Careful He Might Hear You [1983]   (85) 130
  Mad Max Beyond Thunderdome   (86) 223
FRANK, PETER
  Compromising Positions   (86) 120
  Verdict, The   (83) 377
FRATICELLI, FRANCO
  Joke of Destiny, A [1983]   (85) 259
FRAZER, LINDSAY
  Test of Love   (86) 462
FRECHE, LUC
  Je tu il elle [1974]   (86) 447
FREEMAN-FOX, LOIS
  Teen Wolf   (86) 462

FREUND, JAY
  Trip to Bountiful, The   (86) 383
FRICKE, RON
  Chronos   (86) 440
  Koyaanisqatsi   (84) 197
FRIEDGEN, BUD
  This Is Elvis   (82) 360
FRUCHTMAN, LISA
  Heaven's Gate   (82) 195
  Right Stuff, The   (84) 342

GAILLING, HANS
  Céleste [1981]   (83) 104
GANCE, ABEL
  Napoleon [1927]   (82) 461
GARFIELD, DAVID
  All the Right Moves   (84) 41
  Chosen, The   (83) 116
  Sylvester   (86) 462
GARRONE, MIRCO
  Henry IV [1983]   (86) 446
GARSON, ARLINE
  Nightmare on Elm Street, Part 2, A   (86) 454
GAY, NORMAN
  Lily in Love   (86) 450
GEE, TIMOTHY
  Clash of the Titans   (82) 111
  Ordeal by Innocence [1984]   (86) 455
GIBBS, ANTONY
  Agnes of God   (86) 56
  Dune   (85) 171
  Ragtime   (82) 304
GILMORE, STUART
  World of Henry Orient, The [1964]   (84) 600
GLATSTEIN, BERT
  Rappin'   (86) 457
GODARD, JEAN-LUC
  Every Man for Himself [1979]   (82) 139
  Passion   (84) 289
GOLDBLATT, MARK
  Commando   (86) 111
  Howling, The   (82) 207
  Rambo: First Blood Part II   (86) 299
  Terminator, The   (85) 478
GOLDMAN, MIA
  Choose Me   (85) 135
GONZALEZ, CONRAD M.
  Krush Groove   (86) 449
GORDEAN, WILLIAM
  Sharky's Machine   (82) 324
  Stick   (86) 460
GORDON, ROBERT
  Return of the Living Dead, The   (86) 314
GORDOS, EVA
  Valley Girl   (84) 447
GOURSAUD, ANNE
  One from the Heart   (83) 250
  Outsiders, The   (84) 282
GOURSON, JEFF
  Perfect   (86) 456
  TRON   (83) 371
GOW, JOHN
  Gregory's Girl [1981]   (83) 193

GREEN, PAUL
  Brimstone and Treacle   (83) 91
  Missionary, The   (83) 233
GREENBERG, JERRY
  Heaven's Gate   (82) 195
  Scarface   (84) 361
  Still of the Night   (83) 326
  They Might Be Giants [1971]   (83) 515
GREENBURY, CHRISTOPHER
  Heavenly Kid, The   (86) 445
GREENE, WENDY
  Love Letters   (85) 288
GRENVILLE, GEORGE
  Wrong Is Right   (83) 403
GROSS, ROLAND
  Woman on the Beach, The [1947]   (83) 519
GROSSMAN, MARC
  Once Bitten   (86) 455
  Tuff Turf   (86) 464
GROVER, JOHN
  For Your Eyes Only   (82) 155
  Lifeforce   (86) 450
GRUNENWALDT, LUCE
  Fool for Love   (86) 172
GUIDO, ELISABETH
  My Other Husband   (86) 453
GUILLEMOT, AGNES
  Dangerous Moves [1984]   (86) 129
GUNEY, YILMAZ
  Yol   (83) 411
GUNTEN, MATHIAS VON
  Taxi Zum Klo   (82) 346
GUTHRIDGE, JOHN
  Victim [1961]   (85) 649
GUYOT, RAYMONDE
  Peril   (86) 456

HAINES, RICHARD
  Clue   (86) 440
HALE, WANDA
  "Obituaries"   (83) 537
HALSEY, RICHARD
  Dreamscape   (85) 166
  Moscow on the Hudson   (85) 321
  Next Stop, Greenwich Village [1976]   (85) 592
  That Championship Season   (83) 338
HAMBLING, GERRY
  Birdy   (85) 93
  Heartaches [1981]   (83) 197
  Pink Floyd the Wall [1981]   (83) 258
  Shoot the Moon   (83) 295
HANLEY, DANIEL
  Cocoon   (86) 96
  Splash   (85) 434
HARRIS, RICHARD A.
  Fletch   (86) 169
  Toy, The   (83) 358
HARRISON, DOANE
  Take a Letter, Darling [1942]   (85) 632
HARTZELL, DUANE
  Aviator, The   (86) 437
HARVEY, JOAN
  Matter of Struggle, A   (86) 451
HAUGSE, WILLIAM
  Cattle Annie and Little Britches   (82) 97

HEICK, SUSAN
Hard Traveling (86) 445
HEIM, ALAN
Goodbye, New York (86) 444
Star 80 (84) 374
HEISLER, STUART
Peter Ibbetson [1935] (86) 527
HELFRICH, MARK
Rambo: First Blood Part II (86) 299
HENNESY, DALE
"Obituaries" (82) 491
HEREDIA, LISA
Beau Mariage, Le (83) 65
HERRING, PEMBROKE
Best Little Whorehouse in Texas, The (83) 72
National Lampoon's European Vacation (86) 453
National Lampoon's Vacation (84) 241
Out of Africa (86) 255
HERZNER, NORBERT
Out of Order (86) 455
HILL, MICHAEL J.
Cocoon (86) 96
Splash (85) 434
HIRSCH, PAUL
Blow Out (82) 83
Footloose (85) 198
Protocol (85) 383
HIRSCH, TINA
Explorers (86) 442
Gremlins (85) 230
Twilight Zone—The Movie (84) 435
HIRTZ, DAGMAR
Sheer Madness [1983] (86) 459
HOAGLAND, GELSWORTH
Holiday Inn [1942] (82) 443
HODGSON, LESLIE
Return to Oz (86) 458
HOENIG, DOV
Thief (82) 356
HOFFMAN, BUD
Torn Curtain [1966] (85) 644
HOFSTRA, JACK
Best Little Whorehouse in Texas, The (83) 72
HOLDEN, DAVID
Journey of Natty Gann, The (86) 203
HOLLAND, RODNEY
Company of Wolves, The [1984] (86) 115
HOLLYWOOD, PETER
Santa Claus (86) 334
HOLMES, CHRISTOPHER
Berry Gordy's The Last Dragon (86) 438
Code of Silence (86) 440
Nighthawks (82) 259
HOLZMAN, ALLAN
Out of Control (86) 455
HONESS, PETER
Plenty (86) 271
HORNBECK, WILLIAM
Barefoot Contessa, The [1954] (82) 399
"Obituaries" (84) 624
HORTON, KIM
28 Up [1984] (86) 392

HORTON, MICHAEL
Beyond Reasonable Doubt [1980] (84) 74
Quiet Earth, The (86) 295
Smash Palce [1981] (83) 302
Sylvia (86) 462
Utu [1983] (85) 504
HORVITCH, ANDY
Rappin' (86) 457
HUGGINS, JERE
Personal Best (83) 254
HUMPHREYS, NED
Personal Best (83) 254
HYDE, GLENN
Hound of the Baskervilles, The [1978] (82) 203

INGEMARSSON, SYLVIA
After the Rehearsal (85) 52
Fanny and Alexander [1982] (84) 146
Montenegro (82) 250
IRVINE, FRANK
Grey Fox, The (84) 168

JACKSON, ARMETTA
Black Cauldron, The (86) 75
JACOBI, MICHAEL
When Nature Calls (86) 465
JAGLOM, HENRY
Always (86) 60
Can She Bake a Cherry Pie? (84) 95
JARMUSCH, JIM
Stranger than Paradise (85) 455
JAVET, FRANÇOISE
Balance, La [1982] (84) 52
JAYNES, RODERICK
Blood Simple (86) 438
JENKINS, ERIC
Fast Times at Ridgemont High (83) 156
JENKINS, SUSAN
Party Animal (86) 455
JOHN, IAN
Utu [1983] (85) 504
JOHNSON, KEN
That Was Then . . . This Is Now (86) 463
JONES, ALAN
Bullshot [1983] (86) 439
JONES, JEFF
Fever Pitch (86) 443
JONES, ROBERT
Twice in a Lifetime (86) 397
JORDAN, BERT
Our Relations [1936] (86) 523
JURGENSON, ALBERT
Adolescente, L' [1979] (83) 53
Garde à vue [1981] (83) 189
Goat, The [1981] (86) 444
JYMPSON, JOHN
Bad Medicine (86) 437

KAHN, MICHAEL
Color Purple, The (86) 105
Goonies, The (86) 176
Indiana Jones and the Temple of Doom (85) 253
Poltergeist (83) 263

Raiders of the Lost Ark   (82) 308
Table for Five   (84) 404
Twilight Zone—The Movie   (84) 435
KAHN, SHELDON
  Absence of Malice   (82) 57
  Ghostbusters   (85) 219
  Kiss Me Goodbye   (83) 209
  Out of Africa   (86) 255
KAMEN, JAY
  Split Image   (83) 317
KANY, ZSUZSA ZSA
  Mephisto   (82) 237
KARR, GARRY
  Crossover Dreams   (86) 441
KEATING, ARTHUR
  James Joyce's Women   (86) 193
KELLER, HARRY
  Fast Forward   (86) 442
  Specter of the Rose [1943]   (83) 504
  Stripes   (82) 336
  Transylvania 6-5000   (86) 463
KELLY, MICHAEL
  Honkytonk Man   (83) 200
KEMP, JACK
  Light Ahead, The [1939]   (83) 460
KEMPLEN, RALPH
  Dark Crystal, The   (83) 130
  Freud [1962]   (84) 535
  Great Muppet Caper, The   (82) 187
KENT, TED J.
  Bedtime for Bonzo [1951]   (84) 512
  Creature from the Black Lagoon, The
    [1954]   (82) 422
KERAMIDAS, HARRY
  Back to the Future   (86) 65
KERN, HAL C.
  Beloved Rogue [1927]   (84) 368
  "Obituaries"   (86) 573
KIZER, ROBERT
  City Limits   (86) 440
KLINGMAN, LYNZEE
  Maxie   (86) 452
  True Confessions   (82) 368
KLOTZ, GEORGES
  Little Jerk [1984]   (86) 450
KONG, JACKIE
  Night Patrol   (86) 454
KOSLOWSKI, ALAN J.
  Krush Groove   (86) 449
KOULAGRINE, VALENTINA
  Siberiade [1977]   (83) 299
KRESS, HAROLD F.
  H.M. Pulham, Esq. [1941]   (82) 439
KUKLOWSKY, VAL
  Gringo   (86) 445
KUROIWA, YOSHITAMI
  Godzilla 1985   (86) 444
KUROSAWA, AKIRA
  Ran   (86) 304
KURSON, JANE
  Pumping Iron II   (86) 456

LAMBERT, ROBERT K.
  Bring on the Night   (86) 439
  Hotel New Hampshire, The   (85) 243

LANDIS, EVAN
  Sesame Street Presents: Follow That Bird
    459
LANGLOIS, YVES
  Quest for Fire   (83) 271
LANG-WILLAR, SUZANNE
  First Name, Carmen [1983]   (85) 186
LAUB, MARC
  Four Friends   (82) 167
  Hammett   (84) 174
LAWRENCE, ROBERT
  Never Say Never Again   (84) 252
  Warning Sign   (86) 465
LAWSON, TONY
  Dragonslayer   (82) 125
  Eureka   (86) 442
  Insignificance   (86) 447
LEAN, DAVID
  Passage to India, A   (85) 365
LEBENZON, CHRISTOPHER
  Weird Science   (86) 465
  Wolfen   (82) 382
LEBOWITZ, ARMOND
  Stuff, The   (86) 461
LEEDS, ROBERT M.
  Pete Kelly's Blues [1955]   (83) 481
LEIGHTON, ROBERT
  Sure Thing, The   (86) 369
  This Is Spinal Tap   (85) 484
LERNER, IRVING
  New York, New York [1977]   (84) 567
LEVIN, SIDNEY
  Cross Creek   (84) 116
  Front, The [1976]   (86) 502
  Murphy's Romance   (86) 242
  River, The   (85) 416
LEWIS, TIM
  Lonely Hearts [1982]   (84) 212
  My First Wife   (86) 453
LEWIS, VICTORIA
  Louis Bluie   (86) 450
LINDER, STU
  Diner   (83) 142
  Natural, The   (85) 329
  Young Sherlock Holmes   (86) 431
LITTLETON, CAROL
  Big Chill, The   (84) 78
  Body Heat   (82) 87
  E.T.: The Extra-Terrestrial   (83) 151
  Places in the Heart   (85) 371
  Silverado   (86) 349
LOEFFLER, LOUIS
  My Cousin Rachel   (82) 458
LOEWENTHAL, DANIEL
  Invasion U.S.A.   (86) 447
  Stephen King's Silver Bullet   (86) 460
LOMBARDO, LOUIS
  Brewster McCloud [1970]   (86) 484
  Just One of the Guys   (86) 448
LONDON, ANDREW
  Psycho II   (84) 307
LONDON, MELODY
  Stranger than Paradise   (85) 455
LORENZ, JULIANE
  Berlin Alexanderplatz [1980]   (84) 57

Lili Marleen (82) 222
Lola [1981] (83) 215
Querelle [1982] (84) 313
Veronika Voss (83) 382
LOTTMAN, EVAN
Sophie's Choice (83) 311
LOVEJOY, RAY
Dresser, The (84) 130
Eleni (86) 151
LOVETT, ROBERT Q.
Cotton Club, The (85) 150
Hammett (84) 174
LOVITT, B.
New York, New York [1977] (84) 567
LUCAS, GEORGE
THX 1138 [1971] (85) 638
LUCAS, MARCIA
New York, New York [1977] (84) 567
Return of the Jedi (84) 326
LUCIANO, MICHAEL
Flight of the Phoenix, The [1966] (85) 549
Stripes (82) 336
LUSK, SKIP
Reuben, Reuben (84) 337
LYON, WILLIAM A.
Cowboy [1958] (82) 417
Long Gray Line, The [1955] (82) 447

MCGUIRE, GEORGE
Detour [1946] (86) 498
MACIAS, JUAN CARLOS
Official Story, The (86) 249
MCINTYRE, ALASTAIR
Tess [1980] (82) 47
MACK, STEPHEN
Angelo My Love (84) 47
MCKAY, CRAIG
Melvin and Howard [1980] (82) 453
MCLEAN, BARBARA
Snows of Kilimanjaro, The [1952] (83) 498
MCNEIL, ALLEN
Man Hunt [1941] (85) 570
MCSWEENEY, JOHN, JR.
Mutiny on the Bounty [1962] (85) 581
MAGNOLI, ALBERT
Purple Rain (85) 389
MAINKA-JELLINGHAUS, BEATE
Fitzcarraldo (83) 167
Where the Green Ants Dream [1984] (86) 465
MALKIN, BARRY
Cotton Club, The (85) 150
Four Friends (82) 167
Hammett (84) 174
MANDELL, DANIEL
Animal Kingdom, The [1932] (86) 469
North Star, The [1943] (83) 476
MANSFIELD, DUNCAN
Arch of Triumph [1948] (84) 501
MANTON, MARCUS
Missing in Action 2 (86) 452
MARANI, ERMINIA
Nostalgia [1983] (85) 340
MARDEN, RICHARD
Falcon and the Snowman, The (86) 165

Hound of the Baskervilles, The
[1978] (82) 203
MARKS, OWEN
Colorado Territory [1949] (86) 489
Disraeli [1929] (82) 426
Hatchet Man, The [1932] (83) 447
MARKS, RICHARD
Adventures of Buckaroo Banzai, The
(85) 47
Max Dugan Returns (84) 228
Pennies from Heaven (82) 276
St. Elmo's Fire (86) 330
Terms of Endearment (84) 414
MARSHALL, A. DAVID
Fire and Ice (84) 153
MARSHEK, ARCHIE
Becky Sharp [1935] (82) 403
Most Dangerous Game, The [1932] (86) 519
MARTIN, DAVID
Ploughman's Lunch, The [1983] (85) 377
MASTROIANNI, RUGGERO
And the Ship Sails On [1983] (85) 69
Bizet's Carmen [1983] (85) 98
City of Women (82) 106
Three Brothers [1980] (83) 349
MELNICK, MARK
Remo Williams (86) 457
MELTON, JAMES
Black Cauldron, The (86) 75
MERLIN, CLAUDINE
Beau Pere (82) 78
My Best Friend's Girl [1983] (85) 326
MERY-CLARK, LAURENCE
Doctor and the Devils, The (86) 442
Secret Places [1984] (86) 459
MEYER, RICHARD C.
"Obituaries" (86) 576
MIEVILLE, ANNE-MARIE
Every Man for Himself [1979] (82) 139
MITCHELL, JAMES
2010 (85) 494
MOLIN, BUD
All of Me (85) 58
Dead Men Don't Wear Plaid (83) 134
Man with One Red Shoe, The (86) 451
Man with Two Brains, The (84) 223
Summer Rental (86) 462
MONDSHEIN, ANDREW
Desperately Seeking Susan (86) 137
MONTANARI, SERGIO
Hercules II (86) 446
MORRISS, FRANK
American Flyers (86) 436
Blue Thunder (84) 84
Earthling, The [1980] (82) 130
Romancing the Stone (85) 421
Whose Life Is It Anyway? (82) 378
MORSE, SUSAN E.
Arthur (82) 71
Broadway Danny Rose (85) 112
Midsummer Night's Sex Comedy, A (83)
228
Purple Rose of Cairo, The (86) 290
Stardust Memories [1980] (85) 626
Zelig (84) 473
MUELLER, FRITZ
Falstaff [1967] (83) 443

MULCONERY, WALT
  Flashdance (84) 158
  Karate Kid, The   (85) 264
  Personal Best   (83) 254
MURRAY, JACK
  Fort Apache [1948]   (84) 530

NAGATA, CHIZUKO
  Makioka Sisters, The [1983]   (86) 451
NAKASHIMA, MARSHA
  Blade Runner   (83) 76
NAUDON, JEAN-FRANÇOIS
  Argent, L' [1983]   (85) 74
NEDD, PRISCILLA
  Flamingo Kid, The   (85) 192
NELSON, ARGYLE
  Buddy Buddy   (82) 93
  Lady Sings the Blues [1972]   (85) 565
NELSON, CHARLES
  Solid Gold Cadillac, The [1956]   (85) 615
NEUBURGER, JON
  Tokyo-Ga   (86) 463
NEWTON, ANGUS
  Dreamchild   (86) 146
NIKEL, HANNES
  Boot, Das [1981]   (83) 86
  Enemy Mine   (86) 161
NOBLE, THOM
  First Blood   (83) 164
  Improper Channels   (82) 218
  Witness   (86) 421
NUNEZ, VICTOR
  Flash of Green, A   (86) 443

O'BANNON, DAN
  Dark Star [1975]   (86) 494
O'MEARA, C. TIMOTHY
  Last Starfighter, The   (85) 277
  My Science Project   (86) 453
ORDONEZ, VICTOR
  9 Deaths of the Ninja   (86) 454
OSHIMA, TOMOYO
  Merry Christmas, Mr. Lawrence   (84) 231
  Mishima   (86) 236
O'STEEN, SAM
  Silkwood   (84) 367
OTTIE, OREL NORRIE
  28 Up [1984]   (86) 392

PALMER, KEITH
  Wild Geese II   (86) 466
PARASHELES, PETER
  Code of Silence   (86) 440
  Never Cry Wolf   (84) 247
PARRINELLO, WILL
  Kerouac, the Movie   (86) 448
PATCH, JEFFREY
  Secret of NIMH, The   (83) 288
PELETIER, KENOUT
  Erendira [1983]   (85) 181
PERCY, LEE
  Re-Animator   (86) 457
PERPIGNANI, ROBERT O.
  Night of the Shooting Stars, The [1982]
   (84) 258

PERRY, DAN
  James Joyce's Women   (86) 193
PETTIT, SUZANNE
  Sylvester   (86) 462
  Testament   (84) 420
PINGITORE, CARL
  Play Misty for Me [1971]   (86) 532
PIROUÉ, JEAN-CLAUDE
  Sugarbaby   (86) 461
PIVAR, MAURICE
  King of Jazz [1930]   (86) 515
  "Obituaries"   (83) 548
POLIVKA, STEVEN
  Volunteers   (86) 464
POSTEC, ZIVA
  Shoah   (86) 339
POTTER, MARK
  Bostonians, The   (85) 105
POULTON, RAYMOND
  Invitation to the Dance [1956]   (86) 507
PRATT, THOMAS
  Hard Way, The [1942]   (85) 555
PRESSBURGER, FRED
  It Happened Tomorrow [1944]   (84) 552
PRIESTLY, TOM
  1984   (85) 335
  Tess [1980]   (82) 471
PRIM, MONIQUE
  Diva [1980]   (82) 147
PRUGAR, HALINA
  Danton [1982]   (84) 121
  Love in Germany, A [1983]   (85) 283
  Man of Iron   (82) 230
  Man of Marble [1977]   (82) 234
PRUGAR-KETLING, HALINA. See PRUGAR,
  HALINA
PRZYGODDA, PETER
  Paris, Texas   (85) 359
PSENNY, ARMAND
  Coup de torchon [1981]   (83) 124
  Sunday in the Country, A   (85) 466

RAMIREZ, DAVID
  American Pop   (82) 62
  Barbarosa   (83) 60
  New York, New York   (82) 567
RAMSAY, TODD
  Escape from New York [1977]   (82) 133
  Thing, The   (83) 343
RAND, PATRICK
  Streetwalkin'   (86) 461
RAWLINGS, TERRY
  Blade Runner   (83) 76
  Chariots of Fire   (82) 101
  Yentl   (84) 468
REITANO, ROBERT
  Grace Quigley   (86) 444
RELPH, SIMON
  Reds   (82) 312
REYNOLDS, WILLIAM
  Heaven's Gate   (82) 195
RICHARDS, THOMAS
  They Drive by Night [1940]   (83) 508
RICHARDSON, ED
  Cat People   (83) 100

RICHARDSON, HENRY
  Octopussy (84) 276
  Runaway Train (86) 324
RIPPS, MICHAEL
  Brewster's Millions (86) 438
ROBERTS, RANDY
  Hammett (84) 174
  One from the Heart (83) 250
ROBINSON, KEN
  Purple Rain (85) 389
ROBSON, MARK
  Journey into Fear [1943] (86) 511
RODRUEZ, LEAL
  Bar Esperanza [1983] (86) 437
ROLAND, RITA
  Fort Apache, the Bronx (82) 159
ROLF, TOM
  Ghost Story (82) 183
  Heaven's Gate (82) 195
  New York, New York [1977] (84) 567
  Right Stuff, The (84) 342
  WarGames (84) 458
ROOSE, RONALD
  Volunteers (86) 464
ROSENFIELD, JASON
  Come Back to the 5 & Dime Jimmy Dean,
    Jimmy Dean (83) 120
ROTHMAN, MARION
  Christine (84) 106
  Starman (85) 445
ROTTER, STEPHEN A.
  Heaven Help Us (86) 445
  Right Stuff, The (84) 342
  Target (86) 462
  World According to Garp, The (83) 397
RUBELL, PAUL
  Stone Boy, The (85) 450
RUGGIERO, EVA
  Stripes (82) 336
RUNNE, GELA-MARINA
  Taxi Zum Klo (82) 346

SALCEDO, JOSE
  Only Emptiness Remains (86) 455
SALFA, AMADEO
  Nostalgia [1983] (85) 340
SANDERS, RONALD
  Videodrome (84) 452
SAUNDERS, DON
  Silver City [1984] (86) 460
  Wild Duck, The [1983] (86) 466
SAUNIER, NICOLE
  My New Partner [1984] (86) 246
SAVITT, JILL
  Key Exchange (86) 448
SAYLES, JOHN
  Brother from Another Planet, The (85) 118
  Lianna (84) 201
  Return of the Secaucus 7 [1980] (83) 484
SCHENKKAN, INE
  Flesh and Blood (86) 443
  4th Man, The [1983] (85) 203
SCHLESINGER, REVA
  Tomorrow [1972] (84) 589

SCHMIDT, ARTHUR
  Back to the Future (86) 65
  Fandango (86) 442
SCHMIDT, SOPHIE
  Subway (86) 461
SCHMITT-KLINK, LIESGRET
  Imperative [1982] (86) 447
SCHNEIDER, CYNTHIA
  Legend of Billie Jean, The (86) 450
SCHOONMAKER, THELMA
  After Hours (86) 51
  King of Comedy, The (84) 192
SCOTT, JOHN
  Coca-Cola Kid, The (86) 440
SEABOURNE, JOHN
  I Know Where I'm Going [1945] (83) 456
SECRIST, KIM
  This Is Spinal Tap (85) 484
SEIDELMAN, SUSAN
  Smithereens (83) 307
SEITH, LEON
  1918 (86) 454
SEMEL, STEPHEN
  Fandango (86) 442
SEMPRUN, COLETTE
  Bizet's Carmen [1983] (85) 98
SHANKS, SUSAN
  Bad Boy, The (86) 437
SHAPIRO, MELVIN
  Bring on the Night (86) 439
SHELDON, RALPH
  Holcroft Covenant, The (86) 446
SHIRLEY, JOHN
  Experience Preferred…but Not Essential
    [1982] (84) 141
  King Solomon's Mines (86) 449
  Nate and Hayes (84) 236
SHUGRU, ROBERT F.
  Star Trek III—The Search for
    Spock (85) 439
SICILIANO, ANTONIO
  Water and Soap (86) 465
SILVI, ROBERTO
  Under the Volcano (85) 499
  Victory (82) 374
SIMONCELLI, CARA
  Macaroni (86) 451
SINDE, MIGUEL GONZALES
  Volver a empezar (83) 393
SMITH, BUD
  Flashdance (84) 158
  Karate Kid, The (85) 264
SMITH, HOWARD
  Baby (86) 437
  Sylvester (86) 462
  Tex (83) 335
  Twilight Zone—The Movie (84) 435
SMITH, JOHN VICTOR
  Rustler's Rhapsody (86) 458
  Superman II (82) 339
  Superman III (84) 399
SMITH, NORMAN
  Streamers (84) 391
SMITH, SCOTT
  To Live and Die in L.A. (86) 379

SONES, SONYA
  School Spirit (86) 458
SPANG, RON
  Firefox (83) 160
SPENCE, MICHAEL
  Kid Colter (86) 449
STEINKAMP, FREDRIC
  Out of Africa (86) 255
  Tootsie (83) 353
  White Nights (86) 416
STEINKAMP, WILLIAM
  Out of Africa (86) 255
  Tootsie (83) 353
  White Nights (86) 416
STEVENSON, MICHAEL A.
  Annie (83) 56
  Gotcha! (86) 444
  Toy, The (83) 358
STEWARD, DOUG
  Jinxed (83) 206
STEWART, DOUGLAS
  Right Stuff, The (84) 342
STIVEN, DAVID
  Road Warrior, The [1981] (83) 277
SULLIVAN, FRANK
  Guy Named Joe, A [1943] (82) 435
  Too Hot to Handle [1938] (84) 596
SWINK, ROBERT E.
  Boys from Brazil, The [1978] (86) 480
SYLVI, FRANCA
  Traviata, La (83) 366

TAGG, BRIAN
  Crimes of Passion (85) 161
TANNER, PETER
  Turtle Diary (86) 464
TAVERES, MAIR
  Xica [1976] (83) 407
TAYLOR, MIKE
  Long Good Friday, The (83) 220
TAYLOR, PETER
  Traviata, La (83) 366
TINTORI, JOHN
  Sudden Death (86) 461
TOMASINI, GEORGE
  Time Machine, The [1960] (84) 585
TOMSKI, MICHELLE
  Savage Island (86) 458
TOOMAYAN, ALAN
  Lust in the Dust (86) 450
TRAVIS, NEIL
  Marie (86) 227
TSURBUSHI, MASATOSHI
  Here Come the Littles (86) 446

URIOSTE, FRANK O.
  Red Sonja (86) 457
UYS, JAMIE
  Gods Must Be Crazy, The [1980] (85) 224

VAN EFFENTERRE, JOELE
  Entre nous [1983] (85) 176
VICKREY, SCOTT
  Flanagan (86) 443

Invasion U.S.A. (86) 447
Mixed Blood (86) 452
They All Laughed (82) 350
VILLASENOR, GEORGE
  Love Streams (85) 293
  Neil Simon's The Slugger's Wife (86) 454
VINCE, BARRIE
  Moonlighting (83) 237
  Private Function, A [1984] (86) 280
VIRKLER, DENNIS
  Continental Divide (82) 115
  Gorky Park (82) 162
  Secret Admirer (86) 459
VOYOTTE, MARIE-JOSEPH
  Sugar Cane Alley [1983] (85) 461

WAELCHLI, ELISABETH
  Yol (83) 411
WALKER, LESLEY
  Richard's Things (82) 321
WALLACE, SCOTT
  Weird Science (86) 465
WALLS, TOM
  Trouble in Mind (86) 388
WALPOLE, ALTON
  Koyaanisqatsi (84) 197
WALSCH, FRANZ
  Lili Marleen (82) 222
WARNER, MARK
  48 HRS. (83) 173
  Rocky III (83) 283
  Soldier's Story, A (85) 427
  Staying Alive (84) 386
  Weird Science (86) 465
WARNOW, STANLEY
  Ragtime (82) 304
WARSCHLIKA, EDWARD
  Raggedy Man (82) 300
WATERS, ROBERT
  9 Deaths of the Ninja (86) 454
WATTS, ROBERT
  Invitation to the Dance [1956] (86) 507
WEBER, BILLY
  Beverly Hills Cop (85) 88
  48 HRS. (83) 173
  Iceman (85) 248
  Pee-wee's Big Adventure (86) 265
WEBSTER, FERRIS
  Firefox (83) 160
  Honkytonk Man (83) 200
WEISBART DAVID
  My Reputation [1946] (85) 586
  Roughly Speaking [1945] (83) 490
WEITERHAUSEN, BARBARA VON
  State of Things, The (84) 379
WELLBURN, TIM
  Caddie [1976] (83) 439
  Road Warrior, The [1981] (83) 277
WELLS, TOM
  Moving Violations (86) 453
WENDERS, WIM
  Tokyo-Ga (86) 463
WENNING, KATHERINE
  Bostonians, The (85) 105

WHEELER, JOHN W.
 Challenge, The   (83) 109
 Rocky IV   (86) 319
WHYTOCK, GRANT
 "Obituaries"   (82) 506
WIEGMANN, DON
 Blood Simple   (86) 438
WIKKE, RALPH
 Dim Sum   (86) 141
WILSON, JOHN
 Draughtsman's Contract, The [1982]
  (84) 126
WIMBLE, CHRIS
 Wetherby   (86) 406
WINETROBE, MAURY
 Taps   (82) 343
 Vision Quest   (86) 464
WINTERS, RALPH E.
 Man Who Loved Women, The   (84) 218
 Micki & Maude   (85) 308
 S.O.B.   (82) 328
 Victor/Victoria   (83) 387
WISMAN, RON
 Joshua Then and Now   (86) 198
WITTA, JACQUES
 Patsy, The   (86) 456
WOLFE, ROBERT L.
 On Golden Pond   (82) 263
WOLINSKY, SIDNEY
 One Magic Christmas   (86) 455
WOOD, TRUMAN K.
 Divorcée, The [1930]   (82) 429
WRIGHT, JOHN
 Frances   (83) 178
 Mass Appeal   (85) 303
 Only When I Laugh   (82) 268

WRIGHT, MAURICE
 Miracle Woman, The [1931]   (83) 473
WYMAN, BOB
 Police Academy 2   (86) 276
WYNN, HUGH
 Divorcée, The [1930]   (82) 429
 Scarlet Letter, The [1927]   (85) 602

YAHRAUS, BILL
 Country   (85) 156
 Heartland   (82) 191
YAMAJI, SACHIKO
 MacArthur's Children   (86) 451
YOYOTTE, MARIE-JOSEPHE
 Diva [1980]   (83) 147

ZÁFRANOVIC, ANDRIJA
 When Father Was Away on Business
  [1984]   (86) 411
ZEMKE, KEN
 Came a Hot Friday   (86) 440
ZIHNER, PETER
 War and Love   (86) 465
ZIMMERMAN, DON
 Barbarosa   (83) 60
 Best Friends   (83) 68
 Rocky III   (83) 283
 Rocky IV   (86) 319
 Staying Alive   (84) 386
ZINNER, PETER
 Officer and a Gentleman, An   (83) 246
 Running Brave   (84) 354
ZITA, LUIGI
 Softly Softly [1984]   (86) 460

ART DIRECTOR INDEX

ABRAMSON, PHILIP
  Real Genius (86) 309
  Stick (86) 460
ACHMANN, WERNER
  Berlin Alexanderplatz [1980] (84) 57
ACKLAND-SNOW, BRIAN
  Doctor and the Devils, The (86) 442
  Superman III (84) 399
ACKLAND-SNOW, TERRY
  King David (86) 449
  Superman II (82) 339
  Superman III (84) 399
ADAM, KEN
  Agnes of God (86) 56
  King David (86) 449
ALEXANDER, BRANDY
  Remo Williams (86) 457
ALLEN, GENE
  Star Is Born, A [1954] (84) 573
ALLEN, JAMES
  Weird Science (86) 465
ALLEY, WILLIAM
  D.A.R.Y.L. (86) 441
ALTMAN, KATE
  Paris, Texas (85) 359
ALTMAN, STEVE
  Fool for Love (86) 172
  Streamers (84) 391
ALVES, JOE
  Escape from New York (82) 133
AMES, PRESTON
  Bells Are Ringing [1960] (84) 517
  Brewster McCloud [1970] (86) 484
  "Obituaries" (84) 608
AMMON, RUTH
  Flanagan (86) 443
ANANIA, MICHAEL
  I Sent a Letter to My Love [1980] (82) 214
ANDERSON, CARL
  Lady Sings the Blues [1972] (85) 565
ANDERSON, CLETUS
  Day of the Dead (86) 441
ANDERSON, ROLAND
  Holiday Inn [1942] (82) 443
  Take a Letter, Darling [1942] (85) 632
ANDRE, DOMINIQUE
  Little Jerk [1984] (86) 450
ANGWIN, NEIL
  Lonely Hearts [1982] (84) 212
ARCHER, ERNEST
  Pirates of Penzance, The (84) 301
  Superman II (82) 339
ARRIGHI, LUCIANA
  Mrs. Soffel (85) 314
  Ploughman's Lunch, The [1983] (85) 377
  Return of the Soldier, The [1982] (84) 332
ARRIGO, FRANK
  Torn Curtain [1966] (85) 644
ASP, ANNA
  After the Rehearsal (85) 52
  Fanny and Alexander [1982] (84) 146

ATKINSON, ADRIENNE
  Comfort and Joy (85) 146
  Gregory's Girl [1981] (83) 193
  Local Hero (84) 206
AUSTIN, JOHN P.
  Mikey and Nicky [1976] (85) 576
AUSTIN, LEO
  Bostonians, The (85) 105
  Turtle Diary (86) 464
AVCHEN, ALAN
  Cease Fire (86) 440

BAER, HARRY
  Berlin Alexanderplatz [1980] (84) 57
BAILEY, CHARLES
  Front, The [1976] (86) 502
BASEVI, JAMES
  Fort Apache [1948] (84) 530
BASILE, PIERLUIGI
  Dune (85) 171
BATO, JOSEPH
  Sound Barrier, The [1952] (85) 621
BEARD, JOHN
  Brazil (86) 80
BELLAH, ROSS
  Solid Gold Cadillac, The [1956] (85) 615
BENTON, ROBERT
  Starman (85) 445
BERGFELDER, ULRICH
  Fitzcarraldo (83) 167
  Where the Green Ants Dream [1984] (86) 465
BERT, ALLEN
  Star Is Born, A [1954] (84) 573
BERT, MALCOLM C.
  Arrangement, The [1969] (86) 474
BERTO, MAX
  Loulou [1980] (82) 226
BIDDLE, MARYANN
  All the Right Moves (84) 41
BIRNIE, CAMERON
  Star Trek III—The Search for Spock (85) 439
BISHOP, CHARLES
  Return to Oz (86) 458
  Superman II (82) 339
  Superman III (84) 399
  Young Sherlock Holmes (86) 431
BISHOP, ERNIE
  Mischief (86) 452
  Pale Rider (86) 261
  Tightrope (85) 489
BISSELL, JAMES D.
  E.T.: The Extra-Terrestrial (83) 151
  Falcon and the Snowman, The (86) 165
  Last Starfighter, The (85) 277
BLASDEL, AUDREY
  Arrangement, The [1969] (86) 474
BOLTON, GREGORY
  Cotton Club, The (85) 150
BOLTON, MICHAEL
  Star 80 (84) 374
BORUSESCU, RADU
  Montenegro (82) 250

BOSE, ASHOKE
Home and the World, The [1984]   (86) 447
BOURNE, MEL
Broadway Danny Rose   (85) 118
Natural, The   (85) 329
Stardust Memories [1980]   (85) 626
BOUSMAN, TRACY
Prizzi's Honor   (86) 285
Protocol   (85) 383
BOX, JOHN
Passage to India, A   (85) 365
BOXIN, CLAUDE
Bob le Flambeur [1955]   (84) 526
BOYLE, ROBERT F.
Explorers   (86) 442
Table for Five   (84) 404
BRANDENBERG, ROSEMARY
Teen Wolf   (86) 462
BRENNER, ALBERT
Only When I Laugh   (82) 268
Sweet Dreams   (86) 374
2010   (85) 494
BRITO, ARTURO
Volunteers   (86) 464
BROCKHURST, DAVID
Insignificance   (86) 447
Priest of Love   (82) 288
BRODIE, BILL
One Magic Christmas   (86) 455
BROWN, HILYARD
Cutter's Way   (82) 119
BROWNING, ANNI
Mad Max Beyond Thunderdome   (86) 223
BUENO, CLOVIS
Kiss of the Spider Woman   (86) 209
Pixote [1980]   (82) 280
BUFNOIR, JACQUES
Entre nous [1983]   (85) 176
Goat, The [1981]   (86) 444
BUMSTEAD, HENRY
Slap Shot [1977]   (82) 467
Warning Sign   (86) 465
BURBANK, LINDA
Repo Man   (85) 408
BURIAN-MOHR, CHRISTOPHER
Jagged Edge   (86) 190
St. Elmo's Fire   (86) 330
BURKE, CHRIS
Pink Floyd the Wall [1981]   (83) 258
BURLS, CAROLINE
Gods Must Be Crazy, The [1980]   (85) 224
BURNS, MILLY
Brimstone and Treacle   (83) 91
BURNS, ROBERT A.
Howling, The   (82) 207
Re-Animator   (86) 457

CADIOU, PIERRE
Erendira [1983]   (85) 181
CAGLI, LEONARDO COEN
King Solomon's Mines   (86) 449
CAIN, MAURICE
Nate and Hayes   (84) 236

CAIN, ROGER
Indiana Jones and the Temple of Doom   (85)
253
CAIN, SYD
Wild Geese II   (86) 466
CALLAHAN, GENE
Arrangement, The [1969]   (86) 474
Jagged Edge   (86) 190
Places in the Heart   (85) 371
Whose Life Is It Anyway?   (82) 378
CAMERON, ALAN
French Lieutenant's Woman, The   (82) 174
1984   (85) 335
CAMPBELL, DIANE
Stitches   (86) 461
CAMPBELL, W. STEWART
Birdy   (85) 93
Right Stuff, The   (84) 342
Shoot the Moon   (83) 295
True Confessions   (82) 368
CARFAGNO, EDWARD
All of Me   (85) 58
City Heat   (85) 141
Honkytonk Man   (83) 200
Pale Rider   (86) 261
Sudden Impact   (84) 395
Tightrope   (85) 489
Time After Time [1979]   (84) 579
Wrong Is Right   (83) 403
CARPENTIER, DON
Bostonians, The   (85) 105
CARTER, RICHARD
Adventures of Buckaroo Banzai, The   (85) 47
Goonies, The   (86) 176
CARTWRIGHT, BOB
Lifeforce   (86) 450
National Lampoon's European Vacation   (86)
453
CARTWRIGHT, JACK .
Officer and a Gentleman, An   (83) 246
CASO, MARIA REBMAN
Terminator, The   (85) 478
CASSIE, ALAN
D.A.R.Y.L.   (86) 441
Dragonslayer   (82) 125
Indiana Jones and the Temple of Doom   (85)
253
Pirates of Penzance, The   (84) 301
CAVERS, CLINTON
Pink Floyd the Wall [1981]   (83) 258
CAZIOT, JEAN-JACQUES
Quartet   (82) 296
CEDER, ELAYNE
Firefox   (83) 160
CERNY, KAREL
Amadeus   (85) 63
CESARI, BRUNO
Once upon a Time in America   (85) 345
CHAPER, RAINER
Erendira [1983]   (85) 181
CHAPMAN, DAVID
Cotton Club, The   (85) 150
Four Friends   (82) 167
Wolfen   (82) 382
CHAVOOSIAN, NORA
Brother from Another Planet, The   (85) 118

CHILBERG, JOHN E., II
Star Trek III—The Search for Spock (85) 439
CLARK, CARROLL
Most Dangerous Game, The [1932] (86) 519
COBB, RON
Last Starfighter, The (85) 277
CODRICK, THOMAS H.
Bambi [1942] (85) 543
COLLIS, JACK
Cocoon (86) 96
Four Seasons, The (82) 171
National Lampoon's Vacation (84) 241
Splash (85) 434
Tex (83) 335
COMMON, TONY
Company of Wolves, The [1984] (86) 115
COMTOIS, GUY
Quest for Fire (83) 271
CONE, BUDDY
To Live and Die in L.A. (86) 379
CONLEY, DAN
Mrs. Soffel (85) 314
COPELAND, CARL
Heartland (82) 191
CORMACK, ROBERT C.
Bambi [1942] (85) 543
CORSO, JOHN W.
Breakfast Club, The (86) 85
Psycho II (84) 307
Weird Science (86) 465
COSTELLO, GEORGE
Terminator, The (85) 478
COUTZEN, ALEXANDER
Play Misty for Me [1971] (86) 532
CRABBE, BYRON L.
Most Dangerous Game, The [1932] (86) 519
CRAIG, STUART
Cal (85) 124
Gandhi (83) 183
Greystoke (85) 236
CREBER, WILLIAM
Twice in a Lifetime (86) 397
CRESCENTI, FELIPE
Kiss of the Spider Woman (86) 209
CRIKSANTI, ANDREA
Nostalgia [1983] (85) 340
Three Brothers [1980] (83) 349
CRUZ, RODELL
9 Deaths of the Ninja (86) 454
CUTLER, BERNIE
Pennies from Heaven (82) 276

D'AGOSTINO, ALBERT S.
Journey into Fear [1943] (86) 511
Woman on the Beach, The [1947] (83) 519
DALTON, NINKY
Improper Channels (82) 218
DANE, STEPHEN
Adventures of Buckaroo Banzai, The (85) 47
DANKLEFSEN, DIANE
Turtle Diary (86) 464
DAPPER, JOHN
Chorus Line, A (86) 91

DAVIES, TESSA
Bride, The (86) 438
Yentl (84) 468
DAVIS, GEORGE W.
Bells Are Ringing [1960] (84) 517
Brewster McCloud [1970] (86) 484
Mutiny on the Bounty [1962] (85) 581
Time Machine, The [1960] (84) 585
DAWKING, RICHARD
Jewel of the Nile, The (86) 448
White Nights (86) 416
DAY, RICHARD
Barbary Coast [1935] (84) 506
Come and Get It [1936] (82) 412
Man Hunt [1941] (85) 570
DECINCES, RICHARD J.
Mask (86) 231
DECUIR, JOHN, JR.
Dead Men Don't Wear Plaid (83) 134
Fright Night (86) 444
Ghostbusters (85) 219
DE GOVIA, JACKSON
Remo Williams (86) 457
DE GROOT, ROLAND
4th Man, The [1983] (85) 203
DE LA GUERRA, JOSÉ ANTONIO
Falstaff [1967] (83) 443
My Cousin Rachel [1952] (82) 458
Snows of Kilimanjaro, The [1952] (83) 498
DELEU, FRANÇOIS
My New Partner [1984] (86) 246
DESCENNA, LINDA
Color Purple, The (86) 105
Falcon and the Snowman, The (86) 165
Goonies, The (86) 176
DESIDERI, GIORGIO
Dune (85) 171
DESIDERI, OSVALDO
Once upon a Time in America (85) 345
DESPOTOVIC, VELJKO
Gymkata (86) 445
Out of Control (86) 455
DETITTA, GEORGE
Chorus Line, A (86) 91
King of Comedy, The (84) 192
DEVERILL, SPENCER
Heaven's Gate (82) 195
DILLEY, LESLIE
American Werewolf in London, An (82) 66
Bad Medicine (86) 437
Never Say Never Again (84) 252
Raiders of the Lost Ark (82) 308
DI MONTI, EZIO
Macaroni (86) 451
DISS, EILEEN
Betrayal (84) 67
DIXON, VERNON
Boys from Brazil, The [1978] (86) 480
Victim [1961] (85) 649
DODSON, MARY
Thief (82) 356
DONATI, DANILO
Red Sonja (86) 457
DORME, NORMAN
French Lieutenant's Woman, The (82) 174

DOWD, ROSS
  Journey into Fear [1943]   (86) 511
DREIER, HANS
  Holiday Inn [1942]   (82) 443
  I'm No Angel [1933]   (85) 561
  Peter Ibbetson [1935]   (86) 527
  Take a Letter, Darling [1942]   (85) 632
DRUMHELLER, ROBERT
  Front, The [1976]   (86) 502
  Ghostbusters   (85) 219
  Year of the Dragon   (86) 426
DUFFY, JIM
  Cocoon   (86) 96
DUNLOP, CHARLES
  Improper Channels   (82) 218
DUNPHY, BARBARA
  Running Brave   (84) 354
DURFEE, DUKE
  Flamingo Kid, The   (85) 192
DURRELL, WILLIAM JOSEPH, JR.
  Legend of Billie Jean, The   (86) 450
  Starman   (85) 445
DWYER, JOHN M.
  Fever Pitch   (86) 443

EADS, PAUL
  Turk 182   (86) 464
EAGAN, BEVERLI
  Jagged Edge   (86) 190
EATSWELL, BRIAN
  Man Who Fell to Earth, The [1975]   (83) 469
EDGAR, CRAIG
  Right Stuff, The   (84) 342
EDWARDS, BEN
  Fort Apache, the Bronx   (82) 159
EICHBAUER, HELIO
  Gabriela [1983]   (85) 213
EISENMAN, AL
  Lust in the Dust   (86) 450
ELTON, RICHARD
  Bostonians, The   (85) 105
ENEI, EVGENI
  New Babylon, The [1929]   (84) 561
EQUINI, ARRIGO
  Barefoot Contessa, The [1954]   (82) 399
ERDORZA, MARIANO
  Falstaff [1967]   (83) 443
ERICKSEN, LEON
  Iceman   (85) 248
ESTEVEZ, ENRIQUE
  Romancing the Stone   (85) 421
EXSHAW, DENISE
  Lifeforce   (86) 450

FACELLO, ABEL
  Official Story, The   (86) 249
FENNER, JOHN
  Octopussy   (84) 276
  View to a Kill, A   (86) 402
FERGUSON, DON
  Trouble in Mind   (86) 388
FERGUSON, PERRY
  North Star, The [1943]   (83) 476
  Secret Life of Walter Mitty, The [1947]   (86) 540

FERNANDES, AGNES
  Heat and Dust [1982]   (84) 187
FERNANDEZ, BENJAMIN
  Dune   (85) 171
FERRARI, WILLIAM
  Time Machine, The [1960]   (84) 585
FERRETTI, DANTE
  And the Ship Sails On [1983]   (85) 69
  City of Women   (82) 106
FETTIS, GARY
  Nuit de Varennes, La [1982]   (84) 270
  Outsiders, The   (84) 282
FIELD, VIRGINIA
  Moving Violations   (86) 453
FISCHER, LISA
  Sure Thing, The   (86) 369
FLACKSMAN, MARCOS
  Emerald Forest, The   (86) 156
FLANNERY, SEAMUS
  Wicker Man, The [1974]   (86) 555
FLANNERY, WILLIAM E.
  Arch of Triumph [1948]   (84) 501
FLATING, JANICE
  Movers and Shakers   (86) 453
FORD, JO
  Nate and Hayes   (84) 236
FORD, MARIANNE
  Dreamchild   (86) 146
FORD, MICHAEL
  Return to Oz   (86) 458
  Young Sherlock Holmes   (86) 431
FOREMAN, RONALD KENT
  Marie   (86) 227
  Rocky III   (83) 283
FOWLER, MAURICE
  Educating Rita   (84) 136
  Heat and Dust [1982]   (84) 187
  Heaven's Gate   (82) 195
  Superman II   (82) 339
FOX, J. RAE
  Repo Man   (85) 408
FOX, K.C.
  Trouble in Mind   (86) 388
FRANCO, JOHN, JR.
  Country   (85) 156
FREEBORN, MARK
  Christmas Story, A   (84) 110
FREED, REUBEN
  Porky's   (83) 267
FULLER, RHILEY
  Alamo Bay   (86) 436
FURGINSON, BOB
  Police Academy 2   (86) 276
FURST, ANTON
  Company of Wolves, The [1984]   (86) 115

GAILLING, HANS
  Céleste [1981]   (83) 104
GAINES, GEORGE
  City Heat   (85) 141
GALBRAITH, ELINOR ROSE
  Sesame Street Presents: Follow That Bird   (86) 459

GALLAND, NOEL
  Adolescente, L' [1979]   (83) 53
GANZ, ARMIN
  Birdy   (85) 93
GARNES, GEORGE
  Maxie   (86) 452
GARRITY, JOSEPH
  Runaway Train   (86) 324
GARWOOD, NORMAN
  Brazil   (86) 80
  Bullshot [1983]   (86) 439
  Missionary, The   (83) 223
  Time Bandits [1980]   (82) 364
GASSNER, HELMUT
  Berlin Alexanderplatz [1980]   (84) 57
GAUCHET, PIERRE
  My New Partner [1984]   (86) 246
GAUDRY, ALAIN
  My Other Husband   (86) 453
GAUSMAN, HAL
  Back to the Future   (86) 65
GELLENG, TONY
  Hercules II   (86) 446
GENTZ, RICK
  Murphy's Romance   (86) 242
GERZSO, GUNTHER
  Under the Volcano   (85) 499
GIBBONS, CEDRIC
  Bridge of San Luis Rey, The [1929]   (82) 408
  Divorcée, The [1930]   (82) 429
  Guy Named Joe, A [1943]   (82) 435
  H. M. Pulham, Esq. [1941]   (82) 439
  Royal Wedding [1951]   (86) 536
  Scarlet Letter, The [1927]   (85) 602
  Too Hot to Handle [1938]   (84) 596
GIERKE, HENNING VON
  Fitzcarraldo   (83) 167
GIORGETTI, NELLO
  King Solomon's Mines   (86) 449
GIOVAGNONI, GIANNI
  Bizet's Carmen [1983]   (85) 98
  Red Sonja   (86) 457
  Softly Softly [1984]   (86) 460
GIRAUD, JEAN "MOEBIUS"
  TRON   (83) 371
GLASGOW, WILLIAM
  Flight of the Phoenix, The [1966]   (85) 549
GOLDSTEIN, BOB
  Hammett   (84) 174
GOLITZEN, ALEXANDER
  Lost Moment, The [1947]   (83) 465
GORTON, ADRIAN H.
  American Ninja   (86) 436
GOULD, ROBERT
  Commando   (86) 111
GOUPIL, ROMAIN
  Every Man for Himself [1979]   (82) 139
GRACE, HENRY
  Mutiny on the Bounty [1962]   (85) 581
GRAHAM, ANGELO
  Beverly Hills Cop   (85) 88
  Natural, The   (85) 329
  One from the Heart   (83) 250

GRANADA, JOSE RODRIGUEZ
  Under the Volcano   (85) 499
  Volunteers   (86) 464
GRAY, FIELD
  Pete Kelly's Blues [1955]   (83) 481
GRAY, MAGGIE
  Brazil   (86) 80
GRAYSMARK, JOHN
  Firefox   (83) 159
GRIFFIN, HAYDEN
  Wetherby   (86) 406
GRIFFITHS, RESTON
  Smash Palace [1981]   (83) 302
GRIMES, COLIN
  Dresser, The   (84) 130
GRIMES, STEPHEN
  Dresser, The   (84) 130
  Freud [1962]   (84) 535
  On Golden Pond   (82) 263
  Out of Africa   (86) 255
  Way We Were, The [1973]   (82) 474
GROPMAN, DAVID
  Come Back to the 5 & Dime Jimmy Dean, Jimmy
    Dean   (83) 120
  Key Exchange   (86) 448
GROT, ANTON
  Hatchet Man, The [1932]   (83) 447
  My Reputation [1946]   (85) 586
GUFFROY, PIERRE
  Argent, L' [1983]   (85) 74
  Hanna K.   (84) 177
GUZMAN, PATO
  Moscow on the Hudson   (85) 321
  Tempest   (83) 331

HAAS, ROBERT
  Roughly Speaking [1945]   (83) 490
HABER, DAVID M.
  Max Dugan Returns   (84) 228
  Sweet Dreams   (86) 374
HALEY, JAFF
  Vision Quest   (86) 464
HALL, RALPH
  Risky Business   (84) 349
HALL, ROGER
  Chariots of Fire   (82) 101
  Dreamchild   (86) 146
HALL, TONY
  One Magic Christmas   (86) 455
HALLER, MICHAEL
  Perfect   (86) 456
  THX 1138 [1971]   (85) 638
HALLOWELL, TODD
  Back to the Future   (86) 65
HANSEN, GARY
  Sylvia   (86) 462
HARLAND, FRANZ
  Smithereens   (83) 307
HARPMAN, FRED
  Rich and Famous   (82) 316
HARRIS, ANDY
  Comfort and Joy   (85) 146
HARRIS, DONALD L.
  Movers and Shakers   (86) 453

HARRIS, LEON
  Diner (83) 142
HARRISON, PHILIP
  Razor's Edge, The (85) 402
  White Nights (86) 416
HARTING, LLOYD
  Bambi [1942] (85) 543
HAUSMAN, MICHAEL
  Taking Off [1971] (86) 545
HAWKESWORTH, JOHN
  Sound Barrier, The [1952] (85) 621
HAWKINS, KAI
  Beyond Reasonable Doubt [1980] (84) 74
HAWORTH, TED
  Jinxed (83) 206
  Legend of Billie Jean, The (86) 450
HAY, JOHN
  Fool for Love (86) 172
HELMY, MICHAEL
  Prizzi's Honor (86) 285
HENDRICKSON, STEPHEN
  Arthur (82) 71
HENNAH, DAN
  Nate and Hayes (84) 236
HENNESY, DALE
  Annie (83) 56
HENZE, JURGEN
  Berlin Alexanderplatz [1980] (84) 57
  Love in Germany, A [1983] (85) 283
HERBERT, JOCELYN
  Hotel New Hampshire, The (85) 243
HERBERT, MARTIN
  1984 (85) 335
HERNDON, WALTER SCOTT
  Cross Creek (84) 116
  River, The (85) 416
  Sharky's Machine (82) 324
HERZBRUN, BERNARD
  Bedtime for Bonzo [1951] (84) 512
  Creature from the Black Lagoon, The
    [1954] (82) 422
  Cutter's Way (82) 119
  I'm No Angel [1933] (85) 561
HEYMANN, GOTZ
  Love in Germany, A [1983] (85) 283
HICKS, GRANT
  1984 (85) 335
HIGHFIELD, RON
  Utu [1983] (85) 504
HILBERMAN, DAVID
  Bambi [1942] (85) 543
HILDITCH, BOB
  Earthling, The [1980] (82) 130
HILL, DEREK R.
  Places in the Heart (85) 371
  Trip to Bountiful, The (86) 383
HILLIARD, MARY
  Quiet Earth, The (86) 295
HINTON, VICTORIA L.
  That Was Then . . . This Is Now (86) 463
HIREM, WILLIAM, JR.
  Brewster's Millions (86) 438
HOANG THANH AT
  Sugar Cane Alley [1983] (85) 461

HOBBS, RON
  Country (85) 156
  Footloose (85) 198
  Heavenly Kid, The (86) 445
  Personal Best (83) 254
HODJIS, YANKO
  Death of Mario Ricci, The [1983] (86) 133
HOLE, FRED
  Return of the Jedi (84) 326
  Return to Oz (86) 458
  Young Sherlock Holmes (86) 431
HOLLAND, SIMON
  Emerald Forest, The (86) 156
HOLT, WILLY
  Target (86) 462
HOPKINS, SPEED
  Desperately Seeking Susan (86) 137
  Midsummer Night's Sex Comedy, A (83) 228
  Natural, The (85) 329
  Zelig (84) 473
HOWITT, PETER
  Indiana Jones and the Temple of Doom (85)
    253
  Pirates of Penzance, The (84) 301
HOWLAND, ROBERT
  Once Bitten (86) 455
  Return of the Living Dead, The (86) 314
HUBLEY, JOHN
  Bambi [1942] (85) 543
HUGHES, JOHN
  They Drive by Night [1940] (83) 508
HUNT, HUGH
  Mutiny on the Bounty [1962] (85) 581
HUNTINGFORD, LEN
  Dreamchild (86) 146
HURST, RALPH
  Play Misty for Me [1971] (86) 532
HUTCHINSON, TIM
  Santa Claus (86) 334
  Victor/Victoria (83) 387

IDEGAWA, MITSUO
  Foster Daddy, Tora! [1980] (82) 163
IHNEN, WIARD B.
  Man Hunt [1941] (85) 570
ISAAC, LUCERO
  Missing (83) 232
ISHEDA, YOSHIYUKI
  Challenge, The (83) 109
ISHIOKA, EIKO
  Mishima (86) 236
ITUARTE, AUGUSTIN
  Romancing the Stone (85) 421

JAMES, PETER
  Doctor and the Devils, The (86) 442
  Plenty (86) 271
JAMES, RICHARD
  Silkwood (84) 367
JAMISON, PETER
  Continental Divide (82) 115
JAVIER, MARY DELIA
  Valley Girl (84) 447
JEFFERIES, PHILIP M.
  First Monday in October (82) 151

Kiss Me Goodbye   (83) 209
Mass Appeal   (85) 303
JENKINS, GEORGE
Postman Always Rings Twice, The   (82) 284
Secret Life of Walter Mitty, The [1947]   (86) 540
JENNINGS, JOSEPH R.
Star Trek II—The Wrath of Khan   (83) 321
JENSEN, JOHN R.
Remo Williams   (86) 457
JERICEVIC, DUSKO
Aviator, The   (86) 437
JEWELL, EDWARD C.
Detour [1946]   (86) 498
JOB, ENRICO
Bizet's Carmen [1983]   (85) 98
Joke of Destiny, A [1983]   (85) 259
JOFFE, CAROL
Purple Rose of Cairo, The   (86) 290
JOHN, TOM H.
Zoot Suit   (82) 389
JOHNSON, J. MCMILLAN
Mutiny on the Bounty [1962]   (85) 581
JOHNSON, RONDI
One Magic Christmas   (86) 455
JOHNSTON, JOE
Indiana Jones and the Temple of Doom   (85) 253
JOLLEY, STAN
Cattle Annie and Little Britches   (82) 97
Taps   (82) 343
Witness   (86) 421
JONES, DRYAN
This Is Spinal Tap   (85) 484
JONES, ROBERT EDMOND
Becky Sharp [1935]   (82) 403
JOYCE, ROBERT
Smooth Talk   (86) 354
JUNGE, ALFRED
I Know Where I'm Going [1945]   (83) 456

KACZENSKI, CHESTER
That Was Then . . . This Is Now   (86) 463
KAHUT-SVELKO, JEAN-PIERRE
Woman Next Door, The   (82) 385
KALUTAS, ERIKOS
Eleni   (86) 151
KARNBACK, RICHARD
Crossover Dreams   (86) 441
KELLY, CHRISTIAN
Alamo Bay   (86) 436
KELLY, ERROL
Indiana Jones and the Temple of Doom   (85) 253
KELSEY, DICK
Bambi [1942]   (85) 543
KELTER, JERIE
Moving Violations   (86) 453
Once Bitten   (86) 455
KEMM, HARRY R.
New York, New York [1977]   (84) 567
KEMPSTER, VICTOR
Compromising Positions   (86) 120
KENNEY, BILL
Body Heat   (82) 87

Rambo: First Blood Part II   (86) 299
Rocky IV   (86) 319
KILBEY, MARGOT
Lust in the Dust   (86) 450
KILVERT, LILLY
Sure Thing, The   (86) 369
To Live and Die in L.A.   (86) 379
Too Scared to Scream   (86) 463
KIRK, MARK-LEE
Journey into Fear [1943]   (86) 511
KIRKLAND, GEOFFREY
Birdy   (85) 93
KNIGHT, TERRY
Jewel of the Nile, The   (86) 448
Lifeforce   (86) 450
KNOWLTON, PETER
School Spirit   (86) 458
KOFOED, RICK
Nate and Hayes   (84) 236
Quiet Earth, The   (86) 295
KORDA, VINCENT
Sound Barrier, The [1952]   (85) 621
KOSEKI, MUTSUO
Here Come the Littles   (86) 446
KRAMS, ARTHUR
"Obituaries"   (86) 573
KROEGER, WOLF
Ladyhawke   (86) 214
Year of the Dragon   (86) 426
KULJIAN, ANNE
Runaway Train   (86) 324
KUTER, LEO K.
Unfaithful, The [1947]   (86) 550

LAFRANCHI, DAMIEN
Jewel of the Nile, The   (86) 448
LAING, BOB
Doctor and the Devils, The   (86) 442
Gandhi   (83) 183
LAKOVIC, PEDRAG
When Father Was Away on Business [1984]   (86) 411
LAMB, PHILIP
Trip to Bountiful, The   (86) 383
LAMONT, PETER
Boys from Brazil, The [1978]   (86) 480
For Your Eyes Only   (82) 155
Octopussy   (84) 276
View to a Kill, A   (86) 402
LANG, JUDITH ARIADNE
Turtle Diary   (86) 464
LANGE, HARRY
Dark Crystal, The   (83) 130
Great Muppet Caper, The   (82) 187
LARCHER, GEOFFREY
Sugar Cane Alley [1983]   (85) 461
LARKIN, PETER
Compromising Positions   (86) 120
Nighthawks   (82) 259
Tootsie   (83) 353
LARRECQ, HENRY
Thing, The   (83) 343
LARRINAGA, MARIO
Most Dangerous Game, The [1932]   (86) 519

LARSEN, TAMBI
  Heaven's Gate   (82) 195
LAWRENCE, JOEL DAVID
  Right Stuff, The   (84) 342
LAWRENCE, RICHARD J.
  Right Stuff, The   (84) 342
LEACH, ROGER MURRAY
  Killing Fields, The   (85) 270
LEE, EUGENE
  Hammett   (84) 174
LEGLER, STEVEN
  Choose Me   (85) 135
  Trouble in Mind   (86) 388
LEISEN, MITCHELL
  Sign of the Cross, The [1932]   (85) 607
LEONARD, JAMIE
  Wetherby   (86) 406
LEVEN, BORIS
  Fletch   (86) 169
  King of Comedy, The   (84) 192
  New York, New York [1977]   (84) 567
LEVESQUE, MICHAEL
  Barbarosa   (83) 60
LEVISEUR, TANTAR
  Marie   (86) 227
LEWIS, GARRETT
  American Flyers   (86) 436
  Sweet Dreams   (86) 374
LINEWEAVER, STEPHEN J.
  After Hours   (86) 51
  Brother from Another Planet, The   (85) 118
LINGHEIM, SUSANNE
  Fanny and Alexander [1982]   (84) 146
LITTLE, THOMAS
  Man Hunt [1941]   (85) 570
LITWACK, SYDNEY Z.
  Blue Thunder   (84) 84
  Places in the Heart   (85) 371
LLOYD, JOHN
  Clue   (86) 440
  Into the Night   (86) 186
  Maxie   (86) 452
  Raggedy Man   (82) 300
  They Might Be Giants [1971]   (83) 515
  TRON   (83) 371
LOMINO, DANIEL A.
  Buddy Buddy   (82) 93
  Christine   (84) 106
  Fast Times at Ridgemont High   (83) 156
  Starman   (85) 445
LOQUASTO, SANTO
  Desperately Seeking Susan   (86) 137
LUCAS, ROBERT
  Moving Violations   (86) 453
  Return of the Living Dead, The   (86) 314
LUDI, TONI
  Out of Control   (86) 455
LUNDELL, KERT
  They All Laughed   (82) 350

MACAVIN, JOSIE
  Cal   (85) 124
  Dresser, The   (84) 130
  Out of Africa   (86) 255

MCCAPE, STEPHEN
  My Dinner with André   (82) 255
MCCONNICO, HILTON
  Diva [1980]   (83) 147
MCCULLEY, ANNE D.
  Purple Rain   (85) 389
  Silverado   (86) 349
MACDONALD, RICHARD
  Plenty   (86) 271
MCDONNEL, JEANNE
  Lianna   (84) 201
MACKINTOSH, WOODS
  Remo Williams   (86) 457
  World According to Garp, The   (83) 397
MACLEAN, FRED M.
  Colorado Territory [1949]   (86) 489
MCMILLAN, STEPHANIE
  Santa Claus   (86) 334
MCSHERRY, ROSIE-MARIE
  Joshua Then and Now   (86) 198
MALLEY, BILL
  Vision Quest   (86) 464
MALTESE, DAN
  Commando   (86) 111
MANSBRIDGE, JOHN B.
  Baby   (86) 437
  Country   (85) 156
  My Science Project   (86) 453
  Splash   (85) 434
  TRON   (83) 371
MANSBRIDGE, MARK
  Man with Two Brains, The   (84) 223
MARCH, MARVIN
  Ghostbusters   (85) 219
MARSH, STEPHEN
  Crimes of Passion   (85) 161
  Runaway Train   (86) 324
MARSH, TERENCE
  Absence of Malice   (82) 57
MARTA, MARLEEN
  Stuff, The   (86) 461
MARTIN, JANE
  Experience Preferred ... but Not Essential
  [1982]   (84) 141
MARTY, JACK
  Split Image   (83) 317
MASTERS, ANTHONY
  Dune   (85) 171
MAUS, ROGER
  Man Who Loved Women, The   (84) 218
  S.O.B.   (82) 328
MAYNARD, WILLIAM
  Gymkata   (86) 445
MEAD, SYD
  TRON   (83) 371
MEIGHEN, JOHN
  Hotel New Hampshire, The   (85) 243
MELVILLE, JEAN-PIERRE
  Bob le Flambeur [1955]   (84) 526
MENZIES, WILLIAM CAMERON
  Arch of Triumph [1948]   (84) 501
  Beloved Rogue [1927]   (84) 522
MERCIER, PATRICE
  Sunday in the Country, A   (85) 466

METZNER, ERNO
  It Happened Tomorrow [1944]   (84) 552
MEURISSE, THEOBALD
  Beau Pere   (82) 78
  My Best Friend's Girl [1983]   (85) 326
MICHAEL, MICKEY S.
  Warning Sign   (86) 465
MICHELSON, HAROLD
  Mommie Dearest   (82) 245
  Terms of Endearment   (84) 414
MIDDLETON, MALCOLM
  Outland   (82) 272
  Razor's Edge, The   (85) 402
  White Nights   (86) 416
MILLER, BRUCE
  Day of the Dead   (86) 441
MILLER, LAWRENCE
  King of Comedy, The   (84) 192
MILO, GEORGE
  Torn Curtain [1966]   (85) 644
MINOR, MICHAEL
  Remo Williams   (86) 457
MITCHELL, GAVIN
  Christmas Story, A   (84) 110
MITZNER, DEAN E.
  Man with One Red Shoe, The   (86) 451
MOLLO, ANDREW
  Dance with a Stranger [1984]   (86) 125
MOLLY, MICHAEL
  Still of the Night   (83) 326
MONDELLO, ANTONY
  Terms of Endearment   (84) 414
  Twice in a Lifetime   (86) 397
MOORE, JOHN J.
  D.A.R.Y.L.   (86) 441
  Ghostbusters   (85) 219
  Sophie's Choice   (83) 311
MORENO, GARY
  Better Off Dead   (86) 438
  Summer Rental   (86) 462
MOULARD, ERIC
  Balance, La [1982]   (84) 52
  Garde à vue [1981]   (83) 189
MULLINS, PETER
  Death Wish III   (86) 441
MURAKAMI, JAMES
  Beverly Hills Cop   (85) 88
  Hammett   (84) 174
  Natural, The   (85) 329
  WarGames   (84) 458
MURAKI, SHINOBU
  Ran   (86) 304
MURAKI, YOSHIRO
  Ran   (86) 304
MURCIA, FÉLIX
  Carmen   (84) 101
  Flesh and Blood   (86) 443
MURRAY, GRAEME
  Never Cry Wolf   (84) 247
MURTON, PETER
  Spies like Us   (86) 360

NATALLUCCI, GIOVANNI
  Ladyhawke   (86) 214
  Once upon a Time in America   (85) 345

NAVARRO, NICANOR
  Right Stuff, The   (84) 342
NEGRÉ, ALAIN
  Return of Martin Guerre, The   (84) 318
NELSON, GEORGE R.
  Explorers   (86) 442
  Right Stuff, The   (84) 342
NEMEC, JOSEPH
  American Flyers   (86) 436
NEWBERRY, NORMAN
  Best Little Whorehouse in Texas, The   (83) 7
  Ghost Story   (82) 183
  Mask   (86) 231
  River, The   (85) 416
  Staying Alive   (84) 386
  Table for Five   (84) 404
NEWPORT, JAMES WILLIAM
  Heart Like a Wheel   (84) 182
  Sylvester   (86) 462
NISHIOKA, YOSHINOBU
  MacArthur's Children   (86) 451

O'BANNON, DAN
  Dark Star [1975]   (86) 494
O'BRIEN, WILLIAM F.
  Cannery Row   (83) 95
ODELL, CARY
  Cowboy [1958]   (82) 417
O'DONOVAN, EDWIN
  Honky Tonk Freeway   (82) 199
OPPEWALL, JEANNINE
  Love Letters   (85) 288
  Racing with the Moon   (85) 397
  Tender Mercies   (84) 409
ORBOM, ERIC
  Bedtime for Bonzo [1951]   (84) 512
O'SULLIVAN, MICHAEL
  1918   (86) 454

PACELLI, JOSEPH G.
  Stone Boy, The   (85) 450
PAIGE, MONICA
  Invasion U.S.A.   (86) 447
PAIN, KEITH
  Brazil   (86) 80
PAPAMICHAEL, PHEDON
  Love Streams   (85) 293
PARADISE, LYNDA
  Perfect   (86) 456
PARKER, ARTHUR
  Silverado   (86) 349
  Table for Five   (84) 404
PARKER, MAX
  Hard Way, The [1942]   (85) 555
PARRONDO, GIL
  Boys from Brazil, The [1978]   (86) 480
  Rustler's Rhapsody   (86) 458
  Volver a empezar   (83) 393
PATON, RAUL
  Rustler's Rhapsody   (86) 458
PAUL, VICKI
  Year of the Dragon   (86) 426
PAULL, LAURENCE G.
  American Flyers   (86) 436
  Back to the Future   (86) 65

PEARL, LINDA
  Testament   (84) 420
PEDIGO, TOM
  Star Trek III—The Search for Spock   (85) 439
  Terms of Endearment   (84) 414
PEEPLES, DENNIS
  Police Academy 2   (86) 276
PENDING, PAT
  Right Stuff, The   (84) 342
PEREIRA, HAL
  "Obituaries"   (84) 631
PETERS, PAUL
  Just One of the Guys   (86) 448
  Mischief   (86) 452
PETERSON, ROBERT
  Long Gray Line, The [1955]   (82) 447
PETROVIC, NEMANJA
  Gymkata   (86) 445
  Out of Control   (86) 455
PETROW, MISCHA
  Krush Groove   (86) 449
PICKETTE, WALTER
  Lust in the Dust   (86) 450
PICKWOAD, MICHAEL
  Ploughman's Lunch, The [1983]   (85) 377
PIERCE, CHUCK
  Protocol   (85) 383
PINTER, HERBERT
  Gallipoli [1980]   (82) 179
  Year of Living Dangerously, The [1982]   (84)
    462
PISONI, EDWARD
  Deathtrap   (83) 137
  King of Comedy, The   (84) 192
  Prince of the City   (82) 292
  Purple Rose of Cairo, The   (86) 290
  Verdict, The   (83) 377
PLATT, POLLY
  Man with Two Brains, The   (84) 223
  Terms of Endearment   (84) 414
POLGLASE, VAN NEST
  Animal Kingdom, The [1932]   (86) 469
POLITO, JENNIFER
  Breakfast Club, The   (86) 85
POLL, LEE
  Places in the Heart   (85) 371
POPE, LESLIE
  After Hours   (86) 51
POSTIGLIONE, GIORGIO
  Stephen King's Silver Bullet   (86) 460
POTTLE, HARRY
  Turk 182   (86) 464
PRATT, ANTHONY
  Excalibur   (82) 144
  Santa Claus   (86) 334
PRESTON, WARD
  Purple Rain   (85) 389
  That Championship Season   (83) 338
PRITCHARD, ANNE
  Atlantic City   (82) 74
  Joshua Then and Now   (86) 198
PRITCHARD, TERRY
  French Lieutenant's Woman, The   (82) 174

RAFELSON, TOBY
  Under Fire   (84) 441
RAGGETT, MARK
  1984   (85) 335
RANDOLF, VIRGINIA
  Adventures of Buckaroo Banzai, The   (85) 47
RANDOM, IDA
  Big Chill, The   (84) 78
  Frances   (83) 178
  Silverado   (86) 349
RAU, GRETCHEN
  Once upon a Time in America   (85) 345
READING, TONY
  Lifeforce   (86) 450
  Plenty   (86) 271
  Ragtime   (82) 304
REAMS, RICHARD
  Just One of the Guys   (86) 448
REICHEL, STEPHANE
  First Blood   (83) 164
REISS, STUART A.
  Micki & Maude   (85) 308
REMISOFF, NICOLAI
  Apache [1954]   (82) 395
REYNOLDS, NORMAN
  Raiders of the Lost Ark   (82) 308
  Return to Oz   (86) 458
  Superman II   (82) 339
  Young Sherlock Holmes   (86) 431
RICCERI, LUCIANO
  Bal, Le [1983]   (85) 80
  Macaroni   (86) 451
RICHARDSON, EDWARD
  Cat People   (83) 100
  Modern Romance   (82) 241
  Scarface   (84) 361
  Stick   (86) 460
RICHWOOD, FRANK
  Explorers   (86) 442
RINGWOOD, BOB
  Draughtsman's Contract, The [1982]   (84) 126
RIPPER, LUIS CARLOS
  Xica [1976]   (83) 407
RIVA, J. MICHAEL
  Adventures of Buckaroo Banzai, The   (85) 47
  Color Purple, The   (86) 105
  Goonies, The   (86) 176
ROBERS, TERISE
  D.A.R.Y.L.   (86) 441
ROBERT, DANIEL
  King of Comedy, The   (84) 192
ROBERTS, CASEY
  Secret Life of Walter Mitty, The [1947]   (86) 540
ROCKETT, NORMAN
  Splash   (85) 434
ROELOFS, AL
  TRON   (83) 371
ROMANAC, NICHOLAS
  Heavenly Kid, The   (86) 445
ROMERO, PETER
  Right Stuff, The   (84) 342
ROMVÁRI, JÓZSEF
  Colonel Redl [1984]   (86) 100

ROSE, STUART
Company of Wolves, The [1984]   (86) 115
Razor's Edge, The   (85) 402
ROSEMARIN, HILTON
Joshua Then and Now   (86) 198
Mrs. Soffel   (85) 314
ROSEN, CHARLES
Flashdance   (84) 158
My Favorite Year   (83) 241
River, The   (85) 416
Toy, The   (83) 358
ROSENBERG, PHILIP
Next Stop, Greenwich Village [1976]   (85) 592
ROSSE, HERMAN
King of Jazz [1930]   (86) 515
ROSSO, JOSAN
Iceman   (85) 248
ROWLAND, CRICKET
To Live and Die in L.A.   (86) 379
ROYCE, ARTHUR I.
Our Relations [1936]   (86) 523
ROYSDEN, THOMAS L.
Clue   (86) 440
Perfect   (86) 456
RUDOLF, GENE
Once Bitten   (86) 455
Trading Places   (84) 430
RUSSELL, BLAKE
Star Trek III—The Search for Spock   (85) 439
RUSSELL, SHIRLEY
Agatha [1979]   (83) 435
RUSSO, JOE
Best Friends   (83) 68
RUSSO, JOSAN F.
Creator   (86) 441
Real Genius   (86) 309

SALLES, JOSE JOAQUIN
Gabriela [1983]   (85) 213
SALLIS, CRISPIAN
View to a Kill, A   (86) 402
SANDELL, WILLIAM
St. Elmo's Fire   (86) 330
SANDERS, ANDREW
Merry Christmas, Mr. Lawrence   (84) 231
SASAKI, KYOJI
Mishima   (86) 236
SAULNIER, JACQUES
Swann in Love   (85) 471
SAWYER, RICHARD
Lost in America   (86) 219
Melvin and Howard [1980]   (82) 453
Twilight Zone—The Movie   (84) 435
SBARRA, GIANNI
Night of the Shooting Stars, The [1982]   (84) 258
SCAIFE, HUGH
Passage to India, A   (85) 365
SCARFIOTTI, FERNANDO
Bring on the Night   (86) 439
SCHEIBEL, K. C.
Choose Me   (85) 135
SCHOPPE, JAMES
Return of the Jedi   (84) 326
Volunteers   (86) 464

SCOTT, ELLIOT
Pirates of Penzance, The   (84) 301
SCOTT, JAN
World of Henry Orient, The [1964]   (84) 600
SENECIC, ZELJKO
Transylvania 6-5000   (86) 463
SENTER, JACK
Man Who Loved Women, The   (84) 218
Micki & Maude   (85) 308
SESSA, BOB
Pale Rider   (86) 261
SEYMOUR, MICHAEL
Bride, The   (86) 438
SHANAHAN, JAMES
Stick   (86) 460
SHINGLETON, WILFRED
Eye of the Needle   (82) 148
SIDDALL, JOHN
D.A.R.Y.L.   (86) 441
SIEGEL, RON
Party Animal   (86) 455
SILVERA, DARRELL
Journey into Fear [1943]   (86) 511
"Obituaries"   (84) 637
SILVESTRI, GIANNI
Tragedy of a Ridiculous Man [1981]   (83) 361
SIMI, CARLO
Once upon a Time in America   (85) 345
SIMPSON, RICK
2010   (85) 494
SINCLAIR, KIM
Quiet Earth, The   (86) 295
SINGELLIS, JAMES
Once upon a Time in America   (85) 345
SMILIE, CYD
City Limits   (86) 440
SMITH, ADRIAN
Plenty   (86) 271
SMITH, JACK MARTIN
Hombre [1967]   (84) 547
Royal Wedding [1951]   (86) 536
SMITH, MORLEY
Shooting Party, The [1984]   (86) 344
SMITH, PETER J.
Jagged Edge   (86) 190
SMITH, PETER LANSDOWN
Fandango   (86) 442
SMITH, PHILIP
Splash   (85) 434
SMITH, ROBERT E.
Hombre [1967]   (84) 547
SMITH, ROY FORGE
Hound of the Baskervilles, The [1978]   (82) 203
Mrs. Soffel   (85) 314
SMITH, TED
Colorado Territory [1949]   (86) 489
SMITH, WILLIAM CRAIG
Victor/Victoria   (83) 387
SNYDER, DAVID L.
Blade Runner   (83) 76
My Science Project   (86) 453
Pee-wee's Big Adventure   (86) 265
Racing with the Moon   (85) 397

SOLER, OCTAVIO
  Crossover Dreams   (86) 441
SPADONI, LUCIANO
  King Solomon's Mines   (86) 449
SPASOJEVIC, VLADIMR
  Out of Control   (86) 455
SPENCE, STEVE
  Baby   (86) 437
  Eleni   (86) 151
  Killing Fields, The   (85) 270
SPENCER, ALFRED E.
  Royal Wedding [1951]   (86) 536
SPENCER, JAMES H.
  Gremlins   (85) 230
  Poltergeist   (83) 263
  Stripes   (82) 336
  Twilight Zone—The Movie   (84) 435
SPHEERIS, LINDA
  Last Starfighter, The   (85) 277
SPIER, CAROL
  Running Brave   (84) 354
  Sesame Street Presents: Follow That Bird   (86)
  459
  Videodrome   (84) 452
SPISAK, NEIL
  Trip to Bountiful, The   (86) 383
SPRIGGS, AUSTEN
  White Nights   (86) 416
STAGGS, JEFF
  Dreamscape   (85) 166
STAHELI, PAUL
  Kid Colter   (86) 449
STARSKI, ALLAN
  Danton [1982]   (84) 121
  Love in Germany, A [1983]   (85) 283
  Man of Iron   (82) 230
  Man of Marble [1977]   (82) 234
STEPHENS, JACK
  Octopussy   (84) 276
  Tess [1980]   (82) 471
STEVENS, WILLIAM L.
  Our Relations [1936]   (86) 523
STEWART, MCLAREN
  Bambi [1942]   (85) 543
STODDART, JOHN
  Careful He Might Hear You [1983]   (85) 130
STOLL, GEORGE
  Stuff, The   (86) 461
STOREY, RAYMOND G.
  Baby   (86) 437
  Fever Pitch   (86) 443
STOUT, WILLIAM
  Return of the Living Dead, The   (86) 314
STUBENRAUCH, MAX
  Boat Is Full, The [1981]   (83) 82
SWANSON, MARY OLIVIA
  Footloose   (85) 198
  Protocol   (85) 383
SWEENEY, ALFRED
  Taps   (82) 343
SWIFT, BRENTON
  Aviator, The   (86) 437
SYLBERT, PAUL
  Blow Out   (82) 83
  Gorky Park   (84) 162

Journey of Natty Gann, The   (86) 203
  Mikey and Nicky [1976]   (85) 576
SYLBERT, RICHARD
  Breathless   (84) 89
  Cotton Club, The   (85) 150
  Frances   (83) 178
  Reds   (82) 312
SYMONDS, VIC
  Long Good Friday, The   (83) 220
SZOLLÁR, TIBOR
  Colonel Redl [1984]   (86) 100

TAKENAKA, KAZUO
  Mishima   (86) 236
TANJI, LYDIA
  Dim Sum   (86) 141
TAVOULARIS, DEAN
  Hammett   (84) 174
  Outsiders, The   (84) 282
TAYLOR, JACK G., JR.
  Real Genius   (86) 309
  Star 80   (84) 374
TAYLOR, JAMES A.
  Rich and Famous   (82) 316
TESTER, TED
  Priest of Love   (82) 288
THALER, FRIEDER
  Enemy Mine   (86) 161
THEVENET, PIERRE
  Bizet's Carmen [1983]   (85) 98
THOMAS, IAN
  Grey Fox, The   (84) 168
THOMPSON, GLENN P.
  Detour [1946]   (86) 498
THRASHER, HAROLD
  Joshua Then and Now   (86) 198
TILFORD, WALTER F.
  Hard Way, The [1942]   (85) 555
TOCCI, JAMES E.
  Pee-wee's Big Adventure   (86) 265
  St. Elmo's Fire   (86) 330
TOLUBOFF, ALEXANDER
  History Is Made at Night [1937]   (84) 542
TOMKINS, ALAN
  Lifeforce   (86) 450
TOMKINS, LESLIE
  Jewel of the Nile, The   (86) 448
TOWNSEND, JEFFREY
  After Hours   (86) 51
TRAUNER, ALEXANDER
  Coup de torchon [1981]   (83) 124
  Subway   (86) 461
TUCH, FRED
  Pennies from Heaven   (82) 276

ULLMAN, SIDNEY
  Scarlet Letter, The [1927]   (85) 602
USHER, ROBERT
  Peter Ibbetson [1935]   (86) 527

VALLONE, JOHN
  Brewster's Millions   (86) 438
  Commando   (86) 111
  48 HRS.   (83) 173
  Southern Comfort   (82) 332

VETCHINSKY, ALEX
  Victim [1961]   (85) 649
VON BRANDENSTEIN, PATRIZIA
  Amadeus   (85) 63
  Chorus Line, A   (86) 91
  Ragtime   (82) 304
VON GIERKE, HENNING. See GIERKE,
  HENNING VON.

WAKEFIELD, SIMON
  D.A.R.Y.L.   (86) 441
  Lifeforce   (86) 450
WAKHÉVITCH, GEORGES
  "Obituaries"   (85) 697
WALDEN, TOM
  Bostonians, The   (85) 105
WALKER, GRAHAM
  Coca-Cola Kid, The   (86) 440
  Mad Max Beyond Thunderdome   (86) 223
  Road Warrior, The [1981]   (83) 277
WALKER, ROY
  Eleni   (86) 151
  Killing Fields, The   (85) 270
  Yentl   (84) 468
WALKER, STUART
  Private Function, A [1984]   (86) 280
WALLACE, WILLIAM
  Unfaithful, The [1947]   (86) 550
WALSH, FRANK
  Local Hero   (84) 206
WARNKE, JOHN
  Jagged Edge   (86) 190
WASCO, DAVID
  Smooth Talk   (86) 354
WASHINGTON, J. DENNIS
  Prizzi's Honor   (86) 285
  To Be or Not to Be   (84) 426
  Victory   (82) 374
WATSON, DAN
  Local Hero   (84) 206
WEAVER, CHARLES
  Sudden Death   (86) 461
WEIDNER, GÖTZ
  Boot, Das [1981]   (83) 86
WEINTRAUB, BRUCE
  Prizzi's Honor   (86) 285
WELCH, ROBERT W.
  Color Purple, The   (86) 105
WELLES, ORSON
  Falstaff [1967]   (83) 443
WESTLUND, ROBERT CHRISTOPHER
  Legend of Billie Jean, The   (86) 450
WHEELER, LYLE
  My Cousin Rachel [1952]   (82) 458
  Snows of Kilimanjaro, The [1952]   (83) 498
WHITE, FRANK
  Clash of the Titans   (82) 111
WHITTAKER, IAN
  Bad Medicine   (86) 437
  Emerald Forest, The   (86) 156

Razor's Edge, The   (85) 402
  Return of the Soldier, The [1982]   (84) 332
  Richard's Things   (82) 321
WIGHTMAN, ROBERT
  Taking Off [1971]   (86) 545
WILHEIM, LADISLAV
  Invasion U.S.A.   (86) 447
WILLIAMS, L. P.
  Nell Gwyn [1934]   (84) 557
WILLIAMS, OWEN
  Caddie [1976]   (83) 439
WILLIAMS, PETER
  Wild Geese II   (86) 466
WILLIAMS, TREVOR
  Alamo Bay   (86) 436
  Police Academy 2   (86) 276
  Pretty Baby [1978]   (85) 597
WILLIS, EDWIN B.
  Royal Wedding [1951]   (86) 536
WOLLARD, JOAN
  White Nights   (86) 416
WOLLARD, TONY
  Moonlighting   (83) 237
WOODRUFF, DON
  Mass Appeal   (85) 303
WOOLEY, PETER
  Summer Rental   (86) 462
WOOLEY, STEPHANIE
  Stone Boy, The   (85) 450
WUNDERLICH, JERRY
  My Science Project   (86) 453
  Racing with the Moon   (85) 397
WURTZEL, STUART
  Chosen, The   (83) 116
  Purple Rose of Cairo, The   (86) 290

YADEKAR, RAM
  Heat and Dust [1982]   (84) 187
YBARRA, AL
  Hondo [1953]   (83) 452
YTUARTE, AGUSTIN
  Falcon and the Snowman, The   (86) 165
  Missing   (83) 232
  Under Fire   (84) 441
YUNG, DANNY
  Dim Sum   (86) 141

ZAIDA, SABA
  Razor's Edge, The   (85) 402
ZEFFIRELLI, FRANCO
  Traviata, La   (83) 366
ZEHETBAUER, ROLF
  Enemy Mine   (86) 161
  Lili Marleen   (82) 222
  Lola [1981]   (83) 215
  Querelle [1982]   (84) 313
  Veronika Voss   (83) 382
ZIMMERMAN, HERMAN
  Better Off Dead   (86) 438
ZINNEN, AL
  Bambi [1942]   (85) 543

MUSIC INDEX

ABENE, MICHAEL
  Goodbye, New York   (86) 444
ABRIL, ANTON GARCIA
  Holy Innocents, The   (86) 447
ADDISON, JOHN
  Grace Quigley   (86) 444
  Torn Curtain [1966]   (85) 644
AMFITHEATROF, DANIELE
  Lost Moment, The [1947]   (83) 465
  "Obituaries"   (84) 608
AMRAM, DAVID
  Arrangement, The [1969]   (86) 474
ANTHEIL, GEORGE
  Specter of the Rose [1946]   (83) 504
APOLLONIA 6
  Purple Rain   (85) 389
ARGOL, SEBASTIAN
  Yol   (83) 411
ARLEN, HAROLD
  Star Is Born, A [1954]   (84) 573
ARNOLD, MALCOLM
  Sound Barrier, The [1952]   (85) 621
ARTEMIEV, EDUARD
  Siberiade [1977]   (83) 299
ASKEY, GIL
  Lady Sings the Blues [1972]   (85) 565
AURIC, GEORGES
  "Obituaries"   (84) 609
AUTUMN
  Krush Groove   (86) 449

B., SARA
  Tender Mercies   (84) 409
BACALOV, LUIS
  City of Women   (82) 106
  Entre nous [1983]   (85) 176
BACH, JOHANN SEBASTIAN
  Hail Mary   (86) 182
BACHARACH, BURT
  Arthur   (82) 71
BADINGS, HANK
  Freud [1962]   (84) 535
BAKALEINIKOFF, C.
  Journey into Fear [1943]   (86) 511
BAKER, ARTHUR
  Sudden Death   (86) 461
BAKER, HERBERT
  "Obituaries"   (84) 609
BAKER, MICHAEL CONWAY
  Grey Fox, The   (84) 168
  One Magic Christmas   (86) 455
BAND, RICHARD
  Re-Animator   (86) 457
BARBER, SAMUEL
  Norte, El   (84) 265
BARCLAY, EDDIE
  Bob le Flambeur [1955]   (84) 526
BARRY, JOHN
  Body Heat   (82) 87
  Cotton Club, The   (85) 150
  Frances   (83) 178

Hammett   (84) 174
Jagged Edge   (86) 190
Octopussy   (84) 276
Out of Africa   (86) 255
They Might Be Giants [1971]   (83) 515
View to a Kill, A   (86) 402
BARTON, DEE
  Play Misty for Me [1971]   (86) 532
BATES, BOBO
  Taking Off [1971]   (86) 545
BEASTIE BOYS
  Krush Groove   (86) 449
BEE GEES, THE
  Staying Alive   (84) 386
BEETHOVEN, LUDWIG VAN
  First Name, Carmen [1983]   (85) 186
  Nostalgia [1983]   (85) 340
  Passion [1982]   (84) 289
BELL, DANIEL
  Fanny and Alexander [1982]   (84) 146
BELLING, ANDREW
  Starchaser   (86) 460
BEN, JORGE
  Xica [1976]   (83) 407
BENNET, RICHARD RODNEY
  Return of the Soldier, The [1982]   (84) 332
BERGMAN, ALAN
  Yentl   (84) 468
BERGMAN, MARILYN
  Yentl   (84) 468
BERLIN, IRVING
  Holiday Inn [1942]   (82) 443
BERNSTEIN, ELMER
  American Werewolf in London, An   (82) 66
  Black Cauldron, The   (86) 75
  Chosen, The   (83) 116
  Ghostbusters   (85) 219
  Honky Tonk Freeway   (82) 199
  Slap Shot [1977]   (82) 467
  Spies like Us   (86) 360
  Stripes   (82) 336
  Trading Places   (84) 430
  World of Henry Orient, The [1964]   (84) 600
BERNSTEIN, PETER
  My Science Project   (86) 453
BERTI, SANH
  Cattle Annie and Little Britches   (82) 97
BICKHARDT, CRAIG
  Tender Mercies   (84) 409
BIZET, GEORGES
  Carmen   (84) 101
BLACK, KAREN
  Can She Bake a Cherry Pie?   (84) 95
BLOCH, ERNEST
  Where the Green Ants Dream [1984]   (86) 465
BLOW, KURTIS
  Krush Groove   (86) 449
BOCQUET, ROLAND
  Balance, La [1982]   (84) 52
BODDICKER, MICHAEL
  Adventures of Buckaroo Banzai, The   (85) 47

BOEKELHEIDE, TODD
Dim Sum   (86) 141
BOLLING, CLAUDE
Bad Boy, The   (86) 437
BONNEAU, CHRISTIAN
Death of Mario Ricci, The [1983]   (86) 133
BOSHOFF, JOHN
Gods Must Be Crazy, The [1980]   (85) 224
BOW WOW WOW
Scandalous   (85) 532
BOYER, JEAN
Bob le Flambeur [1955]   (84) 526
BRAHAM, PHILIP
Nell Gwyn [1934]   (84) 557
BRAHMS, JOHANNES
Peril   (86) 456
BREWIS, PETER
Morons from Outer Space   (86) 452
BRICUSSE, LESLIE
Victor/Victoria   (83) 387
BRITTEN, TONY
Wetherby   (86) 406
BROOKS, HARVEY
I'm No Angel [1933]   (85) 561
BROUGHTON, BRUCE
Silverado   (86) 349
Young Sherlock Holmes   (86) 431
BRUNER, TOM
School Spirit   (86) 457
BRUNS, GEORGE E.
"Obituaries"   (84) 610
BUDD, ROY
Wild Geese II   (86) 466
BURGON, GEOFFREY
Turtle Diary   (86) 464
BURNS, RALPH
Annie   (83) 56
Chorus Line, A   (86) 91
Kiss Me Goodbye   (83) 209
Moving Violations   (86) 453
My Favorite Year   (83) 241
National Lampoon's Vacation   (84) 242
New York, New York [1977]   (84) 567
Perfect   (86) 456
Star 80   (84) 374
BURT, GEORGE
Fool for Love   (86) 172
BURWELL, CARTER
Blood Simple   (86) 438
BUTTOLPH, DAVID
Colorado Territory [1949]   (86) 489

CAESAR, SHIRLEY
Gospel   (85) 520
CAHN, SAMMY
Pete Kelly's Blues [1955]   (83) 481
CALE, J. J.
My Best Friend's Girl [1983]   (85) 326
CAMPBELL, DAVID
All the Right Moves   (84) 41
CAMPINA, ENRIQUE GRANADOS
Peril   (86) 456
CARLOS, WENDY
TRON   (83) 371

CARMICHAEL, HOAGY
"Obituaries"   (82) 481
CARNEIRO, NANDO
Kiss of the Spider Woman   (86) 209
CARPENTER, JOHN
Christine   (84) 106
Dark Star [1975]   (86) 494
Escape from New York   (82) 133
CASE, ANNA
"Obituaries"   (85) 658
CHABRIER, EMMANUEL
Detective   (86) 442
CHAD
Krush Groove   (86) 449
CHARLES, JOHN
Quiet Earth, The   (86) 295
Utu [1983]   (85) 504
CHARNIN, MARTIN
Annie   (83) 56
CHATTAWAY, JAY
Invasion U.S.A.   (86) 447
Stephen King's Silver Bullet   (86) 460
CHIHARA, PAUL
Prince of the City   (82) 292
CHOPIN, FRÉDÉRIC
Colonel Redl [1984]   (86) 100
Detective   (86) 442
CHUNG, WANG
To Live and Die in L.A.   (86) 379
CHURCHILL, FRANK
Bambi [1942]   (85) 543
CILLA, MAX
Sugar Cane Alley [1983]   (85) 461
CLARK, TWINKIE AND THE CLARK
SISTERS
Gospel   (85) 520
CLASH, THE
Valley Girl   (84) 447
CLEVELAND, JAMES AND THE SOUTHERN
CALIFORNIA CHOIR
Gospel   (85) 520
CLIFFORD, MATT
Return of the Living Dead, The   (86) 314
COLAYCO, CECILE
9 Deaths of the Ninja   (86) 454
COLEMANN, ORNETTE
Detective   (86) 442
COLOMBIER, MICHEL
Purple Rain   (85) 389
White Nights   (86) 416
COLTRANE, JOHN
Hail Mary   (86) 182
COMDEN, BETTY
Bells Are Ringing [1960]   (84) 517
CONLAN, JOSEPH
Stick   (86) 460
CONLY, PAUL
Kid Colter   (86) 449
CONTE, PAOLO
Joke of Destiny, A [1983]   (85) 259
Softly Softly [1984]   (86) 460
CONTI, BILL
For Your Eyes Only   (82) 155
Gotcha!   (86) 444

Karate Kid, The (85) 264
Mass Appeal (85) 303
Next Stop, Greenwich Village (85) 592
Right Stuff, The (84) 342
Rocky III (83) 283
Split Image (83) 317
That Championship Season (83) 338
Victory (82) 374
COODER, RY
Alamo Bay (86) 436
Brewster's Millions (86) 438
Paris, Texas (85) 359
Southern Comfort (82) 332
COOK, RAY
Careful He Might Hear You [1983] (85) 130
COPLAND, AARON
North Star, The [1943] (83) 476
COPPOLA, CARMINE
Outsiders, The (84) 282
CORIGLIANO, JOHN
Revolution (86) 458
CORNELL, PETER
Taking Off [1971] (86) 545
COSMA, VLADIMIR
Bal, Le [1983] (85) 80
Diva [1981] (83) 147
Goat, The [1981] (86) 444
Little Jerk [1984] (86) 450
COTTON, JOSIE
Valley Girl (84) 447
COURAGE, ALEXANDER
Bells Are Ringing [1960] (84) 517
CRAIG, CHARLIE
Tender Mercies (84) 409
CULTURE CLUB
Valley Girl (84) 447
CUOMO, BILL
That Was Then . . . This Is Now (86) 463
CUSTER, ARTHUR
When Nature Calls (86) 465
CUTTER, MURRAY
Unfaithful, The [1947] (86) 550
CYMBAL, JOHNNY
Tender Mercies (84) 409

DARING, K. MASON
Brother from Another Planet, The (85) 118
Lianna (84) 201
Return of the Secaucus 7 [1980] (83) 484
DAVIES, IVA
Razorback [1984] (86) 457
DAVIES, PHIL
Trancers (86) 463
DAVIS, CARL
French Lieutenant's Woman, The (82) 174
King David (86) 449
DAVIS, JOHNNY "SCATS"
"Obituaries" (84) 617
DE BENEDICTICS, DICK
Earthling, The [1980] (82) 130
DELERUE, GEORGES
Agnes of God (86) 56
Garde à vue [1981] (83) 189
Maxie (86) 452
Rich and Famous (82) 316
Richard's Things (82) 321
Silkwood (84) 367

True Confessions (82) 368
Woman Next Door, The (82) 385
DEL MONACO, MARIO
Carmen (84) 101
DE LUCIA, PACO
Carmen (84) 101
Hit, The (86) 446
DENJEAN, CLAUDE
Plouffe, Les (86) 456
DE VORZON, BARRY
Stick (86) 460
DES INNOCENTS, SIMON
Beau Mariage, Le (83) 65
DESTOCKI, BOB
Fast Times at Ridgemont High (83) 156
DEVIES, PHIL
Savage Island (86) 457
DEVOL, FRANK
Flight of the Phoenix, The [1966] (85) 549
"DICK TRACY"
Tokyo-Ga (86) 463
DICKERSON, DEZ
Purple Rain (85) 389
DICOLA, VINCE
Rocky IV (86) 319
DIETRICH, JAMES
King of Jazz [1930] (86) 515
DIETZ, HOWARD
"Obituaries" (84) 619
DIKKER, LOEK
4th Man, The [1983] (85) 203
DILGE, DOUGLAS
They All Laughed (82) 350
DOLBY, THOMAS
Fever Pitch (86) 443
DOLDINGER, KLAUS
Boot, Das [1981] (83) 86
DONAGGIO, PINO
Blow Out (82) 83
Hercules II (86) 446
Howling, The (82) 207
Tex (83) 335
DORFF, STEVE
Rustler's Rhapsody (86) 458
DORING, MASON
Key Exchange (86) 448
DRAGON, CARMEN
"Obituaries" (85) 664
DREIEIER
Sugarbaby (86) 461
DU BOIS, GLADYS
I'm No Angel [1933] (85) 561
DUNING, GEORGE
Cowboy [1958] (82) 417
Long Gray Line, The [1955] (82) 447
DU PREZ, JOHN
Bullshot [1983] (86) 439
Once Bitten (86) 455
Private Function, A [1984] (86) 280
DUVALL, ROBERT
Tender Mercies (84) 409
DVOŘÁK, ANTONÍN
Hail Mary (86) 182
Passion [1982] (84) 289
Taking Off [1971] (86) 545

ECONOMOU, NICOLAS
Sheer Madness [1983]   (86) 459
EDITIONS SARAVAH
Erendira [1983]   (85) 181
EISLER, HANNS
Woman on the Beach, The [1947]   (83) 522
ELFMAN, DANNY
Pee-wee's Big Adventure   (86) 265
ELIAS, JONATHAN
Almost You   (86) 436
Tuff Turf   (86) 464
ELINOR, CARLI
Bridge of San Luis Rey, The [1929]   (82) 408
ELLI
Full Moon in Paris   (85) 208
ELLISON, BEN
I'm No Angel [1933]   (85) 561
EMERSON, KEITH
Nighthawks   (82) 259
ENDER, MATTHEW
Streetwalkin'   (86) 461
ERBE, MICKY
Improper Channels   (82) 218
EURYTHMICS
1984   (85) 335
EYEN, TOM
Taking Off [1971]   (86) 545

FALTERMEYER, HAROLD
Beverly Hills Cop   (85) 88
Fletch   (86) 169
Sunday in the Country, A   (85) 466
FAT BOYS
Krush Groove   (86) 449
FAURÉ, GABRIEL-URBAIN
Passion [1982]   (84) 289
Where the Green Ants Dream [1984]   (86) 465
FELDMAN, NICK. See CHUNG, WANG
FENTON, ANTHONY
Company of Wolves, The [1984]   (86) 115
FENTON, GEORGE
Gandhi   (83) 183
FENYES, SZABOLES
Lily in Love   (86) 450
FERGUSON, BOB
Tender Mercies   (84) 409
FIEDEL, BRAD
Compromising Positions   (86) 120
Fright Night   (86) 444
Terminator, The   (85) 478
FINSTON, NAT W.
Peter Ibbetson [1935]   (86) 527
FLEISCHER, LOUIS
"Obituaries"   (86) 567
FLOKE, BOB
Stitches   (86) 461
FLYNN, PATRICK
Caddie [1976]   (83) 439
FOLK, ROBERT
Police Academy 2   (86) 276
FOLKLORISTS, THE
Norte, El   (84) 265
FORBSTEIN, LEO F.
Unfaithful, The [1947]   (86) 550

FORCE M.D.'S
Krush Groove   (86) 449
FORREST, GEORGE
Taking Off [1971]   (86) 545
FORSEY, KEITH
Breakfast Club, The   (86) 85
FOSTER, DAVID
St. Elmo's Fire   (86) 330
FOSTER, STEPHEN
Streamers   (84) 391
FOX, CHARLES
National Lampoon's European Vacation   (86) 453
FRANK, DAVID
Code of Silence   (86) 440
FRASER, DAVE
Beyond Reasonable Doubt [1980]   (84) 74
FRASER, IAN
First Monday in October   (82) 151
FRASER, JILL
Personal Best   (83) 254
FRIEDHOFER, HUGH
Hondo [1953]   (83) 452
"Obituaries"   (82) 487
FRIZZELL, LEFTY
Tender Mercies   (84) 409
FRONTIERE, DOMINIC
Aviator, The   (86) 437
FRY, GARY
Cease Fire   (86) 440

GABRIEL, PETER
Birdy   (85) 93
GALLAGHER, RORY
Sense of Freedom, A   (86) 459
GAP BAND
Krush Groove   (86) 449
GARCIA, RUSSELL
Time Machine, The [1960]   (84) 585
GARRETT, SNUFF
Honkytonk Man   (83) 200
Sharky's Machine   (82) 324
GARVARENTZ, GEORGE
Too Scared to Scream   (86) 463
GASCOIGNE, BRIAN
Emerald Forest, The   (86) 156
GERMAN, EDWARD
Nell Gwyn [1934]   (84) 557
GERSHENSON, JOSEPH
Creature from the Black Lagoon, The [1954]   (82) 422
GERSHWIN, GEORGE
"Life Achievement Award"   (86) 7
GERSHWIN, IRA
North Star, The [1943]   (83) 476
"Obituaries"   (84) 621
GILMOUR, DAVID
Pink Floyd the Wall [1981]   (83) 258
GIOVANNI, PAUL
Wicker Man, The [1974]   (86) 555
GIRRE, RONAN
Beau Mariage, Le   (83) 65

MUSIC INDEX

GLASS, PHILIP
  Koyaanisqatsi (84) 197
  Mishima (86) 236
GOLDENBERG, BILLY
  Reuben, Reuben (84) 337
GOLDSMITH, JERRY
  Baby (86) 437
  Boys from Brazil, The [1978] (86) 480
  Challenge, The (83) 109
  Explorers (86) 442
  First Blood (83) 164
  Freud [1962] (84) 535
  Gremlins (85) 230
  King Solomon's Mines (86) 449
  Outland (82) 272
  Poltergeist (83) 263
  Psycho II (84) 307
  Raggedy Man (82) 300
  Rambo: First Blood Part II (86) 299
  Secret of NIMH, The (83) 288
  Twilight Zone—The Movie (84) 435
  Under Fire (84) 441
GOLDSMITH, JOEL
  Man with Two Brains, The (84) 223
GOODMAN, MILES
  Footloose (85) 198
  Jinxed (83) 206
  Table for Five (84) 404
  Teen Wolf (86) 462
GORE, MICHAEL
  Terms of Endearment (84) 414
GRAINER, RON
  "Obituaries" (82) 488
GRAY, ALLAN
  I Know Where I'm Going [1945] (83) 456
GREEN, ADOLPH
  Bells Are Ringing [1960] (84) 517
GREEN, JOHNNY
  Royal Wedding [1951] (86) 536
GREEN, PHILIP
  Victim, The [1961] (85) 649
GROSS, CHARLES
  Country (85) 156
  Heartland (82) 191
  Sweet Dreams (86) 374
GRUENBERG, LOUIS
  Arch of Triumph [1948] (84) 501
GRUSIN, DAVE
  Absence of Malice (82) 57
  Front, The [1976] (86) 502
  Goonies, The (86) 176
  On Golden Pond (82) 263
  Racing with the Moon (85) 397
  Reds (82) 312
  Tootsie (83) 353
GUEST, CHRISTOPHER
  This Is Spinal Tap (85) 484

HAGEMAN, RICHARD
  Fort Apache [1948] (84) 530
HALL, CAROL
  Best Little Whorehouse in Texas, The (83) 72
HAMILTON, ARTHUR
  Pete Kelly's Blues [1955] (83) 481
HAMLISCH, MARVIN
  Chorus Line, A (86) 91
  D.A.R.Y.L. (86) 441

Pennies from Heaven (82) 276
Sophie's Choice (83) 311
Way We Were, The [1973] (82) 474
HAMMER, JAN
  Secret Admirer (86) 459
HANCOCK, HERBIE
  Soldier's Story, A (85) 427
HARRISON, GEORGE
  Time Bandits [1980] (82) 364
HARRISON, JOHN
  Day of the Dead (86) 441
HARRY, DEBBIE
  Krush Groove (86) 449
HART, BOBBY
  Tender Mercies (84) 409
HART, NINA
  Taking Off [1971] (86) 545
HARTLEY, RICHARD
  Dance with a Stranger [1984] (86) 125
HARWOOD, BO
  Love Streams (85) 293
HASKELL, JIMMIE
  Rainy Day Friends (86) 457
HAWKINS, WALTER AND THE HAWKINS
FAMILY WITH THE LOVE CENTER CHOIR
  Gospel (85) 520
HAYES, JACK
  Fast Forward (86) 442
HEARSHEN, IRA
  Transylvania 6-5000 (86) 463
HEINDORF, RAY
  Pete Kelly's Blues [1955] (83) 481
HENTSCHEL, DAVID
  Educating Rita (84) 136
HENZE, HANS-WERNER
  Swann in Love (85) 471
HERIZA, CATHERINE
  Taking Off [1971] (86) 545
HERNANDEZ, ANDY "SUGARCOATED"
  Mixed Blood (86) 452
HERON, MIKE
  Taking Off [1971] (86) 545
HERRMANN, BERNARD
  Snows of Kilimanjaro, The [1952] (83) 498
HINE, RUPERT
  Better Off Dead (86) 438
HOLDRIDGE, LEE
  American Pop (82) 62
  Micki & Maude (85) 308
  Splash (85) 434
  Sylvester (86) 462
  Transylvania 6-5000 (86) 463
HOMRICH, JUNIOR
  Emerald Forest, The (86) 156
HONEGGER, ARTHUR
  Napoleon [1927] (82) 461
HORNER, JAMES
  Cocoon (86) 96
  Commando (86) 111
  Dresser, The (84) 130
  48 HRS. (83) 173
  Gorky Park (84) 162
  Heaven Help Us (86) 445
  Journey of Natty Gann, The (86) 203
  Star Trek II—The Wrath of Khan (83) 321

Star Trek III—The Search for Spock (85) 439
Stone Boy, The (85) 450
Testament (84) 420
Volunteers (86) 464
Wolfen (82) 382
HOWARTH, ALAN
  Christine (84) 106
  Escape from New York (82) 133
HUES, JACK. *See* CHUNG, WANG
HYMAN, DICK
  Broadway Danny Rose (85) 112
  Purple Rose of Cairo, The (86) 290
  Stardust Memories [1980] (85) 626
  Zelig (84) 473

IBERT, JACQUES
  Invitation to the Dance [1956] (86) 507
IKEBE, SHINICHIRO
  MacArthur's Children (86) 451
IMPROTA, THOMAS
  Bar Esperanza [1983] (86) 437
ISHAM, MARK
  Mrs. Soffel (85) 314
  Never Cry Wolf (84) 247
  Trouble in Mind (86) 388
IVERS, PETER
  "Obituaries" (84) 624

JACNO
  Full Moon in Paris (85) 208
JAMES, HARRY
  "Obituaries" (84) 624
JAMES, JOSEPH
  Priest of Love (82) 288
JANSEN, PIERRE
  Horse of Pride, The (86) 447
JARRE, MAURICE
  Bride, The (86) 438
  Dreamscape (85) 166
  Enemy Mine (86) 161
  Firefox (83) 160
  Mad Max Beyond Thunderdome (86) 223
  Passage to India, A (85) 365
  Taps (82) 343
  Witness (86) 421
  Year of Living Dangerously, The [1982] (84) 462
JENKINS, GORDON
  "Obituaries" (85) 674
JESUS, LUCHI DE
  "Obituaries" (85) 674
JOBIM, ANTONIO CARLOS
  Gabriela [1983] (85) 213
JONES, QUINCY
  Color Purple, The (86) 105
JONES, RALPH
  Love Letters (85) 288
JONES, TREVOR
  Dark Crystal, The (83) 130
  Excalibur (82) 144
  Nate and Hayes (84) 236
  Runaway Train (86) 324
JOURNEY
  TRON (83) 371

KABILJO, ALFI
  Gymkata (86) 445
KAHN, CHAKA
  Krush Groove (86) 449
KAMEN, MICHAEL
  Angelo My Love (84) 47
  Brazil (86) 80
KANDER, JOHN
  Places in the Heart (85) 371
  Still of the Night (83) 326
KANE, ARTIE
  Wrong Is Right (83) 403
KAPER, BRONISLAU
  H. M. Pulham, Esq. [1941] (82) 439
  Mutiny on the Bounty [1962] (85) 581
  "Obituaries" (84) 624
KASDAN, MEG
  Big Chill, The (84) 78
KAYE, NORMAN
  Lonely Hearts [1982] (84) 212
KEATING, ARTHUR
  James Joyce's Women (86) 193
KENDAL
  Yol (83) 411
KENTIS, CHUCK
  Gringo (86) 445
KIKUCHI-YNGOJO, ROBERT
  Chan Is Missing (83) 113
KILAR, WOJCIECH
  Imperative [1982] (86) 447
KILDUFF, VINCENT
  James Joyce's Women (86) 193
KING, CAROLE
  Care Bears Movie, The (86) 439
  Murphy's Romance (86) 242
KING, PETE
  Bells Are Ringing [1960] (84) 517
KNIEPER, JURGEN
  State of Things, The (84) 379
KNOPFLER, MARK
  Cal (85) 124
  Comfort and Joy (85) 146
  Local Hero (84) 206
KOPP, RUDOLPH
  Sign of the Cross, The [1932] (85) 607
KOROKU, REIJIRO
  Godzilla 1985 (86) 444
KORZYNSKI, ANDRZEJ
  Man of Iron (82) 230
  Man of Marble [1977] (82) 234
KOVACH, KORNELL
  Montenegro (82) 250
KRAFT, WILLIAM
  Fire and Ice (84) 153
KUBIK, GAIL
  "Obituaries" (85) 677
KYSER, KAY
  "Obituaries" (86) 573

LAI, FRANCIS
  Marie (86) 227
  My New Partner [1984] (86) 246
LANGHORNE, BRUCE
  Melvin and Howard [1980] (82) 453

LAVAGNINO, ANGELO FRANCESCO
  Falstaff [1967] (83) 443
LEANDER, MIKE
  Taking Off [1971] (86) 545
LECOEUR, MAURICE
  Erendira [1983] (85) 181
LE FEVRE, ADAM
  Return of the Secaucus 7 [1980] (83) 484
LEGRAND, MICHEL
  Atlantic City (82) 74
  Best Friends (83) 68
  Lady Sings the Blues [1972] (85) 565
  Love in Germany, A [1983] (85) 283
  Never Say Never Again (84) 252
  Secret Places [1984] (86) 459
  Yentl (84) 468
LEVAY, SYLVESTER
  Creator (86) 441
LEVINE, JAMES
  Traviata, La (83) 366
LEVY, SHUKI
  Here Come the Littles (86) 446
  Rainbow Brite and the Star Stealer (86) 456
LIBERATORI, FABIO
  Water and Soap (86) 465
LINN, MICHAEL
  American Ninja (86) 436
LISZT, FRANZ
  Colonel Redl [1984] (86) 100
  Detective (86) 442
LL COOL J
  Krush Groove (86) 449
LLOYD, MICHAEL
  Tomboy (86) 463
LOJEWSKI, HARRY V.
  Diner (83) 142
LOUIS, ROLAND
  Sugar Cane Alley [1983] (85) 461
LUBIN, SHELLEN
  Taking Off [1971] (86) 545
LUCAS, LEIGHTON
  "Obituaries" (83) 549
LURIE, JOHN
  City Limits (86) 440
  Stranger than Paradise (85) 455

MAAZEL, LORIN
  Bizet's Carmen [1983] (85) 98
MCCURDY, STEPHEN
  Came a Hot Friday (86) 439
MCHUGH, DAVID
  Pumping Iron II (86) 456
MCHUGH, DONALD
  Moscow on the Hudson (85) 321
MCKEAN, MICHAEL
  This Is Spinal Tap (85) 484
MAGNE, MICHEL
  "Obituaries" (85) 682
MAHLER, GUSTAV
  Norte, El (84) 265
  War and Love (86) 465
MALAVOI, GROUPE
  Sugar Cane Alley [1983] (85) 461
MAMECIER, MECHE
  Tokyo-Ga (86) 463

MANCINI, HENRY
  Lifeforce (86) 450
  Man Who Loved Women, The (84) 218
  Mommie Dearest (82) 245
  Santa Claus (86) 334
  S.O.B. (82) 328
  Victor/Victoria (83) 387
MANDEL, JOHNNY
  Agatha [1979] (83) 435
  Deathtrap (83) 134
  Staying Alive (84) 386
  Verdict, The (83) 377
MANNE, SHELLY
  "Obituaries" (85) 682
MANSFIELD, DAVID
  Heaven's Gate (82) 195
  Year of the Dragon (86) 426
MANUEL, VICTOR
  Only Emptiness Remains (86) 455
MARIKA, WANDJUK
  Where the Green Ants Dream [1984] (86) 465
MARTIN, FREDDY
  "Obituaries" (84) 626
MARTIN, GEORGE
  Honky Tonk Freeway (82) 199
MARTIN, SIMON MICHAEL
  Heartaches [1981] (83) 197
MARTINEZ, MALECIO
  Norte, El (84) 265
MASON, NICK
  Pink Floyd the Wall [1981] (83) 258
MATHIESON, GREG
  American Flyers (86) 436
MATZ, PETER
  Lust in the Dust (86) 450
MAY, BILLY
  Pennies from Heaven (82) 276
MAY, BRIAN
  Gallipoli [1980] (82) 197
  Missing in Action 2 (86) 452
  Road Warrior, The [1981] (83) 277
MAYS, LYLE
  Falcon and the Snowman, The (86) 165
MEN AT WORK
  Valley Girl (84) 447
MENDELSSOHN, FELIX
  Midsummer Night's Sex Comedy, A (83) 228
MENESCAL, ROBERTO
  Xica [1976] (83) 407
MERCER, GLENN
  Smithereens (83) 307
MERMAN, ETHEL
  "Obituaries" (85) 684
METHENY, PAT
  Falcon and the Snowman, The (86) 165
  Twice in a Lifetime (86) 397
MIGHTY CLOUDS OF JOY
  Gospel (85) 520
MILLER, FRANKIE
  Sense of Freedom, A (86) 459
MILLION, BILL
  Smithereens (83) 307
MOCKRIDGE, CYRIL J.
  Solid Gold Cadillac, The [1956] (85) 615

MONKMAN, FRANCIS
  Long Good Friday, The   (83) 220
MONTENEGRO, HUGH
  "Obituaries"   (82) 499
MONTES, MICHAEL
  Pumping Iron II   (86) 456
MONTEVERDI, CLAUDIO
  Death of Mario Ricci, The [1983]   (86) 133
MOORE, DUDLEY
  Hound of the Baskervilles, The [1978]   (82) 203
MORAN, MIKE
  Missionary, The   (83) 233
MORODER, GIORGIO
  Cat People   (83) 100
  Flashdance   (84) 158
  Scarface   (84) 361
MOROSS, JEROME
  "Obituaries"   (84) 627
MORRICONE, ENNIO
  Once upon a Time in America   (85) 345
  Red Sonja   (86) 457
  Thing, The   (83) 343
  Tragedy of a Ridiculous Man [1981]   (83) 361
MORRIS, JOHN
  Clue   (86) 440
  Doctor and the Devils, The   (86) 442
  Table for Five   (84) 404
  To Be or Not to Be   (84) 426
MOTZING, WILLIAM
  Coca-Cola Kid, The   (86) 440
  Silver City [1984]   (86) 460
MOZART, WOLFGANG AMADEUS
  Passion [1982]   (84) 289
MULDOWNEY, DOMINIC
  Betrayal   (84) 67
  1984   (85) 335
  Ploughman's Lunch, The [1983]   (85) 377
MYERS, STANLEY
  Dreamchild   (86) 146
  Eureka   (86) 442
  Insignificance   (86) 447
  Moonlighting   (83) 237

NASCIMBENE, MARIO
  Barefoot Contessa, The [1954]   (82) 399
NAYOBE
  Krush Groove   (86) 449
NELSON, WILLIE
  1918   (86) 454
NESCHLING, JOHN
  Kiss of the Spider Woman   (86) 209
  Pixote [1980]   (82) 280
NEW EDITION
  Krush Groove   (86) 449
NEWBORN, IRA
  Into the Night   (86) 186
  Weird Science   (86) 465
NEWMAN, ALFRED
  Barbary Coast [1935]   (84) 506
  Come and Get It [1936]   (82) 412
  History Is Made at Night [1937]   (84) 542
  Man Hunt [1941]   (85) 570
NEWMAN, EMIL
  Hondo [1953]   (83) 452

"Obituaries"   (85) 687
  Secret Life of Walter Mitty, The [1947]   (86) 540
NEWMAN, RANDY
  Natural, The   (85) 329
  Ragtime   (82) 304
NEWMAN, THOMAS
  Desperately Seeking Susan   (86) 137
  Man with One Red Shoe, The   (86) 451
  Real Genius   (86) 309
NIEHAUS, LENNIE
  City Heat   (85) 141
  Pale Rider   (86) 261
  Sesame Street Presents: Follow That
    Bird   (86) 459
  Tightrope   (85) 489
NITZSCHE, JACK
  Breathless   (84) 89
  Cannery Row   (83) 95
  Cutter's Way   (82) 119
  Jewel of the Nile, The   (86) 448
  Officer and a Gentleman, An   (83) 246
  Personal Best   (83) 254
  Razor's Edge, The   (85) 402
  Starman   (85) 445
NORTH, ALEX
  Dragonslayer   (82) 125
  Prizzi's Honor   (86) 285
  Under the Volcano   (85) 499
NYMAN, MICHAEL
  Draughtsman's Contract, The [1982]   (84) 126
NYRO, LAURA
  Broken Rainbow   (86) 439

O'BRIEN, LINDA
  Norte, El   (84) 265
O'CONNER, GARRETT
  James Joyce's Women   (86) 193
OFFENBACH, JACQUES
  Hotel New Hampshire, The   (85) 243
OKAWA, SHINNOSUKE
  Makioka Sisters, The [1983]   (86) 451
OLDFIELD, MIKE
  Killing Fields, The   (85) 270
OLSEN, KEITH
  That Was Then . . . This Is Now   (86) 463
O'NEILL, SHARON
  Smash Palace [1981]   (83) 302
ORDODY, LEO
  Detour [1946]   (86) 498
ORTEGA, CHICO ROJO
  Tokyo-Ga   (86) 463

PACHELBEL, JOHANN
  Volver a empezar   (83) 393
PAGE, GENE
  Brewster McCloud [1970]   (86) 484
PAGE, JIMMY
  Death Wish III   (86) 441
PARKS, VAN DYKE
  Sesame Street Presents: Follow That Bird   (86)
    459
PARLAN, HORSE
  Choose Me   (85) 135
PARTON, DOLLY
  Best Little Whorehouse in Texas, The   (83) 72

MUSIC INDEX

PEERCE, JAN
  "Obituaries"   (85) 689
PENDERGRASS, TEDDY
  Choose Me   (85) 135
PENN, ARTHUR
  Colonel Redl [1984]   (86) 100
PETITGARD, LOORIE
  Tokyo-Ga   (86) 463
PHILLIPS, JOHN
  Man Who Fell to Earth, The   (83) 72
PIAZZOLLA, ASTOR
  Henry IV [1983]   (86) 446
PICCIONI, PIERO
  Three Brothers [1980]   (83) 349
PIOVANI, NICOLA
  Night of the Shooting Stars, The [1982]   (84) 258
PLENIZIO, GIANFRANCO
  And the Ship Sails On [1983]   (85) 69
PLIMSOULS
  Valley Girl   (84) 447
PLUGZ, LOS
  Repo Man   (85) 408
PLUMB, EDWARD
  Bambi [1942]   (85) 543
POLEDOURIS, BASIL
  Flesh and Blood   (86) 443
  Protocol   (85) 383
PORTAL, MICHEL
  Return of Martin Guerre, The   (84) 318
PORTER, COLE
  Volver a empezar   (83) 393
POST, MIKE
  Running Brave   (84) 354
POWELL, ANDREW
  Ladyhawke   (86) 214
PREVIN, ANDRÉ
  Bells Are Ringing [1960]   (84) 517
  Invitation to the Dance [1956]   (86) 507
PRINCE
  Purple Rain   (85) 389
PROOROMIDES, JEAN
  Danton [1982]   (84) 121

RABEN, PEER
  Berlin Alexanderplatz [1980]   (84) 57
  Lili Marleen   (82) 222
  Lola [1981]   (83) 215
  Querelle [1982]   (84) 313
  Veronika Voss   (83) 382
RABIN, BUZZ
  Tender Mercies   (84) 409
RAKSIN, DAVID
  Apache [1954]   (82) 395
  Secret Life of Walter Mitty, The [1947]   (86) 540
RAMSEY, KENNARD
  Heavenly Kid, The   (86) 445
RAPOSO, JOE
  Great Muppet Caper, The   (82) 187
RAVEL, MAURICE
  Passion [1982]   (84) 289
RAY, SATYAJIT
  Home and the World, The [1984]   (86) 447
REDFORD, J.A.C.
  Trip to Bountiful, The   (86) 383

REINER, ROB
  This Is Spinal Tap   (85) 484
REMAL, GARY S.
  Maria's Lovers   (86) 451
RESNIK, REGINA
  Carmen   (84) 101
RICHARDS, EMIL
  Norte, El   (84) 265
RICOTTA, DENNIS
  Mask   (86) 231
RIDDLE, NELSON
  "Obituaries"   (86) 580
RIESMAN, MICHAEL
  Mishima   (86) 236
RIMSKY-KORSAKOV, NIKOLAY
  Invitation to the Dance [1956]   (86) 507
RITENOUR, LEE
  American Flyers   (86) 436
ROBBINS, RICHARD
  Bostonians, The   (85) 105
  Heat and Dust [1982]   (84) 187
ROBERGE, JIM
  Joey   (86) 448
ROBERTS, AUSTIN
  Tender Mercies   (84) 409
ROBERTS, BRUCE
  Jinxed   (83) 206
ROBERTSON, ROBBIE
  King of Comedy, The   (84) 192
ROBIN, LEO
  "Obituaries"   (85) 692
ROEMHELD, HEINZ
  Hard Way, The [1942]   (85) 555
  "Obituaries"   (86) 580
ROGERS, SHORTY
  Zoot Suit   (82) 389
ROSE, DAVID
  Hombre [1967]   (84) 547
ROSENMAN, LEONARD
  Cross Creek   (84) 116
  Sylvia   (86) 462
ROSENTHAL, LAURENCE
  Clash of the Titans   (82) 111
  Heart Like a Wheel   (84) 182
ROZSA, MIKLOS
  Dead Men Don't Wear Plaid   (83) 134
  Eye of the Needle   (82) 148
  Time After Time [1979]   (84) 579
RUBIN, LANCE
  Modern Romance   (82) 241
RUBINSTEIN, ARTHUR B.
  Blue Thunder   (84) 84
  Lost in America   (86) 219
  WarGames   (84) 458
  Whose Life Is It Anyway?   (82) 378
RUDHYAR, DANE
  "Obituaries"   (86) 581
RUN DMC
  Krush Groove   (86) 449
RYDER, MARK
  Savage Island   (86) 457
  Trancers   (86) 463

SABAN, HAIM
  Here Come the Littles   (86) 446
  Rainbow Brite and the Star Stealer   (86) 456

SAFAN, CRAIG
    Last Starfighter, The   (85) 277
    Legend of Billie Jean, The   (86) 450
    Remo Williams   (86) 457
    Warning Sign   (86) 465
ST. JAMES, JON
    Cave Girl   (86) 439
SAITO, ICHIRO
    Flowing [1956]   (86) 444
SAKAMOTO, RYUICHI
    Merry Christmas, Mr. Lawrence   (84) 231
SARDE, PHILIPPE
    Adolescente, L' [1979]   (83) 53
    Beau Pere   (82) 78
    Coup de torchon [1981]   (83) 124
    Ghost Story   (82) 183
    I Sent a Letter to My Love [1980]   (82) 214
    Joshua Then and Now   (86) 198
    Loulou [1980]   (82) 226
    My Other Husband   (86) 453
    Quest for Fire   (83) 271
    Tess [1980]   (82) 471
SAUNDERS, TIM
    Taking Off [1971]   (86) 545
SCHARF, WALTER
    This Is Elvis   (82) 360
SCHIFRIN, LALO
    Bad Medicine   (86) 437
    Buddy Buddy   (82) 93
    Mean Season, The   (86) 452
    New Kids, The   (86) 454
    Sudden Impact   (84) 395
SCHUBERT, FRANZ
    Detective   (86) 442
    Peril   (86) 456
SCHUMANN, GEORGE
    Colonel Redl [1984]   (86) 100
SCHWARTZ, ARTHUR
    "Obituaries"   (85) 694
SCHWARZ, JEAN
    Detective   (86) 442
SCOTT, JOHN
    Experience Preferred ... but Not Essential
      [1982]   (84) 141
    Greystoke   (85) 236
    Shooting Party, The [1984]   (86) 344
SCOTT, TOM
    Fast Forward   (86) 442
    Just One of the Guys   (86) 448
    Sure Thing, The   (86) 369
SEBASTIAN, JOHN
    Care Bears Movie, The   (86) 439
SEGAL, MISHA
    Berry Gordy's The Last Dragon   (86) 438
SERRA, ERIC
    Subway   (86) 461
SHANKAR, RAVI
    Gandhi   (83) 183
SHAWN, ALLEN
    My Dinner with André   (82) 255
SHEARER, HARRY
    This Is Spinal Tap   (85) 484
SHEILA E.
    Krush Groove   (86) 449
SHEILD, LE ROY
    Our Relations [1936]   (86) 523

SHELDON, EMIE
    Hard Traveling   (86) 445
SHEPP, ARCHIE
    Choose Me   (85) 135
SHIRE, DAVID
    Max Dugan Returns   (84) 228
    Only When I Laugh   (82) 268
    Return to Oz   (86) 458
    2010   (85) 494
    World According to Garp, The   (83) 397
SHNITKE, ALFRED
    Rasputin [1975]   (86) 457
SHORE, HOWARD
    After Hours   (86) 51
    Videodrome   (84) 452
SHOSTAKOVICH, DMITRI
    New Babylon, The [1929]   (84) 561
SILVESTRI, ALAN
    Back to the Future   (86) 65
    Romancing the Stone   (85) 421
    Stephen King's Cat's Eye   (86) 460
    Summer Rental   (86) 462
SIMJANOVIC, ZORAN
    When Father Was Away on Business [1984]   (86)
      411
SIMON, CARLY
    Taking Off [1971]   (86) 545
SKINNER, FRANK
    Bedtime for Bonzo [1951]   (84) 512
SLOCUM, TOM
    Cattle Annie and Little Britches   (82) 97
SMALL, MICHAEL
    Continental Divide   (82) 115
    Postman Always Rings Twice, The   (82) 284
    Target   (86) 462
SMEATON, BRUCE
    Barbarosa   (83) 60
    Eleni   (86) 151
    Plenty   (86) 271
SMITH, LARRY
    Rappin'   (86) 457
SMITH, MAURICIO
    Crossover Dreams   (86) 441
SMITH, PETE
    Bring on the Night   (86) 439
SOBEL, CURT
    Flamingo Kid, The   (85) 192
    Iceman   (85) 248
    Young Sherlock Holmes   (86) 431
SOLOMON, MARIBETH
    Improper Channels   (82) 218
SONDHEIM, STEPHEN
    Reds   (82) 312
STAHL, IRWIN
    Tomorrow [1972]   (84) 589
STALLONE, FRANK
    Staying Alive   (84) 386
STAMPONE, ATILIO
    Official Story, The   (86) 249
STANISLAS
    Holcroft Covenant, The   (86) 446
STEARNS, MICHAEL
    Chronos   (86) 440
STEINER, MAX
    Most Dangerous Game, The [1932]   (86) 519

MUSIC INDEX

My Reputation [1946] (85) 586
Roughly Speaking [1945] (83) 490
Unfaithful, The [1947] (86) 550
STIGWOOD, ROBERT
Staying Alive (84) 386
STING
Brimstone and Treacle (83) 91
Bring on the Night (86) 439
STOLTZ, ROBERT
It Happened Tomorrow [1944] (84) 552
STOTHART, HERBERT
Guy Named Joe, A [1943] (82) 435
STRAUSS, JOHANN
Colonel Redl [1984] (86) 100
STRAUSS, JOHN
Amadeus (85) 63
STROUSE, CHARLES
Annie (83) 56
STYNE, JULE
Bells Are Ringing [1960] (84) 517
SUKMAN, HARRY
"Obituaries" (85) 694
SULLIVAN, ARTHUR SEYMOUR
Pirates of Penzance, The (84) 301
SWADOS, ELIZABETH
Four Friends (82) 167

TAKEMITSU, TORU
Ran (86) 304
TALKING HEADS
Stop Making Sense (85) 534
TAMASSY, ZDENKÓ
Colonel Redl [1984] (86) 100
Mephisto (82) 237
TANGERINE DREAM
Risky Business (84) 349
Thief (82) 356
Vision Quest (86) 464
TAYLOR, JAMES
Smooth Talk (86) 354
THORNE, KEN
Superman III (84) 399
TIME, THE
Purple Rain (85) 389
TIMM, DOUG
Streetwalkin' (86) 461
TOCH, ERNST
Peter Ibbetson [1935] (86) 527
TOCNAY, BRUNOY
Sugar Cane Alley [1983] (85) 461
TOTO
Dune (85) 171
TROVAJOLI, ARMANDO
Macaroni (86) 451
Nuit de Varennes, La [1982] (84) 270
TUBB, ERNEST
"Obituaries" (85) 696
TULLY, COLIN
Gregory's Girl [1981] (83) 193
TUNICK, JONATHAN
Fort Apache, the Bronx (82) 159
TURNER, IKE
Taking Off [1971] (86) 545

TURNER, TINA
Taking Off [1971] (86) 545

UTFO
Krush Groove (86) 449

VALDEZ, DANIEL
Zoot Suit (82) 389
VALERO, JEAN-LOUIS
Pauline at the Beach [1982] (84) 296
VANDERSON, V.
Sugar Cane Alley [1983] (85) 461
VANGELIS
Blade Runner (83) 76
Chariots of Fire (82) 101
Missing (83) 232
VENNE, STÉPHANE
Plouffe, Les (86) 456
VERDI, GIUSEPPE
Norte, El (84) 265
Nostalgia [1983] (85) 340
VIVALDI, ANTONIO
Death of Mario Ricci, The [1983] (86) 133
Four Seasons, The (82) 171
VUH, POPOL
Fitzcarraldo (83) 167

WAGNER, RICHARD
Detective (86) 442
Where the Green Ants Dream [1984] (86) 465
WAITS, TOM
One from the Heart (83) 250
Streetwise (86) 364
WAKEMAN, RICK
Crimes of Passion (85) 161
WALKER, SIMON
Test of Love (86) 462
WALSH, MARIA ELENA
Official Story, The (86) 249
WALTON, WILLIAM
"Obituaries" (84) 640
WARING, FRED
"Obituaries" (85) 698
WARREN, HARRY
"Obituaries" (82) 505
WATERS, ROGER
Pink Floyd the Wall [1981] (83) 258
WAXMAN, FRANZ
My Cousin Rachel [1952] (82) 458
Too Hot to Handle [1938] (84) 596
WEBB, ROY
Becky Sharp [1935] (82) 403
Journey into Fear [1943] (86) 511
"Obituaries" (83) 556
WEBSTER, PAUL FRANCIS
"Obituaries" (85) 698
WELCH, KEN
Movers and Shakers (86) 453
WELCH, MITZIE
Movers and Shakers (86) 453
WEXLER, JERRY
Pretty Baby [1978] (85) 597
WIESE, KLAUS-JOCHEN
Where the Green Ants Dream [1984] (86) 465

WILBER, BOB
  Cotton Club, The   (85) 150
WILLIAMS, JOHN
  E.T.: The Extra-Terrestrial   (83) 151
  Indiana Jones and the Temple of Doom   (85)
  253
  Raiders of the Lost Ark   (82) 308
  Return of the Jedi   (84) 326
  River, The   (85) 416
WILLIAMS, PATRICK
  All of Me   (85) 58
  Neil Simon's The Slugger's Wife   (86) 454
  Toy, The   (83) 358
WILLSON, MEREDITH
  "Obituaries"   (85) 701
WITTSTADT, HANS
  Superman II   (82) 339
  Taxi Zum Klo   (82) 346
WOODWARD, WALT
  Care Bears Movie, The   (86) 439
WRIGHT, ROBERT
  Taking Off [1971]   (86) 545

YAMAMOTO, NAOZOMI
  Foster Daddy, Tora! [1980]   (82) 163

YAMASHTA, STOMU
  Tempest   (83) 331
YARED, GABRIEL
  Dangerous Moves [1984]   (86) 129
  Every Man for Himself [1979]   (82) 139
  Hanna K.   (84) 177
YOUNG, CHRISTOPHER
  Avenging Angel   (86) 436
  Def-Con 4   (86) 441
  Nightmare on Elm Street, Part 2, A   (86) 454
YOUNG, VICTOR
  Take a Letter, Darling [1942]   (85) 632

ZAZA, PAUL
  Christmas Story, A   (84) 110
  Porky's   (83) 267
  Turk 182   (86) 464
ZITTRER, CARL
  Christmas Story, A   (84) 110
  Porky's   (83) 267
ZWART, JACQUES
  Out of Order   (86) 455

PERFORMER INDEX

A, FIDELIS CHE
King Solomon's Mines (86) 449

AAKER, LEE
Hondo [1953] (83) 452

AAMES, WILLIE
Paradise (83) 426
Zapped! (83) 431

AARON, CAROLINE
Brother from Another Planet, The (85) 118

ABANES, RICHIE
Rappin' (86) 457

ABBATIELLO, SAL
Krush Groove (86) 449

ABBOTT, BRUCE
Re-Animator (86) 457

ABBOTT, DIAHNNE
King of Comedy, The (84) 192
Love Streams (85) 293
New York, New York [1977] (84) 567

ABBOTT, JOHN
Slapstick (85) 533

ABEL, WALTER
Grace Quigley (86) 444
Holiday Inn [1942] (82) 443

ABERDEIN, KEITH
Smash Palace [1981] (83) 302
Wild Horses [1983] (85) 538

ABRAHAM, F. MURRAY
Amadeus (85) 63

ABRAMOICZ, HALINA
Silver City [1984] (86) 460

ABRIL, VICTORIA
Moon in the Gutter, The (84) 490
Patsy, The (86) 456

ACHORN, JOHN
Night of the Comet (85) 527

ACHTMAN, ARNIE
Heartaches [1981] (83) 197

ACKER, SHARON
Threshold (84) 495

ACKERMAN, LESLIE
Blame It on the Night (85) 512

ACKRIDGE, WILLIAM
Hard Traveling (86) 445

ADAMS, BILL
Cave Girl (86) 439

ADAMS, BROOKE
Almost You (86) 436
Dead Zone, The (84) 481
Key Exchange (86) 448

ADAMS, DIANE
Invitation to the Dance [1956] (86) 507

ADAMS, JULIA
Creature from the Black Lagoon, The [1954] (82) 422

ADAMS, MARGARET
That Sinking Feeling [1979] (85) 536

ADAMS, MARLA
Gotcha! (86) 444

ADAMS, MAUD
Octopussy (84) 276

ADAMS, THOMAS
No Small Affair (85) 527

ADDAMS, DAWN
"Obituaries" (86) 559

ADDIE, ROBERT
Excalibur (82) 144

ADDY, WESLEY
Bostonians, The (85) 105

ADJANI, ISABELLE
Next Year if All Goes Well (84) 490
Quartet (82) 296
Subway (86) 461

ADKINSON, SUZANNE
Racing with the Moon (85) 397

ADLER, LUTHER
Absence of Malice (82) 57
"Obituaries" (85) 655

ADLER, MATT
Teen Wolf (86) 462

ADORF, MARIO
Holcroft Covenant, The (86) 446
Invitation au voyage [1982] (84) 486
Lola [1981] (83) 215

ADRIAN, IRIS
Our Relations [1936] (86) 523

AGAR, JOHN
Fort Apache [1948] (84) 530

AGBAYANI, TETCHIE
Gymkata (86) 445

AGOSTINI, DIDIER
Garde à vue [1981] (83) 189

AGREN, JANET
Red Sonja (86) 457

AGUTTER, JENNY
American Werewolf in London, An (82) 66
Riddle of the Sands, The [1979] (85) 531
Secret Places [1984] (86) 459

AHLSTEDT, BÖRJE
Fanny and Alexander [1982] (84) 146

AICH, GOPA
Home and the World, The [1984] (86) 447

AIDMAN, CHARLES
Zoot Suit (82) 389

AIELLO, DANNY
Fort Apache, the Bronx (82) 159
Key Exchange (86) 448
Once upon a Time in America (85) 345
Purple Rose of Cairo, The (86) 290
Stuff, The (86) 461

AILHAUD, YVELINE
Petite Bande, La [1982] (85) 528

AIMÉE, ANOUK
Tragedy of a Ridiculous Man [1981] (83) 361

AIZAWA, MASATO
Mishima (86) 236

AKAN, TARIK
Yol (83) 411

95

AKÇA, TUNCAY
  Yol (83) 411
AKERMAN, CHANTAL
  Je tu il elle [1974] (86) 447
AKERS, KAREN
  Purple Rose of Cairo, The (86) 290
AKTOLGA, SEVDA
  Yol (83) 411
ALBASINY, JOHN
  Kipperbang [1983] (85) 524
ALBERT, EDDIE
  Dreamscape (85) 166
  Stitches (86) 461
  Yes, Giorgio (83) 431
ALBERT, EDWARD
  House Where Evil Dwells, The (83) 423
ALBERTSON, JACK
  "Obituaries" (82) 478
ALBRIGHT, MAROY
  Bambi [1942] (85) 543
ALDA, ALAN
  Four Seasons, The (82) 171
ALDA, BEATRICE
  Four Seasons, The (82) 171
ALDA, ELIZABETH
  Four Seasons, The (82) 171
ALDA, RUTANYA
  Amityville II (83) 417
  Racing with the Moon (85) 397
ALDERSON, BROOKE
  Mike's Murder (85) 526
ALDON, MARI
  Barefoot Contessa, The [1954] (82) 399
ALDRICH, WILLIAM
  Flight of the Phoenix, The [1966] (85) 549
ALDRIDGE, MICHAEL
  Bullshot [1983] (86) 439
  Turtle Diary (86) 464
ALEANDRO, NORMA
  Official Story, The (86) 249
ALEX, STANLEY
  Bambi [1942] (85) 543
ALEXANDER, JANE
  City Heat (85) 141
  Night Crossing (83) 426
  Testament (84) 420
ALEXANDER, JOHN
  Return to Oz (86) 458
ALEXANDER, KRIS
  Pumping Iron II (86) 456
ALEXANDER, TERRY
  Day of the Dead (86) 441
  Flashpoint (85) 519
ALFIERI, RICHARD
  Echoes (84) 483
ALIGRUDIC, SLOBODAN
  When Father Was Away on Business [1984] (86)
  411
ALLEN, CHESNEY
  "Obituaries" (83) 523
ALLEN, DEBBIE
  Ragtime (82) 304
ALLEN, JOAN
  Compromising Positions (86) 120

ALLEN, KAREN
  Raiders of the Lost Ark (82) 308
  Shoot the Moon (83) 295
  Split Image (83) 317
  Starman (85) 445
  Until September (85) 537
ALLEN, NANCY
  Blow Out (82) 83
  Buddy System, The (85) 514
  Not for Publication (85) 527
  Philadelphia Experiment, The (85) 529
  Strange Invaders (84) 494
ALLEN, SETH
  Key Exchange (86) 448
ALLEN, VALERIE
  Bells Are Ringing [1960] (84) 517
ALLEN, WOODY
  Broadway Danny Rose (85) 112
  Front, The [1976] (86) 502
  Midsummer Night's Sex Comedy, A (83)
  228
  Stardust Memories [1980] (85) 626
  Zelig (84) 473
ALLENBURY, GENEVIEVE
  King David (86) 449
ALLENDE, FERNANDO
  Heartbreaker (84) 485
ALLEY, KIRSTIE
  Champions (85) 515
  Star Trek II—The Wrath of Khan (83)
  321
ALLEY, NORMAN
  "Obituaries" (82) 478
ALLPRESS, BRUCE
  Nate and Hayes (84) 236
ALLWIN, PERNILLA
  Fanny and Alexander [1982] (84) 146
ALLWRIGHT, CHRISTOPHE
  Bal, Le [1983] (85) 80
ALNUTT, WENDY
  Priest of Love (82) 288
ALONSO, MARIA CONCHITA
  Moscow on the Hudson (85) 321
ALTERIO, HECTOR
  Basileus Quartet (85) 511
  Flesh and Blood (86) 443
  Official Story, The (86) 249
ALTON, WALTER GEORGE
  Heavenly Bodies (85) 522
ALVARADO, DON
  Bridge of San Luis Rey, The [1929] (82)
  408
ALVARADO, TRINI
  Mrs. Soffel (85) 314
ALVARO, ANNE
  Danton [1982] (84) 121
ALWOOD, DENNIS
  Starchaser (86) 460
AMECHE, DON
  Cocoon (86) 96
  Trading Places (84) 430
AMES, LEON
  Testament (84) 420
AMIDOU, SOUAD
  Little Jerk [1984] (86) 450

AMIS, SUZY
Fandango (86) 442
AMOS, JOHN
American Flyers (86) 436
Beastmaster, The (83) 418
AMPHOUX, MICHEL
Petite Bande, La [1982] (85) 528
AMPLAS, JOHN
Day of the Dead (86) 441
AMRITRAJ, VIJAY
9 Deaths of the Ninja (86) 454
AMSTUTZ, ROLAND
Every Man for Himself [1979] (82) 139
Petite Bande, La [1982] (85) 528
ANAYA, YANO
Christmas Story, A (84) 110
ANDERS, GLENN
"Obituaries" (82) 478
ANDERSEN, BRIDGETTE
Fever Pitch (86) 443
Nightmares (84) 490
Savannah Smiles (84) 493
ANDERSEN, JURGEN
Riddle of the Sands, The [1979] (85) 531
ANDERSON, ANGRY
Mad Max Beyond Thunderdome (86) 223
ANDERSON, E. ERICH
Friday the 13th—The Final Chapter (85) 520
ANDERSON, INGRID
Hercules (84) 485
ANDERSON, ISABELLE
Careful He Might Hear You [1983] (85) 130
ANDERSON, JOHN
Zoot Suit (82) 389
ANDERSON, JUDITH
Specter of the Rose [1946] (83) 504
Star Trek III—The Search for
Spock (85) 439
ANDERSON, LAWRENCE
Nell Gwyn [1934] (84) 557
ANDERSON, LINDSAY
Chariots of Fire (82) 101
ANDERSON, LOUISE
River Rat, The (85) 531
ANDERSON, MANON
Hail Mary (86) 182
ANDERSON, MELISSA SUE
Chattanooga Choo Choo (85) 515
ANDERSON, MIGNON
"Obituaries" (84) 609
ANDERSON, WARNER
My Reputation [1946] (85) 586
ANDERSSON, DAVID
Gregory's Girl [1981] (83) 193
ANDRE, CAROLE
Yor (84) 498
ANDRE, LONA
Our Relations [1936] (86) 523
ANDREAS, DIMITRI
Top Secret (85) 536
ANDREI, FREDERICK
Diva [1980] (83) 147
ANDRESS, URSULA
Clash of the Titans (82) 111

ANDREU, SIMON
Flesh and Blood (86) 443
ANDREWS, ANTHONY
Holcroft Covenant, The (86) 446
Under the Volcano (85) 499
ANDREWS, DANA
North Star, The [1943] (83) 476
ANDREWS, DAVID
Kerouac, the Movie (86) 448
ANDREWS, EDWARD
"Obituaries" (86) 559
Sixteen Candles (85) 532
ANDREWS, JULIE
Man Who Loved Women, The (84) 218
S.O.B. (82) 323
Torn Curtain [1966] (85) 643
Victor/Victoria (83) 387
ANDREYTSCHENKO, NATALIA
Siberiade [1977] (83) 299
ANEMONE
Peril (86) 456
ANGLADE, JEAN-HUGHES
Dangerous Moves [1984] (86) 129
Subway (86) 461
ANGLIM, PHILIP
Testament (84) 420
ANGWIN, LUCY
My First Wife (86) 453
ANKERS, EVELYN
"Obituaries" (86) 559
ANKRUM, MORRIS
Apache [1954] (82) 395
Colorado Territory [1949] (86) 489
ANN-MARGRET
I Ought to Be in Pictures (83) 423
Lookin' to Get Out (83) 425
Return of the Soldier, The [1982] (84) 332
Twice in a Lifetime (86) 397
ANNIS, FRANCESCA
Dune (85) 171
Krull (84) 487
ANSPACH, SUSAN
Misunderstood (85) 526
Montenegro (82) 250
ANTHONY, LYSETTE
Krull (84) 487
ANTHONY, TONY
Treasure of the Four Crowns (84) 495
ANTIN, STEVE
Goonies, The (86) 176
Last American Virgin, The (83) 424
Sweet Sixteen (85) 535
ANTON, DOROTHY
American Taboo (85) 509
ANTON, MATTHEW
Pretty Baby [1978] (85) 597
ANTON, SUSAN
Cannonball Run II (85) 514
ANTONUTTI, OMERO
Basileus Quartet (85) 511
Night of the Shooting Stars, The
[1982] (84) 258
ANTRIM, PAUL
Lassiter (85) 524
Wild Geese II (86) 466

APICELLA, JOHN
Just One of the Guys   (86) 448
APTEKMAN, JEANNE
Argent, L' [1983]   (85) 74
ARANA, HUGO
Official Story, The   (86) 249
ARAU, ALFONSO
Romancing the Stone   (85) 421
ARBATT, ALEXANDER
Dangerous Moves [1984]   (86) 129
ARBIA, AZIZ
Bal, Le [1983]   (85) 80
ARCAND, GABRIEL
Agnes of God   (86) 56
Plouffe, Les   (86) 456
ARCHER, ANNE
Too Scared to Scream   (86) 463
Waltz Across Texas   (84) 497
ARCHER, JOHN
Colorado Territory [1949]   (86) 489
Lost Moment, The [1947]   (83) 465
ARCHIE, JOHN
Cease Fire   (86) 440
ARDANT, FANNY
Confidentially Yours [1983]   (85) 516
Swann in Love   (85) 471
Woman Next Door, The   (82) 385
ARDEN, EVE
Grease 2   (83) 422
My Reputation [1946]   (85) 586
Unfaithful, The [1947]   (86) 550
ARDITI, PIERRE
Heads or Tails [1980]   (84) 485
AREL, DITA
Drifting   (85) 518
ARESTRUP, NEILS
Je tu il elle [1974]   (86) 447
ARGENZIANO, CARMEN
Starchaser   (86) 460
ARGUE, DAVID
Razorback [1984]   (86) 457
ARHONDIS, TINA
Test of Love   (86) 462
ARIANE
Year of the Dragon   (86) 426
ARIAS, IMANOL
Demons in the Garden [1982]   (85) 517
ARIEL, BRIGITTE
Piaf [1980]   (83) 427
ARIMA, INEKO
Late Chrysanthemums [1954]   (86) 449
ARKIN, ALAN
Bad Medicine   (86) 437
Improper Channels   (82) 218
Joshua Then and Now   (86) 198
ARLISS, FLORENCE
Disraeli [1929]   (82) 426
ARLISS, GEORGE
Disraeli [1929]   (82) 426
ARMENDARIZ, PEDRO, JR.
Goat, The [1981]   (86) 444
ARMSTRONG, BESS
Four Seasons, The   (82) 171

High Road to China   (84) 486
Jaws 3-D   (84) 486
Jekyll and Hyde . . . Together Again   (83) 424
ARMSTRONG, CURTIS
Bad Medicine   (86) 437
Better Off Dead   (86) 438
Risky Business   (84) 349
ARMSTRONG, HOWARD "LOUIS BLUIE"
Louis Bluie   (86) 450
ARMSTRONG, R. G.
Hammett   (84) 174
Raggedy Man   (82) 300
Stephen King's Children of the Corn   (85) 534
ARMSTRONG, ROBERT
Most Dangerous Game, The [1932]   (86) 519
ARMSTRONG, TOM
Louis Bluie   (86) 450
ARNAUD, DANIELE
School Spirit   (86) 458
ARNAZ, LUCIE
Second Thoughts   (84) 493
ARNDT, JURGEN
Céleste [1981]   (83) 104
ARNE, PETER
"Obituaries"   (84) 609
Victor/Victoria   (83) 387
ARNESS, JAMES
Hondo [1953]   (83) 452
ARNOLD, EDWARD
Come and Get It [1936]   (82) 412
I'm No Angel [1933]   (85) 561
ARNOLD, MARK
Teen Wolf   (86) 462
ARNOTT, MARK
Best Defense   (85) 512
Return of the Secaucus 7 [1980]   (83) 484
ARNT, CHARLES E.
Take a Letter, Darling [1942]   (85) 632
ARONSON, JUDIE
American Ninja   (86) 436
Friday the 13th—The Final Chapter   (85) 520
Weird Science   (86) 465
ARQUETTE, ROSANNA
After Hours   (86) 51
Aviator, The   (86) 437
Baby, It's You   (84) 479
Desperately Seeking Susan   (86) 137
Silverado   (86) 349
ARROYO, ALEJANDRO
Toy Soldiers   (85) 536
ARTAUD, ANTONIN
Napoleon [1927]   (82) 461
ARTHUR, JEAN
History Is Made at Night [1937]   (84) 542
ASANTE, CHRISTOPHER
Local Hero   (84) 206
ASCARIDE, PIERRE
Petite Bande, La [1982]   (85) 528
ASH, LESLIE
Curse of the Pink Panther   (84) 481
ASHCROFT, PEGGY
Passage to India, A   (85) 365
ASHER, JANE
Dreamchild   (86) 146

PERFORMER INDEX

ASHKAR, NIDAL
  Misunderstood (85) 526
ASHLEY, ELIZABETH
  Split Image (83) 317
ASHLEY, SUZANNE
  Party Animal (86) 455
ASHTON, JOHN
  Beverly Hills Cop (85) 88
ASHTON-GRIFFITHS, ROGER
  Young Sherlock Holmes (86) 431
ASKEY, ARTHUR
  "Obituaries" (83) 523
ASKIN, LEON
  Savage Island (86) 458
ASLAN, GREGOIRE
  "Obituaries" (83) 523
ASNER, EDWARD
  Daniel (84) 481
  Fort Apache, the Bronx (82) 159
  O'Hara's Wife (83) 426
ASSANTE, ARMAND
  I, the Jury (83) 423
  Unfaithfully Yours (85) 537
ASSYLMURATOVA, ALTYANI
  Backstage at the Kirov (85) 511
ASTAIRE, FRED
  Band Wagon, The [1953] (82) 4
  Gay Divorcée, The [1934] (82) 2
  Ghost Story (82) 183
  Holiday Inn [1942] (82) 443
  "Life Achievement Award" (82) 1
  "Life Achievement Award" (86) 3,4,5
  Royal Wedding [1951] (86) 536
ASTHER, NILS
  "Obituaries" (82) 478
ASTIN, JOHN
  National Lampoon's European Vacation (86) 453
ASTIN, SEAN
  Goonies, The (86) 176
ATHERTON, WILLIAM
  Ghostbusters (85) 219
  Real Genius (86) 309
ATKIN, HARVEY
  Atlantic City (82) 74
  Joshua Then and Now (86) 198
ATKINE, FÉODOR
  Beau Mariage, Le (83) 65
  Pauline at the Beach [1982] (84) 296
ATKINS, CHRISTOPHER
  Night in Heaven, A (84) 490
  Pirate Movie, The (83) 427
ATKINS, EILEEN
  Dresser, The (84) 130
ATKINS, TOM
  Halloween III (83) 422
ATSUMI, KIYOSHI
  Foster Daddy, Tora! [1980] (82) 163
ATSUTA, YUHARU
  Tokyo-Ga (86) 463
ATTENBOROUGH, RICHARD
  Flight of the Phoenix, The [1966] (85) 549
AUBERJONOIS, RENÉ
  Brewster McCloud [1970] (86) 484

AUBREY, JIMMY
  "Obituaries" (84) 609
AUCAMP, EMILE
  Guest, The (85) 520
AUCLAIR, MICHEL
  Bon Plaisir, Le [1983] (85) 513
AUDRAN, STÉPHANE
  Coup de torchon [1981] (83) 124
  Plouffe, Les (86) 456
AUGER, CLAUDINE
  Secret Places [1984] (86) 459
AULD, GEORGIE
  New York, New York [1977] (84) 567
AUMONT, MICHEL
  Dangerous Moves [1984] (86) 129
  Sunday in the Country, A (85) 466
  Vie Continue, La [1981] (83) 430
AUSTIN, ALAN
  Door to Door (85) 518
AUSTIN, KAREN
  Summer Rental (86) 462
AUTEUIL, DANIEL
  Little Jerk [1984] (86) 450
AUTIN, CYRIL
  Detective (86) 442
AVERY, MARGARET
  Color Purple, The (86) 105
AVERY, VAL
  Continental Divide (82) 115
  Jinxed (83) 206
  Pope of Greenwich Village, The (85) 529
AVERYUSKIN, NIKOLAI
  Jazzman (85) 523
AVIDAN, SHIMON
  King David (86) 449
AXELROD, NINA
  Cross Country (84) 481
AXTON, HOYT
  Endangered Species (83) 420
  Gremlins (85) 230
  Heart Like a Wheel (84) 182
  Liar's Moon (83) 424
AYKROYD, DAN
  Doctor Detroit (84) 482
  Ghostbusters (85) 219
  Into the Night (86) 186
  Spies like Us (86) 360
  Trading Places (84) 430
  Twilight Zone—The Movie (84) 435
AYKROYD, PETER
  Funny Farm (84) 484
AYRES, LEAH
  Eddie Macon's Run (84) 483
AYRES, LEW
  "Interview with, An" (86) 1
  Unfaithful, The [1947] (86) 550
AZEMA, SABINE
  Sunday in the Country, A (85) 466
AZITO, TONY
  Chattanooga Choo Choo (85) 515
  Pirates of Penzance, The (84) 301
AZNAVOUR, CHARLES
  Edith and Marcel [1983] (85) 518
AZZARA, CANDY
  Easy Money (84) 482

BAAL, KARIN
Berlin Alexanderplatz [1980]   (84) 57
Lili Marleen   (82) 222
Lola [1981]   (83) 215
BABCOCK, BARBARA
Lords of Discipline, The   (84) 488
That Was Then . . . This Is Now   (86) 463
BABCOCK, NATHAN
World According to Garp, The   (83) 397
BABENCO, HECTOR
Pixote [1980]   (82) 280
BABTIST, JENNIFER
Goodbye, New York   (86) 444
Lily in Love   (86) 450
BACH, BARBARA
Give My Regards to Broad Street   (85) 520
BACH, CATHERINE
Cannonball Run II   (85) 514
BACH, JOHN
Wild Horses [1983]   (85) 538
BACKER, BRIAN
Fast Times at Ridgemont High   (83) 156
Moving Violations   (86) 453
BACKUS, JIM
Slapstick   (85) 533
BACON, KEVIN
Diner   (83) 142
Footloose   (85) 198
BACRI, JEAN-PIERRE
Entre nous [1983]   (85) 176
Subway   (86) 461
BADDELEY, HERMIONE
Secret of NIMH, The   (83) 288
BADEL, ALAN
"Obituaries"   (83) 523
Riddle of the Sands, The [1979]   (85) 531
BADEL, SARAH
Shooting Party, The [1984]   (86) 344
BAFFICO, JAMES A.
Stephen King's Silver Bullet   (86) 460
BAGNERIS, VERNEL
Pennies from Heaven   (82) 276
BAGOT, JEAN-PIERRE
Petite Bande, La [1982]   (85) 528
BAHRS, ILSE
Boat Is Full, The [1981]   (83) 82
BAIL, CHUCK
Rainy Day Friends   (86) 457
BAILEY, G. W.
Police Academy   (85) 529
Rustler's Rhapsody   (86) 458
Warning Sign   (86) 465
BAILEY, SHANE
River, The   (85) 416
BAIN, RON
Experience Preferred ... but Not Essential
[1982]   (84) 141
BAINTER, FAY
Secret Life of Walter Mitty, The [1947]   (86) 540
BAIO, SCOTT
Zapped!   (83) 431
BAIRD, MIKE
Hard to Hold   (85) 521

BAISHO, CHIEKO
Foster Daddy, Tora! [1980]   (82) 163
BAKALYAN, DICK
Blame It on the Night   (85) 512
BAKER, BETSY
Evil Dead, The   (84) 484
BAKER, BLANCHE
Cold Feet   (85) 516
Sixteen Candles   (85) 532
BAKER, CARROLL
Star 80   (84) 374
BAKER, JAY
Toy Soldiers   (85) 536
BAKER, JOE DON
Fletch   (86) 169
Joysticks   (84) 487
Natural, The   (85) 329
BAKER, KENNY
Amadeus   (85) 63
"Obituaries"   (86) 559
Return of the Jedi   (84) 326
Time Bandits [1980]   (82) 364
BAKER, LENNY
Next Stop, Greenwich Village [1976]   (85) 592
BAKER, LOUISE
Running Hot   (85) 531
BAKER, RAY
Silverado   (86) 349
BAKRI, MUHAMAD
Hanna K.   (84) 177
BALABAN, BOB
Absence of Malice   (82) 57
Prince of the City   (82) 292
2010   (85) 494
Whose Life Is It Anyway?   (82) 378
BALASKI, BELINDA
Howling, The   (82) 207
BALASKO, JOSIANE
Little Jerk [1984]   (86) 450
BALDACCINI, ANNA
Every Man for Himself [1979]   (82) 139
BALDAN, BERNARD
Purple Haze   (84) 492
BALDASSARRI, RAF
Hercules II   (86) 446
BALDWIN, ADAM
D. C. Cab   (84) 481
Hadley's Rebellion   (85) 521
Reckless   (85) 530
BALDWIN, BILL
"Obituaries"   (83) 523
BALDWIN, JANIT
Humongous   (83) 423
BALDWIN, JUDY
No Small Affair   (85) 527
BALFOUR, KATHARINE
Teachers   (85) 535
BALGOBIN, JENNIFER
Repo Man   (85) 408
BÁLINT, ANDRÁS
Colonel Redl [1984]   (86) 100
BALINT, ESZTER
Stranger than Paradise   (85) 455

BALK, FRUZA
Return to Oz (86) 458
BALL, NICHOLAS
Lifeforce (86) 450
BALLARD, MICHAEL
Alamo Bay (86) 436
BALLATORE, THOMAS
Once Bitten (86) 455
BALLESTEROS, BELÉN
Holy Innocents, The (86) 447
BALSAM, MARTIN
Death Wish III (86) 441
Hombre [1967] (84) 547
St. Elmo's Fire (86) 330
BALSAN, HUMBERT
Loulou [1980] (82) 226
BANCROFT, ANNE
Agnes of God (86) 56
Garbo Talks (85) 520
To Be or Not to Be (84) 426
BANDE, SILVIA
Bar Esperanza [1983] (86) 437
BANDO, YASOSUKE
Mishima (86) 236
BANERJEE, VICTOR
Home and the World, The [1984] (86) 447
Passage to India, A (85) 365
BANES, LISA
Hotel New Hampshire, The (85) 243
Marie (86) 227
BANKS, JONATHAN
Beverly Hills Cop (85) 88
BANKS, LESLIE
Most Dangerous Game, The [1932] (86) 519
BANNEN, IAN
Eye of the Needle (82) 148
Flight of the Phoenix, The [1966] (85) 549
Gorky Park (84) 162
BÁNSAGI, ILDIKÓ
Brady's Escape (85) 514
Mephisto (82) 237
BAOS, FERENC
Brady's Escape (85) 514
BARASH, OLIVIA
Repo Man (85) 408
Tuff Turf (86) 464
BARBEAU, ADRIENNE
Creepshow (83) 419
Escape from New York (82) 133
Swamp Thing (83) 429
BARBER, ELLEN
Firstborn (85) 519
BARBEY, CLAUDE INGA
Death of Mario Ricci, The [1983] (86) 133
BARBOUR, THOMAS
Arthur (82) 71
BARDSLEY, GRANT
Black Cauldron, The (86) 75
BARENDS, EDDA
Question of Silence, A (85) 530
BARKIN, ELLEN
Adventures of Buckaroo Banzai, The (84) 47

Diner (83) 142
Eddie and the Cruisers (84) 483
Harry and Son (85) 521
Tender Mercies (84) 409
BARKLEY, LUCILLE
Bedtime for Bonzo [1951] (84) 512
BARKWORTH, PETER
Champions (85) 515
BARNER, KLAUS
Secret Places [1984] (86) 459
BARNES, C.B.
American Dreamer (85) 509
BARNES, SUSAN
Repo Man (85) 408
BARNETT, CHARLIE
D. C. Cab (84) 481
BARON, GERALDINE
City Girl, The (85) 516
Time After Time [1979] (84) 579
BARON, JOANNE
Joy of Sex (85) 524
BARON, SANDY
Birdy (85) 93
Broadway Danny Rose (85) 112
BARR, JEAN-MARC
King David (86) 449
BARRAULT, JEAN-CLAUDE
Nuit de Varennes, La [1982] (84) 270
BARRAULT, MARIE-CHRISTINE
Love in Germany, A [1983] (85) 283
Stardust Memories [1980] (85) 626
Swann in Love (85) 471
Table for Five (84) 404
BARRETT, AMY
House Where Evil Dwells, The (83) 423
BARRETT, JOHN
Gymkata (86) 445
BARRETT, RAY
Where the Green Ants Dream [1984] (86) 465
BARRETT, SEAN
Return to Oz (86) 458
BARRETT, TOMI
Rainy Day Friends (86) 457
BARRIE, JOHN
Victim [1961] (85) 647
BARRIER, EDGAR
Journey into Fear [1943] (86) 511
BARRIER, MAURICE
Return of Martin Guerre, The (84) 318
BARRON, DANA
National Lampoon's Vacation (84) 242
BARRY, NEILL
Joey (86) 448
BARRY, PATRICIA
Twilight Zone—The Movie (84) 435
BARRY, TONY
Beyond Reasonable Doubt [1980] (84) 74
Coca-Cola Kid, The (86) 440
BARRYMORE, DREW
E.T.: The Extra-Terrestrial (83) 151
Firestarter (85) 519
Irreconcilable Differences (85) 523
Stephen King's Cat's Eye (86) 460

BARRYMORE, JOHN
  Beloved Rogue [1927]   (84) 522
  Sherlock Holmes [1922]   (83) 494
BARRYMORE, LIONEL
  Guy Named Joe, A [1943]   (82) 435
BARTEL, PAUL
  Eating Raoul   (83) 420
  Heart Like a Wheel   (84) 182
  Sesame Street Presents: Follow That Bird   (86)
  459
BARTLETT, BONNIE
  Love Letters   (85) 288
BARTOLI, LUCIANO
  Henry IV [1983]   (86) 446
  Oedipus Rex [1967]   (85) 528
BARTOLLI, MORENO
  When Father Was Away on Business [1984]   (86)
  411
BARTON, PETER
  Friday the 13th—The Final Chapter   (85) 520
BARTY, BILLY
  Night Patrol   (86) 454
BARYSHNIKOV, MIKHAIL
  White Nights   (86) 416
BASARABA, GARY
  One Magic Christmas   (86) 455
BASEHART, RICHARD
  "Obituaries"   (85) 655
BASINGER, KIM
  Fool for Love   (86) 172
  Man Who Loved Women, The   (84) 218
  Mother Lode   (84) 490
  Natural, The   (85) 329
  Never Say Never Again   (84) 252
BASKIN, ELYA
  Moscow on the Hudson   (85) 321
  2010   (85) 494
BASS, HARRIET
  Madman   (84) 488
BASSETT, STEVE
  Spring Break   (84) 494
BASSETT, WILLIAM H.
  Sam's Son   (85) 531
BATCHIEFF, PIERRE
  Napoleon [1927]   (82) 461
BATES, ALAN
  Quartet   (82) 296
  Return of the Soldier, The [1982]   (84) 332
  Wicked Lady, The   (84) 497
BATES, FLORENCE
  Secret Life of Walter Mitty, The [1947]   (86) 540
BATES, KATHY
  Come Back to the 5 & Dime Jimmy Dean,
  Jimmy Dean   (83) 120
BATINKOFF, RANDALL
  Streetwalkin'   (86) 461
BATTAGLIA, GUILLERMO
  Official Story, The   (86) 249
BAUCHAU, PATRICK
  Choose Me   (85) 135
  Entre nous [1983]   (85) 176
  State of Things, The   (84) 379
  View to a Kill, A   (86) 402
BAUER, BELINDA
  Flashdance   (84) 158
  Timerider   (84) 495

BAUER, ELLE
  Man Who Loved Women, The   (84) 218
BAUER, STEVEN
  Scarface   (84) 361
  Thief of Hearts   (85) 536
BAUMGARTNER, MICHÈLE
  Woman Next Door, The   (82) 385
BAUSCH, PINA
  And the Ship Sails On [1983]   (85) 69
BAUSSY, DIDIER
  Argent, L' [1983]   (84) 74
BAXTER, ANNE
  North Star, The [1943]   (83) 476
  "Obituaries"   (86) 559
BAXTER, KEITH
  Falstaff [1967]   (83) 443
BAXTER, LYNSEY
  French Lieutenant's Woman, The   (82) 174
BAXTON, BILL
  Impulse   (85) 523
BAYE, NATHALIE
  Balance, La [1982]   (84) 52
  Beau Pere   (82) 78
  Detective   (85) 442
  Every Man for Himself [1979]   (82) 139
  I Married a Shadow   (84) 486
  Return of Martin Guerre, The   (84) 318
BAYER, MICHAEL "FLEA"
  Suburbia   (85) 534
BAYLDON, GEOFFREY
  Bullshot [1983]   (86) 439
BAYNE, BEVERLY
  "Obituaries"   (83) 524
BEALS, JENNIFER
  Bride, The   (86) 438
  Flashdance   (84) 158
BEARD, MATTHEW "STYMIE"
  "Obituaries"   (82) 478
BEARSE, AMANDA
  Fraternity Vacation   (86) 444
  Fright Night   (86) 444
BEATTY, NED
  Stroker Ace   (84) 494
  Superman II   (82) 339
  Toy, The   (83) 358
BEATTY, WARREN
  Reds   (82) 312
BEAUMONT, LUCY
  Beloved Rogue [1927]   (84) 522
BEAUNE, MICHEL
  Coup de torchon [1981]   (83) 124
BEAVERS, LOUIS
  Holiday Inn [1942]   (82) 443
BECK, JENNIFER
  Tightrope   (85) 489
BECK, JULIAN
  Cotton Club, The   (85) 150
  Oedipus Rex [1967]   (85) 528
BECK, KIMBERLY
  Friday the 13th—The Final Chapter   (85) 520
BECK, MICHAEL
  Battletruck   (83) 417
  Golden Seal, The   (84) 485
  Megaforce   (83) 425

BECKETT, SCOTTY
  My Reputation [1946]   (85) 586
BECKLEY, TONY
  Falstaff [1967]   (83) 443
BECKMAN, HENRY
  Joshua Then and Now   (86) 198
BECUE, NATHALIE
  Petite Bande, La [1982]   (85) 528
BEDELIA, BONNIE
  Heart Like a Wheel   (84) 182
BEER, ROBERT
  Right Stuff, The   (84) 342
BEGLEY, ED, JR.
  Cat People   (83) 100
  Protocol   (85) 383
  Transylvania 6-5000   (86) 463
BEHN, PETER
  Bambi [1942]   (85) 543
BEHRENS, BERNARD
  Unfaithfully Yours   (85) 537
BEIM, NICKY
  When Nature Calls   (86) 465
BEKASSY, STEPHEN
  Arch of Triumph [1948]   (84) 501
BELEN, ANA
  Demons in the Garden [1982]   (85) 517
BELFORD, CHRISTINE
  Christine   (84) 106
BELITA
  Invitation to the Dance [1956]   (86) 507
BELL, ANN
  Champions   (85) 515
BELL, EDWARD
  Gymkata   (86) 445
BELL, MARSHALL
  Nightmare on Elm Street, Part 2, A   (86) 454
BELLAMY, RALPH
  Trading Places   (84) 430
BELLASHMI, AHMED
  Oedipus Rex [1967]   (85) 528
BELLER, KATHLEEN
  Sword and the Sorcerer, The   (83) 429
BELLIN, OLGA
  Tomorrow [1972]   (84) 589
BELLMAN, GINA
  King David   (86) 449
BELLOW, SAUL
  Zelig   (84) 473
BELTRAN, ROBERT
  Eating Raoul   (83) 420
  Night of the Comet   (85) 527
BELUSHI, JIM
  Man with One Red Shoe, The   (86) 451
  Thief   (82) 356
BELUSHI, JOHN
  Continental Divide   (82) 115
  "Obituaries"   (83) 524
BELVAUX, LUCAS
  Death of Mario Ricci, The [1983]   (86) 133
BENCHLEY, ROBERT
  Take a Letter, Darling [1942]   (85) 632
BENE, CARMELO
  Oedipus Rex [1967]   (85) 528

BENEDICT, LEON
  Kerouac, the Movie   (86) 448
BENEDICT, PAUL
  Man with Two Brains, The   (84) 223
  Taking Off [1971]   (86) 545
BENGSCH, HUBERTUS
  Boot, Das [1981]   (83) 86
BENIAMINOV, ALEXANDER
  Moscow on the Hudson   (85) 321
BENNENT, HEINZ
  Death of Mario Ricci, The [1983]   (86) 133
BENNETT, JILL
  Brittania Hospital   (84) 480
  For Your Eyes Only   (82) 155
BENNETT, JOAN
  Bulldog Drummond [1929]   (83) 17
  Disraeli [1929]   (82) 426
  Father of the Bride [1950]   (83) 20
  "Interview with, An"   (83) 16
  Little Women [1933]   (83) 18
  Macomber Affair, The [1947]   (83) 20
  Man Hunt [1941]   (85) 570
  Me and My Gal [1932]   (83) 17
  Private Worlds [1935]   (83) 18
  Trade Winds [1939]   (83) 18
  We're No Angels [1954]   (83) 21
  Woman on the Beach, The [1947]   (83) 519
BENNETT, MARJORIE
  "Obituaries"   (83) 525
BENNETT, MAUREEN
  Jigsaw Man, The [1983]   (85) 524
BENNETT, NORMAN
  River Rat, The   (85) 531
BENNINSON, ISHIA
  King David   (86) 449
BENSEN, GREG
  Bolero   (85) 513
BENSON, DANNY
  That Sinking Feeling [1979]   (85) 536
BENSON, LUCILLE
  "Obituaries"   (85) 656
BENSON, PATRICIA
  Stephen King's Cat's Eye   (86) 460
BENSON, ROBBY
  Chosen, The   (83) 116
  City Limits   (86) 440
  Harry and Son   (85) 521
  Running Brave   (84) 354
BENSON, ROBERT GREEN, III
  Marie   (86) 227
BENTON, BARBI
  Deathstalker   (85) 517
BENTON, JEROME
  Purple Rain   (85) 389
BENUREAU, DIDIER
  Petite Bande, La [1982]   (85) 528
BENZ, DONNA KEI
  Challenge, The   (83) 109
BENZALLI, DANIEL
  Home Free All   (85) 522
BERANGER, ANDRÉ
  Dulcy [1923]   (82) 432
BERCOVICI, LUCA
  American Flyers   (86) 436
  Parasite   (83) 426

BERENGER, TOM
  Big Chill, The   (84) 78
  Eddie and the Cruisers   (84) 483
  Rustler's Rhapsody   (86) 458
BERENSFORD, MARCUS
  Ladyhawke   (86) 214
BERENSON, MARISA
  S.O.B.   (82) 328
BERESFORD, HARRY
  Sign of the Cross, The [1932]   (85) 607
BERET, DAWN
  Victim [1961]   (85) 647
BEREZIN, TANYA
  Compromising Positions   (86) 120
BERGEN, CANDICE
  Gandhi   (83) 183
  Rich and Famous   (82) 316
  Stick   (86) 460
BERGER, GREGG
  Here Come the Littles   (86) 446
BERGER, TONI
  Sugarbaby   (86) 461
BERGER, WILLIAM
  Hercules II   (86) 446
BERGESE, MICHA
  Company of Wolves, The [1984]   (86) 115
BERGHOF, HERBERT
  Target   (86) 462
BERGMAN, INGRID
  Arch of Triumph [1948]   (84) 501
  "Obituaries"   (83) 525
BERGMAN, MATS
  Fanny and Alexander [1982]   (84) 146
BERGMAN, SANDAHL
  Conan the Barbarian   (83) 419
  Red Sonja   (86) 457
BERGMAN, TRACY
  Funny Farm   (84) 484
BERKELEY, XANDER
  Mommie Dearest   (82) 245
BERKOFF, STEVEN
  Beverly Hills Cop   (85) 88
  Octopussy   (84) 276
  Rambo: First Blood Part II   (86) 299
  Revolution   (86) 458
BERKOWITZ, MYLES
  No Small Affair   (85) 527
BERLE, MILTON
  Broadway Danny Rose   (85) 112
BERLEAND, FRANÇOIS
  Balance, La [1982]   (84) 52
BERLINER, BRIN
  Wild Life, The   (85) 538
BERLING, PETER
  Fitzcarraldo   (83) 167
BERMAN, MARC
  Bal, Le [1983]   (85) 80
BERMAN, SUSAN
  Smithereens   (83) 307
BERNABE, JOBY
  Sugar Cane Alley [1983]   (85) 461
BERNARD, JASON
  All of Me   (85) 58

BERNARDI, HERSCHEL
  Front, The [1976]   (86) 502
BERNARDI, ROBERTO
  Comfort and Joy   (85) 146
BERNARDO, CLAUDIO
  Pixote [1980]   (82) 280
BERNHARD, SANDRA
  King of Comedy, The   (84) 192
  Sesame Street Presents: Follow That Bird   (86) 459
BERR, ULRICH
  Mixed Blood   (86) 452
BERRIDGE, ELIZABETH
  Amadeus   (85) 63
  "Interview with Miloš Forman, An"   (86) 26
  Smooth Talk   (86) 354
BERRY, NOAH
  Waltz Across Texas   (84) 497
BERRY, RICHARD
  Balance, La [1982]   (84) 52
  Patsy, The   (86) 456
  Trace, The [1983]   (85) 537
BERTHIER, EUGÈNE
  Detective   (86) 442
BERTHOMIER, MARCEL
  Dernier Combat, Le [1983]   (85) 517
BERTI, DEHL
  Invasion U.S.A.   (86) 447
BERTIN, PIERRE
  Detective   (86) 442
BERTIN, ROLAND
  Diva [1980]   (83) 147
BERTINI, FRANCESCA
  "Obituaries"   (86) 560
BERTOZZI, GIACOMO
  Henry IV [1983]   (86) 446
BERTRAND, LILIANE
  Petite Bande, La [1982]   (85) 528
BERVAL, PAUL
  Plouffe, Les   (86) 456
BESCH, BIBI
  Beast Within, The   (83) 418
  Lonely Lady, The   (84) 488
  Star Trek II—The Wrath of Khan   (83) 321
BESNEHARD, DOMINIQUE
  À nos amour [1983]   (85) 509
BESSE, ARIEL
  Beau Pere   (82) 78
BESSERER, EUGENIE
  Bridge of San Luis Rey, The [1929]   (82) 408
BESSY, CLAUDE
  Invitation to the Dance [1956]   (86) 507
BETANCOURT, ANNE
  Rainy Day Friends   (86) 457
BETTELHEIM, BRUNO
  Zelig   (84) 473
BETTI, LAURA
  Nuit de Varennes, La [1982]   (84) 270
BEVAR, CAROL
  Waitress   (83) 431
BEVERLY, HELEN
  Light Ahead, The [1939]   (83) 460

BEYMER, RICHARD
  Cross Country   (84) 481
BIALIS, ROSETTE
  Light Ahead, The [1939]   (83) 460
BIANCHINI, ALFREDO
  Softly Softly [1984]   (86) 460
BIAZZA, BEN
  Waltz Across Texas   (84) 497
BICKFORD, CHARLES
  Star Is Born, A [1954]   (84) 573
  Woman on the Beach, The [1947]   (83) 519
BICKNELL, GENE
  They're Playing with Fire   (85) 536
BIEHN, MICHAEL
  Terminator, The   (85) 478
BIERI, RAMON
  Grandview, U.S.A.   (85) 520
BIETTE, JEAN-CLAUDE
  Oedipus Rex [1967]   (85) 528
BIGAGLI, CLAUDIO
  Night of the Shooting Stars, The [1982]   (84) 258
BILAOUL, BERNARD
  My New Partner [1984]   (86) 246
BILL, TONY
  Pee-wee's Big Adventure   (86) 265
BILLETT, DON
  Prince of the City   (82) 292
BILLINGSLEY, PETER
  Christmas Story, A   (84) 110
BILON, MICHAEL (PAT)
  "Obituaries"   (84) 610
BINNS, EDWARD
  Verdict, The   (83) 377
BINOCHE, JULIETTE
  Hail Mary   (86) 182
BIRD, BILLIE
  Sixteen Candles   (85) 532
BIRD, NORMAN
  Victim [1961]   (85) 647
BIRKIN, JANE
  Evil Under the Sun [1981]   (83) 421
BIRNEY, REED
  Four Friends   (82) 167
BISLEY, STEVE
  Silver City [1984]   (86) 460
BISSELL, WHIT
  Creature from the Black Lagoon, The [1954]   (82) 422
BISSET, JACQUELINE
  Class   (84) 480
  Inchon   (83) 424
  Rich and Famous   (82) 316
  Under the Volcano   (85) 499
BISSO, PATRICIO
  Kiss of the Spider Woman   (86) 209
BLACK, GERRY
  Re-Animator   (86) 457
BLACK, JENNIFER
  Local Hero   (84) 206
BLACK, KAREN
  Can She Bake a Cherry Pie?   (84) 95

Come Back to the 5 & Dime Jimmy Dean, Jimmy Dean   (83) 120
BLACKSTONE, SUSAN
  Stone Boy, The   (85) 450
BLADES, RUBEN
  Crossover Dreams   (86) 441
BLAIR, AL
  Hard Traveling   (86) 445
BLAIR, LINDA
  Chained Heat   (84) 480
  Night Patrol   (86) 454
  Savage Island   (86) 458
BLAKE, GEOFFREY
  Secret Admirer   (86) 459
BLAKE, JULIA
  Lonely Hearts [1982]   (84) 212
  My First Wife   (86) 453
BLAKE, LARRY
  "Obituaries"   (83) 526
BLAKE, TIMOTHY
  Finders Keepers   (85) 519
BLAKELY, COLIN
  Evil Under the Sun [1981]   (83) 421
BLAKLEY, RONEE
  Nightmare on Elm Street, A   (85) 527
BLANCHARD, RON
  Caddie [1976]   (83) 439
  Silver City [1984]   (86) 460
BLANCHARD, SAGA
  Entre nous [1983]   (85) 176
BLAND, PETER
  Came a Hot Friday   (86) 439
BLANKFIELD, MARK
  Jekyll and Hyde . . . Together Again   (83) 424
BLECH, HANS-CHRISTIAN
  Colonel Redl [1984]   (86) 100
BLEE, DEBRA
  Beach Girls, The   (83) 417
BLEVINS, MICHAEL
  Chorus Line, A   (86) 91
BLEYER, KEVIN
  Twice in a Lifetime   (86) 397
BLIN, ROGER
  Adolescente, L' [1979]   (83) 53
BLOND, SUSAN
  Mixed Blood   (86) 452
BLONIGAN, COLETTE
  Diner   (83) 142
BLOOM, BRIAN
  Flanagan   (86) 443
  Once upon a Time in America   (85) 345
BLOOM, CLAIRE
  Clash of the Titans   (82) 111
BLOOM, SCOTT
  Stuff, The   (86) 461
BLOOM, VERNA
  After Hours   (86) 51
  Honkytonk Man   (83) 200
  Journey of Natty Gann, The   (86) 203
BLOSSOM, ROBERTS
  Christine   (84) 106
  Reuben, Reuben   (84) 337
BLOT, JACQUES
  Petite Bande, La [1982]   (85) 528

BLOUNT, LISA
Cease Fire   (86) 440
Officer and a Gentleman, An   (83) 246
BLOW, KURTIS
Krush Groove   (86) 449
BLUE, MONTE
Apache [1954]   (82) 395
BLUM, JACK
Funny Farm   (84) 484
BLUM, JOHN MORTON
Zelig   (84) 473
BLUM, MARK
Desperately Seeking Susan   (86) 137
BLYE, MARGARET
Hombre [1967]   (84) 547
Mischief   (86) 452
BLYTHE, ROBERT
Experience Preferred ... but Not Essential
[1982]   (84) 141
BO, VICTOR
Deathstalker   (85) 517
BOCCARDO, DELIA
Nostalgia [1983]   (85) 340
BOCHNER, HART
Rich and Famous   (82) 316
Supergirl   (85) 535
Wild Life, The   (85) 538
BOCHNER, LLOYD
Lonely Lady, The   (84) 488
BODALO, JOSE
Volver a empezar   (83) 393
BOEN, EARL
Movers and Shakers   (86) 453
BOENSCH, PAUL, III
This Is Elvis   (82) 360
BOGAN, TED
Louis Bluie   (86) 450
BOGARDE, DIRK
Victim [1961]   (85) 647
BOGART, HUMPHREY
Barefoot Contessa, The [1954]   (82) 399
They Drive by Night [1940]   (83) 508
BOGART, JOHN PAUL
Bizet's Carmen [1983]   (85) 98
BOHM, HARK
Berlin Alexanderplatz [1980]   (84) 57
Lili Marleen   (82) 222
BOHNEN, ROMAN
Arch of Triumph [1948]   (84) 501
Hard Way, The [1942]   (85) 555
BOHORQUEZ, HUEREQUEQUE ENRIQUÉ
Fitzcarraldo   (83) 167
BOHRER, CORINNE
Surf II   (85) 535
BOHRINGER, RICHARD
Diva [1980]   (83) 147
I Married a Shadow   (84) 486
Patsy, The   (86) 456
Peril   (86) 456
Subway   (86) 461
BOIS, CURT
Arch of Triumph [1948]   (84) 501
Boat Is Full, The [1981]   (83) 82
BOIS, JEAN
Petite Bande, La [1982]   (85) 528

BOITARD, CYR
À nos amour [1983]   (85) 509
BOLAND, EDDIE
Miracle Woman, The [1931]   (83) 473
BOLES, ERIC
Hadley's Rebellion   (85) 521
BOLES, JOHN
King of Jazz [1930]   (86) 515
BOLKAN, FLORINDA
Water and Soap   (86) 465
BOLLING, ANGIE
River Rat, The   (85) 531
BOLOGNA, JOSEPH
Blame It on Rio   (85) 512
My Favorite Year   (83) 241
Transylvania 6-5000   (86) 463
Woman in Red, The   (85) 538
BONACELLI, PAOLO
Henry IV [1983]   (86) 446
BOND, SUDIE
Come Back to the 5 & Dime Jimmy Dean,
Jimmy Dean   (83) 120
"Obituaries"   (85) 656
Silkwood   (84) 367
Swing Shift   (85) 535
Tomorrow [1972]   (84) 589
BOND, WARD
Fort Apache [1948]   (84) 530
Guy Named Joe, A [1943]   (82) 435
Hondo [1953]   (83) 452
Long Gray Line, The [1955]   (82) 447
BONDI, BEULAH
"Obituaries"   (82) 480
BONNAFFÉ, JACQUES
First Name, Carmen [1983]   (85) 186
BONNAIRE, SANDRINE
À nos amour [1983]   (85) 509
BONO, SUSIE
Breakin' 2   (85) 514
BONOMO, JOE
Sign of the Cross, The [1932]   (85) 607
BONOVISIN, BERANGERE
Trace, The [1983]   (85) 537
BOONE, RICHARD
Arrangement, The [1969]   (86) 474
Hombre [1967]   (84) 547
"Obituaries"   (82) 481
BOORMAN, CHARLEY
Emerald Forest, The   (86) 156
BOORMAN, IMOGEN
Dreamchild   (86) 146
BOORMAN, KATRINE
Excalibur   (82) 144
BOOTH, KATHERINE
Take a Letter, Darling [1942]   (85) 632
BOOTHE, POWERS
Emerald Forest, The   (86) 156
Red Dawn   (85) 530
Southern Comfort   (82) 332
BORBONI, PAOLA
Yes, Giorgio   (83) 431
BORGE, RIKKE
Still of the Night   (83) 326
BORGE, VICTOR
King of Comedy, The   (84) 192

BORGENICHT, NANCY
  Silent Night, Deadly Night (85) 532
BORGES, YAMIL
  Chorus Line, A (86) 91
BORGNINE, ERNEST
  Escape from New York (82) 133
  Flight of the Phoenix, The [1966] (85) 549
BOROWITZ, KATHERINE
  Harry and Son (85) 521
BORRELLI, JIM
  Beat Street (85) 512
  Windy City (85) 538
BORROMEL, CHARLES
  Ladyhawke (86) 214
BORTHWICK, JAMES
  Guest, The (85) 520
BOSCO, PHILIP
  Flanagan (86) 443
  Pope of Greenwich Village, The (85) 529
BOSCOLI, TANIA
  Gabriela [1983] (85) 213
BOSIO, ANITA
  Rent Control (85) 530
BOSLEY, TOM
  O'Hara's Wife (83) 426
  World of Henry Orient, The [1964] (84) 600
BOSSON, BARBARA
  Last Starfighter, The (85) 277
BOSTWICK, BARRY
  Megaforce (83) 425
BOSWELL, CHARLES
  Lost in America (86) 219
BOTSFORD, SARA
  By Design (83) 419
  Deadly Eyes (84) 482
  Still of the Night (83) 326
BOUCHER, CHRISTIAN
  Loulou [1980] (82) 226
BOUDET, JACQUES
  Dangerous Moves [1984] (86) 129
BOUISE, JEAN
  Dernier Combat, Le [1983] (85) 517
  Edith and Marcel [1983] (85) 518
  Subway (86) 461
BOUIX, EVELYNE
  Edith and Marcel [1983] (85) 518
BOUQUET, CAROLE
  For Your Eyes Only (82) 155
BOUQUET, RÉGIS
  Bal, Le [1983] (85) 80
BOVASSO, JULIE
  Staying Alive (84) 386
  Verdict, The (83) 377
BOW WOW WOW
  Scandalous (85) 532
BOWEN, MICHAEL
  Night of the Comet (85) 527
  Valley Girl (84) 447
BOWENS, MALICK
  Out of Africa (86) 255
BOWER, ANTOINETTE
  Evil That Men Do, The (85) 518
BOWER, HUGO
  Holcroft Covenant, The (86) 446

BOWIE, DAVID
  Hunger, The (84) 486
  Into the Night (86) 186
  Man Who Fell to Earth, The [1975] (83) 469
  Merry Christmas, Mr. Lawrence (84) 231
BOWKER, JUDI
  Clash of the Titans (82) 111
  Shooting Party, The [1984] (86) 344
BOWMAN, CAL
  Wavelength (84) 497
BOXLEITNER, BRUCE
  TRON (83) 371
BOYD, GUY
  Body Double (85) 513
  Flashpoint (85) 519
  Streamers (84) 391
  Target (86) 462
BOYD, JAN GAN
  Chorus Line, A (86) 91
BOYD, KARIN
  Mephisto (82) 237
BOYD, ROBERT
  Ragtime (82) 304
BOYDEN, PETER
  Blow Out (82) 83
  Cold Feet (85) 516
BOYER, CHANCE
  Night of the Comet (85) 527
BOYER, CHARLES
  Arch of Triumph [1948] (84) 501
  History Is Made at Night [1937] (84) 542
BOYETT, WILLIAM
  Sam's Son (85) 531
BOYLAN, PATRICK
  Stephen King's Children of the Corn (85) 534
BOYLE, PETER
  Hammett (84) 174
  Johnny Dangerously (85) 524
  Outland (82) 272
  Turk 182 (86) 464
  Yellowbeard (84) 498
BRACCONERI, FABRIZIO
  Water and Soap (86) 465
BRACKEN, EDDIE
  National Lampoon's Vacation (84) 242
BRADFORD, ANDREW
  Holcroft Covenant, The (86) 446
BRADFORD, GREG
  Lovelines (85) 525
BRADFORD, RICHARD
  Legend of Billie Jean, The (86) 450
  Mean Season, The (86) 452
  Running Hot (85) 531
  Trip to Bountiful, The (86) 383
BRADSHAW, MELANIE
  Home Free All (85) 522
BRADY, SCOTT
  "Obituaries" (86) 561
BRAGA, SONIA
  Gabriela [1983] (85) 213
  I Love You (83) 423
  Kiss of the Spider Woman (86) 209

BRAILSFORD, MARK
  Kipperbang [1983]   (85) 524
BRANDAUER, KLAUS MARIA
  Colonel Redl [1984]   (86) 100
  Mephisto   (82) 237
  Never Say Never Again   (84) 252
  Out of Africa   (86) 255
BRANDO, JOCELYN
  Mommie Dearest   (82) 245
BRANDO, MARLON
  Mutiny on the Bounty [1962]   (85) 581
BRANDON, CLARK
  My Tutor   (84) 490
BRANDON, RICHARD
  Firstborn   (85) 519
BRANTLEY, BETSY
  Five Days One Summer   (83) 421
BRASSELLE, KEEFE
  "Obituaries"   (82) 481
BRASSEUR, CLAUDE
  Boum, La [1980]   (84) 480
  Detective   (86) 442
BRAVOS, PETER
  Flight of the Phoenix, The [1966]   (85) 549
BRAY, DAWSON
  Under the Volcano   (85) 499
BRAZZI, ROSSANO
  Barefoot Contessa, The [1954]   (82) 399
BREEDING, LARRY
  "Obituaries"   (83) 528
BRELAND, MARK
  Lords of Discipline, The   (84) 488
BRENNAN, EILEEN
  Clue   (86) 440
  Funny Farm   (84) 484
BRENNAN, WALTER
  Barbary Coast [1935]   (84) 506
  Come and Get It [1936]   (82) 412
  North Star, The [1943]   (83) 476
BRENNER, DORI
  Next Stop, Greenwich Village [1976]   (85) 592
  Oasis, The   (85) 528
BRENT, GEORGE
  My Reputation [1946]   (85) 586
BRESTOFF, RICHARD
  Man with Two Brains, The   (84) 223
BRIALY, JEAN-CLAUDE
  Edith and Marcel [1983]   (85) 518
  Nuit de Varennes, La [1982]   (84) 270
BRICKTOP
  Zelig   (84) 473
BRIDGES, BEAU
  Heart Like a Wheel   (84) 182
  Honky Tonk Freeway   (82) 199
  Hotel New Hampshire, The   (85) 243
  Love Child   (83) 425
  Night Crossing   (83) 426
BRIDGES, JEFF
  Against All Odds   (85) 509
  Cutter's Way   (82) 119
  Heaven's Gate   (82) 195
  Jagged Edge   (86) 190
  Kiss Me Goodbye   (83) 209
  Starman   (85) 445
  TRON   (83) 371

BRIDGES, LLOYD
  Airplane II   (83) 417
BRIDGEWATER, DEE DEE
  Brother from Another Planet, The   (85) 118
BRIERS, JANE
  Secrets   (85) 532
BRIEUX, BERNARD
  Little Jerk [1984]   (86) 450
BRIGHT, RICHARD
  Once upon a Time in America   (85) 345
BRIGUET, MICHEL
  Argent, L' [1983]   (85) 74
BRILL, FRANCESCA
  Champions   (85) 515
BRIMLEY, WILFORD
  Absence of Malice   (82) 57
  Cocoon   (86) 96
  Country   (85) 156
  Harry and Son   (85) 521
  High Road to China   (84) 486
  Hotel New Hampshire, The   (85) 243
  Natural, The   (85) 329
  Remo Williams   (86) 457
  Stone Boy, The   (85) 450
  Tender Mercies   (84) 409
  Thing, The   (83) 343
BRINKLEY, CHRISTIE
  National Lampoon's Vacation   (84) 242
BRINKLEY, RITCH
  Man with One Red Shoe, The   (86) 451
  Rhinestone   (85) 531
BRISTOWE, TANIA
  Utu [1983]   (85) 504
BRITT, MELENDY
  Secret of the Sword, The   (86) 459
BRITTS, TONY
  Death Wish III   (86) 441
BROADBENT, JIM
  Hit, The   (86) 446
BROADERUP, BERND
  Taxi Zum Klo   (82) 346
BROADHURST, KENT
  Stephen King's Silver Bullet   (86) 460
BROCK, PHIL
  Tex   (83) 335
BROCKETTE, GARY
  Philadelphia Experiment, The   (85) 529
BROCKMAN, MICHAEL
  Harry and Son   (85) 521
BRODERICK, JAMES
  "Obituaries"   (83) 528
BRODERICK, MATTHEW
  Ladyhawke   (86) 214
  Max Dugan Returns   (84) 228
  1918   (86) 454
  WarGames   (84) 458
BRODIE, DONALD
  Detour [1946]   (86) 498
BROK, EWA
  Silver City [1984]   (86) 460
BROLIN, JAMES
  Pee-wee's Big Adventure   (86) 265
BROLIN, JOSH
  Goonies, The   (86) 176

BROMBERG, J. EDWARD
  Arch of Triumph [1948] (84) 501
BROMLEY, SYDNEY
  Dragonslayer (82) 125
  Neverending Story, The (85) 527
BRON, ELEANOR
  Turtle Diary (86) 464
BRONSON, CHARLES
  Apache [1954] (82) 395
  Death Wish II (83) 420
  Death Wish III (86) 441
  Evil That Men Do, The (85) 518
  10 to Midnight (84) 495
BROOK, FAITH
  Razor's Edge, The (85) 402
BROOKE, PAUL
  Agatha [1979] (83) 435
BROOKER, RICHARD
  Deathstalker (85) 517
  Friday the 13th — Part III (83) 422
BROOKS, ALBERT
  Lost in America (86) 219
  Modern Romance (82) 241
  Twilight Zone — The Movie (84) 435
  Unfaithfully Yours (85) 537
BROOKS, ELISABETH
  Howling, The (82) 207
BROOKS, FOSTER
  Cannonball Run II (85) 514
BROOKS, JAMES L.
  Modern Romance (82) 241
BROOKS, JOEL
  Protocol (85) 383
BROOKS, LOUISE
  "Obituaries" (86) 562
BROOKS, MEL
  To Be or Not to Be (84) 426
BROOKSMITH, ROY
  Rent Control (85) 530
BROTHERS, JOYCE
  King of Comedy, The (84) 192
  Lonely Guy, The (85) 525
BROWN, BLAIR
  Continental Divide (82) 115
  Flash of Green, A (86) 443
BROWN, BRYAN
  Give My Regards to Broad Street (85) 520
  Winter of Our Dreams [1981] (83) 431
BROWN, CARLOS
  Southern Comfort (82) 332
BROWN, CLANCY
  Adventures of Buckaroo Banzai,
    The (85) 47
  Bride, The (86) 438
BROWN, D. W.
  Fast Times at Ridgemont High (83) 156
  Mischief (86) 452
  Weekend Pass (85) 537
BROWN, ERIC
  They're Playing with Fire (85) 536
BROWN, JANET
  For Your Eyes Only (82) 155
BROWN, JUNE
  Misunderstood (85) 526

BROWN, LOU
  King of Comedy, The (84) 192
BROWN, MAX M.
  Wolfen (82) 382
BROWN, OLIVIA M.
  48 HRS. (83) 173
BROWN, OLLIE E.
  Blame It on the Night (85) 512
BROWN, PAMELA
  I Know Where I'm Going [1945] (83) 456
BROWN, PAUL
  Morons from Outer Space (86) 452
BROWN, PHILIP MARTIN
  Bounty, The (85) 513
  Eye of the Needle (82) 148
BROWN, RALPH
  Hit, The (86) 446
BROWN, REB
  Uncommon Valor (84) 496
  Yor (84) 498
BROWN, ROBERT
  View to a Kill, A (86) 402
BROWN, SHARON
  Chorus Line, A (86) 91
BROWN, STEVEN JAMES
  No Small Affair (85) 527
BROWN, TOM
  Silverado (86) 349
BROWNE, CORAL
  American Dreamer (85) 509
  Dreamchild (86) 146
BROWNE, ROBERT ALAN
  Fleshburn (85) 519
BROWNING, ALISTAIR
  Merry Christmas, Mr. Lawrence (84) 231
BROX SISTERS
  King of Jazz [1930] (86) 515
BRUCE, NIGEL
  Becky Sharp [1935] (82) 403
BRUCH, VIRGINIA
  "Obituaries" (83) 528
BRUENGGER, ALICE
  Boat Is Full, The [1981] (83) 82
BRUGMAN, EDDY
  Question of Silence, A (85) 530
BRULL, PAMELA
  Good Bye Cruel World (85) 520
  Philadelphia Experiment, The (85) 529
BRUNCKHORST, NATJA
  Christine F. [1981] (83) 419
BRUNING, ROBERT
  Wild Duck, The [1983] (86) 466
BRYANT, JOSHUA
  First Monday in October (82) 151
BRYANT, TODD
  Lovelines (85) 525
BRYAR, CLAUDIA
  Psycho II (84) 307
BRYER, DENISE
  Return to Oz (86) 458
BRYNE, BARBARA
  Amadeus (85) 63
BRYNNER, YUL
  "Obituaries" (86) 563

BUCHANAN, ROBERT
  Gregory's Girl [1981]   (83) 193
  That Sinking Feeling [1979]   (85) 536
BUCHANAN, RUSSELL
  Rhinestone   (85) 531
BUCHANAN, SHERRY
  Dr. Butcher, M.D. [1980]   (83) 420
BUCHHOLZ, HORST
  Sahara   (85) 531
BUCHINSKY, CHARLES. See BRONSON,
  CHARLES.
BUCHREISER, FRANZ
  Berlin Alexanderplatz [1980]   (84) 57
  Sheer Madness [1983]   (86) 459
BUCK, GEORGE
  Birdy   (85) 93
BUCKLEY, BETTY
  Tender Mercies   (84) 409
BUDAY, HELEN
  Mad Max Beyond Thunderdome   (86) 223
BUDKIN, CELIA
  Light Ahead, The [1939]   (83) 460
BUGGY, MIALL
  King David   (86) 449
BUHR, GERARD
  Bob le Flambeur [1955]   (84) 526
BUJOLD, GENEVIÈVE
  Choose Me   (85) 135
  Monsignor   (83) 425
  Tightrope   (85) 489
  Trouble in Mind   (86) 388
BULL, PETER
  "Obituaries"   (85) 657
BUNTIC, PETER
  Transylvania 6-5000   (86) 463
BUONO, VICTOR
  "Obituaries"   (83) 528
BURGE, GREGG
  Chorus Line, A   (86) 91
BURKLEY, DENNIS
  Mask   (86) 231
BURLINSON, TOM
  Flesh and Blood   (86) 443
  Man from Snowy River, The   (83) 425
  Phar Lap   (85) 528
  River Rat, The   (85) 531
BURNETT, CAROL
  Annie   (83) 56
  Four Seasons, The   (82) 171
BURNETT, STEVE
  Muppets Take Manhattan, The   (85) 526
BURNHAM, JANET
  Home Free All   (85) 522
BURNS, BART
  Frances   (83) 178
BURNS, GEORGE
  Oh God, You Devil   (85) 528
  Solid Gold Cadillac, The [1956]   (85) 615
BURNT, DREW
  That Sinking Feeling [1979]   (85) 536
BURR, RAYMOND
  Godzilla 1985   (86) 444
BURRELL, MARYEDITH
  Kiss Me Goodbye   (83) 209

BURROUGHS, JACKIE
  Grey Fox, The   (84) 168
BURSTYN, ELLEN
  Twice in a Lifetime   (86) 397
BURT, EDDIE
  That Sinking Feeling [1979]   (85) 536
BURTON, BILL
  Romancing the Stone   (85) 421
BURTON, RICHARD
  My Cousin Rachel [1952]   (82) 458
  1984   (85) 335
  "Obituaries"   (85) 657
  Wagner   (84) 497
BURTON, TONY
  Rocky IV   (86) 319
BUSEY, GARY
  Barbarosa   (83) 60
  Bear, The   (85) 511
  D. C. Cab   (84) 481
  Insignificance   (86) 447
  Stephen King's Silver Bullet   (86) 460
BUSH, BETTINA
  Here Come the Littles   (86) 446
BUSH, CHUCK
  Fandango   (86) 442
BUSH, GRAND L.
  Weekend Pass   (85) 537
BUSH, NORMAN
  Muppets Take Manhattan, The   (85) 526
BUSHELL, ANTHONY
  Disraeli [1929]   (82) 426
BUSIA, AKOSUA
  Color Purple, The   (86) 105
BUTHELEZI, JUNE
  King Solomon's Mines   (86) 449
BUTLER, MARK
  Test of Love   (86) 462
BUTRICK, MERRITT
  Star Trek II—The Wrath of Khan   (83)
    321
  Star Trek III—The Search for
    Spock   (85) 439
BUTT, LAWSON
  Beloved Rogue [1927]   (84) 522
BUXTON, SARAH
  Sure Thing, The   (86) 369
BUZZI, RUTH
  Surf II   (85) 535
BYNER, JOHN
  Black Cauldron, The   (86) 75
  Transylvania 6-5000   (86) 463
BYRDE, EDYE
  Rappin'   (86) 457
BYRNE, GABRIEL
  Excalibur   (82) 144
  Hanna K.   (84) 177
BYRON, ANNIE
  Silver City [1984]   (86) 460
BYRON, JEFFREY
  Metalstorm   (84) 489
BYRSKA, IRENE
  Man of Iron   (82) 230

PERFORMER INDEX

CAAN, JAMES
Bolero [1981]   (83) 418
Kiss Me Goodbye   (83) 209
Thief   (82) 356
CABOT, SEBASTIAN
Time Machine, The [1960]   (84) 585
CACCAVO, ROLAND
Home Free All   (85) 522
CADENAT, GARRY
Sugar Cane Alley [1983]   (85) 461
CADMAN, JOSHUA
Sure Thing, The   (86) 369
CAESAR, ADOLPH
Color Purple, The   (86) 105
Soldier's Story, A   (85) 427
CAESAR, HARRY
Breakin' 2   (85) 514
CAESAR, SHIRLEY
Gospel   (85) 520
CAESAR, SID
Cannonball Run II   (85) 514
Grease 2   (83) 422
CAGE, NICOLAS
Birdy   (85) 93
Cotton Club, The   (85) 150
Racing with the Moon   (85) 397
Valley Girl   (84) 447
CAGNEY, JAMES
Ragtime   (82) 304
CAGNEY, JEANNE
"Obituaries"   (85) 658
CAHILL, CATHY
Harry and Son   (85) 521
CAIN, DEAN
Stone Boy, The   (85) 450
CAINE, MICHAEL
Beyond the Limit   (84) 479
Blame It on Rio   (85) 512
Deathtrap   (83) 137
Educating Rita   (84) 136
Holcroft Covenant, The   (86) 446
Jigsaw Man, The [1983]   (85) 524
Victory   (82) 374
CAIRNEY, JOHN
Victim [1961]   (85) 647
CALDERON, SERGIO
Erendira [1983]   (85) 181
CALDWELL, ZOE
Purple Rose of Cairo, The   (86) 290
CALF, ANTHONY
Oxford Blues   (85) 528
CALFA, DON
Return of the Living Dead, The   (86) 314
CALHERN, LOUIS
Arch of Triumph [1948]   (84) 501
CALHOUN, RORY
Angel   (85) 510
Avenging Angel   (86) 436
CALLAHAN, JAMES
Lady Sings the Blues [1972]   (85) 565
CALLOW, SIMON
Amadeus   (85) 63
CALOT, JUAN
Hit, The   (86) 446

CAMERON, DAVID
My First Wife   (86) 453
CAMERON, ROD
"Obituaries"   (84) 612
CAMP, COLLEEN
City Girl, The   (85) 516
Clue   (86) 440
D.A.R.Y.L.   (86) 441
Joy of Sex   (85) 524
Police Academy 2   (86) 276
They All Laughed   (82) 350
Valley Girl   (84) 447
CAMP, HAMILTON
Meatballs Part II   (85) 526
CAMPANELLA, FRANK
Flamingo Kid, The   (85) 192
CAMPBELL, BRUCE
Evil Dead, The   (84) 484
CAMPBELL, CHERYL
Chariots of Fire   (82) 101
Greystoke   (85) 236
Shooting Party, The [1984]   (86) 344
CAMPBELL, J. KENNETH
Sudden Death   (86) 461
CAMPBELL, KEN
Joshua Then and Now   (86) 198
CAMPBELL, TORQUIL
Golden Seal, The   (84) 485
CAMPOS, RAPHAEL
"Obituaries"   (86) 564
CAMPOS, VICTOR
Moving Violations   (86) 453
CANCELIER, JACQUES
Petite Bande, La [1982]   (85) 528
CANDY, JOHN
Brewster's Millions   (86) 438
Going Berserk   (84) 485
National Lampoon's Vacation   (84) 242
Sesame Street Presents: Follow That
   Bird   (86) 459
Splash   (85) 434
Stripes   (82) 336
Summer Rental   (86) 462
Volunteers   (86) 464
CANNON, DYAN
Author! Author!   (83) 417
Deathtrap   (83) 137
CANNON, J. D.
Death-Wish II   (83) 420
CANOVA, JUDY
"Obituaries"   (84) 613
CANTAFORA, ANTONIO
Gabriela [1983]   (85) 213
CANTARELLI, DARIO
Night of the Shooting Stars, The [1982]
   (84) 258
CAPALDI, PETER
Local Hero   (84) 206
CAPELJA, JAD
Puberty Blues [1981]   (84) 492
CAPPETTA, JOE
No Small Affair   (85) 527
CAPRI, HERSON
Kiss of the Spider Woman   (86) 209

111

CAPRON, CHANTAL
  Bal, Le [1983]   (85) 80
CAPSHAW, KATE
  Best Defense   (85) 512
  Dreamscape   (85) 166
  Indiana Jones and the Temple of
    Doom   (85)   253
  Little Sex, A   (83) 424
  Windy City   (85) 538
CARA, IRENE
  Certain Fury   (86) 440
  City Heat   (85) 141
  D. C. Cab   (84) 481
CARAFOTES, PAUL
  All the Right Moves   (84) 41
CARAMASCHI, CLAUDIO
  Death of Mario Ricci, The [1983]   (86) 133
CARAVELLI, TYKE
  Starchaser   (86) 460
CARDILLE, LORI
  Day of the Dead   (86) 441
CARDINALE, CLAUDIA
  Fitzcarraldo   (83) 167
  Gift, The   (84) 484
  Henry IV [1983]   (86) 446
CAREY, GEOFFREY
  State of Things, The   (84) 379
CAREY, HARRY
  Barbary Coast [1935]   (84) 506
CAREY, HARRY, JR.
  Long Gray Line, The [1955]   (82) 447
  Mask   (86) 231
CAREY, MACDONALD
  Take a Letter, Darling [1942]   (85) 632
CAREY, PHIL
  Long Gray Line, The [1955]   (82) 447
CARHART, TIMOTHY
  Party Animal   (86) 455
  Witness   (86) 421
CARIDEO, EDDIE
  "Obituaries"   (86) 564
CARIDI, CARMINE
  Prince of the City   (82) 292
CARILLO, MARY
  Holy Innocents, The   (86) 447
CARIOU, LEN
  Four Seasons, The   (82) 171
CARLE, CYNTHIA
  Warning Sign   (86) 465
CARLIN, LYNN
  Taking Off [1971]   (86) 545
CARLISLE, ANNE
  Liquid Sky   (84) 487
CARLOS, ERIC
  Little Jerk [1984]   (86) 450
CARLSON, JEFF
  Slap Shot [1977]   (82) 467
CARLSON, KAREN
  Fleshburn   (85) 519
CARLSON, LES
  Videodrome   (84) 452
CARLSON, RICHARD
  Creature from the Black Lagoon, The
    [1954]   (82) 422

CARLSON, STEVE
  Slap Shot [1977]   (82) 467
CARLUCCI, MILLY
  Hercules II   (86) 446
CARLYLE, AILEEN
  Miracle Woman, The [1931]   (83) 473
CARMEN, DAWN
  Marie   (86) 227
CARMET, JEAN
  Circle of Deceit [1981]   (83) 419
CARNEY, ART
  Firestarter   (85) 519
CAROL, SUE
  "Obituaries"   (83) 529
CARON, LESLIE
  Dangerous Moves [1984]   (86) 129
  Imperative [1982]   (86) 447
  "Life Achievement Award"   (86) 7
CARR, GEORGIE
  Phar Lap   (85) 528
CARRADINE, DAVID
  Lone Wolf McQuade   (84) 488
CARRADINE, JOHN
  Howling, The   (82) 207
  Ice Pirates, The   (85) 523
  Klynham Summer   (84) 487
  Man Hunt [1941]   (85) 570
  Secret of NIMH, The   (83) 288
CARRADINE, KEITH
  Choose Me   (85) 135
  Maria's Lovers   (86) 451
  Pretty Baby [1978]   (85) 597
  Southern Comfort   (82) 332
  Trouble in Mind   (86) 388
CARRADINE, ROBERT
  Heartaches [1981]   (83) 197
  Just the Way You Are   (85) 524
  Revenge of the Nerds   (85) 530
  Tag   (83) 429
  Wavelength   (84) 497
CARRERA, BARBARA
  I, the Jury   (83) 423
  Lone Wolf McQuade   (84) 488
  Wild Geese II   (86) 466
CARREY, JIM
  Once Bitten   (86) 455
CARRICO, MONICA
  Running Hot   (85) 531
CARRIERE, MATHIEU
  Bad Boy, The   (86) 437
  Woman in Flames, A   (85) 538
CARRILLO, ELPIDIA
  Beyond the Limit   (84) 479
CARRILLO, LEO
  History Is Made at Night [1937]   (84) 542
  Too Hot to Handle [1938]   (84) 596
CARRINGTON, JIM
  City Girl, The   (85) 516
CARRIVE, PIERRE
  Dernier Combat, Le [1983]   (85) 517
CARROLL, LEO G.
  Snows of Kilimanjaro, The [1952]   (83) 498
CARROLL, LISA HART
  Moving Violations   (86) 453
  Terms of Endearment   (84) 414

CARRY, JULIUS J., III
  Berry Gordy's The Last Dragon   (86) 438
CARSON, HUNTER
  Paris, Texas   (85) 359
CARSON, JACK
  Hard Way, The [1942]   (85) 555
  Roughly Speaking [1945]   (83) 490
  Star Is Born, A [1954]   (84) 573
CARTER, JASON
  King David   (86) 449
CARTER, JIM
  Private Function, A [1984]   (86) 280
  Rustler's Rhapsody   (86) 458
  Top Secret   (85) 536
CARTER, THOMAS
  Whose Life Is It Anyway?   (82) 378
CARTER, T. K.
  Southern Comfort   (82) 332
  Thing, The   (83) 343
CARTIER, JACQUES
  King of Jazz [1930]   (86) 515
CARTWRIGHT, LYNN
  Lovelines   (85) 525
CARTWRIGHT, NANCY
  Twilight Zone—The Movie   (84) 435
CARTWRIGHT, VERONICA
  Nightmares   (84) 490
  Right Stuff, The   (84) 342
CARUSO, DAVID
  First Blood   (83) 164
  Thief of Hearts   (85) 536
CARVANA, HUGO
  Bar Esperanza [1983]   (86) 437
CARVER, BRENT
  Cross Country   (84) 481
CASADOS, ELOY
  Cloak and Dagger   (85) 516
CASE, ANNA
  "Obituaries"   (85) 658
CASE, JUSTIN
  Return to Oz   (86) 458
CASEY, BERNIE
  Man Who Fell to Earth, The [1975]   (83) 469
  Never Say Never Again   (84) 252
  Revenge of the Nerds   (85) 530
  Sharky's Machine   (82) 324
CASH, ROSALIND
  Wrong Is Right   (83) 403
CASHIER, ISIDORE
  Light Ahead, The [1939]   (83) 460
CASHIER, JENNY
  Light Ahead, The [1939]   (83) 460
CASSAGNE, MICHEL
  Death of Mario Ricci, The [1983]   (86) 133
CASSAVETES, JOHN
  Incubus, The [1980]   (83) 424
  Love Streams   (85) 293
  Marvin & Tige   (84) 489
  Tempest   (83) 331
  Whose Life Is It Anyway?   (82) 378
CASSEL, JEAN-PIERRE
  Trout, The [1982]   (84) 496
  Vie Continue, La [1981]   (83) 430

CASSEL, SEYMOUR
  Love Streams   (85) 293
CASSIDY, JOANNA
  Blade Runner   (83) 76
  Under Fire   (84) 441
CASSIDY, PATRICK
  Just the Way You Are   (85) 524
CASSINELLI, CLAUDIO
  Hercules II   (86) 446
CASTAINIE, JEAN-MICHEL
  Dernier Combat, Le [1983]   (85) 517
CASTLE, JOHN
  King David   (86) 449
CASTRO, ANALIA
  Official Story, The   (86) 249
CATES, PHOEBE
  Fast Times at Ridgemont High   (83) 1!
  Gremlins   (85) 230
  Paradise   (83) 426
  Private School   (84) 491
CATTRALL, KIM
  City Limits   (86) 440
  Police Academy   (85) 529
  Porky's   (83) 267
  Turk 182   (86) 464
CAUCHY, DANIEL
  Bob le Flambeur [1955]   (84) 526
CAULFIELD, MAXWELL
  Grease 2   (83) 422
CAUSEY, MATTHEW
  Party Animal   (86) 455
CAVALLO, VICTOR
  Tragedy of a Ridiculous Man [1981]   361
CAZENOVE, CHRISTOPHER
  Eye of the Needle   (82) 148
  Heat and Dust [1982]   (84) 187
  Until September   (85) 537
CECCALDI, DANIEL
  Plouffe, Les   (86) 456
CECCHI, NANA
  Ladyhawke   (86) 214
CEDAR, LARRY
  Dreamscape   (85) 166
CEDERNA, GIUSEPPE
  Henry IV [1983]   (86) 446
CEI, PINA
  Joke of Destiny, A [1983]   (85) 259
  Traviata, La   (83) 366
CELIK, HIKMET
  Yol   (83) 411
CELLIER, CAROLINE
  Little Jerk [1984]   (86) 450
CELLIER, PETER
  And the Ship Sails On [1983]   (85) 6!
CERBONNET, FRÉDÉRIQUE
  Loulou [1980]   (82) 226
CERDAN, MARCEL, JR.
  Edith and Marcel [1983]   (85) 518
CERINI, LIVIA
  Joke of Destiny, A [1983]   (85) 259
CERVAL, CLAUDE
  Bob le Flambeur [1955]   (84) 526

CESAK, BRIAN
Fandango (86) 442
CHADWICK, JUNE
Forbidden World (83) 421
This Is Spinal Tap (85) 484
CHAGAS, WALMOR
Xica [1976] (83) 407
CHAMBERLAIN, HOWLAND
"Obituaries" (85) 658
CHAMBERLAIN, RICHARD
King Solomon's Mines (86) 449
CHAMBERLAIN, WILT
Conan the Destroyer (85) 516
CHAMBERLIN, LEE
Beat Street (85) 512
CHAMBERLIN, MARK
Ghost Story (82) 183
CHAMBERS, MICHAEL "BOOGALOO
SHRIMP"
Breakin' (85) 514
Breakin' 2 (85) 514
CHAMPANE, PATRICIA
Entre nous [1983] (85) 176
CHAN, JACKIE
Cannonball Run II (85) 514
CHANDLER, GEORGE
"Obituaries" (86) 565
CHANNING, STOCKARD
Without a Trace (84) 498
CHAPIN, MILES
Buddy Buddy (82) 93
Funny Farm (84) 484
Get Crazy (84) 484
CHAPLIN, GERALDINE
Bolero [1981] (83) 418
CHAPMAN, GRAHAM
Monty Python's The Meaning of Life (84) 489
Yellowbeard (84) 498
CHARBIT, CORYNNE
Goat, The [1981] (86) 444
CHARDIET, JON
Beat Street (85) 512
CHARDONS, LATOU
Henry IV [1983] (86) 446
CHARLES, FRANCISCO
Sugar Cane Alley [1983] (85) 461
CHARLESON, IAN
Chariots of Fire (82) 101
Gandhi (83) 183
CHARNEY, JORDON
Ghostbusters (85) 219
CHARNO, STUART
Christine (84) 106
Just One of the Guys (86) 448
CHASE, BARRIE
Flight of the Phoenix, The [1966] (85) 549
CHASE, CHEVY
Deal of the Century (84) 482
Fletch (86) 169
National Lampoon's European Vacation (86) 453
National Lampoon's Vacation (84) 242
Sesame Street Presents: Follow That Bird (86) 459
Spies like Us (86) 360

CHASE, ILKA
Animal Kingdom, The [1932] (86) 469
CHATTERJEE, BIMAL
Home and the World, The [1984] (86) 447
CHATTERJEE, SOUMITRA
Home and the World, The [1984] (86) 447
CHATTERJEE, SWATIKLEKHA
Home and the World, The [1984] (86) 447
CHATTO, DANIEL
Quartet (82) 296
CHAUMETTE, MONIQUE
Sunday in the Country, A (85) 466
CHAUVEAU, LAETITIA
Adolescente, L' [1979] (83) 53
CHAUVIN, LILYAN
Silent Night, Deadly Night (85) 532
CHAUVIN, MARTINE
Bal, Le [1983] (85) 80
CHAVES, RICHARD
Cease Fire (86) 440
CHAYETTE, JEFF
Cave Girl (86) 439
CHAYKIN, MAURY
Def-Con 4 (86) 441
Harry and Son (85) 521
CHAZEL, MARIE-ANNE
Next Year if All Goes Well (84) 490
CHEKHOV, MICHAEL
Specter of the Rose [1946] (83) 504
CHEMINEAU, SOPHIE
Trace, The [1983] (85) 537
CHENG, LYDIA
Pumping Iron II (86) 456
CHER
Come Back to the 5 & Dime Jimmy Dean,
Jimmy Dean (83) 120
Mask (86) 231
Silkwood (84) 367
CHEREAU, PATRICE
Danton [1982] (84) 121
CHERVIAKOV, EVGENI
New Babylon, The [1929] (84) 561
CHERWIN, TOM
Smithereens (83) 307
CHESHIRE, ELIZABETH
Melvin and Howard [1980] (82) 453
CHEUNG, GEORGE KEE
Rambo: First Blood Part II (86) 299
CHEW, KIM
Dim Sum (86) 141
CHEW, LAUREEN
Dim Sum (86) 141
CHEY, EDWARD ENTERO
Killing Fields, The (85) 270
CHEY, KATHERINE KRAPUM
Killing Fields, The (85) 270
CHIAO, ROY
Indiana Jones and the Temple of
Doom (85) 253
CHIBAS, MARISSA
Cold Feet (85) 516
CHIFFRE, YVAN
Cheech and Chong's The Corsican
Brothers (85) 515

CHILDS, TRACY
Richard's Things (82) 321
CHILES, GEORGE
King of Jazz [1930] (86) 515
CHILES, LINDEN
Cloak and Dagger (85) 516
CHILES, LOIS
Way We Were, The [1973] (82) 474
CHILVERS, SIMON
Test of Love (86) 462
CHIMENTO, ROBERT
Fleshburn (85) 519
CHOATE, TIM
Def-Con 4 (86) 441
Ghost Story (82) 183
CHONG, RAE DAWN
American Flyers (86) 436
Beat Street (85) 512
Cheech and Chong's The Corsican
Brothers (85) 515
Choose Me (85) 135
City Limits (86) 440
Color Purple, The (86) 105
Commando (86) 111
Quest for Fire (83) 271
CHONG, ROBBI
Cheech and Chong's The Corsican
Brothers (85) 515
CHONG, THOMAS
After Hours (86) 51
Cheech and Chong Still Smokin' (84) 480
Cheech and Chong's The Corsican
Brothers (85) 515
Things Are Tough All Over (83) 430
Yellowbeard (84) 498
CHOPEL, FARID
My Best Friend's Girl [1983] (85) 326
Patsy, The (86) 456
CHORNY, ALEXANDER
Jazzman (85) 523
CHOY, KEITH
Dim Sum (86) 141
CHRISTIE, JULIE
Heat and Dust [1982] (84) 187
Return of the Soldier, The [1982] (84)
332
CHRISTIE, MARCIA
Sure Thing, The (86) 369
CHRISTMAS, ERIC
Philadelphia Experiment, The (85) 529
CHRISTOPHER, DENNIS
Chariots of Fire (82) 101
Don't Cry, It's Only Thunder (83) 420
CHRISTOPHER, PASCALE
Piaf [1980] (83) 427
CHUBB, PAUL
Coca-Cola Kid, The (86) 440
CHUNG, IDA F.O.
Dim Sum (86) 141
CHUNG, WONG
Barbary Coast [1935] (84) 506
CHURCHILL, DONALD
Victim [1961] (85) 647
CHURCHILL, SARAH
"Obituaries" (83) 530
Royal Wedding [1951] (86) 536

CIANNELLI, EDUARDO
Lost Moment, The [1947] (83) 465
CIESLAK, PIOTR
Man of Marble [1977] (82) 234
CIFARELLI, LESLIE
Rent Control (85) 530
CILENTO, DIANE
Hombre [1967] (84) 547
Wicker Man, The [1974] (86) 555
CINFRON, MONIQUE
Fast Forward (86) 442
CIOFFI, CHARLES
All the Right Moves (84) 41
Missing (83) 232
Remo Williams (86) 457
Time After Time [1979] (84) 579
CISARANO, PATRICIA
Skyline (85) 533
CITTI, FRANCO
Oedipus Rex [1967] (85) 528
CLAIRE, INA
"Obituaries" (86) 565
CLANTON, RONY
Rappin' (86) 457
CLAPP, GORDON
Return of the Secaucus 7 [1980] (83) 484
CLARIDGE, CHRISTIE
Gotcha! (86) 444
CLARK, CANDY
Amityville 3-D (84) 479
Blue Thunder (84) 84
Man Who Fell to Earth, The [1975] (83)
469
Stephen King's Cat's Eye (86) 460
CLARK, CHRISTIE
Nightmare on Elm Street, Part 2, A (86) 454
CLARK, DORT
Bells Are Ringing [1960] (84) 517
CLARK, FRED
Bells Are Ringing [1960] (84) 517
Solid Gold Cadillac, The [1956] (85) 615
CLARK, GERRY
That Sinking Feeling [1979] (85) 536
CLARK, LIDDY
Kitty and the Bagman [1982] (84) 487
Test of Love (86) 462
CLARK, MATT
Adventures of Buckaroo Banzai,
The (85) 47
Country (85) 156
Honkytonk Man (83) 200
Love Letters (85) 288
Return to Oz (86) 458
Tuff Turf (86) 464
CLARK, ROGER
Detour [1946] (86) 498
CLARK, RUSSELL
Body Rock (85) 513
CLARK, SUSAN
Porky's (83) 267
CLARKE, A. J.
Hit, The (86) 446
CLARKE, BASIL
Where the Green Ants Dream [1984] (86) 465

CLARKE, CAITLIN
Dragonslayer (82) 125
CLARKE, HOPE
Beat Street (85) 512
CLARKE, LOGAN
Sweet Sixteen (85) 535
CLARKE, WARREN
Firefox (83) 160
Lassiter (85) 524
CLARKSON, LANA
Deathstalker (85) 517
CLAY, ANDREW
Making the Grade (85) 526
CLAY, JENNIFER
Suburbia (85) 534
CLAY, JUANIN
WarGames (84) 458
CLAY, NICHOLAS
Excalibur (82) 144
CLAYBURGH, JILL
First Monday in October (82) 151
Hanna K. (84) 177
I'm Dancing as Fast as I Can (83) 423
CLAYTON, JAN
"Obituaries" (84) 614
CLAYTON, MERRY
Blame It on the Night (85) 512
CLEESE, JOHN
Great Muppet Caper, The (82) 187
Monty Python's The Meaning of Life (84) 489
Silverado (86) 349
Time Bandits [1980] (82) 364
CLEMENS, PAUL
Beast Within, The (83) 418
They're Playing with Fire (85) 536
CLEMENT, AURORE
Invitation au voyage [1982] (84) 486
Paris, Texas (85) 359
CLEMENTI, PIERRE
Quartet (82) 296
CLEMENTO, STEVE
Most Dangerous Game, The [1932] (86) 519
CLEMONS, CLARENCE
New York, New York [1977] (84) 187
CLENNON, DAVID
Falling in Love (85) 519
Hanna K. (84) 177
Missing (83) 232
Star 80 (84) 374
Sweet Dreams (86) 374
Thing, The (83) 343
CLER, ANDRE
Argent, L' [1983] (85) 74
CLER, CLAUDE
Argent, L' [1983] (85) 74
CLERY, CORINNE
Yor (84) 498
CLEVELAND, GEORGE
It Happened Tomorrow [1944] (84) 552
CLEVELAND, JAMES, AND THE
SOUTHERN CALIFORNIA CHOIR
Gospel (85) 520
CLEVER, EDITH
Adolescente, L' [1979] (83) 53
Parsifal (84) 491

CLIFFORD, COLLEEN
Careful He Might Hear You [1983] (85) 130
Where the Green Ants Dream [1984] (86) 465
CLIFFORD, VERONICA
Secret Places [1984] (86) 459
CLIFT, MONTGOMERY
Freud [1962] (85) 535
CLINTON, JACK R.
No Small Affair (85) 527
CLIVE, COLIN
History Is Made at Night [1937] (84) 542
CLIVER, AL
Black Cat, The (85) 512
CLOSE, GLENN
Big Chill, The (84) 78
Jagged Edge (86) 190
Maxie (86) 452
Natural, The (85) 329
Stone Boy, The (85) 450
World According to Garp, The (83) 397
CLOUGH, JOHN SCOTT
Fast Forward (86) 442
CLUZET, FRANÇOIS
Horse of Pride, The (86) 447
COAD, JOYCE
Scarlet Letter, The [1927] (85) 602
COBANOIGLU, NECMETTIN
Yol (83) 411
COBBS, BILL
Brother from Another Planet, The (85) 118
COBURN, CHARLES
H. M. Pulham, Esq. [1941] (82) 439
COCA, IMOGENE
National Lampoon's Vacation (84) 242
COCCIOLETTI, PHIL
Love Letters (85) 288
COCHRANE, IAN
Bolero (85) 513
COCKBURN, DAISY
Secrets (85) 532
COCO, JAMES
Only When I Laugh (82) 268
COE, GEORGE
Entity, The (84) 483
Flash of Green, A (86) 443
Micki & Maude (85) 308
Remo Williams (86) 457
COFFEY, DENISE
Another Time, Another Place [1983] (85) 510
COHEN, ALEXANDER H.
Purple Rose of Cairo, The (86) 290
COHEN, JEFF B.
Goonies, The (86) 176
COHEN, JEFFREY JAY
Secret Admirer (86) 459
COHEN, JOEL
Silver City [1984] (86) 460
COHEN, JULIE
Once upon a Time in America (85) 345
COLAS, DANIEL
My Best Friend's Girl [1983] (85) 326
COLASANTO, NICHOLAS
"Obituaries" (86) 565

COLBERT, CLAUDETTE
Sign of the Cross, The [1932]   (85) 607
COLE, ALEXANDRA
Dr. Butcher, M.D. [1980]   (83) 420
COLEMAN, DABNEY
Cloak and Dagger   (85) 516
Man with One Red Shoe, The   (86) 451
On Golden Pond   (82) 263
Tootsie   (83) 353
WarGames   (84) 458
COLEMAN, GARY
Jimmy the Kid   (84) 486
COLEMAN, JOEY
Lost in America   (86) 219
COLERIDGE, SYLVIA
Secret Places [1984]   (86) 459
COLES, CHARLES "HONI"
Cotton Club, The   (85) 150
COLICOS, JOHN
Postman Always Rings Twice, The   (82) 284
COLLET, CHRISTOPHER
Firstborn   (85) 519
COLLEY, KENNETH
And Nothing but the Truth   (85) 510
Firefox   (83) 160
THX 1138 [1971]   (85) 638
COLLIER, PATIENCE
French Lieutenant's Woman, The   (82) 174
COLLIGAN, JOE
Starchaser   (86) 460
COLLIN, JOHN
Tess [1980]   (82) 471
COLLINS, ALAN
Hunters of the Golden Cobra, The [1982]   (85) 523
Last Hunter, The   (85) 525
COLLINS, JOAN
Homework   (83) 422
COLLINS, LEWIS
Final Option, The   (84) 484
COLLINS, RAY
Roughly Speaking [1945]   (83) 490
COLLINS, ROBERTA
Hardbodies   (85) 521
School Spirit   (86) 458
COLLINS, STEPHEN
Brewster's Millions   (86) 438
COLLODEL, DAUREEN
Weekend Pass   (85) 537
COLMAN, RONALD
"Interview with Lillian Gish, An"   (83) 26
White Sister, The [1923]   (83) 26
COLOMBY, SCOTT
Porky's   (83) 267
COLON, ALEX
Invasion U.S.A.   (86) 447
COLUCHE
My Best Friend's Girl [1983]   (85) 326
COMBS, JEFFREY
Re-Animator   (86) 457
COMI, PAUL
Best Defense   (85) 512

CONDE, EDUARDO
Emerald Forest, The   (86) 156
CONLON, NOEL
Fast Forward   (86) 442
CONLON, TOMMY
Sign of the Cross, The [1932]   (85) 607
CONNART, JEAN-PAUL
Balance, La [1982]   (84) 52
CONNELLY, CHRISTOPHER
Liar's Moon   (83) 424
1990   (84) 491
CONNELLY, JENNIFER
Once upon a Time in America   (85) 345
CONNERY, SEAN
Five Days One Summer   (83) 421
Never Say Never Again   (84) 252
Outland   (82) 272
Time Bandits [1980]   (82) 364
Wrong Is Right   (83) 403
CONNOLLY, BILLY
Bullshot [1983]   (86) 439
CONNOLLY, WALTER
Too Hot to Handle [1938]   (84) 596
CONNORS, MIKE
Too Scared to Scream   (86) 463
CONRAD, MICHAEL
Cattle Annie and Little Britches   (82) 97
"Obituaries"   (84) 614
CONRAD, ROBERT
Wrong Is Right   (83) 403
CONROY, JARLATH
Day of the Dead   (86) 441
CONSIDINE, JOHN
Trouble in Mind   (86) 388
CONSTANTINE, EDDIE
Long Good Friday, The [1980]   (83) 220
CONTI, MARIE-CATHERINE
Until September   (85) 537
CONTI, TOM
American Dreamer   (85) 509
Merry Christmas, Mr. Lawrence   (84) 231
Reuben, Reuben   (84) 337
CONTRERAS, PATRICIO
Official Story, The   (86) 249
CONVERSE-ROBERTS, WILLIAM
1918   (86) 454
CONWAY, KEVIN
Flashpoint   (85) 519
CONWAY, LYLE
Return to Oz   (86) 458
CONWAY, TIM
Cannonball Run II   (85) 514
CONWELL, CAROLYN
Torn Curtain [1966]   (85) 644
COOGAN, JACKIE
"Obituaries"   (85) 660
COOK, CAROLE
Grandview, U.S.A.   (85) 520
Sixteen Candles   (85) 532
COOK, CLYDE
Barbary Coast [1935]   (84) 506
"Obituaries"   (85) 661
COOK, ELISHA, JR.
Hammett   (84) 174

COOK, PETER
Hound of the Baskervilles, The
[1978]   (82) 203
Supergirl   (85) 535
Yellowbeard   (84) 498
COOK, RODERICK
Silent Madness   (85) 532
COOLEN, CEES
Question of Silence, A   (85) 530
COOMBES, JAMES
King David   (86) 449
COONEY, KEVIN
Trip to Bountiful, The   (86) 383
COOPER, BOBBY
My Reputation [1946]   (85) 586
COOPER, GARRY
Kipperbang [1983]   (85) 524
COOPER, GARY
Peter Ibbetson [1935]   (86) 527
COOPER, JACKIE
Superman II   (82) 339
Superman III   (84) 399
COOPER, TERENCE
Beyond Reasonable Doubt [1980]   (84) 74
Heart of a Stag   (85) 522
Sylvia   (86) 462
COOPER, THOMAS
"Obituaries"   (83) 530
COOTE, ROBERT
"Obituaries"   (83) 530
COPELAND, MAURICE
Arthur   (82) 71
COPELAND, ROGER
River Rat, The   (85) 531
COPLESTON, GEOFFREY
Black Cat, The   (85) 512
COPLEY, PETER
Victim [1961]   (85) 649
CORBETT, HARRY H.
"Obituaries"   (83) 531
CORBIN, BARRY
Hard Traveling   (86) 445
Honkytonk Man   (83) 200
Man Who Loved Women, The   (84) 218
My Science Project   (86) 453
WarGames   (84) 458
CORDAY, MARCELLE
Scarlet Letter, The [1927]   (85) 602
CORDEN, HENRY
Secret Life of Walter Mitty, The [1947]   (86) 540
COREY, ISABEL
Bob le Flambeur [1955]   (84) 526
COREY, JEFF
Conan the Destroyer   (85) 516
Creator   (86) 441
CORFMAN, CARIS
Dreamchild   (86) 146
CORKILL, DANNY
D.A.R.Y.L.   (86) 441
Mrs. Soffel   (85) 314
CORLEY, PAT
Against All Odds   (85) 509
CORMAN, ROGER
State of Things, The   (84) 379

CORNWALL, ANNE
Dulcy [1923]   (82) 432
CORNWELL, JUDY
Santa Claus   (86) 334
CORRI, NICK
Gotcha!   (86) 444
Nightmare on Elm Street, A   (85) 527
CORT, BUD
Brewster McCloud [1970]   (86) 484
Love Letters   (85) 288
Maria's Lovers   (86) 451
COSTA, COSIE
Missing in Action 2   (86) 452
COSTELLO, MARICLARE
Nightmares   (84) 490
COSTELLO, MARK
Hotdog . . . The Movie   (85) 522
COSTNER, KEVIN
American Flyers   (86) 436
Fandango   (86) 442
Silverado   (86) 349
Testament   (84) 420
COTTEN, JOSEPH
Heaven's Gate   (82) 195
Journey into Fear [1943]   (86) 511
COTTENCON, FANNY
Étoile du nord, L'   (84) 484
COTTERILL, RALPH
Where the Green Ants Dream [1984]   (86) 465
COTTON, OLIVER
Eleni   (86) 151
COULTER, JACK
Kerouac, the Movie   (86) 448
COURBOIS, KITTY
Flesh and Blood   (86) 443
COURTENAY, TOM
Dresser, The   (84) 130
COURTNEY, ALEX
Enter the Ninja   (83) 420
COUSINEAU-ARNDT, MAGGIE
Return of the Secaucus 7 [1980]   (83) 484
COVIC, JELENA
When Father Was Away on Business [1984]   (86) 411
COWAN, CLAUDIA
Lovelines   (85) 525
COWAN, DAVID
Stephen King's Children of the Corn   (85) 534
COWAN, JEROME
Unfaithful, The [1947]   (86) 550
COWARD, DENISE
Sudden Death   (86) 461
COWGILL, BRAD
Gotcha!   (86) 444
COWIE, SUSANNE
Heart of a Stag   (85) 522
COWPER, GERALDINE
Wicker Man, The [1974]   (86) 555
COWPER, NICOLA
Dreamchild   (86) 146
COX, ALAN
Young Sherlock Holmes   (86) 431
COX, PAUL
Where the Green Ants Dream [1984]   (86) 465

COX, RICHARD
  Oasis, The   (85) 528
COX, RONNY
  Beast Within, The   (83) 418
  Beverly Hills Cop   (85) 88
  Some Kind of Hero   (83) 428
  Taps   (82) 343
  Vision Quest   (86) 464
COX, SURA
  Fool for Love   (86) 172
COYNE, BILL
  Suburbia   (85) 534
COYOTE, PETER
  Cross Creek   (84) 116
  E.T.: The Extra-Terrestrial   (83) 151
  Jagged Edge   (86) 190
  Legend of Billie Jean, The   (86) 450
  Slayground [1983]   (85) 533
  Southern Comfort   (82) 332
  Stranger's Kiss   (85) 534
  Timerider   (84) 495
CRABBE, LARRY "BUSTER"
  "Obituaries"   (84) 614
CRAIG, JAMES
  "Obituaries"   (86) 565
CRAMER, GRANT
  Hardbodies   (85) 521
CRAMPTON, BARBARA
  Fraternity Vacation   (86) 444
  Re-Animator   (86) 457
CRANE, STEVEN
  "Obituaries"   (86) 566
CRAVEN, FRANK
  Barbary Coast [1935]   (84) 506
CRAVEN, GEMMA
  Wagner   (84) 497
CRAWFORD, KATHRYN
  King of Jazz [1930]   (86) 515
CRAWFORD, MARTHA
  Fool for Love   (86) 172
CREER, ERICA
  Great Muppet Caper, The   (82) 187
CRELEY, JACK
  Videodrome   (84) 452
CRENNA, RICHARD
  Body Heat   (82) 87
  First Blood   (83) 164
  Flamingo Kid, The   (85) 192
  Rambo: First Blood Part II   (86) 299
  Summer Rental   (86) 462
  Table for Five   (84) 404
CRIMAN, DENIS
  Gregory's Girl [1981]   (83) 193
CRIPPA, MADDALENA
  Three Brothers [1980]   (83) 349
CRISP, DONALD
  Long Gray Line, The [1955]   (82) 447
CRISP, QUENTIN
  Bride, The   (86) 438
CRISTOFER, MICHAEL
  Little Drummer Girl, The   (85) 525
CRITTENDEN, JAMES
  Philadelphia Experiment, The   (85) 529
CROFT, COLIN
  Wild Duck, The [1983]   (86) 466

CROISET, HANS
  Question of Silence, A   (85) 530
CROMWELL, JAMES
  Explorers   (86) 442
  Tank   (85) 535
CRON, CLAUDIA
  Diner   (83) 142
  Running Brave   (84) 354
CRONOGUE, MARK
  Cold Feet   (85) 516
CRONYN, HUME
  Arrangement, The [1969]   (86) 474
  Brewster's Millions   (86) 438
  Cocoon   (86) 96
  Honky Tonk Freeway   (82) 199
  Impulse   (85) 523
  World According to Garp, The   (83) 397
CROSBIE, ANNETTE
  Ordeal by Innocence [1984]   (86) 455
CROSBY, BING
  Holiday Inn [1942]   (82) 443
  King of Jazz [1930]   (86) 515
CROSBY, DON
  "Obituaries"   (86) 566
CROSBY, MARY
  Ice Pirates, The   (85) 523
CROSS, BEN
  Chariots of Fire   (82) 101
CROSS, HARLEY
  Mrs. Soffel   (85) 314
CROSSON, ROBERT
  Mike's Murder   (85) 526
CROTHERS, SCATMAN
  Deadly Eyes   (84) 482
  Journey of Natty Gann, The   (86) 203
  Twilight Zone—The Movie   (84) 435
CROUSE, LINDSAY
  Daniel   (84) 481
  Iceman   (85) 248
  Places in the Heart   (85) 371
  Prince of the City   (82) 292
  Slap Shot [1977]   (82) 467
  Verdict, The   (83) 377
CROWDEN, GRAHAM
  Brittania Hospital   (84) 480
  Company of Wolves,The [1984]   (86) 115
  Missionary, The   (83) 233
CROWLEY, ED
  Witness   (86) 421
CRUISE, TOM
  All the Right Moves   (84) 41
  Losin' It   (84) 488
  Outsiders, The   (84) 282
  Risky Business   (84) 349
  Taps   (82) 343
CRUTCHLEY, ROSALIE
  Freud [1962]   (84) 535
CRUTTENDEN, ABIGAIL
  Kipperbang [1983]   (85) 524
CRUZ, ERNESTO GOMEZ
  Erendira [1983]   (85) 181
  Norte, El   (84) 265
CRYER, JON
  No Small Affair   (85) 527
CSERHALMI, GYÖRGY
  Mephisto   (82) 237

119

CUDNEY, ROGER
Evil That Men Do, The   (85) 518
CULP, ROBERT
Turk 182   (86) 464
CULVER, MICHAEL
Passage to India, A   (85) 365
CULVER, RONALD
Missionary, The   (83) 233
"Obituaries"   (85) 661
CUMMINGS, ROBERT
Lost Moment, The [1947]   (83) 465
CUMMINGS, RUTH
"Obituaries"   (85) 661
CUMMINS, JULIETTE
Running Hot   (85) 531
CUNNINGHAM, NEIL
Draughtsman's Contract, The [1982]   (84) 126
CUNY, ALAIN
Basileus Quartet   (85) 511
Detective   (86) 442
CURRAN, ADRIAN
Once upon a Time in America   (85) 345
CURRIE, CHERIE
Wavelength   (84) 497
CURRIER, TERRENCE
Blow Out   (82) 83
CURRIN, BRENDA
World According to Garp, The   (83) 397
CURRIN, LYNETTE
Caddie [1976]   (83) 439
CURRY, CHRISTOPHER
C.H.U.D.   (85) 515
CURRY, TIM
Annie   (83) 56
Clue   (86) 440
Ploughman's Lunch, The [1983]   (85) 377
CURTIN, ROBERT
Cloak and Dagger   (85) 516
CURTIN, VALERIE
Maxie   (86) 452
CURTIS, JAMIE LEE
Grandview, U.S.A.   (85) 520
Love Letters   (85) 288
Perfect   (86) 456
Trading Places   (84) 430
CURTIS, KEENE
Buddy System, The   (85) 514
CURTIS, LIANA
Sixteen Candles   (85) 532
CURTIS, ROBIN
Star Trek III—The Search for Spock   (85) 439
CURTIS, TONY
Insignificance   (86) 447
CURZI, PIERRE
Plouffe, Les   (86) 456
CUSACK, CYRIL
1984   (85) 335
True Confessions   (82) 368
CUSACK, JOHN
Better Off Dead   (86) 438
Journey of Natty Gann, The   (86) 203

Sixteen Candles   (85) 532
Sure Thing, The   (86) 369
CUSHING, PETER
Top Secret   (85) 536
CUTELL, LOU
Pee-wee's Big Adventure   (86) 265
CUTT, TIMOTHY J.
Alley Cat   (85) 509
CVETKOVIC, SVETOZAR
Montenegro   (82) 250

D'ABO, OLIVIA
Bolero   (85) 513
Conan the Destroyer   (85) 516
DAFOE, WILLEM
Loveless, The   (85) 525
Streets of Fire   (85) 534
To Live and Die in L.A.   (86) 379
D'AGOSTINO, ANTONELLA
Joke of Destiny, A [1983]   (85) 259
DAIKOS, THOMAS PETER
World According to Garp, The   (83) 397
DAILY, ELIZABETH
Fandango   (86) 442
No Small Affair   (85) 527
Pee-wee's Big Adventure   (86) 265
Valley Girl   (84) 447
DALE, CYNTHIA
Heavenly Bodies   (85) 522
DALE, DAPHNE
Invitation to the Dance [1956]   (86) 507
DALE, ESTHER
North Star, The [1943]   (83) 476
DALE, JENNIFER
Of Unknown Origin   (84) 491
DALE, JIM
Scandalous   (85) 532
DALIO, MARCEL
"Obituaries"   (84) 617
DALLESANDRO, JOE
Cotton Club, The   (85) 150
DALTON, AUDREY
My Cousin Rachel [1952]   (82) 458
DALTON, DARREN
Joy of Sex   (85) 524
Outsiders, The   (84) 282
Red Dawn   (85) 530
DALTON, TIMOTHY
Agatha [1979]   (83) 435
Doctor and the Devils, The   (86) 442
DALY, TIMOTHY
Diner   (83) 142
Just the Way You Are   (85) 524
DALY, TYNE
Aviator, The   (86) 437
Movers and Shakers   (86) 453
Zoot Suit   (82) 389
DAMIANI, DONATELLA
City of Women   (82) 106
DAMITA, LILY
Bridge of San Luis Rey, The [1929]   (82) 408
DAMMETT, BLACKIE
9 Deaths of the Ninja   (86) 454

D'AMORE, RENATO
Softly Softly [1984] (86) 460
DANA, ROD
Ladyhawke (86) 214
DANARE, MALCOLM
Christine (84) 106
Heaven Help Us (86) 445
DANCE, CHARLES
Plenty (86) 271
DANE, KARL
Scarlet Letter, The [1927] (85) 602
DANE, LAWRENCE
Of Unknown Origin (84) 491
D'ANGELO, BEVERLY
Finders Keepers (85) 519
Honky Tonk Freeway (82) 199
National Lampoon's European Vacation (86) 453
National Lampoon's Vacation (84) 242
D'ANGELO, MIRELLA
Hercules (84) 485
DANGERFIELD, RODNEY
Easy Money (84) 482
DANIEL, SUSAN
Bizet's Carmen [1983] (85) 98
DANIELI, ISA
Macaroni (86) 451
Softly Softly [1984] (86) 460
DANIELL, HENRY
Mutiny on the Bounty [1962] (85) 581
DANIELS, ANTHONY
Return of the Jedi (84) 326
DANIELS, JEFF
Marie (86) 227
Purple Rose of Cairo, The (86) 290
Terms of Endearment (84) 414
DANIELS, PHIL
Bride, The (86) 438
DANIELS, RUDY
Philadelphia Experiment, The (85) 529
DANKER, ELI
Little Drummer Girl, The (85) 525
DANNA, ANTHONY
Hard Traveling (86) 445
DANNELL, DENNIS
Another State of Mind (85) 510
DANNER, BLYTHE
Man, Woman and Child (84) 489
DANNING, SYBIL
Chained Heat (84) 480
Hercules (84) 485
They're Playing with Fire (85) 536
DANO, ROYAL
Right Stuff, The (84) 342
Teachers (85) 535
DANSON, TED
Body Heat (82) 87
DANTAS, NELSON
Bar Esperanza [1983] (86) 437
DANTINE, HELMUT
"Obituaries" (83) 531
DANZA, TONY
Cannonball Run II (85) 514

D'ARBANVILLE, PATTI
Real Genius (86) 309
DARBY, KIM
Better Off Dead (86) 438
D'ARCY, JAKE
Gregory's Girl [1981] (83) 193
Sense of Freedom, A (86) 459
D'ARCY, MARY
Stephen King's Cat's Eye (86) 460
DARLING, JOSEPH
No Small Affair (85) 527
DARMON, GERARD
Diva [1980] (83) 147
DARNELL, LINDA
It Happened Tomorrow [1944] (84) 552
DARRIEU, GERARD
Little Jerk [1984] (86) 450
DA SILVA, FERNANDO RAMOS
Pixote [1980] (82) 280
DA SILVA, HOWARD
Garbo Talks (85) 520
Mommie Dearest (82) 245
DAVENPORT, NIGEL
Greystoke (85) 236
Nighthawks (82) 259
DAVI, ROBERT
Goonies, The (86) 176
DAVID, ANGEL
Mixed Blood (86) 452
DAVID, ELEANOR
Comfort and Joy (85) 146
Pink Floyd the Wall [1981] (83) 258
Sylvia (86) 462
DAVID, GERD
Boat Is Full, The [1981] (83) 82
DAVID, KEITH
Thing, The (83) 343
DAVIDSON, JACK
Reuben, Reuben (84) 337
DAVIDSON, WILLIAM B.
I'm No Angel [1933] (85) 561
Most Dangerous Game, The [1932] (86) 519
DAVIES, IRVING
Invitation to the Dance [1956] (86) 507
DAVIES, RACHEL
Private Function, A [1984] (86) 280
DAVIES, STEPHEN
Long Good Friday, The [1980] (83) 220
DAVIS, BRAD
Chariots of Fire (82) 101
Querelle [1982] (84) 313
DAVIS, CAROLE R.
Flamingo Kid, The (85) 192
DAVIS, GEENA
Transylvania 6-5000 (86) 463
DAVIS, GENE
10 to Midnight (84) 495
DAVIS, GEORGE
History Is Made at Night [1937] (84) 542
DAVIS, GUY
Beat Street (85) 512
DAVIS, JIM
"Obituaries" (82) 484

DAVIS, JUDY
  Final Option, The   (84) 484
  Heatwave   (84) 485
  Passage to India, A   (85) 365
  Winter of Our Dreams [1981]   (83) 431
DAVIS, MAC
  Sting II, The   (84) 494
DAVIS, NATHAN
  Code of Silence   (86) 440
  Thief   (82) 356
  Windy City   (85) 538
DAVIS, OSSIE
  Avenging Angel   (86) 436
  Harry and Son   (85) 521
DAVIS, PHILIP
  Bounty, The   (85) 513
DAVIS, SAMMY, JR.
  Cannonball Run II   (85) 514
DAVIS, TIM
  Bambi [1942]   (85) 543
DAVIS, VIVEKA
  Shoot the Moon   (83) 295
DAVISON, BRUCE
  Spies like Us   (86) 360
DAVOLI, GIANDOMENICO
  Oedipus Rex [1967]   (85) 528
DAVOLI, NINETTO
  Oedipus Rex [1967]   (85) 528
DAWSON, PADDY
  James Joyce's Women   (86) 193
  Jigsaw Man, The [1983]   (85) 524
DAX, DANIELLE
  Company of Wolves, The [1984]   (86) 115
DAY, CLAYTON
  Deep in the Heart   (85) 517
DAY, MARCELINE
  Beloved Rogue [1927]   (84) 522
DAY, MORRIS
  Purple Rain   (85) 389
DAY-LEWIS, DANIEL
  Bounty, The   (85) 513
DAZAI, HISAO
  Foster Daddy, Tora! [1980]   (82) 163
DEACON, RICHARD
  "Obituaries"   (85) 662
DE AHNA, KERSTIN
  Little Drummer Girl, The   (85) 525
DEAN, LAURA
  Almost You   (86) 436
DE ANDA, RODOLFO
  Toy Soldiers   (85) 536
DEARDEN, ROBIN
  Stitches   (86) 461
DEBAER, JEAN
  Flash of Green, A   (86) 443
DE BANZIE, BRENDA
  "Obituaries"   (82) 484
DEBANZIE, LOIS
  Annie   (83) 56
  Mass Appeal   (85) 303
DEBELL, KRISTINE
  Tag   (83) 429
DE BENITO, MANUEL
  Hit, The   (86) 446

DE BURGH, CELIA
  Phar Lap   (85) 528
DE CAPITANI, GRACE
  My New Partner [1984]   (86) 246
DE CASALIS, JEANNE
  Nell Gwyn [1934]   (84) 557
DECEA, CLAUDIA
  Alley Cat   (85) 509
DECOMBLE, GUY
  Bob le Flambeur [1955]   (84) 526
DE CORDOVA, FRED
  King of Comedy, The   (84) 192
DEE, FRANCES
  Becky Sharp [1935]   (82) 403
DEE, MAURICE
  Kipperbang [1983]   (85) 524
DEE, PROTACIO
  Hunters of the Golden Cobra, The [1982]   (85) 523
DEE, RUBY
  Cat People   (83) 100
DEEZEN, EDDIE
  Sesame Street Presents: Follow That Bird   (86) 459
  Surf II   (85) 535
DEFORE, DON
  Guy Named Joe, A [1943]   (82) 435
DE FUNÈS, LOUIS
  "Obituaries"   (84) 617
DE HAVILLAND, OLIVIA
  My Cousin Rachel [1952]   (82) 458
DEHNER, JOHN
  Apache [1954]   (82) 395
  Creator   (86) 441
  Jagged Edge   (86) 190
DEITRICH, CINDI
  Out of Control   (86) 455
DE JAGER, NIC
  Gods Must Be Crazy, The [1980]   (85) 224
DE JONG, GEERT
  4th Man, The [1983]   (85) 203
DE KEYSER, DAVID
  King David   (86) 449
DE KOVA, FRANK
  American Pop   (82) 62
DE LA BROSSE, SIMON
  Pauline at the Beach [1982]   (84) 296
DELANEY, KIM
  That Was Then . . . This Is Now   (86) 463
DELANY, DANA
  Almost You   (86) 436
DE LA PAZ, DANNY
  Barbarosa   (83) 60
DELAPP, ROBERT
  Lovelines   (85) 525
DE LA TOUR, FRANCES
  Wombling Free [1979]   (85) 538
DEL LAGO, ALICIA
  Norte, El   (84) 265
DELL'ATTE, ANTONIA
  Softly Softly [1984]   (86) 460
DELMAR, KENNY
  "Obituaries"   (85) 663

DELON, ALAIN
Swann in Love (85) 471
DELONGIS, ANTHONY
Starchaser (86) 460
DELPHY, JULIE
Detective (86) 442
DELRICH, HAL
Evil Dead, The (84) 484
DEL RIO, DOLORES
Journey into Fear [1943] (86) 511
"Obituaries" (84) 617
DEL SOL, LAURA
Carmen (84) 101
Hit, The (86) 446
DELUAL, LILIANE
Bal, Le [1983] (85) 80
DELUCA, RUDY
Transylvania 6-5000 (86) 463
DE LUCIA, PACO
Carmen (84) 101
DELUISE, DOM
Best Little Whorehouse in Texas, The (83) 72
Cannonball Run II (85) 514
Secret of NIMH, The (83) 288
DELVAUX, CLAUDINE
Little Jerk [1984] (86) 450
DEMAREST, WILLIAM
"Obituaries" (84) 618
DEMJANENKO, MILAN
Amadeus (85) 63
DE MORNAY, REBECCA
Neil Simon's The Slugger's Wife (86) 454
Risky Business (84) 349
Runaway Train (86) 324
Testament (84) 420
Trip to Bountiful, The (86) 383
DEMOSS, DARCY
Hardbodies (85) 521
DEMPSEY, MARTIN
James Joyce's Women (86) 193
DEMPSTER, CAROL
Sherlock Holmes [1922] (83) 494
DEMPSY, JEROME
Brewster's Millions (86) 438
DEMUNN, JEFFREY
Frances (83) 178
Ragtime (82) 304
Warning Sign (86) 465
Windy City (85) 538
DENCH, JUDI
Wetherby (86) 406
DENEUVE, CATHERINE
Bon Plaisir, Le [1983] (85) 513
Hunger, The (84) 486
DE NIRO, ROBERT
Brazil (86) 80
Falling in Love (85) 519
King of Comedy, The (84) 192
New York, New York [1977] (84) 567
Once upon a Time in America (85) 345
True Confessions (82) 368
DENIS, PRINCE
"Obituaries" (85) 663

DENNEHY, BRIAN
Cocoon (86) 96
Finders Keepers (85) 519
First Blood (83) 164
Gorky Park (84) 162
Never Cry Wolf (84) 247
River Rat, The (85) 531
Silverado (86) 349
Split Image (83) 317
Twice in a Lifetime (86) 397
DENNEN, BARRY
Dark Crystal, The (83) 130
Not for Publication (85) 527
DENNING, RICHARD
Creature from the Black Lagoon, The [1954] (82) 422
DENNIS, SANDY
Come Back to the 5 & Dime Jimmy Dean, Jimmy Dean (83) 120
Four Seasons, The (82) 171
DENNY, REGINALD
Secret Life of Walter Mitty, The [1947] (86) 540
Sherlock Holmes [1922] (83) 494
DENZ, MANUELA
Sugarbaby (86) 461
DEPARDIEU, GERARD
Danton [1982] (84) 121
Goat, The [1981] (86) 444
Loulou [1980] (82) 226
Moon in the Gutter, The (84) 490
Return of Martin Guerre, The (84) 318
Woman Next Door, The (82) 385
DE PIERO, ADRIAN
Deathstalker (85) 517
DEPP, JOHNNY
Nightmare on Elm Street, A (85) 527
DEREK, BO
Bolero (85) 513
Fantasies (83) 421
DE REMER, RUBYE
"Obituaries" (85) 663
DERN, BRUCE
That Championship Season (83) 338
DERN, LAURA
Mask (86) 231
Smooth Talk (86) 354
Teachers (85) 535
DE ROSA, FRANCESCO
Bal, Le [1983] (85) 80
DERRICKS, CLEAVANT
Moscow on the Hudson (85) 321
Neil Simon's The Slugger's Wife (86) 454
DERUAZ, CHANTAL
Diva [1980] (83) 147
DE SALIS, PETER
Wild Duck, The [1983] (86) 466
DE SALVO, ANNE
Arthur (82) 71
Compromising Positions (86) 120
D. C. Cab (84) 481
My Favorite Year (83) 241
Perfect (86) 456
Stardust Memories [1980] (85) 626
DESARTHE, GERARD
Love in Germany, A [1983] (85) 283

DESCAS, MARIE-JO
  Sugar Cane Alley [1983]   (85) 461
DESCHANEL, MARY JO
  Right Stuff, The   (84) 342
DESIDERIO, ROBERT
  Oh God, You Devil   (85) 528
DESMOND, JOHNNY
  "Obituaries"   (86) 566
DESNY, IVAN
  Berlin Alexanderplatz [1980]   (84) 57
DESPIERRE, GERARD
  Death of Mario Ricci, The [1983]   (86) 133
DESPOTOVICH, NADA
  Smithereens   (83) 307
DETMERS, MARUSCHKA
  First Name, Carmen [1983]   (85) 186
DEVANE, WILLIAM
  Hadley's Rebellion   (85) 521
  Honky Tonk Freeway   (82) 199
  Testament   (84) 420
DEVINE, ANDY
  Pete Kelly's Blues [1955]   (83) 481
DEVINNEY, W. SCOTT
  Hard Traveling   (86) 445
DEVITO, DANNY
  Jewel of the Nile, The   (86) 448
  Johnny Dangerously   (85) 524
  Romancing the Stone   (85) 461
DE VRIES, DOLF
  4th Man, The [1983]   (85) 203
  Question of Silence, A   (85) 530
DEVRIES, JON
  Lianna   (84) 201
DEWAERE, PATRICK
  Beau Pere   (82) 78
  Heat of Desire [1981]   (85) 522
  "Obituaries"   (83) 531
DEWHURST, COLLEEN
  Dead Zone, The   (84) 481
DE YOUNG, CLIFF
  Hunger, The   (84) 486
  Protocol   (85) 383
  Reckless   (85) 530
  Secret Admirer   (86) 459
DIAMOND, BARRY
  Bachelor Party   (85) 511
DIAMOND, JOEL
  Crossover Dreams   (86) 441
DIAMOND, SELMA
  "Obituaries"   (86) 566
DIAZ, RAFAEL
  Demons in the Garden [1982]   (85) 517
DIBENEDETTO, TONY
  Pope of Greenwich Village, The   (85) 529
  Splash   (85) 434
DICENZO, GEORGE
  Secret of the Sword, The   (86) 459
DI CICCO, BOBBY
  Philadelphia Experiment, The   (85) 529
  Splash   (85) 434
DICK
  Hail Mary   (86) 182
DICKEY, LUCINDA
  Breakin'   (85) 514
  Breakin' 2   (85) 514

DIEGO, JUAN
  Holy Innocents, The   (86) 447
DIEHL, HANS
  Boat Is Full, The [1981]   (83) 82
DIEHL, JOHN
  Angel   (85) 510
  City Limits   (86) 440
DIEUDONNE, ALBERT
  Napoleon [1927]   (82) 461
DIGGES, DUDLEY
  Hatchet Man, The [1932]   (83) 447
DIGNAM, ARTHUR
  We of the Never Never [1982]   (84) 497
  Wild Duck, The [1983]   (86) 466
DILEO, ANTONE, JR.
  Day of the Dead   (86) 441
DILLMAN, BRADFORD
  Sudden Impact   (84) 395
  Way We Were, The [1973]   (82) 474
DILLON, KEVIN
  Heaven Help Us   (86) 445
DILLON, MATT
  Flamingo Kid, The   (85) 192
  Liar's Moon   (83) 424
  Outsiders, The   (84) 282
  Rumble Fish   (84) 492
  Target   (86) 462
  Tex   (83) 335
DILLON, MELINDA
  Absence of Malice   (82) 57
  Christmas Story, A   (84) 110
  Slap Shot [1977]   (82) 467
  Songwriter   (85) 533
DILLON, MICK
  Champions   (85) 515
DILLOWAY, DONALD
  Animal Kingdom, The [1932]   (86) 469
DI LORENZO, ROSSANA
  Bal, Le [1983]   (85) 80
DINOME, JERRY
  Tomboy   (86) 463
DINSDALE, REECE
  Private Function, A [1984]   (86) 280
DITCHBURN, ANNE
  Curtains   (84) 481
DITSON, HARRY
  Improper Channels   (82) 218
  Top Secret   (85) 536
DIVINE
  Lust in the Dust   (86) 450
  Trouble in Mind   (86) 388
DIXON, DONNA
  Doctor Detroit   (84) 482
  Spies like Us   (86) 360
DIXON, MALCOLM
  Time Bandits [1980]   (82) 364
DOAZAN, AURELLE
  Detective   (86) 442
DOBROWOLSKA, GOSIA
  Silver City [1984]   (86) 460
DOBSON, TAMARA
  Chained Heat   (84) 480
DOCKERY, ERICA
  Hardbodies   (85) 521

DOLAN, DON
Philadelphia Experiment, The   (85) 529
DOLENZ, GEORGE
My Cousin Rachel [1952]   (82) 458
DOLINA, LARISSA
Jazzman   (85) 523
DOLL, DORA
Bastille [1984]   (86) 437
DOMBASLE, ARIELLE
Beau Mariage, Le   (83) 65
Pauline at the Beach [1982]   (84) 296
DOMINGO, PLACIDO
Bizet's Carmen [1983]   (85) 98
Traviata, La   (83) 366
DONAHUE, PATRICIA
Cutter's Way   (82) 119
DONAHUE, TROY
Grandview, U.S.A.   (85) 520
DONALD, JULIANA
Muppets Take Manhattan, The   (85) 526
DONAT, PETER
Bad Boy, The   (86) 437
DONATH, LUDWIG
Torn Curtain [1966]   (85) 644
DONLEVY, BRIAN
Barbary Coast [1935]   (84) 506
Cowboy [1958]   (82) 417
DONNADIEU, BERNARD PIERRE
Return of Martin Guerre, The   (84) 318
DONNELLY, JAMES
And Nothing but the Truth   (85) 510
DONNELLY, PATRICE
Personal Best   (83) 254
DONNELLY, RUTH
"Obituaries"   (83) 532
DONOVAN, ERIN
Homework   (83) 422
DONOVAN, KING
Cowboy [1958]   (82) 417
DONOVAN, TERENCE
Man from Snowy River, The   (83) 425
DOOHAN, JAMES
Star Trek III—The Search for Spock   (85) 439
DOOLEY, PAUL
Endangered Species   (83) 420
Kiss Me Goodbye   (83) 209
Sixteen Candles   (85) 532
DOOLING, LUCINDA
Surf II   (85) 535
DOQUI, ROBERT
Cloak and Dagger   (85) 516
DORAN, ANN
Roughly Speaking [1945]   (83) 490
DORAN, PETER
Experience Preferred … but Not Essential
[1982]   (84) 141
DORCEV, ALEKSANDAR
When Father Was Away on Business [1984]   (86) 411
DORE, CHARLIE
Ploughman's Lunch, The [1983]   (85) 377
DORIO, DANIELA
Black Cat, The   (85) 512

DORNBIERER, OTTO
Boat Is Full, The [1981]   (83) 82
DOROTHÉE
Heads or Tails [1980]   (84) 485
DORS, DIANA
"Obituaries"   (85) 663
D'ORSAY, FIFI
"Obituaries"   (84) 619
DOSET, MICHEL
Dernier Combat, Le [1983]   (85) 517
DOTRICE, KAY
Cheech and Chong's The Corsican
Brothers   (85) 515
DOTRICE, ROY
Amadeus   (85) 63
Cheech and Chong's The Corsican
Brothers   (85) 515
DOTSON, RHONDA
Songwriter   (85) 533
DOUCETTE, PAMELA
Philadelphia Experiment, The   (85) 529
DOUGLAS, DAMON
Reuben, Reuben   (84) 337
DOUGLAS, ERIC
Tomboy   (86) 463
DOUGLAS, GILBERT
Dulcy [1923]   (82) 432
DOUGLAS, KIRK
Arrangement, The [1969]   (86) 474
Eddie Macon's Run   (84) 483
Man from Snowy River, The   (83) 425
DOUGLAS, MALCOLM
Educating Rita   (84) 136
DOUGLAS, MELVYN
Ghost Story   (82) 183
"Obituaries"   (82) 485
DOUGLAS, MICHAEL
Chorus Line, A   (86) 91
Jewel of the Nile, The   (86) 448
Romancing the Stone   (85) 421
Star Chamber, The   (84) 494
DOUGLAS, PAUL
Solid Gold Cadillac, The [1956]   (85) 615
DOUGLAS, SARAH
Conan the Destroyer   (85) 516
Superman II   (82) 339
DOUGLASS, ROBYN
Lonely Guy, The   (85) 525
Partners   (83) 427
DOUKAS, SUSAN
Liquid Sky   (84) 487
DOURIF, BRAD
Dune   (85) 171
Heaven's Gate   (82) 195
Ragtime   (82) 304
DOWLING, KATHRYN
Diner   (83) 142
DOWNES, CATHY
Winter of Our Dreams [1981]   (83) 431
DOWNEY, ROBERT
Firstborn   (85) 519
Tuff Turf   (86) 464
Weird Science   (86) 465
DOYLE, TONY
Final Option, The   (84) 484

DOYLE-MURRAY, BRIAN
  Razor's Edge, The   (85) 402
DOZIER, AARON
  Better Off Dead   (86) 438
DRAGO, BILLY
  Invasion U.S.A.   (86) 447
DRAKE, CAROL
  Waitress   (83) 431
DRAKE, CHARLES
  Arrangement, The [1969]   (86) 474
DRAKE, CLAUDIA
  Detour [1946]   (86) 498
DRAKE, FRANCIS
  Death Wish III   (86) 441
DRAKE, MERVYN
  Razorback [1984]   (86) 457
DRAKE, PAUL
  Sudden Impact   (84) 395
DRAKE, TOM
  "Obituaries"   (83) 532
DREIFUS, ROSE
  Alley Cat   (85) 509
DREMANN, BEAU
  Heavenly Kid, The   (86) 445
DRESCHER, FRAN
  This Is Spinal Tap   (85) 484
DRESS, EVELYNE
  Bastille [1984]   (86) 437
DREWNIAK, JOSEPH
  Silver City [1984]   (86) 460
DREYER, FRED
  Cannonball Run II   (85) 514
DREYFUS, JEAN-CLAUDE
  Cheech and Chong's The Corsican
    Brothers   (85) 515
DREYFUSS, RICHARD
  Buddy System, The   (85) 514
  Whose Life Is It Anyway?   (82) 378
DRIEST, BURKHARD
  Querelle [1982]   (84) 313
DUBAC, BOB
  Stitches   (86) 461
DUBIN, ALEXIS
  Madman   (84) 488
DUBINSKY, YUDEL
  Light Ahead, The [1939]   (83) 460
DUBOIS, JEAN-POL
  Target   (86) 462
DUCHESNE, ROGER
  Bob le Flambeur [1955]   (84) 526
DUCHIN, PETER
  World of Henry Orient, The [1964]   (84) 600
DUCREUX, LOUIS
  Sunday in the Country, A   (85) 466
DUDGEON, ELSPETH
  Becky Sharp [1935]   (82) 403
DUDIKOFF, MICHAEL
  American Ninja   (86) 436
  Bachelor Party   (85) 511
DUELL, WILLIAM
  Grace Quigley   (86) 444
DUFILHO, JACQUES
  Horse of Pride, The   (86) 447

DUGAN, DENNIS
  Howling, The   (82) 207
DUJMOVIC, DAVOR
  When Father Was Away on Business [1984]   (86)
    411
DUKAKIS, OLYMPIA
  Flanagan   (86) 443
DUKE-ASTIN, PATTY
  By Design   (83) 419
DUKES, DAVID
  Only When I Laugh   (82) 268
  Without a Trace   (84) 498
DULLEA, KEIR
  2010   (85) 494
DUMBRILLE, DOUGLASS
  Peter Ibbetson [1935]   (86) 527
DUMMONT, DENISE
  Kiss of the Spider Woman   (86) 209
DUNAWAY, FAYE
  Arrangement, The [1969]   (86) 474
  Mommie Dearest   (82) 245
  Ordeal by Innocence [1984]   (86) 455
  Supergirl   (85) 535
  Wicked Lady, The   (84) 497
DUNCAN, CARMEN
  Escape 2000   (84) 483
DUNDAS, JENNIE
  Heaven Help Us   (86) 445
  Hotel New Hampshire, The   (85) 243
  Mrs. Soffel   (85) 314
DUNLAP, CARLA
  Pumping Iron II   (86) 456
DUNLAP, DAWN
  Forbidden World   (83) 421
  Heartbreaker   (84) 485
DUNN, CONRAD
  Stripes   (82) 336
DUNN, ROBERT
  Breathless   (84) 89
DUNNE, DOMINIQUE
  "Obituaries"   (83) 532
  Poltergeist   (83) 263
DUNNE, GRIFFIN
  After Hours   (86) 51
  Almost You   (86) 436
  American Werewolf in London, An   (82) 66
  Cold Feet   (85) 516
  Johnny Dangerously   (85) 524
DUNNE, IRENE
  Guy Named Joe, A [1943]   (82) 435
  "Interview with DeWitt Bodeen,
    An"   (82) 10
DUPIRE, SERGE
  Plouffe, Les   (86) 456
DUPOIS, STARLETTA
  Pee-wee's Big Adventure   (86) 265
DUPPEZ, JUNE
  "Obituaries"   (85) 664
DUPUIS, JEAN-MICHEL
  Death of Mario Ricci, The [1983]   (86) 133
DURANT, JACK
  Journey into Fear [1943]   (86) 511
DÜRINGER, ANNEMARIE
  Berlin Alexanderplatz [1980]   (84) 57
  Veronika Voss   (83) 382

DURNING, CHARLES
  Best Little Whorehouse in Texas, The (83)
    72
  Hadley's Rebellion (85) 521
  Man with One Red Shoe, The (86) 451
  Mass Appeal (85) 303
  Sharky's Machine (82) 324
  Stick (86) 460
  To Be or Not to Be (84) 426
  Tootsie (83) 353
  True Confessions (82) 368
  Two of a Kind (84) 496
DUROCK, DICK
  Swamp Thing (83) 429
DURYEA, DAN
  Flight of the Phoenix, The [1966] (85) 549
DUSENBERRY, ANN
  Cutter's Way (82) 119
DUSSARRAT, MICHAEL
  Next Year if All Goes Well (84) 490
DUSSOLLIER, ANDRE
  Beau Mariage, Le (83) 65
  Just the Way You Are (85) 524
DUTRONC, JACQUES
  Every Man for Himself [1979] (82) 139
DUVALL, ROBERT
  Natural, The (85) 329
  Stone Boy, The (85) 450
  Tender Mercies (84) 409
  THX 1138 [1971] (85) 638
  Tomorrow [1972] (84) 589
  True Confessions (82) 368
DUVALL, SHELLEY
  Brewster McCloud [1970] (86) 484
  Time Bandits [1980] (82) 364
DUX, PIERRE
  Heat of Desire [1981] (85) 522
  Vie Continue, La [1981] (83) 430
DWORSKY, PETER
  Videodrome (84) 452
DYE, CAMERON
  Body Rock (85) 513
  Fraternity Vacation (86) 444
  Joy of Sex (85) 524
  Valley Girl (84) 447
DYSART, RICHARD
  Falcon and the Snowman, The (86) 165
  Mask (86) 231
  Pale Rider (86) 261
  Thing, The (84) 343
  Warning Sign (86) 465
DZUNDZA, GEORGE
  Best Defense (85) 512
  Honky Tonk Freeway (82) 199
  Streamers (84) 391

EARLE, MERIE
  "Obituaries" (85) 665
EAST, JEFF
  Up the Creek (85) 537
EASTERBROOK, LESLIE
  Police Academy (85) 529
EASTIN, STEVE
  Nightmare on Elm Street, Part 2, A (86) 454
EASTWOOD, ALISON
  Tightrope (85) 489

EASTWOOD, CLINT
  Beguiled, The [1971] (83) 37
  City Heat (85) 141
  Coogan's Bluff [1968] (83) 37
  Dirty Harry [1971] (83) 37
  Escape from Alcatraz [1979] (83) 33, 38
  Firefox (83) 160
  Honkytonk Man (83) 200
  "Interview with Don Siegel, An" (83) 36
  Pale Rider (86) 261
  Play Misty for Me [1971] (86) 532
  Sudden Impact (84) 395
  Tightrope (85) 489
EASTWOOD, KYLE
  Honkytonk Man (83) 200
EATON, GLEN
  Berry Gordy's The Last Dragon (86) 438
EATON, WALLAS
  Test of Love (86) 462
EATWELL, BRIAN
  American Dreamer (85) 509
EBERHARD, FABRICE
  Patsy, The (86) 456
EBERSOLE, CHRISTINE
  Amadeus (85) 63
  Thief of Hearts (85) 536
ECCLES, DONALD
  Young Sherlock Holmes (86) 431
EDE, GEORGE
  World According to Garp, The (83) 397
EDEN, BARBARA
  Chattanooga Choo Choo (85) 515
EDEN, MARK
  Richard's Things (82) 321
EDGE, DEBBIE
  This Is Elvis (82) 360
EDMONDS, ELIZABETH
  Experienced Preferred ... but Not
    Essential [1982] (84) 141
EDMONDS, MIKE
  Time Bandits [1980] (82) 364
EDOLS, MICHAEL
  Where the Green Ants Dream [1984] (86) 465
EDSON, RICHARD
  Stranger than Paradise (85) 455
EDWALL, ALLAN
  Fanny and Alexander [1982] (84) 146
EDWARD, MARION
  Wild Duck, The [1983] (86) 466
EDWARDS, ANNIE JOE
  Purple Rose of Cairo, The (86) 290
EDWARDS, ANTHONY
  Gotcha! (86) 444
  Heart Like a Wheel (84) 182
  Revenge of the Nerds (85) 530
  Sure Thing, The (86) 369
EDWARDS, DARRYL
  Brother from Another Planet, The (85)
    118
EDWARDS, GAIL
  Get Crazy (84) 484
EDWARDS, HILTON
  "Obituaries" (83) 532
EDWARDS, JENNIFER
  Man Who Loved Women, The (84) 218

EDWARDS, PERCY
  Dark Crystal, The   (83) 130
EDWARDS, VINCE
  Deal of the Century   (84) 482
  Seduction, The   (83) 427
EFRON, MARSHALL
  Twice upon a Time   (84) 496
EGAR, MICHAEL
  Next Stop, Greenwich Village [1976]   (85) 592
EGGAR, SAMANTHA
  Curtains   (84) 481
EGI, MOTOSHI
  Makioka Sisters, The [1983]   (86) 451
EGOLF, LOUISE
  Fool for Love   (86) 172
EICHORN, LISA
  Cutter's Way   (82) 119
EIDING, PAUL
  Personals, The   (84) 491
EIKENBERRY, JILL
  Arthur   (82) 71
EILBACHER, LISA
  Beverly Hills Cop   (85) 88
  Officer and a Gentleman, An   (83) 246
  10 to Midnight   (84) 495
EILBER, JANET
  Hard to Hold   (85) 521
  Romantic Comedy   (84) 492
  Whose Life Is It Anyway?   (82) 378
EINSTEIN, BOB
  Modern Romance   (82) 241
EINSTEIN, CLIFF
  Modern Romance   (82) 241
EISENBERG, AVNER
  Jewel of the Nile, The   (86) 448
EISENBERG, NED
  Moving Violations   (86) 453
  Slayground [1983]   (85) 533
EKBLAD, STINA
  Fanny and Alexander [1982]   (84) 146
EKLAND, BRITT
  Wicker Man, The [1974]   (86) 555
ELAM, JACK
  Cannonball Run II   (85) 514
  Jinxed   (83) 206
ELCAR, DANA
  All of Me   (85) 58
  Blue Skies Again   (84) 479
  Buddy Buddy   (82) 93
ELDRIDGE, FLORENCE
  Divorcée, The [1930]   (82) 429
ELIZABETH OF TORO
  Sheena   (85) 532
ELIZONDO, HECTOR
  Flamingo Kid, The   (85) 192
ELIZONDO, HUMBERTO
  Erendira [1983]   (85) 181
ELIZONDO, RENE
  Body Rock   (85) 513
EL-KADI, NAMEER
  Quest for Fire   (83) 271
EL-KADI, NASEER
  Quest for Fire   (83) 271

ELLENSTEIN, PETER
  Weekend Pass   (85) 537
ELLIOT, SHAWN
  Beat Street   (85) 512
  Crossover Dreams   (86) 441
ELLIOTT, DEAN
  Beat Street   (85) 512
ELLIOTT, DENHOLM
  Brimstone and Treacle   (83) 91
  Hound of the Baskervilles, The
    [1978]   (82) 203
  Missionary, The   (83) 233
  Private Function, A [1984]   (86) 280
  Raiders of the Lost Ark   (82) 308
  Razor's Edge, The   (85) 402
  Sound Barrier, The [1952]   (85) 621
  Trading Places   (84) 430
  Wicked Lady, The   (84) 497
ELLIOTT, SAM
  Mask   (86) 231
ELLIOTT, STEPHEN
  Cutter's Way   (82) 119
  Kiss Me Goodbye   (83) 209
ELLIOTT, TIM
  Utu [1983]   (85) 504
ELLIS, BOB
  Where the Green Ants Dream [1984]   (86) 465
ELLIS, PAUL
  Bridge of San Luis Rey, The [1929]   (82)
    408
ELLIS, RICKEY
  Joey   (86) 448
ELLYN, MAURA
  Home Free All   (85) 522
ELPHICK, MICHAEL
  Ordeal by Innocence [1984]   (86) 455
ELSOM, ISOBEL
  "Obituaries"   (82) 486
ELWES, CARY
  Bride, The   (86) 438
  Oxford Blues   (85) 528
EMERSON, FAYE
  "Obituaries"   (84) 620
EMIL, MICHAEL
  Always   (86) 60
  Can She Bake a Cherry Pie?   (84) 95
  Insignificance   (86) 447
EMMANUEL, TAKIS
  Caddie [1976]   (83) 439
ENGEL, GEORGIA
  Care Bears Movie, The   (86) 439
  Taking Off [1971]   (86) 545
ENGEL, TINA
  Boat Is Full, The [1981]   (83) 82
ENGLISH, CAMERON
  Chorus Line, A   (86) 91
ENGLUND, ROBERT
  Nightmare on Elm Street, A   (85) 527
  Nightmare on Elm Street, Part 2, A   (86) 454
ENRIQUEZ, RENE
  Evil That Men Do, The   (85) 518
  Under Fire   (84) 441
ENSIGN, MICHAEL
  Maxie   (86) 452
EPERJES, KÁROLY
  Colonel Redl [1984]   (86) 100

PERFORMER INDEX

ERDMAN, RICHARD
Tomboy (86) 463
ERGÜN, HALIL
Yol (83) 411
ERHARD, BERNARD
Deathstalker (85) 517
ERICKSON, LISA
Power, The (85) 529
ERMEY, LEE
Purple Hearts (85) 529
ERRICKSON, KRISTA
Jekyll and Hyde . . . Together Again (83) 424
ERWIN, JOHN
Secret of the Sword, The (86) 459
ESHAM, FAITH
Bizet's Carmen [1983] (85) 98
ESPOSITO, JOE
This Is Elvis (82) 360
ESPOSTI, PIERA DEGLI
Joke of Destiny, A [1983] (85) 259
ESSEN, VIOLA
Specter of the Rose [1946] (83) 504
ESTABROOK, CHRISTINE
Almost You (86) 436
ESTEVEZ, EMILIO
Breakfast Club, The (86) 85
Nightmares (84) 490
Outsiders, The (84) 282
Repo Man (85) 408
St. Elmo's Fire (86) 330
Tex (83) 335
That Was Then . . . This Is Now (86) 463
EUBA, WOLF
Céleste [1981] (83) 104
EVANS, ANGELO
Angelo My Love (84) 47
EVANS, ART J.
Fright Night (86) 444
Solider's Story, A (85) 427
EVANS, DEBBIE
Angelo My Love (84) 47
EVANS, MADGE
"Obituaries" (82) 487
EVANS, MARY BETH
Lovelines (85) 525
Toy Soldiers (85) 536
EVANS, MICHAEL
Angelo My Love (84) 47
EVANS, MOSTYN
Experience Preferred . . . but Not Essential
[1982] (84) 141
EVANS, RUTHIE
Angelo My Love (84) 47
EVANS, TONY
Angelo My Love (84) 47
EVERETT, CHAD
Fever Pitch (86) 443
EVERETT, RUPERT
Dance with a Stranger [1984] (86) 125
EVISON, PAT
Starstruck (83) 428
EWART, JOHN
Razorback [1984] (86) 457

EWING, JOHN CHRISTY
Breakin' 2 (85) 514
EYRE, PETER
Dragonslayer (82) 125

FABBRI, JACQUES
Diva [1980] (83) 147
FABIANI, JOEL
Reuben, Reuben (84) 337
FABRIZI, ELENA
Softly Softly [1984] (86) 460
Water and Soap (86) 465
FAHEY, JEFF
Silverado (86) 349
FAIRBANKS, DOUGLAS, JR.
Ghost Story (82) 183
FAIRCHILD, MORGAN
Pee-wee's Big Adventure (86) 265
Seduction, The (83) 427
FAISON, SANDY
All the Right Moves (84) 41
FALCO, RUBENS DE
Pixote [1980] (82) 280
FALCON, BRUNO "PUP 'N' TACO"
Breakin' (85) 514
FALCON, PETER GONZALES
Heartbreaker (84) 485
FALK, RON
My First Wife (86) 453
FARGAS, ANTONIO
Pretty Baby [1978] (85) 597
FARMER, BUDDY
Bear, The (85) 511
FARMER, FRANCES
Come and Get It [1936] (82) 412
FARMER, MIMSY
Black Cat, The (85) 512
Death of Mario Ricci, The [1983] (86) 133
FARNSWORTH, RICHARD
Grey Fox, The (84) 168
Into the Night (86) 186
Natural, The (85) 329
Rhinestone (85) 531
Sylvester (86) 462
Waltz Across Texas (84) 497
FAROT, MARIE-ANGE
Sugar Cane Alley [1983] (85) 461
FARR, JAMIE
Cannonball Run II (85) 514
FARRELL, NICHOLAS
Chariots of Fire (82) 101
FARRELL, SHARON
Night of the Comet (85) 527
Sweet Sixteen (85) 535
FARROW, MIA
Broadway Danny Rose (85) 112
Midsummer Night's Sex Comedy, A (83)
228
Purple Rose of Cairo, The (86) 290
Supergirl (85) 535
Zelig (84) 473
FARROW, STEPHANIE
Purple Rose of Cairo, The (86) 290
FARROW, TISA
Last Hunter, The (85) 525

FAUCHER, FRANÇOISE
  Agnes of God   (86) 56
FAULKNER, JAMES
  Priest of Love   (82) 288
FAVILLA, GIAN LUCA
  Another Time, Another Place [1983]   (85) 510
FAY, FRANCES
  Pretty Baby [1978]   (85) 597
FAYLEN, FRANK
  "Obituaries"   (86) 567
FEAST, MICHAEL
  Draughtsman's Contract, The [1982]   (84) 126
FEDOROFF, SERGE
  Cheech and Chong's The Corsican
    Brothers   (85) 515
FEE, MELINDA O.
  Nightmare on Elm Street, Part 2, A   (86) 454
FEGAN, JORGE
  Erendira [1983]   (85) 181
FEINSTEIN, ALAN
  War and Love   (86) 465
FELD, FRITZ
  Secret Life of Walter Mitty, The [1947]   (86) 540
FELDER, CLARENCE
  Slayground [1983]   (85) 533
FELDMAN, COREY
  Friday the 13th—The Final Chapter   (85) 520
  Goonies, The   (86) 176
FELDMAN, MARTY
  "Obituaries"   (83) 533
  Slapstick   (85) 533
  Yellowbeard   (84) 498
FELDSHUH, TOVAH
  Brewster's Millions   (86) 438
  Daniel   (84) 481
FELL, ANDREW
  Champions   (85) 515
FELL, NORMAN
  Transylvania 6-5000   (86) 463
FELLOWES, JULIAN
  Baby   (86) 437
FELMY, HANSJÖERG
  Torn Curtain [1966]   (85) 644
FELTY, L.T.
  1918   (86) 454
FENN, SHERILYN
  Just One of the Guys   (86) 448
  Out of Control   (86) 455
FENTON, LESLIE
  Hatchet Man, The [1932]   (83) 447
FERGUSON, J. DON
  Loveless, The   (85) 525
  Tank   (85) 535
FERNANDES, MIGUEL
  Ghost Story   (82) 183
FERNANDEZ, WILHELMENIA WIGGINS
  Diva [1980]   (83) 147
FERRACHE, RACHID
  My Other Husband   (86) 453
FERRANDIS, ANTONIO
  Volver a empezar   (83) 393
FERRARA, STEPHANE
  Detective   (86) 442

FERRELL, CONCHATA
  Heartland   (82) 191
FERREOL, ANDREA
  Nuit de Varennes, La [1982]   (84) 270
  Three Brothers [1980]   (83) 349
FERRER, JOSÉ
  Dune   (85) 171
  Evil That Men Do, The   (85) 518
  Midsummer Night's Sex Comedy, A   (83) 228
  To Be or Not to Be   (84) 426
FERRER, MEL
  Lili Marleen   (82) 222
FERRER, MIGUEL
  Flashpoint   (85) 519
  Heartbreaker   (84) 485
FERRER, SEAN
  They All Laughed   (82) 350
FERRIER, NOEL
  Escape 2000   (84) 483
  Year of Living Dangerously, The
    [1982]   (84) 462
FERRIGNO, LOU
  Hercules   (84) 485
  Hercules II   (86) 446
FERSEN, CHRISTINE
  Sheer Madness [1983]   (86) 459
FERZETTI, GABRIELE
  Basileus Quartet   (85) 511
FESS, ULLI
  Sophie's Choice   (83) 311
FETCHIT, STEPIN. See PERRY, LINCOLN
  THEODORE.
FEUER, DEBRA
  To Live and Die in L.A.   (86) 379
FEUILLARD, SERGE
  Razor's Edge, The   (85) 402
FIANDER, LEWIS
  Doctor and the Devils, The   (86) 442
FIDDIS, SHELBY
  Cheech and Chong's The Corsican
    Brothers   (85) 515
  Things Are Tough All Over   (83) 430
FIELD, CRYSTAL
  Birdy   (85) 93
FIELD, SALLY
  Absence of Malice   (82) 57
  Kiss Me Goodbye   (83) 209
  Murphy's Romance   (86) 242
  Places in the Heart   (85) 371
FIELDING, DOROTHY
  Fright Night   (86) 444
  Kiss Me Goodbye   (83) 209
FIELDS, TONY
  Chorus Line, A   (86) 91
FIELDSTEEL, ROBERT
  Just One of the Guys   (86) 448
FIERSTEIN, HARVEY
  Garbo Talks   (85) 520
FILHO, DANIEL
  Bar Esperanza [1983]   (86) 437
FILHO, JARDEL
  Pixote [1980]   (82) 280
FILIATRAULT, DENISE
  Plouffe, Les   (86) 456

FILLALI, HAMID
  Jewel of the Nile, The   (86) 448
FILPI, CARMEN
  Pee-wee's Big Adventure   (86) 265
FINCH, JON
  And Nothing but the Truth   (85) 510
FINCH, PETER
  Flight of the Phoenix, The [1966]   (85) 549
FINK, AGNES
  Sheer Madness [1983]   (86) 459
FINKEL, SHIMON
  Hanna K.   (84) 177
  Vulture, The   (86) 464
FINLAY, FRANK
  Lifeforce   (86) 450
  Ploughman's Lunch, The [1983]   (85) 377
  Return of the Soldier, The [1982]   (84) 332
FINLAYSON, JAMES
  Our Relations [1936]   (86) 523
FINLAYSON, JON
  Lonely Hearts [1982]   (84) 212
  My First Wife   (86) 453
FINN, TIM
  Coca-Cola Kid, The   (86) 440
FINNEGAN, JOHN
  Natural, The   (85) 329
  School Spirit   (86) 458
FINNEGAN, TOM
  Repo Man   (85) 408
FINNEY, ALBERT
  Annie   (83) 56
  Dresser, The   (84) 130
  Shoot the Moon   (83) 295
  Under the Volcano   (85) 499
  Wolfen   (82) 382
FIORENTINO, LINDA
  After Hours   (86) 51
  Gotcha!   (86) 444
  Vision Quest   (86) 464
FIRBANK, ANNE
  Passage to India, A   (85) 365
FIRDEVS, EKMEKYEMEZ
  Out of Order   (86) 455
FIRSHMAN, DANIEL
  Lust in the Dust   (86) 450
FIRTH, JULIAN
  Oxford Blues   (85) 528
FIRTH, PETER
  Lifeforce   (86) 450
  Tess [1980]   (82) 471
FISCHER, BRUCE M.
  Journey of Natty Gann, The   (86) 203
FISCHER, GISELA
  Torn Curtain [1966]   (85) 644
FISCHER, VERA
  I Love You   (83) 423
FISH, TONY
  Madman   (84) 488
FISHBURNE, LARRY
  Cotton Club, The   (85) 150
FISHER, CARRIE
  Garbo Talks   (85) 520
  Man with One Red Shoe, The   (86) 451
  Return of the Jedi   (84) 326

FISHER, CINDY
  Liar's Moon   (83) 424
  Stone Boy, The   (85) 450
FISHER, FRANCES
  Can She Bake a Cherry Pie?   (85) 95
FISHER, GREGOR
  Another Time, Another Place [1983]   (85) 510
FISHER, JAY
  Alley Cat   (85) 509
FISHER, TRICIA LEIGH
  Stick   (86) 460
FITE, BOBBY
  Explorers   (86) 442
FITZGERALD, ELLA
  Pete Kelly's Blues [1955]   (83) 481
FITZGERALD, GERALDINE
  Arthur   (82) 71
  Easy Money   (84) 482
FITZ-GERALD, LEWIS
  We of the Never Never [1982]   (84) 497
FITZMAHONY, GERALD
  James Joyce's Women   (86) 193
FITZPATRICK, CHRISTIAN
  Santa Claus   (86) 334
FITZROY, EMILY
  Bridge of San Luis Rey, The [1929]   (82) 408
FITZSIMMONS, MARGOT
  I Know Where I'm Going [1945]   (83) 456
FIX, PAUL
  Hondo [1953]   (83) 452
  "Obituaries"   (84) 620
FLAHERTY, JOE
  Going Berserk   (84) 485
  Sesame Street Presents: Follow That Bird   (86) 459
FLANAGAN, FIONNULA
  James Joyce's Women   (86) 193
FLANDERS, ED
  True Confessions   (82) 368
FLANNERY, ANNE
  Heart of a Stag   (85) 522
FLANNERY, ERIN
  Incubus, The [1980]   (83) 424
FLAVIN, JAMES
  Most Dangerous Game, The [1932]   (86) 519
FLEETWOOD, SUSAN
  Clash of the Titans   (82) 111
  Young Sherlock Holmes   (86) 431
FLEISHER, CHARLES
  Nightmare on Elm Street, A   (85) 527
FLEMING, REBECCA
  Stephen King's Silver Bullet   (86) 460
FLETCHER, DEXTER
  Revolution   (86) 458
FLETCHER, LOUISE
  Brainstorm   (84) 480
  Firestarter   (85) 519
FLEURY, COLETTE
  Bob le Flambeur [1955]   (84) 526
FLOERSHEIM, PATRICK
  Diva [1980]   (83) 147
FLOHE, CHARLES
  Rappin'   (86) 457

FLON, SUSANNE
  Quartet (82) 296
FLORIAN, LUC
  Patsy, The (86) 456
FLOWERS, BESS
  "Obituaries" (85) 665
FLUEGEL, DARLANNE
  Once upon a Time in America (85) 345
  To Live and Die in L.A. (86) 379
FLUET, JANINE
  Agnes of God (86) 56
FLYNN, MIRIAM
  National Lampoon's Class Reunion (83) 426
FOCAS, SPIROS
  Jewel of the Nile, The (86) 448
FOLLOWS, MEGAN
  Stephen King's Silver Bullet (86) 460
FOLSOM, MEGAN
  Heartland (82) 191
FONDA, HENRY
  "American Cinema in 1981, The" (82) 30
  Fort Apache [1948] (84) 530
  "Obituaries" (83) 535
  On Golden Pond (82) 263
FONDA, JANE
  Agnes of God (86) 56
  On Golden Pond (82) 263
FONDA, PETER
  Split Image (83) 317
FONDACARO, PHIL
  Black Cauldron, The (86) 75
FONG, BENSON
  Jinxed (83) 206
FONG, LEO
  Killpoint (85) 524
FONTANNE, LYNN
  "Obituaries" (84) 621
FOODY, RALPH
  Code of Silence (86) 440
FOOTE, HALLIE
  1918 (86) 454
FOOTE, HORTON, JR.
  1918 (86) 454
FORD, GLENN
  Cowboy [1958] (82) 417
FORD, HARRISON
  Blade Runner (83) 76
  Indiana Jones and the Temple of
    Doom (85) 253
  Raiders of the Lost Ark (82) 308
  Return of the Jedi (84) 326
  Witness (86) 421
FORD, RUTH
  Too Scared to Scream (86) 463
FOREMAN, DEBORAH
  Valley Girl (84) 447
FORGEHAM, JOHN
  Sheena (85) 532
FORONJY, RICHARD
  Prince of the City (82) 292
  Repo Man (85) 408
FORREST, FREDERIC
  Hammett (84) 174
  One from the Heart (83) 250

Stone Boy, The (85) 450
Valley Girl (84) 447
FORREST, STEVE
  Mommie Dearest (82) 245
  Sahara (85) 531
  Spies like Us (86) 360
FORSTER, ALLISON
  Gregory's Girl [1981] (83) 193
FORSYTHE, BILL
  Cloak and Dagger (85) 516
FORSYTHE, DREW
  Caddie [1976] (83) 439
  Test of Love (86) 462
FORSYTHE, HENDERSON
  Silkwood (84) 367
FORSYTHE, WILLIAM
  Once upon a Time in America (85) 345
FORTE, NICK APOLLO
  Broadway Danny Rose (85) 112
FOSSE, NICOLE
  Chorus Line, A (86) 91
FOSSEY, BRIGITTE
  Boum, La [1980] (84) 480
  Enigma [1982] (84) 483
  Imperative [1982] (86) 447
FOSTER, JODIE
  Hotel New Hampshire, The (85) 243
  O'Hara's Wife (83) 426
FOSTER, MEG
  Emerald Forest, The (86) 156
FOURNEAU, MARC ERNEST
  Argent, L' [1983] (85) 74
FOX, EDWARD
  Bounty, The (85) 513
  Dresser, The (84) 130
  Gandhi (83) 183
  Never Say Never Again (84) 252
  Shooting Party, The [1984] (86) 344
  Wild Geese II (86) 466
FOX, HUCKLEBERRY
  American Dreamer (85) 509
  Misunderstood (85) 526
FOX, JAMES
  Greystoke (85) 236
  Passage to India, A (85) 365
FOX, MICHAEL J.
  Back to the Future (86) 65
  Teen Wolf (86) 462
FOXX, ELIZABETH
  School Spirit (86) 458
FOY, EDDIE, JR.
  Bells Are Ringing [1960] (84) 517
  "Obituaries" (84) 621
FRANCIS, BEV
  Pumping Iron II (86) 456
FRANCIS, JAN
  Champions (85) 515
FRANCIS, ROBERT
  Long Gray Line, The [1955] (82) 447
FRANCO, ABEL
  Zoot Suit (82) 389
FRANÇOIS, JACQUES
  Gift, The (84) 484
FRANK, CHARLES
  Right Stuff, The (84) 342

FRANK, JOANNA
Always (86) 60
FRANK, TONY
River Rat, The (85) 531
FRANKEL, ART
Lost in America (86) 219
FRANKFATHER, WILLIAM
Alamo Bay (86) 436
FRANKLIN, DIANE
Better Off Dead (86) 438
Last American Virgin, The (83) 424
FRANKLIN, DON
Fast Forward (86) 442
FRANKLIN, JOHN
Stephen King's Children of the Corn (85) 534
FRANKS, JAMES
Tomorrow [1972] (84) 589
FRANZ, DENNIS
Blow Out (82) 83
Body Double (85) 513
Psycho II (84) 307
FRANZ, EDWARD
"Obituaries" (84) 621
FRASER, HUGH
Draughtsman's Contract, The [1982] (84) 126
FRASER, RONALD
Flight of the Phoenix, The [1966] (85)
FRAZEE, JANE
"Obituaries" (86) 567
FRAZER, RUPERT
Shooting Party, The [1984] (86) 344
FRAZIER, RON
D.A.R.Y.L. (86) 441
FREBERG, DONOVAN
Here Come the Littles (86) 446
FRECHETTE, PETER
No Small Affair (85) 527
FREDERICK, VICKI
Body Rock (85) 513
Chorus Line, A (86) 91
FREDERICKS, PETER
They Might Be Giants [1971] (83) 515
FREEMAN, J. E.
Hard Traveling (86) 445
FREEMAN, JOAN
Friday the 13th—The Final Chapter (85) 520
FREEMAN, LISA
Friday the 13th—The Final Chapter (85) 520
FREEMAN, MORGAN
Harry and Son (85) 521
Marie (86) 227
That Was Then . . . This Is Now (86) 463
FREEMAN, PAUL
Long Good Friday, The [1980] (83) 220
Raiders of the Lost Ark (82) 308
Sender, The (83) 427
FREINDLIKH, ALICE
Rasputin [1975] (86) 457
FREITAG, ROBERT
Wild Geese II (86) 466
FREY, SAMI
Little Drummer Girl, The (85) 525

FREYD, BERNARD
Balance, La [1982] (84) 52
FRIEDBERG, MARTIN HARVEY
Can She Bake a Cherry Pie? (84) 95
FRIJDA, NELLY
Question of Silence, A (85) 530
FRITZ, ROGER
Berlin Alexanderplatz [1980] (84) 57
FROBOESS, CORNELIA
Veronika Voss (83) 382
FRÖLING, EWA
Fanny and Alexander [1982] (84) 146
FROMMER, BEN
American Pop (82) 62
FRY, RAY
Target (86) 462
FRYE, VIRGIL
Revenge of the Ninja (84) 492
Running Hot (85) 531
FUCHS, MATTHIAS
Lola [1981] (83) 215
FUENTES, MIGUEL ANGEL
Fitzcarraldo (83) 167
FUGARD, ATHOL
Gandhi (83) 183
Guest, The (85) 520
Killing Fields, The (85) 270
FUHRMANN, ROBERT
Hotdog . . . The Movie (85) 522
FUJIOKA, JOHN
American Ninja (86) 436
FULLER, FRANCES
They Might Be Giants [1971] (83) 515
FULLER, SAMUEL
Slapstick (85) 533
State of Things, The (84) 379
FULLERTON, FIONA
View to a Kill, A (86) 402
FULTON, JOHNNY
King of Jazz [1930] (86) 515
FULTON, RIKKI
Comfort and Joy (85) 146
Gorky Park (84) 162
FURLAN, MIRA
When Father Was Away on Business [1984] (86) 411
FURST, JOSEPH
Freud [1962] (84) 535
FURST, STEPHEN
Up the Creek (85) 537
FURST, TIMOTHY DANIEL
Jewel of the Nile, The (86) 448
FURY, BILLY
"Obituaries" (84) 621
FYODOROVA, VICTORIA
Target (86) 462

GABISON, DAVID
Cheech and Chong's The Corsican
Brothers (85) 515
GABLE, CLARK
Too Hot to Handle [1938] (84) 596
GABRIEL, LARRY
Cave Girl (86) 439

GABRIELSON, CHARLES
Bear, The   (85) 511
GADES, ANTONIO
Blood Wedding [1981]   (83) 418
Carmen   (84) 101
GAIGE, TRUMAN
Grace Quigley   (86) 444
GAINES, BOYD
Porky's   (83) 267
Sure Thing, The   (86) 369
GAINS, COURTNEY
Hardbodies   (85) 521
Lust in the Dust   (86) 450
Secret Admirer   (86) 459
Stephen King's Children of the Corn   (85) 534
GALABRU, MICHEL
Subway   (86) 461
GALATI, FRANK
Party Animal   (86) 455
GALE, DAVID
Re-Animator   (86) 457
GÁLFFI, LÁSZLÓ
Colonel Redl [1984]   (86) 100
Wagner   (84) 497
GALL, AXELLE
Traviata, La   (83) 366
GALLAGHER, PETER
Dreamchild   (86) 146
Summer Lovers   (83) 429
GALLEGO, GINA
Lust in the Dust   (86) 450
GALLIGAN, ZACH
Gremlins   (85) 230
GALLOWAY, DON
Big Chill, The   (84) 78
GALVAO, FLAVIO
Gabriela [1983]   (85) 213
GAMBON, MICHAEL
Turtle Diary   (86) 464
GAMMELL, ROBIN
Nightmares   (84) 490
GAMMON, JAMES
Hard Traveling   (86) 445
GAMPU, KEN
King Solomon's Mines   (86) 449
GANCE, ABEL
Napoleon [1927]   (82) 461
GANIOS, TONY
Body Rock   (85) 513
Continental Divide   (82) 115
Porky's   (83) 267
GANT, KATHRYN
Sheena   (85) 532
GANT, RICHARD E.
Krush Groove   (86) 449
GANZ, BRUNO
Circle of Deceit [1981]   (83) 419
GANZEL, TERESA
Toy, The   (83) 358
Transylvania 6-5000   (86) 463
GARBER, JOHN
American Flyers   (86) 436
GARBER, TERRI
Toy Soldiers   (85) 536

GARCIA, ANDY
Mean Season, The   (86) 452
GARCIA, NICOLE
Beau Pere   (82) 78
Bolero [1981]   (83) 418
Peril   (86) 456
GARCIA, SABRINA
Breakin' 2   (85) 514
GARCIN, HENRI
Woman Next Door, The   (82) 385
GARDENIA, VINCENT
Death Wish II   (83) 420
Movers and Shakers   (86) 453
GARDNER, AVA
Barefoot Contessa, The [1954]   (82) 399
Priest of Love   (82) 288
Snows of Kilimanjaro, The [1952]   (83) 498
GARET, ANDRÉ
Bob le Flambeur [1955]   (84) 526
GARFIELD, ALLEN
Cotton Club, The   (85) 150
Teachers   (85) 535
GARGAN, WILLIAM
Animal Kingdom, The [1932]   (86) 469
GARIJO, ALEXANDRA
Detective   (86) 442
GARLAND, JUDY
"Interview with James Mason, An"   (86) 31
"Life Achievement Award"   (86) 5, 6
Star Is Born, A [1954]   (84) 573
GARLICH, STEPHEN
Dark Crystal, The   (83) 130
GARNER, JAMES
Murphy's Romance   (86) 242
Tank   (85) 535
Victor / Victoria   (83) 387
GARNER, PEGGY ANN
"Obituaries"   (85) 667
GARR, TERI
After Hours   (86) 51
Black Stallion Returns, The   (84) 479
Escape Artist, The   (83) 421
Firstborn   (85) 519
Mr. Mom   (84) 489
One from the Heart   (83) 250
Sting II, The   (84) 494
Tootsie   (83) 353
GARRETT, LEIF
Outsiders, The   (84) 282
GARRISON, ROB
Karate Kid, The   (85) 264
GARRIVIER, VICTOR
Coup de torchon [1981]   (83) 124
GARSON, JOHN
Witness   (86) 421
GARTIN, CHRISTOPHER
Firstborn   (85) 519
GARVIN, GENE
Modern Romance   (82) 241
GARY, LINDA
Secret of the Sword, The   (86) 459
GASSMAN, VITTORIO
Sharky's Machine   (82) 324
Tempest   (83) 331

GAUL, PATRICIA
Silverado (86) 349
GAUTHIER, ANNE
Hail Mary (86) 182
GAYLE, JACKIE
Broadway Danny Rose (85) 112
Tempest (83) 331
GAYNES, GEORGE
Dead Men Don't Wear Plaid (83) 134
Micki & Maude (85) 308
Police Academy (85) 529
Police Academy 2 (86) 276
GAYNOR, JANET
"Obituaries" (85) 667
GAZZARA, BEN
Inchon (83) 424
Tales of Ordinary Madness (84) 495
They All Laughed (82) 350
GAZZO, MICHAEL
Cannonball Run II (85) 514
GEDRICK, JASON
Heavenly Kid, The (86) 445
GEER, ELLEN
Creator (86) 441
GEHMAN, MARTHA
Flamingo Kid, The (85) 192
Legend of Billie Jean, The (86) 450
GELDART, ED
Raggedy Man (82) 300
GELDOF, BOB
Pink Floyd the Wall [1981] (83) 258
GELIC, TOMISLAV
When Father Was Away on Business [1984] (86)
411
GELIN, DANIEL
Nuit de Varennes, La [1982] (84) 270
GELIN, PATRICIA
Montenegro (82) 250
GÉLINAS, GRATIEN
Agnes of God (86) 56
GELMAN, LARRY
Dreamscape (85) 166
GEMPART, MICHAEL
Boat Is Full, The [1981] (83) 82
GENEST, EMILE
Plouffe, Les (86) 456
GENEST, VERONIQUE
Basileus Quartet (85) 511
GENOVESE, MIKE
Code of Silence (86) 440
GEOFFREY, PAUL
Excalibur (82) 144
Greystoke (85) 236
GEOFFREYS, STEPHEN
Fraternity Vacation (86) 444
Fright Night (86) 444
GEORGE, CHRISTOPHER
"Obituaries" (84) 621
GEORGE, GLADYS
Hard Way, The [1942] (85) 555
GEORGE, GÖTZ
Out of Order (86) 455
GEORGE, JOE
Running Hot (85) 531

GEORGE, MURIEL
Nell Gwyn [1934] (84) 557
GEORGE, SUSAN
Enter the Ninja (83) 420
House Where Evil Dwells, The (83) 423
Jigsaw Man, The [1983] (85) 524
GEORGE, TRICIA
Missionary, The (83) 233
GER, AVIVA
Goodbye, New York (86) 444
GERARD, CHARLES
Edith and Marcel [1983] (85) 518
GERASIMOV, SERGEI
New Babylon, The [1929] (84) 561
GERAY, STEVEN
Unfaithful, The [1947] (86) 550
GERE, RICHARD
Beyond the Limit (84) 479
Breathless (84) 89
Cotton Club, The (85) 150
King David (86) 449
Officer and a Gentleman, An (83) 246
GERRITSEN, GUSTA
Flaxfield, The [1983] (86) 443
GERTZ, JAMIE
Alphabet City (85) 509
Mischief (86) 452
GETTY, ESTELLE
Mask (86) 231
GETTY, PAUL, III
State of Things, The (84) 379
GETZ, JOHN
Blood Simple (86) 438
Thief of Hearts (85) 536
GHOSTLEY, ALICE
Not for Publication (85) 527
GIAMBALVO, LOUIS
Nightmares (84) 490
GIANINI, CHERYL
War and Love (86) 465
GIANNINI, GIANCARLO
American Dreamer (85) 509
Fever Pitch (86) 443
Lili Marleen (82) 222
GIBB, DONALD
Lost in America (86) 219
Transylvania 6-5000 (86) 463
GIBBES, ROBYN
Wild Horses [1983] (85) 538
GIBSON, KITTY
Cal (85) 124
GIBSON, MEL
Bounty, The (85) 513
Gallipoli [1980] (82) 179
Mad Max Beyond Thunderdome (86) 223
Mrs. Soffel (85) 314
River, The (85) 416
Road Warrior, The [1981] (83) 277
Year of Living Dangerously, The
[1982] (84) 462
GIELGUD, JOHN
Arthur (82) 71
Chariots of Fire (82) 101
Falstaff [1967] (83) 443
Gandhi (83) 183
Plenty (86) 271

Priest of Love   (82) 288
Scandalous   (85) 532
Shooting Party, The [1984]   (86) 344
Wagner   (84) 497
Wicked Lady, The   (84) 497
GIGLIOTTI, LUPE
Blame It on Rio   (85) 512
GIL, JORGE
Cease Fire   (86) 440
GILAN, YVONNE
Agatha [1979]   (83) 435
Another Time, Another Place [1983]   (85) 510
GILBERT, MELISSA
Sylvester   (86) 462
GILFORD, JACK
Cocoon   (86) 96
They Might Be Giants [1971]   (83) 515
GILLESPIE, DANA
Hound of the Baskervilles, The
[1978]   (82) 203
GILLIAM, TERRY
Monty Python's The Meaning of Life   (84) 489
GILLIES, CAROL
Secrets   (85) 532
GILLIES, MAX
Coca-Cola Kid, The   (86) 440
GILLIN, HUGH
Psycho II   (84) 307
GILLINGWATER, CLAUDE
Dulcy [1923]   (82) 432
GILLIS, ANN
Bambi [1942]   (85) 543
GILMAN, SAM
"Obituaries"   (86) 567
GINGOLD, HERMIONE
Garbo Talks   (85) 520
GIORDANO, DOMIZIANA
Nostalgia [1983]   (85) 340
GIRADEAU, BERNARD
Hecate   (85) 522
GIRARDOT, ANNIE
Vie Continue, La [1981]   (83) 430
GIRARDOT, HIPPOLYTE
Bon Plaisir, Le [1983]   (85) 513
GISH, DOROTHY
"Interview with Lillian Gish, An"   (83) 23
"Life Achievement Award"   (85) 1
GISH, LILLIAN
Birth of a Nation, The [1915]   (83) 25
Bohème, La [1926]   (83) 27
Duel in the Sun [1946]   (83) 29
Grass Harp, The   (83) 30
"Interview with, An"   (83) 23
"Life Achievement Award"   (85) 1
Scarlet Letter, The [1927]   (83) 28; (85)
602
Trip to Bountiful, A [1953]   (83) 29
Wedding, A [1978]   (83) 31
White Sister, The [1923]   (83) 26
GITTLER, DAVID
Taking Off [1971]   (86) 545
GIUSHENKO, YEYGENIYA
Unfinished Piece for Piano Player, An
[1977]   (83) 430

GLASS, ANNE GISELE
Detective   (86) 442
GLAUDINI, ROBERT
Parasite   (83) 426
GLEASON, JACKIE
Smokey and the Bandit—Part 3   (84) 493
Sting II, The   (84) 494
Toy, The   (83) 358
GLEASON, JAMES
Guy Named Joe, A [1943]   (82) 435
GLEASON, PAT
Detour [1946]   (86) 498
GLEASON, PAUL
Breakfast Club, The   (86) 85
Tender Mercies   (84) 409
GLEDHILL, NICHOLAS
Careful He Might Hear You [1983]   (83) 130
GLEESON, REDMOND
Dreamscape   (85) 166
GLENN, SCOTT
Challenge, The   (83) 109
Keep, The   (84) 487
Personal Best   (83) 254
Right Stuff, The   (84) 342
River, The   (85) 416
Silverado   (86) 349
Wild Geese II   (86) 466
GLESS, SHARON
Star Chamber, The   (84) 494
GLOVER, BRIAN
American Werewolf in London, An   (82) 66
Company of Wolves, The [1984]   (86) 115
GLOVER, CRISPIN
Back to the Future   (86) 65
Friday the 13th—The Final Chapter   (85) 520
Teachers   (85) 535
GLOVER, DANNY
Color Purple, The   (86) 105
Iceman   (85) 248
Places in the Heart   (85) 371
Silverado   (86) 349
Witness   (86) 421
GLOVER, JOHN
Evil That Men Do, The   (85) 518
Flash of Green, A   (86) 443
White Nights   (86) 416
GLOVER, JULIAN
For Your Eyes Only   (82) 155
GLUCHKOVA, A.
New Babylon, The [1929]   (84) 561
GLYNN, CARLIN
Continental Divide   (82) 115
Sixteen Candles   (85) 532
Trip to Bountiful, The   (86) 383
GNAEDINGER, MATHIAS
Boat Is Full, The [1981]   (83) 82
GO, HIROMI
MacArthur's Children   (86) 451
GODARD, JEAN-LUC
First Name, Carmen [1983]   (85) 186
GODFREY, ARTHUR
"Obituaries"   (84) 622
GODUNOV, ALEXANDER
Witness   (86) 421

GODWIN, CHRISTOPHER
Bullshot [1983] (86) 439
GOELZ, DAVE
Great Muppet Caper, The (82) 187
Muppets Take Manhattan, The (85) 526
GOETZ, PETER MICHAEL
Best Defense (85) 512
GOLD, HARVEY
Sam's Son (85) 531
GOLD, TRACEY
Shoot the Moon (83) 295
GOLDBERG, WHOOPI
Color Purple, The (86) 105
GOLDBLUM, JEFF
Adventures of Buckaroo Banzai,
The (85) 47
Big Chill, The (84) 78
Into the Night (86) 186
Next Stop, Greenwich Village [1976] (85) 592
Right Stuff, The (84) 342
Silverado (86) 349
Threshold (84) 495
Transylvania 6-5000 (86) 463
GOLDEN, ANNIE
Streetwalkin' (86) 461
GOLDMAN, LORRY
Home Free All (85) 522
GOLDOI, LELIA
Rainy Day Friends (86) 457
GOLDSMITH, CLIO
Gift, The (84) 484
Heat of Desire [1981] (85) 522
GOLDSMITH, MERWIN
Lily in Love (86) 450
GOLDSTEIN, SETH
Kerouac, the Movie (86) 448
GOLDTHWAIT, BOB
Police Academy 2 (86) 276
GOLINO, VALERIA
Joke of Destiny, A [1983] (85) 259
GOLONKA, ARLENE
My Tutor (84) 490
GOMEZ, MIKE
Norte, El (84) 265
Zoot Suit (82) 389
GOMEZ, PALOMA
Valentina [1982] (84) 496
GOMEZ, PANCHITO
Tuff Turf (86) 464
GONCALVES, MILTON
Kiss of the Spider Woman (86) 209
GONZALEZ, AUGUSTIN
Holy Innocents, The (86) 447
Volver a empezar (83) 393
GONZALEZ, JOSEPH
Death Wish III (86) 441
GONZALEZ-GONZALEZ, PEDRO
Lust in the Dust (86) 450
GOOD, CHRISTOPHER
Bullshot [1983] (86) 439
GOODE, LUCY
Secrets (85) 532
GOODFELLOW, JOAN
Flash of Green, A (86) 443

GOODMAN, DODY
Splash (85) 434
GOODMAN, JOHN
Maria's Lovers (86) 451
GOODMAN, ROBERT
Harry and Son (85) 521
GOODRICH, DEBORAH
Just One of the Guys (86) 448
GOODROW, GARRY
Breathless (84) 89
Sure Thing, The (86) 369
GOORWITZ, ALLEN
Black Stallion Returns, The (84) **479**
Continental Divide (82) 115
Get Crazy (84) 484
State of Things, The (84) 379
GORCEY, DAVID
"Obituaries" (85) 669
GORDON, DON
Beast Within, The (83) 418
GORDON, GAVIN
"Obituaries" (84) 623
GORDON, KEITH
Christine (84) 106
Legend of Billie Jean, The (86) 450
GORDON, LEE
Fire and Ice (84) 153
GORDON, PHILIP
Came a Hot Friday (86) 439
GORDON, ROBERT
Loveless, The (85) 525
GORDON, RUTH
Jimmy the Kid (84) 486
Maxie (86) 452
"Obituaries" (86) 567
GORDON, VIC
Lonely Hearts [1982] (84) 212
GORING, MARIUS
Barefoot Contessa, The [1954] (82) 399
GORMAN, CLIFF
Angel (85) 510
Videodrome (84) 452
GORSHIN, FRANK
Bells Are Ringing [1960] (84) 517
Lonely Hearts [1982] (84) 212
GOSDEN, FREEMAN F.
"Obituaries" (83) 536
GOSSETT, LOUIS, JR.
Enemy Mine (86) 161
Finders Keepers (85) 519
Jaws 3-D (84) 486
Officer and a Gentleman, An (83) 246
GOTHARD, MICHAEL
Lifeforce (86) 450
GOTTSCHALK, FERDINAND
Sign of the Cross, The [1932] (85) 607
GOUDAL, JETTA
"Obituaries" (86) 568
GOUGH, LLOYD
Front, The [1976] (86) 502
GOUGH, MICHAEL
Oxford Blues (85) 528
Top Secret (85) 536
GOULART, PAULO
Gabriela [1983] (85) 213

GOULD, HAROLD
  Arrangement, The [1969]   (86) 474
GOULD-PORTER, ARTHUR
  Torn Curtain [1966]   (85) 644
GOUTMAN, CHRISTOPHER
  Goodbye, New York   (86) 444
GOWEN, LORI
  Pumping Iron II   (86) 456
GOZ, HARRY
  Mommie Dearest   (82) 245
  Rappin'   (86) 457
GRACE, NICKOLAS
  Heat and Dust [1982]   (84) 187
GRAF, DAVID
  Police Academy   (85) 529
  Police Academy 2   (86) 276
GRAFASI, JOE
  Bad Medicine   (86) 437
GRAHAM, GARY
  All the Right Moves   (84) 41
GRAHAM, GERRIT
  Man with One Red Shoe, The   (86) 451
  National Lampoon's Class Reunion   (83) 426
GRAHAM, RONNY
  To Be or Not to Be   (84) 426
GRAHAM, THERESE
  Country   (85) 156
GRAHAME, GLORIA
  "Obituaries"   (82) 488
GRAHAME, MARGOT
  "Obituaries"   (83) 536
GRAINER, DOROTHY
  Take a Letter, Darling [1942]   (85) 632
GRANGER, FARLEY
  North Star, The [1943]   (83) 476
GRANGER, LEEYAN
  Blame It on the Night   (85) 512
GRANOTIER, SYLVIE
  Dangerous Moves [1984]   (86) 129
GRANT, CARY
  I'm No Angel [1933]   (85) 561
GRANT, DAVID
  American Flyers   (86) 436
GRANT, KIRBY
  "Obituaries"   (86) 568
GRANT, LEE
  Teachers   (85) 535
  Visiting Hours   (83) 431
GRANT, LEON W.
  Beat Street   (85) 512
GRAVES, PETER
  Airplane II   (83) 417
  Savannah Smiles   (84) 493
GRAY, CHARLES
  Jigsaw Man, The [1983]   (85) 524
GRAY, ERIN
  Six Pack   (83) 428
GRAY, ROGER
  Barbary Coast [1935]   (84) 506
GRAY, SPALDING
  Almost You   (86) 436
  Killing Fields, The   (85) 270

GRAY, WILLOUGHBY
  Hit, The   (86) 446
  View to a Kill, A   (86) 402
GREEN, ADOLPH
  My Favorite Year   (83) 241
GREEN, CARLOTTA
  Hercules II   (86) 446
GREEN, KERRI
  Goonies, The   (86) 176
  Summer Rental   (86) 462
GREEN, LEIF
  Joysticks   (84) 487
GREEN, SETH
  Hotel New Hampshire, The   (85) 243
GREENAN, DAVID
  Silent Madness   (85) 532
GREENE, GRAHAM
  Running Brave   (84) 354
GREENE, JANICE
  City Girl, The   (85) 516
GREENE, JON
  Alley Cat   (85) 509
GREENE, MICHAEL
  Lost in America   (86) 219
GREENE, RICHARD
  "Obituaries"   (86) 568
GREENE, SHECKY
  Splash   (85) 434
GREENLEAF, JIM
  Joysticks   (84) 487
  Toy Soldiers   (85) 536
GREENLEES, WILLIAM
  Gregory's Girl [1981]   (83) 193
  That Sinking Feeling [1979]   (85) 536
GREENSPUN, HANK
  Fever Pitch   (86) 443
GREENSTEIN, STEVE
  Bear, The   (85) 511
GREENWOOD, JOAN
  Hound of the Baskervilles, The
    [1978]   (82) 203
GREENWOOD, ROSAMUND
  Missionary, The   (83) 233
GREER, ELLEN
  Hard Traveling   (86) 445
GREER, JANE
  Against All Odds   (85) 509
GREGG, SHARON
  Repo Man   (85) 408
GREGGORY, PASCAL
  Pauline at the Beach [1982]   (84) 296
GREGORIO, ROSE
  True Confessions   (82) 368
GREGORY, ANDRÉ
  Always   (86) 60
  My Dinner with André   (82) 255
  Protocol   (85) 383
GREGORY, CELIA
  Agatha [1979]   (83) 435
GREGORY, MARK
  1990   (84) 491
GREGORY, SHAREE
  Mass Appeal   (85) 303

GREGORY, STEPHEN
Heavenly Kid, The   (86) 445
GREIST, KIM
C.H.U.D.   (85) 515
GRESS, GOOGY
Maxie   (86) 452
GREY, DENISE
Boum, La [1980]   (84) 480
GREY, JENNIFER
American Flyers   (86) 436
Red Dawn   (85) 530
GREY, JOEL
Remo Williams   (86) 457
GREYBE, VALERIE
Cave Girl   (86) 439
GRIER, DAVID ALAN
Soldier's Story, A   (85) 427
Streamers   (84) 391
GRIER, PAM
Fort Apache, the Bronx   (82) 159
Something Wicked This Way Comes   (84) 493
Tough Enough   (84) 495
GRIES, JONATHAN
Real Genius   (86) 309
GRIEST, KIM
Brazil   (86) 80
GRIFASI, JOE
Brewster's Millions   (86) 438
Honky Tonk Freeway   (82) 199
Pope of Greenwich Village, The   (85) 529
Still of the Night   (83) 326
GRIFFIN, LORIE
Teen Wolf   (86) 462
GRIFFIN, LYNNE
Strange Brew   (84) 494
GRIFFIN, MERV
Lonely Guy, The   (85) 525
Man with Two Brains, The   (84) 223
Slapstick   (85) 533
GRIFFITH, ANDY
Rustler's Rhapsody   (86) 458
GRIFFITH, ED
Pee-wee's Big Adventure   (86) 265
GRIFFITH, GERALDINE
Experience Preferred ... but Not Essential
[1982]   (84) 141
GRIFFITH, HUGH
Hound of the Baskervilles, The
[1978]   (82) 203
Mutiny on the Bounty [1962]   (85) 581
GRIFFITH, MELANIE
Body Double   (85) 513
GRIFFITHS, LINDA
Lianna   (84) 201
GRIFFITHS, RICHARD
Greystoke   (85) 236
Private Function, A [1984]   (86) 280
GRIMALDI, DAN
Joey   (86) 448
GRIZZARD, GEORGE
Bachelor Party   (85) 511
Wrong Is Right   (83) 403
GRODIN, CHARLES
Great Muppet Caper, The   (82) 187
Lonely Guy, The   (85) 525

Movers and Shakers   (86) 453
Woman in Red, The   (85) 538
GROGAN, CLARE
Comfort and Joy   (85) 146
Gregory's Girl [1981]   (83) 193
GRÖNEMEYER, HERBERT-ARTHUR
Boot, Das [1981]   (83) 86
GROOM, SAM
Deadly Eyes   (84) 482
GROSS, ARYE
Just One of the Guys   (86) 448
GROSSMAN, GARY
Bachelor Party   (85) 511
GROTH, JAN
Out of Order   (86) 455
GROUTAS, XENIA
My First Wife   (86) 453
GROVES, ROBIN
Stephen King's Silver Bullet   (86) 460
GRUBB, ROBERT
Phar Lap   (85) 528
GRUBEL, ILONA
Target   (86) 462
GUARDIOLA, JOSÉ
Holy Innocents, The   (86) 447
GUERRA, BLANCA
Erendira [1983]   (85) 181
GUERRA, CASTULO
Stick   (86) 460
GUEST, CHRISTOPHER
This Is Spinal Tap   (85) 484
GUEST, LANCE
Just the Way You Are   (85) 524
Last Starfighter, The   (85) 277
GUFFEY, CARY
Bear, The   (85) 511
GUICHARD, ETIENNE
Bal, Le [1983]   (85) 80
GUIDELLI, MICOL
Night of the Shooting Stars, The
[1982]   (84) 258
GUIDELLI, MIRIAM
Night of the Shooting Stars, The
[1982]   (84) 258
GUILFOYLE, PAUL
Apache [1954]   (82) 395
GUINNESS, ALEC
Lovesick   (84) 488
Passage to India, A   (85) 365
Return of the Jedi   (84) 326
GULAGER, CLU
Chattanooga Choo Choo   (85) 515
Into the Night   (86) 186
Nightmare on Elm Street, Part 2, A   (86) 454
Return of the Living Dead, The   (86) 314
GULP, EISI
Sugarbaby   (86) 461
GUNDEN, ERIK
Secret of the Sword, The   (86) 459
GUNN, MOSES
Firestarter   (85) 519
Neverending Story, The   (85) 527
Ragtime   (82) 304
GUNTY, MORTY
Broadway Danny Rose   (85) 112

GURCHENKO, LUDMILLA
  Siberiade [1977]   (83) 299
  Waiting for Gavrilov [1982]   (84) 497
GURRY, ERIC
  Bad Boys   (84) 479
GUSEV, S.
  New Babylon, The [1929]   (84) 561
GUSKIN, ANNA
  Light Ahead, The [1939]   (83) 460
GUTHRIE, CAROLINE
  Gregory's Girl [1981]   (83) 193
GUTIERREZ, ZAIDE SILVA
  Norte, El   (84) 265
GUTMAN, DAVID
  New Babylon, The [1929]   (84) 561
GUTTENBERG, STEVE
  Bad Medicine   (86) 437
  Boys from Brazil, The [1978]   (86) 480
  Cocoon   (86) 96
  Diner   (83) 142
  Man Who Wasn't There, The   (84) 489
  Police Academy   (85) 529
  Police Academy 2   (86) 276
GUTTERIDGE, LUCY
  Top Secret   (85) 536
GUVE, BERTIL
  After the Rehearsal   (85) 52
  Fanny and Alexander [1982]   (84) 146
GUZALDO, JOSEPH
  Code of Silence   (86) 440
GWATKIN, ANN-MARIE
  Secret Places [1984]   (86) 459
GWILLIM, JACK
  Clash of the Titans   (82) 111
GWILYM, MIKE
  Priest of Love   (82) 288
GWILYM, ROBERT
  Experience Preferred . . . but Not Essential
    [1982]   (84) 141
GWYNNE, FRED
  Cotton Club, The   (85) 150

HAAKE, JAMES
  To Be or Not to Be   (84) 426
HAAS, LUKAS
  Testament   (84) 420
  Witness   (86) 421
HABEMA, COX
  Question of Silence, A   (85) 530
HABICH, MATTHIAS
  Imperative [1982]   (86) 447
HACK, SHELLEY
  King of Comedy, The   (84) 192
HACKETT, JOAN
  Escape Artist, The   (83) 421
  "Obituaries"   (84) 623
  Only When I Laugh   (82) 268
HACKETT, SANDY
  Hotdog . . . The Movie   (85) 522
HACKMAN, GENE
  Eureka   (86) 442
  Misunderstood   (85) 526
  Superman II   (82) 339
  Target   (86) 462
  Twice in a Lifetime   (86) 397

Uncommon Valor   (84) 496
Under Fire   (84) 441
HACZKIEWICZ, EUGENIUSZ
  Moonlighting   (83) 237
HADEN, SARA
  "Obituaries"   (82) 489
HADZIHAFISBEGOVIC, EMIR
  When Father Was Away on Business [1984]   (86)
    411
HAGEN, UTA
  Boys from Brazil, The [1978]   (86) 480
HAGERTY, JULIE
  Airplane II   (83) 417
  Bad Medicine   (86) 437
  Goodbye, New York   (86) 444
  Lost in America   (86) 219
  Midsummer Night's Sex Comedy, A   (83)
    228
HAGGERTY, H. B.
  Micki & Maude   (85) 308
HAGMAN, LARRY
  S.O.B.   (82) 328
HAGUE, ALBERT
  Nightmares   (84) 490
HAHN, ARCHIE
  Meatballs Part II   (85) 526
HAIG, MICHAEL
  Wild Horses [1983]   (85) 538
HAIGH, KENNETH
  Wild Geese II   (86) 466
HAIM, COREY
  Firstborn   (85) 519
  Murphy's Romance   (86) 242
  Stephen King's Silver Bullet   (86) 460
HAKIM, OMAR
  Bring on the Night   (86) 439
HALE, ALAN, SR.
  Our Relations [1936]   (86) 523
  Roughly Speaking [1945]   (83) 490
  They Drive by Night [1940]   (83) 508
HALEY, JACKIE EARLE
  Losin' It   (84) 488
HALEY, PAUL
  Experience Preferred ... but Not Essential
    [1982]   (84) 141
HALL, AMELIA
  Iceman   (85) 248
HALL, ANTHONY MICHAEL
  Breakfast Club, The   (86) 85
  National Lampoon's Vacation   (84) 242
  Sixteen Candles   (85) 532
  Weird Science   (86) 465
HALL, GRAYSON
  "Obituaries"   (86) 569
HALL, ROBERT DAVID
  Here Come the Littles   (86) 446
HALL, THURSTON
  Secret Life of Walter Mitty, The [1947]   (86) 540
HALL, WILBUR
  King of Jazz [1930]   (86) 515
HALLAHAN, CHARLES
  Pale Rider   (86) 261
  Silkwood   (84) 367
  Thing, The   (83) 343
  Vision Quest   (86) 464

HALLAM, JOHN
  Dragonslayer (82) 125
  Lifeforce (86) 450
HALLAREN, JANE
  Lianna (84) 201
  Modern Romance (82) 241
  Unfaithfully Yours (85) 537
HALLIDAY, JOHN
  Peter Ibbetson [1935] (86) 527
HALLYDAY, JOHNNY
  Detective (86) 442
HALMER, GUNTHER MARIA
  Sophie's Choice (83) 311
HAMAMURA, JUN
  Cruel Story of Youth [1960] (85) 517
HAMILL, MARK
  Return of the Jedi (84) 326
HAMILTON, ALLEN
  Code of Silence (86) 440
HAMILTON, FRANK
  Man with One Red Shoe, The (86) 451
HAMILTON, HALE
  Most Dangerous Game, The [1932] (86) 519
HAMILTON, KIT
  Hardbodies (85) 521
HAMILTON, LINDA
  Stephen King's Children of the Corn (85) 534
  Tag (83) 429
  Terminator, The (85) 478
HAMILTON, LISA GAY
  Krush Groove (86) 449
HAMILTON, MARGARET
  Brewster McCloud [1970] (86) 484
  "Obituaries" (86) 569
HAMILTON, MURRAY
  Too Scared to Scream (86) 463
HAMILTON, NEIL
  Animal Kingdom, The [1932] (86) 469
  "Obituaries" (85) 670
HAMILTON, SUZANNA
  Brimstone and Treacle (83) 91
  1984 (85) 335
  Out of Africa (86) 255
  Wetherby (86) 406
HAMILTON, TED
  Pirate Movie, The (83) 427
HAMLIN, HARRY
  Blue Skies Again (84) 479
  Clash of the Titans (82) 111
  Making Love (83) 425
HAMLIN, JOANNE
  Muppets Take Manhattan, The (85) 526
HAMMER, BEN
  Running Hot (85) 531
HAMMILL, ELLEN
  Joey (86) 448
HAMMONG, JOHN
  Cross Creek (84) 116
HAMNETT, OLIVIA
  Earthling, The [1980] (82) 130
HAMPTON, HOPE
  "Obituaries" (83) 537
HAMPTON, JAMES
  Teen Wolf (86) 462

HAMPTON, PAUL
  Lady Sings the Blues [1972] (85) 565
HANDL, IRENE
  Hound of the Baskervilles, The
    [1978] (82) 203
HANDY, JAMES
  Verdict, The (83) 377
HANEY, CAROL
  Invitation to the Dance [1956] (86) 507
HANFT, HELEN
  Next Stop, Greenwich Village [1976] (85) 592
  Stardust Memories [1980] (85) 626
HANIN, ROGER
  My Other Husband (86) 453
HANKS, TOM
  Bachelor Party (85) 511
  Man with One Red Shoe, The (86) 451
  Splash (85) 434
  Volunteers (86) 464
HANLEY, BRIDGET
  Chattanooga Choo Choo (85) 515
HANNAH, DARYL
  Blade Runner (83) 76
  Pope of Greenwich Village, The (85) 529
  Reckless (85) 530
  Splash (85) 434
  Summer Lovers (83) 429
HANNON, SEAN
  Fire and Ice (84) 153
HANSEN, ARNE
  Zappa (85) 539
HANSEN, PATTI
  Hard to Hold (85) 521
  They All Laughed (82) 350
HANSON, DAVID
  Slap Shot [1977] (82) 467
HANSON, LARS
  Scarlet Letter, The [1927] (85) 602
HARADA, ERNEST
  Volunteers (86) 464
HARADA, MIEKO
  Ran (86) 304
HARBOR, GAYLE
  Firstborn (85) 519
HARBORT, CHRISTINE
  Mephisto (82) 237
HARDESTER, CROFTON
  Android (85) 510
HARDIMAN, TERENCE
  Sahara (85) 531
HARDIN, JERRY
  Heartland (82) 191
  Honky Tonk Freeway (82) 199
  Mass Appeal (85) 303
  Warning Sign (86) 465
HARDING, ANN
  Animal Kingdom, The [1932] (86) 469
  North Star, The [1943] (83) 476
  "Obituaries" (82) 489
  Peter Ibbetson [1935] (86) 527
HARDISON KADEEM
  Rappin' (86) 457
HARDWICKE, CEDRIC
  Becky Sharp [1935] (82) 403
  Nell Gwyn [1934] (84) 557

HARDY, JONATHAN
  Lonely Hearts [1982]   (84) 212
HARDY, OLIVER
  Our Relations [1936]   (86) 523
HARDY, ROBERT
  Shooting Party, The [1984]   (86) 344
HARDY, SAM
  Miracle Woman, The [1931]   (83) 473
HARE, WILL
  Aviator, The   (86) 437
  Silent Night, Deadly Night   (85) 532
HAREWOOD, DORIAN
  Against All Odds   (85) 509
  Falcon and the Snowman, The   (86) 165
HARGREAVES, CHRISTINE
  Pink Floyd the Wall [1981]   (83) 258
HARGREAVES, JOHN
  Beyond Reasonable Doubt [1980]   (84) 74
  Careful He Might Hear You [1983]   (85)
    130
  My First Wife   (86) 453
HARKINS, JOHN
  Absence of Malice   (82) 57
  Birdy   (85) 93
HARLAN, OTIS
  King of Jazz [1930]   (86) 515
HARLAN, ROBIN
  Party Animal   (86) 455
HARNOIS, ELIZABETH
  One Magic Christmas   (86) 455
HAROLDE, RALF
  Our Relations [1936]   (86) 523
HAROLDS, ROLF
  I'm No Angel [1933]   (85) 561
HARPAZ, SHRAGA
  Vulture, The   (86) 464
HARPER, JAMES
  Firstborn   (85) 519
HARPER, JESSICA
  My Favorite Year   (83) 241
  Pennies from Heaven   (82) 276
  Stardust Memories [1980]   (85) 626
HARPER, SHARI BELAFONTE
  If You Could See What I Hear   (83) 423
HARPER, TESS
  Amityville 3-D   (84) 479
  Flashpoint   (85) 519
  Tender Mercies   (84) 409
HARPER, VALERIE
  Blame It on Rio   (85) 512
HARRA, JOHNNY
  This Is Elvis   (82) 360
HARRINGTON, LAURA
  City Girl, The   (85) 516
HARRIS, BOB
  Flash of Green, A   (86) 443
HARRIS, CYNTHIA
  Reuben, Reuben   (84) 337
HARRIS, DARREN
  Sixteen Candles   (85) 532
HARRIS, DAVID
  Purple Hearts   (85) 529
  Soldier's Story, A   (85) 427

HARRIS, ED
  Alamo Bay   (86) 436
  Flash of Green, A   (86) 443
  Places in the Heart   (85) 371
  Right Stuff, The   (84) 342
  Sweet Dreams   (86) 374
  Swing Shift   (85) 535
  Under Fire   (84) 441
HARRIS, FOX
  Repo Man   (85) 408
HARRIS, JIM
  Waitress   (83) 431
HARRIS, JON
  Pee-wee's Big Adventure   (86) 265
HARRIS, MARY LOU
  Muppets Take Manhattan, The   (85) 526
HARRIS, RICHARD
  Mutiny on the Bounty [1962]   (85) 581
HARRIS, ROBERT H.
  "Obituaries"   (82) 490
HARRIS, ROSEMARY
  Ploughman's Lunch, The [1983]   (85) 377
HARRIS, ROSS
  Testament   (84) 420
HARRISON, CATHRYN
  Dresser, The   (84) 130
HARRISON, GREGORY
  Razorback [1984]   (86) 457
HARRISON, JENILEE
  Tank   (85) 535
HARRISON, NICOLE
  American Taboo   (85) 509
HARROLD, KATHRYN
  Into the Night   (86) 186
  Modern Romance   (82) 241
  Sender, The   (83) 427
  Yes, Giorgio   (83) 431
HARRY, DEBORAH
  Videodrome   (84) 452
HART, CHUCK
  Hardbodies   (85) 521
HART, ROXANNE
  Oh God, You Devil   (85) 528
  Verdict, The   (83) 377
HARTLEY, MARIETTE
  Improper Channels   (82) 218
  O'Hara's Wife   (83) 426
HARTLEY, TAMARA
  River Rat, The   (85) 531
HARTMAN, ELIZABETH
  Secret of NIMH, The   (83) 288
HARTMAN, LISA
  Where the Boys Are '84   (85) 537
HARVEY, ALEX
  Country   (85) 156
HARVEY, HARRY, SR.
  "Obituaries"   (86) 569
HARVEY, RODNEY
  Mixed Blood   (86) 452
HARVEY, TONY
  Taking Off [1971]   (86) 545
HASKELL, DAVID
  Body Double   (85) 513

HASMANN, MARK
  Drifting (85) 518
HASSEL, KARL HEINZ VON
  Lili Marleen (82) 222
HASSELL, GEORGE
  Becky Sharp [1935] (82) 403
HASTINGS, IAN
  Give My Regards to Broad Street (85) 520
HATFIELD, HURD
  King David (86) 449
HATHAWAY, NOAH
  Neverending Story, The (85) 527
HATTANGADY, ROHINI
  Gandhi (83) 183
HATTEN, TOM
  Spies like Us (86) 360
HATTEN, YANKTON
  Places in the Heart (85) 371
  Sylvester (86) 462
HAUER, RUTGER
  Blade Runner (83) 76
  Eureka (86) 442
  Flesh and Blood (86) 443
  Ladyhawke (86) 214
  Nighthawks (82) 259
  Osterman Weekend, The (84) 491
HAUFRECT, ALAN
  Kiss Me Goodbye (83) 209
HAUGE, DENNIS
  Hadley's Rebellion (85) 521
HAUGLAND, AAGE
  Parsifal (84) 491
HAUSER, PATRICK
  Weekend Pass (85) 537
HAUSER, WINGS
  Deadly Force (84) 482
  Soldier's Story, A (85) 427
  Vice Squad (83) 430
HAUSSERMAN, MISCHA
  Evil That Men Do, The (85) 518
HAUSTEIN, THOMAS
  Christine F. [1981] (83) 419
HAVENS, RICHIE
  Matter of Struggle, A (86) 451
HAVERS, NIGEL
  Chariots of Fire (82) 101
  Passage to India, A (85) 365
HAVET, BERNARD
  Dernier Combat, Le [1983] (85) 517
HAWES, MARY
  Scarlet Letter, The [1927] (85) 602
HAWKE, ETHAN
  Explorers (86) 442
HAWLEY, WILLIAM
  Tomorrow [1972] (84) 589
HAWN, GOLDIE
  Best Friends (83) 68
  Protocol (85) 383
  Swing Shift (85) 535
HAWTHORNE, NIGEL
  Black Cauldron, The (86) 75
  Firefox (83) 160
  Turtle Diary (86) 464

HAYASHI, MARC
  Chan Is Missing (83) 113
HAYDEN, JAMES
  Once upon a Time in America (85) 345
HAYDEN, RUSSELL
  "Obituaries" (82) 490
HAYDN, RICHARD
  Mutiny on the Bounty [1962] (85) 581
  "Obituaries" (86) 570
HAYES, ALAN
  Friday the 13th—The Final Chapter (85) 520
  Sam's Son (85) 531
HAYES, BILLIE
  Black Cauldron, The (86) 75
HAYES, GRACE
  King of Jazz [1930] (86) 515
HAYES, HELEN
  "Interview with Lillian Gish, An" (83) 30
HAYES, ISAAC
  Escape from New York (82) 133
HAYES, PATRICIA
  Neverending Story, The (85) 527
HAYGARTH, TONY
  Private Function, A [1984] (86) 280
HAYMAN, DAVID
  Sense of Freedom, A (86) 459
HAYNIE, JIM
  Country (85) 156
  Hard Traveling (86) 445
HAYS, ROBERT
  Airplane II (83) 417
  Scandalous (85) 532
  Stephen King's Cat's Eye (86) 460
  Trenchcoat (84) 496
HAYTER, JAMES
  "Obituaries" (84) 623
HAYWARD, DAVID
  Slayground [1983] (85) 533
HAYWARD, LOUIS
  "Obituaries" (86) 570
HAYWARD, SUSAN
  Lost Moment, The [1947] (83) 465
  Snows of Kilimanjaro, The [1952] (83) 498
HAYWOOD, CHRIS
  Coca-Cola Kid, The (86) 440
  Heatwave (84) 485
  Razorback [1984] (86) 457
HEACOCK, LINNEA
  Taking Off [1971] (86) 545
HEADLY, GLENN
  Fandango (86) 442
HEALY, BETTY
  Our Relations [1936] (86) 523
HEALY, DAVID
  Supergirl (85) 535
HEALY, HAROLD
  Sign of the Cross, The [1932] (85) 607
HEALY, KATHERINE
  Six Weeks (83) 428
HEARD, JOHN
  After Hours (86) 51
  Cat People (83) 100
  C.H.U.D. (85) 515

Cutter's Way   (82) 119
Heaven Help Us   (86) 445
Too Scared to Scream   (86) 463
Trip to Bountiful, The   (86) 383
HEARN, LEW
  Specter of the Rose [1946]   (83) 504
HECHT, PAUL
  Joshua Then and Now   (86) 198
HEDAYA, DAN
  Blood Simple   (86) 438
  Commando   (86) 111
  Reckless   (85) 530
  Tightrope   (85) 489
HEDLEY, JACK
  For Your Eyes Only   (82) 155
HEFFERNAN, HONOR
  Danny Boy   (85) 517
HEFFNER, KYLE T.
  Flashdance   (84) 158
  Runaway Train   (86) 324
  Woman in Red, The   (85) 538
HEFLIN, MARTA
  Come Back to the 5 & Dime Jimmy Dean,
    Jimmy Dean   (83) 120
HEFLIN, VAN
  H. M. Pulham, Esq. [1941]   (82) 439
HEFNER, KEITH
  Fever Pitch   (86) 443
HEGIRA, ANNE
  Arrangement, The [1969]   (86) 474
HEIGH, HELENE
  Mass Appeal   (85) 303
HEIM, CARRIE KEI
  Santa Claus   (86) 334
HEINSOHN, ELISA
  Joey   (86) 448
HELBERG, SANDY
  Up the Creek   (85) 537
HELFER, BRITT
  Alley Cat   (85) 509
HELL, RICHARD
  Smithereens   (83) 307
HELLBERG, MARTIN
  Mephisto   (82) 237
HELLER, RANDEE
  Karate Kid, The   (85) 264
HELLMAN, IRVING
  Pee-wee's Big Adventure   (86) 265
HELM, LEVON
  Smooth Talk   (86) 354
HELMOND, KATHERINE
  Brazil   (86) 80
  Time Bandits [1980]   (82) 364
HEMINGWAY, MARGAUX
  They Call Me Bruce   (83) 429
HEMINGWAY, MARIEL
  Creator   (86) 441
  Mean Season, The   (86) 452
  Personal Best   (83) 254
  Star 80   (84) 374
HEMMINGS, DAVID
  Beyond Reasonable Doubt [1980]   (84) 74
  Man, Woman and Child   (84) 489
HENDERSON, ALBERT
  Modern Romance   (82) 241

HENDERSON, BILL
  Clue   (86) 440
HENDERSON, JO
  Lianna   (84) 201
HENDRA, TONY
  This Is Spinal Tap   (85) 484
HENDRIAN, DUTCH
  Most Dangerous Game, The [1932]   (86) 519
HENDRIX, WANDA
  "Obituaries"   (82) 491
HENDRY, IAN
  "Obituaries"   (85) 672
HENNER, MARILU
  Cannonball Run II   (85) 514
  Hammett   (84) 174
  Johnny Dangerously   (85) 524
  Man Who Loved Women, The   (84) 218
  Perfect   (86) 456
  Rustler's Rhapsody   (86) 458
HENRIKSEN, LANCE
  Nightmares   (84) 490
  Right Stuff, The   (84) 342
  Terminator, The   (85) 478
HENRIQUES, DARRYL
  Best Defense   (85) 512
HENRIQUEZ, RON
  Code of Silence   (86) 440
HENRY, BUCK
  Man Who Fell to Earth, The [1975]   (83)
    469
  Taking Off [1971]   (86) 545
HENRY, GREGG
  Body Double   (85) 513
HENRY, JUSTIN
  Sixteen Candles   (85) 532
HENRY, LAURA
  Heavenly Bodies   (85) 522
HENSON, BRIAN
  Return to Oz   (86) 458
HENSON, JIM
  Great Muppet Caper, The   (82) 187
  Muppets Take Manhattan, The   (85) 526
  Sesame Street Presents: Follow That Bird   (86)
    459
HEPBURN, AUDREY
  They All Laughed   (82) 350
HEPBURN, DEE
  Gregory's Girl [1981]   (83) 193
HEPBURN, KATHARINE
  "American Cinema in 1981, The"   (82) 30
  Grace Quigley   (86) 444
  On Golden Pond   (82) 263
HEPTON, BERNARD
  Holcroft Covenant, The   (86) 446
HERBERT, CHRIS
  Last Starfighter, The   (85) 277
HERD, RICHARD
  Trancers   (86) 463
HERLIE, EILEEN
  Freud [1962]   (84) 535
HERLIHY, ED
  King of Comedy, The   (84) 192
  Pee-wee's Big Adventure   (86) 265
HERLIHY, JAMES LEO
  Four Friends   (82) 167

HERLITZKA, ROBERTO
Joke of Destiny, A [1983] (85) 259
HERMAN, PEE-WEE. *See* REUBENS, PAUL.
HERMANN, IRM
Berlin Alexanderplatz [1980] (84) 56
HERNANDEZ, GÉRARD
Coup de torchon [1981] (83) 124
HERRIER, MARK
Porky's (83) 267
Porky's II (84) 491
Tank (85) 535
HERRIN, KYM
Romancing the Stone (85) 421
HERRMANN, EDWARD
Annie (83) 56
Compromising Positions (86) 120
Death Valley (83) 419
Little Sex, A (83) 424
Man with One Red Shoe, The (86) 451
Mrs. Soffel (85) 314
Purple Rose of Cairo, The (86) 290
Reds (82) 312
HERSHEY, BARBARA
Entity, The (84) 483
Natural, The (85) 329
Right Stuff, The (84) 342
HERZOG, WERNER
Tokyo-Ga (86) 463
HESSEMAN, HOWARD
Clue (86) 440
Doctor Detroit (84) 482
Police Academy 2 (86) 276
HESTON, CHARLTON
Mother Lode (84) 490
HEUDÉLINE, RAYMONDE
Bal, Le [1983] (85) 80
HEWITT, MARTIN
Out of Control (86) 455
HEXUM, JON-ERIK
Bear, The (85) 511
"Obituaries" (85) 672
HEY, VIRGINIA
Road Warrior, The [1981] (83) 277
HEYES, HERBERT
Bedtime for Bonzo [1951] (84) 512
HICKEY, WILLIAM
Flanagan (86) 443
Prizzi's Honor (86) 285
HICKS, BARBARA
Brazil (86) 80
HICKS, CATHERINE
Death Valley (83) 419
Fever Pitch (86) 443
Garbo Talks (85) 520
Razor's Edge, The (85) 402
HIDARI, SACHIKO
Mishima (86) 236
HIGGINS, ANTHONY
Bride, The (86) 438
Draughtsman's Contract, The [1982] (84) 126
Quartet (82) 296
Raiders of the Lost Ark (82) 308
Young Sherlock Holmes (86) 431
HIGGINS, MICHAEL
Arrangement, The [1969] (86) 474

HIGSON, CHRISTOPHER
Gregory's Girl [1981] (83) 193
HILARY, JENNIFER
Five Days One Summer (83) 421
HILL, AMY
Dim Sum (86) 141
HILL, ARTHUR
Amateur, The (83) 417
One Magic Christmas (86) 455
HILL, BERNARD
Bounty, The (85) 513
HILL, DANA
Cross Creek (84) 116
National Lampoon's European Vacation (86) 453
Shoot the Moon (83) 295
HILL, DAVE
Draughtsman's Contract, The [1982] (84) 126
HILL, LON
Fool for Love (86) 172
HILL, RICHARD
Deathstalker (85) 517
HILL, STEVEN
Garbo Talks (85) 520
Rich and Famous (82) 316
Yentl (84) 468
HILL, THELMA
Miracle Woman, The [1931] (83) 473
HILL, THOMAS
Neverending Story, The (85) 527
True Confessions (82) 368
HILLBECK, FERNANDO
Flesh and Blood (86) 443
HILLER, WENDY
I Know Where I'm Going [1945] (83) 456
Making Love (83) 425
HILLERMAN, JOHN
Up the Creek (85) 537
HILLS, DENNIS
Amin—The Rise and Fall (84) 479
HINCHLEY, PIPPA
Secret Places [1984] (86) 459
HINDLE, ART
Man Who Wasn't There, The (84) 489
Porky's (83) 267
HINDMAN, EARL
Silverado (86) 349
HINES, GRAINGER
Protocol (85) 383
HINES, GREGORY
Cotton Club, The (85) 150
Deal of the Century (84) 482
White Nights (86) 416
Wolfen (82) 382
HINES, MAURICE
Cotton Club, The (85) 150
HINES, ROBERT
Wetherby (86) 406
HINGLE, PAT
Brewster's Millions (86) 438
Falcon and the Snowman, The (86) 165
Going Berserk (84) 485
Running Brave (84) 354
Sudden Impact (84) 395

HINTON, PHILLIP
Caddie [1976]   (83) 439
HINTON, SEAN
Caddie [1976]   (83) 439
HINTON, SIMON
Caddie [1976]   (83) 439
HINZ, MICHAEL
Death of Mario Ricci, The [1983]   (86) 133
HIRSCH, JUDD
Teachers   (85) 535
Without a Trace   (84) 498
HIRSON, ALICE
Mass Appeal   (85) 303
HITTSCHER, PAUL
Fitzcarraldo   (83) 167
HOBEL, MARA
Mommie Dearest   (82) 245
HODDER, KANE
Hardbodies   (85) 521
HODGE, PATRICIA
Betrayal   (84) 67
HOFF, MORTEN
Zappa   (85) 539
HOFFMAN, DUSTIN
Agatha [1979]   (83) 435
Tootsie   (83) 353
HOFFMAN, GUY
Agnes of God   (86) 56
HOFFMAN, OTTO
Barbary Coast [1935]   (84) 506
HOFFMAN, ROY
Skyline   (85) 533
HOFFMAN, THOM
4th Man, The [1983]   (85) 203
HOFFMEISTER, JOHN
Blow Out   (82) 83
HOGAN, HULK
Rocky III   (83) 283
HOHL, ARTHUR
Sign of the Cross, The [1932]   (85) 607
HOHLFELD, BRIAN
Sesame Street Presents: Follow That Bird   (86)
459
HOJFELDT, SOLBJORN
Zappa   (85) 539
HOLBROOK, HAL
Creepshow   (83) 419
Star Chamber, The   (84) 494
HOLBY, KRISTIN
Trading Places   (84) 430
HOLDEN, WILLIAM
Earthling, The [1980]   (82) 130
"Obituaries"   (82) 492
S.O.B.   (82) 328
HOLDER, GEOFFREY
Annie   (83) 56
HOLDER, PHILLIP
Came a Hot Friday   (86) 439
HOLICKER, HEIDI
Valley Girl   (84) 447
HOLIDAY, HOPE
Killpoint   (85) 524
HOLLAND, JERRY
American Pop   (82) 62

HOLLAND, JOHN
Take a Letter, Darling [1942]   (85) 632
HOLLAND, PAMELA
Dorm That Dripped Blood, The   (84) 482
HOLLEN, REBECCA
Sudden Death   (86) 461
HOLLIDAY, JUDY
Bells Are Ringing [1960]   (84) 517
Solid Gold Cadillac, The [1956]   (85) 615
HOLLIDAY, KENE
No Small Affair   (85) 527
Philadelphia Experiment, The   (85) 529
HOLLIDAY, POLLY
Gremlins   (85) 230
HOLLIMAN, EARL
Sharky's Machine   (82) 324
HOLLIS, CAREY, JR.
Raggedy Man   (82) 300
HOLLOWAY, STANLEY
"Obituaries"   (83) 537
HOLLOWAY, STERLING
Bambi [1942]   (85) 543
HOLM, ARWEN
Experience Preferred . . . but Not Essential
[1982]   (84) 141
HOLM, IAN
Brazil   (86) 80
Chariots of Fire   (82) 101
Dance with a Stranger [1984]   (86) 125
Dreamchild   (86) 146
Greystoke   (85) 236
Return of the Soldier, The [1982]   (84)
332
Time Bandits [1980]   (82) 364
Wetherby   (86) 406
HOLTON, MARK
Pee-wee's Big Adventure   (86) 265
Teen Wolf   (86) 462
HONG, JAMES
Missing in Action   (85) 526
HONZE, MIMI
Door to Door   (85) 518
HOOD, DON
Absence of Malice   (82) 57
Marie   (86) 227
River, The   (85) 416
HOOL, CONSTANZA
Evil That Men Do, The   (85) 518
HOOTEN, PETER
Fantasies   (83) 421
HOPKINS, ANTHONY
Bounty, The   (85) 513
HOPKINS, BO
Sweet Sixteen   (85) 535
HOPKINS, CHARLES
Repo Man   (85) 408
HOPKINS, LINDA
Honkytonk Man   (83) 200
HOPKINS, MIRIAM
Barbary Coast [1935]   (84) 507
Becky Sharp [1935]   (82) 403
HOPPE, ROLF
Mephisto   (82) 237
HOPPER, DENNIS
My Science Project   (86) 453

Osterman Weekend, The (84) 491
Rumble Fish (84) 492
HOPPER, HEDDA
Sherlock Holmes [1922] (83) 494
HOPTON, RUSSELL
I'm No Angel [1933] (85) 561
Miracle Woman, The [1931] (83) 473
HORAN, JAMES
Chattanooga Choo Choo (85) 515
HORDERN, MICHAEL
Missionary, The (83) 233
HORENSTEIN, JAY
American Taboo (85) 509
HORGAN, PATRICK
Zelig (84) 473
HORMEL, GREGORY
Mike's Murder (85) 526
HORN, LANNY
Homework (83) 422
HOROWITZO, STEFANO
Ladyhawke (86) 214
HORSLEY, JOHN
Secrets (85) 532
HORSLEY, LEE
Sword and the Sorcerer, The (83) 429
HORTON, PETER
Stephen King's Children of the Corn (85) 534
HORTON, RUSSELL
Stephen King's Cat's Eye (86) 460
HORVATH, LASZLO
Brady's Escape (85) 514
HOSKINS, BOB
Beyond the Limit (84) 479
Cotton Club, The (85) 150
Lassiter (85) 524
Long Good Friday, The [1980] (83) 220
HOSOKAWA, CHIKAKO
Late Chrysanthemums [1954] (86) 449
HOSSEIN, ROBERT
Bolero [1981] (83) 418
HOURICAN, DEE
Joey (86) 448
HOUSE, RON
Bullshot [1983] (86) 439
HOUSEMAN, JOHN
Ghost Story (82) 183
HOUSER, JERRY
Slap Shot [1977] (82) 467
HOUSER, PATRICK
Hotdog . . . The Movie (85) 522
HOUSMAN, ARTHUR
Our Relations [1936] (86) 523
HOUSTON, DONALD
Clash of the Titans (82) 111
HOVEY, NATASHA
Water and Soap (86) 465
HOWARD, ALAN
Oxford Blues (85) 528
Victim [1961] (85) 649
HOWARD, ARLISS
Door to Door (85) 518
HOWARD, BARBARA
Friday the 13th—The Final Chapter (85) 520

HOWARD, BREE
Android (85) 510
HOWARD, ESTHER
Detour [1946] (86) 498
HOWARD, FRANK
That Was Then . . . This Is Now (86) 463
HOWARD, GERTRUDE
I'm No Angel [1933] (85) 561
HOWARD, JOHN
Razorback [1984] (86) 457
HOWARD, KEN
Second Thoughts (84) 493
HOWARD, LESLIE
Animal Kingdom, The [1932] (86) 469
HOWARD, MARIANNE
Caddie [1976] (83) 439
HOWARD, PAUL
King of Jazz [1930] (86) 515
HOWARD, RANCE
Love Letters (85) 288
HOWARD, TREVOR
Gandhi (83) 183
Missionary, The (83) 233
Mutiny on the Bounty [1962] (85) 581
Sea Wolves, The [1981] (83) 427
HOWE, IRVING
Zelig (84) 473
HOWELL, C. THOMAS
Grandview, U.S.A. (85) 520
Outsiders, The (84) 282
Red Dawn (85) 530
Secret Admirer (86) 459
Tank (85) 535
HOXIE, AL
"Obituaries" (83) 538
HOYO, PABLO
Volver a empezar (83) 393
HOYOS, CHRISTINA
Blood Wedding [1981] (83) 418
Carmen (84) 101
HOYT, JOHN
Unfaithful, The [1947] (86) 550
HUBBARD, ALLAN
Tender Mercies (84) 409
HUBBERT, CORK
Not for Publication (85) 527
HUBLEY, SEASON
Escape from New York (82) 133
Vice Squad (83) 430
HUDDLESTON, DAVID
Santa Claus (86) 334
HUDDLESTON, MICHAEL
Four Friends (82) 167
Woman in Red, The (85) 538
HUDSON, DON
Ladyhawke (86) 214
HUDSON, ERNIE
Ghostbusters (85) 219
Joy of Sex (85) 524
Penitentiary II (83) 427
Spacehunter (84) 493
HUDSON, ROCK
"Obituaries" (86) 571

HUDSON, TONI
  Cross Creek   (84) 116
  Just One of the Guys   (86) 448
HUFF, BRENT
  Gwendoline [1983]   (85) 521
  9 Deaths of the Ninja   (86) 454
HUFFMAN, DAVID
  Firefox   (83) 160
HUGGER, JONATHAN
  Repo Man   (85) 408
HUGH-KELLY, DANIEL
  Cujo   (84) 481
HUGHES, BARNARD
  Best Friends   (83) 68
  Maxie   (86) 452
  TRON   (83) 371
HUGHES, FINOLA
  Staying Alive   (84) 386
HUGHES, JOHN
  That Sinking Feeling [1979]   (85) 536
HUGHES, TONY
  Puberty Blues [1981]   (84) 492
HUGHES, WENDY
  Careful He Might Hear You [1983]   (85) 130
  Lonely Hearts [1982]   (84) 212
  My First Wife   (86) 453
HULCE, TOM
  Amadeus   (85) 63
HULL, DIANNE
  Arrangement, The [1969]   (86) 474
HULL, HENRY
  Colorado Territory [1949]   (86) 489
HUMANN, HELENA
  Deep in the Heart   (85) 517
HUMPHREYS, SUZIE
  Deep in the Heart   (85) 517
HUNNICUTT, GAYLE
  Target   (86) 462
HUNT, HELEN
  Trancers   (86) 463
HUNT, LINDA
  Bostonians, The   (85) 105
  Eleni   (86) 151
  Silverado   (86) 349
  Year of Living Dangerously, The
    [1982]   (84) 462
HUNT, RICHARD
  Muppets Take Manhattan, The   (85) 526
HUNTER, BILL
  Gallipoli [1980]   (82) 179
  Heatwave   (84) 485
  Hit, The   (86) 446
HUNTER, HOLLY
  Swing Shift   (85) 535
HUNTER, KAKI
  Just the Way You Are   (85) 524
  Porky's   (83) 267
  Whose Life Is It Anyway?   (82) 378
HUNTER, TAB
  Lust in the Dust   (86) 450
HUNTINGTON, PAM
  They Call Me Bruce   (83) 429
HUNTLEY, G. P., JR.
  Becky Sharp [1935]   (82) 403

HUOT, JULIETTE
  Plouffe, Les   (86) 456
HUPPERT, ISABELLE
  Coup de torchon [1981]   (83) 124
  Entre nous [1983]   (85) 176
  Every Man for Himself   (82) 139
  Heaven's Gate   (82) 195
  Loulou [1980]   (82) 226
  My Best Friend's Girl [1983]   (85) 326
  Passion [1982]   (84) 289
  Trout, The [1982]   (84) 496
HURT, JOHN
  Black Cauldron, The   (86) 75
  Champions   (85) 515
  Heaven's Gate   (82) 195
  Hit, The   (86) 446
  Night Crossing   (83) 426
  1984   (85) 335
  Osterman Weekend, The   (84) 491
  Partners   (83) 427
HURT, MARY BETH
  Compromising Positions   (86) 120
  D.A.R.Y.L.   (86) 441
  World According to Garp, The   (83) 397
HURT, WILLIAM
  Big Chill, The   (84) 78
  Body Heat   (82) 87
  Gorky Park   (84) 78
  Kiss of the Spider Woman   (86) 209
HUSSAIN, ZAKIR
  Heat and Dust [1982]   (84) 187
HUSSEY, OLIVIA
  Escape 2000   (84) 483
HUSSEY, RUTH
  H. M. Pulham, Esq. [1941]   (82) 439
HUSTER, FRANCIS
  Adolescente, L' [1979]   (83) 53
  Edith and Marcel [1983]   (85) 518
  I Married a Shadow   (84) 486
HUSTON, ANJELICA
  Ice Pirates, The   (85) 523
  Postman Always Rings Twice, The   (82)
    284
  Prizzi's Honor   (86) 285
HUSTON, JOHN
  Cannery Row   (83) 95
  Freud [1962]   (84) 535
  "Life Achievement Award"   (84) 1
  Lovesick   (84) 488
HUSTON, WALTER
  North Star, The [1943]   (83) 476
HUTCHISON, KEN
  Ladyhawke   (86) 214
HUTTON, LAUREN
  Hecate   (85) 522
  Lassiter   (85) 524
  Once Bitten   (86) 454
HUTTON, TIMOTHY
  Daniel   (84) 481
  Falcon and the Snowman, The   (86) 165
  Iceman   (85) 248
  Taps   (82) 343
  Turk 182   (86) 464
HUY-QUAN, KE
  Goonies, The   (86) 176
  Indiana Jones and the Temple of Doom   (85)
    253

HYDE-WHITE, WILFRED
Toy, The (83) 358
HYLANDS, SCOTT
Oasis, The (85) 528
HYSER, JOYCE
Just One of the Guys (86) 448

IDLE, ERIC
Monty Python's The Meaning of Life (84) 489
National Lampoon's European Vacation (86) 453
IGAWA, HISASHI
Ran (86) 304
IGLESIAS, EUGENE
Cowboy [1958] (82) 417
IMPARATO, GIANFELICE
Henry IV [1983] (86) 446
IMPERT, MARGIE
Howling, The (82) 207
INCE, RALPH
Hatchet Man, The [1932] (83) 447
INESCROT, IRENE
Lonely Hearts [1982] (84) 212
INGALLS, JOYCE
Deadly Force (84) 482
INGLIS, SARAH
Smooth Talk (86) 354
INGRAHAM, AMO
Take a Letter, Darling [1942] (85) 632
INWOOD, STEVE
Prince of the City (82) 292
Staying Alive (84) 386
IPALE, AHARON
Shooting Party, The [1984] (86) 344
IRELAND, JILL
Death Wish II (83) 420
IRELAND, JOHN
Incubus, The [1980] (83) 424
IRONS, JEREMY
Betrayal (84) 67
French Lieutenant's Woman, The (82) 174
Moonlighting (83) 237
Swann in Love (85) 471
Wild Duck, The [1983] (86) 466
IRONSIDE, MICHAEL
Cross Country (84) 481
Visiting Hours (83) 431
IRVING, AMY
Micki & Maude (85) 308
Yentl (84) 468
IRWIN, CHARLES
King of Jazz [1930] (86) 515
ISACKSEN, PETER
Surf II (85) 535
ISHIZAKA, KOJI
Makioka Sisters, The [1983] (86) 451
ISIMOTO, DALE
Cannonball Run II (85) 514
ITAMI, JYUZO
MacArthur's Children (86) 451
Makioka Sisters, The [1983] (86) 451
ITO, RAN
Foster Daddy, Tora! [1980] (82) 163

ITO, ROBERT
Adventures of Buckaroo Banzai, The (85) 47
ITO, TOSHIYA
Ran (86) 304
ITTIMANGNAQ, MARTHA
Never Cry Wolf (84) 247
ITZEN, GREGORY
Hard to Hold (85) 521
IVANEK, ZELJKO
Mass Appeal (85) 303
Sender, The (83) 427
IVEY, DANA
Color Purple, The (86) 105
Explorers (86) 442
IVEY, JUDITH
Compromising Positions (86) 120
Harry and Son (85) 521
Lonely Guy, The (85) 525
Woman in Red, The (85) 538
IWASHITA, SHIMA
MacArthur's Children (86) 451

JACKLEY, JOLYON
Sound Barrier, The [1952] (85) 621
JACKLEY, NAT
Ploughman's Lunch, The [1983] (85) 377
JACKSON, ANNE
Sam's Son (85) 531
JACKSON, CERI
Champions (85) 515
JACKSON, DESRETA
Color Purple, The (86) 105
JACKSON, FREDA
Clash of the Titans (82) 111
JACKSON, GLENDA
And Nothing but the Truth (85) 510
Return of the Soldier, The [1982] (84) 332
Turtle Diary (86) 464
JACKSON, GORDON
Shooting Party, The [1984] (86) 344
JACKSON, KATE
Making Love (83) 425
JACKSON, LEONARD
Brother from Another Planet, The (85) 118
Color Purple, The (86) 105
JACOBI, DEREK
Enigma [1982] (84) 483
Secret of NIMH, The (83) 288
JACOBI, LOU
Next Stop, Greenwich Village [1976] (85) 592
JACOBI, MARIANNA
Montenegro (82) 250
JACOBS, OLU
Baby (86) 437
JACOBS, RUSTY
Once upon a Time in America (85) 345
JACOBS, STEVE
Silver City [1984] (86) 460
JACOBSSON, ULLA
"Obituaries" (83) 538
JACOBY, BILLY
Just One of the Guys (86) 448
Reckless (85) 530

JACQUEMONT, MAURICE
  Return of Martin Guerre, The   (84) 318
JAECKEL, RICHARD
  Cowboy [1958]   (82) 417
  Starman   (85) 445
JAENICKE, HANNES
  Out of Order   (86) 455
JAFFE, SAM
  "Obituaries"   (85) 673
JAFFE, TALIESIN
  Mr. Mom   (84) 489
JAFFREY, MADHUR
  Heat and Dust [1982]   (84) 187
JAFFREY, SAEED
  Passage to India, A   (85) 365
JAGGER, DEAN
  North Star, The [1943]   (83) 476
JAGLOM, HENRY
  Always   (86) 60
JAMES ANTHONY
  Nightmares   (84) 490
JAMES, BILLY T.
  Came a Hot Friday   (86) 439
JAMES, BRION
  Blade Runner   (83) 76
  Enemy Mine   (86) 161
  Flesh and Blood   (86) 443
  Southern Comfort   (82) 332
JAMES, EMRYS
  And Nothing but the Truth   (85) 510
  Dragonslayer   (82) 125
JAMES, GENNIE
  Places in the Heart   (85) 371
JAMES, GERALDINE
  Gandhi   (83) 183
JAMES, STEVE
  American Ninja   (86) 436
  Brother from Another Planet, The   (85) 118
JAMIESON, MALCOLM
  Victor/Victoria   (83) 387
JANDA, KRYSTYNA
  Man of Iron   (82) 230
  Man of Marble [1977]   (82) 234
  Mephisto   (82) 237
JANNACCI, ENZO
  Joke of Destiny, A [1983]   (85) 259
JARRET, GABE
  Real Genius   (86) 309
JARVIS, GRAHAM P.
  Mischief   (86) 452
JASON, PETER
  Brewster's Millions   (86) 438
  Dreamscape   (85) 166
JASTROW, TERRY
  Waltz Across Texas   (84) 497
JEANNERET, ANAIS
  Peril   (86) 456
JEANS, ISABEL
  "Obituaries"   (86) 572
JEFFORD, BARBARA
  And the Ship Sails On [1983]   (85) 69
JEIMO, JANINA
  New Babylon, The [1929]   (84) 561

JELLISON, JOHN
  Cold Feet   (85) 516
JEMISON, ANNA
  My First Wife   (86) 453
  Silver City [1984]   (86) 460
  Smash Palace [1981]   (83) 302
JENE, AUBREY
  Summer Rental   (86) 462
JENKINS, MARGO
  Experience Preferred . . . but Not Essential [1982]   (84) 141
JENNINGS, BRENT
  Witness   (86) 421
JENNINGS, TOM
  Mad Max Beyond Thunderdome   (86) 223
JENNINGS, WAYLON
  Sesame Street Presents: Follow That Bird   (86) 459
JENSEN, BILL
  MacArthur's Children   (86) 451
JENSON, ROY
  Red Dawn   (85) 530
JEQUIER, MARBLUM
  Death of Mario Ricci, The [1983]   (86) 133
JESSEL, GEORGE
  "Obituaries"   (82) 492
JETT, ROGER
  Smithereens   (83) 307
JEZEQUEL, JULIE
  Étoile du nord, L'   (84) 484
JIMINEZ, JUAN ANTONIO
  Carmen   (84) 101
JODE, GARRY
  Dernier Combat, Le [1983]   (85) 517
JOHN, ERROL
  Sheena   (85) 532
JOHN, GOTTFRIED
  Berlin Alexanderplatz [1980]   (84) 57
  Lili Marleen   (82) 222
JOHNS, STRATFORD
  Wild Geese II   (86) 466
JOHNSON, ARTE
  Cannonball Run II   (85) 514
JOHNSON, BEN
  Champions   (85) 515
  Red Dawn   (85) 530
  Tex   (83) 335
JOHNSON, CELIA
  "Obituaries"   (83) 539
JOHNSON, D. G.
  Stephen King's Children of the Corn   (85) 534
JOHNSON, DOI
  American Flyers   (86) 436
JOHNSON, DON
  Cease Fire   (86) 440
JOHNSON, HELEN
  Divorcée, The [1930]   (82) 429
JOHNSON, JUSTINE
  Arthur   (82) 71
JOHNSON, KELLY
  Utu [1983]   (85) 504
JOHNSON, KURT
  Ghost Story   (82) 183

JOHNSON, LYNN-HOLLY
For Your Eyes Only   (82) 155
Where the Boys Are '84   (85) 537
JOHNSON, MICHAEL
Plenty   (86) 271
JOHNSON, MICHELLE
Blame It on Rio   (85) 512
JOHNSON, NOBLE
Most Dangerous Game, The [1932]   (86) 519
JOHNSON, REBECCA
Secrets   (85) 532
JOHNSON, RICHARD
Turtle Diary   (86) 464
JOHNSON, SUNNY
Flashdance   (84) 158
"Obituaries"   (85) 675
JOHNSON, VAN
Guy Named Joe, A [1943]   (82) 435
Purple Rose of Cairo, The   (86) 290
JOHNSTON, JOHN DENNIS
Flesh and Blood   (86) 443
JOHNSTON, MICHELLE
Chorus Line, A   (86) 91
JOHNSTONE, SHANE
Company of Wolves, The [1984]   (86) 115
JOLIVET, PIERRE
Dernier Combat, Le [1983]   (85) 517
JONES, ANNA CAMPBELL
Secrets   (85) 532
JONES, BEN
Deep in the Heart   (85) 517
JONES, CAROLYN
"Obituaries"   (84) 624
JONES, CLAUDE EARL
Impulse   (85) 523
JONES, CLIFTON
Sheena   (85) 532
JONES, DARRYL
Bring on the Night   (86) 439
JONES, DUANE
Beat Street   (85) 512
JONES, EDDIE
C.H.U.D.   (85) 515
New Kids, The   (86) 454
JONES, FREDDIE
And the Ship Sails On [1983]   (85) 69
Black Cauldron, The   (86) 75
Dune   (85) 171
Firefox   (83) 160
Firestarter   (85) 519
Krull   (84) 487
Young Sherlock Holmes   (86) 431
JONES, GORDON
Secret Life of Walter Mitty, The [1947]   (86) 540
JONES, GRACE
Conan the Destroyer   (85) 516
View to a Kill, A   (86) 402
JONES, GREGORY
Champions   (85) 515
JONES, GRIFF RHYS
Morons from Outer Space   (86) 452
JONES, HENRY
Deathtrap   (83) 137

JONES, JAMES EARL
City Limits   (86) 440
Conan the Barbarian   (83) 419
Return of the Jedi   (84) 326
JONES, JANET
Chorus Line, A   (86) 91
Flamingo Kid, The   (85) 192
JONES, JEFFREY
Amadeus   (85) 63
Transylvania 6-5000   (86) 463
JONES, JERRY
Party Animal   (86) 455
JONES, JOHN RANDOLPH
Arrangement, The [1969]   (86) 474
JONES, LUCINDA
Wild Duck, The [1983]   (86) 466
JONES, SETH
Madman   (84) 488
JONES, SHIRLEY
Tank   (85) 535
JONES, TERRY
Monty Python's The Meaning of Life   (84) 489
JONES, TOMMY LEE
Nate and Hayes   (84) 236
River Rat, The   (85) 531
JONG, GEERT DE
Bastille [1984]   (86) 437
JORAH, SAMSON
Never Cry Wolf   (84) 247
JORDAN, ARMIN
Parsifal   (84) 491
JORDAN, RICHARD
Flash of Green, A   (86) 443
Mean Season, The   (86) 452
JORDAN, WILL
Broadway Danny Rose   (85) 112
JORDANO, DANIEL
Alphabet City   (85) 509
JORY, VICTOR
"Obituaries"   (83) 540
JOSEPH, ERIC
That Sinking Feeling [1979]   (85) 536
JOSEPHSON, ERLAND
After the Rehearsal   (85) 58
Fanny and Alexander [1982]   (84) 146
Montenegro   (82) 250
Nostalgia [1983]   (85) 340
JOSLYN, ALLYN
"Obituaries"   (82) 493
JOURDAN, LOUIS
Octopussy   (84) 276
Swamp Thing   (83) 429
JOY, LEATRICE
"Obituaries"   (86) 573
JOY, ROBERT
Amityville 3-D   (84) 479
Atlantic City   (82) 74
Desperately Seeking Susan   (86) 137
Joshua Then and Now   (86) 198
Ragtime   (82) 304
JOYNER, JOYZELLE
Sign of the Cross, The [1932]   (85) 607
JUARBE, ISRAEL
Hadley's Rebellion   (85) 521

JULIA, RAUL
  Compromising Positions (86) 120
  Escape Artist, The (83) 421
  Kiss of the Spider Woman (86) 209
  One from the Heart (83) 250
  Tempest (83) 331
JULIAN, JANET
  Humongous (83) 423
JULIAO, JORGE
  Pixote [1980] (82) 280
JUMP, GORDON
  Making the Grade (85) 526
JUNG, CALVIN
  Challenge, The (83) 109
JUNKIN, JOHN
  Wombling Free [1979] (85) 538
JURADO, KATY
  Under the Volcano (85) 499
JURASIK, PETER
  TRON (83) 371
JURGENS, CURT
  "Obituaries" (83) 540
JUSTIN, JOHN
  Sound Barrier, The [1952] (85) 621

KAA, WI KUKI
  Bounty, The (85) 513
  Utu [1983] (85) 504
KACZMAREK, JANE
  Door to Door (85) 518
  Falling in Love (85) 519
  Heavenly Kid, The (86) 445
KAHAM, JUDITH
  Twice upon a Time (84) 496
KAHARA, NATSUKO
  Flowing [1956] (86) 444
KAHLER, WOLF
  Raiders of the Lost Ark (82) 308
KAHN, MADELINE
  City Heat (85) 141
  Clue (86) 440
  Slapstick (85) 533
KALAIGIN, ALEKSANDR
  Unfinished Piece for Piano Player, An
    [1977] (83) 430
KALINOWSKI, WALDEMAR
  Breathless (84) 89
KAMPMANN, STEVEN
  Twice upon a Time (84) 496
KANALY, STEVE
  Fleshburn (85) 519
KANE, CAROL
  Racing with the Moon (85) 397
  Transylvania 6-5000 (86) 463
KANIN, FAY
  Rich and Famous (82) 316
KANTER, MARIN
  Loveless, The (85) 525
KANTOR, RICHARD
  Out of Control (86) 455
KANTS, IVAR
  Silver City [1984] (86) 460
KAPELOS, JOHN
  Breakfast Club, The (86) 85

KAPOOR, JENNEFER
  Home and the World, The [1984] (86) 447
KAPOOR, SHASHI
  Heat and Dust [1982] (84) 187
KAPRISKY, VALERIE
  Breathless (84) 89
KARABATSOS, RON
  Flashdance (84) 158
KARALLIS, CHRIS
  Kipperbang [1983] (85) 524
KARANOVIC, MIRJANA
  When Father Was Away on Business [1984] (86)
    411
KARAPIET, RASHID
  Passage to India, A (85) 365
KAREN, JAMES
  Return of the Living Dead, The (86) 314
  Sam's Son (85) 531
KARIN, RITA
  Sophie's Choice (83) 311
KARLATOS, OLGA
  Purple Rain (85) 389
KARLEN, JOHN
  Impulse (85) 523
  Racing with the Moon (85) 397
KARLOFF, BORIS
  Secret Life of Walter Mitty, The [1947] (86) 540
KARMANN, SAM
  Balance, La [1982] (84) 52
KARNS, ROSCOE
  They Drive by Night [1940] (83) 508
KARRAS, ALEX
  Against All Odds (85) 509
  Porky's (83) 267
  Victor/Victoria (83) 387
KARTALIAN, BUCK
  Gymkata (86) 445
KARYO, TCHEKY
  Balance, La [1982] (84) 52
  Full Moon in Paris (85) 208
KASDAY, DAVID
  Invitation to the Dance [1956] (86) 507
KASDORF, LENORE
  Missing in Action (85) 526
KASE, RUSSELL
  Ladyhawke (86) 214
KASHFI, ANNA
  Cowboy [1958] (82) 417
KATO, DAISUKE
  Flowing [1956] (86) 444
KATO, HARUKO
  MacArthur's Children (86) 451
  Mishima (86) 236
KATO, KAZUO
  Ran (86) 304
KATO, TAKESHI
  Ran (86) 304
KATON, ROSANNE
  City Girl, The (85) 516
KATSUNO, HIROSHI
  Mishima (86) 236
KATSURA, KOBAICHO
  Makioka Sisters, The [1983] (86) 451

KATT, WILLIAM
Baby (86) 437
KATZOFF, MARVIN
Hardbodies (85) 521
KAUFER, JONATHAN
Always (86) 60
KAUFMAN, ANDY
"Obituaries" (85) 675
KAUFMAN, SETH
Body Rock (85) 513
KAUFMANN, CHRISTINE
Lili Marleen (82) 222
KAUFMANN, GUNTHER
Querelle [1982] (84) 313
KAVA, CAROLINE
Year of the Dragon (86) 426
KAVANAGH, JOHN
Cal (85) 124
KAVNER, JULIE
Bad Medicine (86) 437
KAWAYE, JANICE
Night of the Comet (85) 527
KAWAZU, YUSUKE
Cruel Story of Youth [1960] (85) 517
KAY, CHARLES
Amadeus (85) 63
KAY, PAMELA
Weekend Pass (85) 537
KAYE, CAREN
My Tutor (84) 490
KAYE, DANNY
Secret Life of Walter Mitty, The [1947] (86) 540
KAYE, LILA
American Werewolf in London, An (82) 66
KAYE, NORMAN
Lonely Hearts [1982] (84) 212
Where the Green Ants Dream [1984] (86) 465
KAZAN, LAINIE
Journey of Natty Gann, The (86) 203
Lust in the Dust (86) 450
My Favorite Year (83) 241
One from the Heart (83) 250
KEACH, JAMES
Love Letters (85) 288
Moving Violations (86) 453
Razor's Edge, The (85) 402
KEACH, STACY
Brewster McCloud [1970] (86) 484
That Championship Season (83) 338
KEAN, MARIE
Danny Boy (85) 517
KEANE, JAMES
Cannery Row (83) 95
KEANE, KERRI
Incubus, The [1980] (83) 424
KEATON, DIANE
Little Drummer Girl, The (85) 525
Mrs. Soffel (85) 314
Reds (82) 312
Shoot the Moon (83) 295
KEATON, MICHAEL
Johnny Dangerously (85) 524
Mr. Mom (84) 489
Night Shift (83) 426

KEATS, STEVEN
Silent Rage (83) 428
Turk 182 (86) 464
KEAYS-BYRNE, HUGH
Where the Green Ants Dream [1984] (86) 465
KEDROVA, LILA
Torn Curtain [1966] (85) 644
KEEGAN, JIMMY E.
Here Come the Littles (86) 446
KEEN, GEOFFREY
For Your Eyes Only (82) 155
KEHOE, JACK
Melvin and Howard [1980] (82) 453
Pope of Greenwich Village, The (85) 529
Wild Life, The (85) 538
KEITEL, HARVEY
Border, The (83) 418
Exposed (84) 484
Falling in Love (85) 519
Nuit de Varennes, La [1982] (84) 270
KEITH, BRIAN
Sharky's Machine (82) 324
KEITH, DAVID
Firestarter (85) 519
Lords of Discipline, The (84) 488
Officer and a Gentleman, An (83) 246
KEITH, IAN
Sign of the Cross, The [1932] (85) 607
KEITH, PENELOPE
Priest of Love (82) 288
KELLAWAY, CECIL
Take a Letter, Darling [1942] (85) 632
KELLER, MARTHE
Amateur, The (83) 417
KELLERMAN, SALLY
Brewster McCloud [1970] (86) 484
Moving Violations (86) 453
Sesame Street Presents: Follow That Bird (86) 459
KELLEY, DEFOREST
Star Trek II—The Wrath of Khan (83) 321
Star Trek III—The Search for Spock (85) 439
KELLIN, MIKE
Next Stop, Greenwich Village [1976] (85) 592
KELLJAN, ROBERT
"Obituaries" (83) 540
KELLY, DAVID
Jigsaw Man, The [1983] (85) 524
KELLY, DAVID PATRICK
Commando (86) 111
Dreamscape (85) 166
48 HRS. (83) 173
Hammett (84) 174
KELLY, GENE
Invitation to the Dance [1956] (86) 507
"Life Achievement Award" (86) 1
KELLY, GRACE
"Obituaries" (83) 540
KELLY, KAREN LEE
Hardbodies (85) 521
KELLY, PATSY
"Obituaries" (82) 493

KELLY, ROZ
  American Pop (82) 62
KEMBER, PAUL
  American Werewolf in London, An (82) 66
KEMP, BRANDIS
  Surf II (85) 535
KEMP, JEREMY
  Top Secret (85) 536
KEMP, LINDSEY
  Wicker Man, The [1974] (86) 555
KENDE, JANOS
  Lily in Love (86) 450
KENEAS, SEBASTIAN
  War and Love (86) 465
KENIN, ALEXA
  Honkytonk Man (83) 200
KENNE, GEOFFREY
  Amin—The Rise and Fall (84) 479
KENNEDY, DOUGLAS
  Unfaithful, The [1947] (86) 550
KENNEDY, EDGAR
  It Happened Tomorrow [1944] (84) 552
KENNEDY, GEORGE
  Bolero (85) 513
  Chattanooga Choo Choo (85) 515
  Flight of the Phoenix, The [1966] (85) 549
  Modern Romance (82) 241
KENNEDY, GRAHAM
  Killing Fields, The (85) 270
KENNEDY, JAYNE
  Body and Soul (83) 418
KENNEDY, JO
  Starstruck (83) 428
KENNEDY, LEON ISAAC
  Body and Soul (83) 418
  Lone Wolf McQuade (84) 488
  Penitentiary II (83) 427
  Too Scared to Scream (86) 463
KENNEDY, MERNA
  King of Jazz [1930] (86) 515
KENT, WILLIAM
  King of Jazz [1930] (86) 515
KENYON, SANDY
  Blame It on the Night (85) 512
KER, EVELYN
  À nos amour [1983] (85) 509
KER, LILLIAN
  Deathstalker (85) 517
KERR, BILL
  Coca-Cola Kid, The (86) 440
  Gallipoli [1980] (82) 179
  Razorback [1984] (86) 457
  Year of Living Dangerously, The
    [1982] (84) 462
KERR, BRUCE
  Man from Snowy River, The (83) 425
KERR, DEBORAH
  Arrangement, The [1969] (86) 474
KERR, E. KATHERINE
  Reuben, Reuben (84) 337
  Silkwood (84) 367
KERRIDGE, LINDA
  Mixed Blood (86) 452
  Stranger's Kiss (85) 534
  Surf II (85) 535

KERRIGAN, J. M.
  Barbary Coast [1935] (84) 506
  My Cousin Rachel [1952] (82) 458
KERST, ALEXANDER
  Holcroft Covenant, The (86) 446
KERWIN, BRIAN
  Murphy's Romance (86) 242
KERWIN, MAUREEN
  Misunderstood (85) 526
KESSLER, LEE
  Creator (86) 441
KESSLER, WULF
  White Rose, The (84) 497
KEYLOUN, MARK
  Mike's Murder (85) 526
KHAMBATTA, PERSIS
  Megaforce (83) 425
  Nighthawks (82) 259
KHANER, JULIE
  Videodrome (84) 452
KHORSAND, PHILIPPE
  Little Jerk [1984] (86) 450
KIBBEE, GUY
  Fort Apache [1948] (84) 530
KIDDER, MARGOT
  Heartaches [1981] (83) 197
  Some Kind of Hero (83) 428
  Superman II (82) 339
  Superman III (84) 399
  Trenchcoat (84) 496
KIEL, RICHARD
  Cannonball Run II (85) 514
  Pale Rider (86) 261
KIELING, WOLFGANG
  Out of Order (86) 455
  Torn Curtain [1966] (85) 644
KIGER, ROBBY
  Stephen King's Children of the Corn (85) 534
  Table for Five (84) 404
KILMER, VAL
  Real Genius (86) 309
  Top Secret (85) 536
KIMBROUGH, CHARLES
  Front, The [1976] (86) 502
KIME, JEFFREY
  State of Things, The (84) 379
KIMMEL, ERIC
  Joshua Then and Now (86) 198
KIMMELL, DANA
  Friday the 13th—Part III (83) 422
  Sweet Sixteen (85) 535
KING, ALAN
  Author! Author! (83) 417
  I, the Jury (83) 423
  Stephen King's Cat's Eye (86) 460
KING, CAMMIE
  Bambi [1942] (85) 543
KING, DAVE
  Long Good Friday, The [1980] (83) 220
  Revolution (86) 458
KING, EMMA
  Dreamchild (86) 146
KING, KATHERINE
  American Taboo (85) 509

KING, KEVIN
Def-Con 4   (86) 441
KING, L. CRAIG
Mask   (86) 231
KING, PERRY
Class of 1984   (83) 419
KING, TONY
Last Hunter, The   (85) 525
KING, WALTER WOOLF
"Obituaries"   (85) 676
KINGSLEY, BEN
Betrayal   (84) 67
Gandhi   (83) 183
Turtle Diary   (86) 464
KINMONT, KATHLEEN
Fraternity Vacation   (86) 444
KINNEAR, ROY
Hammett   (84) 174
Hound of the Baskervilles, The
[1978]   (82) 203
KINSKA, PETO
Color Purple, The   (86) 105
KINSKI, KLAUS
Android   (85) 510
Buddy Buddy   (82) 93
Fitzcarraldo   (83) 167
Little Drummer Girl, The   (85) 525
Soldier, The   (83) 428
Venom [1981]   (83) 430
KINSKI, NASTASSJA
Cat People   (83) 100
Exposed   (84) 484
Hotel New Hampshire, The   (85) 243
Maria's Lovers   (86) 451
Moon in the Gutter, The   (84) 490
One from the Heart   (83) 250
Paris, Texas   (85) 359
Revolution   (86) 458
Tess [1980]   (82) 471
Unfaithfully Yours   (85) 537
KINYANJUI, STEPHEN
Out of Africa   (86) 255
KIRBY, BRUNO
Flesh and Blood   (86) 443
Modern Romance   (82) 241
KIRBY, GEORGE
Trouble in Mind   (86) 388
KIRCHLECHNER, DIETER
Love in Germany, A [1983]   (85) 283
KIRKLAND, KENNY
Bring on the Night   (86) 439
KIRKLAND, SALLY
Love Letters   (85) 288
KIROV, IVAN
Specter of the Rose [1946]   (83) 504
KIRSCH, NANCY
Muppets Take Manhattan, The   (85) 526
KISER, TERRY
Surf II   (85) 535
KISHI, KEIKO
Makioka Sisters, The [1983]   (86) 451
KISHIBE, ITTOKU
Makioka Sisters, The [1983]   (86) 451
KITAEN, TAWNY
Bachelor Party   (85) 511
Gwendoline [1983]   (85) 521

KITCHEN, MICHAEL
Out of Africa   (86) 255
KLAFF, JACK
King David   (86) 449
KLAR, GARY HOWARD
Day of the Dead   (86) 441
KLINE, KEVIN
Big Chill, The   (84) 78
Pirates of Penzance, The   (84) 301
Silverado   (86) 349
Sophie's Choice   (83) 311
KLINE, VAL
Beach Girls, The   (83) 417
KLINGER, PAM
Chorus Line, A   (86) 91
KNEBEL, LEVI L.
Country   (85) 156
KNELL, DAVID
Spring Break   (84) 494
KNIGHT, CAPTAIN C. W. R.
I Know Where I'm Going [1945]   (83) 456
KNIGHT, SHIRLEY
Sender, The   (83) 427
KNIGHT, WYATT
Porky's   (83) 267
Porky's II   (84) 491
KNOTTS, DON
Cannonball Run II   (85) 514
KNOX, ALEXANDER
Joshua Then and Now   (86) 198
KNUDSON, KURT
Cold Feet   (85) 516
KOBAYASHI, KEIJU
Godzilla 1985   (86) 444
KOBAYASHI, SHOJI
Makioka Sisters, The [1983]   (86) 451
KOBAYASHI, TOSHIKO
Cruel Story of Youth [1960]   (85) 517
KOBER, MARTA
School Spirit   (86) 458
KOCH, MONIKA
Boat Is Full, The [1981]   (83) 82
KODAMA, KENJI
Ran   (86) 304
KOEHLER, FREDERICK
Mr. Mom   (84) 489
KOENIG, TOMMY
Stitches   (86) 461
KOENIG, WALTER
Star Trek II—The Wrath of Khan   (83)
321
Star Trek III—The Search for
Spock   (85) 439
KOHAN, MALACHI JARA
Hail Mary   (86) 182
KOHNER, SUSAN
Freud [1962]   (84) 535
KOLLEK, AMOS
Goodbye, New York   (86) 444
KOLLER, LAWRENCE
This Is Elvis   (82) 360
KOOCK, GUICH
American Ninja   (86) 436

KOPINS, KAREN
  Creator   (86) 441
  Once Bitten   (86) 455
KOPPOLA, FRANK
  Hotdog . . . The Movie   (85) 522
KORZEN, ANNI
  Rent Control   (85) 530
KOS, JENNIE C.
  Cheech and Chong's The Corsican
  Brothers   (85) 515
KOSINSKI, JERZY
  Reds   (82) 312
KOSLECK, MARTIN
  North Star, The [1943]   (83) 476
KOSMALSKA, WIESLAWA
  Man of Iron   (82) 230
KOSSOFF, DAVID
  Freud [1962]   (84) 535
KOSTRICHKIN, ANDREI
  New Babylon, The [1929]   (84) 561
KOSUGI, SHO
  Enter the Ninja   (83) 420
  9 Deaths of the Ninja   (86) 454
  Revenge of the Ninja   (84) 492
KOTEAS, ELIAS
  One Magic Christmas   (86) 455
KOTEGAWA, YUKO
  Makioka Sisters, The [1983]   (86) 451
KOTERO, APOLLONIA
  Purple Rain   (85) 389
KOTTO, YAPHET
  Fighting Back   (83) 421
  Star Chamber, The   (84) 494
  Warning Sign   (86) 465
KOUBITZKY, ALEXANDRE
  Napoleon [1927]   (82) 461
KOUNNAS, DEBORAH
  Caddie [1976]   (83) 439
KOVE, MARTIN
  Karate Kid, The   (85) 264
  Rambo: First Blood Part II   (86) 299
KOWANKO, PETE
  Sylvester   (86) 462
KRABBE, JEROEN
  4th Man, The [1983]   (85) 203
  Turtle Diary   (86) 464
KRAKOFF, ROCKY
  Rocky IV   (86) 319
KRAMER, JEFFREY
  Clue   (86) 440
  Santa Claus   (86) 334
KRIEGER, ROBIN
  Philadelphia Experiment, The   (85) 529
KRIGE, ALICE
  Chariots of Fire   (82) 101
  Ghost Story   (82) 183
  King David   (86) 449
KRIMER, HARRY
  Napoleon [1927]   (82) 461
KRISTOFFERSON, KRIS
  Flashpoint   (85) 519
  Heaven's Gate   (82) 195
  Songwriter   (85) 533
  Trouble in Mind   (86) 388

KRUEUZER, LISA
  Basileus Quartet   (85) 511
KRUGER, CHRISTIANE
  Dernier Combat, Le [1983]   (85) 517
KRUGER, HARDY
  Flight of the Phoenix, The [1966]   (85) 549
  Wrong Is Right   (83) 403
KRUPKA, ELISKA
  Pennies from Heaven   (82) 276
KUGA, YOSHIKO
  Cruel Story of Youth [1960]   (85) 517
KULLE, JARL
  Fanny and Alexander [1982]   (84) 146
KUNIHOLM, CARL
  Dark Star [1975]   (86) 494
KUPHAL, JENS
  Christine F. [1981]   (83) 419
KURISHIMA, SUMIKO
  Flowing [1956]   (86) 444
KURTZ, MARCIA JEAN
  Cold Feet   (85) 516
KURTZ, SWOOSIE
  Against All Odds   (85) 509
  World According to Garp, The   (83) 397
KURUPPU, DHARMADASA
  Indiana Jones and the Temple of
  Doom   (85)   253
KUSATSU, CLYDE
  Challenge, The   (83) 109
KUWANO, MIYUKI
  Cruel Story of Youth [1960]   (85) 517
KUZMINA, ELENA
  New Babylon, The [1929]   (84) 561
KWOUK, BURT
  Plenty   (86) 271
KYDD, SAM
  "Obituaries"   (83) 543

LABIOSA, DAVID
  Entity, The   (84) 483
LACEY, RONALD
  Firefox   (83) 160
  Flesh and Blood   (86) 443
  Making the Grade   (85) 526
  Raiders of the Lost Art   (82) 308
  Red Sonja   (86) 457
  Sahara   (85) 531
LACK, SUSANNA
  Purple Haze   (84) 492
LACKEY, SKIP
  Once Bitten   (86) 455
LACOSTE, PHILIPPE
  Hail Mary   (86) 182
LACROIX, DENIX
  Running Brave   (84) 354
LADD, CHERYL
  Purple Hearts   (85) 529
LADD, DIANE
  Something Wicked This Way Comes   (84) 493
LAFARI, GABRIELE
  Woman in Flames, A   (85) 538
LA FLEUR, ART
  Trancers   (86) 463

LAFONT, BERNADETE
Gwendoline [1983] (85) 521
LAGO, ALICIA DEL
Norte, El (84) 265
LAHTI, CHRISTINE
Swing Shift (85) 535
Whose Life Is It Anyway? (82) 378
LAI, CHRISTINA
Savage Island (86) 458
LAIKEN, CHARLES
Rent Control (85) 530
LAINE, JENNIFER
Caged Fury (85) 514
LAKOVIC, PEDRAG
When Father Was Away on Business [1984] (86) 411
LAMARR, HEDY
H. M. Pulham, Esq. [1941] (82) 439
LAMAS, FERNANDO
"Obituaries" (83) 543
LAMAS, LORENZO
Body Rock (85) 513
LAMBERT, ANNE LOUISE
Draughtsman's Contract, The [1982] (84) 126
LAMBERT, CHRISTOPHER
Greystoke (85) 236
Subway (86) 461
LAMBIE, JOE
Nightmares (84) 490
LA MOTTA, JOHN
American Ninja (86) 436
LAMPERT, ZOHRA
Alphabet City (85) 509
Teachers (85) 535
LAMPRECHT, GUNTER
Berlin Alexanderplatz [1980] (84) 57
LAMY, MAURICE
Dernier Combat, Le [1983] (85) 517
LANCASTER, BURT
Apache [1954] (82) 395
Atlantic City (82) 74
Cattle Annie and Little Britches (82) 97
Local Hero (84) 206
Osterman Weekend, The (84) 491
LANCILOTI, LOUIE
Windy City (85) 538
LAND, PAUL
Spring Break (84) 494
LANDA, ALFREDO
Holy Innocents, The (86) 447
LANDEN, DINSDALE
Morons from Outer Space (86) 452
LANDERS, AUDREY
Chorus Line, A (86) 91
LANDGREBE, GUDRUN
Colonel Redl [1984] (86) 100
Woman in Flames, A (85) 538
LANDHAM, SONNY
Fleshburn (85) 519
48 HRS. (83) 173
LANDI, ELISSA
Sign of the Cross, The [1932] (85) 607

LANDIS, MONTE
Pee-wee's Big Adventure (86) 265
LANDON, MICHAEL
Sam's Son (85) 531
LANDRY, KAREN
Personals, The (84) 491
LANE, DIANE
Cattle Annie and Little Britches (82) 97
Cotton Club, The (85) 150
Outsiders, The (84) 282
Rumble Fish (84) 492
Six Pack (83) 428
Streets of Fire (85) 534
LANE, LOLA
"Obituaries" (82) 495
LANE, MICHAEL
Stryker (84) 494
LANE, RICHARD
"Obituaries" (83) 543
LANG, CAROLINE
Argent, L' [1983] (85) 74
LANG, JEANIE
King of Jazz [1930] (86) 515
LANG, PERRY
Body and Soul (83) 418
Sahara (85) 531
Spring Break (84) 494
Tag (83) 429
LANG, STEPHEN
Twice in a Lifetime (86) 397
LANGE, HOPE
Nightmare on Elm Street, Part 2, A (86) 454
LANGE, JESSICA
Country (85) 156
Frances (83) 178
Postman Always Rings Twice, The (82) 284
Sweet Dreams (86) 374
Tootsie (83) 353
LANGENKAMP, HEATHER
Nightmare on Elm Street, A (85) 527
LANGFORD, BONNIE
Wombling Free [1979] (85) 538
LANGLET, AMANDA
Pauline at the Beach [1982] (84) 296
LANGLOIS, LISA
Deadly Eyes (84) 482
Joy of Sex (85) 524
Man Who Wasn't There, The (84) 489
Neil Simon's The Slugger's Wife (86) 454
LANGSTON, MURRAY
Night Patrol (86) 454
LANNOM, LES
Southern Comfort (82) 332
LANOUX, VICTOR
National Lampoon's European Vacation (86) 453
LANSBURY, ANGELA
Company of Wolves, The [1984] (86) 115
Pirates of Penzance, The (84) 301
World of Henry Orient, The [1964] (84) 600
LANTEAU, WILLIAM
On Golden Pond (82) 263
LANZ, FRANKIE
Joey (86) 448

LAPARÉ, LOUISE
  Plouffe, Les   (86) 456
LAPEYRE, BRUNO
  Argent, L' [1983]   (85) 74
LAPINSKI, LAURIE
  Dorm That Dripped Blood, The   (84) 482
LAPLANTE, LAURA
  King of Jazz [1930]   (86) 515
LAPOTAIRE, JANE
  Eureka   (86) 442
LARANGE, STEWART
  Return to Oz   (86) 458
LARCH, JOHN
  Play Misty for Me [1971]   (86) 532
LARIO, VERONICA
  Softly Softly [1984]   (86) 460
LARRETA, AUGUSTO
  Deathstalker   (85) 517
  Official Story, The   (86) 249
LARROQUETTE, JOHN
  Choose Me   (85) 135
  Meatballs Part II   (85) 526
LARSEN, ERNA
  Came a Hot Friday   (86) 439
LARSON, DARRELL
  City Limits   (86) 440
  Mike's Murder   (85) 526
  Twice in a Lifetime   (86) 397
LARSSON, PAUL
  Mad Max Beyond Thunderdome   (86) 223
LARUE, JACK
  "Obituaries"   (85) 677
LA SALLE, ERIQ
  Rappin'   (86) 457
LASALLE, MARTINO
  Alamo Bay   (86) 436
  Missing   (83) 228
LASKIN, MICHAEL
  Maxie   (86) 452
  Personals, The   (84) 491
LASSANDER, DAGMAR
  Black Cat, The   (85) 512
LASSICK, SYDNEY
  Night Patrol   (86) 454
  Silent Madness   (85) 532
  Stitches   (86) 461
LATHAM, LOUISE
  Mass Appeal   (85) 303
LATHOURIS, NICHOLAS
  Where the Green Ants Dream [1984]   (86) 465
LATTANZI, MATT
  My Tutor   (84) 490
LAU, CHARLEY
  Max Dugan Returns   (84) 228
LAU, WESLEY
  "Obituaries"   (85) 677
LAUDENBACH, PHILIPPE
  Confidentially Yours [1983]   (85) 516
LAUGHLIN, JOHN
  Crimes of Passion   (85) 161
LAUGHTON, CHARLES
  Arch of Triumph [1948]   (84) 501
  Sign of the Cross, The [1932]   (85) 607

LAURANCE, MATTHEW
  Best Defense   (85) 512
LAURE, CAROLE
  Dirty Dishes [1978]   (84) 482
LAUREL, STAN
  Our Relations [1936]   (86) 523
LAURENSON, JAMES
  Pink Floyd the Wall [1981]   (83) 258
LAURENT
  Boat Is Full, The [1981]   (83) 82
LAURENT, RÉMI
  Plouffe, Les   (86) 456
LAURIE, PIPER
  Return to Oz   (86) 458
LAUTER, ED
  Death Wish III   (86) 441
  Eureka   (86) 442
  Finders Keepers   (85) 519
  Lassiter   (85) 524
  Timerider   (84) 495
LAVANANT, DOMINIQUE
  My Other Husband   (86) 453
LAW, JOHN PHILLIP
  Rainy Day Friends   (86) 458
LAWFORD, PETER
  Body and Soul   (83) 418
  Royal Wedding [1951]   (86) 536
  "Obituaries"   (85) 678
LAWRANCE, DEBRA
  Silver City [1984]   (86) 460
LAWRENCE, BRUNO
  Heart of a Stag   (85) 522
  Quiet Earth, The   (86) 295
  Smash Palace [1981]   (83) 302
  Utu [1983]   (85) 504
  Wild Horses [1983]   (85) 538
LAWRENCE, ELIZABETH
  Four Friends   (82) 167
LAWRENCE, JOEY
  Summer Rental   (86) 462
LAWRENCE, MICHAEL
  Came a Hot Friday   (86) 439
LAWRENCE, STEVE
  Lonely Guy, The   (85) 525
LAWSON, DENIS
  Local Hero   (84) 206
LAWSON, LEIGH
  Tess [1980]   (82) 471
LAWSON, RICHARD
  Stick   (86) 460
  Streets of Fire   (85) 534
LAZARO, EUSEBIO
  Demons in the Garden [1982]   (85) 517
LAZER, PETER
  Hombre [1967]   (84) 547
LAZURE, GABRIELLE
  Joshua Then and Now   (86) 198
LEACH, ROSEMARY
  Turtle Diary   (86) 464
LEADBETTER, CINDY
  Hercules II   (86) 446
LEAKE, CYNTHIA
  Bear, The   (85) 511
  Fire and Ice   (84) 153

LEAND, JEAN-PIERRE
Detective (86) 442
LEANDER, ZARAH
"Obituaries" (82) 495
LEBEDEFF, IVAN
History Is Made at Night [1937] (84) 542
LE BROCK, KELLY
Weird Science (86) 465
Woman in Red, The (85) 538
LECARPENTIER, ARNAULT
Bal, Le [1983] (85) 80
LEDER, ERWIN
Boot, Das [1981] (83) 86
LEDERER, ANDREW J.
Out of Control (86) 455
LEDOUX, FERNAND
Freud [1962] (84) 535
LEE, BERNARD
"Obituaries" (82) 495
LEE, CHRISTOPHER
Wicker Man, The [1974] (86) 555
LEE, JONNA
Lovelines (85) 525
Making the Grade (85) 526
Sam's Son (85) 531
LEE, MARGO
Starstruck (83) 428
LEE, MARK
Gallipoli [1980] (82) 179
LEE, PEGGY
Pete Kelly's Blues [1955] (83) 481
LEE, REISEN
Mishima (86) 236
LEE, STEPHEN
Purple Hearts (85) 529
LEEDS, ANDREA
"Obituaries" (85) 679
LE FEVER, KIT
Grace Quigley (86) 444
LEFEVRE, ADAM
Return of the Secaucus 7 [1980] (83) 484
LEGAULT, LANCE
Stripes (82) 336
LEGITIMUS, DARLING
Sugar Cane Alley [1983] (85) 461
LE GUELLEC, GUILLAUME
Entre nous [1983] (85) 176
LEHMAN, VAL
Kitty and the Bagman [1982] (84) 487
LEI, LINDA
Cannonball Run II (85) 514
LEI, LYDIA
Doctor Detroit (84) 482
Hammett (84) 174
LEIBMAN, RON
Door to Door (85) 518
Phar Lap (85) 528
Rhinestone (85) 531
Romantic Comedy (84) 492
LEIGH, DIANA
Killpoint (85) 524
LEIGH, JANET
Pete Kelly's Blues [1955] (83) 481

LEIGH, JENNIFER JASON
Fast Times at Ridgemont High (83) 156
Flesh and Blood (86) 443
Grandview, U.S.A. (85) 520
LE MAT, PAUL
Death Valley (83) 419
Jimmy the Kid (84) 486
Melvin and Howard [1980] (82) 453
Strange Invaders (84) 494
LE MESURIER, JOHN
"Obituaries" (84) 625
LEMMON, CHRIS
Cannonball Run II (85) 514
LEMMON, JACK
Buddy Buddy (82) 93
Cowboy [1958] (82) 417
Macaroni (86) 451
Mass Appeal (85) 303
Missing (83) 232
LENARD, MARK
Star Trek III—The Search for Spock (85) 439
LENAUER, JEAN
My Dinner with André (82) 255
LENNOX, ANNIE
Revolution (86) 458
LENOIRE, ROSETTA
Lily in Love (86) 450
LENYA, LOTTE
"Obituaries" (82) 495
LENZ, RICH
Melvin and Howard [1980] (82) 453
LENZI, LAURA
Hercules II (86) 446
LEO, MELISSA
Always (86) 60
Streetwalkin' (86) 461
LEON, JOE
Almost You (86) 436
Cold Feet (85) 516
LEONARD, LU
Breakin' 2 (85) 514
Micki & Maude (85) 308
LEONETTI, FRANCESCO
Oedipus Rex [1967] (85) 528
LEOTARD, PHILIPPE
Balance, La [1982] (84) 52
LE POGAM, PIERRE-ANGE
Subway (86) 461
LERNER, MICHAEL
Movers and Shakers (86) 453
National Lampoon's Class Reunion (83) 426
Postman Always Rings Twice, The (82) 284
Strange Invaders (84) 494
LE SACHE, BERNADETTE
Horse of Pride, The (86) 447
LESLIE, FRANK
King of Jazz [1930] (86) 515
LESLIE, JOAN
Hard Way, The [1942] (85) 555
LESLIE, NAN
Veronika Voss (83) 382
LESLIE, WILLIAM
Long Gray Line, The [1955] (82) 447

LESNIAK, EMILIA
9 Deaths of the Ninja   (86) 454
LETCH, DAVID
Sylvia   (86) 462
LEUSTIG, JACK
Breathless   (84) 89
LEVERINGTON, SHELBY
Cloak and Dagger   (85) 516
Love Letters   (85) 288
LEVIN, BEN
Drifting   (85) 518
LEVINE, ANNA
Desperately Seeking Susan   (86) 137
LEVINE, JERRY
Teen Wolf   (86) 462
LEVY, EUGENE
Going Berserk   (84) 485
National Lampoon's Vacation   (84) 242
Splash   (85) 434
LEWGOY, JOSÉ
Blame It on Rio   (85) 512
Fitzcarraldo   (83) 167
Kiss of the Spider Woman   (86) 209
LEWIS, ALUN
Experience Preferred ... but Not Essential
[1982]   (84) 141
LEWIS, FURRY
This Is Elvis   (82) 360
LEWIS, GEOFFREY
Lust in the Dust   (86) 450
Night of the Comet   (85) 527
Stitches   (86) 461
LEWIS, JARMA
"Obituaries"   (86) 574
LEWIS, JERRY
King of Comedy, The   (84) 192
Play Misty for Me [1971]   (86) 532
Slapstick   (85) 533
LEWIS, MITCHELL
Bridge of San Luis Rey, The [1929]   (82)
408
LEYSEN, JOHANN
Girl with the Red Hair, The   (84) 485
Hail Mary   (86) 182
LHERMITTE, THIERRY
My Best Friend's Girl [1983]   (85) 326
My New Partner [1984]   (86) 246
Next Year if All Goes Well   (84) 490
Until September   (85) 537
L'HOTSKY, TINA
Loveless, The   (85) 525
LIBERTINI, RICHARD
All of Me   (85) 58
Fletch   (86) 169
Unfaithfully Yours   (85) 537
LIBERTY, RICHARD
Day of the Dead   (86) 441
LICHT, JEREMY
Twilight Zone—The Movie   (84) 435
LICHTENSTEIN, MITCHELL
Streamers   (84) 391
LICHTERMAN, MARVIN
Front, The [1976]   (86) 502
LIEBMAN, RITON
Patsy, The   (86) 456

LIGHTLE, LORRIE
Sure Thing, The   (86) 369
LINCOLN, WARREN
Power, The   (85) 529
LINDA, BOGUSŁAW
Danton [1982]   (84) 121
Man of Iron   (82) 230
LINDFORS, VIVECA
Creepshow   (83) 419
Silent Madness   (85) 532
Sure Thing, The   (86) 369
LINDLEY, AUDRA
Best Friends   (83) 68
Cannery Row   (83) 95
Taking Off [1971]   (86) 545
LINDORFF, LONE
Zappa   (85) 539
LINDSAY, HELEN
Secrets   (85) 532
LINDSAY, KIRSTY
Sheena   (85) 532
LINDSAY, MARGARET
"Obituaries"   (82) 495
LINDSEY, GEORGE
Cannonball Run II   (85) 514
LINHARES, LUIZ
Gabriela [1983]   (85) 213
LINN-BAKER, MARK
My Favorite Year   (83) 241
LINNE, VELTA
Rasputin [1975]   (86) 457
LINO, EDILSON
Pixote [1980]   (82) 280
LINT, DEREK DE
Bastille [1984]   (86) 437
LINVILLE, LARRY
School Spirit   (86) 458
LIOTARD, ANNE-SÉVERINE
Full Moon in Paris   (85) 208
LIPINSKI, EUGENE
Moonlighting   (83) 237
LIPMAN, JENNY
King David   (86) 449
LIPMAN, MAUREEN
Educating Rita   (84) 136
LIPPA, JEFFRY
American Pop   (82) 62
LIPSCOMB, DENNIS
Soldier's Story, A   (85) 427
LITEL, JOHN
They Drive by Night [1940]   (83) 508
LITHGOW, JOHN
Adventures of Buckaroo Banzai,
The   (85) 47
Blow Out   (82) 83
Footloose   (85) 198
Santa Claus   (86) 334
Terms of Endearment   (84) 414
Twilight Zone—The Movie   (84) 435
2010   (85) 494
World According to Garp, The   (83) 397
LITTLE, ANN
"Obituaries"   (85) 679

LITTLE, CLEAVON
   Once Bitten (86) 455
   Surf II (85) 535
   Toy Soldiers (85) 536
LIVELY, JASON
   National Lampoon's European Vacation (86)
   453
LIVESEY, ROGER
   I Know Where I'm Going [1945] (83) 456
LIVINGSTONE, MARY
   "Obituaries" (84) 626
LIZER, KARI
   Gotcha! (86) 444
LLEWELLYN-JONES, TONY
   Where the Green Ants Dream [1984] (86) 465
LLEWELYN, DESMOND
   Octopussy (84) 276
   View to a Kill, A (86) 402
LLOYD, CHRISTOPHER
   Adventures of Buckaroo Banzai,
     The (85) 47
   Back to the Future (86) 65
   Clue (86) 440
   Star Trek III—The Search for Spock
     (85) 439
LLOYD, DORIS
   Becky Sharp [1935] (82) 403
   Disraeli [1929] (82) 426
LLOYD, ROBERT
   Parsifal (84) 491
LLOYD, ROLLO
   Barbary Coast [1935] (84) 506
LOBIANCO, TONY
   City Heat (85) 141
LOCKE, SONDRA
   Sudden Impact (84) 395
LOCKHART, ANNE
   Oasis, The (85) 528
LOCKHART, KATHLEEN
   Roughly Speaking [1945] (83) 490
LOCKLEAR, HEATHER
   Firestarter (85) 519
LODDI, LORIS
   Ladyhawke (86) 214
LODGE, JOHN
   "Obituaries" (86) 574
LOEWITSCH, KLAUS
   Gotcha! (86) 444
LOFF, JEANETTE
   King of Jazz [1930] (86) 515
LOGAN, JACQUELINE
   "Obituaries" (84) 626
LOGAN, PHYLLIS
   Another Time, Another Place [1983] (85) 510
   Doctor and the Devils, The (86) 442
LOGAN, ROBERT
   Night in Heaven, A (84) 490
LOGGIA, ROBERT
   Jagged Edge (86) 190
   Officer and a Gentleman, An (83) 246
   Psycho II (84) 307
   Scarface (84) 361
LOISEAU, OLIVIER
   Bal, Le [1983] (85) 80

LOKEY, BEN
   Breakin' (85) 514
LOM, HERBERT
   Dead Zone, The (84) 481
   King Solomon's Mines (86) 449
   Trail of the Pink Panther (83) 430
LOMITA, SAL
   Zelig (84) 473
LOMNICKI, JACEK
   Man of Marble [1977] (82) 234
   Man of Marble [1977] (82) 234
LONDER, DAVID L.
   Man with One Red Shoe, The (86) 451
LONDON, LAURENE
   I, the Jury (83) 423
LONE, JOHN
   Iceman (85) 248
   Year of the Dragon (86) 426
LONG, SHELLEY
   Irreconcilable Differences (85) 523
   Losin' It (84) 488
   Night Shift (83) 426
LONSDALE, MICHAEL
   Erendira [1983] (85) 181
   Holcroft Covenant, The (86) 446
LOO, RICHARD
   "Obituaries" (84) 626
LOPERT, TANYA
   Tales of Ordinary Madness (84) 495
LOPEZ, IRENE OLGA
   Gotcha! (86) 444
LORRAINE, LOUISE
   "Obituaries" (82) 497
LORRING, JOAN
   Lost Moment, The [1947] (83) 465
LOUDON, DOROTHY
   Garbo Talks (85) 520
LOUGHLIN, LORI
   New Kids, The (86) 454
   Secret Admirer (86) 459
LOUREIRO, OSWALDO
   Bar Esperanza [1983] (86) 437
LOVE, ALAN
   Gregory's Girl [1981] (83) 193
   That Sinking Feeling [1979] (85) 536
LOVEJOY, ROBIN
   My First Wife (86) 453
LOWE, ARTHUR
   "Obituaries" (83) 543
LOWE, OLGA
   Riddle of the Sands, The [1979] (85) 531
LOWE, ROB
   Class (84) 480
   Hotel New Hampshire, The (85) 243
   Outsiders, The (84) 282
   Oxford Blues (85) 528
   St. Elmo's Fire (86) 330
LOWE, STANJA
   Silent Madness (85) 532
LOWITSCH, KLAUS
   Firefox (83) 160
LOY, MYRNA
   Animal Kingdom, The [1932] (86) 469
   "Interview with, An" (84) 18
   Too Hot to Handle [1938] (84) 596

LOZANO, MARGARITA
  Night of the Shooting Stars, The
    [1982] (84) 258
LU, LISA
  Don't Cry, It's Only Thunder   (83) 420
LUCA, LOES
  Girl with the Red Hair, The   (84) 485
LUCAS, BETTY
  My First Wife   (86) 453
LUCAS, LISA
  Hadley's Rebellion   (85) 521
LUCENA, CARLOS
  Hit, The   (86) 446
LUCERO, ENRIQUE
  Evil That Men Do, The   (85) 518
LUCHINI, FABRICE
  Full Moon in Paris   (85) 208
LUCKINBILL, LAURENCE
  Not for Publication   (85) 527
LUDLUM, ANNE
  Twice in a Lifetime   (86) 397
LUDWICK, REX
  Blame It on the Night   (85) 512
LUDWIG, PAMELA
  Split Image   (83) 317
LUFT, LORNA
  Where the Boys Are '84   (85) 537
LUHRS, BILL
  Slayground [1983]   (85) 533
LUKE, JORGE
  Evil That Men Do, The   (85) 518
LUKE, KEYE
  Gremlins   (85) 230
LUMBLY, CARL
  Adventures of Buckaroo Banzai,
    The   (85) 47
LUNDGREN, DOLPH
  Rocky IV   (86) 319
LUNGHI, CHERIE
  Excalibur   (82) 144
  King David   (86) 449
LUNGHINI, ELSA
  Garde à vue [1981]   (83) 189
LUPINO, IDA
  Hard Way, The [1942]   (85) 555
  Peter Ibbetson [1935]   (86) 527
  They Drive by Night [1940]   (83) 508
LUPONE, PATTI
  Fighting Back   (83) 421
  Witness   (86) 421
LURIE, JOHN
  Paris, Texas   (85) 359
  Stranger than Paradise   (85) 455
LUU, THUY AN
  Diva [1980]   (83) 147
LYE, REG
  Wombling Free [1979]   (85) 538
LYLE, BRENT
  Another State of Mind   (85) 510
LYN, RHONDA
  This Is Elvis   (82) 360
LYNCH, BECKY JO
  River, The   (85) 416

LYNCH, JOHN
  Cal   (85) 124
LYNCH, KATE
  Def-Con 4   (86) 441
LYNCH, RAYMOND
  Night of the Comet   (85) 527
LYNCH, RICHARD
  Invasion U.S.A.   (86) 447
LYNDE, PAUL
  "Obituaries"   (83) 544
LYNN, DIANA
  Bedtime for Bonzo [1951]   (84) 512
LYONS, ROBERT F.
  Avenging Angel   (86) 436
  Cease Fire   (86) 440
LYONS, TONY
  James Joyce's Women   (86) 193
LYS, AGATA
  Holy Innocents, The   (86) 447
LYSAK, PIOTR
  Love in Germany, A [1983]   (85) 283

MCALLISTER, CHIP
  Weekend Pass   (85) 537
MCANALLY, RAY
  Cal   (85) 124
  Danny Boy   (85) 517
MACARTNEY, CAROL
  Gregory's Girl [1981]   (83) 193
MCAVOY, MAY
  "Obituaries"   (85) 681
MCCAIN, FRANCES LEE
  Gremlins   (85) 230
  Tex   (83) 335
MCCALL, JAMES
  World According to Garp, The   (83) 397
MCCALLUM, DAVID
  Freud [1962]   (84) 535
MCCALMAN, MACON
  Fleshburn   (85) 519
MCCAMBRIDGE, MERCEDES
  Echoes   (84) 483
MCCAMEY, SHANE
  Invasion U.S.A.   (86) 447
MCCANN, DONAL
  Cal   (85) 124
  Danny Boy   (85) 517
MCCARREN, FRED
  National Lampoon's Class Reunion   (83) 426
MCCARTHY, ANDREW
  Class   (84) 480
  Heaven Help Us   (86) 445
  St. Elmo's Fire   (86) 330
MCCARTHY, JEANNIE
  1918   (86) 454
MCCARTHY, JIM
  Under the Volcano   (85) 499
MCCARTHY, KEVIN
  My Tutor   (84) 490
MCCARTHY, MOLLY
  Flamingo Kid, The   (85) 192
MCCARTHY, NEIL
  Clash of the Titans   (82) 111

MCCARTNEY, LINDA
  Give My Regards to Broad Street   (85) 520
MCCARTNEY, PAUL
  Give My Regards to Broad Street   (85) 520
MCCAUGHAN, CHARLES
  Heat and Dust [1982]   (84) 187
MACCHIO, RALPH
  Karate Kid, The   (85) 264
  Outsiders, The   (84) 282
  Teachers   (85) 535
MACCIANTELLI, FABRICIO
  Henry IV [1983]   (86) 446
MCCLANAHAN, RUE
  They Might Be Giants [1971]   (83) 515
MCCLORY, SEAN
  Long Gray Line, The [1955]   (82) 447
MCCLOSKEY, LEIGH
  Fraternity Vacation   (86) 444
  Just One of the Guys   (86) 448
MCCLURE, DOUG
  Cannonball Run II   (85) 514
  House Where Evil Dwells, The   (83) 423
MCCLURE, MARC
  Back to the Future   (86) 65
  Supergirl   (85) 535
  Superman III   (84) 399
MCCLURG, EDIE
  Cheech and Chong's The Corsican
    Brothers   (85) 515
MCCOLL, BILLY
  Ordeal by Innocence [1984]   (86) 455
MACCONE, RONALD
  Pope of Greenwich Village, The   (85) 529
MCCONNELL, RICHARD
  Tomorrow [1972]   (84) 589
MCCONNOCHIE, RHYS
  Wild Duck, The [1983]   (86) 466
MACCORKINDALE, SIMON
  Jaws 3-D   (84) 486
  Riddle of the Sands, The [1979]   (85) 531
  Sword and the Sorcerer, The   (83) 429
MCCORMICK, CAROLYN
  Enemy Mine   (86) 161
MCCORMICK, GILMER
  Silent Night, Deadly Night   (85) 532
MCCORMICK, PAT
  Smokey and the Bandit—Part 3   (84) 493
MCCOWEN, ALEC
  Never Say Never Again   (84) 252
MCCOY, MATT
  Fraternity Vacation   (86) 444
MCCRACKEN, JEFF
  Running Brave   (84) 354
MCCRANE, PAUL
  Hotel New Hampshire, The   (85) 243
  Purple Hearts   (85) 529
MCCREA, JOEL
  Barbary Coast [1935]   (84) 506
  Colorado Territory [1949]   (86) 489
  Come and Get It [1936]   (82) 412
  Most Dangerous Game, The [1932]   (86) 519
MCCRINDLE, ALEX
  Eye of the Needle   (82) 148
MCCULLOCH, IAN
  Dr. Butcher, M.D. [1980]   (83) 420

MCCULLOUGH, PHILO
  "Obituaries" [1982]   (82) 497
MCCURRY, JOHN
  Atlantic City   (82) 74
MCDANIELS, DARYLL
  Krush Groove   (86) 449
MCDIARMID, IAN
  Return of the Jedi   (84) 326
MACDONALD, BRUCE
  Return of the Secaucus 7 [1980]   (83) 484
MCDONALD, CHRISTOPHER
  Breakin'   (85) 514
  Chattanooga Choo Choo   (85) 515
MCDONALD, DANIEL
  Where the Boys Are '84   (85) 537
MCDONALD, DAVID H.
  Joy of Sex   (85) 524
MCDONALD, DOLETTE
  Bring on the Night   (86) 439
MACDONALD, EDMUND
  Detour [1946]   (86) 498
MACDONALD, IAN
  Apache [1954]   (82) 395
MACDONALD, JESSICA WIGHT
  Lianna   (84) 201
MCDORMAND, FRANCES
  Blood Simple   (86) 438
MCDOWALL, RODDY
  Class of 1984   (83) 419
  Fright Night   (86) 444
  Man Hunt [1941]   (85) 570
MACDOWELL, ANDIE
  Greystoke   (85) 236
  St. Elmo's Fire   (86) 330
MCDOWELL, MALCOLM
  Blue Thunder   (84) 84
  Brittania Hospital   (84) 480
  Cat People   (83) 100
  Cross Creek   (84) 116
  Get Crazy   (84) 484
  Time After Time [1979]   (84) 579
MCEACHIN, JAMES
  Play Misty for Me [1971]   (86) 532
MCENERY, PETER
  Victim [1961]   (85) 649
MCENROE, ANNIE
  Battletruck   (83) 417
  Purple Hearts   (85) 529
MCEVOY, ANNEMARIE
  Stephen King's Children of the Corn   (85) 534
MACEWEN, LINDA
  They All Laughed   (82) 350
MCFADDEN, CHERYL
  Muppets Take Manhattan, The   (85) 526
MCFADDEN, THOM
  Nightmare on Elm Street, Part 2, A   (86) 454
MCGARTH, DOUG
  Porky's   (83) 267
MCGAVIN, DARREN
  Christmas Story, A   (84) 110
  Natural, The   (85) 329
  Turk 182   (86) 464
MCGAVIN, GRAEM
  Weekend Pass   (85) 537

MCGEE, BILL
  1918 (86) 454
MCGEE, CINDY
  Fast Forward (86) 442
MCGEE, VONETTA
  Repo Man (85) 408
MCGILL, BRUCE
  Into the Night (86) 186
  Silkwood (84) 367
MCGILL, CAROLE
  City Girl, The (85) 516
MCGILL, EVERETT
  Quest for Fire (83) 271
  Stephen King's Silver Bullet (86) 460
MCGILLIS, KELLY
  Reuben, Reuben (84) 337
  Witness (86) 421
MCGINLEY, TED
  Revenge of the Nerds (85) 530
MCGINNIS, SCOTT
  Joysticks (84) 487
  Making the Grade (85) 526
MCGOOHAN, PATRICK
  Baby (86) 437
MCGOVERN, ELIZABETH
  Lovesick (84) 488
  Once upon a Time in America (85) 345
  Racing with the Moon (85) 397
  Ragtime (82) 304
MCGOWAN, CHARLES
  Chorus Line, A (86) 91
MACGOWRAN, TARA
  Secret Places [1984] (86) 459
MCGRADY, MICHAEL
  Bear, The (85) 511
MCGRATH, DOUG
  Pale Rider (86) 261
MCGREGOR, ANGELA PUNCH
  Test of Love (86) 462
  We of the Never Never [1982] (84) 497
MACGREGOR, IAN
  World According to Garp, The (83) 397
MCGUIRE, GERARD
  Kitty and the Bagman [1982] (84) 487
MCHATTIE, STEPHEN
  Death Valley (83) 419
MCHUGH, FRANK
  "Obituaries" (82) 497
MCHUGH, MATT
  Barbary Coast [1935] (84) 506
MCINNERNY, TIM
  Wetherby (86) 406
MACINNES, ANGUS
  Strange Brew (84) 494
  Witness (86) 421
MCINTIRE, JOHN
  Apache [1954] (82) 395
  Cloak and Dagger (85) 516
  Honkytonk Man (83) 200
MACINTOSH, JOAN
  Flash of Green, A (86) 443
MCINTYRE, CHRISTINE
  "Obituaries" (85) 681

MCINTYRE, MARVIN J.
  Fandango (86) 442
MACKAY, DANA
  This Is Elvis (82) 360
MACKAY, FULTON
  Local Hero (84) 206
  Sense of Freedom, A (86) 459
MCKEAN, MICHAEL
  Clue (86) 440
  D.A.R.Y.L. (86) 441
  This Is Spinal Tap (85) 484
  Young Doctors in Love (83) 431
MCKEE, LONETTE
  Brewster's Millions (86) 438
  Cotton Club, The (85) 150
MCKELLEN, IAN
  Plenty (86) 271
  Priest of Love (82) 288
MCKENZIE, TIM
  Silver City [1984] (86) 460
MCKEON, DOUG
  Mischief (86) 452
  On Golden Pond (82) 263
MCKEON, KEVIN
  Pink Floyd the Wall [1981] (83) 258
MCKERN, LEO
  French Lieutenant's Woman, The (82) 174
  Ladyhawke (86) 214
MCKILLOP, DON
  American Werewolf in London, An (82) 66
MCKINNEY, BILL
  Against All Odds (85) 509
  First Blood (83) 164
  Heart Like a Wheel (84) 182
  Tex (83) 335
MCKINNEY, FLORINE
  Take a Letter, Darling [1942] (85) 632
MACKINNON, JANE
  Bad Boy, The (86) 437
MACKRELL, JIM
  Teen Wolf (86) 462
MACLACHLAN, KYLE
  Dune (85) 171
MCLAGLEN, VICTOR
  Fort Apache [1948] (84) 530
MACLAINE, SHIRLEY
  Cannonball Run II (85) 514
  Terms of Endearment (84) 414
MCLAREN, DANIEL
  Klynham Summer (84) 487
MCLAREN, HOLLIS
  Atlantic City (82) 74
MACLAREN, MARY
  "Obituaries" (86) 575
MACLEAN, PETER
  Breakin' 2 (85) 514
MACLENNAN, SUSAN
  Guest, The (85) 520
MACLEOD, MARY
  Brimstone and Treacle (83) 91
MCLISH, RACHEL
  Pumping Iron II (86) 456
MCMARTIN, JOHN
  Pennies from Heaven (82) 276

MCMASTER, NILES
Windy City (85) 538
MCMILLAN, KENNETH
Blue Skies Again (84) 479
Dune (85) 171
Partners (83) 427
Pope of Greenwich Village, The (85) 529
Protocol (85) 383
Ragtime (82) 304
Reckless (85) 530
Runaway Train (86) 324
Stephen King's Cat's Eye (86) 460
True Confessions (82) 368
Whose Life Is It Anyway? (82) 378
MACMURRAY, FRED
Take a Letter, Darling [1942] (85) 632
MCNAMARA, BRIAN
Flamingo Kid, The (85) 192
MCNAMARA, ED
Stitches (86) 461
MACNAUGHTAN, ALAN
Victim [1961] (85) 649
MCNAUGHTON, DEBORAH
Fool for Love (86) 172
MCNAUGHTON, ROBERT
E. T.: The Extra-Terrestrial (83) 151
MACNEE, PATRICK
Howling, The (82) 207
Sweet Sixteen (85) 535
This Is Spinal Tap (85) 484
View to a Kill, A (86) 402
Young Doctors in Love (83) 431
MACNEIL, CORNELL
Traviata, La (83) 366
MACNICOL, PETER
Dragonslayer (82) 125
Sophie's Choice (83) 311
MCNICHOL, KRISTY
Just the Way You Are (85) 524
Only When I Laugh (82) 268
Pirate Movie, The (83) 427
MCOMIE, MAGGIE
THX 1138 [1971] (85) 638
MCQUADE, KRIS
Coca-Cola Kid, The (86) 440
MCQUARY, CHUCK
Purple Haze (84) 492
MCQUEEN, ARMELIA
Quartet (82) 296
MCQUEEN, CHAD
Hadley's Rebellion (85) 521
Karate Kid, The (85) 264
MCRAE, FRANK
Cannery Row (83) 95
48 HRS. (83) 173
Red Dawn (85) 530
MCRAE, HILTON
French Lieutenant's Woman, The (82) 174
Greystoke (85) 236
MCRANEY, GERALD
Neverending Story, The (85) 527
MCSHANE, IAN
Exposed (84) 484
Ordeal by Innocence [1984] (86) 455
Too Scared to Scream (86) 463

MACY, BILL
Bad Medicine (86) 437
Movers and Shakers (86) 453
My Favorite Year (83) 241
MADDALENA, JULIE
Stephen King's Children of the Corn (85) 534
MADIGAN, AMY
Alamo Bay (86) 436
Love Child (83) 425
Love Letters (85) 288
Places in the Heart (85) 371
Streets of Fire (85) 534
Twice in a Lifetime (86) 397
MADISON, NOEL
Our Relations [1936] (86) 523
MADONNA
Desperately Seeking Susan (86) 137
"Interview with Susan Seidelman, An" (86) 33,
34
Vision Quest (86) 464
MADSEN, MICHAEL
Natural, The (85) 329
MADSEN, VIRGINIA
Creator (86) 441
Electric Dreams (85) 518
MAEDA, GIN
Foster Daddy, Tora! [1980] (82) 163
MAGARILL, SOPHIE
New Babylon, The [1929] (84) 561
MAGEE, PATRICK
Black Cat, The (85) 512
"Obituaries" (83) 544
MAGGART, BRANDON
World According to Garp, The (83) 397
MAGID, PAUL DAVID
Jewel of the Nile, The (86) 448
MAGILL, JIM
Scandalous (85) 532
MAGWOOD, ROBBIE
One Magic Christmas (86) 455
MAHAR, CHRISTOPHER
Best Defense (85) 512
MAHARIS, GEORGE
Sword and the Sorcerer, The (83) 429
MAHER, JOSEPH
Evil That Men Do, The (85) 518
MAHLER, BRUCE
Friday the 13th—The Final Chapter (85) 520
Police Academy 2 (86) 276
MAHONEY, TOM
Cannery Row (83) 95
MAIA, NUÑO LEAL
Gabriela [1983] (85) 213
Kiss of the Spider Woman (86) 209
MAILER, NORMAN
Ragtime (82) 304
MAJIAS, ISABELLE
Bad Boy, The (86) 437
MAKEPEACE, CHRIS
Oasis, The (85) 528
MAKO
Conan the Destroyer (85) 516
Testament (84) 420
MAL, ARTHUR
Black Cauldron, The (86) 75

MALAHIDE, PATRICK
  Comfort and Joy   (85) 146
MALAVOY, CHRISTOPHE
  Balance, La [1982]   (84) 52
  Peril   (86) 456
MALCOLM, CHRISTOPHER
  Rustler's Rhapsody   (86) 458
MALCOLM, JAMES
  Merry Christmas, Mr. Lawrence   (84) 231
MALDEN, KARL
  Sting II, The   (84) 494
MALET, ARTHUR
  Secret of NIMH, The   (83) 288
MALET, LAURENT
  Invitation au voyage [1982]   (84) 486
  Querelle [1982]   (84) 313
MALET, PIERRE
  Basileus Quartet   (85) 511
MALIS-MOREY, ADELE
  Black Cauldron, The   (86) 75
MALKOVICH, JOHN
  Eleni   (86) 151
  Killing Fields, The   (85) 270
  Places in the Heart   (85) 371
MALLESON, MILES
  Nell Gwyn [1934]   (84) 557
MALLOY, JOHN
  Cannery Row   (83) 95
MALM, MONA
  Fanny and Alexander [1982]   (84) 146
MALMSJÖ, JAN
  Fanny and Alexander [1982]   (84) 146
MALONE, DOROTHY
  Colorado Territory [1949]   (86) 489
MALONEY, MICHAEL
  Ordeal by Innocence [1984]   (86) 455
  Richard's Things   (82) 321
MALONEY, PATTY
  Swing Shift   (85) 535
MALONEY, PETER
  Thing, The   (83) 343
MANAHAN, ANNA
  Clash of the Titans   (82) 111
MANARD, BIFF
  Trancers   (86) 463
MANCUSO, NICK
  Blame It on the Night   (85) 512
  Mother Lode   (84) 490
MANDA, HISAKO
  Mishima   (86) 236
MANE, SAMBA
  Coup de torchon [1981]   (83) 124
MANES, GINA
  Napoleon [1927]   (82) 461
MANGANO, SILVANA
  Oedipus Rex [1967]   (85) 528
MANI, KARIN
  Alley Cat   (85) 509
MANN, MARGARET
  Disraeli [1929]   (82) 426
MANN, TERRENCE
  Chorus Line, A   (86) 91
MANN, TRACY
  Klynham Summer   (84) 487

MANNERS, DAVID
  Miracle Woman, The [1931]   (83) 473
MANNI, ETTORE
  City of Women   (82) 106
MANNING, ROBERT
  Sign of the Cross, The [1932]   (85) 607
MANOFF, DINAH
  I Ought to Be in Pictures   (83) 423
MANOJLOVIC, MIKI
  When Father Was Away on Business [1984]   (86) 411
MANSON, JEAN
  Trace, The [1983]   (85) 537
MANTELL, JOE
  Movers and Shakers   (86) 453
MAPES, TED
  "Obituaries"   (85) 682
MARANNE, ANDRE
  Plenty   (86) 271
MARASSI, HORACE
  Deathstalker   (85) 517
MARCEAU, SOPHIE
  Boum, La [1980]   (84) 480
MARCH, CATHERINE
  Caged Fury   (85) 514
MARCH, FREDRIC
  Hombre [1967]   (84) 547
  Sign of the Cross, The [1932]   (85) 607
MARCH, TONY
  Wrong Is Right   (83) 403
MARCHAND, GUY
  Coup de torchon [1981]   (83) 124
  Entre nous [1983]   (85) 176
  Garde à vue [1981]   (83) 189
  Heat of Desire [1981]   (85) 522
  Little Jerk [1984]   (86) 450
  Loulou [1980]   (82) 226
MARCHAND, NANCY
  Bostonians, The   (85) 105
MARCOVICCI, ANDREA
  Front, The [1976]   (86) 502
  Spacehunter   (84) 493
  Stuff, The   (86) 461
MARCUCCI, ROBERT ANTHONY
  Sure Thing, The   (86) 369
MARCUS, RICHARD
  Enemy Mine   (86) 161
MAREIKURA, MATIU
  Wild Horses [1983]   (85) 538
MARGOLIN, STUART
  Running Hot   (85) 531
  S.O.B.   (82) 328
MARGOTTA, MICHAEL
  Can She Bake a Cherry Pie?   (84) 95
MARGULIES, DAVID
  Front, The [1976]   (86) 502
MARICLE, LEONA
  Hard Way, The [1942]   (85) 555
MARIELLE, JEAN-PIERRE
  Coup de torchon [1981]   (83) 124
MARIKA, DHUNGULA
  Where the Green Ants Dream [1984]   (86) 465
MARIKA, ROAY
  Where the Green Ants Dream [1984]   (86) 465

MARIKA, WANDJUK
Where the Green Ants Dream [1984] (86) 465
MARIN, CHEECH
After Hours (86) 51
Cheech and Chong Still Smokin' (84) 480
Cheech and Chong's The Corsican
Brothers (85) 515
Things Are Tough All Over (83) 430
Yellowbeard (84) 498
MARIN, RIKKI
Cheech and Chong's The Corsican
Brothers (85) 515
Things Are Tough All Over (83) 430
MARIN, RUSS
Stitches (86) 461
MARINO, KENNY
Alphabet City (85) 509
Prince of the City (82) 292
MARK, TAMARA
Fast Forward (86) 442
MARKEY, ENID
"Obituaries" (82) 497
MARKHAM, DAVID
Richard's Things (82) 321
MARKHAM, KIKKA
Outland (82) 272
MARLEY, JOHN
Mother Lode (84) 490
"Obituaries" (85) 682
Threshold (84) 495
MARLOWE, HUGH
"Obituaries" (83) 544
MARLOWE, JONAS
Stephen King's Children of the Corn (85) 534
MARLOWE, JUNE
"Obituaries" (85) 683
MARON, HANNAH
Vulture, The (86) 464
MARONEY, KELLI
Night of the Comet (85) 527
Slayground [1983] (85) 533
MARQUAND, CHRISTIAN
Flight of the Phoenix, The [1966] (85) 549
MARRERO, RALPH
Day of the Dead (86) 441
MARS, KENNETH
Protocol (85) 383
MARSALIS, BRANFORD
Bring on the Night (86) 439
MARSH, GARY
"Obituaries" (82) 497
MARSH, JAMIE
Montenegro (82) 250
MARSH, JEAN
Return to Oz (86) 458
MARSH, MAE
Fort Apache [1948] (84) 530
MARSHALL, BRYAN
Long Good Friday, The [1980] (83) 220
MARSHALL, CHARLES "RED"
Specter of the Rose [1946] (83) 504
MARSHALL, CLIVE
Wild Duck, The [1983] (86) 466

MARSHALL, E. G.
Creepshow (83) 419
Superman II (82) 339
MARSHALL, GARRY K.
Lost in America (86) 219
MARSHALL, KEN
Krull (84) 487
MARSHALL, LARRY
Cotton Club, The (85) 150
MARSHALL, MONA
Here Come the Littles (86) 446
Starchaser (86) 460
MARSHALL, PENNY
Movers and Shakers (86) 453
MARSHALL, RAY
Where the Green Ants Dream [1984] (86) 465
MARSHALL, TULLY
Bridge of San Luis Rey, The [1929] (82)
408
MARSILLACH, BLANCA
Flesh and Blood (86) 443
MARTIN, BARNEY
Arthur (82) 71
MARTIN, DAMON
Pee-wee's Big Adventure (86) 265
MARTIN, DEAN
Bells Are Ringing [1960] (84) 517
Cannonball Run II (85) 514
MARTIN, DEAN PAUL
Heart Like a Wheel (84) 182
MARTIN, GEORGE
C.H.U.D. (85) 515
Falling in Love (85) 519
MARTIN, JARED
Lonely Lady, The (84) 488
MARTIN, MARIBEL
Holy Innocents, The (86) 447
MARTIN, MARION
"Obituaries" (86) 575
MARTIN, ROSEMARY
Secret Places [1984] (86) 459
MARTIN, STEVE
All of Me (85) 58
Dead Men Don't Wear Plaid (83) 134
Lonely Guy, The (85) 525
Man with Two Brains, The (84) 223
Movers and Shakers (86) 453
Pennies from Heaven (82) 276
MARTIN, STROTHER
Cowboy [1958] (82) 417
Slap Shot [1977] (82) 467
MARTINEZ, ALMA ROSE
Zoot Suit (82) 389
MARUZZO, JOE
Sudden Death (86) 461
MARVIN, LEE
Gorky Park (84) 162
Pete Kelly's Blues [1955] (83) 481
MARX, SOLLY
Silent Madness (85) 532
MASAMBA, LELO
Color Purple, The (86) 105
MASCARINO, PIERRINO
Missing in Action (85) 526

MASK, JOHNNY
  Tomorrow [1972]   (84) 589
MASON, JAMES
  Boys from Brazil, The [1978]   (86) 480
  Evil Under the Sun [1981]   (83) 421
  "Interview with, An"   (86) 27
  "Obituaries"   (85) 683
  Shooting Party, The [1984]   (86) 344
  Star Is Born, A [1954]   (84) 573
  Verdict, The   (83) 377
MASON, MARSHA
  Max Dugan Returns   (84) 228
  Only When I Laugh   (82) 268
MASSEY, ANNA
  Little Drummer Girl, The   (85) 525
MASSEY, DANIEL
  Victory   (82) 374
MASSEY, EDITH
  "Obituaries"   (85) 684
MASSEY, RAYMOND
  "Obituaries"   (84) 626
MASTERS, BEN
  Key Exchange   (86) 448
MASTERS, MARIE
  Slayground [1983]   (85) 533
MASTERSON, MARY STUART
  Heaven Help Us   (86) 445
MASTERSON, PETER
  Tomorrow [1972]   (84) 589
MASTERTON, KIM
  That Sinking Feeling [1979]   (85) 536
MASTRANTONIO, MARY ELIZABETH
  Scarface   (84) 361
MASTROIANNI, JOE
  City Girl, The   (85) 516
MASTROIANNI, MARCELLO
  City of Women   (82) 106
  Gabriela [1983]   (85) 213
  Henry IV [1983]   (86) 446
  Macaroni   (86) 451
  Nuit de Varennes, La [1982]   (84) 270
MASUR, RICHARD
  Mean Season, The   (86) 452
  Nightmares   (84) 490
  Risky Business   (84) 349
  Thing, The   (83) 343
  Under Fire   (84) 441
MATEGNA, JOE
  Compromising Positions   (86) 120
MATHESON, MURRAY
  "Obituaries"   (86) 576
  Twilight Zone—The Movie   (84) 435
MATHESON, TIM
  Fletch   (86) 169
  Impulse   (85) 523
  Little Sex, A   (83) 424
  To Be or Not to Be   (84) 426
  Up the Creek   (85) 537
MATHEWS, THOM
  Return of the Living Dead, The   (86) 314
MATIVO, KYALO
  Baby   (86) 437
MATSUI, NORIO
  Ran   (86) 304

MATSUMURA, TATSUO
  Foster Daddy, Tora! [1980]   (82) 163
MATSUYAMA, NATSUKO
  Flowing [1956]   (86) 444
MATSUZAKI, SHINJIRO
  Cruel Story of Youth [1960]   (85) 517
MATTES, EVA
  Céleste [1981]   (83) 104
MATTHAU, WALTER
  Buddy Buddy   (82) 93
  First Monday in October   (82) 151
  I Ought to Be in Pictures   (83) 423
  Movers and Shakers   (86) 453
  Survivors, The   (84) 495
MATTHEWS, JESSIE
  Hound of the Baskervilles, The
    [1978]   (82) 203
  "Obituaries"   (82) 498
MATUSZAK, JOHN
  Goonies, The   (86) 176
  Ice Pirates, The   (85) 523
MAUGHAN, MONICA
  Test of Love   (86) 462
MAUNDER, WAYNE
  Porky's   (83) 267
MAURI, FRANCISCO
  Erendira [1983]   (85) 181
MAURIELLO, GIOVANNI
  Another Time, Another Place [1983]   (85) 510
MAURIER-GENOUD, PHILIPPE
  Confidentially Yours [1983]   (85) 516
MAUSER, RICHARD
  My Science Project   (86) 453
MAXWELL, LISA
  Dark Crystal, The   (83) 130
MAXWELL, LOIS
  View to a Kill, A   (86) 402
MAY, BEVERLY
  Witness   (86) 421
MAY, CURT
  Blow Out   (82) 83
MAY, DORIS
  "Obituaries"   (85) 684
MAY, MATHILDA
  Lifeforce   (86) 450
MAYHEW, PETER
  Return of the Jedi   (84) 326
MAYNARD, BIFF
  Surf II   (85) 535
MAYNE, FERDINAND
  Conan the Destroyer   (85) 516
MAYO, VIRGINIA
  Colorado Territory [1949]   (86) 489
  Secret Life of Walter Mitty, The [1947]   (86) 540
MAYRON, MELANIE
  Missing   (83) 232
MAZER, ARNOLD
  Sudden Death   (86) 461
MAZURSKY, PAUL
  Into the Night   (86) 186
  Tempest   (83) 331
MEAGHER, KAREN
  Experience Preferred ... but Not Essential
    [1982]   (84) 141

MEARA, ANNE
In Our Hands (84) 486
MEDWIN, MICHAEL
Jigsaw Man, The [1983] (85) 524
MEEK, DONALD
Barbary Coast [1935] (84) 506
Peter Ibbetson [1935] (86) 527
MEEKER, GEORGE
History Is Made at Night [1937] (84) 542
MEIJER, ISCHA
Bastille [1984] (86) 437
MEILLON, JOHN
Wild Duck, The [1983] (86) 466
MELFI, LEONARD
Rent Control (85) 530
MELON, HENRI
Sugar Cane Alley [1983] (85) 461
MELTON, SID
Lady Sings the Blues [1972] (85) 565
MENDEL, STEPHEN
Fire and Ice (84) 153
MENDOZA, VICTOR MANUEL
Cowboy [1958] (82) 417
MENGATTI, JOHN
Hadley's Rebellion (85) 521
Meatballs Part II (85) 526
MENKEN, ROBIN
Body Rock (85) 513
MENSÁROS, LÁSZLÓ
Brady's Escape (85) 514
Colonel Redl [1984] (86) 100
MERCER, BERYL
Miracle Woman, The [1931] (83) 473
MERCER, JACK
"Obituaries" (85) 684
MERCHANT, VIVIEN
"Obituaries" (83) 544
MERCUR, WOLF
Light Ahead, The [1939] (83) 460
MERCURIO, MICOLE
Mask (86) 231
MEREDITH, BURGESS
Broken Rainbow (86) 439
Clash of the Titans (82) 111
Rocky III (83) 283
Santa Claus (86) 334
True Confessions (82) 368
MERIN, EDA REISS
Black Cauldron, The (86) 75
MERINO, FRANCISCO
Demons in the Garden [1982] (85) 517
MERLI, MAURIZIO
Priest of Love (82) 288
MERMAN, ETHEL
"Obituaries" (85) 684
MERRITT, THERESA
Best Little Whorehouse in Texas, The (83) 72
MESGUICH, DANIEL
Quartet (82) 296
METCALF, KEN
Caged Fury (85) 514
METCALF, LAURIE
Desperately Seeking Susan (86) 137

METCALF, MARK
Heavenly Kid, The (86) 445
Oasis, The (85) 528
METRANO, ART
Police Academy 2 (86) 276
Teachers (85) 535
METTE, NANCY
Key Exchange (86) 448
METZLER, JIM
Four Friends (82) 167
Tex (83) 335
METZMAN, IRVING
Man with One Red Shoe, The (86) 451
MEYERS, RUSTY
Silverado (86) 349
MEYRINK, MICHELLE
Joy of Sex (85) 524
One Magic Christmas (86) 455
Outsiders, The (84) 282
Real Genius (86) 309
Valley Girl (84) 447
MEZBAH, THAMILE
Beau Mariage, Le (83) 65
MEZENTSEVA, GALINA
Backstage at the Kirov (85) 511
MEZZOGIORNO, VITTORIO
Moon in the Gutter, The (84) 490
Three Brothers [1980] (83) 349
MIAKE, BONTARO
Late Chrysanthemums [1954] (86) 449
MIAO, CORA
Dim Sum (86) 141
MICHAEL, GERTRUDE
I'm No Angel [1933] (85) 561
MICHAEL, PIERRE
Dangerous Moves [1984] (86) 129
MICHALIK, STEVE
Pumping Iron II (86) 456
MICHAN, CHERIE
Wrong Is Right (83) 403
MIDDLETON, CHARLES
Miracle Woman, The [1931] (83) 473
MIDKIFF, DALE
Streetwalkin' (86) 461
MIDLER, BETTE
"Interview with Don Siegel, An" (83) 33
Jinxed (83) 33, 206
MIFUNE, TOSHIRO
Challenge, The (83) 109
Inchon (83) 424
MIGENES-JOHNSON, JULIA
Bizet's Carmen [1983] (85) 98
MIGHTY CLOUDS OF JOY
Gospel (85) 520
MIKHALKOV, NIKITA
Siberiade [1977] (83) 299
MIKSAK, JOE
Hard Traveling (86) 445
MILANO, ALYSSA
Commando (86) 111
MILES, JOANNA
Cross Creek (84) 116
MILES, SARAH
Ordeal by Innocence [1984] (86) 455
Venom [1981] (83) 430

MILES, VERA
Into the Night   (86) 186
Psycho II   (84) 307
MILFORD, PENELOPE
Golden Seal, The   (84) 485
MILLARD, HELENE
Divorcée, The [1930]   (82) 429
MILLER, BARRY
Chosen, The   (83) 116
Journey of Natty Gann, The   (86) 203
MILLER, BETTY
Pope of Greenwich Village, The   (85) 529
MILLER, COURT
Stephen King's Cat's Eye   (86) 460
MILLER, DEAN R.
Hadley's Rebellion   (85) 521
MILLER, DENNIS
Silver City [1984]   (86) 460
MILLER, DEREK
That Sinking Feeling [1979]   (85) 536
MILLER, DICK
After Hours   (86) 51
Explorers   (86) 442
Howling, The   (82) 207
MILLER, JASON
Monsignor   (83) 425
Toy Soldiers   (85) 536
MILLER, MARK
Savannah Smiles   (84) 493
MILLER, MARVIN
"Obituaries"   (86) 576
MILLER, MICHAEL
Hardbodies   (85) 521
MILLER, MIRTA
Bolero   (85) 513
MILLER, WARREN
Ski Country   (85) 533
MILLIGAN, SPIKE
Hound of the Baskervilles, The
   [1978]   (82) 203
MILLS, ALLEY
Going Berserk   (84) 485
MILLS, DONNA
Play Misty for Me [1971]   (86) 532
MILLS, JOHN
Gandhi   (83) 183
Sahara   (85) 531
MILLS, MORT
Torn Curtain [1966]   (85) 643
MILNER, MARTIN
Pete Kelly's Blues [1955]   (83) 481
MILO, CANDY
Bad Medicine   (86) 437
MIMIEUX, YVETTE
Time Machine, The [1960]   (84) 585
MINAMI, ROGER
Annie   (83) 56
MINER, GRANT
Suburbia   (85) 534
MINER, WORTHINGTON
They Might Be Giants [1971]   (83) 515
MINNELLI, LIZA
Arthur   (82) 71
New York, New York [1977]   (84) 567

MINTER, KELLY
Mask   (86) 231
MINTER, MARY MILES
"Obituaries"   (85) 685
MINTY, EMIL
Road Warrior, The [1981]   (83) 277
MIOU-MIOU
Entre nous [1983]   (85) 176
My Other Husband   (86) 453
MIRA, BRIGITTE
Berlin Alexanderplatz [1980]   (84) 57
MIRANDA, ISA
"Obituaries"   (83) 545
MIRREN, HELEN
Cal   (85) 124
Excalibur   (82) 144
Long Good Friday, The [1980]   (83) 220
2010   (85) 494
White Nights   (86) 416
MISAKI, CHIEKO
Foster Daddy, Tora! [1980]   (82) 163
MR. T.
D. C. Cab   (84) 481
Penitentiary II   (83) 427
Rocky III   (83) 283
MITA, MERATA
Utu [1983]   (85) 504
MITCHELL, BILLY J.
Rustler's Rhapsody   (86) 458
Top Secret   (85) 536
MITCHELL, CAMERON
Killpoint   (85) 524
My Favorite Year   (83) 241
MITCHELL, CHUCK
Porky's   (83) 267
MITCHELL, EDDY
Coup de torchon [1981]   (83) 124
My Other Husband   (86) 453
MITCHELL, JAMES
Colorado Territory [1949]   (86) 489
MITCHELL-SMITH, ILAN
Weird Science   (86) 465
MITCHUM, ROBERT
Maria's Lovers   (86) 451
That Championship Season   (83) 338
MITRA, MANOJ
Home and the World, The [1984]   (86) 447
MITROVICH, MARTA
Unfaithful, The [1947]   (86) 550
MITTLEMAN, BEN
Moving Violations   (86) 453
MIYAGUCHI, SEIJI
Flowing [1956]   (86) 444
MIYAZAKI, YOSHIKO
Ran   (86) 304
MIZELL, JASON
Krush Groove   (86) 449
MNICH, GENEVIÈVE
Sunday in the Country, A   (85) 466
MOAZEZI, NOAH
Hotel New Hampshire, The   (85) 243
Once upon a Time in America   (85) 345
MOCHIZUKI, YUKO
Late Chrysanthemums [1954]   (86) 449

MODINE, MATTHEW
  Birdy (85) 93
  Mrs. Soffel (85) 314
  Private School (84) 491
  Streamers (84) 391
  Vision Quest (86) 464
MOEREMANS, VIC
  Flaxfield, The [1983] (86) 443
MOFFAT, DONALD
  Right Stuff, The (84) 342
  Thing, The (83) 343
MOIR, RICHARD
  Heatwave (84) 485
MOLENKAMP, ONNO
  Question of Silence, A (85) 530
MOLINA, ALFRED
  Ladyhawke (86) 214
  Raiders of the Lost Ark (82) 308
MOLINA, ANGELA
  Demons in the Garden [1982] (85) 517
MÖLLER, FELIX
  Sheer Madness [1983] (86) 459
MONA, EUGENE
  Sugar Cane Alley [1983] (85) 461
MONAHAN, DAN
  Porky's (83) 267
  Porky's II (84) 491
  Up the Creek (85) 537
MONDY, PIERRE
  Gift, The (84) 484
MONES, PAUL
  Tuff Turf (86) 464
MONETTI, MIKE
  Once upon a Time in America (85) 345
MONG, WILLIAM V.
  Sign of the Cross, The [1932] (85) 607
MONICA, CORBETT
  Broadway Danny Rose (85) 112
MONK
  Another State of Mind (85) 510
MONK, ALAN
  Traviata, La (83) 366
MONOSON, LAWRENCE
  Friday the 13th—The Final Chapter (85) 520
  Last American Virgin, The (83) 424
  Mask (86) 231
MONTAGNANI, RENZO
  Joke of Destiny, A [1983] (85) 259
MONTALBAN, RICARDO
  Cannonball Run II (85) 514
  Star Trek II—The Wrath of Khan (83) 321
MONTEFIORI, LUIGI
  King David (86) 449
MONTESANO, ENRICO
  Softly Softly [1984] (86) 460
MONTGOMERY, BELINDA
  Silent Madness (85) 532
MONTGOMERY, JULIE
  Revenge of the Nerds (85) 530
MONTGOMERY, ROBERT
  Divorcée, The [1930] (82) 429
  "Obituaries" (82) 499

MONTOYA, ALEX
  Flight of the Phoenix, The [1966] (85) 549
MOODY, JIM
  Bad Boys (84) 479
  Berry Gordy's The Last Dragon (86) 438
MOODY, RON
  Wrong Is Right (83) 403
MOONEY, WILLIAM
  Flash of Green, A (86) 443
MOORE, ALVY
  Here Come the Littles (86) 446
MOORE, BOBBY
  Victory (82) 374
MOORE, CONSTANCE
  Take a Letter, Darling [1942] (85) 632
MOORE, DEMI
  No Small Affair (85) 527
  Parasite (83) 426
  St. Elmo's Fire (86) 330
MOORE, DICKIE
  Peter Ibbetson [1935] (86) 527
MOORE, DUDLEY
  Arthur (82) 71
  Best Defense (85) 512
  Hound of the Baskervilles, The [1978] (82) 203
  Lovesick (84) 488
  Micki & Maude (85) 308
  Romantic Comedy (84) 492
  Santa Claus (86) 334
  Six Weeks (83) 428
  Unfaithfully Yours (85) 537
MOORE, KENNY
  Personal Best (83) 254
MOORE, MARY TYLER
  Six Weeks (83) 428
MOORE, ROBERT
  "Obituaries" (85) 687
MOORE, ROGER
  For Your Eyes Only (82) 155
  Octopussy (84) 276
  Sea Wolves, The [1981] (83) 427
  View to a Kill, A (86) 402
MOORE, SABRINA
  World According to Garp, The (83) 397
MOOREHEAD, AGNES
  Journey into Fear [1943] (86) 511
  Lost Moment, The [1947] (83) 465
MORALES, ESAI
  Bad Boys (84) 479
  Rainy Day Friends (86) 457
MORALES, MARK
  Krush Groove (86) 449
MORALES, SANTOS
  Cannery Row (83) 95
MORAN, JIM
  Specter of the Rose [1946] (83) 504
MORANIS, RICK
  Ghostbusters (85) 219
  Strange Brew (84) 494
  Streets of Fire (85) 534
  Wild Life, The (85) 538
MORANTE, LAURA
  Tragedy of a Ridiculous Man [1981] (83) 361

MORE, CAMILLA
  Friday the 13th—The Final Chapter   (85) 520
MORE, CARY
  Friday the 13th—The Final Chapter   (85) 520
MORE, KENNETH
  "Obituaries"   (83) 545
MOREAU, JEANNE
  Falstaff [1967]   (83) 443
  Heat of Desire [1981]   (85) 522
  Querelle [1982]   (84) 313
  Trout, The [1982]   (84) 496
MORECAMBE, ERIC
  "Obituaries"   (85) 687
MORENO, ANTONIO
  Creature from the Black Lagoon, The
  [1954]   (82) 422
MORENO, CLAUDIO
  Emerald Forest, The   (86) 156
MORENO, RITA
  Four Seasons, The   (82) 171
MORFOGEN, GEORGE
  They All Laughed   (82) 350
MORGAN, CINDY
  TRON   (83) 371
MORGAN, DENNIS
  Hard Way, The [1942]   (85) 555
MORGAN, EMILY
  French Lieutenant's Woman, The   (82) 174
MORGAN, JAYE P.
  Night Patrol   (86) 454
MORGAN, MICHAEL
  Homework   (83) 422
MORGAN, RICHARD
  Phar Lap   (85) 528
MORIARTY, MICHAEL
  Pale Rider   (86) 261
  Stuff, The   (86) 461
MORINEAU, BARBARA
  When Nature Calls   (86) 465
MORITA, NORIYUKI "PAT"
  Karate Kid, The   (85) 264
  Night Patrol   (86) 454
  Slapstick   (85) 533
MORLEY, ROBERT
  Great Muppet Caper, The   (82) 187
MORRIS, ANITA
  Maria's Lovers   (86) 451
MORRIS, AUBREY
  Lifeforce   (86) 450
  Oxford Blues   (85) 528
MORRIS, CHESTER
  Divorcée, The [1930]   (82) 429
MORRIS, GARRET
  Stuff, The   (86) 461
MORRIS, HAVILAND
  Sixteen Candles   (85) 532
MORRIS, HOWARD
  Splash   (85) 434
MORRIS, JUDY
  Phar Lap   (85) 528
  Razorback [1984]   (86) 457
MORRISON, MURDO
  I Know Where I'm Going [1945]   (83) 456

MORROW, VIC
  1990   (84) 491
  "Obituaries"   (83) 546
  Twilight Zone—The Movie   (84) 435
MORSE, HELEN
  Agatha [1979]   (83) 435
  Caddie [1976]   (83) 439
MORSHOWER, GLENN
  Philadelphia Experiment, The   (85) 529
MORTENSEN, VIGGO
  Witness   (86) 421
MORTH, NOELLE
  Starchaser   (86) 460
MORTON, JOE
  Brother from Another Planet, The   (85)
  118
  Trouble in Mind   (86) 388
MORTON, MICKEY
  Fire and Ice   (84) 153
  Starchaser   (86) 460
MOSCHIN, GASTONE
  Joke of Destiny, A [1983]   (85) 259
MOSCHITTA, JOHN, JR.
  Starchaser   (86) 460
MOSLEY, LUCKY
  Alamo Bay   (86) 436
MOSQUINI, MARIE
  "Obituaries"   (84) 628
MOSS, JACK
  Journey into Fear [1943]   (86) 511
MOSTEL, JOSH
  Almost You   (86) 436
  Compromising Positions   (86) 120
  Sophie's Choice   (83) 311
  Windy City   (85) 538
MOSTEL, ZERO
  Front, The [1976]   (86) 502
MOTTA, BESS
  Terminator, The   (85) 478
MOTTA, ZEZE
  Xica [1976]   (83) 407
MOURA, GILBERTO
  Pixote [1980]   (82) 280
MOWBRAY, ALAN
  Becky Sharp [1935]   (82) 403
MOY, WOOD
  Chan Is Missing   (83) 113
MUELLER-STAHL, ARMIN
  Colonel Redl [1984]   (86) 100
  Lola [1981]   (83) 215
  Love in Germany, A [1983]   (85) 283
MULGREW, KATE
  Remo Williams   (86) 457
  Stranger Is Watching, A   (83) 429
MULHALL, JACK
  Dulcy [1923]   (82) 432
MULHARE, EDWARD
  Megaforce   (83) 425
MULL, MARTIN
  Clue   (86) 440
MULLER, PETRA
  Dernier Combat, Le [1983]   (85) 517
MULLIGAN, BARRET
  Slayground [1983]   (85) 533

MULLIGAN, GERRY
Bells Are Ringing [1960]   (84) 517
MULLIGAN, RICHARD
Heavenly Kid, The   (86) 445
Meatballs Part II   (85) 526
Micki & Maude   (85) 308
S.O.B.   (82) 328
Teachers   (85) 535
Trail of the Pink Panther   (83) 430
MUMY, BILL
Hard to Hold   (85) 521
MUNATO, TONY
Stephen King's Cat's Eye   (86) 460
MUNCH, RICHARD
Holcroft Covenant, The   (86) 446
Target   (86) 462
MURCH, BOB
Flash of Green, A   (86) 443
MURDOCK, GEORGE
Shoot the Moon   (83) 295
MURET, PAULE
Every Man for Himself [1979]   (82) 139
MURILLO, GERRY
Testament   (84) 420
MURNEY, CHRISTOPHER
Berry Gordy's The Last Dragon   (86) 438
Grace Quigley   (86) 444
MURO, MARTA FERNANDEZ
Volver a empezar   (83) 393
MURPHY, EDDIE
Best Defense   (85) 512
Beverly Hills Cop   (85) 88
48 HRS.   (83) 173
Trading Places   (84) 430
MURPHY, MICHAEL
Brewster McCloud [1970]   (86) 484
Cloak and Dagger   (85) 516
Front, The [1976]   (86) 502
Year of Living Dangerously, The
[1982]   (84) 462
MURPHY, TIMOTHY PATRICK
Sam's Son   (85) 531
MURRAY, BILL
Ghostbusters   (85) 219
Razor's Edge, The   (85) 402
Stripes   (82) 336
Tootsie   (83) 353
MURRAY, CHIC
Gregory's Girl [1981]   (83) 193
MURRAY, JOHN
Moving Violations   (86) 453
MURRAY, JULIA
Four Friends   (82) 167
MURRAY, STEPHEN
"Obituaries"   (84) 628
MURREL, TOM
1918   (86) 454
MUSANTE, TONY
Pope of Greenwich Village, The   (85) 529
MUSIC, LORENZO
Twice upon a Time   (84) 496
MUTI, ORNELLA
Swann in Love   (85) 471
Tales of Ordinary Madness   (84) 495

MYERS, KIM
Nightmare on Elm Street, Part 2, A   (86) 454
MYRTETUS, J. DINAN
Power, The   (85) 529

NABORS, JIM
Best Little Whorehouse in Texas, The   (83)
72
Cannonball Run II   (85) 514
Stroker Ace   (84) 494
NADAREVIC, MUSTAFA
When Father Was Away on Business [1984]   (86)
411
NAGAHARA, YUKI
Mishima   (86) 236
NAGASHIMA, TOSHIYUKI
Mishima   (86) 236
NAGAZUMI, YASUKO
Wombling Free [1979]   (85) 538
NAGEL, CONRAD
Divorcée, The [1930]   (82) 429
NAIL, JIMMY
Morons from Outer Space   (86) 452
NAISH, J. CARROLL
Hatchet Man, The [1932]   (83) 447
NAITO, TAKETOSHI
MacArthur's Children   (86) 451
NAKADAI, TATSUYA
Ran   (86) 304
NAKAHARA, KELLYE
Clue   (86) 440
NAKAKITA, CHIEKO
Flowing [1956]   (86) 444
NAKAMURA, ATSUO
Challenge, The   (83) 109
NAKAYA, NOBORU
Flowing [1956]   (86) 444
NAMATH, JOE
Chattanooga Choo Choo   (85) 515
NANAYAKKARU, D. R.
Indiana Jones and the Temple of
Doom   (85) 253
NANCE, JACK
Hammett   (84) 174
NAPIER, CHARLES
Rambo: First Blood Part II   (86) 299
NAPIER, DIANA
"Obituaries"   (83) 546
NAPIER, MARSHALL
Came a Hot Friday   (86) 439
Wild Horses [1983]   (85) 538
NARELLE, BRIAN
Dark Star [1975]   (86) 494
NASH, CHRIS
Mischief   (86) 452
NASH, CLARENCE
"Obituaries"   (86) 576
NATSUME, MASAKO
Antarctica   (85) 511
MacArthur's Children   (86) 451
NAUGHTON, DAVID
American Werewolf in London, An   (82) 66
Hotdog . . . The Movie   (85) 522
Not for Publication   (85) 527

NAUGHTON, JAMES
  Stephen King's Cat's Eye   (86) 460
  Stranger Is Watching, A   (83) 429
NAYAR, HARSH
  Gandhi   (83) 183
NAZAROVA, NATASHA
  Waiting for Gavrilov [1982]   (84) 497
NEAGLE, ANNA
  "Interview with, An"   (84) 24
  Nell Gwyn [1934]   (84) 557
NEAL, PATRICIA
  Ghost Story   (82) 183
NEAL, TOM
  Detour [1946]   (86) 498
NEESON, LIAM
  Bounty, The   (85) 513
NEFF, HILDEGARDE
  Snows of Kilimanjaro, The [1952]   (83) 498
NEGRON, TAYLOR
  Bad Medicine   (86) 437
NEIGHBORS, WILLIAM WESLEY, JR.
  Bear, The   (85) 511
NEILL, SAM
  Enigma [1982]   (84) 483
  Plenty   (86) 271
NELKIN, STACEY
  Halloween III   (83) 422
NELL, NATHALIE
  Echoes   (84) 483
NELLIGAN, KATE
  Eleni   (86) 151
  Eye of the Needle   (82) 148
  Without a Trace   (84) 498
NELSON, BARRY
  Guy Named Joe, A [1943]   (82) 435
NELSON, BERNIE
  Killpoint   (85) 524
NELSON, CRAIG T.
  All the Right Moves   (84) 41
  Killing Fields, The   (85) 270
  Man, Woman and Child   (84) 489
  Osterman Weekend, The   (84) 491
  Poltergeist   (83) 263
  Silkwood   (84) 367
NELSON, DAVID LLOYD
  Sam's Son   (85) 531
NELSON, JERRY
  Great Muppet Caper, The   (82) 187
  Muppets Take Manhattan, The   (85) 526
NELSON, JUDD
  Breakfast Club, The   (86) 85
  Fandango   (86) 442
  Making the Grade   (85) 526
  St. Elmo's Fire   (86) 330
NELSON, NOVELLA
  Cotton Club, The   (85) 150
NELSON, PETER
  Purple Haze   (84) 492
NELSON, RANDALL EDWIN
  Jewel of the Nile, The   (86) 448
NELSON, RICK
  "Obituaries"   (86) 576
NELSON, RUTH
  Arch of Triumph [1948]   (84) 501

NELSON, TRACY
  Maria's Lovers   (86) 451
NELSON, WILLIE
  Barbarosa   (83) 60
  Songwriter   (85) 533
  Thief   (82) 356
NERO, FRANCO
  Enter the Ninja   (83) 420
  Querelle [1982]   (84) 313
NERO, TONI
  Silent Night, Deadly Night   (85) 532
NESBITT, CATHLEEN
  "Obituaries"   (83) 546
NESBITT, DERREN
  Victim [1961]   (85) 647
NESS, MIKE
  Another State of Mind   (85) 510
NETTLETON, LOIS
  Best Little Whorehouse in Texas, The   (83)
  72
NEUDORFER, SONJA
  Lola [1981]   (83) 215
NEUMAN, JOAN
  Stardust Memories [1980]   (85) 626
NEVIN, ROBYN
  Careful He Might Hear You [1983]   (85) 130
NEVINS, CLAUDETTE
  Tuff Turf   (85) 464
NEW, NANCY
  Bostonians, The   (85) 105
NEWBORN, PHINEAS, III
  Breakin'   (85) 514
NEWELL, PATRICK
  Young Sherlock Holmes   (86) 431
NEWMAN, LARAINE
  Perfect   (86) 456
  Sesame Street Presents: Follow That
  Bird   (86) 459
NEWMAN, PAUL
  Absence of Malice   (82) 57
  Fort Apache, the Bronx   (82) 159
  Harry and Son   (85) 521
  Hombre [1967]   (84) 547
  Slap Shot [1977]   (82) 467
  Torn Curtain [1966]   (85) 643
  Verdict, The   (83) 377
NEWMAN, STEPHEN D.
  Sophie's Choice   (83) 311
NEWMAR, JULIE
  Streetwalkin'   (86) 461
NEWTH, JONATHAN
  Champions   (85) 515
NEWTON, MARGIT EVELYN
  Hercules II   (86) 446
  Last Hunter, The   (85) 525
NEWTON-JOHN, OLIVIA
  Two of a Kind   (84) 496
NEZU, JINPACHI
  Ran   (86) 304
NGOR, HAING S.
  Killing Fields, The   (85) 270
NICASTRO, MICHELLE
  Body Rock   (85) 513
NICHOLAS-HILL, DENISE
  Marvin & Tige   (84) 489

NICHOLLS, ALLAN
Home Free All (85) 522
NICHOLLS, ANTHONY
Victim [1961] (85) 647
NICHOLLS, PHOEBE
Ordeal by Innocence [1984] (86) 455
NICHOLS, MICHELLE
Star Trek II—The Wrath of Khan (83) 321
Star Trek III—The Search for Spock (85) 439
NICHOLSON, JACK
Border, The (83) 418
Postman Always Rings Twice, The (82) 284
Prizzi's Honor (86) 285
Reds (82) 312
Terms of Endearment (84) 414
NICKSON, JULIA
Rambo: First Blood Part II (86) 299
NICOLODI, DARIA
Macaroni (86) 451
NIELSEN, BRIGITTE
Red Sonja (86) 457
Rocky IV (86) 319
NIELSEN, SCOTT
Wrong Is Right (83) 403
NIELSEN, THOMAS
Zappa (85) 539
NIGRA, CHRISTINA
Cloak and Dagger (85) 516
NIJHOFF, LOUDI
Bastille [1984] (86) 437
NIKLAS, JAN
Colonel Redl [1984] (86) 100
NILSSON, KJELL
Road Warrior, The [1981] (83) 277
NIMOY, LEONARD
Star Trek II—The Wrath of Khan (83) 321
Star Trek III—The Search for Spock (85) 439
NISHIO, JOHN
Dim Sum (86) 141
NISSEN, JULIET
Jigsaw Man, The [1983] (85) 524
NIVEN, DAVID
Barbary Coast [1935] (84) 506
Curse of the Pink Panther (84) 481
"Obituaries" (84) 628
Sea Wolves, The [1981] (83) 427
Trail of the Pink Panther (83) 430
NIXON, MARIAN (MARION)
"Obituaries" (84) 629
NOEL, CHRIS
Cease Fire (86) 440
NOËL, MAGALI
Death of Mario Ricci, The [1983] (86) 133
NOËL, NANI
Bal, Le [1983] (85) 80
NOIRET, PHILIPPE
Coup de torchon [1981] (83) 124
Étoile du nord, L' (84) 484
Heads or Tails [1980] (84) 485
My New Partner [1984] (86) 246
Three Brothers [1980] (83) 349

NOLAN, JEANETTE
Cloak and Dagger (85) 516
True Confessions (82) 368
NOLAN, KIRRILI
Caddie [1976] (83) 439
NOLAN, LLOYD
"Obituaries" (86) 577
NOLAN, TOM
School Spirit (86) 458
NOLTE, NICK
Cannery Row (83) 95
48 HRS. (83) 173
Grace Quigley (86) 444
Teachers (85) 535
Under Fire (84) 441
NOMURA, TAKESHI
Ran (86) 304
NOONAN, TOM
Best Defense (85) 512
Man with One Red Shoe, The (86) 451
Star Is Born, A [1954] (84) 573
Wolfen (82) 382
NORMAN, AL
King of Jazz [1930] (86) 515
NORMAN, ZACK
Romancing the Stone (85) 421
NORMINGTON, JOHN
Private Function, A [1984] (86) 280
NORRINGTON, STEVE
Return to Oz (86) 458
NORRIS, CHUCK
Code of Silence (86) 440
Forced Vengeance (83) 421
Invasion U.S.A. (86) 447
Lone Wolf McQuade (84) 488
Missing in Action (85) 526
Missing in Action 2 (86) 452
Silent Rage (83) 428
NORRIS, KEN
Too Scared to Scream (86) 463
NORTON, ALEX
Comfort and Joy (85) 146
Sense of Freedom, A (86) 459
NORTON, RANDY
Fire and Ice (84) 153
NORTON, RICHARD
Gymkata (86) 445
NOS, JAIME
Skyline (85) 533
NOTARIO, STEVE "SUGARFOOT"
Breakin' 2 (85) 514
NOURI, MICHAEL
Flashdance (84) 158
NOVAK, BLAINE
Stranger's Kiss (85) 534
They All Laughed (82) 350
Up the Creek (85) 537
NOVELLO, JAY
"Obituaries" (83) 547
NOVIKOFF, RASHEL
Next Stop, Greenwich Village [1976] (85) 592
NOWICKI, TOM
Harry and Son (85) 521
NUNEZ, MIGUEL
Return of the Living Dead, The (86) 314

NUNN, ALICE
Pee-wee's Big Adventure   (86) 265
NUREYEV, RUDOLF
Exposed   (84) 484
NYE, CARRIE
Too Scared to Scream   (86) 463
NYE, LOUIS
Cannonball Run II   (85) 514
NYPE, RUSSELL
Stuff, The   (86) 461

OAKIE, JACK
It Happened Tomorrow [1944]   (84) 552
OAKLAND, SIMON
"Obituaries"   (84) 630
OATES, WARREN
Blue Thunder   (84) 84
Border, The   (83) 418
"Obituaries"   (83) 547
Stripes   (82) 336
Tough Enough   (84) 495
OBER, PHILIP
"Obituaries"   (83) 547
OBREGON, ANA
Bolero   (85) 513
Treasure of the Four Crowns   (84) 495
O'BANNON, DAN
Dark Star [1975]   (86) 494
O'BRIEN, DEREK
Another State of Mind   (85) 510
O'BRIEN, EDMOND
Barefoot Contessa, The [1954]   (82) 399
"Obituaries"   (86) 577
Pete Kelly's Blues [1955]   (83) 481
O'BRIEN, EILEEN
Private Function, A [1984]   (86) 280
O'BRIEN, GEORGE
Fort Apache [1948]   (84) 530
"Obituaries"   (86) 578
O'BRIEN, LEO
Berry Gordy's The Last Dragon   (86) 438
Rappin'   (86) 457
O'BRIEN, MARIA
Protocol   (85) 383
O'BRIEN, PAT
"Obituaries"   (84) 630
Ragtime   (82) 304
O'BRIEN, TIMOTHY
Suburbia   (85) 534
O'BRIEN, VALERIE
Ladyhawke   (86) 214
O'BYRNE, PADDY
Gods Must Be Crazy, The [1980]   (85) 224
OCCHIPINTI, ANDREA
Bolero   (85) 513
O'CONNELL, ARTHUR
Solid Gold Cadillac, The [1956]   (85) 615
O'CONNELL, TAFFY
Caged Fury   (85) 514
O'CONNOR, DONALD
Ragtime   (82) 304
O'CONNOR, GLYNNIS
Night Crossing   (83) 426

O'DAY, NELL
King of Jazz [1930]   (86) 515
ODENT, CHRISTOPHE
First Name, Carmen [1983]   (85) 186
ODERSTROM, ELMER
Stephen King's Children of the Corn   (85) 534
O'DONOVAN, ROSS
Starstruck   (83) 428
OGATA, KEN
Mishima   (86) 236
OGIER, PASCALE
Full Moon in Paris   (85) 208
"Obituaries"   (85) 687
OGINOME, KEIKO
Antarctica   (85) 511
O'GRADY, TIMOTHY E.
James Joyce's Women   (86) 193
O'HALLORAN, JACK
Superman II   (82) 339
OHANA, CLAUDIA
Erendira [1983]   (85) 181
O'HARA, CATHERINE
After Hours   (86) 51
O'HARA, MAUREEN
Long Gray Line, The [1955]   (82) 447
O'HERLIHY, DAN
Halloween III   (83) 422
Last Starfighter, The   (85) 277
O'HERLIHY, GAVAN
Never Say Never Again   (84) 252
OHTA, BENNETT
Missing in Action 2   (86) 452
OJEDA, MANUEL
Romancing the Stone   (85) 421
OKADA, MARIKO
Flowing [1956]   (86) 444
O'KEEFE, MICHAEL
Finders Keepers   (85) 519
Nate and Hayes   (84) 236
Neil Simon's The Slugger's Wife   (86) 454
Split Image   (83) 317
OKKING, JENS
Zappa   (85) 539
OKURA, JOHNNY
Merry Christmas, Mr. Lawrence   (84) 231
OLBRYCHSKI, DANIEL
Dangerous Moves [1984]   (86) 129
Love in Germany, A [1983]   (85) 283
Trout, The [1982]   (84) 496
OLFSON, KEN
Breakin' 2   (85) 514
OLIN, KEN
Ghost Story   (82) 183
OLIN, LENA
After the Rehearsal   (85) 52
OLITA, JOSEPH
Amin—The Rise and Fall   (84) 479
OLIVER, BARRET
D.A.R.Y.L.   (86) 441
Neverending Story, The   (85) 527
OLIVER, ROCHELL
Next Stop, Greenwich Village [1976]   (85) 592
1918   (86) 454

OLIVIER, LAURENCE
  Bounty, The   (85) 513
  Boys from Brazil, The [1978]   (86) 480
  Clash of the Titans   (82) 111
  Inchon   (83) 424
  Jigsaw Man, The [1983]   (85) 524
  Wagner   (84) 497
  Wild Geese II   (86) 466
OLKEWICZ, WALTER
  Making the Grade   (85) 526
OLMI, BOY
  Deathstalker   (85) 517
OLMOS, EDWARD JAMES
  Blade Runner   (83) 76
  Wolfen   (82) 382
  Zoot Suit   (82) 389
OLMOS, MICO
  Testament   (84) 420
OLSEN, DANA
  Making the Grade   (85) 526
OLSON, JAMES
  Amityville II   (83) 417
  Commando   (86) 111
  Ragtime   (82) 304
OMAGGIO, MARIA ROSARIA
  Hercules II   (86) 446
O'MALLEY, J. PAT
  "Obituaries"   (86) 578
OMEN, JUDD
  Pee-wee's Big Adventure   (86) 265
OMENS, ESTELLE
  Unfaithfully Yours   (85) 537
OMORI, YOSHIYUKI
  MacArthur's Children   (86) 451
OMS, ALBA
  Whose Life Is It Anyway?   (82) 378
O'NEAL, GRIFFIN
  Escape Artist, The   (83) 421
  Hadley's Rebellion   (85) 521
O'NEAL, PETER
  Dr. Butcher, M.D. [1980]   (83) 420
O'NEAL, RON
  Red Dawn   (85) 530
O'NEAL, RYAN
  Fever Pitch   (86) 443
  Irreconcilable Differences   (85) 523
  Partners   (83) 427
O'NEAL, TATUM
  Certain Fury   (86) 440
O'NEILL, CHRIS
  James Joyce's Women   (86) 193
O'NEILL, DICK
  Turk 182   (86) 464
ONTIVEROS, LUPE
  Goonies, The   (86) 176
  Norte, El   (84) 265
ONTKEAN, MICHAEL
  Just the Way You Are   (85) 524
  Making Love   (83) 425
  Slap Shot [1977]   (82) 467
OPANIA, MARIAN
  Man of Iron   (82) 230
OPATOSHU, DAVID
  Forced Vengeance   (83) 422

  Light Ahead, The [1939]   (83) 460
  Torn Curtain [1966]   (85) 644
OPHIR, SHAI K.
  King Solomon's Mines   (86) 449
OPPENHEIMER, ALAN
  Secret of the Sword, The   (86) 459
O'QUINN, TERRY
  Mischief   (86) 452
  Mrs. Soffel   (85) 314
  Places in the Heart   (85) 371
  Stephen King's Silver Bullet   (86) 460
ORANGE, DAVID
  When Nature Calls   (86) 465
ORBACH, JERRY
  Brewster's Millions   (86) 438
  Prince of the City   (82) 292
O'REILL, EILEEN
  Fire and Ice   (84) 153
O'REILLY, CYRIL
  Porky's   (83) 267
  Purple Hearts   (85) 529
ORHONSOY, MERAL
  Yol   (83) 411
ORIMOTO, JUNKICHI
  Mishima   (86) 236
O'ROURKE, HEATHER
  Poltergeist   (83) 263
ORR, OWEN E.
  Bear, The   (85) 511
ORTEGA, ERNIE
  Missing in Action   (85) 526
OSCARSSON, PER
  Montenegro   (82) 250
O'SHEA, MILO
  Purple Rose of Cairo, The   (86) 290
  Verdict, The   (83) 377
OSSOM, ROBERTS
  Flashpoint   (85) 519
OSTERCAMP, JIM
  Country   (85) 156
OSTERWALD, BIBI
  World of Henry Orient, The [1964]   (84) 600
OSTRANDER, WILLIAM
  Christine   (84) 106
  Fire and Ice   (84) 153
  Mike's Murder   (85) 526
  Stryker   (84) 494
O'SULLIVAN, MAUREEN
  Too Scared to Scream   (86) 463
OTAKI, SHUJI
  MacArthur's Children   (86) 451
OTANI, NAOKO
  Mishima   (86) 236
OTHELO, GRANDE
  Fitzcarraldo   (83) 167
O'TOOLE, ANNETTE
  Cat People   (83) 100
  48 HRS.   (83) 173
  Superman III   (84) 399
O'TOOLE, PETER
  Creator   (86) 441
  My Favorite Year   (83) 241
  Supergirl   (85) 535
OWEN, NANCY LEA
  River Rat, The   (85) 531

OWEN, SID
Revolution (86) 458
OWEN, SIONTUDOR
Experience Preferred ... but Not Essential
[1982] (84) 141
OWENS, TUDOR
My Cousin Rachel [1952] (82) 458
OZ, FRANK
American Werewolf in London, An (82) 66
Great Muppet Caper, The (82) 187
Muppets Take Manhattan, The (85) 526
Return of the Jedi (84) 326
Sesame Street Presents: Follow That Bird (86)
459

PACINO, AL
Author
Revolution (86) 458
Scarface (84) 361
PACULA, JOANNA
Gorky Park (84) 162
PADAMSEE, ALYQUE
Gandhi (83) 183
PAGE, GALE
"Obituaries" (84) 631
They Drive by Night [1940] (83) 508
PAGE, GERALDINE
Bride, The (86) 438
Flanagan (86) 443
Hondo [1953] (83) 452
Honky Tonk Freeway (82) 199
I'm Dancing as Fast as I Can (83) 423
Pope of Greenwich Village, The (85) 529
Trip to Bountiful, The (86) 383
White Nights (86) 416
PAGE, LAWANDA
Good Bye Cruel World (85) 520
PAGE, TONY
Prince of the City (82) 292
PAGEN, ANTONE
Stripes (82) 336
PAGNY, FLORENT
Balance, La [1982] (84) 52
PAHICH, ANDREIJAH
Dark Star [1975] (86) 494
PAIVA, NESTOR
Creature from the Black Lagoon, The
[1954] (82) 422
PALCY, JOEL
Sugar Cane Alley [1983] (85) 461
PALIN, MICHAEL
Brazil (86) 80
Missionary, The (83) 233
Monty Python's The Meaning of Life (84) 489
Private Function, A [1984] (86) 280
Time Bandits [1980] (82) 364
PALMER, BETSY
Long Gray Line, The [1955] (82) 447
PALMER, GRETCHEN F.
Fast Forward (86) 442
PALMER, JOHN
Mean Season, The (86) 452
PALMER, LILLI
Boys from Brazil, The [1978] (86) 480
Holcroft Covenant, The (86) 446

PALMSTJERNA-WEISWS, NADJA
After the Rehearsal (85) 52
PALOMINO, CARLOS
Stranger's Kiss (85) 534
PANALLE, JUAN
Specter of the Rose [1946] (83) 504
PANKOW, JOHN
To Live and Die in L.A. (86) 379
PANTOLIANO, JOE
Goonies, The (86) 176
Mean Season, The (86) 452
Risky Business (84) 349
PAOLONI, PAOLO
And the Ship Sails On [1983] (85) 69
PAPAS, IRENE
Erendira [1983] (85) 181
Into the Night (86) 186
PAPETTI, NICOLINA
Ladyhawke (86) 214
PARE, MICHAEL
Eddie and the Cruisers (84) 483
Philadelphia Experiment, The (85) 529
Streets of Fire (85) 534
PARENTE, NILDO
Kiss of the Spider Woman (86) 209
PARFITT, JUDY
Champions (85) 515
PARIS, SIMONE
Bob le Flambeur [1955] (84) 526
PARKER, CHRIS
Twice in a Lifetime (86) 397
PARKER, JOHNNY
Dulcy [1923] (82) 432
PARKER, MONICA
Improper Channels (82) 218
PARKER, NORMAN
Prince of the City (82) 292
Turk 182 (86) 464
PARKER, SARAH JESSICA
Firstborn (85) 519
Footloose (85) 198
PARKER, SUNSHINE
Cannery Row (83) 95
PARKS, CATHERINE
Friday the 13th—Part III (83) 422
PARKS, LARRY
Freud [1962] (84) 535
PARRIS, PATRICIA
Here Come the Littles (86) 446
PARRY, HARVEY
"Obituaries" (86) 578
PARSONS, NANCY
Porky's (83) 267
PARTON, DOLLY
Best Little Whorehouse in Texas, The (83)
72
Rhinestone (85) 531
PASO, ENCARNA
Demons in the Garden [1982] (85) 517
Volver a empezar (83) 393
PASOLINI, PIER PAOLO
Oedipus Rex [1967] (85) 528
PASSANANTE, JEAN
Return of the Secaucus 7 [1980] (83) 484

PATAKI, MICHAEL
Rocky IV   (86) 319
Sweet Sixteen   (85) 535
PATE, MICHAEL
Hondo [1953]   (83) 452
Wild Duck, The [1983]   (86) 466
PATENGHI, DAVID
Invitation to the Dance [1956]   (86) 507
PATERSON, BILL
Comfort and Joy   (85) 146
Killing Fields, The   (85) 270
Private Function, A [1984]   (86) 280
PATEY, CHRISTIAN
Argent, L' [1983]   (85) 74
PATHAK, RATNA
Heat and Dust [1982]   (84) 187
PATINKIN, MANDY
Daniel   (84) 481
Maxie   (86) 452
Ragtime   (82) 304
Yentl   (84) 468
PATRICK, LAUREL
Running Hot   (85) 531
PATRICK, LEE
"Obituaries"   (83) 548
PATRICK, NIGEL
"Obituaries"   (82) 500
Sound Barrier, The [1952]   (85) 621
PATTERSON, HOWARD JAY
Jewel of the Nile, The   (86) 448
PATTERSON, JAY
Heaven Help Us   (86) 445
PATTERSON, NEVA
Solid Gold Cadillac, The [1956]   (85) 615
PATTERSON, SARAH
Company of Wolves, The [1984]   (86) 115
PATTERSON, WILLIAM
Hard Traveling   (86) 445
PATTON, MARK
Come Back to the 5 & Dime Jimmy Dean,
  Jimmy Dean   (83) 120
Nightmare on Elm Street, Part 2, A   (86) 454
PATTON, WILL
After Hours   (86) 51
PAUL, ALEXANDRA
American Flyers   (86) 436
Christine   (84) 106
Just the Way You Are   (85) 524
PAUL, DON MICHAEL
Lovelines   (85) 525
PAUL, NANCY
Lifeforce   (86) 450
Sheena   (85) 532
PAUL, RICHARD
Not for Publication   (85) 527
PAULIN, SCOTT
Right Stuff, The   (84) 342
Soldier's Story, A   (85) 427
Teen Wolf   (86) 462
PAULL, MORGAN
Surf II   (85) 535
PAULSEN, PAT
Night Patrol   (86) 454
PAULY, REBECCA
State of Things, The   (84) 379

PAVAROTTI, LUCIANO
Yes, Giorgio   (83) 431
PÁVEZ, TERELE
Holy Innocents, The   (86) 447
PAXTON, BILL
Streets of Fire   (85) 534
Weird Science   (86) 465
PAYNE, BRUCE
Oxford Blues   (85) 528
PAYNE, JULIE
Fraternity Vacation   (86) 444
PAYS, AMANDA
Oxford Blues   (85) 528
PEACOCKE, THOMAS
Bad Boy, The   (86) 437
PEARCE, JOANNE
Morons from Outer Space   (86) 452
PEARL, JACK
"Obituaries"   (83) 548
PEARSON, JONAH
Kerouac, the Movie   (86) 448
PEARSON, RODNEY
Secret Admirer   (86) 459
PEC, STEVEN ASPOSTLE
Rhinestone   (85) 531
PECE, ANDREW
Suburbia   (85) 534
PECK, BRIAN
Return of the Living Dead, The   (86) 314
PECK, GREGORY
Boys from Brazil, The [1978]   (86) 480
Sea Wolves, The [1981]   (83) 427
Snows of Kilimanjaro, The [1952]   (83) 498
PECK, STEVEN
Bells Are Ringing [1960]   (84) 517
PEDERSEN, CHRIS
Suburbia   (85) 534
Sylvester   (86) 462
PEDRO, ANTONIO
Bar Esperanza [1983]   (86) 437
PEEL, EDWARD
Lassiter   (85) 524
PEERCE, JAN
"Obituaries"   (85) 689
PELIKAN, LISA
Swing Shift   (85) 535
PELLER, CLARA
Moving Violations   (86) 453
PELÉ
Victory   (82) 374
PEMBER, RON
Bullshot [1983]   (86) 439
PEMBERTON, ANTONIA
Passage to India, A   (85) 365
PENA, ELIZABETH
Crossover Dreams   (86) 441
PENCHENAT, JEAN-CLAUDE
Bal, Le [1983]   (85) 80
Garde à vue [1981]   (83) 189
PENDARVIS, JANICE
Bring on the Night   (86) 439
PENDELTON, NAT
Sign of the Cross, The [1932]   (85) 607

PENN, CHRISTOPHER
 All the Right Moves   (84) 41
 Footloose   (85) 198
 Pale Rider   (86) 261
 Wild Life, The   (85) 538
PENN, SEAN
 Bad Boys   (84) 479
 Crackers   (85) 516
 Falcon and the Snowman, The   (86) 165
 Fast Times at Ridgemont High   (83) 156
 Racing with the Moon   (85) 397
PENNELL, LARRY
 Personal Best   (83) 254
PENNOCK, CHRISTOPHER
 Frances   (83) 178
PENNY, SYDNEY
 Pale Rider   (86) 261
PENVERN, ANDRE
 Holcroft Covenant, The   (86) 446
PEPPER, MARTIN
 Cheech and Chong's The Corsican
  Brothers   (85) 515
PERA, MARILIA
 Bar Esperanza [1983]   (86) 437
 Mixed Blood   (86) 452
 Pixote [1980]   (82) 280
PERCY, ESME
 Nell Gwyn [1934]   (84) 557
PEREIO, PAULO CESAR
 Bar Esperanza [1983]   (86) 437
 I Love You   (83) 423
PERENO, ROBERT
 Little Drummer Girl, The   (85) 525
PERETZ, SUSAN
 Swing Shift   (85) 535
PEREZ, JOSE
 Stick   (86) 460
PEREZ, VICTOR
 Mike's Murder   (85) 526
PEREZ-PORRO, BEATRIZ
 Skyline   (85) 533
PERKINS, ANTHONY
 Crimes of Passion   (85) 161
 Psycho II   (84) 307
PERKINS, MILLIE
 Table for Five   (84) 404
PERLE, REBECCA
 Stitches   (86) 461
PERLMAN, RON
 Quest for Fire   (83) 271
PERLOW, BOB
 Night of the Comet   (85) 527
PERLMAN, JOHN
 Ice Pirates, The   (85) 523
PERRIER, JEAN-FRANÇOIS
 Bal, Le [1983]   (85) 80
PERRIN, JEAN-CLAUDE
 Death of Mario Ricci, The [1983]   (86) 133
PERRINE, VALERIE
 Border, The   (83) 418
 Superman II   (82) 339
PERRONE, MARC
 Trace, The [1983]   (85) 537
PERROT, FRANÇOIS
 My Best Friend's Girl [1983]   (85) 326

PERRY, KATHRYN
 "Obituaries"   (84) 632
PERRY, LINCOLN THEODORE
 "Obituaries"   (86) 578
PERSKY, LISA JANE
 American Pop   (82) 62
 Cotton Club, The   (85) 150
 Sure Thing, The   (86) 369
PERSOFF, NEHEMIAH
 Yentl   (84) 468
PERSONNE, FRED
 Every Man for Himself [1979]   (82) 139
PESCI, JOE
 Easy Money   (84) 482
 Eureka   (86) 442
 Once upon a Time in America   (85) 345
PETER
 Ran   (86) 304
PETERS, BERNADETTE
 Annie   (83) 56
 Pennies from Heaven   (82) 276
PETERS, JEAN
 Apache [1954]   (82) 395
PETERS, LENNIE
 Hit, The   (86) 446
PETERSEN, WILLIAM L.
 To Live and Die in L.A.   (86) 379
PETERSON, AMANDA
 Explorers   (86) 442
PETRAGLIA, JORGE
 Official Story, The   (86) 249
PETRAGLIA, RICARDO
 Gabriela [1983]   (85) 213
PETRELLA, IAN
 Christmas Story, A   (84) 110
PETRENKO, ALEXEI
 Rasputin [1975]   (86) 457
PFEIFFER, MICHELLE
 Grease 2   (83) 422
 Into the Night   (86) 186
 Ladyhawke   (86) 214
 Scarface   (84) 361
PHILBIN, JAMES
 New Kids, The   (86) 454
PHILBIN, JOHN
 Grandview, U.S.A.   (85) 520
 Return of the Living Dead, The   (86) 314
 Stephen King's Children of the Corn   (85) 534
PHILIP, JOHN VAN NESS
 Bostonians, The   (85) 105
PHILLIBER, JOHN
 It Happened Tomorrow [1944]   (84) 552
PHILLIPS, KNOX
 This Is Elvis   (82) 360
PHILLIPS, LAWRENCE
 City Girl, The   (85) 516
PHILLIPS, MACKENZIE
 Love Child   (83) 425
PHILLIPS, PATRICIA
 Came a Hot Friday   (86) 439
PHILLIPS, SIAN
 Clash of the Titans   (82) 111
 Dune   (85) 171

PHIPPS, MAX
  Nate and Hayes (84) 236
  Road Warrior, The [1981] (83) 277
PHOENIX, RIVER
  Explorers (86) 442
PHOTAMO, ANNE MARRE
  Wolfen (82) 382
PIALAT, MAURICE
  À nos amour [1983] (85) 509
PIANKA, MELANIE
  Sophie's Choice (83) 311
PIAZZA, BEN
  Mask (86) 231
PICARDO, ROBERT
  Explorers (86) 442
  Howling, The (82) 207
PICCHIARINI, ANITA
  Bal, Le [1983] (85) 80
PICCOLI, MICHEL
  Atlantic City (82) 74
  Dangerous Moves [1984] (86) 129
  Peril (86) 456
PICHEL, IRVING
  I'm No Angel [1933] (85) 561
PICK, FRANÇOIS
  Bal, Le [1983] (85) 80
PICKARD, HELENA
  Nell Gwyn [1934] (84) 557
  Passion [1982] (84) 289
PICKARD, SORRELLS
  Hardbodies (85) 521
  Running Hot (85) 531
PICKENS, SLIM
  Howling, The (82) 207
  "Obituaries" (84) 632
PICKFORD, MARY
  "Interview with Lillian Gish, An" (83) 24
PICKLES, CAROLYN
  Agatha [1979] (83) 435
  Champions (85) 515
PICKREN, STACEY
  Into the Night (86) 186
PICON, MOLLY
  Cannonball Run II (85) 514
PIDGEON, WALTER
  Man Hunt [1941] (85) 570
  "Obituaries" (85) 689
  Too Hot to Handle [1938] (84) 596
PIERCE, STACK
  Killpoint (85) 524
PIERCEY, JENNIFER
  Another Time, Another Place [1983] (85) 510
PIERPAOLI, OLIVER
  Killing Fields, The (85) 270
PIERPOINT, ERIC
  Windy City (85) 538
PIERSE, SARAH
  Sylvia (86) 462
PIETREK, NICHOLAS
  Shooting Party, The [1984] (86) 344
PIGOTT-SMITH, TIM
  Clash of the Titans (82) 111
  Richard's Things (82) 321

PIK SEN LIM
  Plenty (86) 271
PILATO, JOSEPH
  Day of the Dead (86) 441
PILLSBURY, MATTHEW
  Bon Plaisir, Le [1983] (85) 513
PINCHOT, BRONSON
  After Hours (86) 51
  Flamingo Kid, The (85) 192
  Risky Business (84) 349
PINERO, MIGUEL
  Almost You (86) 436
PINON, DOMINIQUE
  Diva [1980] (83) 147
PINSENT, LEAH
  Bad Boy, The (86) 437
PINTAURO, DANNY
  Cujo (84) 481
PIRES, MIRIAM
  Kiss of the Spider Woman (86) 209
PISCOPO, JOE
  Johnny Dangerously (85) 524
PITONIAK, ANNE
  Agnes of God (86) 56
PITT, INGRID
  Wicker Man, The [1974] (86) 555
  Wild Geese II (86) 466
PLACE, MARY KAY
  Big Chill, The (84) 78
  Explorers (86) 442
  New York, New York [1977] (84) 567
  Smooth Talk (86) 354
  Waltz Across Texas (84) 497
PLACIDO, MICHELE
  Three Brothers [1980] (83) 349
PLAKINGER, TINA
  Pumping Iron II (86) 456
PLANA, TONY
  Nightmares (84) 490
PLANCHON, ROGER
  Return of Martin Guerre, The (84) 318
PLEASENCE, DONALD
  Escape from New York (82) 133
  THX 1138 [1971] (85) 638
PLIMPTON, GEORGE
  Volunteers (86) 464
PLIMPTON, MARTHA
  Goonies, The (86) 176
  River Rat, The (85) 531
PLOWDEN, MELVIN
  Rappin' (86) 457
PLOWRIGHT, JOAN
  Brimstone and Treacle (83) 91
  Brittania Hospital (84) 480
  Revolution (86) 458
PLUMMER, AMANDA
  Cattle Annie and Little Britches (82) 97
  Hotel New Hampshire, The (85) 243
  World According to Garp, The (83) 397
PLUMMER, CHRISTOPHER
  Amateur, The (83) 417
  Dreamscape (85) 166
  Lily in Love (86) 450
  Ordeal by Innocence [1984] (86) 455

PLUNKET, ROBERT
After Hours   (86) 51
POATA, TOM
Wild Horses [1983]   (85) 538
PODELL, RICK
Oasis, The   (85) 528
POGGI, NANDO
Hercules II   (86) 446
POGREBIN, ABIGAIL
Rent Control   (85) 530
POGREBIN, ROBIN
Rent Control   (85) 530
POGSON, KATHRYN
Company of Wolves, The [1984]   (86) 115
POGUE, KEN
Grey Fox, The   (84) 168
POINDEXTER, LARRY
Toy Soldiers   (85) 536
POINTER, PRISCILLA
Micki & Maude   (85) 308
POLANH, RUI
Bar Esperanza [1983]   (86) 437
POLE, FRANCIS
Grace Quigley   (86) 444
POLETTI, VICTOR
And the Ship Sails On [1983]   (85) 69
POLIS, JOEL
Best Defense   (85) 512
Thing, The   (83) 343
POLLACK, DEBORAH
Sixteen Candles   (85) 532
POLLACK, SYDNEY
Tootsie   (83) 353
POLLARD, DAPHNE
Our Relations [1936]   (86) 523
POLONAH, RUI
Emerald Forest, The   (86) 156
PONZINI, ANTONY
Hardbodies   (85) 521
POORE, RICHARD
Wild Horses [1983]   (85) 538
POPWELL, ALBERT
Sudden Impact   (84) 395
PORRETT, SUSAN
Company of Wolves, The [1984]   (86) 115
PORTER, BEATRIX
Lily in Love   (86) 450
PORTILLO, ROSE
Mean Season, The   (86) 452
Zoot Suit   (82) 389
PORTMAN, ERIC
Freud [1962]   (84) 535
POSCHLK, HANNO
Querelle [1982]   (84) 313
POSTLETHWAITE, PETE
Private Function, A [1984]   (86) 280
POTTER, JERRY
Rhinestone   (85) 531
POTTER, MADELEINE
Bostonians, The   (85) 105
POTTS, ANNIE
Crimes of Passion   (85) 161
Ghostbusters   (85) 219
Heartaches [1981]   (83) 197

POTTS, CLIFF
Sahara   (85) 531
POWELL, DICK
It Happened Tomorrow [1944]   (84) 552
POWELL, ELEANOR
"Obituaries"   (83) 549
POWELL, JANE
Royal Wedding [1951]   (86) 536
POWELL, ROBERT
Imperative [1982]   (86) 447
Jigsaw Man, The [1983]   (85) 524
POWELL, RUSS
Barbary Coast [1935]   (84) 506
POWELL, WILLIAM H.
"Obituaries"   (85) 690
Sherlock Holmes [1922]   (83) 494
POWER, TYRONE
Long Gray Line, The [1955]   (82) 447
POWERS, ALEXANDRA
Mask   (86) 231
PREECE, TIM
Brimstone and Treacle   (83) 91
PREISSER, JUNE
"Obituaries"   (85) 691
PRENTISS, PAULA
Buddy Buddy   (82) 93
World of Henry Orient, The [1964]   (84) 600
PRESBY, SHANNON
New Kids, The   (86) 454
PRESCOTT, ROBERT
Bachelor Party   (85) 511
Real Genius   (86) 309
PRESLEY, ELVIS
Flaming Star [1960]   (83) 36
"Interview with Don Siegel, An"   (83) 36
PRESSON, JASON
Explorers   (86) 442
Stone Boy, The   (85) 450
PRESTON, BILLY
Blame It on the Night   (85) 512
PRESTON, J. A.
Body Heat   (82) 87
Remo Williams   (86) 457
PRESTON, KELLY
Metalstorm   (84) 452
Mischief   (86) 452
Secret Admirer   (86) 459
PRESTON, MIKE
Metalstorm   (84) 45
Road Warrior, The [1981]   (83) 277
PRESTON, ROBERT
Last Starfighter, The   (85) 272
S.O.B.   (82) 328
Victor/Victoria   (83) 387
PRETE, GIANCARLO
Ladyhawke   (86) 214
PRICE, DENNIS
Victim [1961]   (85) 647
PRICE, LONNY
Muppets Take Manhattan, The   (85) 526
PRICE, PAGE
All the Right Moves   (84) 41
PRIMUS, BARRY
Absence of Malice   (82) 57

Heartland (82) 191
New York, New York [1977] (84) 567
PRINCE
Purple Rain (85) 389
PRINCE, FAITH
Berry Gordy's The Last Dragon (86) 438
PRICE, WILLIAM
Movers and Shakers (86) 453
Spies like Us (86) 360
PRINE, ANDREW
They're Playing with Fire (85) 536
PRINSLOO, SANDRA
Gods Must Be Crazy, The [1980] (85) 224
PRIVAL, LUCIEN
History Is Made at Night [1937] (84) 542
PROCHNOW, JÜRGEN
Boot, Das [1981] (83) 86
Dune (85) 171
Keep, The (84) 487
PROPHET, MELISSA
Blame It on the Night (85) 512
Invasion U.S.A. (86) 447
PROSKY, ROBERT
Christine (84) 106
Keep, The (84) 487
Lords of Discipline, The (84) 488
Natural, The (85) 329
Thief (82) 356
PROWSE, DAVID
Return of the Jedi (84) 326
PRUCKNER, TILO
Neverending Story, The (85) 527
PRUCNAL, ANNA
City of Women (82) 106
PRYCE, JONATHAN
Brazil (86) 80
Doctor and the Devils, The (86) 442
Ploughman's Lunch, The [1983] (85) 377
Something Wicked This Way Comes (84) 493
PRYOR, NICHOLAS
Risky Business (84) 349
PRYOR, RICHARD
Brewster's Millions (86) 438
Lady Sings the Blues [1972] (85) 565
Richard Pryor Here and Now (84) 492
Some Kind of Hero (83) 428
Superman III (84) 399
Toy, The (83) 358
PSZONIAK, WOJTEK
Dangerous Moves [1984] (86) 129
Danton [1982] (84) 121
PUDOVKIN, VSEVOLOD
New Babylon, The [1929] (84) 561
PUGH, WILLARD
Color Purple, The (86) 105
Moving Violations (85) 453
Toy Soldiers (85) 536
PUGLIA, FRANK
Colorado Territory [1949] (86) 489
PURCELL, LEE
Eddie Macon's Run (84) 483
PURDHAM, DAVID
Lily in Love (86) 450
PURI, AMRISH
Indiana Jones and the Temple of Doom (85) 253

PURL, LINDA
Visiting Hours (83) 431
PUZZI, NICOLE
Gabriela [1983] (85) 213
PYANT, DANENE
Killpoint (85) 524

QUAID, DENNIS
Dreamscape (85) 166
Enemy Mine (86) 161
Jaws 3-D (84) 486
Right Stuff, The (84) 342
Tough Enough (84) 495
QUAID, RANDY
Fool for Love (86) 172
National Lampoon's Vacation (84) 242
Neil Simon's The Slugger's Wife (86) 454
Wild Life, The (85) 538
QUARSHIE, HUGH
Baby (86) 437
QUENNESSEN, VALERIE
Summer Lovers (83) 429
QUICK, DIANA
Ordeal by Innocence [1984] (86) 455
QUIGLEY, LINNEA
Return of the Living Dead, The (86) 314
Silent Night, Deadly Night (85) 532
QUILLEY, DENIS
King David (86) 449
QUINLAN, KATHLEEN
Hanky Panky (83) 422
Twilight Zone—The Movie (84) 435
Warning Sign (86) 465
QUINN, AIDAN
Desperately Seeking Susan (86) 137
Reckless (85) 530
QUINN, AILEEN
Annie (83) 56
QUINN, ANTHONY
Valentina [1982] (84) 496
QUINN, BILL
Twilight Zone—The Movie (84) 435
QUINN, J. C.
Vision Quest (86) 464
QUINN, JAMES
Joey (86) 448
QUINN, THOMAS
Turk 182 (86) 464
QUINONES, ADOLFO "SHABBA-DOO"
Breakin' (85) 514
Breakin' 2 (85) 514
QUINTANO, GENE
Treasure of the Four Crowns (84) 495

RAAB, KURT
Out of Order (86) 455
RAAHAUGE, BENT
Zappa (85) 539
RABAL, FRANCISCO
Holy Innocents, The (86) 447
Treasure of the Four Crowns (84) 495
RABINER, MARK
American Taboo (85) 509
RABINOWITZ, TILLIE
Light Ahead, The [1939] (83) 460

RACHELL, YANK
Louis Bluie (86) 450
RACHINS, ALAN
Always (86) 60
RADMILOVIC, ZORAN
When Father Was Away on Business [1984] (86) 411
RADNER, GILDA
Hanky Panky (83) 422
Movers and Shakers (86) 453
Woman in Red, The (85) 538
RADZIWILOWICZ, JERZY
Man of Iron (82) 230
Man of Marble [1977] (82) 234
Passion [1982] (84) 289
RAFELSON, BOB
Always (86) 60
RAFFIN, DEBORAH
Death Wish III (86) 441
RAFT, GEORGE
They Drive by Night [1940] (83) 508
RAGSDALE, WILLIAM
Fright Night (86) 444
Smooth Talk (86) 354
RAILSBACK, STEVE
Escape 2000 (84) 483
Golden Seal, The (84) 485
Lifeforce (86) 450
RAIMONDI, RUGGERO
Bizet's Carmen [1983] (85) 98
RAIN, LESLIE
Cheech and Chong's The Corsican Brothers (85) 515
RAINES, CRISTINA
Nightmares (84) 490
RALL, TOMMY
Invitation to the Dance [1956] (86) 507
RAMIS, HAROLD
Ghostbusters (85) 219
Stripes (82) 336
RAMPLING, CHARLOTTE
Stardust Memories [1980] (85) 626
Verdict, The (83) 377
RAMSAY, REMAK
Front, The [1976] (86) 502
RAMSEY, ANNE
Goonies, The (86) 176
RAMSEY, JAMES
That Sinking Feeling [1979] (85) 536
RAMSEY, JOHN
C.H.U.D. (85) 515
RAMSEY, MARION
Police Academy (85) 529
Police Academy 2 (86) 276
RANDALL, TONY
King of Comedy, The (84) 192
RANDOLF, ANDERS
Sherlock Holmes [1922] (83) 494
RANDOLPH, BEVERLY
Return of the Living Dead, The (86) 314
RANDOLPH, DONALD
Cowboy [1958] (82) 417
RANDOLPH, ELSIE
"Obituaries" (83) 550

RANDOLPH, JOHN
Prizzi's Honor (86) 285
RANKIN, JANETTE
That Sinking Feeling [1979] (85) 536
RAPHAEL, MICKEY
Songwriter (85) 533
RAPP, LARRY
Once upon a Time in America (85) 345
RAPPAPORT, DAVID
Bride, The (86) 438
Time Bandits [1980] (82) 364
RAPPORT, MICHAEL
Hardbodies (85) 521
RAS, EVA
When Father Was Away on Business [1984] (86) 411
RASCHE, DAVID
Best Defense (85) 512
RATOFF, GREGORY
I'm No Angel [1933] (85) 561
RAVEN, ELSA
American Pop (82) 62
Creator (86) 441
RAWLINGS, KATHY
Wild Horses [1983] (85) 538
RAWLINS, LESTER
They Might Be Giants [1971] (83) 515
RAY, ANTONIA
Beat Street (85) 512
RAY, JAMES
Mass Appeal (85) 303
REA, STEPHEN
Company of Wolves, The [1984] (86) 115
Doctor and the Devils, The (86) 442
READICK, FRANK
Journey into Fear [1943] (86) 511
REAGAN, RONALD
Bedtime for Bonzo [1951] (84) 512
REBIERE, RICHARD
Heavenly Bodies (85) 522
REDFORD, H.E.D.
Silent Night, Deadly Night (85) 532
REDFORD, ROBERT
Natural, The (85) 329
Out of Africa (86) 255
Way We Were, The [1973] (82) 474
REDGRAVE, MICHAEL
"Obituaries" (86) 579
REDGRAVE, VANESSA
Agatha [1979] (83) 435
Bostonians, The (85) 105
Wagner (84) 497
Wetherby (86) 406
REDMAN, AMANDA
Richard's Things (82) 321
REED, ALYSON
Chorus Line, A (86) 91
REED, JERRY
Smokey and the Bandit—Part 3 (84) 493
Survivors, The (84) 495
REED, MATTHEW
Perfect (86) 456
REED, OLIVER
Venom [1981] (83) 430

REED, PAMELA
  Melvin and Howard [1980]   (82) 453
  Right Stuff, The   (84) 342
REES, ROGER
  Star 80   (84) 374
REEVE, CHRISTOPHER
  Aviator, The   (86) 437
  Bostonians, The   (85) 105
  Deathtrap   (83) 137
  Monsignor   (83) 425
  Superman II   (82) 339
  Superman III   (84) 399
REGALBUTO, JE
  Lassiter   (85) 524
  Missing   (83) 232
REGAN, MARY
  Heart of a Stag   (85) 522
  Sylvia   (86) 462
REGENT, BENOIT
  Dangerous Moves [1984]   (86) 129
REGER, JOHN PATRICK
  Hotdog . . . The Movie   (85) 522
REGGIANI, SIMON
  Patsy, The   (86) 456
REGINE
  My New Partner [1984]   (86) 246
REICHARDT, PETER
  Zappa   (85) 539
REICHER, FRANK
  Secret Life of Walter Mitty, The [1947]   (86) 540
REID, CARL BENTON
  North Star, The [1943]   (83) 476
REID, KATE
  Atlantic City   (82) 74
  Heaven Help Us   (86) 445
REILLY, CHARLES NELSON
  Cannonball Run II   (85) 514
REINBOLT, JEREMY SCOTT
  Mommie Dearest   (82) 245
REINEKE, GARY
  Grey Fox, The   (84) 168
REINER, CARL
  Dead Men Don't Wear Plaid   (83) 134
REINER, ROB
  This Is Spinal Tap   (85) 484
REINHOLD, JUDGE
  Beverly Hills Cop   (85) 88
  Fast Times at Ridgemont High   (83) 156
REINKING, ANN
  Annie   (83) 56
  Micki & Maude   (85) 308
REISER, PAUL
  Diner   (83) 142
REKERT, WINSTON
  Agnes of God   (86) 56
  Heartaches [1981]   (83) 197
RELIN, MARIE-THERES
  Secret Places [1984]   (86) 459
REMAR, JAMES
  Cotton Club, The   (85) 150
  48 HRS.   (83) 173
REMSEN, BERT
  Code of Silence   (86) 440

RENALDO, DUNCAN
  Bridge of San Luis Rey, The [1929]   (82) 408
RENICK, RUTH
  "Obituaries"   (85) 691
RENO, JEAN
  Dernier Combat, Le [1983]   (85) 517
  Subway   .(86) 461
RENO, KELLY
  Black Stallion Returns, The   (84) 479
  Brady's Escape   (85) 514
RENUCCI, ROBIN
  Trace, The [1983]   (85) 537
RENZI, MAGGIE
  Brother from Another Planet, The   (85) 118
  Lianna   (84) 201
  Return of the Secaucus 7 [1980]   (83) 484
REQUELME, CARLOS
  Under the Volcano   (85) 499
RESINES, ANTONIO
  Skyline   (85) 533
RESTON, TELMA
  Bar Esperanza [1983]   (86) 437
REUBENS, PAUL
  Pee-wee's Big Adventure   (86) 265
REY, ALEJANDRO
  Moscow on the Hudson   (85) 321
REY, FERNANDO
  Hit, The   (86) 446
  Monsignor   (83) 425
  Rustler's Rhapsody   (86) 458
REY, LEAL
  Official Story, The   (86) 249
REY-PENCHENAT, GENEVIÈVE
  Bal, Le [1983]   (85) 80
REYES, ERNIE, JR.
  Berry Gordy's The Last Dragon   (86) 438
  Red Sonja   (86) 457
REYES, FRANC
  Beat Street   (85) 512
REYNOLDS, BURT
  Best Friends   (83) 68
  Best Little Whorehouse in Texas,
    The   (83) 72
  Cannonball Run II   (85) 514
  City Heat   (85) 141
  Man Who Loved Women, The   (84) 218
  Sharky's Machine   (82) 324
  Smokey and the Bandit—Part 3   (84) 493
  Stick   (86) 460
  Stroker Ace   (84) 494
REYNOLDS, HERB
  Broadway Danny Rose   (85) 112
REYNOLDS, MARJORIE
  Holiday Inn [1942]   (82) 443
REYNOLDS, MICHAEL J.
  Running Brave   (84) 354
RHEA, STEPHEN
  Danny Boy   (85) 517
RHODES, BOBBY
  Last Hunter, The   (85) 525
RHODES, CYNTHIA
  Staying Alive   (84) 386

RHODES, EARL
   Young Sherlock Holmes   (86) 431
RHOE, GEOFF
   Puberty Blues [1981]   (84) 492
RHYS-DAVIES, JOHN
   King Solomon's Mines   (86) 449
   Raiders of the Lost Ark   (82) 308
   Sahara   (85) 531
   Victor/Victoria   (83) 387
RHYTHM BOYS, THE
   King of Jazz [1930]   (86) 515
RIBRAKA, KATERINA
   Angelo My Love   (84) 47
RICE, BRETT
   Bear, The   (85) 511
RICE, RANDY
   Pumping Iron II   (86) 456
RICH, IRENE
   Fort Apache [1948]   (84) 530
RICHARD, PIERRE
   Goat, The [1981]   (86) 444
RICHARDS, KIM
   Meatballs Part II   (85) 526
   Tuff Turf   (86) 464
RICHARDS, MICHAEL
   Transylvania 6-5000   (86) 463
RICHARDS, RICK
   Cease Fire   (86) 440
RICHARDS, TERRY
   Red Sonja   (86) 457
RICHARDSON, ADAM
   Secret Places [1984]   (86) 459
RICHARDSON, IAN
   Brazil   (86) 80
RICHARDSON, JOELY
   Wetherby   (86) 406
RICHARDSON, LEE
   Prizzi's Honor   (86) 285
RICHARDSON, MIRANDA
   Dance with a Stranger [1984]   (86) 125
RICHARDSON, RALPH
   Dragonslayer   (82) 125
   Falstaff [1967]   (83) 443
   Give My Regards to Broad Street   (85) 520
   Greystoke   (85) 236
   "Obituaries"   (84) 633
   Sound Barrier, The [1952]   (85) 621
   Time Bandits [1980]   (82) 364
   Wagner   (84) 497
RICHARDSON, REGINA
   9 Deaths of the Ninja   (86) 454
RICHARDSON, SY
   Repo Man   (85) 408
RICHMAN, ANDY
   Vulture, The   (86) 464
RICHMAN, SANDY
   Broadway Danny Rose   (85) 112
RICHTER, RALPH
   Out of Order   (86) 455
RICKERT, LESLIE
   Explorers   (86) 442
RICKETSON, JAMES
   Where the Green Ants Dream [1984]   (86) 465

RIDGELY, JOHN
   My Reputation [1946]   (85) 586
RIDGELY, ROBERT
   Melvin and Howard [1980]   (82) 453
RIDLEY, EMMA
   Return to Oz   (86) 458
RIEGERT, PETER
   City Girl, The   (85) 516
   Local Hero   (84) 206
RIGG, CARL
   Holcroft Covenant, The   (86) 446
RIGG, DIANA
   Evil Under the Sun [1981]   (83) 421
   Great Muppet Caper, The   (82) 187
RIJU, GO
   Mishima   (86) 236
RILEY, JACK
   Finders Keepers   (85) 519
   Night Patrol   (86) 454
RILEY, LARRY
   Crackers   (85) 516
   Soldier's Story, A   (85) 427
RIMKUS, STEVAN
   Cal   (85) 124
RIMMER, SHANE
   Holcroft Covenant, The   (86) 446
   White Nights   (86) 416
RINGELMANN, THOMAS
   Love in Germany, A [1983]   (85) 283
RINGWALD, MOLLY
   Breakfast Club, The   (86) 85
   Sixteen Candles   (85) 532
   Spacehunter   (84) 493
   Tempest   (83) 331
RINN, BRAD
   Smithereens   (83) 307
RIPPLOH, FRANK
   Taxi Zum Klo   (82) 346
RISTERUCCI, VINCENT
   Argent, L' [1983]   (85) 74
RITT, MARTIN
   Neil Simon's The Slugger's Wife   (86) 454
RITTER, JOHN
   They All Laughed   (82) 350
RITZ, JIMMY
   "Obituaries"   (86) 580
RIVERA, MARCELINO
   Mixed Blood   (86) 452
RIVERO, JORGE
   Priest of Love   (82) 288
RIVIN, LUCILLE
   Home Free All   (85) 522
RIZZO, JILLY
   Cannonball Run II   (85) 514
ROACH, DARYL
   Pee-wee's Big Adventure   (86) 265
ROACH, PAT
   Clash of the Titans   (82) 111
   Conan the Destroyer   (85) 516
   Indiana Jones and the Temple of
      Doom   (85) 253
   Red Sonja   (86) 457
ROBARDS, JASON
   Max Dugan Returns   (84) 228

Melvin and Howard [1980]   (82) 453
Something Wicked This Way Comes   (84) 493
ROBARDS, SAM
  Fandango   (86) 442
  Tempest   (83) 331
ROBBINS, MARTY
  Honkytonk Man   (83) 200
ROBBINS, REX
  Reuben, Reuben   (84) 337
ROBBINS, TIM
  Fraternity Vacation   (86) 444
  Sure Thing, The   (86) 369
  Toy Soldiers   (85) 536
ROBERTS, ARTHUR
  Revenge of the Ninja   (84) 492
ROBERTS, ERIC
  Coca-Cola Kid, The   (86) 440
  North Star, The [1943]   (83) 476
  Pope of Greenwich Village, The   (85) 529
  Raggedy Man   (82) 300
  Runaway Train   (86) 324
  Star 80   (84) 374
ROBERTS, MICHAEL D.
  Ice Pirates, The   (85) 523
ROBERTS, RALPH
  Bells Are Ringing [1960]   (84) 517
ROBERTS, TANYA
  Beastmaster, The   (83) 418
  Sheena   (85) 532
  View to a Kill, A   (86) 402
ROBERTS, TEAL
  Hardbodies   (85) 521
ROBERTS, TONY
  Amityville 3-D   (84) 479
  Key Exchange   (86) 448
  Midsummer Night's Sex Comedy, A   (83) 228
  Stardust Memories [1980]   (85) 626
ROBERTSON, CLIFF
  Brainstorm   (84) 480
  Class   (84) 480
  Star 80   (84) 374
ROBIN, MICHEL
  Death of Mario Ricci, The [1983]   (86) 133
  Goat, The [1981]   (86) 444
ROBINS, OLIVER
  Poltergeist   (83) 263
ROBINSON, BUMPER
  Enemy Mine   (86) 161
ROBINSON, DAR
  Stick   (86) 460
ROBINSON, DARREN (BUFFY)
  Krush Groove   (86) 449
ROBINSON, EDWARD G.
  Barbary Coast [1935]   (84) 506
  Hatchet Man, The [1932]   (83) 447
ROBINSON, IKEY
  Louis Bluie   (86) 450
ROBINSON, LEON
  Flamingo Kid, The   (85) 192
  Streetwalkin'   (86) 461
ROBINSON, MADELEINE
  I Married a Shadow   (84) 486
ROBLEDO, MARIA LUISA
  Official Story, The   (86) 249

ROBLES, FRANK
  Crossover Dreams   (86) 441
ROBSON, FLORA
  Clash of the Titans   (82) 111
  "Obituaries"   (85) 692
ROBSON, GREER
  Smash Palace [1981]   (83) 302
ROBSON, WAYNE
  Grey Fox, The   (84) 168
  One Magic Christmas   (86) 455
ROCCO, ALEX
  Cannonball Run II   (85) 514
  Gotcha!   (86) 444
  Stick   (86) 460
ROCHARD, DANIELLE
  Bal, Le [1983]   (85) 80
ROCHE, EUGENE
  Oh God, You Devil   (85) 528
ROCHEFORT, JEAN
  I Sent a Letter to My Love [1980]   (82) 214
ROCK, OZ
  Body Rock   (85) 513
ROCO, BEMBOL
  Year of Living Dangerously, The [1982]   (84) 462
RODE, THIERRY
  Hail Mary   (86) 182
RODGERS, ILONA
  Utu [1983]   (85) 504
RODGERS, JEFFREY
  Surf II   (85) 535
RODRIQUEZ, WILLIAM
  Emerald Forest, The   (86) 156
RODWAY, NORMAN
  Falstaff [1967]   (83) 443
ROEBLING, PAUL
  Blue Thunder   (84) 84
  Prince of the City   (82) 292
ROEBUCK, DANIEL
  Cave Girl   (86) 439
ROGERS, KENNY
  Six Pack   (83) 428
ROGERS, MIMI
  Blue Skies Again   (84) 479
ROHNER, CLAYTON
  Just One of the Guys   (86) 448
ROLAND, GILBERT
  Barbarosa   (83) 60
ROLF, FREDERICK
  Witness   (86) 421
ROLLING STONES, THE
  Let's Spend the Night Together   (84) 487
ROLLINS, HOWARD E.
  Ragtime   (82) 304
  Soldier's Story, A   (85) 427
ROLLINS, JACK
  Broadway Danny Rose   (85) 112
ROLSTON, LOUIS
  Cal   (85) 124
ROMAN, RUTH
  Echoes   (84) 483
ROMAND, ANNY
  Diva [1980]   (83) 147

ROMAND, BEATRICE
  Beau Mariage, Le   (83) 65
ROMANUS, RICHARD
  Protocol   (85) 383
  Stranger's Kiss   (85) 534
ROMANUS, ROBERT
  Bad Medicine   (86) 437
  Fast Times at Ridgemont High   (83) 156
ROMANUS, TINA
  Starchaser   (86) 360
ROMASHIN, ANATOLY
  Rasputin [1975]   (86) 457
ROMERO, CESAR
  Lust in the Dust   (86) 450
RONET, MAURICE
  Balance, La [1982]   (84) 52
  Beau Pere   (82) 78
  "Obituaries"   (84) 634
RONSTADT, LINDA
  Pirates of Penzance, The   (84) 301
ROONEY, MICKEY
  Care Bears Movie, The   (86) 439
ROSARIO, JOSE RAMON
  Home Free All   (85) 522
ROSATO, TONY
  Improper Channels   (82) 218
ROSE, DON
  King of Jazz [1930]   (86) 515
ROSE, GEORGE
  Pirates of Penzance, The   (84) 301
ROSE, NORMAN
  Front, The [1976]   (86) 502
ROSE, ROBYN
  Fandango   (86) 442
ROSE, TIM
  Return to Oz   (86) 458
ROSELIUS, JOHN
  Love Streams   (85) 293
ROSEN, DANNY
  Stranger than Paradise   (85) 455
ROSENBERG, ARTHUR
  Cutter's Way   (82) 119
ROSETTE
  Pauline at the Beach [1982]   (84) 296
ROSIC, DZSOKO
  Brady's Escape   (85) 514
ROSINI, CLAUDIO
  Another Time, Another Place [1983]   (85) 510
ROSS, ANNIE
  Superman III   (84) 399
ROSS, DIANA
  Lady Sings the Blues [1972]   (85) 565
ROSS, JUSTIN
  Chorus Line, A   (86) 91
ROSS, KATHARINE
  Wrong Is Right   (83) 403
ROSS, MERRIE LYNN
  Class of 1984   (83) 419
ROSS, RICCO
  Death Wish III   (86) 441
ROSS, TINY
  Time Bandits [1980]   (82) 364
ROSSELLINI, ISABELLA
  White Nights   (86) 416

ROSSEN, CAROL
  Arrangement, The [1969]   (86) 474
ROSSI, GEORGE
  Comfort and Joy   (85) 146
ROSSI, LEO
  Heart Like a Wheel   (84) 182
ROSSI, PETER
  Comfort and Joy   (85) 146
ROSSITER, LEONARD
  Brittania Hospital   (84) 480
  "Obituaries"   (85) 693
ROSSITTO, ANGELO
  Mad Max Beyond Thunderdome   (86) 223
ROSSOVICH, RICK
  Streets of Fire   (85) 534
  Warning Sign   (86) 465
ROSSOVICH, TIM
  Cloak and Dagger   (85) 516
ROSSWELL, MAGGIE
  Fire and Ice   (84) 153
ROTH, IVAN
  Night of the Comet   (85) 527
ROTH, TIM
  Hit, The   (86) 446
ROTHMAN, JOHN
  Stardust Memories [1980]   (85) 626
ROUCIS, LUCI
  Party Animal   (86) 455
ROUDENKO, VLADIMIR
  Napoleon [1927]   (82) 461
ROUGERIE, JEAN
  American Dreamer   (85) 509
  Gwendoline [1983]   (85) 521
ROUNDS, DAVID
  "Obituaries"   (84) 634
ROUNDTREE, RICHARD
  City Heat   (85) 141
  Killpoint   (85) 524
ROURKE, MICKEY
  Body Heat   (82) 87
  Diner   (83) 142
  Eureka   (86) 442
  Pope of Greenwich Village, The   (85) 529
  Rumble Fish   (84) 492
  Year of the Dragon   (86) 426
ROUSSEAU, JOHN
  Kerouac, the Movie   (86) 448
ROUSSEL, MYRIEM
  First Name, Carmen [1983]   (85) 186
  Hail Mary   (86) 182
ROUTLEDGE, ALISON
  Quiet Earth, The   (86) 295
ROVEYRE, LILIANE
  Dirty Dishes [1978]   (84) 482
ROWAN, DIANA
  Beyond Reasonable Doubt [1980]   (84) 74
ROWE, NICHOLAS
  Young Sherlock Holmes   (86) 431
ROWLANDS, GENA
  Love Streams   (85) 293
  Tempest   (83) 331
ROY, DEEP
  Neverending Story, The   (85) 527
  Return to Oz   (86) 458

ROY, INDAPRAMIT
Home and the World, The [1984] (86) 447
ROYAL, BRIAN
Hit, The (86) 446
ROYLE, SELENA
"Obituaries" (84) 635
ROZYCKI, CHRISTOPHER
Local Hero (84) 206
RUB, CHRISTIAN
Peter Ibbetson [1935] (86) 527
RUBES, JAN
One Magic Christmas (86) 455
Witness (86) 421
RUBIE, LES
Mrs. Soffel (85) 314
RUBIN, ANDREW
Police Academy (85) 529
RUBIN, RICK
Krush Groove (86) 449
RUBINEK, SAUL
Against All Odds (85) 509
By Design (83) 419
RUBINSTEIN, ZELDA
Poltergeist (83) 263
RUDE, DICK
Repo Man (85) 408
RUDHYAR, DANE
"Obituaries" (86) 580
RUFUS
Erendira [1983] (85) 181
RUIZ, CHELA
Official Story, The (86) 249
RUIZ, RENE
Under the Volcano (85) 499
RULE, JANICE
Rainy Day Friends (86) 457
RUMAN, SIG
It Happened Tomorrow [1944] (84) 552
RUNYEON, FRANK
Sudden Death (86) 461
RUNYON, JENNIFER
Up the Creek (85) 537
RUSCIO, AL
Deadly Force (84) 482
RUSH, BARBARA
Hombre [1967] (84) 547
Summer Lovers (83) 429
RUSH, DEBORAH
Compromising Positions (86) 120
Honky Tonk Freeway (82) 199
Night in Heaven, A (84) 490
Purple Rose of Cairo, The (86) 290
Split Image (83) 317
RUSKIN, JEANNE
Rent Control (85) 530
RUSKIN, JOSEPH
Prizzi's Honor (86) 285
RUSLER, ROBERT
Nightmare on Elm Street, Part 2, A (86) 454
Weird Science (86) 465
RUSSELL, APRIL
Fool for Love (86) 172
RUSSELL, BETSY
Avenging Angel (86) 436

Out of Control (86) 455
Private School (84) 49
Tomboy (86) 463
RUSSELL, JOHN
Pale Rider (86) 261
RUSSELL, KURT
Escape from New York (82) 133
Mean Season, The (86) 452
Silkwood (84) 367
Swing Shift (85) 535
Thing, The (83) 343
RUSSELL, ROSALIND
Roughly Speaking [1945] (83) 490
Take a Letter, Darling [1942] (85) 632
RUSSELL, THERESA
Eureka (86) 442
Insignificance (86) 447
Razor's Edge, The (85) 402
RUSSO, GAETANO
Ladyhawke (86) 214
RUSSO, JAMES
Beverly Hills Cop (85) 88
Once upon a Time in America (85) 345
RUSSOM, LEON
Stephen King's Silver Bullet (86) 460
RUTHERFORD, ANN
Secret Life of Walter Mitty, The [1947] (86) 540
RUTHERFORD, MARGARET
Falstaff [1967] (83) 443
RUYSDAEL, BASIL
Colorado Territory [1949] (86) 489
RYAN, HELEN
Misunderstood (85) 526
RYAN, JOHN P.
Breathless (84) 89
Cotton Club, The (85) 150
Postman Always Rings Twice, The (82) 284
Right Stuff, The (84) 342
Runaway Train (86) 324
RYAN, MARI KAREN
Caged Fury (85) 514
RYAN, MEG
Rich and Famous (82) 316
RYAN, MICHAEL
Slayground [1983] (85) 533
RYAN, ROBERT
Veronika Voss (83) 382
RYAN, STEVE
D.A.R.Y.L. (86) 441
RYAN, TIM
Detour [1946] (86) 498
RYDELL, CHRISTOPHER
Gotcha! (86) 444
RYDER, AMY
Once upon a Time in America (85) 345
RYU, CHISHU
Foster Daddy, Tora! [1980] (82) 163
Tokyo-Ga (86) 463
RYU, DAISUKE
Ran (86) 304

SACHS, STEPHEN
Dorm That Dripped Blood, The (84) 482
SACKS, MICHAEL
Split Image (83) 317

SADOYAN, ISABELLE
　Return of Martin Guerre, The　(84) 318
SAGALLE, JONATHAN
　Drifting　(85) 518
SAGE, DOLORES
　Birdy　(85) 93
SÄGEBRECHT, MARIANNE
　Sugarbaby　(86) 461
SAINT-CYR, RENEE
　My Other Husband　(86) 453
SAINTE-MARIE, BUFFY
　Broken Rainbow　(86) 439
ST. JACQUES, RAYMOND
　Evil That Men Do, The　(85) 518
SAINT JAMES, SUSAN
　Don't Cry, It's Only Thunder　(83) 420
ST. JOHN, MARCO
　Tightrope　(85) 489
SAINT MACARY, XAVIER
　Detective　(86) 442
ST. SYR, LAURENT
　Sugar Cane Alley [1983]　(85) 461
SAITO, JAMES
　Hotdog . . . The Movie　(85) 522
SAKAMOTO, RYUICHI
　Merry Christmas, Mr. Lawrence　(84) 231
SAKUMA, YOSHIKO
　Makioka Sisters, The [1983]　(86) 451
SAKURA, SHIORI
　MacArthur's Children　(86) 451
SALAMAN, CHLOE
　Dragonslayer　(82) 125
SALDANA, THERESA
　Evil That Men Do, The　(85) 518
SALENGER, MEREDITH
　Journey of Natty Gann, The　(86) 203
SALES, TONY FOX
　Hard to Hold　(85) 521
SALIMO, ANNE-CLAUDE
　Balance, La [1982]　(84) 52
SALINGER, DIANE
　Pee-wee's Big Adventure　(86) 265
SALMI, ALBERT
　Dragonslayer　(82) 125
　Hard to Hold　(85) 521
　Love Child　(83) 425
SALVIAT, CATHERINE
　Just the Way You Are　(85) 524
SAMOILOV, VLADIMIR
　Siberiade [1977]　(83) 299
SAMPSON, ROBERT
　Re-Animator　(86) 457
SAMPSON, WILL
　Insignificance　(86) 447
SANCHEZ, ANA "LOLLIPOP"
　Breakin'　(85) 514
SÁNCHEZ, JUAN
　Holy Innocents, The　(86) 447
SANCHEZ, PEDRO
　Mixed Blood　(86) 452
SANCHEZ, SUSANA
　Holy Innocents, The　(86) 447

SANCHEZ-PRIETO, ALVARO
　Demons in the Garden [1982]　(85) 517
SANDE, WALTER
　Apache [1954]　(82) 395
SANDER, OTTO
　Boot, Das [1981]　(83) 86
SANDERS, GEORGE
　Love in Germany, A [1983]　(85) 283
　Man Hunt [1941]　(85) 570
SANDERSON, MARTYN
　Beyond Reasonable Doubt [1980]　(84) 74
　Sylvia　(86) 462
　Utu [1983]　(85) 504
　Wild Horses [1983]　(85) 538
SANDERSON, WILLIAM
　Blade Runner　(83) 76
　City Heat　(85) 141
　Nightmares　(84) 490
　Raggedy Man　(82) 300
SANDOR, STEVE
　Fire and Ice　(84) 153
　Stryker　(84) 494
SANDOR, SZABO
　Lily in Love　(86) 450
SANDOVAL, MICHAEL
　Repo Man　(85) 408
SANDS, JULIAN
　Doctor and the Devils, The　(86) 442
　Killing Fields, The　(85) 270
　Oxford Blues　(85) 528
SANDWEISS, ELLEN
　Evil Dead, The　(84) 484
SANNACHAN, DOUGLAS
　That Sinking Feeling [1979]　(85) 536
SANSOM, KEN
　Starchaser　(86) 460
SANTANA, ARNALDO
　Scarface　(84) 361
SANTIAGO, SAUNDRA
　Beat Street　(85) 512
SANTINI, PIERRE
　American Dreamer　(85) 509
　Dirty Dishes [1978]　(84) 482
SANTIS, LUISA DE
　Softly Softly [1984]　(86) 460
SANTON, PENNY
　Rhinestone　(85) 531
SANTONI, RENI
　Bad Boys　(84) 479
　Dead Men Don't Wear Plaid　(83) 134
SANTOS, JOSE NILSON DOS
　Pixote [1980]　(82) 280
SANTOS, ZENILDO OLIVEIRA
　Pixote [1980]　(82) 280
SANTUCCI, JOHN
　Thief　(82) 356
SANVIDO, GUY
　Heartaches [1981]　(83) 197
SANZ, JORGE
　Valentina [1982]　(84) 496
SARAFIAN, RICHARD C.
　Songwriter　(85) 533
SARANDON, CHRIS
　Fright Night　(86) 444
　Protocol　(85) 383

SARANDON, SUSAN
Atlantic City (82) 74
Buddy System, The (85) 514
Compromising Positions (86) 120
Hunger, The (84) 486
Pretty Baby [1978] (85) 597
Tempest (83) 331
SARCHIELLI, MASSIMO
Ladyhawke (86) 214
SARKY, DANIEL
Patsy, The (86) 456
SARRAZIN, MICHAEL
Fighting Back (83) 421
Joshua Then and Now (86) 198
Seduction, The (83) 427
SARTAIN, GAILARD
Outsiders, The (84) 282
SASSOON, CATYA
Tuff Turf (86) 464
SAUL, NITZA
Until September (85) 537
SAUNDERS, JOE
Dark Star [1975] (86) 494
SAURA, MARINA
Flesh and Blood (86) 443
SAVAGE, ANN
Detour [1946] (86) 498
SAVAGE, BLANE
Chorus Line, A (86) 91
SAVAGE, BRAD
Red Dawn (85) 530
SAVAGE, JOHN
Amateur, The (83) 417
Brady's Escape (85) 514
Cattle Annie and Little Britches (82) 97
Maria's Lovers (86) 451
SAVALAS, GEORGE
"Obituaries" (86) 581
SAVALAS, TELLY
Cannonball Run II (85) 514
SAVIO, ANDRIAN
Stryker (84) 494
SAWADA, KENJI
Mishima (86) 236
SAWAGUCHI, YASUKO
Godzilla 1985 (86) 444
SAWALHA, NADIM
Misunderstood (85) 526
SAWAMURA, SADAKO
Late Chrysanthemums [1954] (86) 449
SAWYER, ANNE
Heavenly Kid, The (86) 445
SAWYER, JOSEPH
"Obituaries" (83) 551
SAXON, JOHN
Fever Pitch (86) 443
Nightmare on Elm Street, A (85) 527
Wrong Is Right (83) 403
SAYER, PHILIP
Slayground [1983] (85) 533
SAYLE, ALEXI
Bride, The (86) 438
SAYLES, JOHN
Brother from Another Planet, The (85) 118

Lianna (84) 201
Return of the Secaucus 7 [1980] (83) 484
SAYYAD, PARVIZ
Mission, The (84) 489
SBARGE, RAPHAEL
My Science Project (86) 453
Risky Business (84) 349
SCACCHI, GRETA
Coca-Cola Kid, The (86) 440
Heat and Dust [1982] (84) 187
SCALES, PRUNELLA
Hound of the Baskervilles, The [1978] (82) 203
SCANLAN, SEAN
Sense of Freedom, A (86) 459
SCARFE, ALAN
Bad Boy, The (86) 437
Joshua Then and Now (86) 198
SCARPETTA, MARIO
Softly Softly [1984] (86) 460
SCARWID, DIANA
Mommie Dearest (82) 245
Pretty Baby [1978] (85) 597
Silkwood (84) 367
Strange Invaders (84) 494
SCHAAL, WENDY
Where the Boys Are '84 (85) 537
SCHACHTER, FELICE
Zapped! (82) 431
SCHALLERT, WILLIAM
Teachers (85) 535
Twilight Zone—The Movie (84) 435
SCHEDEEN, ANNE
Second Thoughts (84) 493
SCHEIDER, ROY
Blue Thunder (84) 84
Mishima (86) 236
Still of the Night (83) 326
2010 (85) 494
SCHEIMER, ERIKA
Secret of the Sword, The (86) 459
SCHELL, MAXIMILIAN
Chosen, The (83) 116
SCHELLENBERG, AUGUST
Running Brave (84) 354
SCHEPPS, SHAWN
Racing with the Moon (85) 397
SCHERBAKOV, PYOTR
Jazzman (85) 523
SCHIAVELLI, VINCENT
Adventures of Buckaroo Banzai, The (85) 47
Taking Off [1971] (86) 545
SCHIDOR, DIETER
Querelle [1982] (84) 313
SCHLOSS, VANDER
Repo Man (85) 408
SCHNEIDER, DAVID
Better Off Dead (86) 438
SCHNEIDER, HELEN
Eddie and the Cruisers (84) 483
SCHNEIDER, JOHN
Eddie Macon's Run (84) 483

SCHNEIDER, ROMY
  Garde à vue [1981]   (83) 189
  "Obituaries"   (83) 551
SCHOEFFLING, MICHAEL
  Sixteen Candles   (85) 532
  Sylvester   (86) 462
  Vision Quest   (86) 464
SCHOELEN, JILL
  That Was Then . . . This Is Now   (86) 463
SCHOFIELD, DAVID
  American Werewolf in London, An   (82) 66
SCHOFIELD, NELL
  Puberty Blues [1981]   (84) 492
SCHOLLIN, CHRISTINA
  Fanny and Alexander [1982]   (84) 146
SCHOPPERT, BILL
  Personals, The   (84) 491
SCHOTT, BOB
  Gymkata   (86) 445
SCHRODER, RICKY
  Earthling, The [1980]   (82) 130
SCHUMANN, ERIK
  Lili Marleen   (82) 222
SCHWARTZ, DAN
  Cheech and Chong's The Corsican
    Brothers   (85) 515
SCHWARTZ, GARY
  Quest for Fire   (83) 271
SCHWARTZ, SCOTT
  Toy, The   (83) 358
SCHWARZENEGGER, ARNOLD
  Commando   (86) 111
  Conan the Barbarian   (83) 419
  Conan the Destroyer   (85) 516
  Red Sonja   (86) 457
  Terminator, The   (85) 478
SCHYGULLA, HANNA
  Berlin Alexanderplatz [1980]   (84) 57
  Circle of Deceit [1981]   (83) 419
  Lili Marleen   (82) 222
  Love in Germany, A [1983]   (85) 283
  Nuit de Varennes, La [1982]   (84) 270
  Passion [1982]   (84) 289
  Sheer Madness [1983]   (86) 459
SCOGGINS, TRACY
  Toy Soldiers   (85) 536
SCORSESE, MARTIN
  King of Comedy, The   (84) 192
SCOTT, CAREY
  Making the Grade   (85) 526
SCOTT, DAVID
  This Is Elvis   (82) 360
SCOTT, DONOVAN
  Police Academy   (85) 529
  Savannah Smiles   (84) 493
  Sheena   (85) 532
SCOTT, GEORGE C.
  Firestarter   (85) 519
  Taps   (82) 343
  They Might Be Giants [1971]   (83) 515
SCOTT, LARRY B.
  That Was Then . . . This Is Now   (86) 463
SCOTT, NINA
  Invitation au voyage [1982]   (84) 486

SCOTT, TIMOTHY
  Nightmares   (84) 490
SCOTT, ZACHARY
  Unfaithful, The [1947]   (86) 550
SCOURBY, ALEXANDER
  "Obituaries"   (86) 581
  Stuff, The   (86) 461
SCRIBNER, RONNIE
  Split Image   (83) 317
SEACAT, SANDRA
  Country   (85) 156
SEAGROVE, JENNY
  Local Hero   (84) 206
  Nate and Hayes   (84) 236
SEALES, FRANKLYN
  Southern Comfort   (82) 332
SEARL, BERNIE
  Hit, The   (86) 446
SEARS, IAN
  King David   (86) 449
SEATTINI, MONICA
  Bal, Le [1983]   (85) 80
SEDGWICK, KYRA
  War and Love   (86) 465
SEGAL, GEORGE
  Stick   (86) 460
SEIGNER, EMMANUELLE
  Detective   (86) 442
SELBY, DAVID
  Rich and Famous   (82) 316
SELLECK, TOM
  High Road to China   (84) 486
  Lassiter   (85) 524
SELLERS, PETER
  Trail of the Pink Panther   (83) 430
  World of Henry Orient, The [1964]   (84) 600
SELWYN, DON
  Came a Hot Friday   (86) 439
SEMMELROGGE, MARTIN
  Boot, Das [1981]   (83) 86
SENECA, JOE
  Evil That Men Do, The   (85) 518
  Silverado   (86) 349
SEREYS, JACQUES
  Patsy, The   (86) 456
SERNA, PEPE
  Adventures of Buckaroo Banzai,
    The   (85) 47
  Fandango   (86) 442
SERRA, ALESSANDRO
  Ladyhawke   (86) 214
SERRA, FIORENZO
  And the Ship Sails On [1983]   (85) 69
SERRA, RAYMOND
  Alphabet City   (85) 509
SERRAULT, MICHEL
  Bon Plaisir, Le [1983]   (85) 513
  Garde à vue [1981]   (83) 189
  Heads or Tails [1980]   (84) 485
SERWIN, SHANE
  Sylvester   (86) 462
SETH, ROSHAN
  Gandhi   (83) 183

Indiana Jones and the Temple of
  Doom (85) 253
SEWERYN, ANDRZEJ
  Man of Iron (82) 230
SEYMOUR, ANNE
  Trancers (86) 463
SEYMOUR, JANE
  Lassiter (85) 524
SEYMOUR, RALPH
  Meatballs Part II (85) 526
  Surf II (85) 535
SEYRIG, DELPHINE
  I Sent a Letter to My Love [1980] (82) 214
SEZER, SERIF
  Yol (83) 411
SHAFFER, PAUL
  This Is Spinal Tap (85) 484
SHAMATA, CHUCK
  Joshua Then and Now (86) 198
SHAMOS, JEREMY
  Kid Colter (86) 449
SHANKLEY, AMELIA
  Dreamchild (86) 146
SHANKS, DON
  Sweet Sixteen (85) 535
SHANNON, MICHAEL
  Sheena (85) 532
SHAPIRO, HILARY
  Weekend Pass (85) 537
SHARIF, OMAR
  Top Secret (85) 536
SHARKEY, RAY
  Body Rock (85) 513
  Some Kind of Hero (83) 428
SHATNER, WILLIAM
  Star Trek II—The Wrath of Khan (83)
  321
  Star Trek III—The Search for
  Spock (85) 439
  Visiting Hours (83) 431
SHAUGHNESSY, MICKEY
  "Obituaries" (86) 581
SHAUL, NITZA
  Vulture, The (86) 464
SHAVER, HELEN
  Best Defense (85) 512
SHAW, ANTHONY
  Jigsaw Man, The [1983] (85) 524
SHAW, CRYSTAL
  Hardbodies (85) 521
SHAW, ELIZABETH LLOYD
  Fire and Ice (84) 153
SHAW, JACOB
  Love Streams (85) 293
SHAW, SEBASTIAN
  Return of the Jedi (84) 326
SHAW, STAN
  Tough Enough (84) 495
SHAW, WINI
  "Obituaries" (83) 551
SHAWLEE, JOAN
  Buddy Buddy (82) 93
SHAWN, DICK
  Angel (85) 510
  Good Bye Cruel World (85) 520

SHAWN, WALLACE
  Bostonians, The (85) 105
  Crackers (85) 516
  Heaven Help Us (86) 445
  Hotel New Hampshire, The (85) 243
  Micki & Maude (85) 308
  My Dinner with André (82) 255
SHAYNE, KONSTANTIN
  Secret Life of Walter Mitty, The [1947] (86) 540
SHAYNE, TAMARA
  "Obituaries" (84) 636
SHDANOFF, GEORGE
  Specter of the Rose [1946] (83) 504
SHEA, JOHN
  Missing (83) 232
  Windy City (85) 538
SHEARER, HARRY
  Right Stuff, The (84) 342
  This Is Spinal Tap (85) 484
SHEARER, NORMA
  Divorcée, The [1930] (82) 429
  "Obituaries" (84) 636
SHEARMAN, ALAN
  Bullshot [1983] (86) 439
SHEEDY, ALLY
  Bad Boys (84) 479
  Breakfast Club, The (86) 85
  Oxford Blues (85) 528
  St. Elmo's Fire (86) 330
  Twice in a Lifetime (86) 397
  WarGames (84) 458
SHEEN, CHARLIE
  Red Dawn (85) 530
SHEEN, MARTIN
  Broken Rainbow (86) 439
  Dead Zone, The (84) 481
  Enigma [1982] (84) 483
  Firestarter (85) 519
  Gandhi (83) 183
  Man, Woman and Child (84) 489
  That Championship Season (83) 338
SHEFFER, CRAIG
  That Was Then . . . This Is Now (86) 463
SHEILA E.
  Krush Groove (86) 449
SHEINER, DAVID S.
  Blue Thunder (84) 84
SHELLEY, JOSHUA
  Front, The [1976] (86) 502
SHELTON, DEBORAH
  Body Double (85) 513
SHENAR, PAUL
  Deadly Force (84) 482
  Scarface (84) 361
  Secret of NIMH, The (83) 288
SHEPARD, JEWEL
  Return of the Living Dead, The (86) 314
SHEPARD, SAM
  Country (85) 156
  Fool for Love (86) 172
  Frances (83)·178
  Raggedy Man (82) 300
  Right Stuff, The (84) 342
SHEPPARD, PAULA E.
  Liquid Sky (84) 487

SHERIDAN, ANN
  They Drive by Night [1940] (83) 508
  Unfaithful, The [1947] (86) 550
SHERIDAN, DINAH
  Sound Barrier, The [1952] (85) 621
SHERIDAN, NICOLLETTE
  Sure Thing, The (86) 369
SHERIDAN, SUSAN
  Black Cauldron, The (86) 75
SHERMAN, BOB
  Sheena (85) 532
SHERMAN, HIRAM
  Solid Gold Cadillac, The [1956] (85) 615
SHERMAN, HOWARD
  Day of the Dead (86) 441
SHERMAN, KERRY
  48 HRS. (83) 173
SHEYBAL, VLADEK
  Red Dawn (85) 530
SHIELDS, BROOKE
  Pretty Baby [1978] (85) 597
  Sahara (85) 531
SHIELDS, FRED
  Bambi [1942] (85) 543
SHILOH, SHMUEL
  Goodbye, New York (86) 444
SHILOVSKI, VSEVOLOD
  Waiting for Gavrilov [1982] (84) 497
SHIMADA, SHINSUKE
  MacArthur's Children (86) 451
SHIMOJO, MASAMI
  Foster Daddy, Tora! [1980] (82) 163
SHIMONO, SAB
  Challenge, The (83) 109
SHINAGAWA, ERNIE
  Lust in the Dust (86) 450
SHIONOYA, MASAYUKI
  Mishima (86) 236
SHIRE, TALIA
  Rocky III (83) 283
  Rocky IV (86) 319
SHIRIN, MOTI
  Little Drummer Girl, The (85) 525
SHIRLEY, ALEISA
  Sweet Sixteen (85) 535
SHOR, DANIEL
  Mike's Murder (85) 526
  Stranger's Kiss (85) 534
  TRON (83) 371
SHOWALTER, MAX
  Sixteen Candles (85) 532
SHUCK, JOHN
  Brewster McCloud [1970] (86) 484
SHUE, ELISABETH
  Karate Kid, The (85) 264
SHUKURI, CHIHARU
  MacArthur's Children (86) 451
SHULL, RICHARD B.
  Unfaithfully Yours (85) 537
SIDNEY, SYLVIA
  Hammett (84) 174
SIEBERT, OLIVER
  White Rose, The (84) 497

SIEGEL, DON
  Play Misty for Me [1971] (86) 532
SIEMASZKO, CASEY
  Secret Admirer (86) 459
SIGIMURA, HARUKO
  Flowing [1956] (86) 444
SIGNORELLI, TOM
  Crossover Dreams (86) 441
SIGNORET, SIMONE
  Adolescente, L' [1979] (83) 53
  Étoile du nord, L' (84) 484
  I Sent a Letter to My Love [1980] (82) 214
  "Obituaries" (86) 581
SIHOL, CAROLINE
  Confidentially Yours [1983] (85) 516
SIKES, CYNTHIA
  Good Bye Cruel World (85) 520
  Man Who Loved Women, The (84) 218
SIKKING, JAMES B.
  Morons from Outer Space (86) 452
  Outland (82) 272
  Up the Creek (85) 537
SILBERG, TUSSE
  Company of Wolves, The [1984] (86) 115
SILVA, HENRY
  Cannonball Run II (85) 514
  Code of Silence (86) 440
  Lust in the Dust (86) 450
  Sharky's Machine (82) 324
  Wrong Is Right (83) 403
SILVANI, JOLE
  City of Women (82) 106
SILVER, CINDY
  Hardbodies (85) 521
SILVER, JOE
  Almost You (86) 436
SILVER, RON
  Best Friends (83) 68
  Entity, The (84) 483
  Garbo Talks (85) 520
  Oh God, You Devil (85) 528
  Silent Rage (83) 428
  Silkwood (84) 367
SILVER, TRACY
  Fast Forward (86) 442
SILVER, VÉRONIQUE
  Woman Next Door, The (82) 385
SILVERS, CATHY
  Sesame Street Presents: Follow That Bird (86) 459
SILVERS, PHIL
  "Obituaries" (86) 582
SIMMONS, DANIEL
  Krush Groove (86) 449
SIMMONS, HEATHER
  Stephen King's Silver Bullet (86) 460
SIMMONS, JOSEPH
  Krush Groove (86) 449
SIMON, FRANÇOIS
  Basileus Quartet (85) 511
SIMON, MIKLOS
  Four Friends (82) 167
SIMONE
  Boat Is Full, The [1981] (83) 82

SIMONO
  Cheech and Chong's The Corsican
    Brothers (85) 515
SIMPSON, IVAN
  Disraeli [1929] (82) 426
SINATRA, FRANK
  Cannonball Run II (85) 514
SINCLAIR, ANNETTE
  Weekend Pass (85) 537
SINCLAIR, GORDON JOHN
  Gregory's Girl [1981] (83) 193
  That Sinking Feeling [1979] (85) 536
SINGER, LORI
  Falcon and the Snowman, The (86) 165
  Footloose (85) 198
  Man with One Red Shoe, The (86) 451
  Trouble in Mind (86) 388
SINGER, MARC
  Beastmaster, The (83) 418
  If You Could See What I Hear (83) 423
SINGER, RICHARD
  American Pop (82) 62
SINGH, RAJ
  Indiana Jones and the Temple of
    Doom (85) 253
SIRTIS, MARINA
  Death Wish III (86) 441
SISTERS "G"
  King of Jazz [1930] (86) 515
SKALA, LILIA
  Flashdance (84) 158
  Heartland (82) 191
  Testament (84) 420
SKERRITT, TOM
  Dead Zone, The (84) 481
  Fighting Back (83) 421
SKINNER, JONATHAN
  Fool for Love (86) 172
SKINNER, KI
  American Taboo (85) 509
SKIPWORTH, ALISON
  Becky Sharp [1935] (82) 403
SKLYAR, IGOR
  Jazzman (85) 523
SKOBLINE, IRÈNE
  Coup de torchon [1981] (83) 124
SKOLIMOWSKI, JERZY
  Circle of Deceit [1981] (83) 419
  White Nights (86) 416
SLACK, BEN
  Oasis, The (85) 528
SLADE, DEMIAN
  Better Off Dead (86) 438
SLADE, MARK
  Flashpoint (85) 519
SLATER, CHRISTIAN
  Legend of Billie Jean, The (86) 450
SLATER, HELEN
  Legend of Billie Jean, The (86) 450
  Supergirl (85) 535
SLEEPER, MARTHA
  "Obituaries" (84) 637
SLEZAK, WALTER
  Bedtime for Bonzo [1951] (84) 512
  "Obituaries" (84) 638

SLINGSBY, DAVID
  Coca-Cola Kid, The (86) 440
SLOANE, EVERETT
  Journey into Fear [1943] (86) 511
SLOWE, GEORGIA
  Company of Wolves, The [1984] (86) 115
SMALL, MARYA
  American Pop (82) 62
SMART, JEAN
  Flashpoint (85) 519
  Protocol (85) 383
SMITH, BUBBA
  Police Academy (85) 529
  Police Academy 2 (86) 276
SMITH, CHARLES MARTIN
  Never Cry Wolf (84) 247
  Starman (85) 445
SMITH, CRYSTAL
  Hotdog . . . The Movie (85) 522
SMITH, DON
  Razorback [1984] (86) 457
SMITH, GERALDINE
  Mixed Blood (86) 452
SMITH, HAL
  Here Come the Littles (86) 446
SMITH, ILAN-MITCHELL
  Wild Life, The (85) 538
SMITH, JONATHAN
  Klynham Summer (84) 487
SMITH, KENT
  "Obituaries" (86) 583
SMITH, KURTWOOD
  Flashpoint (85) 519
SMITH, LA RON A.
  Body Rock (85) 513
SMITH, LANE
  Places in the Heart (85) 371
  Purple Hearts (85) 529
SMITH, LEWIS
  Adventures of Buckaroo Banzai,
    The (85) 47
  Heavenly Kid, The (86) 445
  Southern Comfort (82) 332
SMITH, LIZ
  Private Function, A [1984] (86) 280
SMITH, LOIS
  Four Friends (82) 167
  Next Stop, Greenwich Village [1976] (85) 592
  Reckless (85) 530
  Reuben, Reuben (84) 337
SMITH, MADOLYN
  All of Me (85) 58
  2010 (85) 494
SMITH, MAGGIE
  Clash of the Titans (82) 111
  Evil Under the Sun [1981] (83) 421
  Lily in Love (86) 450
  Missionary, The (83) 233
  Private Function, A [1984] (86) 280
  Quartet (82) 296
(SMITH), MARY ALICE
  Beat Street (85) 512
SMITH, MEL
  Bullshot [1983] (86) 439

Morons from Outer Space   (86) 452
Slayground [1983]   (85) 533
SMITH, PAUL
   Red Sonja   (86) 457
SMITH, PETER
   Quiet Earth, The   (86) 295
SMITH, PHILLIP
   1918   (86) 454
SMITH, REX
   Pirates of Penzance, The   (84) 301
SMITH, SHAWN
   River Rat, The   (85) 531
SMITH, STANLEY
   King of Jazz [1930]   (86) 515
SMITH, TRACY N.
   Hotdog . . . The Movie   (85) 522
SMITH, WILLIAM
   Fever Pitch   (86) 443
   Mean Season, The   (86) 452
   Outsiders, The   (84) 282
   Red Dawn   (85) 530
SMITH, WYNONNA
   Cotton Club, The   (85) 150
SMITH, YEARDLEY
   Legend of Billie Jean, The   (86) 450
SMITROVICH, BILL
   Stephen King's Silver Bullet   (86) 460
SMITS, SONJA
   Videodrome   (84) 452
SNEGOFF, GREGORY
   Ladyhawke   (86) 214
SNODGRESS, CARRIE
   Night in Heaven, A   (84) 490
   Pale Rider   (86) 261
   Rainy Day Friends   (86) 457
SNOOK, DAN
   Stephen King's Children of the Corn   (85) 534
SNOW, DAVID
   Dorm That Dripped Blood, The   (84) 482
SNOW, NORMAN
   Last Starfighter, The   (85) 277
SNYDER, DREW
   Purple Hearts   (85) 529
SNYDER, SUZANNE
   Oasis, The   (85) 528
   Weird Science   (86) 465
SOARES, JOFRE
   Gabriela [1983]   (85) 213
SOBOLESKII, PIOTR
   New Babylon, The [1929]   (84) 561
SOLES, P. J.
   Stripes   (82) 336
SOLOMON, JESSE
   Lianna   (84) 201
SOLOMON, TIMOTHY "POPPIN' PETE"
   Breakin'   (85) 514
SOLOMON, VITALY
   Siberiade [1977]   (83) 299
SOLOVEI, YELENA
   Unfinished Piece for Piano Player, An
      [1977]   (83) 430
SOMBERT, CLAIRE
   Invitation to the Dance [1956]   (86) 507

SOMERS, KRISTI
   Hardbodies   (85) 521
   Tomboy   (86) 463
SOMMER, ELKE
   Lily in Love   (86) 450
SOMMER, JOSEF
   Absence of Malice   (82) 57
   D.A.R.Y.L.   (86) 441
   Front, The [1976]   (86) 502
   Iceman   (85) 248
   Silkwood   (84) 367
   Sophie's Choice   (83) 311
   Still of the Night   (83) 326
   Target   (86) 462
   Witness   (86) 421
SON HOANG BUI
   Table for Five   (84) 404
SONDERGAARD, GALE
   Echoes   (84) 483
   "Obituaries"   (86) 583
SONKKILA, PAUL
   Year of Living Dangerously, The
      [1982]   (84) 462
SONTAG, SUSAN
   Zelig   (84) 473
SOON-TECK, OH
   Missing in Action 2   (86) 452
SOPER, MARK
   World According to Garp, The   (83) 397
SORENSEN, LINDA
   Joshua Then and Now   (86) 198
SORINA, SVETLANA
   Waiting for Gavrilov [1982]   (84) 497
SORVIC, GEORGE
   Deathstalker   (85) 517
SORVINO, PAUL
   Reds   (82) 312
   Stuff, The   (86) 461
   That Championship Season   (83) 338
   Turk 182   (86) 464
SOUTENDIJK, RENÉE
   4th Man, The [1983]   (85) 203
   Girl with the Red Hair, The   (84) 485
   Out of Order   (86) 455
SOUTHAN, SUZY
   Stephen King's Children of the Corn   (85) 534
SPACEK, SISSY
   Marie   (86) 227
   Missing   (83) 232
   Raggedy Man   (82) 300
   River, The   (85) 416
SPACELY, JOHN
   Gringo   (86) 445
SPADARO, CLAUDIO
   Henry IV [1983]   (86) 446
SPADER, JAMES
   New Kids, The   (86) 454
   Tuff Turf   (86) 464
SPAETH, MERRIE
   World of Henry Orient, The [1964]   (84) 600
SPANO, VINCENT
   Alphabet City   (85) 509
   Baby, It's You   (84) 479
   Black Stallion Returns, The   (84) 479
   Creator   (86) 441

SPARKS, BILLY
  Purple Rain   (85) 389
SPEAR, BERNARD
  Wombling Free [1979]   (85) 538
SPEED, PAMELA
  Smithereens   (83) 307
SPELVIN, GEORGINA
  Police Academy   (85) 529
SPENCE, BRUCE
  Mad Max Beyond Thunderdome   (86) 223
  Road Warrior, The [1981]   (83) 277
  Where the Green Ants Dream [1984]   (86) 465
SPERBER, WENDIE JO
  Bachelor Party   (85) 511
  Back to the Future   (86) 65
  Moving Violations   (86) 453
SPIELBERG, DAVID
  War and Love   (86) 465
SPINDLER, WILL
  Sugarbaby   (86) 461
SPINER, BRENT
  Rent Control   (85) 530
SPINNELL, JOE
  Next Stop, Greenwich Village [1976]   (85) 592
SPINNEY, CAROLL
  Sesame Street Presents: Follow That Bird   (86)
  459
SPIRIDAKIS, TONY
  Death Wish III   (86) 441
SPRADLIN, G. D.
  Wrong Is Right   (83) 403
  Lords of Discipline, The   (84) 488
  Tank   (85) 535
SPRAGER, HART
  Nightmare on Elm Street, Part 2, A   (86) 454
SPRIGGS, ELIZABETH
  Richard's Things   (82) 321
SPRINGFIELD, RICK
  Hard to Hold   (85) 521
SQUIRE, RONALD
  My Cousin Rachel [1952]   (82) 458
STACK, ELIZABETH
  Rent Control   (85) 530
STACK, ROBERT
  Uncommon Valor   (84) 496
STACK, WILLIAM
  Becky Sharp [1935]   (82) 403
STADBAUER, HANS
  Sugarbaby   (86) 461
STADLEN, LEWIS J.
  Windy City   (85) 538
STAFFORD, JIM
  Kid Colter   (86) 449
STAIANO, TINA MARIE
  When Nature Calls   (86) 465
STALEY, JAMES
  American Dreamer   (85) 509
  Protocol   (85) 383
STALLONE, SYLVESTER
  First Blood   (83) 164
  Nighthawks   (82) 259
  Rambo: First Blood Part II   (86) 299
  Rhinestone   (85) 531
  Rocky III   (83) 283

Rocky IV   (86) 319
  Victory   (82) 374
STAMP, TERENCE
  Company of Wolves, The [1984]   (86) 115
  Hit, The   (86) 446
  Superman II   (82) 339
STANDER, LIONEL
  New York, New York [1977]   (84) 567
  Specter of the Rose [1946]   (83) 504
STANISLAW, JIRI
  Moonlighting   (83) 237
STANLEY, KIM
  Frances   (83) 178
  Right Stuff, The   (84) 302
STANLEY, REBECCA
  Body Double   (85) 513
STANTON, HARRY DEAN
  Bear, The   (85) 511
  Care Bears Movie, The   (86) 439
  Christine   (84) 106
  Escape from New York   (82) 133
  Fool for Love   (86) 172
  One from the Heart   (83) 250
  One Magic Christmas   (86) 455
  Paris, Texas   (85) 359
  Red Dawn   (85) 530
  Repo Man   (85) 408
  Young Doctors in Love   (83) 431
STANTON, JOHN
  Kitty and the Bagman [1982]   (84) 487
STANWYCK, BARBARA
  Miracle Woman, The [1931]   (83) 473
  My Reputation [1946]   (85) 586
STAPLETON, JEAN
  Bells Are Ringing [1960]   (84) 517
  Buddy System, The   (85) 514
STAPLETON, MAUREEN
  Cocoon   (86) 96
  Johnny Dangerously   (85) 524
  Reds   (82) 312
STARK, JONATHAN
  Fright Night   (86) 444
STARR, MIKE
  Berry Gordy's The Last Dragon   (86) 438
STARR, RINGO
  Give My Regards to Broad Street   (85) 520
STARRETT, JACK
  First Blood   (83) 164
STATLER, MARIAN
  King of Jazz [1930]   (86) 515
STEADMAN, ALISON
  Champions   (85) 515
  Kipperbang [1983]   (85) 524
  Private Function, A [1984]   (86) 280
STEENBURGEN, MARY
  Cross Creek   (84) 116
  Melvin and Howard [1980]   (82) 453
  Midsummer Night's Sex Comedy, A   (83)
  228
  One Magic Christmas   (86) 455
  Ragtime   (82) 304
  Romantic Comedy   (84) 492
  Time After Time [1979]   (84) 579
STEFANI, MICHAEL
  Trancers   (86) 463
STEFFEN, ANTHONY
  Savage Island   (86) 458

STEGERS, BERNICE
City of Women (82) 106
STEIGER, KLAUS
Boat Is Full, The [1981] (83) 82
STEIGER, RENATE
Boat Is Full, The [1981] (83) 82
STEIGER, ROD
Cattle Annie and Little Britches (82) 97
Chosen, The (83) 116
STEINER, JOHN
Hunters of the Golden Cobra, The [1982] (85) 523
Last Hunter, The (85) 525
Yor (84) 498
STEINER, SIGFRIT
Imperative [1982] (86) 447
Love in Germany, A [1983] (85) 283
STEINFELD, JAKE
Into the Night (86) 186
STENBORG, HELEN
Flash of Green, A (86) 443
STENGEL, LENI
Animal Kingdom, The [1932] 469
STEPHANO, TONY
TRON (83) 371
STEPHENSON, HENRY
Animal Kingdom, The [1932] (86) 469
STEPHENSON, PAMELA
Finders Keepers (85) 519
Scandalous (85) 532
Superman III (84) 399
STERLING, JAN
First Monday in October (82) 151
STERLING, PHILIP
Tomboy (86) 463
STERN, ADAM
Another State of Mind (85) 510
STERN, DANIEL
Blue Thunder (84) 84
C.H.U.D. (85) 515
Diner (83) 142
Get Crazy (84) 484
Honky Tonk Freeway (82) 199
Key Exchange (86) 448
Stardust Memories [1980] (85) 626
STERN, KIMBERLY
Rent Control (85) 530
STERN, MARK
Another State of Mind (85) 510
STERN, SHAWN
Another State of Mind (85) 510
STERNHAGEN, FRANCES
Outland (82) 272
STETTLER, CHARLES
Krush Groove (86) 449
STEVEN, MARGARET
Lonely Hearts [1982] (84) 212
STEVENS, ANDREW
Seduction, The (83) 427
10 to Midnight (84) 495
STEVENS, FISHER
Brother from Another Planet, The (85) 118
Flamingo Kid, The (85) 192
My Science Project (86) 453

STEVENS, K. T.
They're Playing with Fire (85) 536
STEVENS, LANDERS
Most Dangerous Game, The [1932] (86) 519
STEVENS, SARAH
Improper Channels (82) 218
STEVENS, SCOOTER
Better Off Dead (86) 438
STEVENS, WARREN
Barefoot Contessa, The [1954] (82) 399
STEVENSON, PARKER
Stitches (86) 461
Stroker Ace (84) 494
STEWART, ALEXANDRE
Bon Plaisir, Le [1983] (85) 513
STEWART, CATHERINE MARY
Last Starfighter, The (85) 277
Mischief (86) 452
Night of the Comet (85) 527
STEWART, DON
American Ninja (86) 436
STEWART, JAMES
Flight of the Phoenix, The [1966] (85) 549
STEWART, JOHN MICHAEL
Mike's Murder (85) 526
STEWART, PATRICK
Dune (85) 171
Lifeforce (86) 450
STEWART, PAUL
Tempest (83) 331
STIEFEL, ERNST
Boat Is Full, The [1981] (83) 82
STIERS, DAVID OGDEN
Better Off Dead (86) 438
Creator (86) 441
STILLER, JERRY
In Our Hands (84) 486
STING
Bride, The (86) 438
Brimstone and Treacle (83) 91
Bring on the Night (86) 439
Dune (85) 171
Plenty (86) 271
STOCK, NIGEL
Young Sherlock Holmes (86) 431
STOCKENSTROM, WILMA
Guest, The (85) 520
STOCKWELL, DEAN
Dune (85) 171
To Live and Die in L.A. (86) 379
Wrong Is Right (83) 403
STOCKWELL, JOHN
Christine (84) 106
City Limits (86) 440
Losin' It (84) 488
My Science Project (86) 453
Paris, Texas (85) 359
STOKEY, SUSAN
Power, The (85) 529
STOLTZ, ERIC
Mask (86) 231
Running Hot (85) 531
Surf II (85) 535
Wild Life, The (85) 538

PERFORMER INDEX

STOLZE, LENA
  White Rose, The   (84) 497
STONE, CHRISTOPHER
  Cujo   (84) 481
  Howling, The   (82) 207
STONE, DANTON
  Joy of Sex   (85) 524
  Maria's Lovers   (86) 451
STONE, DEE WALLACE
  Secret Admirer   (86) 459
STONE, PHILIP
  Indiana Jones and the Temple of
    Doom   (85) 253
STONE, SHARON
  King Solomon's Mines   (86) 449
STORCH, LARRY
  Sweet Sixteen   (85) 535
STOREY, RUTH
  Bells Are Ringing [1960]   (84) 517
STOVITZ, KEN
  Stitches   (86) 461
STRACK, GÜNTHER
  Torn Curtain [1966]   (85) 644
STRAIGHT, BEATRICE
  Poltergeist   (83) 263
  Two of a Kind   (84) 496
STRASBERG, SUSAN
  Sweet Sixteen   (85) 535
STRASSMAN, MARCIA
  Aviator, The   (86) 437
STRATAS, TERESA
  Traviata, La   (83) 366
STRATHAIRN, DAVID
  Brother from Another Planet, The   (85)
   118
  Return of the Secaucus 7 [1980]   (83)
   484
  Silkwood   (84) 367
  When Nature Calls   (86) 465
STRATTEN, DOROTHY
  They All Laughed   (82) 350
STRAUSS, PETER
  Secret of NIMH, The   (83) 288
  Spacehunter   (84) 493
STREEP, MERYL
  Falling in Love   (85) 519
  French Lieutenant's Woman, The   (82) 174
  In Our Hands   (84) 486
  Out of Africa   (86) 255
  Plenty   (86) 271
  Silkwood   (84) 367
  Sophie's Choice   (83) 311
  Still of the Night   (83) 326
STREET, RACHEL
  Twice in a Lifetime   (86) 397
STREISAND, BARBRA
  Way We Were, The [1973]   (82) 474
  Yentl   (84) 468
STRICKLAND, GAIL
  Oxford Blues   (85) 528
  Protocol   (85) 383
STRICKLER, DAN
  Cold Feet   (85) 516
STRIEBECK, JOCHEN
  Sheer Madness [1983]   (86) 459

STRIEBECK, PETER
  Sheer Madness [1983]   (86) 459
STRODE, WOODY
  Cotton Club, The   (85) 150
  Lust in the Dust   (86) 450
STRONACH, TAMI
  Neverending Story, The   (85) 527
STRONG, PHILLIP
  Color Purple, The   (86) 105
STROUD, DON
  Sweet Sixteen   (85) 535
STROUD, DUKE
  Fleshburn   (85) 519
STRUDWICK, SHEPPERD
  "Obituaries"   (84) 638
STRYKER, AMY
  Impulse   (85) 523
STUART, BARBARA
  Bachelor Party   (85) 511
STUART, CASSIE
  Ordeal by Innocence [1984]   (86) 455
  Secret Places [1984]   (86) 459
STUART, FREDDIE
  Hit, The   (86) 446
STUYCK, JORIS
  Razor's Edge, The   (85) 402
  Shooting Party, The [1984]   (86) 344
SUCHET, DAVID
  Falcon and the Snowman, The   (86) 165
  Little Drummer Girl, The   (85) 525
  Missionary, The   (83) 233
  Trenchcoat   (84) 496
SUGIMURA, HARUKO
  Late Chrysanthemums [1954]   (86) 449
SUKOWA, BARBARA
  Berlin Alexanderplatz [1980]   (84) 57
  Lola [1981]   (83) 215
SULLIVAN, JEREMIAH
  Soldier, The   (83) 428
SULLIVAN, SEAN
  Mrs. Soffel   (85) 314
SUMMERALL, KITTY
  Smithereens   (83) 307
SUMMERVILLE, SLIM
  Beloved Rogue [1927]   (84) 522
  King of Jazz [1930]   (86) 515
SUNDIN, MICHAEL
  Return to Oz   (86) 458
SUSKA, ALMANTA
  Hunters of the Golden Cobra, The [1982]   (85)
   523
SUTHERLAND, DONALD
  Crackers   (85) 516
  Eye of the Needle   (82) 148
  Heaven Help Us   (86) 445
  Max Dugan Returns   (84) 228
  Ordeal by Innocence [1984]   (86) 455
  Revolution   (86) 458
  Threshold   (84) 495
SUTHERLAND, JOHN
  Bambi [1942]   (85) 543
SUTHERLAND, KIEFER
  Bad Boy, The   (86) 437
SUTORIUS, JAMES
  Windy City   (85) 538

199

SUTTON, DUDLEY
  Brimstone and Treacle   (83) 91
SUTTON, JOHN
  My Cousin Rachel [1952]   (82) 458
SUZMAN, JANET
  And the Ship Sails On [1983]   (85) 69
  Draughtsman's Contract, The
    [1982]   (84) 126
  Priest of Love   (82) 288
SUZUKI, HIROSHI
  Late Chrysanthemums [1954]   (86) 449
SWAIN, MACK
  Beloved Rogue [1927]   (84) 522
SWANSON, GARY
  Vice Squad   (83) 430
SWANSON, GLORIA
  "Obituaries"   (84) 638
SWAYZE, PATRICK
  Grandview, U.S.A.   (85) 520
  Outsiders, The   (84) 282
  Red Dawn   (85) 530
SWEET, DOLPH
  "Obituaries"   (86) 584
SWIFT, CLIVE
  Passage to India, A   (85) 365
SWIT, LORETTA
  S.O.B.   (82) 328
SYDOW, MAX VON
  Conan the Barbarian   (83) 419
  Dreamscape   (85) 166
  Strange Brew   (84) 494
  Victory   (82) 374
SYLVESTER, HAROLD
  Vision Quest   (86) 464
SYMONDS, ROBERT
  Micki & Maude   (85) 308
SYMS, SYLVIA
  Victim [1961]   (85) 649
SZABO, ALBERT
  Lovelines   (85) 525
SZABO, BERNARD
  Cheech and Chong's The Corsican
    Brothers   (85) 515
SZABO, LAZLO
  Passion [1982]   (84) 289
SZARABAJKA, KEITH
  Marie   (86) 227
  Protocol   (85) 383
SZLASA, RICHARD E.
  Firstborn   (85) 519

TABLIAN, VIC
  Raiders of the Lost Ark   (82) 308
TABOURIN, BEATRICE
  Argent, L' [1983]   (85) 74
TAGOE, EDDIE
  Baby   (86) 437
  Top Secret   (85) 536
TAIMAK
  Berry Gordy's The Last Dragon   (86) 438
TAIT, PETER
  Wild Horses [1983]   (85) 538
TAKAKURA, KEN
  Antarctica   (85) 511

TAKAMINE, HIDEKO
  Flowing [1956]   (86) 444
TAKEI, GEORGE
  Star Trek II—The Wrath of Khan   (83)
    321
  Star Trek III—The Search for
    Spock   (85) 439
TAKESHI
  Merry Christmas, Mr. Lawrence   (84) 231
TAKUMA, SHIN
  Godzilla 1985   (86) 444
TALBERT, PIERRE
  Good Bye Cruel World   (85) 520
TALBOT, NITA
  Fraternity Vacation   (86) 444
  Movers and Shakers   (86) 453
TALKING HEADS
  Stop Making Sense   (85) 534
TALMADGE, CONSTANCE
  Dulcy [1923]   (82) 432
TALMADGE, RICHARD
  "Obituaries"   (82) 503
TAMBOR, JEFFREY
  Man Who Wasn't There, The   (84) 489
  No Small Affair   (85) 527
TANAKA, KEN
  Godzilla 1985   (86) 444
TANAKA, KINUYO
  Flowing [1956]   (86) 444
TANAKA, SHINJI
  Cruel Story of Youth [1960]   (85) 517
TANAKA, TORU
  Chattanooga Choo Choo   (85) 515
  Pee-wee's Big Adventure   (86) 265
TANDY, JESSICA
  Best Friends   (83) 68
  Bostonians, The   (85) 105
  Cocoon   (86) 96
  Honky Tonk Freeway   (82) 199
  Still of the Night   (83) 326
  World According to Garp, The   (83) 397
TANNER, CECILE
  Every Man for Himself [1979]   (82) 139
TANUGI, SASKIA COHEN
  Never Say Never Again   (84) 252
TAPLEY, COLIN
  Becky Sharp [1935]   (82) 403
TARITA
  Mutiny on the Bounty [1962]   (85) 581
TARKOWSKI, MICHAL
  Man of Marble [1977]   (82) 234
TARPEY, TOM
  Lost in America   (86) 219
TARSES, JAY
  Teen Wolf   (86) 462
TARSO, IGNACIO LOPEZ
  Under the Volcano   (85) 499
TASH, STEVEN
  Christine   (84) 106
TATE, JACK
  Hard Traveling   (86) 445
TATI, JACQUES
  "Obituaries"   (83) 552

PERFORMER INDEX

TAUBER, BERND
  Boot, Das [1981]   (83) 86
TAYLOR, CLARICE
  Play Misty for Me [1971]   (86) 532
TAYLOR, GWEN
  Richard's Things   (82) 321
TAYLOR, HOLLAND
  Jewel of the Nile, The   (86) 448
  Romancing the Stone   (85) 421
TAYLOR, JOSEPH
  James Joyce's Women   (86) 193
TAYLOR, JOSH
  Waltz Across Texas   (84) 497
TAYLOR, KENT
  I'm No Angel [1933]   (85) 561
TAYLOR, KIRK
  Death Wish III   (86) 441
TAYLOR, LISA
  Windy City   (85) 538
TAYLOR, MARCIA
  Hard Traveling   (86) 445
TAYLOR, ROBERT
  Beat Street   (85) 512
TAYLOR, ROD
  Time Machine, The [1960]   (84) 585
TAYLOR, RUTH
  "Obituaries"   (85) 695
TAYLOR, SUZETTE
  American Taboo   (85) 509
TAYLOR, TAMMY
  Lovelines   (85) 525
  Meatballs Part II   (85) 526
TAYLOR, VAUGHN
  Cowboy [1958]   (82) 417
TAYLOR, VIDA
  Clash of the Titans   (82) 111
TAYLOR-YOUNG, LEIGH
  Secret Admirer   (86) 459
TAZAKI, JUN
  Ran   (86) 304
TEEFY, MAUREEN
  Supergirl   (85) 535
TEKA, TUI
  Nate and Hayes   (84) 236
TEMPLE, SHIRLEY
  Fort Apache [1948]   (84) 530
TENNANT, VICTORIA
  All of Me   (85) 58
  Holcroft Covenant, The   (86) 446
  Stranger's Kiss   (85) 534
TEPPER, WILLIAM
  Bachelor Party   (85) 511
  Breathless   (84) 89
TERAO, AKIRA
  Ran   (86) 304
TERRENCE, HAL
  Kid Colter   (86) 449
TERRENO, PATRIZIA
  Nostalgia [1983]   (85) 340
TERRY, JOE MICHAEL
  Missing in Action 2   (86) 452
TERRY, JOHN
  Wild Geese II   (86) 466

TERRY, NIGEL
  Excalibur   (82) 144
  Sylvia   (86) 462
TERRY-THOMAS
  Hound of the Baskervilles, The
    [1978]   (82) 203
TERZIEFF, LAURENT
  Detective   (86) 442
THALBACH, KATHARINE
  Sophie's Choice   (83) 311
THAMES, BYRON
  Blame It on the Night   (85) 512
THATCHER, TORIN
  Snows of Kilimanjaro, The [1952]   (83) 498
THATE, HILMAR
  Veronika Voss   (83) 382
  World of Henry Orient, The [1964]   (84)
    600
THEISMAN, JOE
  Cannonball Run II   (85) 514
THELEN, JODI
  Four Friends   (82) 167
THEOBALD, GEORGE
  Hotdog . . . The Movie   (85) 522
THIAKA, JOSEPH
  Out of Africa   (86) 255
THOMAS, CARMEN
  Bear, The   (85) 511
THOMAS, DAVE
  Sesame Street Presents: Follow That Bird   (86)
    459
  Strange Brew   (84) 494
THOMAS, HENRY
  Cloak and Dagger   (85) 516
  E.T.: The Extra-Terrestrial   (83) 151
  Misunderstood   (85) 526
  Raggedy Man   (82) 300
THOMAS, ISA
  Flash of Green, A   (86) 443
THOMAS, KURT
  Gymkata   (86) 445
THOMAS, RON
  Karate Kid, The   (85) 264
THOMAS, TREVOR
  Sheena   (85) 532
THOMERSON, TIM
  Metalstorm   (84) 45
  Rhinestone   (85) 531
  Trancers   (86) 463
  Volunteers   (86) 464
THOMPSON, CINDY ANN
  Cave Girl   (86) 439
THOMPSON, DEREK
  Long Good Friday, The [1980]   (83) 220
  Wild Geese II   (86) 466
THOMPSON, FRED
  Marie   (86) 227
THOMPSON, JACK
  Caddie [1976]   (83) 439
  Earthling, The [1980]   (82) 130
  Flesh and Blood   (86) 443
  Merry Christmas, Mr. Lawrence   (84)
    231
THOMPSON, LEA
  All the Right Moves   (84) 41

Back to the Future   (86) 65
Red Dawn   (85) 530
Wild Life, The   (85) 538
THOMPSON, RON
American Pop   (82) 62
THOMPSON, T. J.
Hard Traveling   (86) 445
THOMSON, R. H.
If You Could See What I Hear   (83) 423
THOMSON, SCOTT
Police Academy   (85) 529
THORPE, GORDON
Bridge of San Luis Rey, The [1929]   (82)
  408
THORSON, LINDA
Curtains   (84) 481
Flanagan   (86) 443
Joey   (86) 448
THRING, FRANK
Mad Max Beyond Thunderdome   (86) 223
THULIN, INGRID
After the Rehearsal   (85) 52
THURMAN, BILL
Alamo Bay   (86) 436
Raggedy Man   (82) 300
THYS, MICHAEL
Gods Must Be Crazy, The [1980]   (85) 224
TICOTIN, RACHEL
Fort Apache, the Bronx   (82) 159
TIDELIUS, KERSTIN
Fanny and Alexander [1982]   (84) 146
TIERNEY, LAWRENCE
Stephen King's Silver Bullet   (86) 460
TIGAR, KENNETH
Creator   (86) 441
Just One of the Guys   (86) 448
TILER, SCOTT
Once upon a Time in America   (85) 345
TILLIS, MEL
Cannonball Run II   (85) 514
TILLY, GRANT
Beyond Reasonable Doubt [1980]   (84) 74
Nate and Hayes   (84) 236
TILLY, JENNIFER
Moving Violations   (86) 453
No Small Affair   (85) 527
TILLY, MEG
Agnes of God   (86) 56
Big Chill, The   (84) 78
Impulse   (85) 523
"Interview with Miloš Forman, An"   (86) 26
Psycho II   (84) 307
Tex   (83) 335
TINGWELL, CHARLES
My First Wife   (86) 453
TINTI, GABRIELE
Flight of the Phoenix, The [1966]   (85) 549
TIRELLI, JAMIE
Brother from Another Planet, The   (85)
  118
Sudden Death   (86) 461
TOBIN, DAN
"Obituaries"   (83) 553
TOBIN, VIVIAN
Sign of the Cross, The [1932]   (85) 607

TOBOLOWSKY, STEPHEN
Philadelphia Experiment, The   (85) 529
TOBY, DOUG
Red Dawn   (85) 530
TOCHI, BRIAN
Stitches   (86) 461
TODD, ANN
Sound Barrier, The [1952]   (85) 621
TODD, HALLIE
Sam's Son   (85) 531
TODD, RUSSELL
Where the Boys Are '84   (85) 537
TODOROVIC, BORA
Montenegro   (82) 250
TOGNAZZI, RICARDO
Tragedy of a Ridiculous Man [1981]   (83)
  361
TOGNAZZI, UGO
Joke of Destiny, A [1983]   (85) 259
Tragedy of a Ridiculous Man
  [1981]   (83) 361
TOIGO, TERESA
Stephen King's Children of the Corn   (85) 534
TOL, HENRIETTE
Question of Silence, A   (85) 530
TOLAN, RICHARD
Secrets   (85) 532
TOLER, SIDNEY
Our Relations [1936]   (86) 523
TOLKAN, JAMES
Iceman   (85) 248
Prince of the City   (82) 292
TOLL, BETSY
Love Letters   (85) 288
TOMASINA, JEANA
Beach Girls, The   (83) 417
TOMELTY, FRANCES
Bullshot [1983]   (86) 439
TOMELTY, JOSEPH
Sound Barrier, The [1952]   (85) 621
TOMLIN, LILY
All of Me   (85) 58
TOMLINSON, DAVID
Wombling Free [1979]   (85) 538
TOMMY ATKINS SEXTETTE
King of Jazz [1930]   (86) 515
TONSBERG, ADAM
Zappa   (85) 539
TOOKER, WILLIAM H.
Scarlet Letter, The [1927]   (85) 602
TOPAZ, DAVID
Goodbye, New York   (86) 444
TOPOL
For Your Eyes Only   (82) 155
TORGOV, SARAH
If You Could See What I Hear   (83) 423
TORJEMANN, BOAZ
Drifting   (85) 518
TORN, RIP
Beastmaster, The   (83) 418
City Heat   (85) 141
Cross Creek   (84) 116
Flashpoint   (85) 519
Heartland   (82) 191

Jinxed (83) 206
Man Who Fell to Earth, The [1975] (83) 469
Misunderstood (85) 526
Songwriter (85) 533
Stranger Is Watching, A (83) 429
Summer Rental (86) 462
TORNADO, TONY
Pixote [1980] (82) 280
TORRENCE, DAVID
Disraeli [1929] (82) 426
Sherlock Holmes [1922] (83) 494
TORRENCE, ERNEST
Bridge of San Luis Rey, The [1929] (82) 408
TORRENS, PIP
Oxford Blues (85) 528
TORRES, FERNANDO
Kiss of the Spider Woman (86) 209
TORRES, RAQUEL
Bridge of San Luis Rey, The [1929] (82) 408
TORTI, ROBERT
Alley Cat (85) 509
TOTEN, STACEY
Lovelines (85) 525
TOTY, MICHEL
Bal, Le [1983] (85) 80
TOULIATOS, GEORGE
Heartaches [1981] (83) 197
TOUMANOVA, TAMARA
Invitation to the Dance [1956] (86) 507
Torn Curtain [1966] (85) 644
TOURANGEAU, JACQUES
Agnes of God (86) 56
TOUZIE, HOOSHANG
Mission, The (84) 489
TOWERS, CONSTANCE
Sylvester (86) 462
TOWNSEND, BUD
Always (86) 60
TOWNSEND, PATRICE
Always (86) 60
TOWNSEND, ROBERT
American Flyers (86) 436
TRACY, SPENCER
Guy Named Joe, A [1943] (82) 435
TRAINOR, MARY ELLEN
Romancing the Stone (85) 421
Stone Boy, The (85) 450
TRASK, KATHRYN
Hard Traveling (86) 445
TRAUB, AMI
Drifting (85) 518
TRAVOLTA, JOHN
Blow Out (82) 83
Perfect (86) 456
Staying Alive (84) 386
Two of a Kind (84) 496
TREJAN, GUY
Piaf [1980] (83) 427
TREMAYNE, LES
Starchaser (86) 460
TRESS, DAVID
Missing in Action (85) 526

TREVOR, CLAIRE
Kiss Me Goodbye (83) 209
TRIESTE, LEOPOLDO
Henry IV [1983] (86) 446
TRINTIGNANT, JEAN-LOUIS
Bon Plaisir, Le [1983] (85) 513
Confidentially Yours [1983] (85) 516
Nuit de Varennes, La [1982] (84) 270
Under Fire (84) 441
TRIPPET, WAYNE
Taps (82) 343
TRISKA, JAN
Unfaithfully Yours (85) 537
TRISSENAAR, ELISABETH
Berlin Alexanderplatz [1980] (84) 57
Love in Germany, A [1983] (85) 283
TROLLEY, LEONARD
Amin—The Rise and Fall (84) 479
TRONCZAK, BERNARD
Loulou [1980] (82) 226
TROTT, KAREN
Return of the Secaucus 7 [1980] (83) 484
TROTTER, KATE
Joshua Then and Now (86) 198
TROY, HECTOR
Muppets Take Manhattan, The (85) 526
TROYER, DEBRA
Philadelphia Experiment, The (85) 529
TRUEMAN, PAULA
Grace Quigley (86) 444
Mrs. Soffel (85) 314
TRUMAN, JEFF
Wild Duck, The [1983] (86) 466
TRUMBULL, ROBERT
Sudden Death (86) 461
TRYON, GLENN
King of Jazz [1930] (86) 515
TSIGONOFF, MILLIE
Angelo My Love (84) 47
TSIGONOFF, STEVE "PATALAY"
Angelo My Love (84) 47
TSIPLAKOVA, ELENA
Jazzman (85) 523
TSUMURA, TAKASHI
MacArthur's Children (86) 451
TUBB, ERNEST
"Obituaries" (85) 696
TUCKER, MICHAEL
Diner (83) 142
TUERPE, PAUL
Ladyhawke (86) 214
TUINMAN, PETER
Girl with the Red Hair, The (84) 485
TUKER, ULRICH
White Rose, The (84) 497
TULLEY, PAUL
Joy of Sex (85) 524
TULLY, TOM
"Obituaries" (83) 553
TURCKHEIM, CHARLOTTE DE
Edith and Marcel [1983] (85) 518
My Other Husband (86) 453
TURKEL, JOE
Blade Runner (83) 76

TURKEN, GRETA
Sophie's Choice (83) 311
TURMAN, GLYNN
Gremlins (85) 230
TURNER, GERALDINE
Careful He Might Hear You [1983] (85) 130
TURNER, IKE
Taking Off [1971] (86) 545
TURNER, JIM
Kid Colter (86) 449
TURNER, KATHLEEN
Body Heat (82) 87
Crimes of Passion (85) 161
Jewel of the Nile, The (86) 448
Man with Two Brains, The (84) 223
Prizzi's Honor (86) 285
Romancing the Stone (85) 421
TURNER, PATRICK
Kerouac, the Movie (86) 448
TURNER, TINA
Mad Max Beyond Thunderdome (86) 223
Taking Off [1971] (86) 545
TURTURRO, JOHN
To Live and Die in L.A. (86) 379
TUTIN, DOROTHY
Shooting Party, The [1984] (86) 344
TUTTLE, LURENE
Testament (84) 420
TWEED, SHANNON
Hotdog . . . The Movie (85) 522
TWIGGY
Doctor and the Devils, The (86) 442
TWINKIE CLARK AND THE CLARK SISTERS
Gospel (85) 520
TYRELL, SUSAN
Angel (85) 510
Avenging Angel (86) 436
Fire and Ice (84) 153
Flesh and Blood (86) 443
Tales of Ordinary Madness (84) 495

UDVAROS, DOROTTYA
Colonel Redl [1984] (86) 100
UDY, CLAUDIAL
Out of Control (86) 455
UEHARA, KEN
Late Chrysanthemums [1954] (86) 449
UEKI, HITOSHI
Ran (86) 304
ULACI, RICHARD
Mixed Blood (86) 452
ULLMAN, TRACEY
Give My Regards to Broad Street (85) 520
Plenty (86) 271
ULLMANN, LIV
Bad Boy, The (86) 437
Dangerous Moves [1984] (86) 129
Richard's Things (82) 321
Wild Duck, The [1983] (86) 466
UMBERS, MARGARET
Smash Palace [1981] (83) 302
UNDERWOOD, BLAIR
Krush Groove (86) 449
URALOV, LUCY
My First Wife (86) 453

URICH, ROBERT
Endangered Species (83) 420
Ice Pirates, The (85) 523
Turk 182 (86) 464
URQUHART, ROBERT
Kipperbang [1983] (85) 524
URSITTI, SUSAN
Teen Wolf (86) 462
USTINOV, PETER
Evil Under the Sun [1981] (83) 421
USZTICS, MATYAS
Brady's Escape (85) 514

VACCARO, BRENDA
Supergirl (85) 535
VADIM, CHRISTIAN
Full Moon in Paris (85) 208
VALARDY, ANDRE
Goat, The [1981] (86) 444
VALDEZ, DANIEL
Zoot Suit (82) 389
VALDEZ, SOCORRO
Paris, Texas (85) 359
VALEN, NANCY
Heavenly Kid, The (86) 445
VALENTIN, BARBARA
Berlin Alexanderplatz [1980] (84) 57
VALENZA, TASIA
Rappin' (86) 457
VALLI, ALIDA
Oedipus Rex [1967] (85) 528
VANCE, MARC
Hotdog . . . The Movie (85) 522
VAN CLEEF, LEE
Escape from New York (82) 133
VAN DAELE, EDMOND
Napoleon [1927] (82) 461
VAN DAM, GWEN
True Confessions (82) 368
VANDENBURGH, CRAIG
Broadway Danny Rose (85) 112
VAN DEN ELSEN, SYLVIE
Argent, L' [1983] (85) 74
VAN DER GROEN, DORA
Flaxfield, The [1983] (86) 443
VAN DER VELDE, NADINE
Moving Violations (86) 453
VAN DOHLEN, LENNY
Electric Dreams (85) 518
VANEAU, YARA
Emerald Forest, The (86) 156
VANECK, PIERRE
Erendira [1983] (85) 181
VANEL, CHARLES
Three Brothers [1980] (83) 349
VAN EMAN, CHARLES
Joy of Sex (85) 524
VAN HOFFMAN, BRANT
Police Academy (85) 529
Rustler's Rhapsody (86) 458
VAN HOOL, ROGER
Woman Next Door, The (82) 385

VAN IN'T VELD, HANS
Cheech and Chong Still Smokin' (84) 480
VANITY
Berry Gordy's The Last Dragon (86) 438
VAN J. HERWIJEN, CAROL
Cheech and Chong Still Smokin' (84) 480
VAN NORDEN, PETER
Hard to Hold (85) 521
Police Academy 2 (86) 276
VAN NUYS, ED
Silent Madness (85) 532
VAN PALLANDT, NINA
Cutter's Way (82) 364
VAN PATTEN, JOYCE
St. Elmo's Fire (86) 330
VAN PATTEN, TIMOTHY
Class of 1984 (83) 419
VAN PEEBLES, MARIO
Rappin' (86) 457
VAN SAMBEEK, RENE
Flaxfield, The [1983] (86) 443
VAN SPEYBROECK, MICHEL
Bal, Le [1983] (85) 80
VAN VALKENBURGH, DEBORAH
Streets of Fire (85) 534
VARNADO, DEBRA
Fast Forward (86) 442
VASCONCELLOS, ANSELMO
Bar Esperanza [1983] (86) 437
VASQUEZ, JOSE-LUIS LOPEZ
Heat of Desire [1981] (85) 522
VAUGHAN, MARTIN
Phar Lap (85) 528
We of the Never Never [1982] (84) 497
VAUGHAN, PETER
Brazil (86) 80
Time Bandits [1980] (82) 364
VAUGHN, ROBERT
S.O.B. (82) 399
VAVITCH, MICHAEL
Bridge of San Luis Rey, The [1929] (82) 408
VEERMAN, HANS
Flesh and Blood (86) 443
VEGA, ISELA
Barbarosa (83) 60
VEIDT, CONRAD
Beloved Rogue [1927] (84) 522
VELEZ, EDDIE
Repo Man (85) 408
VENANTINI, VENANTINO
Ladyhawke (86) 214
VENORA, DIANE
Wolfen (82) 382
VENTURA, LINO
Garde à vue [1981] (83) 189
VENTURE, RICHARD
Missing (83) 232
VENTURINI, MARK
Return of the Living Dead, The (86) 314
VERA-ELLEN
"Obituaries" (82) 504

VERDON, GWEN
Cocoon (86) 96
Cotton Club, The (85) 150
VERDONE, CARLO
Water and Soap (86) 465
VERITE, DANIEL
Patsy, The (86) 456
VERNAC, DENISE
"Obituaries" (85) 697
VERNETTE, TEVAITE
Bounty, The (85) 513
VERNON, JOHN
Chained Heat (84) 480
Curtains (84) 481
Fraternity Vacation (86) 444
VERNON, KATE
Alphabet City (85) 509
VERUSCHKA
Bride, The (86) 438
VERWEY, LOUW
Gods Must Be Crazy, The [1980] (85) 224
VIAL, PIERRE
Dangerous Moves [1984] (86) 129
VICK, JOHN ALLEN
Hard Traveling (86) 445
VICTOR, HENRY
Beloved Rogue [1927] (84) 522
VICTORIA, S. P.
Caged Fury (85) 514
VICTORY, FIONA
Champions (85) 515
Return to Oz (86) 458
VIDOR, KING
"Interview with Lillian Gish, An" (83) 27
VIGO, ULRIKE
Lola [1981] (83) 215
VIGODA, ABE
Cannonball Run II (85) 514
VILLAFANE, CHUNCHUNA
Official Story, The (86) 249
VILLALPANDO, DAVID
Norte, El (84) 265
VILLARD, TOM
Surf II (85) 535
VILLERET, JACQUES
Edith and Marcel [1983] (85) 518
VILLIERS, CHRISTOPHER
Top Secret (85) 536
VILLIERS, JAMES
Under the Volcano (85) 499
VILLIERS, MAVIS
Victim [1961] (85) 649
VINANTINI, VENANTINO
Hercules II (86) 446
VINE, JOHN
Richard's Things (82) 321
VING, LEE
Clue (86) 440
Streets of Fire (85) 534
Wild Life, The (85) 538
VINT, JESSE
Forbidden World (83) 421
VIRGAN, HERB
Starchaser (86) 460

VITALI, KEITH
Revenge of the Ninja   (84) 492

VITOLD, MICHEL
Basileus Quartet   (85) 511
Nuit de Varennes, La [1982]   (84) 270

VITTE, RAYMOND
"Obituaries"   (84) 640

VIVA
State of Things, The   (84) 379

VIVIANI, SONIA
Hercules II   (86) 446

VOGT, PETER
Hotdog . . . The Movie   (85) 522

VOIGHT, JON
Lookin' to Get Out   (83) 425
Runaway Train   (86) 324
Table for Five   (84) 404

VOLONTÉ, GIAN-MARIA
Death of Mario Ricci, The [1983]   (86) 133

VOLZ, NEDRA
Lust in the Dust   (86) 450
Moving Violations   (86) 453

VONDOHLEN, LENNY
Tender Mercies   (84) 409

VON SEYFFERTITZ, GUSTAV
Sherlock Holmes [1922]   (83) 494

VON STROHEIM, ERICH
North Star, The [1943]   (83) 476

VORSTER, GORDON
Guest, The   (85) 520

VOYAGIS, YORGO
Little Drummer Girl, The   (85) 525

VOZOFF, LORINNE
Impulse   (85) 523

VUJISIC, PAVLE
When Father Was Away on Business [1984]   (86)
411

WACKERNAGEL, ERIKA
Love in Germany, A [1983]   (85) 283

WAGGNER, GEORGE
"Obituaries"   (85) 697

WAGGONER, LYLE
Surf II   (85) 535

WAGNER, DANNY
Silent Night, Deadly Night   (85) 532

WAGNER, LINDSAY
Nighthawks   (82) 259

WAGNER, ROBERT
Curse of the Pink Panther   (84) 481

WAHL, KEN
Fort Apache, the Bronx   (82) 159
Jinxed   (83) 206
Purple Hearts   (85) 529
Soldier, The   (83) 428

WAINWRIGHT, JAMES
Battletruck   (83) 417
Survivors, The   (84) 495

WAINWRIGHT, RUPERT
Dreamchild   (86) 146

WAITES, THOMAS
Thing, The   (83) 343

WAITS, TOM
Cotton Club, The   (85) 150
Outsiders, The   (84) 282

WAKELY, JIMMY
"Obituaries"   (83) 554

WALCUTT, JOHN
Sam's Son   (85) 531

WALDO, KIP
Hardbodies   (85) 521

WALENTYNOWICZ, ANNA
Man of Iron   (82) 230

WALESA, LECH
Man of Iron   (82) 230

WALKEN, CHRISTOPHER
Brainstorm   (84) 480
Dead Zone, The   (84) 481
Heaven's Gate   (82) 276
Next Stop, Greenwich Village [1976]   (85) 592
View to a Kill, A   (86) 402

WALKER, HARRIET
Turtle Diary   (86) 464

WALKER, KATHRYN
D.A.R.Y.L.   (86) 441
Slap Shot [1977]   (82) 467

WALKER, TIPPY
World of Henry Orient, The [1964]   (84) 600

WALKER, WALTER
I'm No Angel [1933]   (85) 561

WALKER, ZENA
Dresser, The   (84) 130

WALL, MAX
Hound of the Baskervilles, The
[1978]   (82) 203

WALLACE, ANZAC
Utu [1983]   (85) 504

WALLACE, DAVID
Humongous   (83) 423

WALLACE, DEE
Cujo   (84) 481
E.T.: The Extra-Terrestrial   (83) 151
Howling, The   (82) 207
Jimmy the Kid   (84) 486

WALLACE, IAN
Plenty   (86) 271

WALLACE, LEE
War and Love   (86) 465

WALLACE, SUE
Experience Preferred ... but Not Essential
[1982]   (84) 141

WALLACH, ELI
Sam's Son   (85) 531

WALLGREN, PERNILLA
Fanny and Alexander [1982]   (84) 146

WALSCH, JOHN
Def-Con 4   (86) 441

WALSH, GEORGE
"Obituaries"   (82) 505

WALSH, M. EMMET
Blade Runner   (83) 76
Blood Simple   (86) 438
Cannery Row   (83) 95
Missing in Action   (85) 526
Pope of Greenwich Village, The   (85) 529
Scandalous   (85) 532

WALSH, SYDNEY
Nightmare on Elm Street, Part 2, A   (86) 454

WALSTON, RAY
Fast Times at Ridgemont High   (83) 156

WALTER HAWKINS AND THE HAWKINS
    FAMILY WITH THE LOVE CENTER CHOIR
  Gospel   (85) 520
WALTER, JESSICA
  Flamingo Kid, The   (85) 192
  Play Misty for Me [1971]   (86) 532
WALTER, TRACEY
  Conan the Destroyer   (85) 516
  Raggedy Man   (82) 300
  Repo Man   (85) 408
WALTERS, CHARLES
  "Obituaries"   (83) 554
WALTERS, JULIE
  Educating Rita   (84) 136
WALTERS, THORLEY
  Little Drummer Girl, The   (85) 525
WALTHALL, HENRY B.
  Bridge of San Luis Rey, The [1929]   (82)
    408
  Scarlet Letter, The [1927]   (85) 602
WALZ, MARTIN
  Boat Is Full, The [1981]   (83) 82
WANAMAKER, SAM
  Aviator, The   (86) 437
  Irreconcilable Differences   (85) 523
WARBECK, DAVID
  Black Cat, The   (85) 512
  Hunters of the Golden Cobra, The [1982]   (85)
    523
  Last Hunter, The   (85) 525
WARBURTON, JOHN
  "Obituaries"   (82) 505
WARD, BRENDAN
  Taps   (82) 343
WARD, FRED
  Remo Williams   (86) 457
  Right Stuff, The   (84) 342
  Secret Admirer   (86) 459
  Silkwood   (84) 367
  Southern Comfort   (82) 332
  Swing Shift   (85) 535
  Timerider   (84) 495
  Uncommon Valor   (84) 496
WARD, GREG
  Kid Colter   (86) 449
WARD, RACHEL
  Against All Odds   (85) 509
  Dead Men Don't Wear Plaid   (83) 134
  Sharky's Machine   (82) 324
WARD, SANDY
  Police Academy 2   (86) 276
  Tank   (85) 535
WARD, SELA
  Rustler's Rhapsody   (86) 458
WARD, SIMON
  Supergirl   (85) 535
WARD, SOPHIE
  Return to Oz   (86) 458
  Young Sherlock Holmes   (86) 431
WARDEN, JACK
  Aviator, The   (86) 437
  Crackers   (85) 516
  Great Muppet Caper, The   (82) 187
  Verdict, The   (83) 377
WARE, HERTA
  Cocoon   (86) 96

WARHIT, DOUGLAS
  Toy Soldiers   (85) 536
WARING, FRED
  "Obituaries"   (85) 698
WARNER, DAVID
  Company of Wolves, The [1984]   (86) 115
  Man with Two Brains, The   (84) 223
  Time After Time [1979]   (84) 579
  Time Bandits [1980]   (82) 364
  TRON   (83) 371
WARNER, JACK
  "Obituaries"   (82) 505
WARNER, MICHAEL
  Kerouac, the Movie   (86) 448
WARNOCK, CRAIG
  Time Bandits [1980]   (82) 364
WARREN, JENNIFER
  Slap Shot [1977]   (82) 467
WARREN, LESLEY ANN
  Choose Me   (85) 135
  Clue   (86) 440
  Night in Heaven, A   (84) 490
  Songwriter   (85) 533
  Victor / Victoria   (83) 387
WARREN, RUTH
  Our Relations [1936]   (86) 523
WARRICK, RUTH
  Journey into Fear [1943]   (86) 511
WARTHA, NORBERT
  Céleste [1981]   (83) 104
WASHINGTON, DENZEL
  Soldier's Story, A   (85) 427
WASS, TED
  Curse of the Pink Panther   (84) 481
  Oh God, You Devil   (85) 528
  Sheena   (85) 532
WASSON, CRAIG
  Body Double   (85) 513
  Four Friends   (82) 167
  Ghost Story   (82) 183
  Second Thoughts   (84) 493
WATANABA, FUMIO
  Cruel Story of Youth [1960]   (85) 517
WATANABE, GEDDE
  Sixteen Candles   (85) 532
  Volunteers   (86) 464
WATANABE, KEN
  MacArthur's Children   (86) 451
WATASE, TSUNEHIKO
  Antarctica   (85) 511
WATERBURY, LAURA
  Better Off Dead   (86) 438
WATERS, HARRY, JR.
  Back to the Future   (86) 65
WATERSTON, SAM
  Heaven's Gate   (82) 195
  Killing Fields, The   (85) 270
  Warning Sign   (86) 465
WATKIN, IAN
  Beyond Reasonable Doubt [1980]   (84) 74
WATKINS, CARLENE
  Tough Enough   (84) 495
WATKINS, ROBIN
  Lovelines   (85) 525

WATSON, ALBERTA
  Keep, The (84) 487
  Soldier, The (83) 428
WATSON, ERIK
  Hotdog . . . The Movie (85) 522
WATSON, LILIAN
  Bizet's Carmen [1983] (85) 98
WATSON, LUCILE
  My Reputation [1946] (85) 586
WATSON, TOM
  Another Time, Another Place [1983] (85) 510
WATT, MARTY
  Almost You (86) 436
WAUTHION, CLAIRE
  Je tu il elle [1974] (86) 447
WAYBORN, KRISTINA
  Octopussy (84) 276
WAYNE, CAROL
  Surf II (85) 535
WAYNE, DAVID
  Finders Keepers (85) 519
WAYNE, JOHN
  Fort Apache [1948] (84) 530
  Hondo [1953] (83) 452
  "Interview with Don Siegel, An" (83) 38
  Shootist, The [1976] (83) 38
WAYNE, MICHAEL
  Alley Cat (85) 509
WAYNE, PATRICK
  Rustler's Rhapsody (86) 458
WEATHERS, CARL
  Rocky III (83) 283
  Rocky IV (86) 319
WEAVER, DOODLES
  "Obituaries" (84) 640
WEAVER, SIGOURNEY
  Deal of the Century (84) 482
  Ghostbusters (85) 219
  Year of Living Dangerously, The
   [1982] (84) 462
WEBB, ALAN
  Falstaff [1967] (83) 443
WEBB, JACK
  "Obituaries" (83) 555
  Pete Kelly's Blues [1955] (83) 481
WEBB, RITA
  Hound of the Baskervilles, The
   [1978] (82) 203
WEBBER, ROBERT
  S.O.B. (82) 328
  Wild Geese II (86) 466
  Wrong Is Right (83) 403
WEBBER, TIMOTHY
  Grey Fox, The (84) 168
WEBER, JACQUES
  Adolescente, L' [1979] (83) 53
WEBER, STEVE
  Flanagan (86) 443
WEDGEWORTH, ANN
  My Science Project (86) 453
  No Small Affair (85) 527
  Sweet Dreams (86) 374
WEHE, OLIVER
  Erendira [1983] (85) 181

WEIDLER, VIRGINIA
  Peter Ibbetson [1935] (86) 527
WEINBERGER, STEVE
  Pumping Iron II (86) 456
WEINGARTEN, ISABELLE
  State of Things, The (84) 379
WEISSER, NORBERT
  Android (85) 510
  City Limits (86) 440
WEISSMULLER, JOHNNY
  "Obituaries" (85) 699
WEITERSHAUSEN, GILDA VON
  Trenchcoat (84) 496
WELCH, MARGARET
  Smooth Talk (86) 354
WELCH, TAHNEE
  Cocoon (86) 96
WELD, TUESDAY
  Author! Author! (83) 417
  Once upon a Time in America (85) 345
  Thief (82) 356
WELLER, MARY LOUISE
  Forced Vengeance (83) 422
WELLER, PETER
  Adventures of Buckaroo Banzai,
   The (85) 47
  Firstborn (85) 519
  Of Unknown Origin (84) 491
  Shoot the Moon (83) 295
WELLES, JESSE
  Rhinestone (85) 531
WELLES, ORSON
  Falstaff [1967] (83) 443
  Journey into Fear [1943] (86) 511
  "Obituaries" (86) 585
  Slapstick (85) 533
WELLS, CLAUDIA
  Back to the Future (86) 65
WELLS, JOHN
  Greystoke (85) 236
  Revolution (86) 458
WELLS, VERNON
  Commando (86) 111
  Road Warrior, The [1981] (83) 277
WELSH, KENNETH
  Of Unknown Origin (84) 491
WENDT, GEORGE
  Dreamscape (85) 166
  Fletch (86) 169
  No Small Affair (85) 527
  Thief of Hearts (85) 536
WENNEMANN, KLAUS
  Boot, Das [1981] (83) 86
  Out of Order (86) 455
WENNER, JANN
  Perfect (86) 456
WEPPER, FRITZ
  Dernier Combat, Le [1983] (85) 517
WERNER, OSKAR
  "Obituaries" (85) 699
WERNHERR, OTTO VON
  Liquid Sky (84) 487
WERTMULLER, MASSIMO
  Joke of Destiny, A [1983] (85) 259
  Softly Softly [1984] (86) 460

WESLEY, JOHN
Missing in Action 2 (86) 452
WEST, BERNIE
Bells Are Ringing [1960] (84) 517
WEST, LOCKWOOD
Dresser, The (84) 130
WEST, MADGE
"Obituaries" (86) 586
WEST, MAE
I'm No Angel [1933] (85) 561
WEST, MATT
Chorus Line, A (86) 91
WEST, TIMOTHY
Agatha [1979] (83) 435
WESTON, JACK
Four Seasons, The (82) 171
High Road to China (84) 486
WEXEL, SHANE
Marie (86) 227
WEYERS, MARIUS
Gods Must Be Crazy, The [1980] (85) 224
Guest, The (85) 520
WHEATON, WIL
Buddy System, The (85) 514
WHEELER-NICHOLSON, DANA
Fletch (86) 169
Little Drummer Girl, The (85) 525
Mrs. Soffel (85) 314
WHIPP, JOSEPH
Body Rock (85) 513
Nightmare on Elm Street, A (85) 527
WHITAKER, FOREST
Fast Times at Ridgemont High (83) 156
WHITE, ALICE
"Obituaries" (84) 641
WHITE, CAROLE ITA
Body Rock (85) 513
WHITE, DAVID
Brewster's Millions (86) 438
WHITE, DIZ
Bullshot [1983] (86) 439
WHITE, ROBYNNE
Smithereens (83) 307
WHITE, TED
Friday the 13th—The Final Chapter (85) 520
WHITELAW, BILLIE
Dark Crystal, The (83) 130
Slayground [1983] (85) 533
WHITELEY, ARKIE
Razorback [1984] (86) 457
WHITEMAN, PAUL
King of Jazz [1930] (86) 515
WHITFIELD, LYNN
Silverado (86) 349
WHITFORD, PETER
Careful He Might Hear You [1983] (85) 130
WHITMAN, PETER
Scandalous (85) 532
WHITMIRE, STEVE
Muppets Take Manhattan, The (85) 526
WHITMORE, JAMES, JR.
Purple Hearts (85) 529
WHITROW, BENJAMIN
Brimstone and Treacle (83) 91

WHITTINGTON, VALERIE
Missionary, The (83) 233
WICKI, BERNHARD
Dangerous Moves [1984] (86) 129
Love in Germany, A [1983] (85) 283
Paris, Texas (85) 359
WIDMARK, RICHARD
Against All Odds (85) 509
Final Option, The (84) 484
Hanky Panky (83) 422
WIEDLIN, JANE
Clue (86) 440
WIELAND, LYNN
Hotdog . . . The Movie (85) 522
WIEST, DIANNE
Falling in Love (85) 519
I'm Dancing as Fast as I Can (83) 423
Purple Rose of Cairo, The (86) 290
WIGGINS, CHRIS
Bad Boy, The (86) 437
WIGHTMAN, ROBERT
Impulse (85) 523
WILCOX, CLAYTON
Philadelphia Experiment, The (85) 529
WILCOX, FRANK
North Star, The [1943] (83) 476
WILCOXON, HENRY
"Obituaries" (85) 701
Sweet Sixteen (85) 535
WILDE, ANDREW
Champions (85) 515
WILDER, GENE
Hanky Panky (83) 422
Woman in Red, The (85) 538
WILKER, JOSE
Xica [1976] (83) 407
WILKES, DONNA
Angel (85) 510
WILKINSON, MAGGIE
Experience Preferred ... but Not Essential [1982] (84) 141
WILKINSON, TOM
Sylvia (86) 462
Wetherby (86) 406
WILLARD, FRED
Moving Violations (86) 453
WILLIAMS, ALLEN
Against All Odds (85) 509
WILLIAMS, BARBARA
Thief of Hearts (85) 536
WILLIAMS, BERNADETTE
Caged Fury (85) 514
WILLIAMS, BILLY DEE
Lady Sings the Blues [1972] (85) 565
Marvin & Tige (84) 489
Nighthawks (82) 259
WILLIAMS, CLARENCE, III
Purple Rain (85) 389
WILLIAMS, GARY
Where the Green Ants Dream [1984] (86) 465
WILLIAMS, GRANT
"Obituaries" (86) 587
WILLIAMS, JOBETH
American Dreamer (85) 509

Big Chill, The   (84) 78
Endangered Species   (83) 420
Poltergeist   (83) 263
Teachers   (85) 535
WILLIAMS, JOHN
"Obituaries"   (84) 641
Solid Gold Cadillac, The [1956]   (85) 615
WILLIAMS, KENNETH
Hound of the Baskervilles, The
[1978]   (82) 203
WILLIAMS, MICHAEL
Educating Rita   (84) 136
WILLIAMS, PAUL
Smokey and the Bandit—Part 3   (84) 493
WILLIAMS, ROBIN
Moscow on the Hudson   (85) 321
Survivors, The   (84) 495
World According to Garp, The   (83) 397
WILLIAMS, SAM
King Solomon's Mines   (86) 449
WILLIAMS, SAMM-ART
Blood Simple   (86) 438
WILLIAMS, SAMUEL ROSS
Jewel of the Nile, The   (86) 448
WILLIAMS, STEVEN
Missing in Action 2   (86) 452
WILLIAMS, SYLVESTER
Sheena   (85) 532
WILLIAMS, TEX
"Obituaries"   (86) 587
WILLIAMS, TREAT
Flashpoint   (85) 519
Once upon a Time in America   (85) 345
Prince of the City   (82) 292
Smooth Talk   (86) 354
WILLIAMSON, FRED
1990   (84) 491
WILLIAMSON, KATE
Racing with the Moon   (85) 397
WILLIAMSON, NICOL
Excalibur   (82) 144
I'm Dancing as Fast as I Can   (83) 423
Return to Oz   (86) 458
Venom [1981]   (83) 430
WILSON, AJITA
Savage Island   (86) 458
WILSON, BRIAN
Beach Boys, The   (86) 438
WILSON, CARL
Beach Boys, The   (86) 438
WILSON, DENNIS
Beach Boys, The   (86) 438
WILSON, DOOLEY
Take a Letter, Darling [1942]   (85) 632
WILSON, ELIZABETH
Grace Quigley   (86) 444
WILSON, HELENA
Wild Horses [1983]   (85) 538
WILSON, KARA
Reuben, Reuben   (84) 337
WILSON, KEVIN
Wild Horses [1983]   (85) 538
WILSON, LAMBERT
Five Days One Summer   (83) 421
Sahara   (85) 531

WILSON, MAK
Return to Oz   (86) 458
WILSON, MARY LOUISE
Zelig   (84) 473
WILSON, MAY
Dulcy [1923]   (83) 432
WILSON, MICHAEL
Heart of a Stag   (85) 522
WILSON, RICHARD
Passage to India, A   (85) 365
WILSON, RITA
Volunteers   (86) 464
WILSON, ROBERT BRIAN
Silent Night, Deadly Night   (85) 532
WILSON, ROGER
Porky's   (83) 267
Porky's II   (84) 491
WILSON, SCOTT
Aviator, The   (86) 437
Right Stuff, The   (84) 342
WILSON, SHEREE J.
Fraternity Vacation   (86) 444
WILSON, STUART
Wetherby   (86) 406
WILSON, THOMAS F.
Back to the Future   (86) 65
WILSON, TREY
Solider's Story, A   (85) 427
WIMBLEY, DAMON
Krush Groove   (86) 449
WINDER, JO DE
Breakin' 2   (85) 514
WINDOM, WILLIAM
Brewster McCloud [1970]   (86) 484
Grandview, U.S.A.   (85) 520
WINFIELD, PAUL
Mike's Murder   (85) 526
Star Trek II—The Wrath of Khan   (83)
321
Terminator, The   (85) 478
WINFREY, OPRAH
Color Purple, The   (86) 105
WINGER, DEBRA
Cannery Row   (83) 95
Mike's Murder   (85) 526
Officer and a Gentleman, An   (83) 246
Terms of Endearment   (84) 414
WINKLER, ANGELA
Danton [1982]   (84) 121
Sheer Madness [1983]   (86) 459
WINKLER, HENRY
Night Shift   (83) 426
WINN, KITTY
They Might Be Giants [1971]   (83) 515
WINNINGHAM, MARE
St. Elmo's Fire   (86) 330
Threshold   (84) 495
WINSLOW, MICHAEL
Alphabet City   (85) 509
Lovelines   (85) 525
Police Academy   (85) 529
Police Academy 2   (86) 276
WINTER, ALEX
Death Wish III   (86) 441

WINTER, CLAUDE
  Bon Plaisir, Le [1983]   (85) 513
  Sunday in the Country, A   (85) 466
WINTER, EDWARD
  Buddy System, The   (85) 514
WINTERS, SHELLEY
  Next Stop, Greenwich Village [1976]   (85) 592
  S.O.B.   (82) 328
WINTON, JANE
  Bridge of San Luis Rey, The [1929] (82) 408
WINWOOD, ESTELLE
  "Obituaries"   (85) 701
WIPANI, MARISE
  Came a Hot Friday   (86) 439
WISE, RAY
  Journey of Natty Gann, The   (86) 203
  Swamp Thing   (83) 429
WITHERS, JANE
  North Star, The [1943]   (83) 476
WITHROW, GLENN
  Outsiders, The   (84) 282
WITT, HOWARD
  Sam's Son   (85) 531
WOHL, DAVID
  Gotcha!   (86) 444
WOINSKY, MARCOS
  Deathstalker   (85) 517
WOLF, MICHAEL
  Holcroft Covenant, The   (86) 446
WOLFE, IAN
  Colorado Territory [1949]   (86) 489
  THX 1138 [1971]   (85) 638
WONG, VICTOR
  Dim Sum   (86) 141
WOOD, GARY
  Hardbodies   (85) 521
WOOD, JAKE
  Flesh and Blood   (86) 443
WOOD, JOHN
  Ladyhawke   (86) 214
  Purple Rose of Cairo, The   (86) 290
  WarGames   (84) 458
WOOD, NATALIE
  Brainstorm   (84) 480
  "Obituaries"   (82) 506
WOODARD, ALFRE
  Cross Creek   (84) 116
WOODINGTON, ALBIE
  Hit, The   (86) 446
WOODS, DONALD
  Roughly Speaking [1945]   (83) 490
WOODS, JAMES
  Against All Odds   (85) 509
  Joshua Then and Now   (86) 198
  Once upon a Time in America   (85) 345
  Split Image   (83) 317
  Stephen King's Cat's Eye   (86) 460
  Videodrome   (84) 452
WOODVINE, JOHN
  American Werewolf in London, An   (82) 66
WOODWARD, EDWARD
  Champions   (85) 515
  King David   (86) 449
  Wicker Man, The [1974]   (86) 555

WOODWARD, JOANNE
  Harry and Son   (85) 521
  They Might Be Giants [1971]   (83) 515
WOODWARD, TIM
  King David   (86) 449
WORONOV, MARY
  Eating Raoul   (83) 420
  Night of the Comet   (85) 527
WORTH, IRENE
  Deathtrap   (83) 137
  Fast Forward   (86) 442
WRAY, FAY
  "Interview with, An"   (82) 16
  King Kong [1933]   (82) 20
  Most Dangerous Game, The [1932]   (86) 519
  Wedding March, The [1928]   (82) 18
WRIGHT, AMY
  Stardust Memories [1980]   (85) 626
WRIGHT, BILL
  Bambi [1942]   (85) 543
WRIGHT, DORSEY
  Hotel New Hampshire, The   (85) 243
WRIGHT, JENNY
  Pink Floyd the Wall [1981]   (83) 258
  St. Elmo's Fire   (86) 330
  Wild Life, The   (85) 538
WRIGHT, JOE
  Stephen King's Silver Bullet   (86) 460
WRIGHT, MAX
  Fraternity Vacation   (86) 444
  Reds   (82) 312
WRIGHT, MICHAEL
  Streamers   (84) 391
WRIGHT, TOM
  Brother from Another Planet, The   (85) 118
WUNUNGMURRA, MARRARU
  Where the Green Ants Dream [1984]   (86) 465
WYANT, SHELLEY
  Home Free All   (85) 522
WYATT, EUSTACE
  Journey into Fear [1943]   (86) 511
WYLE, MICHAEL
  Tuff Turf   (86) 464
WYNN, KEENAN
  Best Friends   (83) 68
  Wavelength   (84) 497
WYSS, AMANDA
  Better Off Dead   (86) 438
  Nightmare on Elm Street, A   (85) 527

XAU, N!
  Gods Must Be Crazy, The [1980]   (85) 224

YAGHLANE, RAOUF BEN
  Balance, La [1982]   (84) 52
YAMADA, ISUZ
  Flowing [1956]   (86) 444
YAMANCHI, TAKAYA
  MacArthur's Children   (86) 451
YAMASAKI, EMILY
  Chan Is Missing   (83) 113
YAMASHITA, TADASHI
  American Ninja   (86) 436

YAMMOTO, YUKIO
  Mixed Blood   (86) 452
YANKOVSKY, OLEG
  Nostalgia [1983]   (85) 340
YANNE, JEAN
  Hanna K.   (84) 177
YATES, CASSIE
  Unfaithfully Yours   (85) 537
YATES, MARJORIE
  Priest of Love   (82) 288
  Wetherby   (86) 406
YELLAND, DAVID
  Chariots of Fire   (82) 101
YEUNG, ELLEN
  Chan Is Missing   (83) 113
YIP, DAVID
  Indiana Jones and the Temple of
    Doom   (85) 253
  View to a Kill, A   (86) 402
YOHN, ERICA
  Pee-wee's Big Adventure   (86) 265
YORDANOFF, WLADIMIR
  Sheer Madness [1983]   (86) 459
YORK, DICK
  Cowboy [1958]   (82) 417
YORK, MICHAEL
  Riddle of the Sands, The [1979]   (85) 531
YORK, SUSANNAH
  Freud [1962]   (84) 535
YOSHINAGA, SAYURI
  Makioka Sisters, The [1983]   (86) 451
YOTHERS, CORY "BUMPERS"
  Dreamscape   (85) 166
YOTHERS, TINA
  Shoot the Moon   (83) 295
YOUNG, ALAN
  Time Machine, The [1960]   (84) 585
YOUNG, BURT
  Amityville II   (83) 417
  Lookin' to Get Out   (83) 425
  Once upon a Time in America   (85) 345
  Pope of Greenwich Village, The   (85) 529
  Rocky III   (83) 283
  Rocky IV   (86) 319
YOUNG, KAREN
  Almost You   (86) 436
  Deep in the Heart   (85) 517
  Maria's Lovers   (86) 451
YOUNG, LORETTA
  Hatchet Man, The [1932]   (83) 447
YOUNG, PAUL
  Another Time, Another Place [1983]   (85) 510
YOUNG, ROBERT
  H.M. Pulham, Esq. [1941]   (82) 439
YOUNG, ROLAND
  Sherlock Holmes [1922]   (83) 494
YOUNG, SEAN
  Baby   (86) 437
  Blade Runner   (83) 76
  Stripes   (82) 336
  Young Doctors in Love   (83) 431
YOUNG, WILLIAM ALLEN
  Soldier's Story, A   (85) 427
YOUNGS, GAIL
  Stone Boy, The   (85) 450

YOUNGS, JIM
  Footloose   (85) 198
  Out of Control   (86) 455
YOUSEKEVITCH, IGOR
  Invitation to the Dance [1956]   (86) 507
YUI, MASAYUKI
  Ran   (86) 304
YULIN, HARRIS
  Scarface   (84) 361
YUNE, JOHNNY
  They Call Me Bruce   (83) 429

ZABKA, WILLIAM
  Just One of the Guys   (86) 448
  Karate Kid, The   (85) 264
ZABOU
  Gwendoline [1983]   (85) 521
ZABRISKIE, GRACE
  Body Rock   (85) 513
ZACHARIAS, JOHN
  Montenegro   (82) 250
ZACHRISSON, LISBETH
  Montenegro   (82) 250
ZACHWATOWICZ, KRYSTYNA
  Man of Marble [1977]   (82) 234
ZADORA, PIA
  Lonely Lady, The   (84) 488
ZAGARINO, FRANK
  Lovelines   (85) 525
ZAKLINSKY, KONSTANTIN
  Backstage at the Kirov   (85) 511
ZAL, ROXANA
  Table for Five   (84) 404
  Testament   (84) 420
ZALE, ALEXANDER
  Invasion U.S.A.   (86) 447
ZAMORA, DEL
  Repo Man   (85) 408
ZANN, LENORE
  Def-Con 4   (86) 441
ZANUCK, VIRGINIA FOX
  "Obituaries"   (83) 556
ZAPPA, MOON
  Nightmares   (84) 490
ZARAZHINSKAIA, ANNA
  New Babylon, The [1929]   (84) 561
ZARZO, MANUEL
  Holy Innocents, The   (86) 447
ZECH, ROSEL
  Veronika Voss   (83) 382
ZEE, JOHN A.
  Best Defense   (85) 512
ZERBE, ANTHONY
  Dead Zone, The   (84) 481
ZERNECK, DANIELLE VON
  My Science Project   (86) 453
ZIEN, CHIP
  Grace Quigley   (86) 444
ZIMMER, KIM
  Body Heat   (82) 87
ZISCHLER, HANNS
  Woman in Flames, A   (85) 538
ZITO, PASQUALE
  And the Ship Sails On [1983]   (85) 69

PERFORMER INDEX

ZITRONE, LEON
 American Dreamer (85) 509
ZMED, ADRIAN
 Bachelor Party (85) 511
ZOBDA, FRANCE
 Sheena (85) 532
ZOFFOLI, MARTA
 Three Brothers [1980] (83) 349

ZOREK, MICHAEL
 Private School (84) 491
 Woman in Red, The (85) 538
ZUNIGA, DAPHNE
 Sure Thing, The (86) 369
 Vision Quest (86) 464
ZWERENZ, GERHARD
 Berlin Alexanderplatz [1980] (84) 57

SUBJECT INDEX

The selection of subject headings combines standard Library of Congress Subject Headings and common usage in order to aid the film researcher. Cross references, listed as *See* and *See also*, are provided when appropriate. While all major themes, locales, and time periods have been indexed, some minor subjects covered in a particular film have not been included.

ABORTION
Agnes of God (86) 56
Arch of Triumph [1948] (84) 501
Bon Plaisir, Le [1983] (85) 513
Heartaches [1981] (83) 197
Loulou [1980] (82) 226
Next Stop, Greenwich Village [1976] (85) 592
Racing with the Moon (85) 397
Second Thoughts (84) 493
Streetwise (86) 364

ACTORS AND ACTRESSES (*See also*
FILMMAKERS AND FILMMAKING *and*
THEATER)
After the Rehearsal (85) 52
Always (86) 60
Barbary Coast [1935] (84) 506
Barefoot Contessa, The [1954] (82) 399
Bells Are Ringing [1960] (84) 517
Bridge of San Luis Rey, The [1929] (82) 408
Broadway Danny Rose (85) 112
Chorus Line, A (86) 91
Come Back to the 5 & Dime Jimmy Dean, Jimmy
  Dean (83) 120
Curtains (84) 481
Dresser, The (84) 130
Entre nous [1983] (85) 176
Fanny and Alexander [1982] (84) 146
Frances (83) 178
French Lieutenant's Woman, The (82) 174
Front, The [1976] (86) 502
Hard Way, The [1942] (85) 555
I Love You (83) 423
I Ought to Be in Pictures (83) 423
Little Drummer Girl, The (85) 525
Marie (86) 227
Maxie (86) 452
Mephisto (82) 237
Mommie Dearest (82) 245
My Favorite Year (83) 241
Nell Gwyn [1934] (84) 557
New York, New York [1977] (84) 567
Next Stop, Greenwich Village [1976] (85) 592
Once upon a Time in America (85) 345
Only When I Laugh (82) 268
Purple Rose of Cairo, The (86) 290
Snows of Kilimanjaro, The [1952] (83) 498
S.O.B. (82) 328
Star 80 (84) 374
Star Is Born, A [1954] (84) 573
Stardust Memories [1980] (85) 626
State of Things, The (84) 379
Still of the Night (83) 326
Stranger's Kiss (85) 534
Tempest (83) 331
Tootsie (83) 353
Torn Curtain [1966] (85) 644
Under the Volcano (85) 499
Veronika Voss (83) 387
ADOLESCENTS
A nos amour [1983] (85) 509

Adolescente, L' [1979] (83) 53
All the Right Moves (84) 41
American Taboo (85) 509
Angel (85) 510
Argent, L' [1983] (85) 74
Baby, It's You (84) 479
Back to the Future (86) 65
Bad Boy, The (86) 436
Bad Boys (84) 479
Beach Girls, The (83) 417
Birdy (85) 93
Blame It on Rio (85) 512
Blue Skies Again (84) 479
Breakfast Club, The (86) 85
Chorus Line, A (86) 91
Chosen, The (83) 116
Christine (84) 106
Christine F. [1981] (83) 419
Class (84) 480
Class of 1984 (83) 419
Cocoon (86) 96
Company of Wolves, The [1984] (86) 115
Cruel Story of Youth [1960] (85) 517
Diner (83) 142
Dreamchild (86) 146
Emerald Forest, The (86) 156
Fast Forward (86) 443
Fast Times at Ridgemont High (83) 156
Flamingo Kid, The (85) 192
Flashdance (84) 158
Footloose (85) 198
Friday the 13th—Part III (83) 422
Goonies, The (86) 176
Grease 2 (83) 422
Gregory's Girl [1981] (83) 193
Hadley's Rebellion (85) 521
Hardbodies (85) 521
Heart Like a Wheel (84) 182
Heavenly Kid, The (86) 445
Homework (83) 422
Humongous (83) 423
I Ought to Be in Pictures (83) 423
Journey of Natty Gann, The (86) 203
Joy of Sex (85) 524
Joysticks (84) 487
Karate Kid, The (85) 264
Kid Colter (86) 449
Kipperbang [1983] (85) 524
Last American Virgin, The (83) 424
Last Starfighter, The (85) 277
Legend of Billie Jean, The (86) 450
Losin' It (84) 488
Lovelines (85) 525
Mad Max Beyond Thunderdome (86) 223
Making the Grade (85) 526
Mask (86) 231
Max Dugan Returns (84) 228
Mischief (86) 452
My Science Project (86) 453
My Tutor (84) 490
New Kids, The (86) 454

Nightmare on Elm Street, A   (85) 527
No Small Affair   (85) 527
Once upon a Time in America   (85) 345
Out of Control   (86) 455
Outsiders, The   (84) 282
Pale Rider   (86) 261
Paradise   (83) 426
Pee-wee's Big Adventure   (86) 265
Porky's   (83) 267
Porky's II   (84) 491
Pretty Baby [1978]   (85) 597
Private School   (84) 491
Puberty Blues [1981]   (84) 492
Racing with the Moon   (85) 397
Reckless   (85) 530
Red Dawn   (85) 530
Repo Man   (85) 408
Return of the Living Dead, The   (86) 314
Risky Business   (84) 349
Rumble Fish   (84) 492
Running Brave   (84) 354
St. Elmo's Fire   (86) 330
Secret Admirer   (86) 459
Secrets   (85) 532
Silverado   (86) 349
Six Weeks   (83) 428
Sixteen Candles   (85) 532
Smooth Talk   (86) 354
Spring Break   (84) 494
Stranger than Paradise   (85) 455
Streetwise   (86) 364
Sugar Cane Alley [1983]   (85) 461
Sure Thing, The   (86) 369
Table for Five   (84) 404
Taking Off [1971]   (86) 545
Taps   (82) 343
Teen Wolf   (86) 402
Tex   (83) 335
That Sinking Feeling [1979]   (85) 536
That Was Then . . . This Is Now   (86) 463
28 Up [1984]   (86) 392
Valley Girl   (84) 447
WarGames   (84) 458
Weird Science   (86) 465
Wild Life, The   (85) 538
World of Henry Orient, The [1964]   (84) 600
Young Sherlock Holmes   (86) 431
Zapped!   (83) 431

ADULTERY
Adolescente, L' [1979]   (83) 53
Agatha [1979]   (83) 435
Animal Kingdom, The [1932]   (86) 469
Arrangement, The [1969]   (86) 474
Barefoot Contessa, The [1954]   (82) 399
Becky Sharp [1935]   (82) 403
Best Friends   (83) 68
Betrayal   (84) 67
Blood Wedding [1981]   (83) 418
Body Heat   (82) 87
Choose Me   (85) 135
Circle of Deceit [1981]   (83) 419
Compromising Positions   (86) 120
Confidentially Yours [1983]   (85) 516
Coup de torchon [1981]   (83) 124
Divorcée, The [1930]   (82) 429
Educating Rita   (84) 136
Entre nous [1983]   (85) 176
Excalibur   (82) 144
Eye of the Needle   (82) 148
Falling in Love   (85) 519
Fool for Love   (86) 172
Frances   (83) 178

French Lieutenant's Woman, The   (82) 174
Full Moon in Paris   (85) 208
Gabriela [1983]   (85) 213
Goodbye, New York   (86) 444
Heart Like a Wheel   (84) 192
Heartaches [1981]   (83) 97
Heat and Dust [1982]   (84) 187
History Is Made at Night [1937]   (84) 452
I'm No Angel [1933]   (85) 561
Jagged Edge, The   (86) 190
James Joyce's Women   (86) 193
Kiss Me Goodbye   (83) 209
Lianna   (84) 201
Little Sex, A   (83) 424
Love in Germany, A [1983]   (85) 283
Love Letters   (85) 288
Man with Two Brains, The   (84) 223
Micki & Maude   (85) 308
Midsummer Night's Sex Comedy, A   (83) 228
My First Wife   (86) 453
Nell Gwyn [1934]   (84) 557
Night of the Shooting Stars, The [1982]   (84) 258
Out of Africa   (86) 255
Places in the Heart   (85) 371
Ploughman's Lunch, The [1983]   (85) 377
Postman Always Rings Twice, The   (82) 284
Priest of Love   (82) 288
Purple Rose of Cairo, The   (86) 290
Quartet   (82) 296
Raggedy Man   (82) 300
Return of Martin Guerre, The   (84) 318
Return of the Secaucus 7 [1980]   (83) 484
St. Elmo's Fire   (86) 330
Scarlet Letter, The [1927]   (85) 602
Shooting Party, The [1984]   (86) 344
Six Weeks   (83) 428
Star 80   (84) 374
Swann in Love   (85) 471
Swing Shift   (85) 535
Tempest   (83) 331
Terms of Endearment   (84) 414
That Championship Season   (83) 338
They All Laughed   (82) 350
Twice in a Lifetime   (86) 397
Under the Volcano   (85) 499
Unfaithful, The [1947]   (86) 550
Until September   (85) 537
Victim [1961]   (85) 649
When Father Was Away on Business [1984]   (86) 411
Woman Next Door, The   (82) 385
Woman on the Beach, The [1947]   (83) 519
World According to Garp, The   (83) 397
World of Henry Orient, The [1964]   (84) 600

ADVERTISING
Arrangement, The [1969]   (86) 474
Brother from Another Planet, The   (85) 118
Comfort and Joy   (85) 146
Front, The [1976]   (86) 502
Lost in America   (86) 219
Rocky III   (83) 283
Take a Letter, Darling [1942]   (85) 632

AFRICA
Amin—The Rise and Fall   (84) 479
Coup de torchon [1981]   (83) 124
Gods Must Be Crazy, The [1980]   (85) 224
Greystoke   (85) 236
King Solomon's Mines   (86) 449
Out of Africa   (86) 255
Raiders of the Lost Ark   (82) 308
Snows of Kilimanjaro, The [1952]   (83) 498
Under Fire   (84) 441

SUBJECT INDEX

AGING
After the Rehearsal   (85) 52
Atlantic City   (82) 74
Cattle Annie and Little Britches   (82) 97
Chorus Line, A   (86) 91
Cocoon   (86) 96
Comfort and Joy   (85) 146
Dangerous Moves [1984]   (86) 129
Dim Sum   (86) 141
Dreamchild   (86) 146
Dresser, The   (84) 130
Fanny and Alexander [1982]   (84) 146
Gandhi   (83) 183
Ghost Story   (82) 183
Grace Quigley   (86) 444
Grey Fox, The   (84) 168
Long Gray Line, The [1955]   (82) 447
Max Dugan Returns   (84) 228
Natural, The   (85) 329
Night of the Shooting Stars, The [1982]   (84) 258
Nuit de Varennes, La [1982]   (84) 270
On Golden Pond   (82) 263
Once upon a Time in America   (85) 345
Only When I Laugh   (82) 268
Private Function, A [1984]   (86) 280
Return of the Secaucus 7 [1980]   (83) 484
Rich and Famous   (82) 316
St. Elmo's Fire   (86) 330
Shoot the Moon   (83) 295
Shooting Party, The [1984]   (86) 344
Tempest   (83) 331
That Championship Season   (83) 338
Trip to Bountiful, The   (86) 383
Trouble in Mind   (86) 388
Twilight Zone—The Movie   (84) 435
ALCOHOLISM
After the Rehearsal   (85) 52
Annie   (83) 56
Arthur   (82) 71
Beloved Rogue [1927]   (84) 522
Berlin Alexanderplatz [1980]   (84) 57
Country   (85) 156
Educating Rita   (84) 136
48 HRS.   (83) 173
4th Man, The [1983]   (85) 203
Mommie Dearest   (82) 245
My Favorite Year   (83) 241
Only When I Laugh   (82) 268
Reuben, Reuben   (84) 337
Running Brave   (84) 354
St. Elmo's Fire   (86) 330
Sophie's Choice   (83) 311
Star Is Born, A [1954]   (84) 573
Streetwise   (86) 364
Tales of Ordinary Madness   (84) 495
Tender Mercies   (84) 409
Under the Volcano   (85) 499
Verdict, The   (83) 377
AMERICAN SOUTH
Bostonians, The   (85) 105
Come Back to the 5 & Dime Jimmy Dean, Jimmy
   Dean   (83) 120
Cross Creek   (84) 116
Honkytonk Man   (83) 200
Pete Kelly's Blues [1955]   (82) 481
Places in the Heart   (85) 371
Pretty Baby [1978]   (85) 597
River, The   (85) 416
Sharky's Machine   (82) 324
Soldier's Story, A   (85) 427
Southern Comfort   (82) 332

Tender Mercies   (84) 409
This Is Elvis   (82) 360
Tomorrow [1972]   (84) 589
Twilight Zone—The Movie   (84) **435**
AMPUTATION
Berlin Alexanderplatz [1980]   **(84) 57**
Return of the Living Dead, The   (86) 314
ANIMALS
American Werewolf in London, An   (82) 66
Antarctica   (85) 511
Aviator, The   (86) 437
Bambi [1942]   (85) 543
Bedtime for Bonzo [1951]   (84) 512
Black Cat, The   (85) 512
Cat People [1942]   (82) 13
Company of Wolves, The [1984]   (86) 115
Cujo   (84) 481
Deadly Eyes   (84) 482
Emerald Forest, The   (86) 156
Falcon and the Snowman, The   (86) 165
4th Man, The [1983]   (85) 203
Gods Must Be Crazy, The [1980]   (85) 224
Golden Seal, The   (84) 485
Greystoke   (85) 236
Hotel New Hampshire, The   (85) 243
I'm No Angel [1933]   (85) 561
Jaws 3-D   (84) 486
Ladyhawke   (86) 214
Of Unknown Origin   (84) 491
Out of Africa   (86) 255
Police Academy 2   (86) 276
Private Function, A [1984]   (86) 280
Razorback [1984]   (86) 457
Romancing the Stone   (85) 421
Secret of NIMH, The   (83) 288
Shooting Party, The [1984]   (86) 344
Sign of the Cross, The [1932]   (85) 607
Silverado   (86) 349
Turtle Diary   (86) 464
Venom [1981]   (83) 430
Wolfen   (82) 382
ANIMATION
Bambi [1942]   (85) 543
Black Cauldron, The   (86) 75
Care Bears Movie, The   (86) 439
Fire and Ice   (84) 153
Here Come the Littles   (86) 446
Invitation to the Dance [1956]   (86) 507
Neverending Story, The   (85) 527
Rainbow Brite and the Star Stealer   (86) 456
Secret of the Sword, The   (86) 459
Starchaser   (86) 460
Smurfs and the Magic Flute, The   **(84) 493**
TRON   (83) 371
Twice upon a Time   (84) 496
ANTHROPOLOGY
Dr. Butcher, M.D. [1980]   (83) 420
ANTI-SEMITISM (See also JEWS AND JEWISH
   LIFE)
Boat Is Full, The [1981]   (83) 82
Boys from Brazil, The [1978]   (86) 480
Chariots of Fire   (82) 101
Chosen, The   (83) 116
Entre nous [1983]   (85) 176
Fanny and Alexander [1982]   (84) 146
Lili Marleen   (82) 222
Shoah   (86) 339
Sophie's Choice   (83) 311
Twilight Zone—The Movie   (84) **435**
ARCTIC
Antarctica   (85) 511

Iceman   (85) 248
Never Cry Wolf   (84) 247
White Nights   (86) 416
ARIZONA
Running Hot   (85) 531
ART AND ARTISTS
After Hours   (86) 51
After the Rehearsal   (85) 52
And the Ship Sails On [1983]   (85) 69
Animal Kingdom, The [1932]   (86) 469
Beau Mariage, Le   (83) 65
Death of Mario Ricci, The [1983]   (86) 133
Dreamchild   (86) 146
Dresser, The   (84) 130
Echoes   (84) 483
Entre nous [1983]   (85) 176
First Name, Carmen [1983]   (85) 186
Lonely Hearts [1982]   (84) 212
Mishima   (86) 236
Nostalgia [1983]   (85) 340
Passion [1982]   (84) 289
Pretty Baby [1978]   (85) 597
Quartet   (82) 296
Running Brave   (84) 354
Secret Life of Walter Mitty, The [1947]   (86) 540
Still of the Night   (83) 326
Sunday in the Country, A   (85) 466
Take a Letter, Darling [1942]   (85) 632
Tempest   (83) 331
Whose Life Is It Anyway?   (82) 378
Woman on the Beach, The [1947]   (83) 519
ASIANS AND ASIAN AMERICANS
Adventures of Buckaroo Banzai, The   (85) 47
Chan Is Missing   (83) 113
Dim Sum   (86) 141
Gremlins   (85) 230
Hatchet Man, The [1932]   (83) 447
Killing Fields, The   (85) 270
Merry Christmas, Mr. Lawrence   (84) 231
Mishima   (86) 236
Rambo: First Blood Part II   (86) 299
Year of the Dragon   (86) 426
Year of Living Dangerously, The [1982]   (84) 462
ASTROLOGY
Beloved Rogue [1927]   (84) 522
I'm No Angel [1933]   (85) 561
ASTRONAUTS
Enemy Mine   (86) 161
Right Stuff, The   (84) 342
Terms of Endearment   (84) 414
AUSTRALIA
Caddie [1976]   (83) 439
Careful He Might Hear You [1983]   (85) 130
Coca-Cola Kid, The   (86) 440
Earthling, The [1980]   (82) 130
Heatwave   (84) 485
Kitty and the Bagman [1982]   (84) 487
Lonely Hearts [1982]   (84) 212
Mad Max Beyond Thunderdome   (86) 223
Man from Snowy River, The   (83) 425
Phar Lap   (85) 528
Pirate Movie, The   (83) 427
Puberty Blues [1981]   (84) 492
Razorback [1984]   (86) 457
Road Warrior, The [1981]   (83) 277
Silver City [1984]   (86) 460
28 Up [1984]   (86) 392
We of the Never Never [1982]   (84) 497
Where the Green Ants Dream [1984]   (86) 465

Year of Living Dangerously, The [1982]   (84) 462
AUTHORS AND WRITERS (See also NEWSPAPERS, REPORTERS, AND JOURNALISTS)
Agatha [1979]   (83) 435
Animal Kingdom, The [1932]   (86) 469
Author! Author!   (83) 417
Barbary Coast [1935]   (84) 506
Bells Are Ringing [1960]   (84) 517
Best Friends   (83) 68
Betrayal   (84) 67
Buddy System, The   (85) 514
Cannery Row   (83) 95
Céleste [1981]   (83) 104
Chosen, The   (83) 116
Cross Creek   (84) 116
Deathtrap   (83) 137
Dreamchild   (86) 146
Fanny and Alexander [1982]   (84) 146
4th Man, The [1983]   (85) 203
Frances   (83) 178
Front, The [1976]   (86) 502
Home Free All   (85) 522
I Ought to Be in Pictures   (83) 423
Jagged Edge   (86) 190
James Joyce's Women   (86) 193
Joshua Then and Now   (86) 198
Lonely Lady, The   (84) 488
Lost Moment, The [1947]   (83) 465
Love Streams   (85) 293
Marie   (86) 227
Mishima   (86) 236
Next Stop, Greenwich Village [1976]   (85) 592
Nuit de Varennes, La [1982]   (84) 270
Out of Africa   (86) 255
Perfect   (86) 456
Ploughman's Lunch, The [1983]   (85) 377
Priest of Love   (82) 288
Rent Control   (85) 530
Rich and Famous   (82) 316
Romancing the Stone   (85) 421
Romantic Comedy   (84) 492
St. Elmo's Fire   (86) 330
Shoot the Moon   (83) 295
Snows of Kilimanjaro, The [1952]   (83) 498
Sophie's Choice   (83) 311
Time After Time [1979]   (84) 579
Trenchcoat   (84) 496
Volver a empezar   (83) 393
Way We Were, The [1973]   (82) 474
Windy City   (85) 538
World According to Garp, The   (83) 393
AUTOMOBILES AND AUTOMOBILE RACING
Adventures of Buckaroo Banzai, The   (85) 47
Back to the Future   (86) 65
Cannonball Run II   (85) 514
Christine   (84) 106
Comfort and Joy   (85) 146
Eddie and the Cruisers   (84) 483
Fast Times at Ridgemont High   (83) 156
48 HRS.   (83) 173
Heart Like a Wheel   (84) 182
Heavenly Kid, The   (86) 445
Joke of Destiny, A [1983]   (85) 259
Mad Max Beyond Thunderdome   (86) 223
Paris, Texas   (85) 359
Repo Man   (85) 408
Road Warrior, The [1981]   (83) 277
Sahara   (85) 531
Six Pack   (83) 428

Smash Palace [1981] (83) 302
Smokey and the Bandit—Part 3 (84) 493
Stroker Ace (84) 494
Sunday in the Country, A (85) 466
Tomboy (86) 463
TRON (83) 371

AVANT-GARDE
After Hours (86) 51
Always (86) 60
Invitation au voyage [1982] (84) 486
James Joyce's Women (86) 193
Koyaanisqatsi (84) 197
Repo Man (85) 408
Trouble in Mind (86) 388

AVIATION AND AVIATORS
Adventures of Buckaroo Banzai, The (85) 47
Airplane II (83) 417
Birdy (85) 93
Firefox (83) 160
Flight of the Phoenix, The [1966] (85) 549
Guy Named Joe, A [1943] (82) 435
High Road to China (84) 486
Oasis, The (85) 528
Officer and a Gentleman, An (83) 246
Out of Africa (86) 255
Return of the Jedi (84) 326
Right Stuff, The (84) 342
Secret Life of Walter Mitty, The [1947] (86) 540
Sound Barrier, The [1952] (85) 621
Star Trek II—The Wrath of Khan (83) 321
Too Hot to Handle [1938] (84) 596
Toy Soldiers (85) 536
Uncommon Valor (84) 496
When Father Was Away on Business [1984] (86) 411
White Nights (86) 416
Young Sherlock Holmes (86) 431
Zelig (84) 473

BANK ROBBERY
Cattle Annie and Little Britches (82) 97
First Name, Carmen [1983] (85) 186
Runaway Train (86) 324
Two of a Kind (84) 496

BASEBALL
Blue Skies Again (84) 479
Chosen, The (83) 116
D.A.R.Y.L. (86) 441
Mask (86) 231
Max Dugan Returns (84) 228
Natural, The (85) 329
Neil Simon's The Slugger's Wife (86) 454
Soldier's Story, A (85) 427

BIBLICAL TIMES
King David (86) 449

BIG-CITY LIFE
After Hours (86) 51
Berlin Alexanderplatz [1980] (84) 57
Blade Runner (83) 76
Broadway Danny Rose (85) 112
Brother from Another Planet, The (85) 118
Can She Bake A Cherry Pie? (84) 95
Choose Me (85) 135
City Heat (85) 141
Comfort and Joy (85) 146
Crimes of Passion (85) 161
Detour [1946] (86) 498
Every Man for Himself [1979] (82) 139
48 HRS. (83) 173
Front, The [1976] (86) 502

Full Moon in Paris (85) 208
Gods Must Be Crazy, The [1980] (85) 224
Heartaches [1981] (83) 197
I'm No Angel [1933] (85) 561
Into the Night (86) 186
Local Hero (84) 205
Lonely Hearts [1982] (84) 212
Lost in America (86) 219
Moonlighting (83) 237
Moscow on the Hudson (85) 321
My New Partner [1984] (86) 246
Natural, The (85) 329
New Babylon, The [1929] (84) 561
New York, New York [1977] (84) 567
Next Stop, Greenwich Village [1976] (85) 592
Norte, El (84) 265
Once upon a Time in America (85) 345
Police Academy 2 (86) 276
Protocol (85) 383
Purple Rose of Cairo, The (86) 290
Repo Man (85) 408
Return of the Living Dead, The (86) 314
Rocky III (83) 283
St. Elmo's Fire (86) 330
Sesame Street Presents: Follow That Bird (86) 459
Stranger than Paradise (85) 455
Streetwise (86) 364
Superman III (84) 399
Swann in Love (85) 471
Tempest (83) 331
To Live and Die in L.A. (86) 379
Tootsie (83) 353
Trading Places (84) 430
TRON (83) 371
Trouble in Mind (86) 388
28 Up [1984] (86) 392
Verdict, The (83) 377
Witness (86) 421
World According to Garp, The (83) 397
World of Henry Orient, The [1964] (84) 600

BIOGRAPHY
Agatha [1979] (83) 435
Amadeus (85) 63
Bear, The (85) 511
Céleste (83) 104
Chariots of Fire (82) 101
Chorus Line, A (86) 91
Colonel Redl [1984] (86) 100
Disraeli [1929] (82) 426
Dreamchild (86) 146
Edith and Marcel [1983] (85) 518
Entre nous [1983] (85) 176
Frances (83) 178
Front, The [1976] (86) 502
Gandhi (83) 183
Grey Fox, The (84) 168
Hammett (84) 174
Heart Like a Wheel (84) 182
If You Could See What I Hear (83) 423
James Joyce's Women (86) 193
Kerouac, the Movie (86) 448
Louis Bluie (86) 450
Marie (86) 227
Mask (86) 231
Mishima (86) 236
Mommie Dearest (82) 245
My Dinner with André (82) 255
Napoleon [1927] (82) 461
Nate and Hayes (84) 236
Nell Gwyn [1934] (84) 557
Next Stop, Greenwich Village [1976] (85) 592

Nuit de Varennes, La [1982]   (84) 270
Out of Africa   (86) 255
Pee-wee's Big Adventure   (86) 265
Piaf [1980]   (83) 427
Pretty Baby [1978]   (85) 597
Priest of Love   (82) 288
Rasputin [1975]   (86) 457
Reds   (82) 312
Reuben, Reuben   (84) 337
Right Stuff, The   (84) 342
Roughly Speaking [1945]   (83) 490
Running Brave   (84) 354
Sense of Freedom, A   (86) 459
Silkwood   (84) 367
Star 80   (84) 374
Sweet Dreams   (86) 374
Sylvia   (86) 462
This Is Elvis   (82) 360
Wagner   (84) 497
World According to Garp, The   (83) 397
Zelig   (84) 473

BIRDS
Berlin Alexanderplatz [1980]   (84) 57
Birdy   (85) 93
Brewster McCloud [1970]   (86) 480
Falcon and the Snowman, The   (86) 165
Ladyhawke   (86) 214
Sesame Street Presents: Follow That Bird   (86) 459

BLACK COMEDY
After Hours   (86) 51
Brazil   (86) 80
Comfort and Joy   (85) 146
Eating Raoul   (83) 420
Erendira [1983]   (85) 181
Evil Dead, The   (84) 484
First Name, Carmen [1983]   (85) 186
Gremlins   (85) 230
Hotel New Hampshire, The   (85) 243
Into the Night   (86) 186
Jinxed   (83) 206
Joke of Destiny, A [1983]   (85) 259
Man with Two Brains, The   (84) 223
Night Shift   (83) 426
Prizzi's Honor   (86) 285
Repo Man   (85) 408
Return of the Living Dead, The   (86) 314
Reuben, Reuben   (84) 337
Stardust Memories [1980]   (85) 626
Stranger than Paradise   (85) 455
Teachers   (85) 535
Trouble in Mind   (86) 388
Under the Volcano   (85) 499

BLACKMAIL
Berlin Alexanderplatz [1980]   (84) 57
Compromising Positions   (86) 120
Cutter's Way   (82) 119
Detour [1946]   (86) 498
Draughtsman's Contract, The [1982]   (84) 126
Flash of Green, A   (86) 443
Front, The [1976]   (86) 502
Hammett   (84) 174
History Is Made at Night [1937]   (84) 542
Joke of Destiny, A [1983]   (85) 259
King of Comedy, The   (84) 192
Official Story, The   (86) 249
Risky Business   (84) 349
Sherlock Holmes [1922]   (83) 494
They Might Be Giants [1971]   (83) 515
Too Hot to Handle [1938]   (84) 596
Unfaithful, The [1947]   (86) 550
Victim [1961]   (85) 649

BLACKS
Adventures of Buckaroo Banzai, The   (85) 47
Beverly Hills Cop   (85) 88
Body and Soul   (83) 418
Brother from Another Planet, The   (85) 118
City Heat   (85) 141
Color Purple, The   (86) 105
Cotton Club, The   (85) 150
48 HRS.   (83) 173
Gods Must Be Crazy, The [1980]   (85) 224
I'm No Angel [1933]   (85) 561
Lady Sings the Blues [1972]   (85) 565
New York, New York [1977]   (84) 567
Next Stop, Greenwich Village [1976]   (85) 592
Officer and a Gentleman, An   (83) 246
Out of Africa   (86) 255
Pretty Baby [1978]   (85) 597
Purple Rain   (85) 389
Ragtime   (82) 304
Repo Man   (85) 408
Rocky III   (83) 277
Silverado   (86) 349
Soldier's Story, A   (85) 427
Streamers   (84) 391
Toy, The   (83) 358
Trading Places   (84) 430
Utu [1983]   (85) 504
White Nights   (86) 416

BLINDNESS
Cannery Row   (83) 95
Draughtsman's Contract, The [1982]   (84) 126
If You Could See What I Hear   (83) 423
Places in the Heart   (85) 371
Woman on the Beach, The [1947]   (83) 519

BOXING AND FIGHTS
Animal Kingdom, The [1932]   (86) 469
Body and Soul   (83) 418
Edith and Marcel [1983]   (85) 518
Joshua Then and Now   (86) 198
Karate Kid, The   (85) 264
Penitentiary II   (83) 427
Rocky III   (83) 283
Rocky IV   (86) 319
Sting II, The   (84) 494
Tough Enough   (84) 495

BRAZIL
Bar Esperanza [1983]   (86) 437
Brazil   (86) 80
Emerald Forest, The   (86) 156
Gabriela [1983]   (85) 213

BULLFIGHTING
Bizet's Carmen [1983]   (85) 98
Under the Volcano   (85) 499

BUREAUCRACY
Absence of Malice   (82) 57
After Hours   (86) 51
Blue Thunder   (84) 84
Brazil   (86) 80
Brother from Another Planet, The   (85) 118
Country   (85) 156
Front, The [1976]   (86) 502
Improper Channels   (82) 218
Joke of Destiny, A [1983]   (85) 259
Marie   (86) 227
Missing   (83) 228
Moscow on the Hudson   (85) 321
1984   (85) 335
Official Story, The   (86) 249
Protocol   (85) 383
Real Genius   (86) 309
Solid Gold Cadillac, The [1956]   (85) 615

Verdict, The   (83) 377
WarGames   (84) 458
When Father Was Away on Business [1984]   (86) 411

BUSINESS EXECUTIVES
Brother from Another Planet, The   (85) 118
Comfort and Joy   (85) 146
Dulcy [1923]   (82) 432
Front, The [1976]   (86) 502
Local Hero   (84) 206
Lost in America   (86) 219
Official Story, The   (86) 249
Prizzi's Honor   (86) 285
Rocky III   (83) 283
Running Brave   (84) 354
St. Elmo's Fire   (86) 330
Sea Wolves, The [1981]   (83) 427
Solid Gold Cadillac, The [1956]   (85) 615
Take a Letter, Darling [1942]   (85) 632
Tootsie   (83) 353
Toy, The   (83) 358
Trading Places   (84) 430
TRON   (83) 371
Unfaithful, The [1947]   (86) 550
Victor/Victoria   (83) 387

CANADA
Agnes of God   (86) 56
Angelo My Love   (84) 47
Bad Boy, The   (86) 436
Grey Fox, The   (84) 168
Heartaches [1981]   (83) 197
Joshua Then and Now   (86) 198
Plouffe, Les   (86) 456
Running Brave   (84) 354
Star 80   (84) 374

CAREER WOMEN
Animal Kingdom, The [1932]   (86) 469
Choose Me   (85) 135
City Girl, The   (85) 516
Continental Divide   (82) 115
Crimes of Passion   (85) 161
Entre nous [1983]   (85) 176
First Monday in October   (82) 151
Frances   (83) 178
Front, The [1976]   (86) 502
Grace Quigley   (86) 444
Grey Fox, The   (84) 168
Guy Named Joe, A [1943]   (82) 435
Hard Way, The [1942]   (85) 555
Heart Like a Wheel   (84) 182
Heat and Dust [1982]   (84) 187
Jagged Edge   (86) 190
James Joyce's Women   (86) 193
Jinxed   (83) 206
Late Chrysanthemums [1954]   (86) 449
Lola [1981]   (83) 215
Lost in America   (86) 219
Marie   (86) 227
Micki & Maude   (85) 308
Mommie Dearest   (82) 245
Mr. Mom   (84) 489
New York, New York [1977]   (84) 567
Out of Africa   (86) 255
Ploughman's Lunch, The [1983]   (85) 377
Police Academy 2   (86) 276
Pretty Baby [1978]   (85) 597
Prizzi's Honor   (86) 285
Rich and Famous   (82) 316
Romancing the Stone   (85) 421
Roughly Speaking [1945]   (83) 490

Royal Wedding [1951]   (86) 536
St. Elmo's Fire   (86) 330
Second Thoughts   (84) 493
S.O.B.   (82) 328
Solid Gold Cadillac, The [1956]   (85) 615
Star 80   (84) 374
Star Is Born, A [1954]   (84) 573
Sweet Dreams   (86) 374
Swing Shift   (85) 535
Take a Letter, Darling [1942]   (85) 632
Tempest   (83) 331
Too Hot to Handle [1938]   (84) 596
Tootsie   (83) 353
Torn Curtain [1966]   (85) 644
Under Fire   (84) 441
Veronika Voss   (83) 382
Victor/Victoria   (83) 387
World According to Garp, The   (83) 397

CARIBBEAN ISLANDS
Sugar Cane Alley [1983]   (85) 461

CENTRAL AMERICA
Deal of the Century   (84) 482
Norte, El   (84) 265
Toy Soldiers   (85) 536
Under Fire   (84) 441

CHICAGO
Breakfast Club, The   (86) 85
City Heat   (85) 141
Code of Silence   (86) 440
Continental Divide   (82) 115
Cowboy [1958]   (82) 417
Journey of Natty Gann, The   (86) 203
My Reputation [1946]   (85) 586
Natural, The   (85) 329
Purple Haze   (84) 492

CHILDREN AND CHILD REARING (*See also* FAMILIES AND FAMILY LIFE)
After the Rehearsal   (85) 52
Annie   (83) 56
Bambi [1942]   (85) 543
Bedtime for Bonzo [1951]   (84) 512
Betrayal   (84) 67
Blame It on the Night   (85) 512
Bon Plaisir, Le [1983]   (85) 513
Breakfast Club, The   (86) 85
Buddy System, The   (85) 514
By Design   (83) 419
Caddie [1976]   (83) 439
Careful He Might Hear You [1983]   (85) 130
Chosen, The   (83) 116
Country   (85) 156
D.A.R.Y.L.   (86) 441
Dreamchild   (86) 146
E.T.: The Extra-Terrestrial   (83) 151
Earthling, The [1980]   (82) 130
Enemy Mine   (86) 161
Entre nous [1983]   (85) 176
Fanny and Alexander [1982]   (84) 146
Firestarter   (85) 519
Firstborn   (85) 519
Footloose   (85) 198
Frances   (83) 178
Heart Like a Wheel   (84) 182
Heartland   (82) 191
Hondo [1954]   (83) 452
Honkytonk Man   (83) 200
Improper Channels   (82) 218
Irreconcilable Differences   (85) 523
Jimmy the Kid   (84) 486
Lianna   (84) 201
Marie   (86) 227

Micki & Maude   (85) 308
Missing   (83) 228
Mommie Dearest   (82) 245
Mr. Mom   (84) 489
Mrs. Soffel   (85) 314
Murphy's Romance   (86) 242
My Favorite Year   (83) 241
My Reputation [1946]   (85) 586
Night of the Shooting Stars, The [1982]   (84) 258
Official Story, The   (86) 249
On Golden Pond   (82) 263
Once upon a Time in America   (85) 345
Paris, Texas   (85) 359
Pee-wee's Big Adventure   (86) 265
Peter Ibbetson [1935]   (86) 527
Petite Bande, La [1982]   (85) 528
Pixote [1980]   (82) 280
Places in the Heart   (85) 371
Poltergeist   (83) 263
Pretty Baby [1978]   (85) 597
Raggedy Man   (82) 300
Roughly Speaking [1945]   (83) 490
Santa Claus   (86) 334
Savannah Smiles   (84) 493
Shoot the Moon   (83) 295
Silkwood   (84) 367
Silverado   (86) 349
Six Pack   (83) 428
Smash Palace [1981]   (83) 302
Smooth Talk   (86) 354
Sophie's Choice   (83) 311
St. Elmo's Fire   (86) 330
State of Things, The   (84) 379
Stephen King's Children of the Corn   (85) 534
Streetwise   (86) 364
Superman III   (84) 399
Table for Five   (84) 404
Taking Off [1971]   (86) 545
Tempest   (83) 331
Tender Mercies   (84) 409
Terms of Endearment   (84) 414
Testament   (84) 420
Thief   (82) 356
Time Bandits [1980]   (82) 364
Tomorrow [1972]   (84) 589
Toy, The   (83) 358
28 Up [1984]   (86) 392
When Father Was Away on Business [1984]   (86) 411
World According to Garp, The   (83) 397

CHINA
Dim Sum   (86) 141
Hatchet Man, The [1932]   (83) 447
Too Hot to Handle [1938]   (84) 596
Year of the Dragon   (86) 426

CHRISTIANITY
Sign of the Cross, The [1932]   (85) 607

CHRISTMAS
Christmas Story, A   (84) 110
Comfort and Joy   (85) 146
Dorm That Dripped Blood, The   (84) 482
Fanny and Alexander [1982]   (84) 146
Gremlins   (85) 230
Holiday Inn [1942]   (82) 443
Marie   (86) 227
One Magic Christmas   (86) 455
Racing with the Moon   (85) 397
Santa Claus   (86) 334
Silent Night, Deadly Night   (85) 532

CIRCUS AND CARNIVALS
Gabriela [1983]   (85) 213

I'm No Angel [1933]   (85) 561
Moscow on the Hudson   (85) 321
Octopussy   (84) 276
Under the Volcano   (85) 499

CIVIL WAR
Battletruck   (83) 417
Bostonians, The   (85) 105
Ran   (86) 304

CLASS CONFLICT
Breakfast Club, The   (86) 85
Bullshot [1983]   (86) 438
Dance with a Stranger [1984]   (86) 125
Hard Traveling   (86) 445
Heartbreaker   (84) 485
Holy Innocents, The   (86) 447
Joshua Then and Now   (86) 198
Official Story, The   (86) 249
Private Function, A [1984]   (86) 280
Return of the Soldier, The [1982]   (84) 332
St. Elmo's Fire   (86) 330
Shooting Party, The [1984]   (86) 344
28 Up [1984]   (86) 392
White Nights   (86) 416

CLEVELAND
Stranger than Paradise   (85) 455

COLLEGE LIFE (See also SCHOOLS AND
    SCHOOL LIFE and TEACHERS AND
    TEACHING)
Baby, It's You   (84) 479
Bear, The   (85) 511
Bedtime for Bonzo [1951]   (84) 512
Big Chill, The   (84) 78
Chariots of Fire   (82) 101
Dorm That Dripped Blood, The   (84) 482
Educating Rita   (84) 136
Fandango   (86) 442
Fraternity Vacation   (86) 444
Gotcha!   (86) 444
Heat of Desire [1981]   (85) 522
If You Could See What I Hear   (83) 423
Imperative [1982]   (86) 447
Lianna   (84) 201
Long Gray Line, The [1955]   (82) 447
Marie   (86) 227
Mass Appeal   (85) 303
Night in Heaven, A   (84) 490
Oxford Blues   (85) 528
Party Animal   (86) 455
Running Brave   (84) 354
St. Elmo's Fire   (86) 330
School Spirit   (86) 458
Sure Thing, The   (86) 369
Tag   (83) 429
They're Playing with Fire   (85) 536
Up the Creek   (85) 537
Way We Were, The [1973]   (82) 474
Where the Boys Are '84   (85) 537

COMEDIANS
Broadway Danny Rose   (85) 112
Cheech and Chong Still Smokin'   (84) 480
Front, The [1976]   (86) 502
Funny Farm   (84) 484
King of Comedy, The   (84) 192
Our Relations [1936]   (86) 523
Pee-wee's Big Adventure   (86) 265
Richard Pryor Here and Now   (84) 492
St. Elmo's Fire   (86) 330
Secret Life of Walter Mitty, The [1947]   (86) 540

COMMUNISTS AND COMMUNISM
Eleni   (86) 151

Falcon and the Snowman, The   (86) 165
Firefox   (83) 160
Front, The [1976]   (86) 502
Gorky Park   (84) 162
Joke of Destiny, A [1983]   (85) 259
Killing Fields, The   (85) 270
Moscow on the Hudson   (85) 321
New Babylon, The [1929]   (84) 561
Rambo: First Blood Part II   (86) 299
Reds   (82) 312
Rocky IV   (86) 319
Torn Curtain [1966]   (85) 644
Under Fire   (84) 441
View to a Kill, A   (86) 402
Way We Were, The [1973]   (82) 474
When Father Was Away on Business [1984]   (86)
  411
White Nights   (86) 416
Year of Living Dangerously, The [1982]   (84)
  462

COMPUTERS (See also SCIENCE AND
  SCIENTISTS and SCIENCE FICTION)
Brazil   (86) 80
Electric Dreams   (85) 518
Rocky IV   (86) 319
Spies like Us   (86) 360
Superman III   (84) 399
TRON   (83) 371
2010   (85) 494
WarGames   (84) 458

CORRUPTION
And Nothing but the Truth   (85) 510
Escape Artist, The   (83) 421

COUNTERFEITING
Argent, L' [1983]   (85) 74

COUNTRY AND WESTERN
Fool for Love   (86) 172
Rhinestone   (85) 531
Songwriter   (85) 533
Sweet Dreams   (86) 374
Tender Mercies   (84) 409
Tough Enough   (84) 495

CRIME (See also BANK ROBBERY;
  BLACKMAIL; GANGSTERS; JEWEL
  ROBBERY; MURDER; and ROBBERY)
After Hours   (86) 51
Agnes of God   (86) 56
Argent, L' [1983]   (85) 74
Bad Boys   (84) 479
Beloved Rogue [1927]   (84) 522
Berlin Alexanderplatz [1980]   (84) 57
Beverly Hills Cop   (85) 88
Beyond Reasonable Doubt [1980]   (84) 74
Blue Thunder   (84) 84
Bob le Flambeur [1955]   (84) 526
Breathless   (84) 89
Brother from Another Planet, The   (85) 118
Cal   (85) 124
City Heat   (85) 141
Colorado Territory [1949]   (86) 489
Comfort and Joy   (85) 146
Cotton Club, The   (85) 150
Crimes of Passion   (85) 161
Dance with a Stranger [1984]   (86) 125
Deathtrap   (83) 137
Detour [1946]   (86) 498
Diva [1980]   (83) 147
Draughtsman's Contract, The [1982]   (84) 126
Firefox   (83) 160
First Name, Carmen [1983]   (85) 186

48 HRS.   (83) 173
Goonies, The   (86) 176
Gorky Park   (84) 162
Grey Fox, The   (84) 168
Hard Traveling   (86) 445
History Is Made at Night [1937]   (84) 542
Hit, The   (86) 446
I'm No Angel [1933]   (85) 561
Into the Night   (86) 186
Jagged Edge   (86) 190
Joshua Then and Now   (86) 198
Man Hunt [1941]   (85) 570
Marie   (86) 227
Max Dugan Returns   (84) 228
Mikey and Nicky [1976]   (85) 576
Mrs. Soffel   (85) 314
My New Partner [1984]   (86) 246
Nate and Hayes   (84) 236
Natural, The   (85) 329
Once upon a Time in America   (85) 345
Pale Rider   (86) 261
Patsy, The   (86) 456
Peter Ibbetson [1935]   (86) 527
Pixote [1980]   (82) 280
Police Academy 2   (86) 276
Pope of Greenwich Village, The   (85) 529
Prince of the City   (82) 292
Prizzi's Honor   (86) 285
Querelle [1982]   (84) 313
Repo Man   (85) 408
Return of Martin Guerre, The   (84) 318
Road Warrior, The [1981]   (83) 277
Romancing the Stone   (85) 421
Runaway Train   (86) 324
Scarface   (84) 361
Secret Life of Walter Mitty, The [1947]   (86) 540
Sense of Freedom, A   (86) 459
Silverado   (86) 349
Soldier's Story, A   (85) 427
Star 80   (84) 374
Star Chamber, The   (84) 494
Stick   (86) 460
Streetwise   (86) 364
Sudden Impact   (84) 395
Superman II   (82) 339
Superman III   (84) 399
Thief   (82) 356
Tightrope   (85) 489
To Live and Die in L.A.   (86) 379
Trouble in Mind   (86) 388
True Confessions   (82) 368
Victim [1961]   (85) 649
View to a Kill, A   (86) 402
Witness   (86) 421
Year of the Dragon   (86) 426
Young Sherlock Holmes   (86) 431

DANCERS AND DANCING
Backstage at the Kirov   (85) 511
Bal, Le [1983]   (85) 80
Beat Street   (85) 512
Blood Wedding [1981]   (83) 418
Body Rock   (85) 513
Breakin'   (85) 514
Breakin' 2   (85) 514
Carmen   (84) 101
Chorus Line, A   (86) 91
Cotton Club, The   (85) 150
Flashdance   (84) 158
Footloose   (85) 198
History Is Made At Night [1937]   (84) 542

Holiday Inn [1942]   (82) 443
I'm No Angel [1933]   (85) 561
Invitation to the Dance [1956]   (86) 507
King of Jazz [1930]   (86) 515
Kiss Me Goodbye   (83) 209
Pee-wee's Big Adventure   (86) 265
Purple Rain   (85) 389
Royal Wedding [1951]   (86) 536
Six Weeks   (83) 428
Specter of the Rose [1946]   (83) 504
Staying Alive   (84) 386
White Nights   (86) 416
DEATH AND DYING
After the Rehearsal   (85) 52
All of Me   (85) 58
Arthur   (82) 71
Bambi [1942]   (85) 543
Beau Pere   (82) 78
Berlin Alexanderplatz [1980]   (84) 57
Big Chill, The   (84) 78
Bizet's Carmen [1983]   (85) 98
Black Cat, The   (85) 512
Blade Runner   (83) 76
Boot, Das [1981]   (83) 86
Brazil   (86) 80
Brewster McCloud [1970]   (86) 484
Cannery Row   (83) 95
Careful He Might Hear You [1983]   (85) 130
Cocoon   (86) 96
Colorado Territory [1949]   (86) 489
Cowboy [1958]   (82) 417
Dangerous Moves [1984]   (86) 129
Death of Mario Ricci, The [1983]   (86) 133
Deathtrap   (83) 137
Detour [1946]   (86) 498
Dreamchild   (86) 146
Earthling, The [1980]   (82) 130
Eddie and the Cruisers   (84) 483
E.T.: The Extra-Terrestrial   (83) 151
Fanny and Alexander [1982]   (84) 146
Fort Apache, the Bronx   (82) 159
48 HRS.   (83) 173
Four Friends   (82) 167
Four Seasons, The   (82) 171
Front, The [1976]   (86) 502
Gandhi   (83) 183
Ghost Story   (82) 183
Guy Named Joe, A [1943]   (82) 435
Heavenly Kid, The   (86) 445
Honkytonk Man   (83) 200
Into the Night   (86) 186
Invitation au Voyage [1982]   (84) 486
Killing Fields, The   (85) 270
Kiss Me Goodbye   (83) 460
Light Ahead, The [1939]   (83) 460
Lonely Hearts [1982]   (84) 212
Long Gray Line, The [1955]   (82) 447
Love Streams   (85) 293
Man with Two Brains, The   (84) 223
Marie   (86) 227
Mask   (86) 231
Max Dugan Returns   (84) 228
Merry Christmas, Mr. Lawrence   (84) 231
Mishima   (86) 236
Missing   (83) 232
Misunderstood   (85) 526
My Reputation [1946]   (85) 586
Next Stop, Greenwich Village [1976]   (85) 592
Night of the Comet   (85) 527
North Star, The [1943]   (83) 476
O'Hara's Wife   (83) 426
On Golden Pond   (82) 263

Pale Rider   (86) 261
Peter Ibbetson [1935]   (86) 527
Phar Lap   (85) 528
Postman Always Rings Twice, The   (82) 284
Quiet Earth, The   (86) 295
Racing with the Moon   (85) 397
Raggedy Man   (82) 300
Ran   (86) 304
Repo Man   (85) 408
Return of the Jedi   (84) 326
Return of the Living Dead, The   (86) 314
Rocky III   (83) 283
Rocky IV   (86) 319
Runaway Train   (86) 324
Running Brave   (84) 354
St. Elmo's Fire   (86) 330
Shoah   (86) 339
Shoot the Moon   (83) 295
Shooting Party, The [1984]   (86) 344
Sign of the Cross, The [1932]   (85) 607
Silkwood   (84) 367
Silverado   (86) 349
Snows of Kilimanjaro, The [1952]   (83) 498
S.O.B.   (82) 328
Sophie's Choice   (83) 311
Sound Barrier, The [1952]   (85) 621
Star 80   (82) 374
Star Trek II—The Wrath of Khan   (83) 321
Star Trek III—The Search for Spock   (85) 439
Stardust Memories [1980]   (85) 626
State of Things, The   (84) 379
Still of the Night   (83) 326
Stone Boy, The   (85) 450
Streamers   (84) 391
Streetwise   (86) 364
Sunday in the Country, A   (85) 466
Swann in Love   (85) 471
Sweet Dreams   (86) 374
Table for Five   (84) 404
Taps   (82) 343
Tender Mercies   (84) 409
Terms of Endearment   (84) 414
Testament   (84) 420
Thing, The   (83) 343
This Is Elvis   (82) 360
Three Brothers [1980]   (83) 349
Time Bandits [1980]   (82) 364
To Live and Die in L.A.   (86) 379
Traviata, La   (83) 366
Under Fire   (84) 441
Under the Volcano   (85) 499
Valentina   (84) 496
Vie continue, La [1981]   (83) 430
Volver a empezar   (83) 393
Wetherby   (86) 406
Whose Life Is It Anyway?   (82) 378
World According to Garp, The   (83) 397
DENMARK
Out of Africa   (86) 255
DENTISTS
Bells Are Ringing [1960]   (84) 517
Compromising Positions   (86) 120
Reuben, Reuben   (84) 337
DEPARTMENT STORES
Comfort and Joy   (85) 146
Commando   (86) 111
Fast Times at Ridgemont High   (83) 156
Moscow on the Hudson   (85) 321
New Babylon, The [1929]   (84) 561
Secret Life of Walter Mitty, The [1947]   (86) 540
Toy, The   (83) 358

SUBJECT INDEX

THE DEPRESSION
Animal Kingdom, The [1932]   (86) 469
Annie   (83) 56
Bad Boy, The   (86) 436
Cannery Row   (83) 95
Careful He Might Hear You [1983]   (85) 130
Dreamchild   (86) 146
Honkytonk Man   (83) 200
I'm No Angel [1933]   (85) 561
Journey of Natty Gann, The   (86) 203
Miracle Woman, The [1931]   (83) 473
Natural, The   (85) 329
Pennies from Heaven   (82) 52
Places in the Heart   (85) 371
Roughly Speaking [1945]   (83) 490

DESERTS
Paradise   (83) 426
Sahara   (85) 531

DETECTIVES (See also POLICE)
Balance, La [1982]   (84) 52
Bells Are Ringing [1960]   (84) 517
Beverly Hills Cop   (85) 88
Beyond Reasonable Doubt [1980]   (84) 74
Blade Runner   (83) 76
Blood Simple   (86) 438
Brewster McCloud [1970]   (86) 484
Chan Is Missing   (83) 113
City Heat   (85) 141
Compromising Positions   (86) 120
Cross Country   (84) 481
Curse of the Pink Panther   (84) 481
Dead Men Don't Wear Plaid   (83) 134
Detective   (86) 442
Endangered Species   (83) 420
Evil Under the Sun [1981]   (83) 421
48 HRS.   (83) 173
Front, The [1976]   (86) 502
Goat, The [1981]   (86) 444
Gorky Park   (84) 162
Grey Fox, The   (84) 168
Hammett   (84) 174
Heads or Tails [1980]   (84) 485
Hound of the Baskervilles, The [1978]   (82) 203
I, the Jury   (83) 423
Jagged Edge   (86) 190
My New Partner [1984]   (86) 246
Sherlock Holmes [1922]   (83) 494
Soldier's Story, A   (85) 427
Specter of the Rose [1946]   (83) 504
Star 80   (84) 374
They All Laughed   (82) 350
They Might Be Giants [1971]   (83) 515
Tightrope   (85) 489
Trail of the Pink Panther   (83) 430
Victim [1961]   (85) 647
Wetherby   (86) 406
Witness   (86) 421
Young Sherlock Holmes   (86) 431

DIVORCE
Always   (86) 60
Caddie [1976]   (83) 439
Can She Bake a Cherry Pie?   (84) 95
Divorcée, The [1930]   (82) 429
Entre nous [1983]   (85) 176
Every Man for Himself [1979]   (82) 139
Fanny and Alexander [1982]   (84) 146
Four Friends   (82) 167
Gabriela [1983]   (85) 213
History Is Made at Night [1937]   (84) 542
Improper Channels   (82) 218
Jagged Edge   (86) 190

Love Streams   (85) 293
Man with Two Brains, The   (84) 223
Marie   (86) 227
Micki & Maude   (85) 308
Out of Africa   (86) 255
Prizzi's Honor   (86) 285
Roughly Speaking [1945]   (83) 490
St. Elmo's Fire   (86) 330
Shoot the Moon   (83) 295
Slap Shot [1977]   (82) 467
Smash Palace [1981]   (83) 302
Star 80   (84) 374
Table for Five   (84) 404
Tender Mercies   (84) 409
Twice in a Lifetime   (86) 397
Unfaithful, The [1947]   (86) 550
World of Henry Orient, The [1964]   (84) 600

DOCTORS AND MEDICINE (See also PSYCHIATRY AND PSYCHIATRISTS)
Adolescente, L' [1979]   (83) 53
Adventures of Buckaroo Banzai, The   (85) 47
American Werewolf in London, An   (82) 66
Arch of Triumph [1948]   (84) 501
Bad Medicine   (86) 437
Brainstorm   (84) 480
Brittania Hospital   (84) 480
Buddy Buddy   (82) 93
Doctor and the Devils, The   (86) 442
Don't Cry, It's Only Thunder   (83) 420
Frances   (83) 178
Freud [1962]   (84) 535
Howling, The   (82) 207
Jekyll and Hyde . . . Together Again   (83) 424
Killing Fields, The   (85) 270
Light Ahead, The [1939]   (83) 460
Man with Two Brains, The   (84) 223
Marie   (86) 227
Mask   (86) 231
North Star, The [1943]   (83) 476
Out of Africa   (86) 255
Private Function, A [1984]   (86) 280
Purple Hearts   (85) 529
Racing with the Moon   (85) 397
Return of the Living Dead, The   (86) 314
Secret Life of Walter Mitty, The [1947]   (86) 540
Spies like Us   (86) 360
Stitches   (86) 461
Threshold   (84) 495
Verdict, The   (83) 377
Veronika Voss   (83) 387
Whose Life Is It Anyway?   (82) 378
World According to Garp, The   (83) 397
Yes, Giorgio   (83) 431
Young Doctors in Love   (83) 431

DOCUMENTARY
Another State of Mind   (85) 510
Beach Boys, The   (86) 438
Blood Wedding [1981]   (83) 418
Broken Rainbow   (86) 439
Gospel   (85) 520
In Our Hands   (84) 486
Let's Spend the Night Together   (84) 487
Richard Pryor Here and Now   (84) 492
Stop Making Sense   (85) 534
Streetwise   (86) 364
28 Up [1984]   (86) 392

DREAMS
After the Rehearsal   (85) 52
Agnes of God   (86) 56
American Dreamer   (85) 509
Berlin Alexanderplatz [1980]   (84) 57

Brazil (86) 80
Breakin' (85) 514
City of Women (82) 106
Cloak and Dagger (85) 516
Comfort and Joy (85) 146
Company of Wolves, The [1984] (86) 115
Dead Zone, The (84) 481
Dreamchild (86) 146
Dreamscape (85) 166
Echoes (84) 483
Emerald Forest, The (86) 156
Erendira [1983] (85) 181
Fanny and Alexander [1982] (84) 146
Flashdance (84) 158
4th Man, The [1983] (85) 203
I Ought to Be in Pictures (83) 423
Love Streams (85) 293
Most Dangerous Game, The [1932] (86) 519
Nightmare on Elm Street, A (85) 527
Nostalgia [1983] (85) 340
Peter Ibbetson [1935] (86) 527
Secret Life of Walter Mitty, The [1947] (86) 540
Stardust Memories [1980] (85) 626
Starstruck (83) 428
Still of the Night (83) 326
Tempest (83) 331
Tender Mercies (84) 409
Under the Volcano (85) 499
Windy City (85) 538
Zelig (84) 473

DRUGS AND DRUG ABUSE
American Pop (82) 62
Atlantic City (82) 74
Balance, La [1982] (84) 52
Beverly Hills Cop (85) 88
Breakfast Club, The (86) 85
Brother from Another Planet, The (85) 118
Cheech and Chong Still Smokin' (84) 480
Christine F. [1981] (83) 419
Class of 1984 (83) 419
Code of Silence (86) 440
Falcon and the Snowman, The (86) 165
Fast Times at Ridgemont High (83) 156
Fletch (86) 169
Fort Apache, the Bronx (82) 159
48 HRS. (83) 173
Frances (83) 178
Gringo (86) 445
Guest, The (85) 520
Hatchet Man, The [1932] (83) 447
Heavenly Kid, The (86) 445
I'm Dancing as Fast as I Can (83) 423
Lady Sings the Blues [1972] (85) 565
Mask (86) 231
Mike's Murder (85) 526
Mixed Blood (86) 452
My New Partner [1984] (86) 246
Nighthawks (82) 259
Once upon a Time in America (85) 345
Prince of the City (82) 292
Querelle [1982] (84) 313
Razor's Edge, The (85) 402
Repo Man (85) 408
St. Elmo's Fire (86) 330
Scarface (84) 361
Sharky's Machine (82) 324
Silkwood (84) 367
S.O.B. (82) 328
Streetwise (86) 364
Taking Off [1971] (86) 545
Things Are Tough All Over (83) 430
This Is Elvis (82) 360

Verdict, The (83) 377
Veronika Voss (83) 382
Year of the Dragon (86) 426
DUBLIN
James Joyce's Women (86) 193

EDUCATION
Educating Rita (84) 136
Marie (86) 227
Mask (86) 231
Monty Python's The Meaning of Life (84) 489
Official Story, The (86) 249
Real Genius (86) 309
St. Elmo's Fire (86) 330
Sure Thing, The (86) 369
Teachers (85) 535
Wetherby (86) 406

EIGHTEENTH CENTURY
Amadeus (85) 63
Bounty, The (85) 513
Bridge of San Luis Rey, The [1929] (82) 408
Danton [1982] (84) 121
Mutiny on the Bounty [1962] (85) 581
Napoleon [1927] (82) 461
Nuit de Varennes, La [1982] (84) 270
Revolution (86) 458
Xica [1976] (83) 407

ENGLAND (See also LONDON)
Agatha [1979] (83) 435
Becky Sharp [1935] (82) 403
Brimstone and Treacle (83) 91
Chariots of Fire (82) 101
Disraeli [1929] (82) 426
Draughtman's Contract, The [1982] (84) 126
Dreamchild (86) 146
Dresser, The (84) 130
Educating Rita (84) 136
Excalibur (82) 148
Falstaff [1967] (83) 443
French Lieutenant's Woman, The (82) 174
Gandhi (83) 183
Greystoke (85) 236
Heat and Dust [1982] (84) 187
Joshua Then and Now (86) 198
Kipperbang [1983] (85) 524
Man Hunt [1941] (85) 570
Missionary, The (83) 233
My Cousin Rachel [1952] (82) 458
Nell Gwyn [1934] (84) 557
Ordeal by Innocence [1984] (86) 455
Oxford Blues (85) 528
Peter Ibbetson [1935] (86) 527
Pirates of Penzance, The (84) 301
Plenty (86) 271
Ploughman's Lunch, The [1983] (85) 377
Priests of Love (82) 288
Private Function, A [1984] (86) 280
Return of the Soldier, The [1982] (84) 332
Royal Wedding [1951] (86) 536
Secret Places [1984] (86) 459
Shooting Party, The [1984] (86) 344
Sound Barrier, The [1952] (85) 621
Tess [1980] (82) 471
28 Up [1984] (86) 392
Victim [1961] (85) 647
Wetherby (86) 406
Young Sherlock Holmes (86) 431

ENTERTAINERS (See ACTORS AND
   ACTRESSES; COMEDIANS; DANCERS
   AND DANCING; FILMMAKERS AND

SUBJECT INDEX

FILMMAKING; MUSIC AND MUSICIANS;
SINGERS; *and* THEATER)

ENVIRONMENTALISM
Emerald Forest, The   (86) 156
Impulse   (85) 523
Koyaanisqatsi   (84) 197
Pale Rider   (86) 261
Silkwood   (84) 367
Where the Green Ants Dream [1984]   (86) 465
Wombling Free [1979]   (85) 538

ESCAPE
After Hours   (86) 51
All the Right Moves   (84) 41
Blood Wedding [1981]   (83) 418
Boat Is Full, The [1981]   (83) 82
Brazil   (86) 80
Dreamchild   (86) 146
Eddie Macon's Run   (84) 483
E.T.: The Extra-Terrestrial   (83) 151
Fire and Ice   (84) 153
Firefox   (83) 160
First Name, Carmen [1983]   (85) 186
Frances   (83) 178
Indiana Jones and the Temple of Doom   (85)
  253
Joke of Destiny, A [1983]   (85) 259
Journey into Fear [1943]   (86) 511
Lost in America   (86) 219
Moscow on the Hudson   (85) 321
Most Dangerous Game, The [1932]   (86) 519
Murphy's Romance   (86) 242
Nate and Hayes   (84) 236
Night Crossing   (83) 426
Night of the Shooting Stars, The [1982]   (84) 258
Norte, El   (84) 265
Nuit de Varennes, La [1982]   (84) 270
Petite Bande, La [1982]   (85) 528
Poltergeist   (83) 263
Purple Rose of Cairo, The   (86) 290
Road Warrior, The [1981]   (83) 277
Romancing the Stone   (85) 421
Runaway Train   (86) 324
Running Hot   (85) 531
St. Elmo's Fire   (86) 330
Secret Life of Walter Mitty, The [1947]   (86) 540
Silverado   (86) 349
Too Hot to Handle [1938]   (84) 596
Torn Curtain [1966]   (85) 643
TRON   (83) 371
White Nights   (86) 416
Yol   (85) 411

ESKIMOS
Golden Seal, The   (84) 485
Iceman   (85) 248

ESPIONAGE
Cloak and Dagger   (83) 516
Colonel Redl [1984]   (86) 100
Daniel   (84) 481
Dune   (85) 171
Enigma [1982]   (84) 483
Eye of the Needle   (82) 148
Falcon and the Snowman, The   (86) 165
Firefox   (83) 160
For Your Eyes Only   (82) 155
Front, The [1976]   (86) 502
Gorky Park   (84) 162
Gotcha!   (86) 444
Holcroft Covenant, The   (86) 446
Invasion U.S.A.   (86) 447
Jigsaw Man, The [1983]   (85) 524
Journey into Fear [1943]   (86) 511

Kiss of the Spider Woman   (86) 209
Little Drummer Girl, The   (85) 525
Man Hunt [1941]   (85) 570
Man with One Red Shoe, The   (86) 451
Never Say Never Again   (84) 252
Octopussy   (84) 276
Osterman Weekend, The   (84) 491
Remo Williams   (86) 457
Soldier, The   (83) 428
Spies like Us   (86) 360
Target   (86) 462
Top Secret   (85) 536
Torn Curtain [1966]   (85) 643
Under Fire   (84) 441
White Nights   (86) 416
Wrong Is Right   (83) 403

EXILE
Beloved Rogue [1927]   (84) 522
Hail Mary   (86) 182
Nostalgia [1983]   (85) 340
Prizzi's Honor   (86) 285
Ran   (86) 304
When Father Was Away on Business [1984]   (86)
  411
White Nights   (86) 416

EXPERIMENTAL
Brewster McCloud [1970]   (86) 484
Dernier Combat, Le [1983]   (85) 517
Good Bye Cruel World   (85) 520
Koyaanisqatsi   (84) 197
Return of the Living Dead, The   (86) 314

FACTORIES
Adventures of Buckaroo Banzai, The   (85) 47
All the Right Moves   (84) 41
Bizet's Carmen [1983]   (85) 98
Comfort and Joy   (85) 146
Flashdance   (84) 158
Officer and a Gentleman, An   (83) 246
Passion [1982]   (84) 289
Silkwood   (84) 367
Sound Barrier, The [1952]   (85) 621
Swing Shift   (85) 535

FAMILIES AND FAMILY LIFE (*See also*
CHILDREN AND CHILD REARING *and*
MARRIAGE)
Adolescente, L' [1979]   (83) 53
After the Rehearsal   (85) 52
All the Right Moves   (84) 41
American Flyers   (86) 436
American Pop   (82) 62
Animal Kingdom, The [1932]   (86) 469
Arrangement, The [1969]   (86) 474
Author! Author!   (83) 417
Back to the Future   (86) 65
Barbarosa   (83) 60
Beau Pere   (82) 78
Beloved Rogue [1927]   (84) 522
Best Friends   (83) 68
Birdy   (85) 93
Bolero [1981]   (83) 418
Breakfast Club, The   (86) 85
Brimstone and Treacle   (83) 91
Careful He Might Hear You [1983]   (85) 130
Cat People [1942]   (82) 13
Cat People   (83) 100
Chan Is Missing   (83) 113
Chosen, The   (83) 116
Christine   (84) 106
Christmas Story, A   (84) 110
Come and Get It [1936]   (82) 412

Comfort and Joy   (85) 146
Country   (85) 156
Cross Creek   (84) 116
Daniel   (84) 481
Demons in the Garden [1982]   (85) 517
Dim Sum   (86) 141
Diner   (83) 142
Easy Money   (84) 482
Eddie Macon's Run   (84) 483
Emerald Forest, The   (86) 156
Entre nous [1983]   (85) 176
Falcon and the Snowman, The   (86) 165
Fanny and Alexander [1982]   (84) 146
Fast Times at Ridgemont High   (83) 156
Firstborn   (85) 519
Flamingo Kid, The   (85) 192
Footloose   (85) 198
Foster Daddy, Tora! [1980]   (82) 163
Four Seasons, The   (82) 171
Frances   (83) 178
Front, The [1976]   (86) 502
Gandhi   (83) 183
Garbo Talks   (85) 520
Goonies, The   (86) 176
Gregory's Girl [1981]   (83) 193
Hard Way, The [1942]   (85) 555
Harry and Son   (85) 521
Heart Like a Wheel   (84) 182
Heart of a Stag   (85) 522
Horse of Pride, The [1984]   (86) 447
Hotel New Hampshire, The   (85) 243
I Sent a Letter to My Love [1980]   (82) 214
Improper Channels   (82) 218
Irreconcilable Differences   (85) 523
James Joyce's Women   (86) 193
Joke of Destiny, A [1983]   (85) 259
Joshua Then and Now   (86) 198
Journey of Natty Gann, The   (86) 203
Kiss of the Spider Woman   (86) 209
Lianna   (84) 201
Little Jerk [1984]   (86) 450
Lonely Hearts [1982]   (84) 212
Long Gray Line, The [1955]   (82) 447
Love Streams   (85) 293
Makioka Sisters, The [1983]   (86) 451
Man, Woman and Child   (84) 489
Marie   (86) 227
Mask   (86) 231
Max Dugan Returns   (84) 228
Melvin and Howard [1980]   (82) 453
Micki & Maude   (85) 308
Missing   (83) 232
Mr. Mom   (84) 489
Misunderstood   (85) 526
Mixed Blood   (86) 452
Montenegro   (82) 250
Moscow on the Hudson   (85) 321
Murphy's Romance   (86) 242
My Favorite Year   (83) 241
My Reputation [1946]   (85) 586
National Lampoon's European Vacation   (86) 453
National Lampoon's Vacation   (84) 241
Natural, The   (85) 329
Next Stop, Greenwich Village [1976]   (85) 592
Norte, El   (84) 265
Officer and a Gentleman, An   (83) 246
Official Story, The   (86) 249
On Golden Pond   (82) 263
One Magic Christmas   (86) 455
Only When I Laugh   (82) 268
Our Relations [1936]   (86) 523

Pale Rider   (86) 261
Paris, Texas   (85) 359
Pirates of Penzance, The   (84) 301
Places in the Heart   (85) 371
Plouffe, Les   (86) 456
Poltergeist   (83) 263
Pretty Baby [1978]   (85) 597
Private Function, A [1984]   (86) 280
Prizzi's Honor   (86) 285
Purple Rain   (85) 389
Racing with the Moon   (85) 397
Raggedy Man   (82) 300
Ran   (86) 304
Repo Man   (85) 408
Return of Martin Guerre, The   (84) 318
Risky Business   (84) 349
River, The   (85) 416
Rocky III   (83) 283
Rocky IV   (86) 319
Roughly Speaking [1945]   (83) 490
Royal Wedding [1951]   (86) 536
St. Elmo's Fire   (86) 330
Sam's Son   (85) 531
Secret Life of Walter Mitty, The [1947]   (86) 540
Secret of NIMH, The   (83) 288
Shoot the Moon   (83) 295
Silverado   (86) 349
Six Weeks   (83) 428
Sixteen Candles   (85) 532
Smash Palace [1981]   (83) 302
Sophie's Choice   (83) 311
Split Image   (83) 317
Star Trek II—The Wrath of Khan   (83) 321
Stone Boy, The   (85) 450
Streetwise   (86) 364
Sugar Cane Alley [1983]   (85) 461
Summer Rental   (86) 462
Sunday in the Country, A   (85) 466
Table for Five   (84) 404
Taking Off [1971]   (86) 545
Target   (86) 462
Tempest   (83) 331
Tender Mercies   (84) 409
Terms of Endearment   (84) 414
Testament   (84) 420
Tex   (83) 335
Three Brothers [1980]   (83) 349
Tough Enough   (84) 495
Toy, The   (83) 358
Tragedy of a Ridiculous Man [1981]   (83) 361
Turk 182   (86) 464
28 Up [1984]   (86) 392
Twice in a Lifetime   (86) 397
Twilight Zone—The Movie   (84) 435
When Father Was Away on Business [1984]   (86) 411
Wild Duck, The [1983]   (86) 466
Witness   (86) 421
Woman in Red, The   (85) 538
World According to Garp, The   (83) 397
World of Henry Orient, The [1964]   (84) 600
FANTASY
After Hours   (86) 51
After the Rehearsal   (85) 52
Agnes of God   (86) 56
Bambi [1942]   (85) 543
Beastmaster, The   (83) 418
Birdy   (85) 93
Black Cauldron, The   (86) 75
Brazil   (86) 80
Brewster McCloud [1970]   (86) 484
Brother from Another Planet, The   (85) 118

SUBJECT INDEX

Choose Me   (85) 135
Clash of the Titans   (82) 111
Cloak and Dagger   (85) 516
Company of Wolves, The [1984]   (86) 115
Crimes of Passion   (85) 161
Dark Crystal, The   (83) 130
Desperately Seeking Susan   (86) 137
Dragonslayer   (82) 125
Dreamchild   (86) 146
Dreamscape   (85) 166
Dune   (85) 171
Erendira [1983]   (85) 181
E.T.: The Extra-Terrestrial   (83) 151
Excalibur   (82) 144
Fanny and Alexander [1982]   (84) 146
Fire and Ice   (84) 153
4th Man, The [1983]   (85) 203
Front, The [1976]   (86) 502
Great Muppet Caper, The   (82) 187
Gremlins   (85) 230
Greystoke   (85) 236
Guy Named Joe, A [1943]   (82) 435
Heavenly Kid, The   (86) 445
I Know Where I'm Going [1945]   (83) 456
I Love You   (83) 423
Iceman   (85) 248
Indiana Jones and the Temple of Doom   (85) 253
It Happened Tomorrow [1944]   (84) 552
Joke of Destiny, A [1983]   (85) 259
Ladyhawke   (86) 214
Last Starfighter, The   (85) 277
Mad Max Beyond Thunderdome   (86) 223
Man with Two Brains, The   (84) 223
Midsummer Night's Sex Comedy, A   (83) 224
Most Dangerous Game, The [1932]   (86) 519
Natural, The   (85) 329
Neverending Story, The   (85) 527
New York, New York [1977]   (84) 567
Night of the Shooting Stars, The [1982]   (84) 258
Pale Rider   (86) 261
Pennies from Heaven   (82) 276
Peter Ibbetson [1935]   (86) 527
Purple Rose of Cairo, The   (86) 290
Red Sonja   (86) 457
Return of the Jedi   (84) 326
Return to Oz   (86) 458
Risky Business   (84) 349
St. Elmo's Fire   (86) 330
Secret Life of Walter Mitty, The [1947]   (86) 540
Secret of NIMH, The   (83) 288
Siberiade [1977]   (83) 299
Smooth Talk   (86) 354
Smurfs and the Magic Flute, The   (84) 493
Splash   (85) 434
Starchaser   (86) 460
Stardust Memories [1980]   (85) 626
Starman   (85) 445
Superman III   (84) 399
Swann in Love   (85) 475
Teen Wolf   (86) 462
Tempest   (83) 331
Time After Time [1979]   (84) 579
Time Bandits [1980]   (82) 364
Timerider   (84) 495
Treasure of the Four Crowns   (84) 495
Twice upon a Time   (84) 496
Twilight Zone—The Movie   (84) 435
Weird Science   (86) 465
Yor   (84) 498
Zapped!   (83) 431

THE FAR EAST
High Road to China   (84) 486
Indiana Jones and the Temple of Doom   (85) 253
Killing Fields, The   (85) 270
Merry Christmas, Mr. Lawrence   (84) 231
Mishima   (86) 236
Nate and Hayes   (84) 236
Ran   (86) 304
Volunteers   (86) 464
Year of Living Dangerously, The [1982]   (84) 462
Year of the Dragon   (86) 426
FARMS AND FARMING
Another Time, Another Place [1983]   (85) 510
Beyond Reasonable Doubt [1980]   (84) 74
Cal   (85) 124
Country   (85) 156
Flaxfield, The [1983]   (86) 440
Heartland   (82) 191
Holiday Inn [1942]   (82) 443
Night of the Shooting Stars, The [1982]   (84) 258
North Star, The [1943]   (83) 476
Out of Africa   (86) 255
Places in the Heart   (85) 371
Return of Martin Guerre, The   (84) 318
River, The   (85) 416
Silverado   (86) 349
Stone Boy, The   (85) 450
Strange Invaders   (84) 494
Tess [1980]   (82) 471
FASCISM
Amin—The Rise and Fall   (84) 479
Boys from Brazil, The [1978]   (86) 480
Escape 2000   (84) 483
Night of the Shooting Stars, The [1982]   (84) 258
Shoah   (86) 339
FASHION AND FASHION DESIGNERS
Animal Kingdom, The [1932]   (86) 469
By Design   (83) 419
Entre nous [1983]   (85) 176
Great Muppet Caper, The   (82) 187
St. Elmo's Fire   (86) 330
Secret Life of Walter Mitty, The [1947]   (86) 540
FEMMES FATALES
Bizet's Carmen [1983]   (85) 98
Mikey and Nicky [1976]   (85) 576
FILM NOIR
After Hours   (86) 51
Blood Simple   (86) 438
Dance with a Stranger [1984]   (86) 125
Detour [1946]   (86) 498
Into the Night   (86) 186
Journey into Fear [1943]   (86) 511
Marie   (86) 227
To Live and Die in L.A.   (86) 379
Trancers   (86) 463
Unfaithful, The [1947]   (86) 550
FILMMAKERS AND FILMMAKING (See also ACTORS AND ACTRESSES)
Always   (86) 60
And the Ship Sails On [1983]   (85) 69
Barbary Coast [1935]   (84) 506
Barefoot Contessa, The [1954]   (82) 399
Best Friends   (83) 68
Blow Out   (82) 83
Cheech and Chong Still Smokin'   (84) 480
Dead Men Don't Wear Plaid   (83) 134
Drifting   (85) 518
First Name, Carmen [1983]   (85) 186

Frances   (83) 178
French Lieutenant's Woman, The   (82) 174
Front, The [1976]   (86) 502
Gremlins   (85) 230
Holiday Inn [1942]   (82) 443
I'm Dancing as Fast as I Can   (83) 423
Insignificance   (86) 447
Into the Night   (86) 186
Man of Iron   (82) 230
Man of Marble [1977]   (82) 234
Modern Romance   (82) 241
Mommie Dearest   (82) 245
Movers and Shakers   (86) 453
New York, New York [1977]   (84) 567
Passion [1982]   (84) 289
Ragtime   (82) 304
S.O.B.   (82) 328
Star 80   (84) 374
State of Things, The   (84) 379
Streamers   (84) 391
This Is Spinal Tap   (85) 484
Tokyo-Ga   (86) 463
Tootsie   (83) 353
True Confessions   (82) 368
Veronika Voss   (83) 382
Way We Were, The [1973]   (82) 474
When Nature Calls   (86) 465

FINANCIAL CRISIS
Argent, L' [1983]   (85) 74
Becky Sharp [1935]   (82) 403
Caddie [1976]   (83) 439
Comfort and Joy   (85) 146
Country   (85) 156
Detour [1946]   (86) 498
Disraeli [1929]   (83) 426
Entre nous [1983]   (85) 176
Front, The [1976]   (86) 502
Long Good Friday, The   (83) 220
Lost in America   (86) 219
Murphy's Romance   (86) 242
Out of Africa   (86) 255
Places in the Heart   (85) 371
Prizzi's Honor   (86) 285
Roughly Speaking [1945]   (83) 490
St. Elmo's Fire   (86) 330
Smithereens   (83) 307
Toy, The   (83) 358
Tragedy of a Ridiculous Man [1981]   (83) 361
Trouble in Mind   (86) 388

FLORIDA
Stranger than Paradise   (85) 455

FOOTBALL
Against All Odds   (85) 509
All the Right Moves   (84) 41
Bear, The   (85) 511
Best Little Whorehouse in Texas, The   (83) 72
Fast Times at Ridgemont High   (83) 156
When Father Was Away on Business [1984]   (86) 411

FORTUNE-TELLING
Bizet's Carmen [1983]   (85) 98
I'm No Angel [1933]   (85) 561
Querelle [1982]   (84) 313

FRANCE (See also PARIS)
Adolescente, L' [1979]   (83) 53
Arch of Triumph [1948]   (84) 501
Bal, Le [1983]   (85) 80
Balance, La [1982]   (84) 52
Beau Mariage, Le   (83) 65
Beau Pere   (82) 78
Beloved Rogue [1927]   (84) 522

Céleste [1981]   (83) 104
Chariots of Fire   (82) 101
Danton [1982]   (84) 121
First Name, Carmen [1983]   (85) 186
Full Moon in Paris   (85) 208
Garde à vue [1981]   (83) 189
History Is Made at Night [1937]   (84) 542
Horse of Pride, The   (86) 447
I Sent a Letter to My Love [1980]   (82) 214
Ladyhawke   (86) 214
My Best Friend's Girl [1983]   (85) 326
My New Partner [1984]   (86) 246
Napoleon [1927]   (82) 461
New Babylon, The [1929]   (84) 561
Nuit de Varennes, La [1982]   (84) 270
Pauline at the Beach [1982]   (84) 296
Return of Martin Guerre, The   (84) 318
Swann in Love   (85) 471
Trace, The [1983]   (85) 537
Woman Next Door, The   (82) 385

FRENCH REVOLUTION
Danton [1982]   (84) 121
Nuit de Varennes, La [1982]   (84) 270

FRIENDSHIP
Animal Kingdom, The [1932]   (86) 469
Berlin Alexanderplatz [1980]   (84) 57
Betrayal   (84) 67
Beverly Hills Cop   (85) 88
Big Chill, The   (84) 78
Birdy   (85) 93
Blame It on Rio   (85) 512
Brady's Escape   (85) 514
Breakfast Club, The   (86) 85
Certain Fury   (86) 440
Cocoon   (86) 96
Dreamchild   (86) 146
Enter the Ninja   (83) 420
Evil That Men Do, The   (85) 518
Falcon and the Snowman, The   (86) 165
Front, The [1976]   (86) 502
Full Moon in Paris   (85) 208
Golden Seal, The   (84) 485
Goonies, The   (86) 176
Heads or Tails [1980]   (84) 485
Home Free All   (85) 522
Joshua Then and Now   (86) 198
Kiss of the Spider Woman   (86) 209
Lianna   (84) 201
Macaroni   (86) 451
Marie   (86) 227
Marvin & Tige   (84) 489
Mask   (86) 231
Mikey and Nicky [1976]   (85) 576
Mischief   (86) 452
Murphy's Romance   (86) 242
My Dinner with André   (82) 255
Official Story, The   (86) 249
Once upon a Time in America   (85) 345
Out of Africa   (86) 255
Pee-Wee's Big Adventure   (86) 265
Pope of Greenwich Village, The   (85) 529
Purple Haze   (84) 492
Quiet Earth, The   (86) 295
Real Genius   (86) 309
Runaway Train   (86) 324
St. Elmo's Fire   (86) 330
Savannah Smiles   (84) 493
Sheer Madness [1983]   (86) 459
Silverado   (86) 349
Spies like Us   (86) 360
State of Things, The   (84) 379
Streetwise   (86) 364

Survivors, The   (84) 495
Unfaithful, The [1947]   (86) 550
Wetherby   (86) 406
White Nights   (86) 416
Woman in Red, The   (85) 538
World of Henry Orient, The [1964]   (84) 600
Yentl   (84) 468
Zappa   (85) 539

FRONTIER LIFE
Colorado Territory [1949]   (86) 489
Grey Fox, The   (84) 168
Pale Rider   (86) 261
Silverado   (86) 349
Timerider   (84) 495
We of the Never Never [1982]   (84) 497

GAMBLING
Atlantic City   (82) 74
Barbary Coast [1935]   (84) 506
Bells Are Ringing [1960]   (84) 517
Choose Me   (85) 135
City Heat   (85) 141
Diner   (83) 142
Fever Pitch   (86) 443
Flamingo Kid, The   (85) 192
Forced Vengeance   (83) 422
Front, The [1976]   (86) 502
Jinxed   (83) 206
Lookin' to Get Out   (83) 425
Lost in America   (86) 219
My New Partner [1984]   (86) 249
Natural, The   (85) 329
Never Say Never Again   (84) 252
Racing with the Moon   (85) 397
Risky Business   (84) 349
Silverado   (86) 349
Stranger than Paradise   (85) 455
Trouble in Mind   (86) 388

GANGS
Alley Cat   (85) 509
Alphabet City   (85) 509
Beat Street   (85) 512
Code of Silence   (86) 440
Death Wish III   (86) 441
First Name, Carmen   (85) 186
Hit, The   (86) 446
Into the Night   (86) 186
Killpoint   (85) 524
1990   (84) 491
Once upon a Time in America   (85) 345
Outsiders, The   (84) 282
Police Academy 2   (86) 276
Prizzi's Honor   (86) 285
Return of the Living Dead, The   (86) 314
Rumble Fish   (84) 492
Silverado   (86) 349
Streets of Fire   (85) 534
Tuff Turf   (86) 464
Year of the Dragon   (86) 426

GANGSTERS
Absence of Malice   (82) 57
Against All Odds   (85) 509
American Pop   (82) 62
Atlantic City   (82) 74
Balance, La [1982]   (84) 52
Beverly Hills Cop   (85) 88
Body and Soul   (83) 418
Breathless   (84) 89
Broadway Danny Rose   (85) 112
Choose Me   (85) 135
City Heat   (85) 141

Comfort and Joy   (85) 146
Continental Divide   (82) 115
Cotton Club, The   (85) 150
Dead Men Don't Wear Plaid   (83) 134
Doctor Detroit   (84) 482
Forced Vengeance   (83) 422
48 HRS.   (83) 173
Hammett   (84) 174
Johnny Dangerously   (85) 524
Kitty and the Bagman [1982]   (84) 487
Long Good Friday, The   (83) 220
Max Dugan Returns   (84) 228
Mikey and Nicky [1976]   (85) 576
Monsignor   (83) 425
Never Say Never Again   (84) 252
Once upon a Time in America   (85) 345
Pete Kelly's Blues [1955]   (83) 481
Scarface   (84) 361
Tempest   (83) 331
They Call Me Bruce   (83) 429
Victor / Victoria   (83) 387

GENERATION GAP
Breakfast Club, The   (86) 85
Dim Sum   (86) 141
National Lampoon's Vacation   (84) 241
Ran   (86) 304
St. Elmo's Fire   (86) 330
Smooth Talk   (86) 354
Taking Off [1971]   (86) 545

GERMANY
Berlin Alexanderplatz [1980]   (84) 57
Boat Is Full, The [1981]   (83) 82
Boot, Das [1981]   (83) 86
Lili Marleen   (82) 222
Lola [1981]   (83) 215
Love in Germany, A [1983]   (85) 283
Man Hunt [1941]   (85) 570
Mephisto   (82) 237
Nate and Hayes   (84) 236
Shoah   (86) 339
Sophie's Choice   (83) 311
Taxi Zum Klo   (82) 346
Torn Curtain [1966]   (85) 644
Veronika Voss   (83) 382
Victory   (82) 374
White Rose, The   (84) 497

GHOSTS
Amityville II   (83) 417
Angelo My Love   (84) 41
Fanny and Alexander [1982]   (84) 146
House Where Evil Dwells, The   (83) 423
Madman   (84) 488
O'Hara's Wife   (83) 426

GOLD AND GOLD MINES
Mother Lode   (84) 490

GREECE
Eleni   (86) 151
Fantasies   (83) 421
Summer Lovers   (83) 429
Tempest   (83) 331

GREEK AND ROMAN TIMES
Clash of the Titans   (82) 111
Sign of the Cross, The [1932]   (85) 607
Time Bandits [1980]   (82) 364

GUILT
After Hours   (86) 51
Agnes of God   (86) 56
Berlin Alexanderplatz [1980]   (84) 57
Breakfast Club, The   (86) 85
Compromising Positions   (86) 120

Dreamchild   (86) 146
Front, The [1976]   (86) 502
Joshua Then and Now   (86) 198
Kiss of the Spider Woman   (86) 209
Man Hunt [1941]   (85) 570
Mission, The   (84) 489
Official Story, The   (86) 249
Ordeal by Innocence [1984]   (86) 455
Plenty   (86) 271
Rocky IV   (86) 319
St. Elmo's Fire   (86) 330
Shoah   (86) 339
Shooting Party, The [1984]   (86) 344
Smooth Talk   (86) 354
Twice in a Lifetime   (86) 397
Unfaithful, The [1947]   (86) 550
Wetherby   (86) 406

GYPSIES
Angelo My Love   (84) 47
Bizet's Carmen [1983]   (85) 98
Carmen   (84) 101

HALLUCINATIONS
Agnes of God   (86) 56
Dreamchild   (86) 146
Emerald Forest, The   (86) 156
Kiss of the Spider Woman   (86) 209
Love Streams   (85) 293
Videodrome   (84) 452
Young Sherlock Holmes   (86) 431

HELICOPTERS
Blue Thunder   (84) 84

HEROISM
Breakfast Club, The   (86) 85
Cheech and Chong's The Corsican
  Brothers   (85) 515
Conan the Barbarian   (83) 419
Conan the Destroyer   (85) 516
Eleni   (86) 151
Front, The [1976]   (86) 502
Girl with the Red Hair, The   (84) 485
Goonies, The   (86) 176
Hercules   (84) 485
Kiss of the Spider Woman   (86) 209
Marie   (86) 227
Official Story, The   (86) 249
Pale Rider   (86) 261
Rambo: First Blood Part II   (86) 299
Right Stuff, The   (84) 342
Rocky IV   (86) 319
Runaway Train   (86) 324
Secret Life of Walter Mitty, The [1947]   (86) 540
Sheena   (85) 532
Silverado   (86) 349
Some Kind of Hero   (83) 428
Spies like Us   (86) 360
Supergirl   (85) 535
Trouble in Mind   (86) 388
White Nights   (86) 416
Zapped!   (83) 431

HISPANICS
Border, The   (83) 418
Brother from Another Planet, The   (85) 118
Cheech and Chong's The Corsican
  Brothers   (85) 515
Erendira [1983]   (85) 181
Heartbreaker   (84) 485
Norte, El   (84) 265
Repo Man   (85) 408
Scarface   (84) 361

Under Fire   (84) 441
Under the Volcano   (85) 499
Zoot Suit   (82) 389

HOLLYWOOD
Front, The [1976]   (86) 502
Into the Night   (86) 186
Pee-wee's Big Adventure   (86) 265
Purple Rose of Cairo, The   (86) 290
S.O.B.   (82) 328
State of Things, The   (84) 379

HOMOSEXUALITY
After Hours   (86) 51
All of Me   (85) 58
Berlin Alexanderplatz [1980]   (84) 57
Bostonians, The   (85) 105
By Design   (83) 419
Chorus Line, A   (86) 91
Colonel Redl [1984]   (86) 100
Color Purple, The   (86) 105
Deathtrap   (83) 137
Dresser, The   (84) 130
Drifting   (85) 518
Entre nous [1983]   (85) 176
Experience Preferred ... but Not Essential
  [1982]   (84) 141
4th Man, The [1983]   (85) 203
Heavenly Kid, The   (86) 445
Hotel New Hampshire, The   (85) 243
Joshua Then and Now   (86) 198
Kiss of the Spider Woman   (86) 209
Lianna   (84) 201
Making Love   (83) 425
Marie   (86) 224
Mass Appeal   (85) 303
Merry Christmas, Mr. Lawrence   (84) 231
Mishima   (86) 236
Next Stop, Greenwich Village [1976]   (85) 592
Nuit de Varennes, La [1982]   (84) 270
Once upon a Time in America   (85) 345
Partners   (83) 427
Personal Best   (83) 254
Police Academy 2   (86) 276
Pretty Baby [1978]   (85) 597
Protocol   (85) 383
Querelle [1982]   (84) 313
St. Elmo's Fire   (86) 330
Sign of the Cross, The [1932]   (85) 607
Spies like Us   (86) 360
Streetwise   (86) 364
Swann in Love   (85) 471
Taxi Zum Klo   (82) 346
Tightrope   (85) 489
To Be or Not to Be   (84) 426
Victor/Victoria   (83) 387

HORROR
Agnes of God   (86) 56
American Werewolf in London, An   (82) 66
Amityville 3-D   (84) 479
Beast Within, The   (83) 418
Black Cat, The   (85) 512
Body Double   (85) 513
Cat People   (83) 100
Christine   (84) 106
Company of Wolves, The [1984]   (86) 115
Creature from the Black Lagoon, The
  [1954]   (82) 422
Creepshow   (83) 419
Cujo   (84) 481
Curtains   (84) 481
Dead Zone, The   (84) 481
Deadly Eyes   (84) 481

Dr. Butcher, M.D. [1980]   (83) 420
Dorm That Dripped Blood, The   (84) 482
Evil Dead, The   (84) 484
Fire and Ice   (84) 153
Forbidden World   (83) 421
4th Man, The [1983]   (85) 203
Friday the 13th — Part III   (83) 422
Friday the 13th — The Final Chapter   (85) 520
Fright Night   (86) 444
Ghost Story   (82) 183
Godzilla 1985   (86) 444
Gremlins   (85) 230
Halloween III   (83) 422
House Where Evil Dwells, The   (83) 423
Howling, The   (82) 207
Humongous   (83) 423
Hunger, The   (84) 486
Jaws 3-D   (84) 486
Madman   (84) 488
Man with Two Brains, The   (84) 223
Most Dangerous Game, The [1932]   (86) 519
Nightmare on Elm Street, A   (85) 527
Nightmare on Elm Street, Part 2, A   (86) 454
Nightmares   (84) 490
Of Unknown Origin   (84) 491
Parasite   (83) 426
Play Misty for Me [1971]   (86) 532
Poltergeist   (83) 263
Re-Animator   (86) 457
Return of the Living Dead, The   (86) 314
Silent Madness   (85) 532
Silent Night, Deadly Night   (85) 532
Silent Rage   (83) 428
Stephen King's Cat's Eye   (86) 460
Stephen King's Children of the Corn   (85) 534
Stephen King's Silver Bullet   (86) 460
Strange Invaders   (84) 494
Stuff, The   (86) 461
Swamp Thing   (83) 429
Thing, The   (83) 343
Time Machine, The [1960]   (84) 585
Twilight Zone — The Movie   (84) 435
Videodrome   (84) 452
Visiting Hours   (83) 431
Wolfen   (82) 382

HORSES AND HORSE RACING
Bells Are Ringing [1960]   (84) 517
Black Stallion Returns, The   (84) 479
Brady's Escape   (85) 514
Came a Hot Friday   (86) 439
Champions   (85) 515
Flamingo Kid, The   (85) 192
Murphy's Romance   (86) 242
My New Partner [1984]   (86) 246
Out of Africa   (86) 255
Phar Lap   (85) 528
Stranger than Paradise   (85) 455
Sylvester   (86) 462
View to a Kill, A   (86) 401
Wild Horses [1983]   (85) 538

HOSPITALS (See DOCTORS AND MEDICINE)

HOTELS AND MOTELS
Agatha [1979]   (83) 435
Buddy Buddy   (82) 93
Cowboy [1958]   (82) 417
Detour [1946]   (86) 498
Experience Preferred ... but Not Essential
   [1982]   (84) 141
Fool for Love   (86) 172
Front, The [1976]   (86) 502
Holiday Inn [1942]   (82) 443

Hotel New Hampshire, The   (85) 243
I'm No Angel [1933]   (85) 561
Local Hero   (84) 206
Lost in America   (86) 219
Marie   (86) 227
National Lampoon's Vacation   (84) 241
Pink Floyd the Wall [1981]   (83) 258
Psycho II   (84) 307
Querelle [1982]   (84) 313
Stranger than Paradise   (85) 455
Tender Mercies   (84) 409

HUNTERS
Man Hunt [1941]   (85) 570
Most Dangerous Game, The [1932]   (86) 519
Never Cry Wolf   (84) 247
Out of Africa   (86) 255
Shooting Party, The [1984]   (86) 344

ILLEGAL ALIENS
Arch of Triumph [1948]   (84) 501
Border, The   (85) 418
My New Partner [1984]   (86) 246
Norte, El   (84) 265

ILLNESS (See also MENTAL ILLNESS and
   PHYSICAL HANDICAPS)
American Flyers   (86) 436
Brimstone and Treacle   (83) 91
Céleste [1981]   (83) 104
Champions   (85) 515
Honkytonk Man   (83) 200
Marie   (86) 227
Mask   (86) 231
My Cousin Rachel   (82) 458
Natural, The   (85) 329
Out of Africa   (86) 255
Rainy Day Friends   (86) 457
Return of the Living Dead, The   (86) 314
St. Elmo's Fire   (86) 330
Taxi Zum Klo   (82) 346
Terms of Endearment   (84) 414
Test of Love   (86) 462
Traviata, La   (83) 366
Turk 182   (86) 464
When Father Was Away on Business [1984]   (86)
   411
Whose Life Is It Anyway?   (82) 378

INCEST
Fantasies   (83) 421
Hotel New Hampshire, The   (85) 243
Heart of a Stag   (85) 522
Liar's Moon   (83) 424

INDIA
Gandhi   (83) 183
Heat and Dust [1982]   (84) 187
Home and the World, The [1984]   (86) 447
Indiana Jones and the Temple of Doom   (85)
   253
Passage to India, A   (85) 365
Razor's Edge, The   (85) 402
Sea Wolves, The [1981]   (83) 427

INDIANS (See NATIVE AMERICANS)

INSANITY (See MENTAL ILLNESS)

IRELAND
Cal   (85) 124
James Joyce's Women   (86) 193

IRISH REPUBLICAN ARMY
Cal   (85) 124

ISOLATION
Detour [1946]   (86) 498

Dreamchild   (86) 146
Front, The [1976]   (86) 502
Love Streams   (85) 288
Never Cry Wolf   (84) 247
Out of Africa   (86) 255
Quiet Earth, The   (86) 295
Rocky IV   (86) 319
Runaway Train   (86) 324
Shooting Party, The [1984]   (86) 344
ISRAEL
Goodbye, New York   (86) 444
Hanna K.   (84) 177
Vulture, The   (86) 464
ITALY
And the Ship Sails On [1983]   (85) 69
Barefoot Contessa, The [1954]   (82) 399
City of Women   (82) 106
Joke of Destiny, A [1983]   (85) 259
Ladyhawke   (86) 214
Macaroni   (86) 451
My Cousin Rachel [1952]   (82) 458
Night of the Shooting Stars, The [1982]   (84) 258
Oedipus Rex [1967]   (85) 528
Priest of Love   (82) 288
Three Brothers [1980]   (83) 349
Trace, The [1983]   (85) 537
Tragedy of a Ridiculous Man [1981]   (83) 361

JAPAN
Challenge, The   (83) 109
Flowing [1956]   (86) 444
Foster Daddy, Tora! [1980]   (82) 163
House Where Evil Dwells, The   (83) 423
Late Chrysanthemums [1954]   (86) 449
MacArthur's Children   (86) 451
Makioka Sisters, The [1983]   (86) 451
Merry Christmas, Mr. Lawrence   (84) 231
Mishima   (86) 236
Ran   (86) 304
Running Brave   (84) 354
Tokyo-Ga   (86) 463
JEWEL ROBBERY
Angelo My Love   (84) 47
Bedtime for Bonzo [1951]   (84) 512
Great Muppet Caper, The   (82) 187
History Is Made at Night [1937]   (84) 542
Into the Night   (86) 186
Octopussy   (84) 276
Romancing the Stone   (85) 421
Trouble in Mind   (86) 388
JEWS AND JEWISH LIFE (*See also* ANTI-
SEMITISM *and* THE MIDDLE EAST)
Bastille [1984]   (86) 437
Boat Is Full, The [1981]   (83) 82
Boys from Brazil, The [1978]   (86) 480
Chariots of Fire   (82) 101
Chosen, The   (83) 116
Dangerous Moves [1984]   (86) 129
Entre nous [1983]   (85) 176
Fanny and Alexander [1982]   (84) 146
Front, The [1976]   (86) 502
Hanna K.   (84) 177
Light Ahead, The [1939]   (83) 460
Lili Marleen   (82) 222
My Favorite Year   (83) 241
Next Stop, Greenwich Village [1976]   (85) 592
Once upon a Time in America   (85) 345
Shoah   (86) 339
Sophie's Choice   (83) 311
Swann in Love   (85) 471
Way We Were, The [1973]   (82) 474

Yentl   (84) 468
Zelig   (84) 473
JOURNALISTS
Perfect   (86) 456
Transylvania 6-5000   (86) 463
JUNGLES
Emerald Forest, The   (86) 156
Sheena   (85) 532

KIDNAPING
Adventures of Buckaroo Banzai, The   (85) 47
Beyond the Limit   (84) 479
Black Stallion Returns, The   (84) 479
Commando   (86) 711
Fire and Ice   (84) 153
First Name, Carmen [1983]   (85) 186
Gods Must Be Crazy, The [1980]   (85) 224
Going Berserk   (84) 485
Jimmy the Kid   (84) 486
Joke of Destiny, A [1983]   (85) 259
Kid Colter   (86) 448
King of Comedy, The   (84) 192
Last Starfighter, The   (85) 277
Missing   (83) 228
Nate and Hayes   (84) 236
Prizzi's Honor   (86) 285
Romancing the Stone   (85) 421
Second Thoughts   (84) 493
Silverado   (86) 349
Spacehunter   (84) 493
Split Image   (83) 317
Stranger Is Watching, A   (83) 429
Tragedy of a Ridiculous Man [1981]   (83) 361
Venom [1981]   (83) 430
Wild Geese II   (86) 465
Without a Trace   (84) 498
KINGS, QUEENS, AND ROYALTY
Beloved Rogue [1927]   (84) 522
Brittania Hospital   (84) 480
Colonel Redl [1984]   (86) 100
Dragonslayer   (82) 125
Excalibur   (82) 144
Falstaff [1967]   (83) 443
Fire and Ice   (84) 153
Heat and Dust [1982]   (84) 187
Napoleon [1927]   (82) 461
Nate and Hayes   (84) 236
Nell Gwyn [1934]   (84) 557
Nuit de Varennes, La [1982]   (84) 270
Oedipus Rex [1967]   (85) 528
Private Function, A [1984]   (86) 280
Protocol   (85) 383
Ran   (86) 304
Raspustin [1975]   (86) 457
Royal Wedding [1951]   (86) 536
Sherlock Holmes [1922]   (83) 494
Sign of the Cross, The [1932]   (85) 607
KOREAN WAR
Inchon   (83) 424

LAS VEGAS
Jinxed   (83) 206
Lost in America   (86) 219
Max Dugan Returns   (84) 228
One from the Heart   (83) 250
Rocky IV   (86) 319
LAW, LAWYERS, AND TRIALS
Absence of Malice   (82) 57
Agnes of God   (86) 51
All of Me   (85) 58

SUBJECT INDEX

Argent, L' [1983] (85) 74
Avenging Angel (86) 436
Barbary Coast [1935] (84) 506
Beau Mariage, Le (83) 65
Beyond Reasonable Doubt [1980] (84) 74
Body Heat (82) 87
Bostonians, The (85) 105
Bounty, The (85) 513
First Monday in October (82) 151
48 HRS. (83) 173
Frances (83) 178
Front, The [1976] (86) 502
Gandhi (83) 183
Garde à vue [1981] (83) 189
Hanna K. (84) 177
I'm No Angel [1933] (85) 561
Improper Channels (82) 218
Irreconcilable Differences (85) 523
Jagged Edge (86) 190
Man Who Fell to Earth, The [1975] (83) 469
Marie (86) 227
Melvin and Howard [1980] (82) 453
Micki & Maude (85) 308
Passage to India, A (85) 365
Postman Always Rings Twice, The (82) 284
Prince of the City (82) 292
Protocol (85) 383
Return of Martin Guerre, The (84) 318
Soldier's Story, A (85) 427
Star Chamber, The (84) 494
They Drive by Night [1940] (83) 508
They Might Be Giants [1971] (83) 515
Tomorrow [1972] (84) 589
Unfaithful, The [1947] (86) 550
Verdict, The (83) 377
Whose Life Is It Anyway? (82) 378
Zoot Suit (82) 389

LIBRARIES AND LIBRARIANS
Breakfast Club, The (86) 85
Ghostbusters (85) 219
Outsiders, The (84) 282

LITERATURE
Doctor Detroit (84) 482
Dreamchild (86) 146
Educating Rita (84) 136
James Joyce's Women (86) 193
Jewel of the Nile, The (86) 448
Kerouac, the Movie (86) 448
Porky's II (84) 491
Ran (86) 304
Sylvia (86) 462

LONDON
American Werewolf in London, An (82) 66
Betrayal (84) 67
Dance with a Stranger [1984] (86) 125
Great Muppet Caper, The (82) 187
Joshua Then and Now (86) 198
Lassiter (85) 524
Lifeforce (86) 450
Long Good Friday, The (83) 220
Man Hunt [1941] (85) 570
Missionary, The (83) 233
Moonlighting (83) 237
Nell Gwyn [1934] (84) 557
Royal Wedding [1951] (86) 536
Sherlock Holmes [1922] (83) 494
Time Machine, The [1960] (84) 585
28 Up [1984] (86) 392
Young Sherlock Holmes (86) 431

LONELINESS
After the Rehearsal (85) 52

Berlin Alexanderplatz [1980] (84) 57
Big Chill, The (84) 78
Birdy (85) 93
Breakfast Club, The (86) 85
Brother from Another Planet, The (85) 118
Can She Bake a Cherry Pie? (84) 95
Come Back to the 5 & Dime Jimmy Dean, Jimmy
  Dean (83) 120
Comfort and Joy (85) 146
Dim Sum (86) 141
Dreamchild (86) 146
Experience Preferred ... but Not Essential
  [1982] (84) 141
Four Seasons, The (82) 171
Front, The [1976] (86) 502
Full Moon in Paris (85) 208
Hail Mary (86) 182
Heartland (82) 191
I Sent a Letter to My Love [1980] (82) 214
Iceman (85) 248
Lonely Guy, The (85) 525
Lonely Hearts [1982] (84) 212
Love Streams (85) 293
Moonlighting (83) 237
Murphy's Romance (86) 242
My Best Friend's Girl [1983] (85) 326
1984 (85) 335
Nostalgia [1983] (85) 340
Once upon a Time in America (85) 345
Outland (82) 272
Personals, The (84) 491
Private Function, A [1984] (86) 280
Purple Rain (85) 389
Purple Rose of Cairo, The (86) 290
Repo Man (85) 408
Road Warrior, The [1981] (83) 277
Running Brave (84) 354
St. Elmo's Fire (86) 330
Sophie's Choice (83) 311
State of Things, The (84) 379
Stranger than Paradise (85) 455
Trouble in Mind (86) 388
Unfaithful, The [1947] (86) 550
Vie continue, La [1981] (83) 430

LOS ANGELES
Always (86) 60
Arrangement, The [1969] (86) 474
Best Friends (83) 68
Beverly Hills Cop (85) 88
Blade Runner (83) 76
Blue Thunder (84) 84
Breathless (84) 89
Crimes of Passion (85) 161
Dead Men Don't Wear Plaid (83) 134
Death Wish II (83) 420
Detour [1946] (86) 498
Fletch (86) 169
Frances (83) 178
Funny Farm (84) 484
I Ought to Be in Pictures (83) 423
Into the Night (86) 186
Jekyll and Hyde . . . Together Again (83) 424
Lost in America (86) 219
Max Dugan Returns (84) 228
Micki & Maude (85) 308
Modern Romance (82) 241
Norte, El (84) 265
Prizzi's Honor (86) 285
Purple Haze (84) 492
Repo Man (85) 408
S.O.B. (82) 328
Star 80 (84) 374

State of Things, The   (84) 379
Sure Thing, The   (86) 369
Terminator, The   (85) 478
To Live and Die in L.A.   (86) 379
Trancers   (86) 463
True Confessions   (82) 368
Tuff Turf   (86) 464
Unfaithful, The [1947]   (86) 550
Valley Girl   (84) 447
Zoot Suit   (82) 389

LOVE (*See also* CHILDREN AND CHILD
REARING; FAMILIES AND FAMILY LIFE;
HOMOSEXUALITY; MARRIAGE;
ROMANCE; *and* SEX AND SEXUALITY)
Agnes of God   (86) 56
Back to the Future   (86) 65
Better Off Dead   (86) 438
Chorus Line, A   (86) 91
Color Purple, The   (86) 105
Fool for Love   (86) 172
Home and the World, The [1984]   (86) 447
Jagged Edge   (86) 190
James Joyce's Women   (86) 193
Jewel of the Nile, The   (86) 448
Joshua Then and Now   (86) 198
Kiss of the Spider Woman   (86) 209
Ladyhawke   (86) 214
Lily in Love   (86) 450
Mask   (86) 231
Murphy's Romance   (86) 242
Out of Africa   (86) 255
Peril   (86) 456
Plenty   (86) 271
Police Academy 2   (86) 276
Prizzi's Honor   (86) 285
Purple Rose of Cairo, The   (86) 290
Runaway Train   (86) 324
St. Elmo's Fire   (86) 330
Silver City [1984]   (86) 460
Subway   (86) 461
Sugarbaby   (86) 461
Sure Thing, The   (86) 369
Turtle Diary   (86) 464
Twice in a Lifetime   (86) 397
War and Love   (86) 465
Wetherby   (86) 406

MAGIC
Black Cauldron, The   (86) 75
Emerald Forest, The   (86) 156
Escape Artist, The   (83) 421
Fire and Ice   (84) 153
Journey into Fear [1943]   (86) 511
Klynham Summer   (84) 487
Smurfs and the Magic Flute, The   (84) 493

MARRIAGE
Adolescente, L' [1979]   (83) 53
After the Rehearsal   (85) 52
Almost You   (86) 436
Always   (86) 60
Arrangement, The [1969]   (86) 474
Author! Author!   (83) 417
Bachelor Party   (85) 511
Bar Esperanza [1983]   (86) 437
Beau Mariage, Le   (83) 65
Becky Sharp [1935]   (82) 403
Best Friends   (83) 68
Betrayal   (84) 67
Big Chill, The   (84) 78
Blood Wedding [1981]   (83) 418
Boat Is Full, The [1981]   (83) 92

Border, The   (83) 418
Can She Bake a Cherry Pie?   (84) 95
Choose Me   (85) 135
Cocoon   (86) 96
Color Purple, The   (86) 105
Compromising Positions   (86) 120
Crimes of Passion   (85) 161
Desperately Seeking Susan   (86) 137
Diner   (83) 142
Dirty Dishes [1978]   (84) 482
Disraeli [1929]   (82) 426
Divorcée, The [1930]   (82) 429
Dulcy [1923]   (82) 432
Educating Rita   (84) 136
Entre nous [1983]   (85) 176
Falling in Love   (85) 519
Fanny and Alexander [1982]   (84) 146
Five Days One Summer   (83) 421
Four Seasons, The   (82) 171
Full Moon in Paris   (85) 208
Gabriela [1983]   (85) 213
Gandhi   (83) 183
Hatchet Man, The [1932]   (83) 447
Heart Like a Wheel   (84) 182
Heartaches [1981]   (83) 197
Heartland   (82) 191
History Is Made at Night [1937]   (84) 542
H. M. Pulham, Esq. [1941]   (82) 439
If You Could See What I Hear   (83) 423
Irreconcilable Differences   (85) 523
Joke of Destiny, A [1983]   (85) 259
Joshua Then and Now   (86) 198
Kiss Me Goodbye   (83) 209
Lianna   (84) 201
Liar's Moon   (83) 424
Lily in Love   (86) 450
Little Sex, A   (83) 424
Long Gray Line, The [1955]   (82) 447
Lost in America   (86) 219
Love Letters   (85) 288
Love Streams   (85) 293
Man with Two Brains, The   (84) 223
Marie   (86) 227
Melvin and Howard [1980]   (82) 453
Micki & Maude   (85) 308
Midsummer Night's Sex Comedy, A   (83) 228
Missing   (83) 232
Monty Python's The Meaning of Life   (84) 489
My Other Husband   (86) 453
My Reputation [1946]   (85) 586
National Lampoon's Vacation   (84) 241
Neil Simon's The Slugger's Wife   (86) 454
New York, New York [1977]   (84) 567
Next Stop, Greenwich Village [1976]   (85) 592
Official Story, The   (86) 249
On Golden Pond   (82) 263
Out of Africa   (86) 255
Paris, Texas   (85) 359
Pink Floyd the Wall [1981]   (83) 258
Police Academy 2   (86) 276
Pretty Baby [1978]   (85) 597
Priest of Love   (82) 288
Private Function, A [1984]   (86) 280
Prizzi's Honor   (86) 285
Protocol   (85) 383
Quartet   (82) 296
Ragtime   (82) 304
Reds   (82) 312
Rent Control   (85) 530
Return of Martin Guerre, The   (84) 318
Return of the Secaucus 7 [1980]   (83) 484
Rich and Famous   (82) 316

Rocky III   (83) 283
Roughly Speaking [1945]   (83) 490
St. Elmo's Fire   (86) 330
Shoot the Moon   (83) 295
Slap Shot [1977]   (82) 467
S.O.B.   (82) 328
Softly Softly [1984]   (86) 460
Solid Gold Cadillac, The [1956]   (85) 615
Star 80   (84) 374
Star Is Born, A [1954]   (84) 573
Swann in Love   (85) 471
Table for Five   (84) 404
Taking Off [1971]   (86) 545
Tender Mercies   (84) 409
Terms of Endearment   (84) 414
Thief   (82) 356
Tragedy of a Ridiculous Man [1981]   (83) 361
Twice in a Lifetime   (86) 397
Under the Volcano   (85) 499
Unfaithful, The [1947]   (86) 550
Unfaithfully Yours   (85) 537
Way We Were, The [1973]   (82) 474
White Nights   (86) 416
Woman in Red, The   (85) 538
Woman Next Door, The   (82) 385
Woman on the Beach, The [1947]   (83) 519
World of Henry Orient, The [1964]   (84) 600
Yol   (83) 411

MARTIAL ARTS
Alley Cat   (85) 509
American Ninja   (86) 436
Berry Gordy's The Last Dragon   (86) 438
Enter the Ninja   (83) 420
Forced Vengeance   (83) 422
Gymkata   (86) 445
Karate Kid, The   (85) 264
Lone Wolf McQuade   (84) 488
Missing in Action   (85) 526
Missing in Action 2   (86) 452
9 Deaths of the Ninja   (86) 454
Revenge of the Ninja   (84) 492
They Call Me Bruce   (83) 429

MATURING
After the Rehearsal   (85) 52
All the Right Moves   (84) 412
Arthur   (82) 71
Aviator, The   (86) 437
Bambi [1942]   (85) 543
Big Chill, The   (84) 78
Breakfast Club, The   (86) 85
Careful He Might Hear You [1983]   (85) 130
Chorus Line, A   (86) 91
Chosen, The   (83) 116
Cocoon   (86) 96
Dance with a Stranger [1984]   (86) 125
Dim Sum   (86) 141
Diner   (83) 142
Dreamchild   (86) 146
Educating Rita   (84) 136
Entre nous [1983]   (85) 176
E.T.: The Extra-Terrestrial   (83) 151
Experience Preferred ... but Not Essential
   [1982]   (84) 141
Fanny and Alexander [1982]   (84) 146
Flamingo Kid, The   (85) 192
Four Friends   (82) 167
Front, The [1976]   (86) 502
Joey   (86) 448
Joke of Destiny, A [1983]   (85) 259
Karate Kid, The   (85) 264
Lianna   (84) 201
Lonely Hearts [1982]   (84) 212

Mask   (86) 231
Mass Appeal   (85) 303
My Best Friend's Girl [1983]   (85) 326
My Reputation [1946]   (85) 586
Natural, The   (85) 329
New York, New York [1977]   (84) 567
Officer and a Gentleman, An   (83) 246
Out of Africa   (86) 255
Pauline at the Beach [1982]   (84) 296
Pretty Baby [1978]   (85) 597
Racing with the Moon   (85) 397
Razor's Edge, The   (85) 402
Repo Man   (85) 408
Return of the Jedi   (84) 326
Risky Business   (84) 349
Smooth Talk   (86) 354
Sophie's Choice   (83) 311
Star Is Born, A [1954]   (84) 573
Stardust Memories [1980]   (85) 626
Sugar Cane Alley [1983]   (85) 461
Sure Thing, The   (86) 369
Taking Off [1971]   (86) 545
Tender Mercies   (84) 409
Trouble in Mind   (86) 388
28 Up [1984]   (86) 392
Wetherby   (86) 406

MEDIEVAL TIMES
Dark Crystal, The   (83) 130
Dragonslayer   (82) 125
Excalibur   (82) 144
Flesh and Blood   (86) 443
Ladyhawke   (86) 214
Ran   (86) 304
Smurfs and the Magic Flute, The   (84) 493
Time Bandits [1980]   (82) 364

MEMORIES
Agnes of God   (86) 56
Berlin Alexanderplatz [1980]   (84) 57
Breakfast Club, The   (86) 85
Chorus Line, A   (86) 91
Cocoon   (86) 96
Dreamchild   (86) 146
It Happened Tomorrow [1944]   (84) 552
James Joyce's Women   (86) 193
Kiss of the Spider Woman   (86) 209
Murphy's Romance   (86) 242
Nostalgia [1983]   (85) 340
Once upon a Time in America   (85) 345
Out of Africa   (86) 255
Peter Ibbetson [1935]   (86) 527
Sender, The   (83) 427
Shoah   (86) 339
Shooting Party, The [1984]   (86) 344
Stardust Memories [1980]   (85) 626
Trip to Bountiful, The   (86) 383
Trouble in Mind   (86) 388
Wetherby   (86) 406
White Nights   (86) 416

MENTAL ILLNESS
Adventures of Buckaroo Banzai, The   (85) 47
Agnes of God   (86) 56
Amityville II   (83) 417
Angel   (85) 510
Berlin Alexanderplatz [1980]   (84) 57
Birdy   (85) 93
Coup de torchon [1981]   (83) 124
Crimes of Passion   (85) 161
Dirty Dishes [1978]   (84) 482
Dreamscape   (85) 166
Fire and Ice   (84) 153
Firefox   (83) 160

Fleshburn   (85) 519
Flight of the Phoenix, The [1966]   (85) 549
Frances   (83) 178
Freud [1962]   (84) 535
Montenegro   (82) 250
Most Dangerous Game, The [1932]   (86) 519
Pink Floyd the Wall [1981]   (83) 258
Play Misty for Me [1971]   (86) 532
Plenty   (86) 271
Psycho II   (84) 307
Repo Man   (85) 408
Return of the Soldier, The [1982]   (84) 332
Richard's Things   (82) 321
Secret Life of Walter Mitty, The [1947]   (86) 540
Seduction, The   (83) 427
Sender, The   (83) 427
Silent Madness   (85) 532
Sophie's Choice   (83) 311
Specter of the Rose [1946]   (83) 504
10 to Midnight   (84) 495
They Might Be Giants [1971]   (83) 515
Wetherby   (86) 406

MEXICO
Cowboy [1958]   (82) 417
Erendira [1983]   (85) 181
Falcon and the Snowman, The   (86) 165
Goat, The [1981]   (86) 444
Norte, El   (84) 265
Priest of Love   (82) 288
Under the Volcano   (85) 499

MIAMI
Scarface   (84) 361
Smokey and the Bandit—Part 3   (84) 493

THE MIDDLE EAST
Flight of the Phoenix, The [1966]   (85) 549
Hanna K.   (84) 177
Jewel of the Nile, The   (86) 448
Journey into Fear [1943]   (86) 511
Protocol   (85) 383
Raiders of the Lost Ark   (82) 308
Spies like Us   (86) 360
Wrong Is Right   (83) 403
Yol   (83) 411
Young Sherlock Holmes   (86) 431

MILITARY LIFE
American Ninja   (86) 436
Bizet's Carmen [1983]   (85) 98
Boot, Das [1981]   (83) 86
Bounty, The   (85) 513
Colonel Redl [1984]   (86) 100
Firefox   (83) 160
Gymkata   (86) 445
Hondo [1954]   (83) 452
Killing Fields, The   (85) 270
Long Gray Line, The [1955]   (82) 447
MacArthur's Children   (86) 451
Megaforce   (83) 425
Merry Christmas, Mr. Lawrence   (84) 231
Mutiny on the Bounty [1962]   (85) 581
Officer and a Gentleman, An   (83) 246
Racing with the Moon   (85) 397
Real Genius   (86) 309
Running Brave   (84) 354
Soldier's Story, A   (85) 427
Southern Comfort   (82) 332
Spies like Us   (86) 360
Streamers   (84) 391
Stripes   (82) 336
Tank   (85) 535
Taps   (82) 336
Under Fire   (84) 441

Vulture, The   (86) 464
Wetherby   (86) 406

MISTAKEN OR SECRET IDENTITY
Agatha [1979]   (83) 435
All of Me   (85) 58
Bells Are Ringing [1960]   (84) 517
Beloved Rogue [1927]   (84) 522
Body Heat   (82) 87
Cannery Row   (83) 95
Cat People   (83) 100
Comfort and Joy   (85) 146
Cross Country   (84) 481
Dead Men Don't Wear Plaid   (83) 134
Desperately Seeking Susan   (86) 137
48 HRS.   (83) 173
Front, The [1976]   (86) 502
Hanky Panky   (83) 422
Henry IV [1983]   (86) 446
History Is Made at Night [1937]   (84) 542
I Married a Shadow   (84) 486
I Sent a Letter to My Love [1980]   (82) 214
It Happened Tomorrow [1944]   (84) 552
Joke of Destiny, A [1983]   (85) 259
Macaroni   (86) 451
Max Dugan Returns   (84) 228
Micki & Maude   (85) 308
Night Patrol   (86) 454
Nighthawks   (82) 259
Our Relations [1936]   (86) 523
Pale Rider   (86) 261
Pirates of Penzance, The   (84) 301
Prizzi's Honor   (86) 285
Purple Rose of Cairo, The   (86) 290
Racing with the Moon   (85) 397
Return of Martin Guerre, The   (84) 318
Return of the Jedi   (84) 326
Sahara   (85) 531
Scarlet Letter, The [1927]   (85) 602
Sophie's Choice   (83) 311
Stranger than Paradise   (85) 455
Superman II   (82) 339
Superman III   (84) 399
They Might Be Giants [1971]   (83) 515
Time After Time [1979]   (84) 579
Tootsie   (83) 353
Trading Places   (84) 430
Victim [1961]   (85) 647
Victor/Victoria   (83) 387
Water and Soap   (86) 465
Zelig   (84) 473

MONSTERS
Bride, The   (86) 438
C.H.U.D.   (85) 515
Creature from the Black Lagoon, The
   [1954]   (82) 422
Dark Star [1975]   (86) 494
Day of the Dead   (86) 441
Dragonslayer   (82) 125
Dreamscape   (85) 166
Enemy Mine   (86) 161
Fire and Ice   (84) 153
Forbidden World   (83) 421
Fright Night   (86) 444
Godzilla 1985   (86) 444
Gremlins   (85) 230
Incubus, The [1980]   (83) 424
Keep, The   (84) 487
Last Starfighter, The   (85) 277
Lifeforce   (86) 450
Once Bitten   (86) 455
Parasite   (83) 426

SUBJECT INDEX

Return of the Jedi   (84) 326
Return of the Living Dead, The   (86) 314
Silent Rage   (83) 428
Stephen King's Cat's Eye   (86) 460
Stephen King's Silver Bullet   (86) 460
Swamp Thing   (83) 429
Teen Wolf   (86) 462
Thing, The   (83) 343
Time Machine, The [1960]   (84) 585
Twilight Zone—The Movie   (84) 435

MOTION PICTURES (*See* FILMMAKERS AND
FILMMAKING)

MURDER
Absence of Malice   (82) 57
Agatha [1979]   (83) 435
Agnes of God   (86) 56
American Werewolf in London, An   (82) 66
Argent, L' [1983]   (85) 74
Atlantic City   (82) 74
Balance, La [1982]   (84) 52
Barbary Coast [1935]   (84) 506
Barefoot Contessa, The [1954]   (82) 399
Beast Within, The   (83) 418
Berlin Alexanderplatz [1980]   (84) 57
Beverly Hills Cop   (85) 88
Beyond Reasonable Doubt [1980]   (84) 74
Bizet's Carmen [1983]   (85) 98
Blade Runner   (83) 76
Blow Out   (82) 83
Body Heat   (82) 87
Boys from Brazil, The [1978]   (86) 480
Brewster McCloud [1970]   (86) 484
Buddy Buddy   (82) 93
Caged Fury   (85) 514
Cal   (85) 124
Carmen   (84) 101
Cat People   (83) 100
Challenge, The   (83) 109
Christine   (84) 106
City Heat   (85) 141
Compromising Positions   (86) 120
Confidentially Yours [1983]   (85) 516
Cotton Club, The   (85) 150
Coup de torchon [1981]   (83) 124
Crimes of Passion   (85) 161
Cross Country   (84) 481
Cujo   (84) 481
Curtains   (84) 481
Cutter's Way   (82) 119
Dance with a Stranger [1984]   (86) 125
Danny Boy   (85) 577
Dead Men Don't Wear Plaid   (83) 134
Death Valley   (83) 419
Deathtrap   (83) 137
Detective   (86) 442
Dorm That Dripped Blood, The   (84) 482
Draughtsman's Contract, The [1982]   (84) 126
Eating Raoul   (83) 420
Endangered Species   (83) 420
Erendira [1983]   (85) 176
Étoile du nord, L'   (84) 484
Evil That Men Do, The   (85) 518
Evil Under the Sun [1981]   (83) 421
Eye of the Needle   (82) 148
Fanny and Alexander [1982]   (84) 146
Fire and Ice   (84) 153
Firefox   (83) 160
First Blood   (83) 164
Fletch   (86) 169
For Your Eyes Only   (82) 155
48 HRS.   (83) 173

Friday the 13th—Part III   (83) 422
Friday the 13th—The Final Chapter   (85) 520
Gandhi   (83) 183
Garde à vue [1981]   (83) 189
Ghost Story   (82) 183
Gorky Park   (84) 162
Hammett   (84) 174
Hatchet Man, The [1932]   (83) 447
Heads or Tails [1980]   (84) 485
History Is Made at Night [1937]   (84) 542
Hound of the Baskervilles, The [1978]   (82) 203
Humongous   (83) 423
I, the Jury   (83) 423
Jagged Edge   (86) 190
Jinxed   (83) 206
Journey into Fear [1943]   (86) 511
Killing Fields, The   (85) 270
Killpoint   (85) 524
Klynham Summer   (84) 487
Long Good Friday, The   (83) 220
Lost Moment, The [1947]   (83) 465
Madman   (84) 488
Man Hunt [1941]   (85) 570
Man with Two Brains, The   (84) 223
Marie   (86) 227
Mean Season, The   (86) 452
Mike's Murder   (85) 526
Missing   (83) 228
Missionary, The   (83) 223
Montenegro   (82) 250
My Cousin Rachel [1952]   (82) 458
Nate and Hayes   (84) 236
Natural, The   (85) 329
Never Say Never Again   (84) 252
Nighthawks   (82) 259
Nightmare on Elm Street, A   (85) 527
Nightmare on Elm Street, Part 2, A   (86) 454
Ordeal by Innocence [1984]   (86) 455
Outland   (82) 272
Pale Rider   (86) 261
Partners   (83) 427
Peril   (86) 456
Pixote [1980]   (82) 280
Places in the Heart   (85) 371
Postman Always Rings Twice, The   (82) 284
Prizzi's Honor   (86) 285
Querelle [1982]   (84) 313
Question of Silence, A   (85) 530
Ragtime   (82) 304
Repo Man   (85) 408
Return of the Living Dead, The   (86) 314
River Rat, The   (85) 531
Road Warrior, The [1981]   (83) 277
Romancing the Stone   (85) 421
Scarface   (84) 361
Secret Life of Walter Mitty, The [1947]   (86) 540
Shoah   (86) 339
Silent Madness   (85) 532
Silent Night, Deadly Night   (85) 532
Silent Rage   (83) 428
Silkwood   (84) 367
Silverado   (86) 349
Slayground [1983]   (85) 533
Soldier's Story, A   (85) 427
Southern Comfort   (82) 332
Specter of the Rose [1946]   (83) 504
Star 80   (84) 374
State of Things, The   (84) 379
Still of the Night   (83) 326
Stranger Is Watching, A   (83) 429
Streamers   (84) 391
Streets of Fire   (85) 534

Sudden Death   (86) 461
Sudden Impact   (84) 395
Sweet Sixteen   (85) 535
Tag   (83) 429
Tess [1980]   (82) 471
They Drive by Night [1940]   (83) 508
Thief   (82) 356
Tightrope   (85) 489
Time After Time [1979]   (84) 579
To Live and Die in L.A.   (86) 379
Tomorrow [1972]   (84) 589
Too Scared to Scream   (86) 463
Torn Curtain [1966]   (85) 644
Trouble in Mind   (86) 388
True Confessions   (82) 368
Under Fire   (84) 441
Vice Squad   (83) 430
Victim [1961]   (85) 647
Videodrome   (84) 452
Visiting Hours   (83) 431
Wetherby   (86) 406
Witness   (86) 421
Wolfen   (82) 382
Woman Next Door, The   (82) 385
World According to Garp, The   (83) 397
Yol   (83) 411
Young Sherlock Holmes   (86) 431
Zoot Suit   (82) 389

MUSIC AND MUSICIANS (*See also* DANCERS
AND DANCING *and* SINGERS)
All of Me   (85) 58
All the Right Moves   (84) 41
Amadeus   (85) 63
American Pop   (82) 62
And the Ship Sails On [1983]   (85) 69
Another State of Mind   (85) 510
Back to the Future   (86) 65
Bal, Le [1983]   (85) 80
Basileus Quartet   (85) 511
Beach Boys, The   (86) 438
Beat Street   (85) 512
Beau Pere   (82) 78
Blame It on the Night   (85) 512
Breakfast Club, The   (86) 85
Bring on the Night   (86) 439
Chorus Line, A   (86) 91
Chronos   (86) 440
Comfort and Joy   (85) 146
Cotton Club, The   (85) 150
Crossover Dreams   (86) 441
Danny Boy   (85) 517
Detour [1946]   (86) 498
Eddie and the Cruisers   (84) 483
Electric Dreams   (85) 518
First Name, Carmen [1983]   (85) 186
Fitzcarraldo   (83) 167
Footloose   (85) 198
Get Crazy   (84) 484
Gospel   (85) 520
Hard to Hold   (85) 521
Heat and Dust [1982]   (84) 187
I'm No Angel [1933]   (85) 561
Jazzman   (85) 523
Joey   (86) 448
King of Jazz [1930]   (86) 515
Krush Groove   (86) 449
Lady Sings the Blues [1972]   (85) 565
Let's Spend the Night Together   (84) 487
Lili Marleen   (82) 222
Lonely Hearts [1982]   (84) 212
Louis Bluie   (86) 450
Man with One Red Shoe, The   (86) 451

Micki & Maude   (85) 308
Morons from Outer Space   (86) 452
Neil Simon's The Slugger's Wife   (86) 454
New York, New York [1977]   (84) 567
Nostalgia [1983]   (85) 340
Pete Kelly's Blues [1955]   (83) 481
Pink Floyd the Wall [1981]   (83) 258
Pirate Movie, The   (83) 427
Pirates of Penzance, The   (84) 301
Pretty Baby [1978]   (85) 597
Purple Rain   (85) 389
Ragtime   (82) 304
Rappin'   (86) 457
Royal Wedding [1951]   (86) 536
Second Thoughts   (84) 493
Smithereens   (83) 307
Starstruck   (83) 428
Stop Making Sense   (85) 534
Streets of Fire   (85) 534
Swann in Love   (85) 471
Sweet Dreams   (86) 374
Tender Mercies   (84) 409
This Is Spinal Tap   (85) 484
Unfaithfully Yours   (85) 537
Wagner   (84) 497
World of Henry Orient, The [1964]   (84) 600

MYSTERY
Agnes of God   (86) 56
Christine   (84) 106
Clue   (86) 440
Compromising Positions   (86) 120
Confidentially Yours [1983]   (85) 516
Death Valley   (83) 419
Detective   (86) 442
Endangered Species   (83) 420
Étoile du nord, L'   (84) 484
Evil Under the Sun [1981]   (83) 421
Flashpoint   (85) 519
Fletch   (86) 169
Ghost Story   (82) 183
Gorky Park   (84) 162
Hanky Panky   (83) 422
Jagged Edge   (86) 190
Keep, The   (84) 487
Klynham Summer   (84) 487
Marie   (86) 227
Pale Rider   (86) 261
Peril   (86) 456
Phar Lap   (85) 528
Question of Silence, A   (85) 530
Riddle of the Sands, The [1979]   (85) 531
Secret Life of Walter Mitty, The [1947]   (86) 540
Tag   (83) 429
Trenchcoat   (84) 496
Unfaithful, The [1947]   (86) 550
Wicker Man, The [1974]   (86) 555

MYTHS, LEGENDS, AND FOLKLORE
Hercules   (84) 485
Hercules II   (86) 446

NATIVE AMERICANS
Apache [1954]   (82) 395
Broken Rainbow   (86) 439
Colorado Territory [1949]   (86) 489
Fort Apache [1948]   (84) 530
Hombre [1967]   (84) 547
Hondo [1954]   (83) 452
Norte, El   (84) 265
Running Brave   (84) 354
Wolfen   (82) 382

NAZI DEATH CAMPS
Front, The [1976]   (86) 502
Shoah   (86) 339
War and Love   (86) 465
NAZISM AND NAZIS (*See also* ANTI-
SEMITISM)
Arch of Triumph [1948]   (84) 501
Bal, Le [1983]   (85) 80
Berlin Alexanderplatz [1980]   (84) 57
Boat Is Full, The [1981]   (83) 82
Boot, Das [1981]   (83) 86
Boys from Brazil, The [1978]   (86) 480
Entre nous [1983]   (85) 176
Girl with the Red Hair, The   (84) 485
Journey into Fear [1943]   (86) 511
Keep, The   (84) 487
Lassiter   (85) 524
Love in Germany, A [1983]   (85) 283
Man Hunt [1941]   (85) 570
Mephisto   (82) 237
North Star, The [1943]   (83) 476
Raiders of the Lost Ark   (82) 308
Secret Places [1984]   (86) 459
Shoah   (86) 339
Sign of the Cross, The [1932]   (85) 607
Sophie's Choice   (83) 311
To Be or Not to Be   (84) 426
Under the Volcano   (85) 499
Victory   (82) 374
War and Love   (86) 465
White Rose, The   (84) 497
Wild Geese II   (86) 466
Zelig   (84) 473
NETHERLANDS
4th Man, The [1983]   (85) 203
NEW ENGLAND
Bostonians, The   (85) 105
H. M. Pulham, Esq. [1941]   (82) 439
Hotel New Hampshire, The   (85) 243
Midsummer Night's Sex Comedy, A   (83) 224
On Golden Pond   (82) 263
Scarlet Letter, The [1927]   (85) 602
Verdict, The   (83) 377
NEW JERSEY
Adventures of Buckaroo Banzai, The   (85) 47
Broadway Danny Rose   (85) 112
Desperately Seeking Susan   (86) 137
NEW MEXICO
Colorado Territory [1949]   (86) 489
NEW ORLEANS
Cat People   (83) 100
Pretty Baby [1978]   (85) 597
Tightrope   (85) 489
NEW WAVE
Bob le Flambeur [1955]   (84) 526
Repo Man   (85) 408
Smithereens   (83) 307
Suburbia   (85) 534
Trouble in Mind   (86) 388
NEW YORK
After Hours   (86) 51
Alphabet City   (85) 509
American Pop   (82) 62
Animal Kingdom, The [1932]   (86) 469
Annie   (83) 56
Arrangement, The [1969]   (86) 474
Arthur   (82) 71
Barbary Coast [1935]   (84) 506
Bells Are Ringing [1960]   (84) 517

Body Rock   (85) 513
Bostonians, The   (85) 105
Broadway Danny Rose   (85) 112
Brother from Another Planet, The   (85) 118
Can She Bake a Cherry Pie?   (84) 95
Chorus Line, A   (86) 91
Chosen, The   (83) 116
C.H.U.D.   (85) 515
Cotton Club, The   (85) 150
Desperately Seeking Susan   (86) 137
Detour [1946]   (86) 498
Dreamchild   (86) 146
Escape from New York   (82) 133
Flamingo Kid, The   (85) 192
Fort Apache, the Bronx   (82) 159
Frances   (83) 178
Front, The [1976]   (86) 502
Ghostbusters   (85) 219
Hard Way, The [1942]   (85) 555
History Is Made at Night [1937]   (84) 542
Home Free All   (85) 522
I'm No Angel [1933]   (85) 561
King of Comedy, The   (84) 192
Kiss Me Goodbye   (83) 209
Lady Sings the Blues [1972]   (85) 565
Little Sex, A   (83) 424
Moscow on the Hudson   (85) 321
My Favorite Year   (83) 41
Natural, The   (85) 329
New York, New York [1977]   (84) 567
Nighthawks   (82) 259
Once upon a Time in America   (85) 345
Only When I Laugh   (82) 268
Pope of Greenwich Village, The   (85) 529
Prince of the City   (82) 292
Prizzi's Honor   (86) 285
Purple Rose of Cairo, The   (86) 290
Ragtime   (82) 304
Rich and Famous   (82) 316
Secret Life of Walter Mitty, The [1947]   (86) 540
Skyline   (85) 533
Smithereens   (83) 307
Sophie's Choice   (83) 311
Splash   (85) 434
Staying Alive   (84) 386
Still of the Night   (83) 326
Streetwalkin'   (86) 461
Tempest   (83) 331
They All Laughed   (82) 350
They Might Be Giants [1971]   (83) 515
Too Scared to Scream   (86) 463
Tootsie   (83) 353
Waitress   (83) 431
Wolfen   (82) 382
World of Henry Orient, The [1964]   (84) 600
Year of the Dragon   (86) 426
NEW ZEALAND
Battletruck   (83) 417
Beyond Reasonable Doubt [1980]   (84) 74
Heart of a Stag   (85) 522
Klynham Summer   (84) 487
Nate and Hayes   (84) 236
Smash Palace [1981]   (83) 302
Utu [1983]   (85) 504
Wild Horses [1983]   (85) 538
NEWSPAPERS, REPORTERS, AND
JOURNALISTS
Absence of Malice   (82) 57
Agatha [1979]   (83) 435
And Nothing but the Truth   (85) 510
Barbary Coast [1935]   (84) 506

Best Little Whorehouse in Texas, The (83) 72
Beyond Reasonable Doubt [1980]   (84) 74
Boot, Das [1981]   (83) 86
Circle of Deceit [1981]   (83) 419
Comfort and Joy   (85) 146
Compromising Positions   (86) 120
Continental Divide   (82) 115
Dreamchild   (86) 146
Fletch   (86) 169
Gandhi   (83) 183
Gods Must Be Crazy, The [1980]   (85) 224
Great Muppet Caper, The   (82) 187
Hanky Panky   (83) 422
Howling, The   (82) 207
It Happened Tomorrow [1944]   (84) 552
Joke of Destiny, A [1983]   (85) 259
Kiss Me Goodbye   (83) 209
Man of Iron   (82) 230
Missing   (83) 232
Mommie Dearest   (82) 245
Natural, The   (85) 329
Not for Publication   (85) 527
Nuit de Varennes, La [1982]   (84) 270
Perfect   (86) 456
Ploughman's Lunch, The [1983]   (85) 377
Protocol   (85) 383
Reds   (82) 312
Rich and Famous   (82) 316
St. Elmo's Fire   (86) 330
Seduction, The   (83) 427
Silkwood   (84) 367
Spies like Us   (86) 360
Star 80   (84) 374
Superman II   (82) 339
Superman III   (84) 399
Tootsie   (83) 353
Toy, The   (83) 358
Under Fire   (84) 441
Under the Volcano   (85) 499
Visiting Hours   (83) 431
Wrong Is Right   (83) 403
Year of Living Dangerously, The [1982]   (84)
  462
NEWSREELS
Front, The [1976]   (86) 502
Purple Rose of Cairo, The   (86) 290
Too Hot to Handle [1938]   (84) 596
Zelig   (84) 473
NIGHTCLUBS
Arch of Triumph [1948]   (84) 501
Choose Me   (85) 135
Detour [1946]   (86) 498
Front, The [1976]   (86) 502
Funny Farm   (84) 484
Love Streams   (85) 293
Our Relations [1936]   (86) 523
Police Academy 2   (86) 276
Purple Rose of Cairo, The   (86) 290
St. Elmo's Fire   (86) 330
Scarface   (84) 361
1920's
Berlin Alexanderplatz [1980]   (84) 501
Zelig   (84) 473
NINETEENTH CENTURY
Apache [1954]   (82) 395
Barbary Coast [1935]   (84) 506
Bizet's Carmen [1983]   (85) 98
Cowboy [1958]   (82) 417
Dreamchild   (86) 146
Flaxfield, The [1983]   (86) 443
Fort Apache [1948]   (84) 530

Heaven's Gate   (82) 195
Nate and Hayes   (84) 236
New Babylon, The [1929]   (84) 561
Pale Rider   (86) 261
Paradise   (83) 426
Pirates of Penzance, The   (84) 301
Silverado   (86) 349
Sunday in the Country, A   (85) 466
Swann in Love   (85) 471
Tess [1980]   (82) 471
Time Machine, The [1960]   (84) 585
Traviata, La   (83) 366
Utu [1983]   (85) 504
Young Sherlock Holmes   (86) 431
NUCLEAR POWER AND WAR
Dreamscape   (85) 166
Front, The [1976]   (86) 502
In Our Hands   (84) 486
Never Say Never Again   (84) 252
Octopussy   (84) 276
Quiet Earth, The   (86) 295
Return of the Living Dead, The   (86) 314
Road Warrior, The [1981]   (83) 277
Silkwood   (84) 367
Stryker   (84) 494
Terminator, The   (85) 478
Testament   (84) 420
Time Machine, The [1960]   (84) 585
WarGames   (84) 458
Wrong Is Right   (83) 403
NURSES (See also DOCTORS AND
  MEDICINE)
Secret Life of Walter Mitty, The [1947]   (86) 540
World According to Garp, The   (83) 397

OBSESSION
Against All Odds   (85) 509
Agnes of God   (86) 56
Bizet's Carmen [1983]   (85) 98
Christine   (84) 106
Colorado Territory [1949]   (86) 489
Danny Boy   (85) 517
Dreamchild   (86) 146
Echoes   (84) 483
Exposed   (84) 484
Garbo Talks   (85) 520
Heat of Desire [1981]   (85) 522
Hecate [1982]   (85) 522
Moon in the Gutter, The   (84) 490
Mother Lode   (84) 490
Night in Heaven, A   (84) 490
Oedipus Rex [1967]   (85) 528
Once upon a Time in America   (85) 345
Play Misty for Me [1971]   (86) 532
Rocky IV   (86) 319
St. Elmo's Fire   (86) 330
Seduction, The   (83) 427
Sender, The   (83) 427
Trouble in Mind   (86) 388
Uncommon Valor   (84) 496
Unfaithful, The [1947]   (86) 550
Videodrome   (84) 452
Woman in Red, The   (85) 538
Zappa   (85) 539
OKLAHOMA
Outsiders, The   (84) 282
Silkwood   (84) 367
OLD AGE
Cocoon   (86) 96
Trip to Bountiful, The   (86) 383

OPERA AND OPERETTA
Carmen   (84) 101
Love Streams   (85) 293
Parsifal   (84) 491
Pirates of Penzance, The   (84) 301
Yes, Giorgio   (83) 431
ORPHANS
Don't Cry, It's Only Thunder   (83) 420
Man from Snowy River, The   (83) 425
Pirates of Penzance, The   (84) 301
Streetwise   (86) 364
OUTLAWS
Argent, L'   [1983]   (85) 74
Barbarosa   (83) 60
Cattle Annie and Little Britches   (82) 97
Colorado Territory [1949]   (86) 489
Gods Must Be Crazy, The [1980]   (85) 224
Grey Fox, The   (84) 168
Heat and Dust [1982]   (84) 187
Hombre [1967]   (84) 547
Joke of Destiny, A [1983]   (85) 259
Mrs. Soffel   (85) 314
Nate and Hayes   (84) 236
1984   (85) 335
Pale Rider   (86) 261
Road Warrior, The [1981]   (83) 277
Romancing the Stone   (85) 421
Silverado   (86) 349
Streetwise   (86) 364
Utu [1983]   (85) 504

PARANOIA
After Hours   (86) 51
Blue Thunder   (84) 84
Detour [1946]   (86) 498
Journey into Fear [1943]   (86) 511
Man Hunt [1941]   (85) 570
Something Wicked This Way Comes   (84) 493
PARIS
American Dreamer   (85) 509
Arch of Triumph [1948]   (84) 501
Balance, La [1982]   (84) 52
Beloved Rogue [1927]   (84) 522
Diva [1980]   (83) 147
Divorcée, The [1930]   (82) 429
Full Moon in Paris   (85) 208
Gotcha!   (86) 444
History Is Made at Night [1937]   (84) 542
Loulou [1980]   (82) 226
My New Partner [1984]   (86) 246
New Babylon, The [1929]   (84) 561
Nuit de Varennes, La [1982]   (84) 270
Piaf [1980]   (83) 427
Quartet   (82) 296
Razor's Edge, The   (85) 402
Secret Life of Walter Mitty, The [1947]   (86) 540
Snows of Kilimanjaro, The [1952]   (83) 498
Swann in Love   (85) 471
Traviata, La   (83) 366
Until September   (85) 537
Victor/Victoria   (83) 387
Victory   (82) 374
Vie continue, La [1981]   (83) 430
PATRIOTISM
Beloved Rogue [1927]   (84) 522
Front, The [1976]   (86) 502
Man Hunt [1941]   (85) 570
Official Story, The   (86) 249
Rambo: First Blood Part II   (86) 299
Rocky IV   (86) 319

Spies like Us   (86) 360
White Nights   (86) 416
PEASANTS
Cheech and Chong's The Corsican
Brothers   (85) 515
Ladyhawke   (86) 214
Night of the Shooting Stars, The [1982]   (84) 258
Trace, The [1983]   (85) 537
Trout, The [1982]   (84) 496
PETS
All of Me   (85) 58
Birdy   (85) 93
Lonely Hearts [1982]   (84) 212
Pee-wee's Big Adventure   (86) 265
Private Function, A [1984]   (86) 280
Sudden Impact   (84) 395
PHILADELPHIA
Birdy   (85) 93
Blow Out   (82) 83
Rocky III   (83) 283
Witness   (86) 421
PHILOSOPHY
Agnes of God   (86) 56
Animal Kingdom, The [1932]   (86) 469
Berlin Alexanderplatz [1980]   (84) 57
Hail Mary   (86) 182
Imperative [1982]   (86) 447
My Dinner with André   (82) 255
PHOBIAS
Nightmares   (84) 490
Twilight Zone — The Movie   (84) 435
Yes, Giorgio   (83) 431
PHYSICAL HANDICAPS
Berlin Alexanderplatz [1980]   (84) 57
Birdy   (85) 93
Brother from Another Planet, The   (85) 118
Death of Mario Ricci, The [1983]   (86) 133
Eye of the Needle   (82) 148
I Sent a Letter to My Love [1980]   (82) 214
Just the Way You Are   (85) 524
Light Ahead, The [1939]   (83) 460
Man with Two Brains, The   (84) 223
Mask   (86) 231
Spies like Us   (86) 360
Whose Life Is It Anyway?   (82) 378
World According to Garp, The   (83) 397
PIONEERS
Barbary Coast [1935]   (84) 506
Heaven's Gate   (82) 18
Silverado   (86) 349
PIRATES
Goonies, The   (86) 176
Nate and Hayes   (84) 236
Pirates of Penzance, The   (84) 301
POETS AND POETRY
Beloved Rogue [1927]   (84) 522
Choose Me   (85) 135
Educating Rita   (84) 136
Guest, The   (85) 520
Out of Africa   (86) 255
Reuben, Reuben   (84) 337
Tales of Ordinary Madness   (84) 495
POLAND
Imperative [1982]   (86) 447
Love in Germany, A [1983]   (85) 283
Man of Iron   (82) 230
Man of Marble [1977]   (82) 234
Moonlighting   (83) 237
Passion [1982]   (84) 289

Shoah   (86) 339
Sophie's Choice   (83) 311
War and Love   (86) 465
POLICE
  Argent, L' [1983]   (85) 74
  Balance, La [1982]   (84) 52
  Beverly Hills Cop   (85) 88
  Beyond Reasonable Doubt [1980]   (84) 74
  Blue Thunder   (84) 84
  Buddy Buddy   (82) 93
  Christine   (84) 106
  Coup de torchon [1981]   (83) 124
  Detour [1946]   (86) 498
  Escape from New York   (82) 133
  Fast Times at Ridgemont High   (83) 156
  First Name, Carmen [1983]   (85) 186
  Flashpoint   (85) 519
  Fletch   (86) 169
  Fort Apache, the Bronx   (82) 159
  48 HRS.   (83) 173
  Front, The [1976]   (86) 502
  Garde à vue [1981]   (83) 189
  Gorky Park   (84) 162
  History Is Made at Night [1937]   (84) 542
  I'm No Angel [1933]   (85) 561
  Joke of Destiny, A [1983]   (85) 259
  Lassiter   (85) 524
  Lonely Hearts [1982]   (84) 212
  Max Dugan Returns   (84) 228
  Moving Violations   (86) 453
  My New Partner [1984]   (86) 246
  Nighthawks   (82) 259
  1984   (85) 335
  Outland   (82) 272
  Partners   (83) 427
  Pirates of Penzance, The   (84) 301
  Police Academy   (85) 529
  Police Academy 2   (86) 276
  Prince of the City   (82) 292
  Private Function, A [1984]   (86) 280
  Prizzi's Honor   (86) 285
  Querelle [1982]   (84) 313
  Ragtime   (82) 304
  Remo Williams   (86) 457
  Return of the Living Dead, The   (86) 314
  Road Warrior, The [1981]   (83) 277
  Romancing the Stone   (85) 421
  Runaway Train   (86) 324
  Sharky's Machine   (82) 324
  Smash Palace [1981]   (83) 302
  Sudden Impact   (84) 395
  Tightrope   (85) 489
  Time After Time [1979]   (84) 579
  To Live and Die in L.A.   (86) 379
  Too Scared to Scream   (86) 463
  Trail of the Pink Panther   (83) 430
  Trouble in Mind   (86) 388
  True Confessions   (82) 368
  Unfaithful, The [1947]   (86) 550
  Venom [1981]   (83) 430
  Victim [1961]   (85) 649
  Wetherby   (86) 406
  Wicker Man, The [1974]   (86) 555
  Wolfen   (82) 382
  Year of the Dragon   (86) 426
  Young Sherlock Holmes   (86) 431
POLITICS AND POLITICIANS
  Adventures of Buckaroo Banzai, The   (85) 47
  Amin—The Rise and Fall   (84) 479
  And Nothing but the Truth   (85) 510
  Best Little Whorehouse in Texas, The   (83) 72
  Beyond the Limit   (84) 479

  Big Chill, The   (84) 78
  Blow Out   (82) 83
  Bon Plaisir, Le [1983]   (85) 513
  Caged Fury   (85) 514
  Colonel Redl [1984]   (86) 100
  Continental Divide   (82) 115
  Daniel   (84) 481
  Danton [1982]   (84) 121
  Disraeli [1929]   (82) 426
  Escape Artist, The   (83) 421
  Firestarter   (85) 519
  First Monday in October   (82) 151
  Flash of Green, A   (86) 443
  Front, The [1976]   (86) 502
  Gabriela [1983]   (85) 213
  Gandhi   (83) 183
  Gods Must Be Crazy, The [1980]   (85) 224
  Going Berserk   (84) 485
  Hanna K.   (84) 177
  Heatwave   (84) 485
  Hecate [1982]   (85) 522
  Home and the World, The [1984]   (86) 447
  Honky Tonk Freeway   (82) 199
  Insignificance   (86) 447
  Joke of Destiny, A [1983]   (85) 259
  Killing Fields, The   (85) 270
  Kiss of the Spider Woman   (86) 209
  Lola [1981]   (83) 215
  Man Hunt [1941]   (85) 570
  Man Who Wasn't There, The   (84) 489
  Marie   (86) 227
  Matter of Struggle, A   (86) 451
  Missing   (83) 232
  Mission, The   (84) 489
  New Babylon, The [1929]   (84) 561
  1984   (85) 335
  Official Story, The   (86) 249
  Ploughman's Lunch, The [1983]   (85) 377
  Protocol   (85) 383
  Purple Haze   (84) 492
  Rambo: First Blood Part II   (86) 299
  Reds   (82) 312
  Return of the Secaucus 7 [1980]   (83) 484
  Rocky IV   (86) 319
  St. Elmo's Fire   (86) 330
  Sharky's Machine   (82) 324
  Six Weeks   (83) 428
  Solid Gold Cadillac, The [1956]   (85) 615
  Under Fire   (84) 441
  Under the Volcano   (85) 499
  Way We Were, The [1973]   (82) 474
  White Nights   (86) 416
  Wrong Is Right   (83) 403
  Year of Living Dangerously, The
    [1982]   (84) 462
PORTUGAL
  State of Things, The   (84) 379
POVERTY
  All the Right Moves   (84) 41
  Annie   (83) 56
  Brother from Another Planet, The   (85) 118
  Cannery Row   (83) 95
  Color Purple, The   (86) 105
  Gandhi   (83) 183
  Heaven's Gate   (82) 195
  Killing Fields, The   (85) 270
  Lady Sings the Blues [1972]   (85) 565
  Norte, El   (84) 265
  Pennies from Heaven   (82) 276
  Piaf [1980]   (83) 427
  Repo Man   (85) 408
  Running Brave   (84) 354

Tess [1980]   (82) 471
Trading Places   (84) 430
Under Fire   (84) 441
Victor/Victoria   (83) 387
Year of Living Dangerously, The [1982]   (84) 462
Yol   (83) 411

PREGNANCY
Color Purple, The   (86) 105
Enemy Mine   (86) 161
Hail Mary   (86) 182
Micki & Maude   (85) 308
Next Year if All Goes Well   (84) 490

PREHISTORIC TIMES
Cave Girl   (86) 439
Iceman   (85) 248
Quest for Fire   (83) 271

PRESIDENTS
Adventures of Buckaroo Banzai, The   (85) 47
Annie   (83) 56
Dreamscape   (85) 166
Escape from New York   (82) 133
Superman II   (82) 339
Wrong Is Right   (83) 403

PRIESTS (See RELIGION AND SPIRITUALITY)

PRISONS
Argent, L' [1983]   (85) 74
Berlin Alexanderplatz [1980]   (84) 57
Bizet's Carmen [1983]   (85) 98
Chained Heat   (84) 480
Escape from New York   (82) 133
Falcon and the Snowman, The   (86) 165
48 HRS.   (83) 173
Gandhi   (83) 183
Joke of Destiny, A [1983]   (85) 259
Kiss of the Spider Woman   (86) 209
Ladyhawke   (86) 214
Love Child   (83) 425
Merry Christmas, Mr. Lawrence   (84) 231
Mrs. Soffel   (85) 314
Missing   (83) 228
My New Partner [1984]   (86) 246
Nate and Hayes   (84) 236
Peter Ibbetson [1935]   (86) 527
Pixote [1980]   (82) 280
Quartet   (82) 296
Rappin'   (86) 457
Runaway Train   (86) 324
Running Hot   (85) 531
St. Elmo's Fire   (86) 330
Sense of Freedom, A   (86) 459
Silverado   (86) 349
Sophie's Choice   (83) 311
Streetwise   (86) 364
Trouble in Mind   (86) 388
Victory   (82) 374
Yol   (83) 411
Zoot Suit   (82) 389

PROHIBITION
City Heat   (85) 141
Once upon a Time in America   (85) 345

PROSTITUTES AND PROSTITUTION
Angel   (85) 510
Arthur   (82) 71
Avenging Angel   (86) 436
Balance, La [1982]   (84) 52
Berlin Alexanderplatz [1980]   (84) 57
Best Little Whorehouse in Texas, The   (83) 72
Cannery Row   (83) 95

Certain Fury   (86) 440
Colorado Territory [1949]   (86) 489
Crimes of Passion   (85) 161
Diva [1980]   (83) 147
Emerald Forest, The   (86) 156
Erendira [1983]   (85) 181
Every Man for Himself [1979]   (82) 139
48 HRS.   (83) 173
Gift, The   (84) 484
Hammett   (84) 174
Heaven's Gate   (82) 195
Honkytonk Man   (83) 200
Lola [1981]   (83) 215
Lonely Hearts [1982]   (84) 212
Love Streams   (85) 293
Man Hunt [1941]   (85) 570
Man with Two Brains, The   (84) 223
Missionary, The   (83) 233
Nate and Hayes   (84) 236
Nell Gwyn [1934]   (84) 557
Night Shift   (83) 426
Once upon a Time in America   (85) 345
Pixote [1980]   (82) 280
Porky's   (83) 267
Pretty Baby [1978]   (85) 597
Purple Rose of Cairo, The   (86) 290
Quartet   (82) 296
Razor's Edge, The   (85) 402
Risky Business   (84) 349
Sharky's Machine   (82) 324
Silverado   (86) 349
Some Kind of Hero   (83) 428
Streetwalkin'   (86) 461
Streetwise   (86) 364
Swann in Love   (85) 471
Tightrope   (85) 489
Time After Time [1979]   (84) 579
Trading Places   (84) 430
Traviata, La   (83) 366
True Confessions   (82) 368
Under the Volcano   (85) 499
Vice Squad   (83) 430
Winter of Our Dreams [1981]   (83) 431
Woman in Flames, A   (85) 538

PSYCHIATRY AND PSYCHIATRISTS
Agnes of God   (86) 56
Birdy   (85) 93
Dreamscape   (85) 166
Frances   (83) 178
Freud [1962]   (84) 535
Howling, The   (82) 207
Lonely Hearts [1982]   (84) 212
Lovesick   (84) 488
Man Who Loved Women, The   (84) 218
Montenegro   (82) 250
Outland   (82) 272
Question of Silence, A   (85) 530
Return of the Soldier, The [1982]   (84) 332
Secret Life of Walter Mitty, The [1947]   (86) 540
Sender, The   (83) 427
Still of the Night   (83) 326
They Might Be Giants [1971]   (83) 515
Videodrome   (84) 452
Zelig   (84) 473

PUPPETS
Muppets Take Manhattan, The   (85) 526
Neverending Story, The   (85) 527

RACIAL PREJUDICE
Alamo Bay   (86) 436
Boys from Brazil, The [1978]   (86) 480

Brother from Another Planet, The   (85) 118
Cotton Club, The   (85) 150
Fort Apache [1948]   (84) 530
48 HRS.   (83) 173
Gandhi   (83) 183
Hombre [1967]   (84) 547
Killing Fields, The   (85) 270
Lady Sings the Blues [1972]   (85) 565
Lords of Discipline, The   (84) 488
Norte, El   (84) 265
Ploughman's Lunch, The [1983]   (85) 377
Police Academy 2   (86) 276
Porky's II   (84) 491
Pretty Baby [1978]   (85) 597
Purple Rain   (85) 389
Ragtime   (82) 304
Rambo: First Blood Part II   (86) 299
Running Brave   (84) 354
Silkwood   (84) 367
Silverado   (86) 349
Soldier's Story, A   (85) 427
Streamers   (84) 391
That Championship Season   (83) 338
Trading Places   (84) 430
Twilight Zone — The Movie   (84) 435
Utu [1983]   (85) 504
White Nights   (86) 416
Zoot Suit   (82) 389

RADIO
Choose Me   (85) 135
Comfort and Joy   (85) 146

RAPE
Agnes of God   (86) 56
Beast Within, The   (83) 418
Brimstone and Treacle   (83) 91
Color Purple, The   (86) 105
Deep in the Heart   (85) 517
Frances   (83) 178
Garde à vue [1981]   (83) 189
Hotel New Hampshire, The   (85) 243
Humongous   (83) 423
Incubus, The [1980]   (83) 424
Jagged Edge   (86) 190
Nuit de Varennes, La [1982]   (84) 270
Official Story, The   (86) 249
Once upon a Time in America   (85) 345
Passage to India, A   (85) 365
Runaway Train   (86) 324
Smooth Talk   (86) 354
Star 80   (84) 374
Stranger Is Watching, A   (83) 429
Sudden Impact   (84) 395
Tightrope   (85) 489
When Father Was Away on Business [1984]   (86) 411
World According to Garp, The   (83) 397

REINCARNATION
All of Me   (85) 58
Echoes   (84) 483

RELIGION AND SPIRITUALITY
After the Rehearsal   (85) 52
Agnes of God   (86) 56
Argent, L' [1983]   (85) 74
Bridge of San Luis Rey, The [1929]   (82) 408
Chariots of Fire   (82) 101
Chosen, The   (83) 116
Clash of the Titans   (82) 111
Color Purple, The   (86) 105
Colorado Territory [1949]   (86) 489
Crimes of Passion   (85) 161
Deathtrap   (83) 137

Emerald Forest, The   (86) 156
Fanny and Alexander [1982]   (84) 146
Fitzcarraldo   (83) 167
Footloose   (85) 198
4th Man, The [1983]   (85) 203
Frances   (83) 178
Gandhi   (83) 183
Hail Mary   (86) 182
Heat and Dust [1982]   (84) 187
Honky Tonk Freeway   (82) 199
Iceman   (85) 248
Ladyhawke   (86) 214
Mass Appeal   (85) 303
Miracle Woman, The [1931]   (83) 473
Missionary, The   (83) 233
Monsignor   (83) 425
Monty Python's The Meaning of Life   (84) 489
Mrs. Soffel   (85) 314
Nate and Hayes   (84) 236
Night of the Shooting Stars, The [1982]   (84) 258
Nostalgia [1983]   (85) 340
Oh God, You Devil   (85) 528
Passion [1982]   (84) 289
Places in the Heart   (85) 371
Raiders of the Lost Ark   (82) 308
Razor's Edge, The   (85) 402
Return of Martin Guerre, The   (84) 318
Return of the Jedi   (84) 326
Scarlet Letter, The [1927]   (85) 602
Sign of the Cross, The [1932]   (85) 607
Softly Softly [1984]   (86) 460
Sophie's Choice   (83) 311
Split Image   (83) 317
Star Trek III — The Search for Spock   (85) 439
Stephen King's Children of the Corn   (85) 534
Tender Mercies   (84) 409
Time Bandits [1980]   (82) 364
Tragedy of a Ridiculous Man [1981]   (83) 361
True Confessions   (82) 368
Wicker Man, The [1974]   (86) 555
Witness   (86) 421
Yentl   (84) 468
Young Sherlock Holmes   (86) 431

THE RESISTANCE
Girl with the Red Hair, The   (84) 485
Plenty   (86) 271
White Rose, The   (84) 497

REPORTERS (See NEWSPAPERS,
REPORTERS, AND JOURNALISTS)

REVENGE
Amateur, The   (83) 417
Balance, La [1982]   (84) 52
Barbarosa   (83) 60
Berlin Alexanderplatz [1980]   (84) 57
Bizet's Carmen [1983]   (85) 98
Blade Runner   (83) 76
Blue Thunder   (84) 84
Challenge, The   (83) 109
Christine   (84) 106
City Heat   (85) 141
Color Purple, The   (86) 105
Comfort and Joy   (85) 146
Conan the Barbarian   (83) 419
Death Wish II   (83) 420
Deep in the Heart   (85) 517
Eleni   (86) 151
Falcon and the Snowman, The   (86) 165
Fighting Back   (83) 421
Fire and Ice   (84) 153
First Blood   (83) 164
Fleshburn   (85) 519

Gabriela [1983]   (85) 213
History Is Made at Night [1937]   (84) 542
Hotel New Hampshire, The   (85) 243
Joke of Destiny, A [1983]   (85) 259
Karate Kid, The   (85) 264
Long Good Friday, The   (83) 220
Man Hunt [1941]   (85) 570
Moon in the Gutter, The   (84) 490
Nate and Hayes   (84) 236
Once upon a Time in America   (85) 345
Pale Rider   (86) 261
Police Academy 2   (86) 276
Prizzi's Honor   (86) 285
Raiders of the Lost Ark   (82) 308
Rambo: First Blood Part II   (86) 299
Road Warrior, The [1981]   (83) 277
Rocky III   (83) 283
Rocky IV   (86) 319
Runaway Train   (86) 324
Savage Island   (86) 458
Star 80   (84) 374
Star Trek II—The Wrath of Khan   (83) 321
Still of the Night   (83) 326
Sudden Impact   (84) 395
Sword and the Sorcerer, The   (83) 429
To Live and Die in L.A.   (86) 379
Utu [1983]   (85) 504
Victim [1961]   (85) 649

REVOLUTION
Cal   (85) 124
Deal of the Century   (84) 482
Killing Fields, The   (85) 270
Megaforce   (83) 425
New Babylon, The [1929]   (84) 561
Protocol   (85) 383
Red Dawn   (85) 530
Under Fire   (84) 441
Year of Living Dangerously, The [1982]   (84) 462

ROBBERY (See also BANK ROBBERY and JEWEL ROBBERY)
After Hours   (86) 51
Berlin Alexanderplatz [1980]   (84) 57
Bon Plaisir, Le [1983]   (85) 513
Challenge, The   (83) 109
Crackers   (85) 516
Detour [1946]   (86) 498
Diva [1980]   (83) 147
48 HRS.   (83) 173
Hombre [1967]   (84) 547
I'm No Angel [1933]   (85) 561
It Happened Tomorrow [1944]   (84) 552
Lassiter   (85) 524
Long Good Friday, The   (83) 220
Marie   (86) 227
Moonlighting   (83) 237
My New Partner [1984]   (86) 246
Once upon a Time in America   (85) 345
Our Relations [1936]   (86) 523
Pee-wee's Big Adventure   (86) 265
Police Academy 2   (86) 276
Prizzi's Honor   (86) 285
Repo Man   (85) 408
Risky Business   (84) 349
River Rat, The   (85) 531
Scandalous   (85) 532
Sherlock Holmes [1922]   (83) 494
Silverado   (86) 349
Streetwise   (86) 364
That Sinking Feeling [1979]   (85) 536
Thief   (82) 356

Thief of Hearts   (85) 536
To Live and Die in L.A.   (86) 379
Trouble in Mind   (86) 388
Under the Volcano   (85) 499
Wicked Lady, The   (84) 497
Xica [1976]   (83) 407

RODEOS AND WESTERN SHOWS
Secret Life of Walter Mitty, The [1947]   (86) 540

ROMANCE
Absence of Malice   (82) 57
Adolescente, L' [1979]   (83) 53
After the Rehearsal   (85) 52
Against All Odds   (85) 509
Agatha [1979]   (83) 435
All the Right Moves   (84) 41
Always   (86) 60
American Dreamer   (85) 509
Animal Kingdom, The [1932]   (86) 469
Annie   (83) 56
Apache [1954]   (82) 395
Arthur   (82) 71
Atlantic City   (82) 74
Baby, It's You   (84) 479
Balance, La [1982]   (84) 52
Beau Mariage, Le   (83) 65
Beau Pere   (82) 78
Beloved Rogue [1927]   (84) 522
Berlin Alexanderplatz [1980]   (84) 57
Best Friends   (83) 68
Best Little Whorehouse in Texas, The   (83) 72
Betrayal   (84) 67
Bizet's Carmen [1983]   (85) 98
Blade Runner   (83) 76
Blame It on Rio   (85) 512
Boum, La [1980]   (84) 480
Breakfast Club, The   (86) 85
Breathless   (84) 89
Bridge of San Luis Rey, The [1929]   (82) 408
Brother from Another Planet, The   (85) 118
Buddy System, The   (85) 514
Bullshot [1983]   (86) 439
Caddie [1976]   (83) 439
Cal   (85) 124
Cannery Row   (83) 95
Cat People [1942]   (82) 137
Cat People   (83) 100
Cattle Annie and Little Britches   (82) 97
Choose Me   (85) 135
Chorus Line, A   (86) 91
City Girl, The   (85) 516
Clash of the Titans   (82) 111
Cold Feet   (85) 516
Colorado Territory [1949]   (86) 489
Come and Get It [1936]   (82) 412
Comfort and Joy   (85) 146
Continental Divide   (82) 115
Creature from the Black Lagoon, The [1954]   (82) 422
Cross Creek   (84) 116
Cruel Story of Youth [1960]   (85) 517
Dance with a Stranger [1984]   (86) 125
Dead Men Don't Wear Plaid   (83) 134
Desperately Seeking Susan   (86) 137
Detour [1946]   (86) 498
Diner   (83) 142
Diva [1980]   (83) 147
Dragonslayer   (82) 125
Dreamchild   (86) 146
Dulcy [1923]   (82) 432
Edith and Marcel [1983]   (85) 518
Electric Dreams   (85) 518

Entre nous [1983]   (85) 176
Every Man for Himself [1979]   (82) 139
Excalibur   (82) 144
Experience Preferred ... but Not Essential
   [1982]   (84) 141
Falling in Love   (85) 519
Fast Times at Ridgemont High   (83) 156
Flamingo Kid, The   (85) 192
Flashdance   (84) 158
Fool for Love   (86) 172
Footloose   (85) 198
For Your Eyes Only   (82) 155
Fort Apache, the Bronx   (82) 159
48 HRS.   (83) 173
Four Friends   (82) 167
Front, The [1976]   (86) 502
Full Moon in Paris   (85) 208
Gabriela [1983]   (85) 213
Ghostbusters   (85) 219
Gorky Park   (84) 162
Grease 2   (83) 422
Great Muppet Caper, The   (82) 187
Gregory's Girl [1981]   (83) 193
Grey Fox, The   (84) 168
Guy Named Joe, A [1943]   (82) 435
Hard to Hold   (85) 521
Hard Traveling   (86) 445
Hard Way, The [1942]   (85) 555
Hatchet Man, The [1932]   (83) 447
Heartaches [1981]   (83) 197
Heartbreaker   (84) 485
Heat and Dust [1982]   (84) 187
Heavenly Bodies   (85) 522
Heaven's Gate   (82) 195
Hecate [1982]   (85) 522
High Road to China   (84) 486
History Is Made at Night [1937]   (84) 542
H. M. Pulham, Esq. [1941]   (82) 439
Holiday Inn [1942]   (82) 443
Hondo [1954]   (83) 452
I Know Where I'm Going [1945]   (83) 456
I Sent a Letter to My Love [1980]   (82) 214
I'm No Angel [1933]   (85) 561
It Happened Tomorrow [1944]   (84) 552
Jewel of the Nile, The   (86) 448
Joy of Sex   (85) 524
Key Exchange   (86) 448
Kiss Me Goodbye   (83) 209
Krull   (84) 487
Lady Sings the Blues [1972]   (85) 565
Ladyhawke   (86) 214
Lianna   (84) 201
Liar's Moon   (83) 424
Light Ahead, The [1939]   (83) 460
Lili Marleen   (82) 222
Lily in Love   (86) 450
Lola [1981]   (83) 215
Lonely Guy, The   (85) 525
Lonely Hearts [1982]   (84) 212
Long Good Friday, The   (83) 220
Lost Moment, The [1947]   (83) 465
Loulou [1980]   (82) 226
Love Child   (83) 425
Love Letters   (85) 288
Love Streams   (85) 293
Lovelines   (85) 525
Lovesick   (84) 488
Man Hunt [1941]   (85) 570
Man Who Loved Women, The   (84) 218
Man with Two Brains, The   (84) 223
Mask   (86) 231
Max Dugan Returns   (84) 228

Maxie   (86) 452
Mephisto   (82) 237
Micki & Maude   (85) 308
Midsummer Night's Sex Comedy, A   (83) 228
Miracle Woman, The [1931]   (83) 473
Mrs. Soffel   (85) 314
Missionary, The   (83) 233
Modern Romance   (82) 241
Moscow on the Hudson   (85) 321
Murphy's Romance   (86) 242
My Best Friend's Girl [1983]   (85) 326
My Cousin Rachel [1952]   (82) 458
My Favorite Year   (83) 241
My New Partner [1984]   (86) 246
My Reputation [1946]   (85) 586
Nate and Hayes   (84) 236
Natural, The   (85) 329
Nell Gwyn [1934]   (84) 557
New York, New York [1977]   (84) 567
Next Year if All Goes Well   (84) 490
Nighthawks   (82) 259
1984   (85) 335
No Small Affair   (85) 527
Officer and a Gentleman, An   (83) 246
Once upon a Time in America   (85) 345
One from the Heart   (83) 250
Out of Africa   (86) 255
Oxford Blues   (85) 528
Paradise   (83) 426
Pauline at the Beach [1982]   (84) 296
Pennies from Heaven   (82) 276
Perfect   (86) 456
Personal Best   (83) 254
Personals, The   (84) 491
Pete Kelly's Blues [1955]   (83) 481
Peter Ibbetson [1935]   (85) 527
Police Academy 2   (86) 276
Pretty Baby [1978]   (85) 597
Prizzi's Honor   (86) 285
Purple Hearts   (85) 529
Purple Rose of Cairo, The   (86) 290
Racing with the Moon   (85) 397
Raggedy Man   (82) 300
Ragtime   (82) 304
Raiders of the Lost Ark   (82) 308
Return of the Secaucus 7 [1980]   (83) 484
Return of the Soldier, The [1982]   (84) 332
Rich and Famous   (82) 316
Risky Business   (84) 349
Romancing the Stone   (85) 421
Romantic Comedy   (84) 492
Royal Wedding [1951]   (86) 536
Runaway Train   (86) 324
St. Elmo's Fire   (86) 330
Scandalous   (85) 532
Secret Admirer   (86) 459
Sharky's Machine   (82) 324
Sherlock Holmes [1922]   (83) 494
Siberiade [1977]   (83) 299
Silkwood   (84) 367
Silverado   (86) 349
Smithereens   (83) 307
Smooth Talk   (86) 354
Snows of Kilimanjaro, The [1952]   (83) 498
Solid Gold Cadillac, The [1956]   (85) 615
Some Kind of Hero   (83) 428
Something Wicked This Way Comes   (84) 493
Sophie's Choice   (83) 311
Spies like Us   (86) 360
Splash   (85) 434
Split Image   (83) 317
Star Trek II—The Wrath of Khan   (83) 321

Star 80   (84) 374
Stardust Memories [1980]   (85) 626
Starman   (85) 445
Staying Alive   (84) 386
Still of the Night   (83) 326
Stranger's Kiss   (85) 534
Stripes   (82) 336
Superman II   (82) 339
Superman III   (84) 399
Sure Thing, The   (86) 369
Swann in Love   (85) 471
Sweet Dreams   (86) 374
Sweet Sixteen   (85) 535
Swing Shift   (85) 535
Table for Five   (84) 404
Take a Letter, Darling [1942]   (85) 632
Tempest   (83) 331
Tender Mercies   (84) 409
Terms of Endearment   (84) 414
Tess [1980]   (82) 471
They All Laughed   (82) 350
They Drive by Night [1940]   (83) 508
They Might Be Giants [1971]   (83) 515
Thief of Hearts   (85) 536
Time After Time [1979]   (84) 579
Time Machine, The [1960]   (84) 585
Too Hot to Handle [1938]   (84) 596
Tootsie   (83) 353
Traviata, La   (83) 366
TRON   (83) 371
Trouble in Mind   (86) 388
Two of a Kind   (84) 496
Under Fire   (84) 441
Until September   (85) 537
Valentina   (84) 496
Valley Girl   (84) 447
Victor / Victoria   (83) 387
Waltz Across Texas   (84) 497
Way We Were, The [1973]   (82) 474
Wetherby   (86) 406
White Nights   (86) 416
Witness   (86) 421
Wolfen   (82) 382
Woman in Flames, A   (85) 538
Woman in Red, The   (85) 538
World of Henry Orient, The [1964]   (84) 600
Xica [1976]   (83) 407
Year of Living Dangerously, The [1982]   (84) 462
Yes, Giorgio   (83) 431
Young Sherlock Holmes   (86) 431
Zapped!   (83) 431
Zoot Suit   (82) 389

ROME
Joke of Destiny, A [1983]   (85) 259
Sign of the Cross, The [1932]   (85) 607

RURAL AMERICA
Color Purple, The   (86) 105
Come and Get It [1936]   (82) 412
Continental Divide   (82) 115
Country   (85) 156
Cross Creek   (84) 116
Heartland   (82) 191
Heaven's Gate   (82) 195
Loveless, The   (85) 525
Melvin and Howard [1980]   (82) 453
Natural, The   (85) 329
Pee-wee's Big Adventure   (86) 265
Places in the Heart   (85) 371
Postman Always Rings Twice, The   (82) 284
River, The   (85) 416

Scarlet Letter, The [1927]   (85) 602
Soldier's Story, A   (85) 427
Southern Comfort   (82) 332
Stone Boy, The   (85) 450
Sure Thing, The   (86) 369
Tender Mercies   (84) 409
Witness   (86) 421

RUSSIA AND THE SOVIET UNION
American Pop   (82) 62
Backstage at the Kirov   (85) 511
Dangerous Moves [1984]   (86) 129
Firefox   (83) 160
Gorky Park   (84) 162
Jazzman   (85) 523
Light Ahead, The [1949]   (83) 460
Man Who Wasn't There, The   (84) 489
Moscow on the Hudson   (85) 321
New Babylon, The [1929]   (84) 561
North Star, The [1943]   (83) 476
Nostalgia [1983]   (85) 340
Rasputin [1975]   (86) 457
Reds   (82) 312
Rocky IV   (86) 319
Siberiade [1977]   (83) 299
Spies like Us   (86) 360
White Nights   (86) 416

SAILORS
Our Relations [1936]   (86) 523
Querelle [1982]   (84) 313
Weekend Pass   (85) 537

SAN FRANCISCO
Barbary Coast [1935]   (84) 506
Chan Is Missing   (83) 113
Dim Sum   (86) 141
48 HRS.   (83) 173
Hatchet Man, The [1932]   (83) 447
Killing Fields, The   (85) 270
Sudden Impact   (84) 395
Time After Time [1979]   (84) 579
View to a Kill, A   (86) 401

SATIRE
Brazil   (86) 80
Brewster McCloud [1970]   (86) 484
Compromising Positions   (86) 120
Dark Star [1975]   (86) 494
Desperately Seeking Susan   (86) 137
Front, The [1976]   (86) 502
I'm No Angel [1933]   (85) 561
Ice Pirates, The   (85) 523
Lost in America   (86) 219
Month Python's The Meaning of Life   (84) 489
9 Deaths of the Ninja   (86) 436
Pee-wee's Big Adventure   (86) 265
Private Function, A [1984]   (86) 280
Prizzi's Honor   (86) 285
Return of the Living Dead, The   (86) 314
Reuben, Reuben   (84) 337
Secret Life of Walter Mitty, The [1947]   (86) 540
They Call Me Bruce   (83) 429
To Be or Not to Be   (84) 426

SCHOOLS AND SCHOOL LIFE
All the Right Moves   (84) 41
Angel   (85) 510
Breakfast Club, The   (86) 85
Christine   (84) 106
Class   (84) 480
Dreamchild   (86) 146
Fast Times at Ridgemont High   (83) 156
Footloose   (85) 198
Foster Daddy, Tora! [1980]   (82) 163

Front, The [1976]   (86) 502
Grease 2   (83) 422
Gregory's Girl [1981]   (83) 193
Heaven Help Us   (86) 445
Kipperbang [1983]   (85) 524
Lords of Discipline, The   (84) 488
Making the Grade   (85) 526
Mask   (86) 231
My Tutor   (84) 490
New Kids, The   (86) 454
Official Story, The   (86) 249
Out of Africa   (86) 255
Porky's   (83) 267
Porky's II   (84) 491
Racing with the Moon   (85) 397
Real Genius   (86) 309
Running Brave   (84) 354
St. Elmo's Fire   (86) 330
Sugar Cane Alley [1983]   (85) 461
Taps   (82) 343
Vision Quest   (86) 464
Water and Soap   (86) 465
Wetherby   (86) 406
World of Henry Orient, The [1964]   (84) 600
Young Sherlock Holmes   (86) 431
Zapped!   (83) 431

SCIENCE AND SCIENTISTS
Adventures of Buckaroo Banzai, The   (85) 47
Android   (85) 510
Baby   (86) 437
Back to the Future   (86) 65
Blade Runner   (83) 76
Brainstorm   (84) 480
Bullshot [1983]   (86) 439
Cannery Row   (83) 95
Creator   (86) 441
Creature from the Black Lagoon, The
[1954]   (82) 422
Dr. Butcher, M.D. [1980]   (83) 420
Dreamscape   (85) 166
E.T.: The Extra-Terrestrial   (83) 151
Gremlins   (85) 230
Greystoke   (85) 236
Iceman   (85) 248
Insignificance   (86) 447
Joke of Destiny, A [1983]   (85) 259
Kiss Me Goodbye   (83) 209
Last Starfighter, The   (85) 277
Lifeforce   (86) 450
Man Who Fell to Earth, The [1975]   (83) 469
Man with Two Brains, The   (84) 223
Midsummer Night's Sex Comedy, A   (83) 224
My Science Project   (86) 543
Parasite   (83) 426
Poltergeist   (83) 263
Real Genius   (86) 309
Re-Animator   (86) 457
Repo Man   (85) 408
Return of the Living Dead, The   (86) 314
Rocky IV   (86) 319
Silkwood   (84) 367
Sound Barrier, The [1952]   (85) 621
Star Trek II—The Wrath of Khan   (83) 321
Strange Brew   (84) 494
Swamp Thing   (83) 429
Thing, The   (83) 343
Torn Curtain [1966]   (85) 644
2010   (85) 494
WarGames   (84) 458
Warning Sign   (86) 465
Wavelength   (84) 497

SCIENCE FICTION
Adventures of Buckaroo Banzai, The   (85) 47
Android   (85) 510
Battletruck   (83) 417
Blade Runner   (83) 76
Brainstorm   (84) 480
Brother from Another Planet, The   (85) 118
Cocoon   (86) 96
Creature from the Black Lagoon, The
[1954]   (82) 422
Dark Star [1975]   (86) 494
Dead Men Don't Wear Plaid   (83) 134
Def-Con 4   (86) 441
Dreamscape   (85) 166
Dune   (85) 171
Enemy Mine   (86) 161
Escape from New York   (82) 133
Escape 2000   (84) 483
E.T.: The Extra-Terrestrial   (83) 151
Explorers   (86) 442
Forbidden World   (83) 421
Gremlins   (85) 230
Hercules   (84) 485
Ice Pirates, The   (85) 523
Iceman   (85) 248
Last Starfighter, The   (85) 277
Liquid Sky   (84) 487
Mad Max Beyond Thunderdome   (86) 223
Man Who Fell to Earth, The [1975]   (83) 469
Man with Two Brains, The   (84) 223
Metalstorm   (84) 489
Morons from Outer Space   (86) 452
My Science Project   (86) 453
Night of the Comet   (85) 527
Outland   (82) 272
Philadelphia Experiment, The   (85) 529
Quiet Earth, The   (86) 295
Re-Animator   (86) 457
Red Dawn   (85) 530
Repo Man   (85) 408
Return of the Jedi   (84) 326
Road Warrior, The [1981]   (83) 277
Secret of the Sword, The   (86) 459
Slapstick   (85) 533
Spacehunter   (84) 493
Star Trek II—The Wrath of Khan   (83) 321
Star Trek III—The Search for Spock   (85) 439
Starman   (85) 445
Strange Invaders   (84) 494
Stuff, The   (86) 461
Superman II   (82) 339
Superman III   (84) 399
Swamp Thing   (83) 429
Terminator, The   (85) 478
Thing, The   (83) 343
THX 1138 [1971]   (85) 638
Time After Time [1979]   (84) 579
Time Machine, The [1960]   (84) 585
Trancers   (86) 463
TRON   (83) 371
2010   (85) 494
Yor   (84) 498

SCOTLAND
Another Time, Another Place [1983]   (85) 510
Comfort and Joy   (85) 146
Gregory's Girl [1981]   (83) 193
Greystoke   (85) 236
I Know Where I'm Going [1945]   (83) 456
Local Hero   (84) 206
That Sinking Feeling [1979]   (85) 536

SCREWBALL COMEDY
  All of Me   (85) 58
  Bachelor Party   (85) 511
  Bedtime for Bonzo [1951]   (84) 512
  Best Defense   (85) 512
  Broadway Danny Rose   (85) 112
  Chattanooga Choo Choo   (85) 515
  Cheech and Chong's The Corsican
    Brothers   (85) 515
  Cocoon   (86) 96
  Comfort and Joy   (85) 146
  Curse of the Pink Panther   (84) 481
  D.C. Cab   (84) 481
  Deal of the Century   (84) 482
  Doctor Detroit   (84) 482
  Dulcy [1923]   (82) 432
  Easy Money   (84) 482
  Gods Must Be Crazy, The [1980]   (85) 224
  Going Berserk   (84) 485
  Good Bye Cruel World   (85) 520
  Meatballs Part II   (85) 526
  Micki & Maude   (85) 308
  Monty Python's The Meaning of Life   (84) 489
  National Lampoon's Class Reunion   (83) 426
  Our Relations [1936]   (86) 523
  Pee-wee's Big Adventure   (86) 265
  Police Academy   (85) 529
  Private Function, A [1984]   (86) 280
  Revenge of the Nerds   (85) 530
  Slapstick   (85) 533
  Stripes   (82) 336
  Surf II   (85) 535
  Survivors, The   (84) 495
  Take a Letter, Darling [1942]   (85) 632
  Things Are Tough All Over   (83) 430
  Top Secret   (85) 536
  Trading Places   (84) 430
  Trail of the Pink Panther   (83) 430
  Young Doctors in Love   (83) 431
SELF-DISCOVERY
  À nos amour [1983]   (85) 509
  Always   (86) 60
  Basileus Quartet   (85) 511
  Boum, La [1980]   (84) 480
  Breakfast Club, The   (86) 85
  Chorus Line, A   (86) 91
  Color Purple, The   (86) 105
  Colorado Territory [1949]   (86) 489
  Dreamchild   (86) 146
  Five Days One Summer   (83) 421
  Front, The [1976]   (86) 502
  Hadley's Rebellion   (85) 521
  Lost in America   (86) 219
  Love Streams   (85) 293
  Making Love   (83) 425
  Mask   (86) 231
  Mission, The   (84) 489
  Never Cry Wolf   (84) 247
  Nostalgia [1983]   (85) 340
  Official Story, The   (86) 249
  Out of Africa   (86) 255
  Purple Rose of Cairo, The   (86) 290
  Querelle [1982]   (84) 313
  Reckless   (85) 530
  Royal Wedding [1951]   (86) 536
  St. Elmo's Fire   (86) 330
  Secrets   (85) 532
  Sixteen Candles   (85) 532
  Smooth Talk   (86) 354
  28 Up [1984]   (86) 392
  Unfinished Piece for Piano Player, An
    [1977]   (83) 430

  White Nights   (86) 416
  Witness   (86) 421
SELLING
  Berlin Alexanderplatz [1980]   (84) 57
  Door to Door   (85) 518
  Dreamchild   (86) 146
  Home Free All   (85) 522
SEVENTEENTH CENTURY
  Draughtsman's Contract, The [1982]   (84) 126
  Nell Gwyn [1934]   (84) 557
  Scarlet Letter, The [1927]   (85) 602
  Wicked Lady, The   (84) 497
SEX AND SEXUALITY (See also
  HOMOSEXUALITY)
  After the Rehearsal   (85) 52
  Agnes of God   (86) 56
  All of Me   (85) 58
  American Taboo   (85) 509
  Animal Kingdom, The [1932]   (86) 469
  Barefoot Contessa, The [1954]   (82) 399
  Beach Girls, The   (83) 417
  Beau Pere   (82) 78
  Beloved Rogue [1927]   (84) 522
  Berlin Alexanderplatz [1980]   (84) 57
  Best Little Whorehouse in Texas, The   (83) 72
  Big Chill, The   (84) 78
  Bizet's Carmen [1983]   (85) 98
  Body Heat   (82) 87
  Bolero   (85) 513
  Breakfast Club, The   (86) 85
  Brother from Another Planet, The   (85) 118
  Buddy Buddy   (82) 93
  Cal   (85) 124
  Can She Bake a Cherry Pie?   (84) 95
  Careful He Might Hear You [1983]   (85) 130
  Carmen   (84) 101
  Cat People [1942]   (82) 13
  Cat People   (83) 100
  Choose Me   (85) 135
  Chorus Line, A   (86) 91
  City of Women   (82) 106
  Class   (84) 480
  Cocoon   (86) 96
  Color Purple, The   (86) 105
  Colorado Territory [1949]   (86) 489
  Come Back to the 5 & Dime Jimmy Dean, Jimmy
    Dean   (83) 120
  Comfort and Joy   (85) 146
  Dance with a Stranger [1984]   (86) 125
  Diner   (83) 142
  Draughtsman's Contract, The [1942]   (84) 126
  Dreamchild   (86) 146
  Enemy Mine   (86) 161
  Erendira [1983]   (85) 181
  Experience Preferred . . . but Not Essential
    [1982]   (84) 141
  Fanny and Alexander [1982]   (84) 146
  Fast Times at Ridgemont High   (83) 156
  Fire and Ice   (84) 153
  First Name, Carmen [1983]   (85) 186
  4th Man, The [1983]   (85) 203
  French Lieutenant's Woman, The   (82) 174
  Freud [1962]   (84) 535
  Front, The [1976]   (86) 502
  Gabriela [1983]   (85) 213
  Gift, The   (84) 484
  Gorky Park   (84) 162
  Hail Mary   (86) 182
  Hardbodies   (85) 521
  Heart of a Stag   (85) 522
  Heat and Dust [1982]   (84) 187

Heat of Desire [1981]   (85) 522
History Is Made at Night [1937]   (84) 542
Homework   (83) 422
Honkytonk Man   (83) 200
Hotel New Hampshire, The   (85) 243
Howling, The   (82) 207
Hunger, The   (84) 486
I Love You   (83) 423
I'm No Angel [1933]   (85) 561
Jagged Edge   (86) 190
James Joyce's Women   (86) 193
Jekyll and Hyde . . . Together Again   (83) 424
Joke of Destiny, A [1983]   (85) 259
Last American Virgin, The   (83) 424
Lianna   (84) 201
Liquid Sky   (84) 487
Lonely Hearts [1982]   (84) 212
Losin' It   (84) 488
Loulou [1980]   (82) 226
Love in Germany, A [1983]   (85) 283
Love Letters   (85) 288
Love Streams   (85) 293
Man Who Loved Women, The   (84) 218
Man with Two Brains, The   (84) 223
Merry Christmas, Mr. Lawrence   (84) 231
Micki & Maude   (85) 308
Midsummer Night's Sex Comedy, A   (83) 228
Mike's Murder   (85) 526
Mikey and Nicky [1976]   (85) 576
Missionary, The   (83) 233
Monsignor   (83) 425
Montenegro   (82) 250
Mutiny on the Bounty [1962]   (85) 581
My Best Friend's Girl [1983]   (85) 326
My New Partner [1984]   (86) 246
My Reputation [1946]   (85) 586
My Tutor   (84) 490
Natural, The   (85) 329
Nell Gwyn [1934]   (84) 557
Next Stop, Greenwich Village [1976]   (85) 592
Night in Heaven, A   (84) 490
Night of the Shooting Stars, The [1982]   (84) 258
1984   (85) 335
No Small Affair   (85) 527
Officer and a Gentleman, An   (83) 246
Once upon a Time in America   (85) 345
Out of Africa   (86) 255
Pale Rider   (86) 261
Pauline at the Beach [1982]   (84) 296
Play Misty for Me [1971]   (86) 532
Porky's   (83) 267
Postman Always Rings Twice, The   (82) 284
Pretty Baby [1978]   (85) 597
Private Function, A [1984]   (86) 280
Private School   (84) 491
Puberty Blues [1981]   (84) 492
Purple Rain   (85) 389
Quartet   (82) 296
Querelle [1982]   (84) 313
Racing with the Moon   (85) 397
Repo Man   (85) 408
Return of Martin Guerre, The   (84) 318
Return of the Living Dead, The   (86) 314
Revenge of the Nerds   (85) 530
Rich and Famous   (82) 316
Romancing the Stone   (85) 421
St. Elmo's Fire   (86) 330
Savage Island   (86) 458
Scarlet Letter, The [1927]   (85) 602
Silkwood   (84) 367
Smooth Talk   (86) 354
Spring Break   (84) 494

Star 80   (84) 374
Starman   (85) 445
State of Things, The   (84) 379
Staying Alive   (84) 386
Still of the Night   (83) 326
Streamers   (84) 391
Streetwise   (86) 364
Summer Lovers   (83) 429
Sure Thing, The   (86) 369
Swann in Love   (85) 471
Taking Off [1971]   (86) 545
Tales of Ordinary Madness   (84) 495
Taxi Zum Klo   (82) 346
Tempest   (83) 331
Terms of Endearment   (84) 414
They're Playing with Fire   (85) 536
Thief of Hearts   (85) 536
Tightrope   (85) 489
Tootsie   (83) 353
Trouble in Mind   (86) 388
Under the Volcano   (85) 499
Up the Creek   (85) 537
Valley Girl   (84) 447
Victim [1961]   (85) 649
Victor/Victoria   (83) 387
Videodrome   (84) 452
Wetherby   (86) 406
Wicker Man, The [1974]   (86) 555
Woman Next Door, The   (82) 385
World According to Garp, The   (83) 397
World of Henry Orient, The [1964]   (84) 600
Yentl   (84) 468

SHERIFFS AND MARSHALS
Best Little Whorehouse in Texas, The   (83) 72
Cattle Annie and Little Britches   (82) 97
Colorado Territory [1949]   (86) 489
First Blood   (83) 164
Heaven's Gate   (82) 195
Mrs. Soffel   (85) 314
Pale Rider   (86) 261
Porky's   (83) 267
Silent Rage   (83) 428
Silverado   (86) 349
Trip to Bountiful, The   (86) 383

SHIPS AND THE SEA
And the Ship Sails On [1983]   (85) 69
Boot, Das [1981]   (83) 86
Bounty, The   (85) 513
Dreamchild   (86) 146
Fitzcarraldo   (83) 167
For Your Eyes Only   (82) 155
History Is Made at Night [1937]   (84) 542
Journey into Fear [1943]   (86) 511
Mutiny on the Bounty [1962]   (85) 581
Nate and Hayes   (84) 236
Never Say Never Again   (84) 252
Pirates of Penzance, The   (84) 301
Riddle of the Sands, The [1979]   (85) 531
Secret Life of Walter Mitty, The [1947]   (86) 540
Splash   (85) 434
Tempest   (83) 331
Under the Volcano   (85) 499
Woman on the Beach, The [1947]   (83) 519

SHOW BUSINESS (See ACTORS AND
ACTRESSES; DANCERS AND DANCING;
MUSIC AND MUSICIANS; SINGERS; and
THEATER)

SINGERS (See also MUSIC AND MUSICIANS)
American Pop   (82) 62
Bal, Le [1983]   (85) 80
Bells Are Ringing [1960]   (84) 517

Broadway Danny Rose   (85) 112
Color Purple, The   (86) 105
Detour [1946]   (86) 498
Diva [1980]   (83) 147
Eddie and the Cruisers   (84) 483
Edith and Marcel [1983]   (85) 518
Front, The [1976]   (86) 502
Give My Regards to Broad Street   (85) 520
Gospel   (85) 520
Holiday Inn [1942]   (82) 443
Honkytonk Man   (83) 200
I'm No Angel [1933]   (85) 561
If You Could See What I Hear   (83) 423
King of Jazz [1930]   (86) 515
Lili Marleen   (82) 222
New York, New York [1977]   (84) 567
Piaf [1980]   (83) 427
Rhinestone   (85) 531
Songwriter   (85) 533
Sweet Dreams   (86) 374
Tender Mercies   (84) 409
This Is Elvis   (82) 360
Top Secret   (85) 536
Tough Enough   (84) 495
Victor/Victoria   (83) 387

SISTERS
Color Purple, The   (86) 105
Company of Wolves, The [1984]   (86) 115
Makioka Sisters, The [1983]   (86) 451
Ran   (86) 304
Return of Martin Guerre, The   (84) 318

SMALL-TOWN LIFE
Adolescente, L' [1979]   (83) 53
All the Right Moves   (84) 41
Best Little Whorehouse in Texas, The   (83) 72
Come Back to the 5 & Dime Jimmy Dean, Jimmy
Dean   (83) 120
Death of Mario Ricci, The [1983]   (86) 133
Footloose   (85) 198
Gabriela [1983]   (85) 213
Ghost Story   (82) 183
Grandview, U.S.A.   (85) 520
Gremlins   (85) 230
Hard Traveling   (86) 445
Hard Way, The [1942]   (85) 555
Heart Like a Wheel   (84) 182
Heaven's Gate   (82) 195
Honky Tonk Freeway   (82) 199
Impulse   (85) 523
Light Ahead, The [1939]   (83) 460
Local Hero   (84) 206
Lola [1980]   (83) 215
Lost in America   (86) 219
Mask   (86) 231
Mrs. Soffel   (85) 314
Night of the Shooting Stars, The [1982]   (84) 258
1918   (86) 454
Officer and a Gentleman, An   (83) 246
Places in the Heart   (85) 371
Porky's   (83) 267
Private Function, A [1984]   (86) 280
Racing with the Moon   (85) 397
Raggedy Man   (82) 300
Red Dawn   (85) 530
Sesame Street Presents: Follow That Bird   (86)
459
Siberiade [1977]   (83) 299
Slap Shot [1977]   (82) 467
Stephen King's Children of the Corn   (85) 534
Superman III   (84) 399
Sweet Sixteen   (85) 535

Tank   (85) 535
Taps   (82) 343
Tender Mercies   (84) 409
Testament   (84) 420
Tex   (83) 335
That Championship Season   (83) 338
Wetherby   (86) 406

SOCIALISM
Berlin Alexanderplatz [1980]   (84) 57
Shooting Party, The [1984]   (86) 344
When Father Was Away on Business [1984]   (86)
411

SONGWRITERS (See also MUSIC AND
MUSICIANS)
Bells Are Ringing [1960]   (84) 517
Color Purple, The   (86) 105
Honkytonk Man   (83) 200
King of Jazz [1930]   (86) 515
Pennies from Heaven   (82) 276
Purple Rain   (85) 389
Songwriter   (85) 533

SOUTH AMERICA
Blame it on Rio   (85) 512
Boys from Brazil, The [1978]   (86) 480
Bridge of San Luis Rey, The [1929]   (82) 408
Commando   (86) 111
Emerald Forest, The   (86) 156
Erendira [1983]   (85) 181
Fitzcarraldo   (83) 167
Gabriela [1983]   (85) 213
Kiss of the Spider Woman   (86) 209
Missing   (83) 232
Norte, El   (84) 265
Official Story, The   (86) 249
Pixote [1980]   (82) 280
Romancing the Stone   (85) 421
Savage Island   (86) 458
Too Hot to Handle [1938]   (84) 596
Xica [1976]   (83) 407

SPACE PROGRAM
Right Stuff, The   (84) 342
Spies like Us   (86) 360

SPACE TRAVEL
Dark Star [1975]   (86) 494
Last Starfighter, The   (85) 277
Return of the Jedi   (84) 326
Star Trek II—The Wrath of Khan   (83) 321
Star Trek III—The Search for Spock   (85) 439
2010   (85) 494

SPAIN
Bizet's Carmen [1983]   (85) 98
Bolero   (85) 513
Carmen   (84) 101
Nate and Hayes   (84) 236
Volver a empezar   (83) 393

SPLIT PERSONALITIES
All of Me   (85) 58
Birdy   (85) 93
Colonel Redl [1984]   (86) 100
Crimes of Passion   (85) 161
Dreamchild   (86) 146
Lost Moment, The [1947]   (83) 465
Love Streams   (85) 293
Psycho II   (84) 307
Sophie's Choice   (83) 311
Superman III   (84) 399
Tightrope   (85) 489
Under the Volcano   (85) 499
Zelig   (84) 473

SPORTS AND SPORTS FIGURES
 All the Right Moves   (84) 41
 American Flyers   (86) 436
 Bear, The   (85) 511
 Berry Gordy's The Last Dragon   (86) 438
 Chariots of Fire   (82) 101
 Continental Divide   (82) 115
 Diner   (83) 142
 Five Days One Summer   (83) 421
 For Your Eyes Only   (82) 155
 Front, The [1976]   (86) 502
 Gregory's Girl [1981]   (83) 193
 Heart Like a Wheel   (84) 182
 Heavenly Bodies   (85) 522
 Hot Dog . . . The Movie   (85) 522
 Joshua Then and Now   (86) 198
 Karate Kid, The   (85) 264
 My Best Friend's Girl [1983]   (85) 326
 Natural, The   (85) 329
 Perfect   (86) 456
 Personal Best   (83) 254
 Pumping Iron II   (86) 456
 Rocky III   (83) 283
 Rocky IV   (86) 319
 Running Brave   (84) 354
 Sam's Son   (85) 531
 Ski Country   (85) 533
 Slap Shot [1977]   (82) 467
 Teen Wolf   (86) 462
 That Championship Season   (83) 338
 Up the Creek   (85) 537
 Victory   (82) 374
 Vision Quest   (86) 464
 World According to Garp, The   (83) 397

STORMS AND NATURAL DISASTERS
 Bambi [1942]   (85) 543
 Bridge of San Luis Rey, The [1929]   (82) 408
 History Is Made at Night [1937]   (84) 542
 I Know Where I'm Going [1945]   (83) 456
 Miracle Woman, The [1931]   (83) 473
 Natural, The   (85) 329
 Places in the Heart   (85) 371
 River, The   (85) 416
 Ran   (86) 304
 Secret Life of Walter Mitty, The [1947]   (86) 540
 Tempest   (83) 331

SUBURBIA
 Compromising Positions   (86) 120
 Desperately Seeking Susan   (86) 137

SUCCESS
 Chorus Line, A   (86) 91
 Color Purple, The   (86) 105
 Front, The [1976]   (86) 502
 Joshua Then and Now   (86) 198
 Just the Way You Are   (85) 524
 Lost in America   (86) 219
 Marie   (86) 227
 Pee-wee's Big Adventure   (86) 265
 Piaf [1980]   (83) 427
 Purple Rain   (85) 389
 St. Elmo's Fire   (86) 330
 Secret Life of Walter Mitty, The [1947]   (86) 540
 Skyline   (85) 533
 Staying Alive   (84) 386
 Trout, The [1982]   (84) 496
 28 Up [1984]   (86) 392
 White Nights   (86) 416

SUICIDE
 Absence of Malice   (82) 57

After Hours   (86) 51
 Big Chill, The   (84) 78
 Breakfast Club, The   (86) 85
 Colonel Redl [1984]   (86) 100
 Colorado Territory [1949]   (86) 489
 Country   (85) 156
 Cutter's Way   (82) 119
 Firefox   (83) 160
 Flight of the Phoenix, The [1966]   (85) 549
 Front, The [1976]   (86) 502
 Goodbye Cruel World   (85) 520
 Hard Way, The [1942]   (85) 555
 History Is Made at Night [1937]   (84) 542
 Jinxed   (83) 206
 Merry Christmas, Mr. Lawrence   (84) 231
 Mishima   (86) 236
 Moon in the Gutter, The   (84) 490
 Natural, The   (85) 329
 Next Stop, Greenwich Village [1976]   (85) 592
 Officer and a Gentleman, An   (83) 246
 Plenty   (86) 271
 Purple Rain   (85) 389
 Ran   (86) 304
 Return of the Living Dead, The   (86) 314
 Runaway Train   (86) 324
 Running Brave   (84) 354
 St. Elmo's Fire   (86) 330
 Soldier's Story, A   (85) 427
 Sophie's Choice   (83) 311
 Specter of the Rose [1946]   (83) 504
 Star 80   (84) 374
 Star Is Born, A [1954]   (84) 573
 Streetwise   (86) 364
 Victim [1961]   (85) 649
 Wetherby   (86) 406
 When Father Was Away on Business [1984]   (86) 411
 Whose Life Is It Anyway?   (82) 378
 Winter of Our Dream [1981]   (83) 431

SUPERNATURAL
 Agnes of God   (86) 56
 Amityville II   (83) 417
 Amityville 3-D   (84) 479
 Brother from Another Planet, The   (85) 118
 Dead Zone, The   (84) 481
 Emerald Forest, The   (86) 156
 Entity, The   (84) 483
 Fanny and Alexander [1982]   (84) 146
 Fire and Ice   (84) 153
 Firestarter   (85) 519
 4th Man, The [1983]   (85) 203
 Ghostbusters   (85) 219
 House Where Evil Dwells, The   (83) 423
 Kiss Me Goodbye   (83) 209
 Ladyhawke   (86) 214
 Nightmares   (84) 490
 Pale Rider   (86) 261
 Poltergeist   (83) 263
 Power, The   (85) 529
 Repo Man   (85) 408
 Time Bandits [1980]   (82) 364
 Twilight Zone—The Movie   (84) 435

SURREALISM
 Agnes of God   (86) 56
 Company of Wolves, The [1984]   (86) 105
 Dreamchild   (86) 146
 4th Man, The [1983]   (85) 203
 Invitation au Voyage [1982]   (84) 486
 Pee-wee's Big Adventure   (86) 265
 Trouble in Mind   (86) 388
 Videodrome   (84) 452

SUBJECT INDEX

SWASHBUCKLERS
Beastmaster, The (83) 418
Conan the Barbarian (83) 419
Conan the Destroyer (85) 516
Deathstalker (85) 517
Gwendoline (85) 521
Hunters of the Golden Cobra, The [1982] (85) 523
Krull (84) 487
Ladyhawke (86) 214
Metalstorm (84) 489
Nate and Hayes (84) 236
Pirate Movie, The (83) 427
Pirates of Penzance, The (84) 301
Romancing the Stone (85) 421
Spacehunter (84) 493
Supergirl (85) 535
Sword and the Sorcerer, The (83) 429
Yellowbeard (84) 498

SWEDEN
After the Rehearsal (85) 52
Fanny and Alexander [1982] (84) 146
Montenegro (82) 250

SWITZERLAND
Boat Is Full, The [1981] (83) 82
Dangerous Moves [1984] (86) 129
Every Man for Himself [1979] (82) 139
Lili Marleen (82) 222

SWORD AND SORCERY
Conan the Barbarian (83) 419
Conan the Destroyer (85) 516
Deathstalker (85) 517
Sword and the Sorcerer, The (83) 429

TEACHERS AND TEACHING (See also COLLEGE LIFE and SCHOOLS AND SCHOOL LIFE)
Bostonians, The (85) 105
Breakfast Club, The (86) 85
Brewster McCloud [1970] (86) 480
Chosen, The (83) 116
Class of 1984 (83) 419
Color Purple, The (86) 105
Doctor Detroit (84) 482
Fast Times at Ridgemont High (83) 156
Gregory's Girl [1981] (83) 193
Mask (86) 231
Max Dugan Returns (84) 228
Night in Heaven, A (84) 490
Official Story, The (86) 249
Out of Africa (86) 255
Porky's II (84) 491
Real Genius (86) 309
Sylvia (86) 462
Taxi Zum Klo (82) 346
Teachers (85) 535
Torn Curtain [1966] (85) 644
Victim [1961] (85) 649
Wetherby (86) 406
White Nights (86) 416
World According to Garp, The (83) 397

TECHNOLOGY
Blue Thunder (84) 84
Emerald Forest, The (86) 156
Enemy Mine (86) 161
Never Cry Wolf (84) 247
Philadelphia Experiment, The (85) 529
Quiet Earth, The (86) 295
Rocky IV (86) 319
Runaway Train (86) 324

Spies like Us (86) 360
Threshold (84) 495
WarGames (84) 458
Young Sherlock Holmes (86) 431

TELEVISION
And Nothing but the Truth (85) 510
Best Little Whorehouse in Texas, The (83) 72
Buddy Buddy (82) 93
Death of Mario Ricci, The [1983] (86) 133
Diner (83) 142
Every Man for Himself [1979] (82) 139
Front, The [1976] (86) 502
Howling, The (82) 207
King of Comedy, The (84) 192
Man of Iron (82) 230
Man of Marble [1977] (82) 234
Man Who Fell to Earth, The [1975] (83) 469
My Favorite Year (83) 241
Ploughman's Lunch, The [1983] (85) 377
Poltergeist (83) 263
Protocol (85) 383
Repo Man (85) 408
Rocky III (83) 283
Tootsie (83) 353
Twilight Zone—The Movie (84) 435
Under Fire (84) 441
Videodrome (84) 452
Wrong Is Right (83) 403

TERRORISM
Final Option, The (84) 484
Hotel New Hampshire, The (85) 243
Mission, The (84) 489
Soldier, The (83) 428

TEXAS
Adventures of Buckaroo Banzai, The (85) 47
Best Little Whorehouse in Texas, The (83) 72
Come Back to the 5 & Dime Jimmy Dean, Jimmy Dean (83) 120
Deep in the Heart (85) 517
Local Hero (84) 206
1918 (86) 454
Paris, Texas (85) 359
Silkwood (84) 367
Smokey and the Bandit—Part 3 (84) 493
Sweet Sixteen (85) 535
Tender Mercies (84) 409
Terms of Endearment (84) 414
Tex (83) 335
Toy, The (83) 358
Trip to Bountiful, The (86) 383
Waltz Across Texas (84) 497

THEATER
After the Rehearsal (85) 52
Bal, Le [1983] (85) 80
Bells Are Ringing [1960] (84) 517
Chorus Line, A (86) 91
Deathtrap (83) 137
Dresser, The (84) 130
Entre nous [1983] (85) 176
Evil Under the Sun [1981] (83) 421
Fanny and Alexander [1982] (84) 146
Flanagan (86) 443
Frances (83) 178
Hard Way, The [1942] (85) 555
King of Jazz [1930] (86) 515
Lonely Hearts [1982] (84) 212
Mephisto (82) 237
Muppets Take Manhattan, The (85) 526
Nell Gwyn [1934] (84) 557
Next Stop, Greenwich Village [1976] (85) 592
Only When I Laugh (82) 268

Star Is Born, A [1954]   (84) 573
To Be or Not to Be   (84) 426
Victor/Victoria   (83) 387
THREE-DIMENSIONAL
   Amityville 3-D   (84) 479
   Jaws 3-D   (84) 486
   Metalstorm   (84) 489
   Parasite   (83) 426
TORTURE
   Beloved Rogue [1927]   (84) 522
   Kiss of the Spider Woman   (86) 209
   Lords of Discipline, The   (84) 488
   Man Hunt [1941]   (85) 570
   Oedipus Rex [1967]   (85) 528
   Official Story, The   (86) 249
   Osterman Weekend, The   (84) 491
   Rambo: First Blood Part II   (86) 299
   Sign of the Cross, The [1932]   (85) 607
   Videodrome   (84) 452
TRAIN ROBBERY
   Colorado Territory [1949]   (86) 489
   Grey Fox, The   (84) 168
TRAINS
   Best Friends   (83) 68
   Étoile du nord, L'   (84) 484
   Grey Fox, The   (84) 168
   Journey of Natty Gann, The   (86) 203
   Natural, The   (85) 329
   Runaway Train   (86) 324
   Sunday in the Country, A   (85) 466
   When Father Was Away on Business [1984]   (86) 411
TREASON
   Beloved Rogue [1927]   (84) 522
   Colonel Redl [1984]   (86) 100
   Daniel   (84) 481
   Falcon and the Snowman, The   (86) 165
   Front, The [1976]   (86) 502
   Ran   (86) 304
   Spies like Us   (86) 360
TRIALS (See LAW, LAWYERS, AND TRIALS)
TRIPS AND TRAVEL
   Best Friends   (83) 68
   Blame It on Rio   (85) 512
   Bolero   (85) 513
   Dark Crystal, The   (83) 130
   Dreamchild   (86) 146
   History Is Made at Night [1937]   (84) 542
   Honky Tonk Freeway   (82) 199
   Honkytonk Man   (83) 200
   Journey of Natty Gann, The   (86) 203
   Lady Sings the Blues [1972]   (85) 565
   Lost in America   (86) 219
   Loveless, The   (85) 525
   Man with Two Brains, The   (84) 223
   Midsummer Night's Sex Comedy, A   (83) 224
   National Lampoon's European Vacation   (86) 453
   National Lampoon's Vacation   (84) 241
   New York, New York [1977]   (84) 567
   Nuit de Varennes, La [1982]   (84) 270
   Paris, Texas   (85) 359
   Petite Bande, La [1982]   (85) 528
   Quest for Fire   (83) 271
   Return of the Jedi   (84) 326
   Romancing the Stone   (85) 421
   Secret of NIMH, The   (83) 288
   Silkwood   (84) 367
   Starman   (85) 445
   Still of the Night   (83) 326

Stranger than Paradise   (85) 455
Sure Thing, The   (86) 369
Table for Five   (84) 404
Too Hot to Handle [1938]   (84) 596
Trip to Bountiful, The   (86) 383
Under Fire   (84) 441
Where the Boys Are '84   (85) 537
White Nights   (86) 416
TROPICAL ISLANDS
   Bounty, The   (85) 513
   Buddy Buddy   (82) 93
   Creature from the Black Lagoon, The [1954]   (82) 422
   Dr. Butcher, M.D. [1980]   (83) 420
   Evil Under the Sun [1981]   (83) 421
   Humongous   (83) 423
   Mutiny on the Bounty [1962]   (85) 581
   Nate and Hayes   (84) 236
   Tempest   (83) 331
   Trading Places   (84) 430
TURN OF THE CENTURY
   Barbarosa   (83) 60
   Cattle Annie and Little Britches   (82) 97
   Colonel Redl [1984]   (86) 100
   Fanny and Alexander [1982]   (84) 146
   Grey Fox, The   (84) 168
   Greystoke   (85) 236
   James Joyce's Women   (86) 193
   Lost Moment, The [1947]   (83) 465
   Midsummer Night's Sex Comedy, A   (83) 228
   Missionary, The   (83) 233
   Ragtime   (82) 304
   Time Machine, The [1960]   (84) 585
   Yentl   (84) 468
TUSCANY
   Night of the Shooting Stars, The [1982]   (84) 258

UNIONS AND UNIONISM
   Man of Iron   (82) 230
   Man of Marble [1977]   (82) 234
   Once upon a Time in America   (85) 345
   Silkwood   (84) 367

VAMPIRES
   Hunger, The   (84) 486
   Once Bitten   (86) 454
VENICE
   Betrayal   (84) 67
   Lost Moment, The [1947]   (83) 465
VETERANS
   Birdy   (85) 93
   Cease Fire   (86) 440
   Cutter's Way   (82) 119
   First Blood   (83) 164
   Front, The [1976]   (86) 502
   Missing in Action 2   (86) 452
   Rambo: First Blood Part II   (86) 299
   Return of the Soldier, The [1982]   (84) 332
   Some Kind of Hero   (83) 428
   Unfaithful, The [1947]   (86) 550
   White Nights   (86) 416
   Woman on the Beach [1947]   (83) 519
VICTORIAN ERA
   Dreamchild   (86) 146
   French Lieutenant's Woman, The   (82) 174
   Hound of the Baskervilles, The [1978]   (82) 203
   Pirates of Penzance, The   (84) 301
   Sherlock Holmes [1922]   (83) 494

Swann in Love (85) 471
Time After Time [1979] (84) 579
Time Machine, The [1960] (84) 585
VIDEOTAPES
Videodrome (84) 452
Joysticks (84) 487
VIENNA
Amadeus (85) 63
Colonel Redl [1984] (86) 100
Freud [1962] (84) 535
Hotel New Hampshire, The (85) 243
Man with Two Brains, The (84) 223
VIETNAM WAR
Birdy (85) 93
Don't Cry, It's Only Thunder (83) 420
First Blood (83) 164
Four Friends (82) 167
Killing Fields, The (85) 270
Last Hunter, The (85) 525
Missing in Action (85) 526
Missing in Action 2 (86) 452
Purple Haze (84) 492
Purple Hearts (85) 529
Rambo: First Blood Part II (86) 299
Streamers (84) 391
10 to Midnight (84) 495
Twilight Zone—The Movie (84) 435
Uncommon Valor (84) 496
White Nights (86) 416
VIGILANTES
After Hours (86) 51
Barbary Coast [1935] (84) 506
Death Wish II (83) 420
Fighting Back (83) 421

WAITERS AND WAITRESSES
Breakin' (85) 514
Death of Mario Ricci, The [1983] (86) 133
Experience Preferred . . . but Not Essential
[1982] (84) 141
Marie (86) 227
Pee-wee's Big Adventure (86) 265
Trouble in Mind (86) 388
Waitress (83) 431
WALES
Experience Preferred . . . but Not Essential
[1982] (84) 141
WASHINGTON, D.C.
D.C. Cab (84) 481
First Monday in October (82) 151
Protocol (85) 383
St. Elmo's Fire (86) 330
Silkwood (84) 367
Solid Gold Cadillac, The [1956] (85) 615
Spies like Us (86) 360
WEALTH
Animal Kingdom, The [1932] (86) 469
Annie (83) 56
Barefoot Contessa, The [1954] (82) 399
Big Chill, The (84) 78
Body Heat (82) 87
Breakfast Club, The (86) 85
Brewster's Millions (86) 438
Careful He Might Hear You [1983] (85) 130
Come and Get It [1936] (82) 412
Cutter's Way (82) 119
Detour [1946] (86) 498
Draughtsman's Contract, The [1982] (84) 126
Eureka (86) 442
Flamingo Kid, The (85) 192

Fletch (86) 169
48 HRS. (83) 173
Front, The [1976] (86) 502
Holy Innocents, The (86) 447
Hound of the Baskervilles, The [1978] (82) 203
I Know Where I'm Going [1945] (83) 456
Local Hero (84) 206
Lost in America (86) 219
Making the Grade (85) 526
Makioka Sisters, The [1983] (86) 451
Man with Two Brains, The (84) 223
Max Dugan Returns (84) 228
Melvin and Howard [1980] (82) 453
My Cousin Rachel [1952] (82) 458
New Babylon, The [1929] (84) 561
Out of Africa (86) 255
Racing with the Moon (85) 397
Ran (86) 304
Risky Business (84) 349
Rocky III (83) 283
St. Elmo's Fire (86) 330
Scarface (84) 361
Shooting Party, The [1984] (86) 344
S.O.B. (82) 328
Star 80 (84) 374
State of Things, The (84) 379
Superman III (84) 399
Toy, The (83) 358
Toy Soldiers (85) 536
Trading Places (84) 430
Trouble in Mind (86) 388
Tuff Turf (86) 464
Under Fire (84) 441
Xica [1976] (83) 407
WEDDINGS
Always (86) 60
Arthur (82) 71
Beau Mariage, Le (83) 65
Best Friends (83) 68
Chosen, The (83) 116
Diner (83) 142
Four Friends (82) 167
Gabriela [1983] (85) 213
I Know Where I'm Going [1945] (83) 456
Micki & Maude (85) 308
Nate and Hayes (84) 236
New York, New York [1977] (84) 567
Out of Africa (86) 255
Police Academy 2 (86) 276
Pretty Baby [1978] (85) 597
Prizzi's Honor (86) 285
Protocol (85) 383
Return of Martin Guerre, The (84) 318
Royal Wedding [1951] (86) 536
Secret Life of Walter Mitty, The [1947] (86) 540
Sixteen Candles (85) 532
Solid Gold Cadillac, The [1956] (85) 615
Twice in a Lifetime (86) 397
Waiting for Gavrilov [1982] (84) 497
When Father Was Away on Business [1984] (86)
411
Yentl (84) 468
WESTERNS
Apache (82) 395
Barbary Coast [1935] (84) 506
Colorado Territory [1949] (86) 489
Grey Fox, The (84) 168
Lone Wolf McQuade (84) 488
Lust in the Dust (86) 450
Pale Rider (86) 261
Rustler's Rhapsody (86) 458

Secret Life of Walter Mitty, The [1947]   (86) 540
Silverado   (86) 349
WOLVES
Company of Wolves, The [1984]   (86) 115
Journey of Natty Gann, The   (86) 203
Ladyhawke   (86) 214
Never Cry Wolf   (84) 247
WOMEN'S RIGHTS
Bostonians, The   (85) 105
City of Women   (82) 106
Color Purple, The   (86) 105
Entre nous [1983]   (85) 176
Heart Like a Wheel   (84) 192
Joke of Destiny, A [1983]   (85) 259
Love Letters   (85) 288
Marie   (86) 227
Mrs. Soffel   (85) 314
Out of Africa   (86) 255
Places in the Heart   (85) 371
Police Academy 2   (86) 276
Protocol   (85) 383
Reds   (82) 312
Roughly Speaking [1945]   (83) 490
Tootsie   (83) 353
World According to Garp, The   (83) 397
Yentl   (84) 468
WORKING CLASS
Breakfast Club, The   (86) 85
Dance with a Stranger [1984]   (86) 125
Educating Rita   (84) 136
Journey of Natty Gann, The   (86) 203
Silkwood   (84) 367
Swing Shift   (85) 535
WORLD WAR I
And the Ship Sails On [1983]   (85) 69
King Solomon's Mines   (86) 449
Long Gray Line, The [1955]   (82) 447

1918   (86) 454
Out of Africa   (86) 255
Pretty Baby [1978]   (85) 597
Priest of Love   (82) 288
Razor's Edge, The   (85) 402
Return of the Soldier, The [1982]   (84) 332
Shooting Party, The [1984]   (86) 344
WORLD WAR II
Arch of Triumph [1948]   (84) 501
Bal, Le [1983]   (85) 80
Boat Is Full, The [1981]   (83) 82
Boot, Das [1981]   (83) 86
Eye of the Needle   (82) 148
Guy Named Joe, A [1943]   (82) 435
Journey into Fear [1943]   (86) 511
Lili Marleen   (82) 222
Long Gray Line, The [1955]   (82) 447
MacArthur's Children   (86) 451
Man Hunt [1941]   (85) 570
Merry Christmas, Mr. Lawrence   (84) 231
My Reputation [1946]   (85) 586
New York, New York [1977]   (84) 567
Night of the Shooting Stars, The [1982]   (84) 258
North Star, The [1943]   (83) 476
Plenty   (86) 271
Racing with the Moon   (85) 397
Raggedy Man   (82) 300
Raiders of the Lost Ark   (82) 308
Roughly Speaking [1945]   (83) 490
Secret Places [1984]   (86) 459
Soldier's Story, A   (85) 427
Sophie's Choice   (83) 311
To Be or Not to Be   (84) 426
Twilight Zone—The Movie   (84) 435
Under the Volcano   (85) 499
Victory   (82) 374
Way We Were, The [1973]   (82) 474
Zoot Suit   (82) 389